Praise for
*Attention Deficit Hyperactivity Disorder:*
*Diagnosis and Management of ADHD in children,*
*young people and adults*

"This book provides a comprehensive and discerning reference that will be of interest to students, clinicians and researchers, not only for its clinical practice guidelines but also for its thorough review of the history, epidemiology and aetiology of ADHD. The guideline development group has tackled thorny issues in a systematic and evidenced-based manner. Readers will find sound answers to the many questions about ADHD that arise in research and practice: Does it remit in adulthood? Is it caused by genes or environment? How should it be diagnosed and treated throughout the lifespan? What impairments afflict patients and families? And what are the costs to society? Although this book was developed to provide a national clinical practice guideline for the UK, that description does not do justice to the breadth and depth of the work. It is most certainly relevant to students and researchers and to clinicians around the world who will likely keep it close at hand as a definitive guide to ADHD."

STEPHEN V. FARAONE,
Professor of Psychiatry and of Neuroscience and Physiology,
SUNY Upstate Medical University

"This NICE clinical guideline provides clear, authoritative advice on the diagnosis and management of ADHD. It is most helpful that there should be such a strong, evidence-based document available to guide practitioners in this controversial field. It should be essential reading for all commissioners, managers, primary care and specialist clinicians who are involved with people with this diagnosis."

PHILIP GRAHAM,
Emeritus Professor of Child Psychiatry,
Institute of Child Health, University of London

# ATTENTION DEFICIT HYPERACTIVITY DISORDER

## Diagnosis and management of ADHD in children, young people and adults

National Clinical Practice Guideline Number 72

National Collaborating Centre for Mental Health

*commissioned by the*

National Institute for Health
& Clinical Excellence

*published by*
The British Psychological Society and The Royal College of Psychiatrists

**British Library Cataloguing-in-Publication Data**

A catalogue record for this book is available from
the British Library.

**ISBN-: 978-1-85433-471-8**

Printed in Great Britain by Alden Press.

Additional material: data CD-Rom created by Pix18
(www.pix18.co.uk)

| | |
|---|---|
| *developed by* | National Collaborating Centre for Mental Health |
| | Royal College of Psychiatrists' Research and Training Unit |
| | 4th Floor, Standon House |
| | 21 Mansell Street |
| | London |
| | E1 8AA |
| | www.nccmh.org.uk |

| | |
|---|---|
| *commissioned by* | National Institute for Health and Clinical Excellence |
| | MidCity Place, 71 High Holborn |
| | London |
| | WCIV 6NA |
| | www.nice.org.uk |

| | |
|---|---|
| *published by* | The British Psychological Society |
| | St Andrews House |
| | 48 Princess Road East |
| | Leicester |
| | LE1 7DR |
| | www.bps.org.uk |

The
British
Psychological
Society

*and*

The Royal College of Psychiatrists
17 Belgrave Square
London
SW1X 8PG
www.rcpsych.ac.uk

RC
PSYCH
ROYAL COLLEGE OF
PSYCHIATRISTS

# CONTENTS

*Contents*

*Contents*

# GUIDELINE DEVELOPMENT GROUP MEMBERS

**Professor Eric Taylor (Chair, Guideline Development Group)**
Head of Department of Child and Adolescent Psychiatry,
Institute of Psychiatry, London

**Dr Tim Kendall (Facilitator, Guideline Development Group)**
Joint Director, The National Collaborating Centre for Mental Health;
Deputy Director, Royal College of Psychiatrists' Research and Training Unit;
Consultant Psychiatrist and Medical Director, Sheffield Health and Social Care Trust

**Professor Philip Asherson**
Professor of Molecular Psychiatry and Honorary Consultant Psychiatrist, Medical
Research Council (MRC) Social, Genetic and Developmental Psychiatry Centre,
Institute of Psychiatry, London

**Mr Simon Bailey (2006–2007)**
Service User Representative

**Dr Karen Bretherton**
Consultant Psychiatrist for Children with Learning Disabilities, Child and
Adolescent Mental Health Services, Leicestershire Partnership NHS Trust

**Ms Amy Brown (2006–2007)**
Research Assistant, The National Collaborating Centre for Mental Health

**Ms Liz Costigan (2006–2007)**
Project Manager, The National Collaborating Centre for Mental Health

**Mr Alan Duncan**
Systematic Reviewer, The National Collaborating Centre for Mental Health

**Dr Val Harpin**
Consultant Paediatrician (Neurodisability), Ryegate Children's Centre,
Sheffield Children's NHS Foundation Trust

**Professor Chris Hollis**
Professor of Child and Adolescent Psychiatry, Division of Psychiatry,
University of Nottingham, Queens Medical Centre, Nottingham

**Dr Daphne Keen**
Consultant Developmental Paediatrician, Developmental Paediatrics,
St George's Hospital, London

**Ms Angela Lewis (2007–2008)**
Research Assistant, The National Collaborating Centre for Mental Health

**Dr Ifigeneia Mavranezouli**
Senior Health Economist, The National Collaborating Centre for Mental Health

**Dr Christine Merrell**
Education Specialist, Curriculum, Evaluation and Management Centre,
Durham University, Durham

**Ms Diane Mulligan**
Carer Representative

**Dr Alejandra Perez**
Systematic Reviewer, The National Collaborating Centre for Mental Health

**Dr Catherine Pettinari (2007–2008)**
Centre Manager, The National Collaborating Centre for Mental Health

**Ms Noreen Ryan**
Nurse Consultant, Child and Adolescent Mental Health Services,
Bolton NHS Hospital Trust, Bolton

**Dr Nicola Salt**
General Practitioner, Thurleigh Road Surgery, London

**Dr Kapil Sayal**
Senior Lecturer in Child and Adolescent Psychiatry, Institute of Mental Health
and University of Nottingham, Nottingham

**Ms Linda Sheppard (2006–2007)**
Carer Representative

**Ms Sarah Stockton**
Senior Information Scientist, The National Collaborating Centre for Mental Health

**Dr Clare Taylor**
Editor, The National Collaborating Centre for Mental Health

**Dr Geoff Thorley**
Head Clinical Child and Adolescent Psychologist, Child and Adolescent Mental
Health Services, Leicestershire Partnership NHS Trust, Leicester

**Ms Jenny Turner (2006–2007)**
Research Assistant, The National Collaborating Centre for Mental Health

**Professor Peter Tymms**
Professor of Education and Director of the Curriculum, Evaluation
and Management Centre, Durham University

**Dr Miranda Wolpert (2006–2007)**
Director, CAMHS Evidence Based Practice Unit, University College London
and Anna Freud Centre, London

**Professor Ian Wong**
Professor of Paediatric Medicine Research, Centre for Paediatric Pharmacy
Research, The School of Pharmacy, London

**Dr Susan Young**
Senior Lecturer in Forensic Clinical Psychology, Institute of Psychiatry, Kings'
College London, Honorary Consultant Clinical and Forensic Psychologist,
Broadmoor Hospital, West London Mental Health Trust

# ACKNOWLEDGEMENTS

The Attention Deficit Hyperactivity Disorder (ADHD) Guideline Development Group and the National Collaborating Centre for Mental Health review team would like to thank those who acted as advisers on specialist topics or have contributed to the development of the guideline by meeting the Guideline Development Group:

**Ms Mary Sainsbury**
Practice Development Manager, Social Care Institute for Excellence (SCIE)

**Dr Ilina Singh**
Wellcome Trust University Lecturer in Bioethics and Society,
London School of Economics

**Dr Miranda Wolpert (2007–2008)**
Director, CAMHS Evidence Based Practice Unit, University College London
and Anna Freud Centre, London

# 1.   PREFACE

This guideline has been developed to advise on the treatment and management of attention deficit hyperactivity disorder (ADHD). The guideline recommendations have been developed by a multidisciplinary team of healthcare professionals, service users and carers, and guideline methodologists after careful consideration of the best available evidence. It is intended that the guideline will be useful to clinicians and service commissioners in providing and planning high-quality care for people with ADHD while also emphasising the importance of the experience of care for them and their carers (see Appendix 1 for more details on the scope of the guideline).

Although the evidence base is rapidly expanding, there are a number of major gaps; future revisions of this guideline will incorporate new scientific evidence as it develops. The guideline makes a number of research recommendations specifically to address gaps in the evidence base. In the meantime, it is hoped that the guideline will assist clinicians, people with ADHD and their carers by identifying the merits of particular treatment approaches where the evidence from research and clinical experience exists.

## 1.1   NATIONAL GUIDELINES

### 1.1.1   What are clinical practice guidelines?

Clinical practice guidelines are 'systematically developed statements that assist clinicians and patients in making decisions about appropriate treatment for specific conditions' (Mann, 1996). They are derived from the best available research evidence, using predetermined and systematic methods to identify and evaluate the evidence relating to the specific condition in question. Where evidence is lacking, the guidelines incorporate statements and recommendations based upon the consensus statements developed by the Guideline Development Group (GDG).

Clinical guidelines are intended to improve the process and outcomes of healthcare in a number of different ways. They can:

● provide up-to-date evidence-based recommendations for the management of conditions and disorders by healthcare professionals
● be used as the basis to set standards to assess the practice of healthcare professionals
● form the basis for education and training of healthcare professionals
● assist patients and carers in making informed decisions about their treatment and care
● improve communication between healthcare professionals, patients and carers
● help identify priority areas for further research.

In addition, when the condition has an impact on another topic area, as in this guideline with education, guidelines are increasingly joint efforts informed by research in those areas and they make recommendations for practice in those areas.

### 1.1.2    Uses and limitations of clinical guidelines

Guidelines are not a substitute for professional knowledge and clinical judgement. They can be limited in their usefulness and applicability by a number of different factors: the availability of high-quality research evidence, the quality of the methodology used in the development of the guideline, the generalisability of research findings and, in this instance, the uniqueness of individuals with ADHD.

Although the quality of research in this field is variable, the methodology used here reflects current international understanding on the appropriate practice for guideline development (AGREE: Appraisal of Guidelines for Research and Evaluation Instrument; www.agreetrust.org; AGREE Collaboration [2003]), ensuring the collection and selection of the best research evidence available and the systematic generation of treatment recommendations applicable to the majority of people with these disorders and situations. However, there will always be some service users for whom clinical guideline recommendations are not appropriate and situations in which the recommendations are not readily applicable. This guideline does not, therefore, override the individual responsibility of healthcare professionals to make appropriate decisions in the circumstances of the individual, in consultation with the person with ADHD or their carer. In addition to the clinical evidence, cost-effectiveness information, where available, is taken into account in the generation of statements and recommendations of the clinical guidelines. While national guidelines are concerned with clinical and cost effectiveness, issues of affordability and implementation costs are to be determined by the National Health Service (NHS).

In using guidelines, it is important to remember that the absence of empirical evidence for the effectiveness of a particular intervention is not the same as evidence for ineffectiveness. In addition, of particular relevance in mental health, evidence-based treatments are often delivered as part of an overall treatment programme including a range of activities, the purpose of which may be to help engage the person and to provide an appropriate context for providing specific interventions. It is important to maintain and enhance the service context in which these interventions are delivered, otherwise the specific benefits of effective interventions will be lost. Indeed, the importance of organising care in order to support and encourage a good therapeutic relationship is at times as important as the specific treatments offered.

### 1.1.3    Why develop national guidelines?

The National Institute for Health and Clinical Excellence (NICE) was established as a Special Health Authority for England and Wales in 1999, with a remit to provide a single source of authoritative and reliable guidance for patients, professionals and the public. NICE guidance aims to improve standards of care, to diminish unacceptable variations in the provision and quality of care across the NHS and to ensure that the health service is patient centred. All guidance is developed in a transparent and collaborative manner using the best available evidence and involving all relevant stakeholders.

NICE generates guidance in a number of different ways, three of which are relevant here. First, national guidance is produced by the NICE Centre for Health Technology

Evaluation to give robust advice about a particular treatment, intervention, procedure or other health technology. Second, the NICE Centre for Public Health Excellence commissions public health guidance focused on both interventions and broader health promotion activities that help to reduce people's risk of developing a disease or condition or help to promote or maintain a healthy lifestyle. Third, the NICE Centre for Clinical Practice commissions the production of national clinical practice guidelines focused upon the overall treatment and management of specific conditions. To enable this latter development, NICE has established seven National Collaborating Centres in conjunction with a range of professional organisations involved in healthcare.

### 1.1.4     The National Collaborating Centre for Mental Health

This guideline has been commissioned by NICE and developed within the National Collaborating Centre for Mental Health (NCCMH). The NCCMH is a collaboration of the professional organisations involved in the field of mental health, national patient and carer organisations, a number of academic institutions and NICE. The NCCMH is funded by NICE and is led by a partnership between the Royal College of Psychiatrists' Research and Training Unit and the British Psychological Society's equivalent unit (Centre for Outcomes Research and Effectiveness).

### 1.1.5     From national guidelines to local protocols

Once a national guideline has been published and disseminated, local healthcare groups will be expected to produce a plan and identify resources for implementation, along with appropriate timetables. Subsequently, a multidisciplinary group involving commissioners of healthcare, primary care and specialist mental health professionals, patients and carers should undertake the translation of the implementation plan into local protocols taking into account both the recommendations set out in this guideline and the priorities set in the National Service Framework (NSF) for Mental Health and related documentation. The nature and pace of the local plan will reflect local healthcare needs and the nature of existing services; full implementation may take a considerable time, especially where substantial training needs are identified. When the guideline is informed by another discipline, such as education, joint efforts to implement the recommendations are undertaken wherever possible.

### 1.1.6     Auditing the implementation of guidelines

This guideline identifies key areas of clinical practice and service delivery for local and national audit in the NHS. Although the generation of audit standards is an important and necessary step in the implementation of this guidance, a more broadly based implementation strategy will be developed. Nevertheless, it should be noted that the Healthcare Commission will monitor the extent to which Primary Care Trusts, trusts responsible for mental health and social care and Health Authorities have implemented these guidelines. Although formal national audit for education is outside the remit for this guideline, the recommendations relevant to education in this guideline would be consistent with a national audit programme or equivalent quality improvement methods.

## 1.2    THE NATIONAL ADHD GUIDELINE

### 1.2.1    Who has developed this guideline?

The GDG was convened by the NCCMH and supported by funding from NICE. The GDG included service users and carers, and professionals from psychiatry, paediatrics, clinical psychology, education, general practice, nursing, and child and adolescent mental health services (CAMHS).

Staff from the NCCMH provided leadership and support throughout the process of guideline development, undertaking systematic searches, information retrieval, appraisal and systematic review of the evidence. Members of the GDG received training in the process of guideline development from NCCMH staff, and the service users and carers received training and support from the NICE Patient and Public Involvement Programme. The NICE Guidelines Technical Advisers provided advice and assistance regarding aspects of the guideline development process.

All GDG members made formal declarations of interest at the outset, which were updated at every GDG meeting. The GDG met a total of 20 times throughout the process of guideline development. It met as a whole, but key topics were led by a national expert in the relevant topics. The GDG was supported by the NCCMH technical team, with additional expert advice from special advisers where needed. The group oversaw the production and synthesis of research evidence before presentation. All statements and recommendations in this guideline have been generated and agreed by the whole GDG.

### 1.2.2    For whom is this guideline intended?

This guideline is relevant for children (over the age of 3 years), young people and adults with ADHD.

The guideline covers the care provided by primary, community, and secondary healthcare professionals and educational services that have direct contact with, and make decisions concerning the care of children, young people and adults with ADHD.

The guideline comments on the interface with other services such as social services, the voluntary sector and young offender institutions, but it will not include recommendations relating to the services exclusively provided by these agencies.

The experience of ADHD can affect the whole family and often the community. The guideline recognises the role of both in the treatment and support of people with ADHD.

### 1.2.3 Specific aims of this guideline

The guideline makes recommendations for the treatment and management of ADHD. It aims to:
- Examine the validity of the diagnostic construct of ADHD
- Evaluate the role of specific pharmacological agents and non-pharmacological, psychological and psychosocial interventions in the treatment and management of ADHD
- Evaluate the role of specific services and systems for providing those services in the treatment and management of ADHD
- Integrate the above to provide best-practice advice on the care of people with a diagnosis of ADHD through the different phases of illness, including the initiation and maintenance of treatment for the chronic condition, the treatment of acute episodes and the promotion of well-being
- Consider economic aspects of various interventions for ADHD.

The guideline does not cover treatments that are not normally available on the NHS.

### 1.2.4 How this guideline is organised

The guideline is divided into chapters, each covering a set of related topics. The first three chapters provide a general introduction to the guideline, to the ADHD condition and to the methods used to develop the guideline. Chapters 4 to 10 provide the evidence that underpins the recommendations.

Each evidence chapter begins with a general introduction to the topic that sets the recommendations in context. Depending on the nature of the evidence, narrative reviews or meta-analyses were conducted, and the structure of the chapters varies accordingly. Where appropriate, details about current practice, the evidence base and any research limitations are provided. Where meta-analyses were conducted, information is given about both the interventions included and the studies considered for review. Clinical summaries are then used to summarise the evidence presented. Finally, recommendations related to each topic are presented at the end of each chapter. On the CD-ROM, full details about the included studies can be found in Appendix 17. Where meta-analyses were conducted, the data are presented using forest plots in Appendix 18 (see Text box 1).

**Text box 1: Appendices on CD-ROM**

| Content | Appendix |
|---|---|
| Included/excluded studies | Appendix 17 |
| Forest plots | Appendix 18 |
| GRADE evidence profiles | Appendix 19 |

# 2. ATTENTION DEFICIT HYPERACTIVITY DISORDER

## 2.1   THE DISORDER

This guideline is concerned with the management of attention deficit hyperactivity disorder (ADHD) as defined in the Diagnostic and Statistical Manual of Mental Disorders, 4th Edition (Text Revision) (DSM-IV-TR) as well as hyperkinetic disorder, as defined in the International Classification of Diseases, 10th revision (ICD-10) in primary, community and secondary care.

### 2.1.1   The concept and its history

The definitions of ADHD and hyperkinetic disorder are based on maladaptively high levels of *impulsivity, hyperactivity* and *inattention*. They are all based on observations about how children behave: 'impulsivity' signifies premature and thoughtless actions; 'hyperactivity' a restless and shifting excess of movement; and 'inattention' is a disorganised style preventing sustained effort. All are shown by individual children to different extents, and are influenced by context as well as by the constitution of the person.

Historically, the origins of the concept were in the idea that some disturbances of behaviour were the result of brain damage or 'minimal brain dysfunction' (MBD), such as were seen in the pandemic of encephalitis in the 1920s or after traumatic birth. These neurological formulations, however, were called into question when epidemiological science examined systematically the causes of behaviour problems in childhood.

In the place of unsubstantiated brain damage theories, the classification of mental disorders emerging in the 1980s in the American Psychiatric Association's diagnostic scheme, DSM-III (later DSM-IV) and the World Health Organization's classification of diseases ICD-9 (now ICD-10), put to one side the aetiological theories and concentrated on the reliable description of problems at a behavioural level. Clinical and statistical studies indicated that impulsivity, hyperactivity and inattention were often associated and were disproportionately common in children referred for psychiatric help. North American and European practice diverged: in North America moderate to severe levels were recognised and termed 'attention deficit hyperactivity disorder'; in most of Europe, only extreme levels were seen as an illness and called 'hyperkinetic disorder'.

More recently, extensive biological investigations of both ADHD and hyperkinetic disorder have yielded some neuroimaging and molecular genetic associations; neurocognitive theories have emerged; and there is a better understanding of the natural history and the risks that hyperactive behaviour imposes. Nevertheless, the disorder remains one that is defined at a behavioural level, and its presence does not imply a neurological disease.

There has also been a large increase in recognition of the problem and a corresponding rise in the numbers treated: from an estimate of 0.5 per 1,000 children diagnosed in the UK 30 years ago (Taylor, 1986), to more than 3 per 1,000 receiving medication for ADHD in the late 1990s (NICE, 2006b). The rates in the US have risen too, but from a much higher base; from about 12 per 1,000 30 years ago to about 35 per 1,000 in the late 1990s, with the increase continuing (Olfson *et al.*, 2003). The terminology in Europe has also changed, and 'ADHD' has become the diagnostic phrase most commonly used in practice, even when more restrictive criteria are being used.

## 2.1.2    Common problems associated with ADHD

It is very common for the core problems of ADHD in children to present together with other developmental impairments and/or mental health problems. There are many rather non-specific problems that are very common in ADHD, and can even be used – incorrectly – as grounds for the diagnosis (see Table 1).

These need recognising, and sometimes intervention, but they are not in themselves grounds for the diagnosis, because they can be the results of many different causes. Similarly, young people and adults may in addition show other associated problems, such as self-harm, a predisposition to road traffic (and other) accidents, substance misuse, delinquency, anxiety states and academic underachievement; similarly they are not in themselves grounds for the diagnosis and may result either from ADHD or from other causes.

**Table 1: Common problems associated with ADHD in children**

| | |
|---|---|
| Non-compliant behaviour | Motor tics |
| Sleep disturbance | Mood swings |
| Aggression | Unpopularity with peers |
| Temper tantrums | Clumsiness |
| Literacy and other learning problems | Immature language |

## 2.1.3    Changes with age

The problems associated with ADHD appear in different ways at different ages, as the individual matures and as the environmental requirements for sustained self-control increase (Taylor & Sonuga-Barke, 2008). Hyperactivity in a pre-school child may involve incessant and demanding extremes of activity; during the school years an affected child may make excess movements during situations where calm is expected rather than on every occasion; during adolescence hyperactivity may present as excessive fidgetiness rather than whole body movement; in adult life it may be a sustained inner sense of restlessness. Inattention too may diminish in absolute terms, and attention span will usually increase with age; but it tends still to lag behind that of unaffected people, and behind the level that is expected and needed for everyday attainments.

### 2.1.4    Course of the disorder

*Onset*

The core behaviours of ADHD are typically present from before the age of 7 years, but at all ages presentation as a problem is very variable (Sayal *et al.*, 2002). Mild forms need not be impairing at all (Mannuzza *et al.*, 1998). Extreme forms are considered to be harmful to the individual's development in most cultures, but there are cultural differences in the level of activity and inattention that is regarded as a problem (Sonuga-Barke *et al.*, 1993). While both teachers and parents can find it hard to deal with or live with a hyperactive child, their tolerance and ability to cope may determine whether the hyperactivity is presented as a problem. Children with hyperactivity rarely ask for help themselves. Inattention without hyperactivity often is not present as a problem even though an inattentive child may have a marked cognitive impairment. The presentation to the clinician therefore depends on a complex blend of the skills and tolerance of adults surrounding the child and the qualities of the children themselves.

*Course and impairment*

The core problems of ADHD and the associated features can persist over time and impair development in children. Several studies have followed diagnosed school-children over periods of 4 to 14 years; all have found that they tend to show, by comparison with people of the same age who have not had mental health problems, persistence of hyperactivity and inattention, poor school achievement and a higher rate of disruptive behaviour disorders. The various studies have been reviewed, successively by Hechtman and Weiss (1983), Klein and Mannuzza (1991), Hill and Schoener (1996) and Faraone and colleagues (2006).

The risk of later maladjustment also affects children not referred to clinics and those not treated at all. Longitudinal population studies have shown that hyperactive-impulsive behaviour is a risk for several kinds of adolescent maladjustment (Moffitt 1990; Taylor *et al.*, 1996). Lack of friends, work and constructive leisure activities are prominent and affect the quality of life. Severe levels of hyperactivity and impulsivity also make children more likely to develop an antisocial adjustment and more likely to show personality dysfunction or substance misuse in later adolescence and adult life.

Although ADHD symptoms persist in the majority of cases, it is important to remember that many young people with ADHD will make a good adjustment to adulthood and be free of mental health problems. A good outcome may be more likely when the main problem is inattention rather than hyperactivity-impulsivity, when antisocial conduct does not develop, and when relationships with family members and other children remain warm. More research is needed on the influences on eventual outcome, and should include enquiry about the possible benefits (and risks) of early diagnosis and treatment.

## 2.2 DIAGNOSIS AND ASSESSMENT

### 2.2.1 Diagnostic systems and criteria

The most commonly used criteria for the diagnosis of both children and adults are those provided in DSM-IV-TR and in ICD-10.

The DSM criteria break down symptoms into two groups: inattentive and hyperactive-impulsive. Six of the nine symptoms in each section must be present for a 'combined type' diagnosis of ADHD. If there are insufficient symptoms for a combined diagnosis then predominantly inattentive (ADHD-I) and hyperactive (ADHD-H) diagnoses are available. Additionally, symptoms must be: chronic (present for 6 months), maladaptive, functionally impairing across two or more contexts, inconsistent with developmental level and differentiated from other mental disorders (see Table 2).

The ICD uses a different nomenclature; the same symptoms are described as part of a group of hyperkinetic disorders of childhood, and inattention, hyperactivity and impulsivity must all be present; so only 'combined-type' ADHD qualifies. In addition, the research diagnostic criteria of the ICD provide an even more restricted set of requirements: the symptom counts must all be met in more than one context. Furthermore, there are quite strict exclusion criteria: whereas coexisting psychiatric disorders are allowed under DSM-IV-TR, the diagnosis of hyperkinetic disorder is not made when criteria for certain other disorders, including anxiety states, are met – unless it is plain that hyperkinetic disorder is additional to the other disorder (see Table 3).

**Table 2: DSM-IV-TR criteria for attention deficit hyperactivity disorder**

| 1. Either A or B. |
| --- |
| A. Inattention – Six or more symptoms persisting for at least 6 months to a degree that is maladaptive and inconsistent with developmental level. |
| Often fails to give close attention to details or makes careless mistakes in schoolwork, work, or other activities |
| Often has difficulty sustaining attention in tasks or play activities |
| Often does not seem to listen when spoken to directly |
| Often does not follow through on instructions; fails to finish schoolwork, chores or workplace duties (not due to oppositional behaviour or failure to understand instructions) |

**Table 2:** (*Continued*)

| | |
|---|---|
| | Often has difficulty organising tasks and activities |
| | Often avoids, dislikes, or is reluctant to do tasks requiring sustained mental effort |
| | Often loses things necessary for tasks or activities |
| | Is often easily distracted by extraneous stimuli |
| | Is often forgetful in daily activities |
| B. Hyperactivity-impulsivity – Six or more symptoms persisting for at least 6 months to a degree that is maladaptive and inconsistent with developmental level. | |
| Hyperactivity | Often fidgets with hands or feet or squirms in seat |
| | Often leaves seat in classroom or in other situations where remaining seated is expected |
| | Often runs or climbs excessively where inappropriate (feelings of restlessness in young people or adults) |
| | Often has difficulty playing or engaging in leisure activities quietly |
| | Is often 'on the go' or often acts as if 'driven by a motor' |
| | Often talks excessively |
| Impulsivity | Often blurts out answers before questions have been completed |
| | Often has difficulty awaiting turn |
| | Often interrupts or intrudes on others (for example, butts into conversations or games) |
| 2. Some hyperactive-impulsive or inattentive symptoms that caused impairment were present before age 7 years. | |
| 3. Some impairment from symptoms is present in two or more settings (for example, at school or work and at home). | |
| 4. There must be clear evidence of significant impairment in social, school or work functioning. | |
| 5. The symptoms do not happen only during the course of a pervasive developmental disorder, schizophrenia or other psychotic disorder. The symptoms are not better accounted for by another mental disorder (for example, mood disorder, anxiety disorder, dissociative disorder, or a personality disorder). | |

Adapted from *Diagnostic and Statistical Manual of Psychiatric Disorders DSM*-IV-TR (2000) with permission from the American Psychiatric Association.

## Table 3: ICD-10 criteria for hyperkinetic disorders

| |
|---|
| 1. Inattention – At least six symptoms of attention have persisted for at least 6 months, to a degree that is maladaptive and inconsistent with the developmental level of the child: |

| |
|---|
| Often fails to give close attention to details, or makes careless errors in school work, work or other activities |
| Often fails to sustain attention in tasks or play activities |
| Often appears not to listen to what is being said to him or her |
| Often fails to follow through on instructions or to finish school work, chores or duties in the workplace (not because of oppositional behaviour or failure to understand instructions) |
| Is often impaired in organising tasks and activities |
| Often avoids or strongly dislikes tasks, such as homework, that require sustained mental effort |
| Often loses things necessary for certain tasks and activities, such as school assignments, pencils, books, toys or tools |
| Is often easily distracted by external stimuli |
| Is often forgetful in the course of daily activities |

| |
|---|
| 2. Hyperactivity – At least three symptoms of hyperactivity have persisted for at least 6 months, to a degree that is maladaptive and inconsistent with the developmental level of the child: |

| |
|---|
| Often fidgets with hands or feet or squirms on seat |
| Often leaves seat in classroom or in other situations in which remaining seated is expected |
| Often runs about or climbs excessively in situations in which it is inappropriate (in adolescents or adults, only feelings of restlessness may be present) |
| Is often unduly noisy in playing or has difficulty in engaging quietly in leisure activities |
| Often exhibits a persistent pattern of excessive motor activity that is not substantially modified by social context or demands |

| |
|---|
| 3. Impulsivity – At least one of the following symptoms of impulsivity has persisted for at least 6 months, to a degree that is maladaptive and inconsistent with the developmental level of the child: |

**Table 3:** (*Continued*)

| |
|---|
| Often blurts out answers before questions have been completed |
| Often fails to wait in lines or await turns in games or group situations |
| Often interrupts or intrudes on others (for example, butts into others' conversations or games) |
| Often talks excessively without appropriate response to social constraints |
| 4. Onset of the disorder is no later than the age of 7 years. |
| 5. Pervasiveness – The criteria should be met for more than a single situation, for example, the combination of inattention and hyperactivity should be present both at home and at school, or at both school and another setting where children are observed, such as a clinic. (Evidence for cross-situationality will ordinarily require information from more than one source; parental reports about classroom behaviour, for instance, are unlikely to be sufficient.) |
| 6. The symptoms in 1 and 3 cause clinically significant distress or impairment in social, academic or occupational functioning. |

Adapted from *ICD10: Classification of Mental and Behavioural Disorders* (1992) with permission from the World Health Organization.

Hyperkinetic disorder (ICD-10) therefore describes a group that forms a severe sub-group of the DSM-IV-TR combined subtype of ADHD. Hyperkinetic disorder is further divided into hyperkinetic disorder with and without conduct disorder.

With regard to adults, strict usage of the full diagnostic criteria may be inappropriate, because the criteria focus on childhood problems and do not take full account of the developmental changes mentioned above. Recommendations for identification in adult life have therefore included lowering of diagnostic thresholds and providing age-appropriate adjustment of the symptoms. Issues such as self-awareness and motivation in adult patients reinforce the importance of taking a thorough developmental and psychiatric history and mental state – though this should be a key feature of any diagnostic process. DSM-IV-TR allows a category of 'ADHD in partial remission' for individuals who no longer meet the full criteria; this criterion is particularly relevant for adults where some of the symptoms may have declined with age but where significant impairments related to the symptoms remain.

In this guideline, 'ADHD' is used as an umbrella term when discussing the disorder more broadly. Some of the earlier literature used the term 'hyperactivity' for the cluster of hyperactive, impulsive and inattentive symptoms. In this guideline 'hyperactivity' is restricted to mean the combination of symptoms that define overactive behaviour. The term 'ADHD symptoms' is used to refer to the combination of hyperactive, impulsive and inattentive symptoms.

Oppositional defiant disorder and conduct disorder are also diagnoses in the ICD and DSM schemes and need to be differentiated from ADHD. Oppositional defiant disorder refers to persistent and frequent disobedience and opposition to authority figures (such as parents, teachers or other adults), characterised by negative, hostile or defiant behaviour. The diagnosis should not be made unless these behaviours persist for more than 6 months and are considerably more frequent than normal for a person of the same developmental age. Conduct disorder represents more severe behavioural problems: a persistent pattern of behaviour that violates the societal rules and the rights of others. This includes aggression that can take the form of bullying or cruelty to animals, destruction of property, stealing and persistent lying (other than to avoid harm). All these oppositional and conduct disorder problems can be seen in some children with ADHD, but they are not essential features and should not be used as grounds for making the diagnosis of ADHD.

### 2.2.2    Differential diagnosis

Features of ADHD often coexist with other problems of mental health; and these other conditions may be both differential diagnoses (because they may produce behaviours superficially similar to those of ADHD) and comorbid disorders that need to be recognised in their own right.

DSM-IV-TR and ICD-10 treat coexisting conditions in different ways. In DSM, symptoms must not exist 'exclusively during the course of' autism spectrum disorders, schizophrenia or other psychotic disorders, and furthermore must not be 'better accounted for' by another mental disorder, such as affective disorders, anxiety disorders, dissociative and personality disorders. ICD-10 research diagnostic criteria go further and make such conditions exclusionary criteria without the need for judgement about whether they account for ADHD features. There is a potential danger in a strict application of these exclusionary criteria: it may lead to the overlooking of ADHD when it coexists with another problem, as described in Chapter 5.

What is clear is that the confounding effect of coexisting conditions needs to be evaluated for each individual, considering especially: global and specific learning disorders, neurological disorders, disorders of motor control, conduct and oppositional disorders, Tourette's syndrome, bipolar illnesses, other affective disorders including anxiety and depression, attachment and post-traumatic disorders, autistic spectrum disorders and borderline and antisocial personality disorders.

The confounding effects of stress, parent/carer/institutional/social intolerance or pressure, and individual or familial drug and alcohol misuse should also be taken into account. Hearing impairment and congenital disorders are particularly common examples of a range of medical conditions that need to be detected if present.

### 2.2.3    Controversies with diagnosis

The diagnosis of ADHD has attracted criticisms from many who challenge several assumptions associated with the process, as described in Chapter 5. Broadly these issues can be summarised into three categories:
● *Technical critiques* focus on the difficulties of diagnosis as a practical accomplishment. These include: the language and specificity of the criteria, accurate differentiation from coexisting conditions, and the lack of criteria and guidance for adult diagnosis in particular.
● *Sociological critiques* cover a broad range of issues, including the present gender, class and ethnicity disproportion in diagnosis, the ideological bases of the practice of psychiatry and the allegedly hegemonic practices of the American Psychiatric Association, and the existence and effects of social pressures, overstated reporting by the media and stereotyping.
● *Validity critiques* question the very existence of the disorder and emphasise the institutional and social conditions upon which they claim the diagnosis is contingent.

### 2.2.4    Assessment – the influence of key clinical characteristics

The assessment of ADHD is best understood when related to the key characteristics of ADHD (including hyperkinetic disorder), as set out in diagnostic schemes. These key features are:
● the presence of the core problems of inattention, hyperactivity and impulsivity
● the inappropriateness of these features in comparison with the qualities of people at a similar developmental level
● long duration of symptoms
● difficulties evident in more than one setting, such as the home, school or workplace and other social settings
● adverse impact on current and/or general development and psychosocial adjustment
● the need to distinguish from neurodevelopmental disorders associated with learning disabilities and cognitive problems, and other mental health disorders or problems – neither using those other problems as evidence for ADHD nor neglecting the presence of ADHD when it coexists with them
● the need to consider whether impairment is attributable solely to ADHD or is caused or exacerbated by other disorders (mental and physical) as well as personal and social circumstances.

### 2.2.5    Key assessment features

There is no single definitive psychological or biological test for ADHD. Diagnosis is the outcome of several strands of investigation that are directed to establishing:
● the extent and severity of the core symptoms and any associated problems

- the characteristics of the symptoms in different situations
- the origins and developmental course of the symptoms
- how any symptoms compare with those seen in other people at the same developmental level
- the presence of other physical, mental health and/or learning disorders.

The complexity of assessment requires cooperation among a number of professionals employed by different agencies and using a wide variety of techniques – in other words, a multi-modal, multi-professional and multi-agency approach.

### 2.2.6    Key approaches

Essential components of a full assessment process include a clinical interview, a medical examination and administration of rating scales to parents and teachers (for example, self-report). Other components such as direct observation in educational settings, cognitive, neuropsychological, developmental and literacy skills assessments may or may not be indicated.

*Clinical interview*
A clinical interview is usually carried out by a paediatrician, psychiatrist, clinical psychologist or specialist nurse; and usually in a semi-structured format so that key issues can be systematically investigated. Although fully structured interview instruments, such as the Diagnostic Interview Schedule for Children (DISC) (Costello *et al.*, 1982), the Diagnostic Interview Scale (DIS) for adults (Robins *et al.*, 1981) and the Conners' ADHD Adult Diagnostic Interview for DSM-IV (Epstein *et al.*, 2001), are often used in research, the length and inflexibility of such instruments has, however, meant that they are seldom employed in clinical practice.

The chief aim of the interview is to detail the full range of problems and their history, together with family, health, social, educational and demographic information. It is also helpful to find out how patients and their families have tried to deal with any problems over the years and the impact of the problems on the family as well as the child. The interview is also designed to highlight any further, more specialist assessments that might be required to facilitate diagnosis and intervention planning.

A detailed clinical interview in child mental health practice will typically take between 2 and 3 hours, often arranged over two sessions. Frequently, persons other than the child are involved in the interview to provide additional information and perspectives. Time is also set aside to see young people individually with a similar opportunity for parents.

*Standardised rating scales*
These help in the evaluation of mental health, social and behavioural problems and possess normative data to enable comparisons with the general population, specific clinical groups or both. There are three main types:
1. Broad-band instruments that evaluate general behavioural and psychosocial functioning: the Strengths and Difficulties Questionnaire (Goodman, 2001) is a widely

available and used example. A longer example is the Achenbach scales (Achenbach, 2003; Achenbach & Rescorla, 2001), which cover the age range 18 months to 59 years with adult, parent, teacher and adolescent self-report versions. Another example is the long version of the Conners' Rating Scales (CRS) (Conners, 1997) for young people, which have versions for parents and teachers.

2. Narrow-band scales that are specific to ADHD symptomatology: examples include the Conners' scales for young people (Conners *et al.*, 1997), the Brown Attention Deficit Disorder Scale (Brown, 2001, 1996) with versions for adults and young people; ADHD Rating Scale (ADHD-RS) IV (DuPaul *et al.*, 1998); the Child Attention Profile (Dulcan & Popper, 1991; Barkley, 1990); and the Home Situations Questionnaire (Barkley & Murphy, 1998).

3. Other rating scales are used to evaluate other types of mental health symptomatology that coexist, or are associated, with ADHD such as anxiety, self-esteem, depression and conduct problems.

The limitations of rating scales include an inter-rater reliability that is at best moderate (Verhulst & van der Ende, 2002) as well as less than complete sensitivity and specificity for the diagnosis compared with a full diagnostic assessment. Many scales describe symptoms only and not their developmental appropriateness or the level of impairment. When developmental appropriateness is included, then it is by asking the rater to judge according to what is considered normal for a child of that age, which may be a difficult task for a non-expert rater and prone to errors of interpretation.

### Educational and occupational adjustment

An understanding of a child or young person's adjustment at school or an adult's functioning in the workplace is an important component of the assessment process. In addition to providing information gathered by questionnaire, teachers may be asked to provide specific information on social and academic functioning. If there are particular problems with functioning at school, direct observation by the assessing clinicians of behaviour in the classroom and in other, less structured situations, may be undertaken.

### Medical assessment

People referred for assessment for ADHD receive a specialist clinical assessment by a psychiatrist or paediatrician. One aim is to rule out undiagnosed disorders with symptoms that in rare instances may mimic or cause some aspects of ADHD, such as hearing impairment, epilepsy, thyroid disorder and iron deficiency anaemia. The possible contribution of prenatal and perinatal factors known to increase the risk of development of ADHD symptoms is noted (and parental questions about risk factors are responded to) and the assessment identifies physical signs of certain genetic conditions that have increased risk of ADHD. There may also be other coexisting physical, neurological and developmental disorders that need to be identified (including developmental coordination disorder, also known as dyspraxia, chronic tic disorders or Tourette's syndrome, and sleep disorders) which will then shape later management. After diagnosis, if ADHD is confirmed, and if drug therapy is being considered, examination involves baseline measurements of height and weight, blood pressure and pulse rate, with continued monitoring of these factors being an ongoing feature.

*Psychological and psychometric assessment*

Educational and clinical psychologists may undertake further assessments if learning difficulties, including poor literacy skills, dyslexia, or other problems such as dyscalculia or non-verbal learning difficulties, are suspected. These may help to explain the presence of attentional problems; and even if ADHD is present as well, they will need addressing as part of the management plan.

Global learning disabilities may also be present, particularly with hyperkinetic disorder; intellectual status needs to be understood so that therapy can be designed to be developmentally appropriate.

Cognitive impairments involving memory, attention or others are very likely to be present and ideally should be investigated further by clinical or educational psychologists. There are many such tests; of particular interest are specific ones to measure attention. One of the best known is the Test of Everyday Attention (Robertson *et al.*, 1994) for adults and the Test of Everyday Attention for Children (Manly *et al.*, 1998). There are also visual and auditory attentional subtests in neuropsychological batteries such as the NEPSY (Korkman *et al.*, 1998) for children. Auditory attention is also a feature of the Auditory Continuous Performance Test for children (Keith, 1994). There are also a number of versions of the Continuous Performance Test (Rosvold *et al.*, 1956) available and helpfully discussed by Barkley and Murphy (1998). Further research is recommended on the extent to which neuropsychological tests can effectively be used to guide psychological interventions.

## 2.3    EPIDEMIOLOGY

ADHD (as defined in DSM-IV-TR) is a common disorder. In the UK, a survey of 10,438 children between the ages of 5 and 15 years found that 3.62% of boys and 0.85% of girls had ADHD (Ford *et al.*, 2003). This survey was founded on careful assessment and included impairment in the diagnosis.

The more restricted diagnosis of hyperkinetic disorder in ICD-10, representing a severe sub-group of DSM-IV-TR combined type ADHD, is naturally less common; prevalence estimates are around 1.5% for boys in the primary school years.

In the international scientific literature, prevalence estimates vary widely across studies. At one extreme, in Colombia, the prevalence rates were estimated to be 19.8% and 12.3% for boys and girls respectively (Pineda *et al.*, 2003). Such a wide range in prevalence estimates is unlikely to reflect true differences in the numbers of individuals with ADHD in various populations. Polanczyk and colleagues (2007) made a systematic review of prevalence studies and concluded that the great majority of variability derived from the methods used, such as the way symptoms were measured and the exact definitions used. There were relatively minor differences in different parts of the world and the review's summary of rates was around 5.3%.

This highlights the difficulties in making direct comparisons between studies and occurs for several reasons. ADHD symptoms are continuously distributed throughout the population with no natural threshold between affected and unaffected individuals (Taylor *et al.*, 1991). This particular problem can be successfully resolved by the application of strictly applied operational diagnostic criteria such as the DSM-IV-TR definition for ADHD or the research ICD-10 criteria for hyperkinetic disorder. However, even where the same diagnostic definitions are applied, there may still be differences in the thresholds applied for individual symptoms, which are rarely operationalised. For example, how severe should be avoidance of tasks requiring sustained attention or levels of fidgetiness before they are considered to be clinically significant?

Key criteria when defining ADHD are not only the presence of sufficient numbers of ADHD symptoms but also, importantly, their association with clinical and social impairments at home, school and in other settings. Surveys that include strict definitions of impairment alongside the symptom count find that prevalence of the syndrome (without evidence of impairment) is around twice the prevalence of the disorder when the syndrome is associated with impairment (Canino *et al.*, 2004). In the UK, a survey in Newcastle found that prevalence was 11% for the syndrome with no impairment, 6.7% when associated with moderately low impairment, 4.2% for moderate impairment and 1.4% for severe pervasive impairment (McArdle *et al.*, 2004).

Taking into account the differences in investigator training and measures used across studies it is not possible to draw firm conclusions from the large variation in prevalence rates cited in the literature. Having said that, small differences are likely to exist. One study from the US using the same diagnostic procedures reported small but significant differences in prevalence rates between African-Americans (5.65%), Hispanics (3.06%) and whites (4.33%) (Cuffe *et al.*, 2005); such differences might, however, be explained by different cultural tolerances for the symptoms of ADHD.

*Adult ADHD*

Prevalence for strictly applied operational definitions of ADHD decline with age. A recent review of longitudinal follow-up studies of individuals diagnosed with ADHD as children found that by age 25 only 15% retained the full ADHD diagnosis. However, a much larger proportion (65%) fulfilled criteria for either ADHD or ADHD in partial remission, indicating the persistence of some symptoms associated with clinical impairments in the majority of cases (Faraone *et al.*, 2006). Applying these figures to the prevalence range commonly seen in children of 4–8%, one would expect to find 0.6–1.2% of adults retaining the full diagnosis by age 25 years and a larger percentage (2–4%) with ADHD in partial remission. This is consistent with population surveys in adult populations that estimate prevalence of ADHD in adults to be between 3 and 4% (Faraone & Biederman, 2005; Kessler *et al.*, 2006).

These data suggest that ADHD in adults will be under identified if the same clinical criteria applied to children is applied to adults. ADHD symptoms follow a developmental decline that parallels the normal change in levels of inattentive, hyperactive and impulsive behaviours seen in the general population. Estimation of prevalence rates will vary unless age-adjusted criteria are applied in a similar way across studies.

## 2.4 AETIOLOGY

The diagnosis of ADHD does not imply a medical or neurological cause. Equally, the presence of psychosocial adversity or risk factors should not exclude the diagnosis of ADHD. The aetiology of ADHD involves the interplay of multiple genetic and environmental factors. ADHD is viewed as a heterogeneous disorder with different sub-types resulting from different combinations of risk factors acting together.

### 2.4.1 Genetic influences

ADHD symptoms show quite strong genetic influences. Twin studies suggest that around 75% of the variation in ADHD symptoms in the population are because of genetic factors (heritability estimate of 0.7 to 0.8) (Faraone *et al.*, 2005). The genetic influences appear to affect the distribution of ADHD symptoms across the whole population and not just in a clinically defined sub-group. No single gene of large effect has been identified in ADHD; rather several DNA variants of small effect – each increasing the susceptibility of ADHD by a small amount – have been associated. These findings have fuelled a controversy over whether ADHD should be considered as part of normal variation or as a categorically defined medical disorder (see Chapter 5). Testing for susceptibility genes is currently not justified in clinical practice given the small predictive value of the associated genes, which therefore lack direct clinical relevance.

### 2.4.2 Environmental influences

*Biological factors*
A range of factors that adversely affect brain development during perinatal life and early childhood are associated with an increase in the risk of ADHD or attention deficit disorder without hyperactivity. These include maternal smoking (Linnet *et al.*, 2003), alcohol consumption (Mick *et al.*, 2002) and heroin during pregnancy (Ornoy *et al.*, 2001), very low birth weight (Botting *et al.*, 1997) and fetal hypoxia, brain injury, exposure to toxins such as lead and deficiency of zinc (Toren *et al.*, 1996). Risk factors do not act in isolation, but interact with one another. For example, the risk of ADHD associated with maternal alcohol consumption in pregnancy may be stronger in those children with a dopamine transporter (DAT) susceptibility gene (Brookes *et al.*, 2006). Further research is required to confirm whether these act as direct risks for ADHD.

There is increased risk of ADHD symptoms in epilepsy and of ADHD in genetic conditions such as neurofibromatosis type 1 (Mautner *et al.*, 2002), and syndromes such as Angelman, Prader-Willi, Smith Magenis, velocardiofacial and fragile X (Hagerman, 1999). Secondary ADHD may follow traumatic brain injury (Gerring *et al.*, 1998).

*Dietary factors*

The influence of dietary factors in ADHD has attracted much public attention: food additives, sugar, colourings and 'E' numbers are often regarded as causes of ADHD, and elimination and supplementation diets are widely used, often without professional advice.

Nevertheless, epidemiological research indicates a link between additives and preservatives in the diet and levels of hyperactivity (McCann *et al.*, 2007); and at least a small proportion of children with ADHD demonstrate idiosyncratic reactions to some natural foods and/or artificial additives, and may be helped by a carefully applied exclusion diet (see Chapter 9).

Richardson (2004) reviewed the evidence on associations between ADHD and long-chain polyunsaturated fatty acids (PUFA) and commented on the brain's need throughout life for adequate supplies, a relative lack of omega-3 PUFA, and a possibility that males may be more vulnerable because testosterone may impair PUFA synthesis. Scientific uncertainties remain, however, concerning the physiological significance of different measures of PUFA metabolism and they are not used in practice.

*Psychosocial factors*

ADHD has been associated with severe early psychosocial adversity, for instance, in children who have survived depriving institutional care (Roy *et al.*, 2000). The mechanisms are not known but may include a failure to acquire cognitive and emotional control.

Disrupted and discordant relationships are more common in the families of young people with ADHD (Biederman *et al.*, 1992). Discordant family relationships, however, may be as much a consequence of living with a child with ADHD as a risk for the disorder itself. In established ADHD, discordant relationships with a harsh parenting style are a risk factor for developing oppositional and conduct problems. Parental hostility and criticism can be reduced in children where ADHD symptoms have been successfully treated with stimulants (Schachar *et al.*, 1997). Parents themselves may also have unrecognised and untreated ADHD, which may adversely affect their ability to manage a child with the disorder.

## 2.5 CURRENT CARE AND TREATMENT OF ADHD FOR CHILDREN IN THE NHS

### 2.5.1 Recognition and treatment strategies

The provision of treatments and interventions for children, young people and their families who have ADHD is varied. The ability to recognise and diagnose the disorder and the way in which services are provided and organised for this identified group are inconsistent as services move towards providing comprehensive child and adolescent mental health services (CAMHS) (Department of Health, 2004). The identification of affected people is unsystematic and driven largely by the extent to which parents are knowledgeable about the condition or recognise that their child might have hyperactive behaviour (Sayal *et al.*, 2002, 2006a). Historically, services for affected children and young people have mostly been provided by CAMHS, psychiatrists with a specialism in learning disability, or paediatricians based in child development centres or in community child health departments.

The willingness of children, young people and their families to seek help has sometimes been compromised by stigma associated with mental health services. Referral pathways can be complicated, and are subject to considerable variation in the local organisation of mental health services for children and young people. There can be difficulties with awareness and recognition of the symptoms by healthcare professionals in schools, primary and secondary care and by the other professionals who come into contact with this group (Schacher & Tannock, 2002).

Treatments and interventions for ADHD are varied and provided in a variety of settings, usually including specialist CAMHS or paediatric clinics.

### Psychological therapies, parent training and other support

Psychological therapies include psychoeducational input, behavioural therapy, cognitive behavioural therapy (CBT) in individual and group formats, interpersonal psychotherapy (IPT), family therapy, school-based interventions, social skills training and parent management training to encourage the development of coping strategies for managing the behavioural disturbance of ADHD (Taylor *et al.*, 2004; Fonagy *et al.*, 2002). Advice is sometimes given to schools and residential institutions.

Remedial disciplines such as occupational therapy and speech and language therapy are sometimes involved in helping the development of individual children.

Families of children and young people who have ADHD may require social support for example, child care relief, help in the home and family support workers.

### Dietary measures

Dietary supplements or restrictions are not commonly provided by health services as interventions for ADHD, but they are nevertheless used by many families, sometimes with advice from voluntary or private sectors. Paediatric dietitians are occasionally involved, especially when potentially hazardous regimes, such as exclusion diets, are contemplated.

### Medication

In the UK, atomoxetine, dexamfetamine and methylphenidate are licensed for the management of ADHD in children and young people. The NICE technology appraisal (TA98) (NICE, 2006b) has concluded that these medications are effective in controlling the symptoms of ADHD relative to no treatment.

Methylphenidate is a central nervous system (CNS) stimulant. Its action has been linked to inhibition of the dopamine transporter, with consequent increases in dopamine available for synaptic transmission (Volkow *et al.*, 1998). It is a Schedule 2 controlled drug and is currently licensed for use in children over 6 years old (see the Summary of Product Characteristics for Ritalin [Novartis Pharmaceuticals UK Ltd, 2007], Equasym [UCB Pharma Limited, 2006], Equasym XL [UCB Pharma

Limited, 2008], Concerta XL [Janssen-Cilag Ltd, 2008a & b], Medikinet (tablets) [Flynn Pharma Ltd, 2007a], Medikinet XL [Flynn Pharma Ltd, 2007b]; all available from http://emc.medicines.org.uk). Both immediate-release (IR) and modified-release (MR) formulations are available in the UK. Common adverse effects include insomnia, nervousness, headache, decreased appetite, abdominal pain and other gastrointestinal symptoms, cardiovascular effects such as tachycardia, palpitations and minor increases in blood pressure. Growth can be affected, at least in the short term, so height and weight are monitored regularly and plotted on growth charts (*BNF for Children*; British Medical Association *et al.*, 2005).

Dexamfetamine is a sympathomimetic amine with a central stimulant and anorectic activity and is licensed as an adjunct in the management of refractory hyperkinetic states in children from 3 years old (see the Summary of Product Characteristics for Dexedrine [UCB Pharma Limited, 2005], available at http://emc.medicines.org.uk). Dexamfetamine is also a Schedule 2 controlled drug. The common adverse effects are similar to those of methylphenidate. Dexamfetamine is unlikely to be used as a first-line treatment for the majority of children or young people with ADHD because of a greater potential for diversion and misuse than the other medications (NICE, 2006b).

Atomoxetine is a selective noradrenaline reuptake inhibitor. It is licensed for the treatment of ADHD in children 6 years and older and in young people (see the Summary of Product Characteristic for Strattera [Eli Lilly and Company Ltd, 2008], available at http://emc.medicines.org.uk). Common adverse effects are abdominal pain, decreased appetite, nausea and vomiting, early morning awakening, irritability and mood swings. Increased heart rate and small increases in blood pressure have been observed in clinical trials. Cases of hepatic disorders associated with atomoxetine have been reported, and patients and parents should be advised of the risk and how to recognise the symptoms of hepatic disorders (*BNF for Children*; British Medical Association *et al.*, 2005). Furthermore, reports of suicidal ideation in a small number of affected children have led to recommendations that clinicians and parents should be alerted to a possible risk of self-harm.

Other medications, including atypical antipsychotics, bupropion, nicotine, clonidine, modafinil, tricyclic and other antidepressants are occasionally prescribed off-label to patients who do not respond to licensed medications. These drugs were not included in the NICE TA98 (NICE, 2006b).

Medications should only be initiated by an appropriately qualified healthcare professional with expertise in ADHD after a comprehensive assessment. Continued prescribing and monitoring of medications may be performed by GPs, under shared care arrangements (NICE, 2006b).


## 2.5.2    Multi-agency working

Multi-agency working in relation to ADHD currently appears to present a number of challenges. There appears to be potential for issues to arise regarding how paediatricians and psychiatrists work together. Both groups of professionals have individuals with ADHD on their caseload, but often there is only an informal arrangement in place regarding who takes which case. This informal approach may lead to disagreements regarding diagnosis and a lack of parity regarding the service provided and treatment options. In addition, while services do report including representatives from education as part of their team or steering group, and a few include representatives from the youth justice service and the voluntary sector, very few report inclusion of representatives from social services. It may be that collaborative working in this area is hampered at times by different models of disability and how to respond to it held by different agencies. Parents and carers also need to be able to be part of steering groups.

A number of successful multi-professional teams for ADHD are emerging with protocols for multi-professional working, including the role of GPs in monitoring aspects of care. There remain, however, difficulties regarding transitional arrangements between CAMHS and adult mental health services (AMHS), and a general lack of support for adults with ADHD because of the difficulties associated with getting a diagnosis and treatment. This is discussed further in Section 2.7. Furthermore, the parents of young people with ADHD often have mental health problems themselves, and find it difficult to get support from AMHS.

### 2.5.3    Health services for children and young people with ADHD

Children and young people with possible ADHD should have access to local services that can provide appropriate assessment and ongoing support. Services nationally remain highly variable regarding the number and range of professionals providing the service, models of service provision, the age of transition into adult provision, waiting times for first appointments and whether the needs of children with a learning disability are met by the service.

Children identified as requiring assessment for ADHD are generally seen by tier 1 services and then referred to more specialist services for full assessment or treatment. Referrals into health services may be made to primary mental health workers, nurses, child psychiatrists, psychologists, and general or specialist paediatricians depending on local protocols and services. Children may therefore be assessed and treated by a range of professionals and there does appear to be a lack of consistent assessment and treatment protocols. In some services there is also a lack of availability of psychosocial approaches or the ability to assess or manage coexisting conditions.

*Transition to adult services*
The age of transition into AMHS continues to vary between the age of 16 and 19 with services working towards age 18 as recommended in the NSF for Children (Department of Health, 2004). The transition between services remains a challenge in some areas because of different thresholds for referral into AMHS and models of service provision. Unfortunately there continue to be gaps in provision for some young people once they have left Children's Services with GPs continuing to monitor and prescribe medication for ADHD without specialist advice or support.

## 2.6     ADHD FROM AN EDUCATIONAL PERSPECTIVE

Many studies (for example, Barkley *et al.*, 1990) have noted that children with ADHD achieve lower grades in academic subjects than their peers. More recently this trend has been found for children with teacher-identified ADHD characteristics (Merrell & Tymms, 2001; McGee *et al.*, 2002; Merrell & Tymms, 2005a). Such children, identified at the end of their first year at school, have significantly lower reading and mathematics attainment at that point than children with no observed behavioural problems. By the end of primary school they have fallen even further behind, in particular those children with symptoms of inattention. Wolraich and colleagues also suggest that inattention is a key ingredient of poor academic achievement (Wolraich *et al.*, 2003). Using rating scales based on the diagnostic criteria published in DSM-IV-TR, the proportion of children observed by their class teachers to be inattentive, hyperactive and/or impulsive in the classroom has been estimated to be between 8.1 and 17% (Wolraich *et al.*, 1996; Gaub & Carlson, 1997; Merrell & Tymms, 2001; Wolraich *et al.*, 2003). A later study by Wolraich and colleagues (2004) found that teachers' screening of elementary pupils gave a higher estimate of 25% of their pupils having a high risk of ADHD.

When children start school, aged 4 or 5 years, their teachers could be very well placed to identify ADHD characteristics. The challenges of the school setting are likely to make those difficulties more obvious and may be picked up by teachers who are experienced in observing a wide range of children's behaviour. However, Bailey (2006) warns that inattentive, hyperactive and impulsive behaviour could be a reaction to the expectations and constraints of the school environment, and it is important to bear in mind that this might be the case for some children.

Theoretically, once children with ADHD symptoms have been identified, further assessment can be undertaken and interventions put in place at an early stage, although Tymms and Merrell's (2006) research did not support screening. Early interventions can be successful in reducing behavioural problems and negative outcomes and the earlier they are implemented, the better (Farrington, 1994). O'Shaughnessy and colleagues (2003) have suggested that coordinated school-wide identification and interventions for children with behavioural problems increase the likelihood of improving their outcomes. Even though many studies have found that classroom-based interventions have a positive impact on the behaviour of children with ADHD and to a lesser extent on their academic progress (Purdie *et al.,* 2002), at the present time teachers in England are not systematically trained to use these classroom management and teaching strategies.

All children and young people, including those with ADHD, have the right to a school experience that provides a broad, balanced and relevant curriculum, including the National Curriculum, which is appropriately differentiated according to their needs. This has implications for the provision of initial teacher training and in-service professional development. Furthermore, a whole school approach to promoting positive behaviour outside as well as inside the classroom is desirable, therefore training should extend to non-teaching members of staff (Philbrick *et al.*, 2004). Several studies have shown that teachers' and student teachers' perceived competence in the management of children with ADHD in the classroom is variable and is correlated with their professional knowledge and experience (Avramidis, 2000; Bekle, 1994; Sciutto *et al.*, 2000). At the present time training is lacking, as illustrated by the report from the Education and Skills Select Committee's inquiry into special educational needs (House of Commons Education and Skills Committee, 2006), which recommended that 'the Government needs to radically increase investment in training its workforce so that all staff, including teaching staff, are fully equipped and resourced to improve outcomes for children with special educational needs (SEN) and disabilities'.

## 2.7    ADULTS WITH ADHD

### 2.7.1    Treatment strategies for adults

The treatment strategies for adults with ADHD are essentially similar to those used in childhood. There are, however, some key differences that need to be taken into account. Identification has been uncommon in the UK, and there are currently very few specialist services in the NHS and only a few that offer diagnostic or treatment services within generic AMHS. Psychological treatment is not routinely offered to adults with ADHD and there have been few attempts to quantify the benefits of such interventions. Adults with ADHD are currently seen in a few specialist clinics and include both transitional cases diagnosed in childhood as well as adults who were not diagnosed during childhood. In many cases adults with ADHD have been diagnosed and treated for coexisting symptoms and syndromes. Because of the increased rates of ADHD among close family members, many have children with ADHD, and need additional help to provide effective support for their children.

*Medication*
While the number of drug trials in adults is far smaller than in children, they consistently demonstrate the effectiveness of stimulants to reduce the level of ADHD symptoms in adults fulfilling diagnostic criteria for ADHD. Treatment regimes in adults are similar to those used in children, although in a few cases higher doses are used. Although stimulants are the most studied and most effective treatment for ADHD in children and adults, their use in adults remains controversial across Europe. In the UK, treatment of ADHD in children has dramatically changed in the last decade with a marked increase in the diagnosis of ADHD and a doubling of stimulant prescriptions between 1998 and 2004 (NICE, 2006b). However, this change in perspective is only slowly filtering through to those engaged in treating the adult population. It remains an anomaly that many drugs that are considered to be safe and effective in children and young people are not licensed for use in adults.

Trial evidence for medication effects on ADHD in adults is described in Chapter 10. Stimulants are usually the first-choice pharmacological treatment for ADHD in both children and adults. In the UK, both methylphenidate and dexamfetamine are available, although as yet remain unlicensed for use in adults. There is some evidence regarding the safety and effectiveness of stimulants in children, and an increasing amount of evidence for efficacy in adults. The effects of stimulants on ADHD symptoms are different from many other psychiatric treatments, as there is an immediate effect, starting within 30 minutes of an initial dose and continuing for 3 to 4 hours in the case of IR preparations. These preparations have to be taken several times throughout the day. MR preparations, which last approximately 8 to 12 hours and are usually taken only once a day, are particularly useful for those who become forgetful or disorganised once the effects of the medication begin to wear off.

The second-line choice of medication for ADHD in adults is usually atomoxetine. Third-line choices include bupropion, modafinil and antidepressants with noradrenergic effects such as imipramine, venlafaxine and reboxetine, although there is less consistent evidence for these medications in the reduction of ADHD symptoms in adults. Trial evidence is described in Chapter 10. Atomoxetine is licensed in the US for the treatment of ADHD in both children and adults, although in the UK it is only licensed for treatment of adults who started atomoxetine in childhood or adolescence.

*Psychological treatments*
Psychotherapeutic interventions that have been used to treat adults with ADHD include psychoeducation, use of support groups, skills training, CBT, coaching and counselling.

Psychological interventions applying a cognitive paradigm to teach strategies to manage ADHD have been used in adults with ADHD (Stevenson *et al.*, 2003; Stevenson *et al.*, 2002; Wilens *et al.*, 1999), usually as a complementary treatment to the use of stimulant medication, although they may be sufficient for adults where considerable moderation of symptoms has occurred with age. Qualitative research has suggested that psychological support begins at the time of diagnosis, following which adults with ADHD go through a process of adjustment in coming to terms with their diagnosis and the impact of the disorder on their lives (Young *et al.*, 2008a). Psychological treatment can then shift to focus on the treatment of coexisting psychiatric problems, psychological problems and skills deficits (Young, 1999, 2002; Young & Bramham, 2007). The aim is to help people develop methods to give structure to daily living and to improve interpersonal skills so they may function more successfully and achieve their potential. Indeed there is a strong evidence base for psychological treatment of many psychiatric problems that are associated with ADHD.

Other forms of psychotherapy such as counselling or client-based psychotherapies have had a role in helping some individuals come to terms with and better understand the way ADHD has influenced their personal and emotional lives. Coaching interventions parallel a mentoring paradigm by supporting people with ADHD to rehearse newly learned skills on a daily basis; these have been used as an adjunct to cognitive group programmes for adults with ADHD (Stevenson *et al.*, 2002, 2003). Formal studies of the effectiveness of psychotherapy and coaching have not yet been carried out, but many adults with ADHD report that they gain benefit from these approaches.

## 2.7.2    Special issues for adults diagnosed with ADHD

*Educational and occupational disadvantage*

Adults with ADHD commonly report a history of erratic academic performance and underachievement. These problems begin in primary school years and often continue into adolescence and young adulthood. This is a time when young people have important decisions to make regarding their future, yet, compared with their peers, young people with ADHD are less likely to make plans (Young *et al.*, 2005a). Academic difficulties are most likely strongly associated with ADHD symptoms. Individual or small group tuition, additional time in examinations (in a separate room if necessary), help with time management, goal setting, task prioritisation and study techniques, may help reduce their impact.

With increasing age, in further education and/or the workplace, young people are expected to take greater personal responsibility for structuring and organising their time, prioritising tasks and meeting deadlines. This may explain why adults with ADHD often underachieve academically compared with the expectations and achievements of their family members. They often deviate from family expectations of job status by being employed in significantly lower-ranking jobs than those of their siblings. While some individuals with ADHD find work that is compatible with their symptoms, many report higher rates of employment problems, including a higher turnover of jobs and periods of unemployment. They also try out many different types of occupations as opposed to developing a career (Young *et al.*, 2003).

*Substance misuse*

The reason for the increased level of substance use disorders among individuals with ADHD is complex. ADHD is a risk factor for substance use disorders through three potential mechanisms: (1) increased levels of reward-seeking (risk-taking) behaviours; (2) increased level of psychosocial impairments (oppositional defiant disorder and conduct disorder in childhood that are themselves associated with substance misuse); and (3) self-medication for ADHD symptoms.

In most cases severe substance use disorders should be treated first because of the known risks and impairments associated with such behaviour. Ongoing substance misuse will interfere with evaluation of ADHD treatment response – interactions will emerge and side effects can be intensified. While all substance use should be minimised before the start of pharmacological treatment, it should be recognised that the persistence of ADHD symptoms may maintain substance misuse in order to supplement medication to treat symptoms. Self-treatment with stimulants is however infrequent, while use of alcohol and cannabis to dampen down symptoms associated with adult ADHD is far more common.

The concerns of some professionals that the use of stimulants in ADHD may lead to drug misuse either by sensitisation or as gateway to other drugs is not supported by available evidence. Although there may be a risk that some individuals with drug misuse problems may sell stimulants, it is important to note that when stimulants are used appropriately by adults they are not habit forming or addictive, and they do not cause euphoria. Furthermore, there is evidence from follow-up studies that the appropriate treatment of ADHD with stimulants is associated with a reduction in substance abuse disorders (Wilens *et al.*, 2008).

*Association with crime*

Early onset and persistent antisocial behaviour is commonly associated with ADHD. Longitudinal studies have shown that ADHD independently predicts the development of antisocial behaviour, a developmental trajectory thought to be mediated by familial environmental influences (Bambinski *et al.*, 1999; Taylor *et al.*, 1996).

The association between ADHD and crime is becoming increasingly recognised and regarded with concern. Studies conducted in the US, Canada, Sweden, Germany, Finland and Norway suggest that around two-thirds of young offender institutions and up to half of the adult prison population screened positively for ADHD in childhood and many continued to be symptomatic (for review see Young, 2007b). A sizeable number of individuals may have mild symptoms, and are in partial remission from their ADHD symptoms. All these studies have limitations in their methodologies, nevertheless it seems that the rate of young people and adults with ADHD in the prison population far exceeds that reported in the general population (that is, 3–4% of children and 1% of adults).

ADHD has been associated with early onset of criminal behaviour, even before the age of 11, and high rates of recidivism have been found in studies of young people with ADHD detained in institutions (Rosler *et al.*, 2004). Young people are likely to have more severe and pervasive symptoms than older offenders detained in adult prisons, and this most likely accounts for the much higher prevalence of ADHD reported in young offender institutions. For such young people the 'revolving door' between prison and probation and the community is most likely strongly associated with the severity of their ADHD symptoms.

A meta-analysis of 20 ADHD studies reported a strong association between measures of ADHD and criminal/delinquent behaviour (Pratt *et al.*, 2002) and concluded that ADHD is a factor that should be considered in the delivery of treatment services for offenders, starting with early intervention programmes and going on to rehabilitation and supervision of adult offenders.

*Differential diagnosis and mistaken diagnosis*

In adulthood, coexisting conditions include personality disorder (particularly antisocial and borderline), bipolar disorder, obsessive-compulsive disorder and, to a lesser extent, psychotic disorders. Adults with severe mental illness, such as schizophrenia, or severe learning disability often have problems with attention and activity levels yet these disorders do not occur any more frequently in people with ADHD than in the normal population (Mannuzza *et al.*, 1998).

However, there is a difficulty in that attentional problems are common to many psychiatric disorders; thus adults with other psychiatric problems may appear to have symptoms of ADHD. On the other hand this also means that there is a pool of adult psychiatric patients in whom the diagnosis of ADHD has been unidentified and where ineffective treatments have been put in place for alternative diagnoses such as anxiety, depression, cyclothymia and personality disorder. This may account for the high rates of contact reported with mental health services for adults with ADHD (Dalsgaard *et al.*, 2002), which in turn has associated cost implications.

ADHD in adults is frequently misdiagnosed because there are potential 'traps' for the inexperienced ADHD diagnostician. ADHD in adulthood does not present in the same way as ADHD in children who, for example, have more symptoms of hyperactivity. The age criterion is crucial to distinguish ADHD from later onset conditions and, unless care is taken to rule out the existence of the other conditions, there may be a high rate of falsely identified cases.

Psychopathology overlaps with other psychiatric conditions in two main ways. First, the chronic trait-like characteristics of ADHD symptoms that start in early childhood and persist into adulthood are frequently mistaken for traits of a personality disorder. This occurs, in particular, for cluster B personality disorders (that is, antisocial, borderline and emotionally unstable personality disorders) as these include symptoms that are commonly associated with adult ADHD such as mood instability, impulsivity and anger outbursts. Second, the volatile and irritable mood frequently reported by adults with ADHD is a symptom that overlaps with that seen in major affective disorders. Both bipolar disorder and ADHD are characterised by hyperactivity, distractibility, inattentiveness and mood changes. The distinction, however, is that the mood state of ADHD is irritable and volatile, rather than containing elements of euphoria and grandiosity. More recently, it has been argued that 'juvenile mania' of very early onset is characterised by a mood of irritability rather than euphoria, and by chronicity rather than fluctuation. If this change of definition is accepted, then this distinction from ADHD in young people will become highly problematic.

## 2.8    THE ECONOMIC COST OF ADHD

The current estimated prevalence of children and young people with ADHD in the UK is 3.62% in boys and 0.85% in girls (Ford *et al.*, 2003). Based on these figures and national population statistics (Office for National Statistics, 2007) it can be estimated that about 210,000 children aged 5 to 18 years are affected by ADHD in England and Wales, although only a minority of them will seek or receive medical treatment (Sayal *et al.*, 2002, 2006a). It has been estimated that in England and Wales, children with ADHD place a significant cost on health, social and education services, reaching £23 million for initial specialist assessment, and £14 million annually for follow-up care, excluding medication (King *et al.*, 2006). These figures do not include costs incurred by adults with ADHD to health and social services.

In 2006, the total annual cost of prescribed stimulants and other drugs for ADHD in England was roughly £29 million, comprising a 20% increase from the previous year (NHS Health and Social Care Information Centre, 2006; NHS Information Centre, 2007). This increase in cost is attributed in part to the increased numbers of individuals being treated, and in part to a shift in prescribing towards more expensive MR formulations. Schlander (2007) estimated that, in 2012, the ADHD pharmacotherapy expenditures for children and young people may exceed £78 million in England, owing to an increase in the number of diagnosed cases, growing acceptance and intensity of pharmacotherapy, and higher unit costs of novel medications. Nevertheless, the current £29 million annual cost of prescribed drugs for ADHD in England is rather low compared with annual costs of drugs prescribed for other chronic conditions such as depression (£292 million) and diabetes (£562 million) (The Information Centre, 2006).

UK data on the economic cost of ADHD are limited; since figures from the US relate to a very different pattern of service provision they cannot be generalised to the UK. Costs in the US have increased over the years due to a constantly increasing rate of identification by clinicians, with identification by paediatricians from 1.4% of children in 1979 to 9.2% in 1996 (Kelleher *et al.*, 2000). Birnbaum and colleagues (2005) estimated that the total cost of ADHD in the US was $31.6 billion in 2000 prices, using a prevalence of 8% for boys, 4% for girls, 5% for male adults and 3.5% for female adults. Of this cost, only 5% ($1.6 billion) related directly to treatment of the condition; the rest constituted other healthcare costs of children and adults with ADHD ($12.1 billion or 38%), healthcare costs of family members of individuals with ADHD (a striking $14.2 billion or 45%), and productivity losses of adults with ADHD and adult family members of persons with ADHD ($3.7 billion or 12%). These figures express excess costs, that is, additional costs of people with ADHD and their families, over and above respective costs of comparable control individuals. Pelham and colleagues (2007) reported an estimated annual cost of ADHD in children and young people approximately $14,600 per individual in 2005 prices (range from $12,000 to $17,500), consisting of healthcare costs (18%), costs to the education system (34%), as well as costs associated with crime and delinquency (48%). Using a prevalence rate of 5%, the authors estimated a total cost of children and people with ADHD in the US reaching $42.5 billion (range from $36 to $52.5 billion).

Children with ADHD have been found to incur similar healthcare costs in the US to children with asthma (Chan *et al.*, 2002; Kelleher *et al.*, 2001) and significantly higher than those of children without ADHD (Chan *et al.*, 2002; Burd *et al.*, 2003a; DeBar *et al.*, 2004; de Ridder & de Graeve, 2006; Leibson *et al.*, 2001; Swensen *et al.*, 2003; Hakkaart-van Roijen *et al.*, 2007; Guevara *et al.*, 2001). This difference in costs was found to be related to a higher frequency in contacts with general practitioners (GPs) and outpatient mental health services, visits to emergency departments and hospitalisations (DeBar *et al.*, 2004; de Ridder & de Graeve, 2006; Leibson *et al.*, 2001; Guevara *et al.*, 2001). Moreover, children with ADHD are more likely to have other psychiatric coexisting conditions such as conduct disorder, oppositional defiant disorder, depression and so on, compared with children without ADHD (Burd *et al.*, 2003b), which significantly increase use of healthcare services and associated costs (Burd *et al.*, 2003b; Hakkaart-van Roijen *et al.*, 2007; Guevara *et al.*, 2001; DeBar *et al.*, 2004). Children with ADHD are also much more likely to have learning difficulties and to incur higher educational costs than children without ADHD; these costs may include costs of special education and the cost of either a school nurse or office staff administering medication to children with ADHD (Guevara & Mandell, 2003).

Adults with ADHD also incur high healthcare costs relative to matched adults without ADHD (Secnik *et al.*, 2005a), despite the relatively low treatment rates of ADHD in this age cohort, estimated roughly at 25% in the US (Birnbaum *et al.*, 2005).

Adults with ADHD are more likely to have a comorbid diagnosis of asthma, depression, anxiety, bipolar disorder, antisocial personality disorder and alcohol or drug misuse, which contributes further to the magnitude of medical expenses (Secnik *et al.*, 2005a). However, even after controlling for the impact of coexisting conditions, adults with ADHD have been found to have higher inpatient and outpatient costs, as well as prescription drug costs. The annual estimated cost of an adult with ADHD in the US was $5,600 in 2001 prices, versus $2,700 for a matched adult without ADHD (Secnik *et al.*, 2005a). It must be noted, however, that adult ADHD incurs lower healthcare costs per person compared with other chronic conditions, such as depression or diabetes (Hinnenthal *et al.*, 2005). Further to the increase in healthcare costs, the presence of ADHD in adults is associated with increased productivity losses because of absenteeism (Kessler *et al.*, 2005; Secnik *et al.*, 2005a) and decrements in work performance (Kessler *et al.*, 2005).

Apart from affected individuals, the carers and families of people with ADHD also bear substantial costs in terms of out-of-pocket expenses as well as productivity losses related to reduced ability to work and absenteeism (de Ridder & de Graeve, 2006; Hakkaart-van Roijen *et al.*, 2007; Swensen *et al.*, 2003). In addition, families of children with ADHD suffer a significant emotional burden, comprising strained family relationships (parent-child or sibling interactions), parenting distress and worry, and marital discord (Hankin *et al.*, 2001). Additional costs are related to increased accident rates (Jerome *et al.*, 2006).

It is evident, from the above review, that ADHD is associated with a significant financial and emotional costs to the healthcare system, education services, carers and families and society as a whole. Providing effective treatment will improve the quality of life of individuals with ADHD, their carers and their families, and at the same time will reduce the financial implications and psychological burden of ADHD to society.

# 3. METHODS USED TO DEVELOP THIS GUIDELINE

## 3.1 OVERVIEW

The development of this guideline drew upon methods outlined by NICE (*The Guidelines Manual*[1] [NICE, 2006c]). A team of healthcare professionals, lay representatives and technical experts known as the Guideline Development Group (GDG), with support from the NCCMH staff, undertook the development of a patient-centred, evidence-based guideline. There are six basic steps in the process of developing a guideline:

- define the scope, which sets the parameters of the guideline and provides a focus and steer for the development work
- define clinical questions considered important for practitioners and service users
- develop criteria for evidence searching and search for evidence
- design validated protocols for systematic review and apply to evidence recovered by search
- synthesise and (meta-) analyse data retrieved, guided by the clinical questions, and produce evidence summaries and profiles
- answer clinical questions with evidence-based recommendations for clinical practice.

The clinical practice recommendations made by the GDG are therefore derived from the most up-to-date and robust evidence base for the clinical and cost effectiveness of the treatments and services used in the treatment and management of ADHD. In addition, to ensure a service user and carer focus, the concerns of service users and carers regarding health and social care have been highlighted and addressed by recommendations agreed by the whole GDG.

## 3.2 THE SCOPE

Guideline topics are selected by the Department of Health and the Welsh Assembly Government, which identify the main areas to be covered by the guideline in a specific remit (for further information see *The Guidelines Manual*[2] [NICE, 2006c]). The remit for this guideline was translated into a scope document by staff at the NCCMH (see Appendix 1).

---

[1] Available from: www.nice.org.uk
[2] Available from: www.nice.org.uk

The purpose of the scope was to:

- provide an overview of what the guideline will include and exclude
- identify the key aspects of care that must be included
- set the boundaries of the development work and provide a clear framework to enable work to stay within the priorities agreed by NICE and the NCCMH and the remit from the Department of Health/Welsh Assembly Government
- inform the development of the clinical questions and search strategy
- inform professionals and the public about the expected content of the guideline
- keep the guideline to a reasonable size to ensure that its development can be carried out within the allocated period.

The draft scope was subject to consultation with registered stakeholders over a 4-week period. During the consultation period, the scope was posted on the NICE website (www.nice.org.uk). Comments were invited from stakeholder organisations and the Guideline Review Panel (GRP). Further information about the GRP can also be found on the NICE website. The NCCMH and NICE reviewed the scope in light of comments received, and the revised scope was signed off by the GRP.

## 3.3     THE GUIDELINE DEVELOPMENT GROUP

The GDG consisted of: professionals in clinical child and adolescent psychiatry, clinical child and adolescent psychology (and neuropsychology), psychiatry for learning disorders, developmental paediatrics, paediatrics (neurodisability), general practice and nursing; academic experts in child and adolescent psychiatry, paediatric medicine research, forensic clinical psychology, and education; service users and carers. In order to ascertain the experiences of children and young people of stimulant medication for ADHD, the NCCMH commissioned a focus group study. The guideline development process was supported by staff from the NCCMH, who undertook the clinical and health economics literature searches, reviewed and presented the evidence to the GDG, managed the process and contributed to drafting the guideline.

### 3.3.1    Guideline Development Group meetings

Twenty GDG meetings were held between March 2006 and May 2008. During each day-long GDG meeting, in a plenary session, clinical questions and clinical evidence were reviewed and assessed and recommendations formulated and reviewed. At each meeting, all GDG members declared any potential conflicts of interest, and the concerns of the service users and carers were routinely discussed as part of a standing agenda.

### 3.3.2    Topic groups

The GDG divided its workload along clinically relevant lines to simplify the guideline development process, and GDG members formed smaller topic groups to undertake guideline work in that area of clinical practice. Topic group 1 covered questions relating to diagnosis and assessment; topic group 2 covered psychological interventions; topic group 3 covered pharmacological interventions; topic group 4 covered education interventions; and topic group 5 covered dietary interventions. These groups were designed to manage the large volume of evidence appraisal efficiently before presenting it to the GDG as a whole. Each topic group was chaired by a GDG member with expert knowledge of the topic area (one of the healthcare professionals). Topic groups refined the clinical definitions of treatment interventions, reviewed and prepared the evidence with the systematic reviewer before presenting it to the GDG as a whole, and helped the GDG to identify further exper-tise in the topic. Topic group leaders reported the status of the group's work as part of the standing agenda. They also introduced and led the GDG discussion of the evidence review for that topic and assisted the GDG Chair in drafting that section of the guideline relevant to the work of each topic group.

### 3.3.3    Service users and carers

Individuals with direct experience of services gave an integral service-user focus to the GDG and the guideline. The GDG included carers and a service user. They contributed as full GDG members to writing the clinical questions, helping to ensure that the evidence addressed their views and preferences, highlighting sensitive issues and terminology associated with ADHD, and bringing service-user research to the attention of the GDG. In drafting the guideline, they contributed to the editing of the first draft of the guideline's introduction and to the writing of Chapter 4, and identified recommendations from the perspective of service users and carers.

### 3.3.4    Special advisers

Special advisers, who had specific expertise in one or more aspects of treatment and management relevant to the guideline, assisted the GDG, commenting on specific aspects of the developing guideline and making presentations to the GDG. Appendix 3 lists those who agreed to act as special advisers.

### 3.3.5    National and international experts

National and international experts in the area under review were identified through the literature search and through the experience of the GDG members. These experts were contacted to recommend unpublished or soon-to-be published studies in order to ensure up-to-date evidence was included in the development of the guideline. They informed the group about completed trials at the pre-publication stage, systematic reviews in the process of being published, studies relating to the cost effectiveness of treatment and trial data if the GDG could be provided with full access to the complete trial report. Appendix 5 lists researchers who were contacted.

## 3.4    CLINICAL QUESTIONS

Clinical questions were used to guide the identification and interrogation of the evidence base relevant to the topic of the guideline. The questions were developed using a modified nominal group technique. The process began by asking each topic group of the GDG to submit as many questions as possible. The questions were then collated and refined by the review team. The GDG members were then asked to rate each question for importance. At a subsequent meeting, the GDG Chair facilitated a discussion to further refine the questions. The results of this process were then discussed and consensus reached about which questions would be of primary importance and which would be secondary. The GDG aimed to address all primary questions, while secondary questions would only be covered time permitting. The PICO (patient, intervention, comparison and outcome) framework was used to help formulate questions about interventions. This structured approach divides each question into four components: the patients (the population under study); the interventions (what is being done; or test/risk factor); the comparisons (other main treatment options); and the outcomes (the measures of how effective the interventions have been; or what is being predicted/prevented). Appendix 6 lists the clinical questions.

To help facilitate the literature review, a note was made of the best study design type to answer each question. There are four main types of clinical question of relevance to NICE guidelines. These are listed in Text box 2. For each type of question

**Text box 2: Best study design to answer each type of question**

| Type of question | Best primary study design |
|---|---|
| Effectiveness or other impact of an intervention | Randomised controlled trial (RCT); other studies that may be considered in the absence of an RCT are the following: internally/externally controlled before and after trial, interrupted time-series |
| Accuracy of information (for example, risk factor, test, or prediction rule) | Comparing the information against a valid gold standard in a randomised trial inception cohort study |
| Rates (of disease, patient experience, rare side effects) | Cohort, registry, cross-sectional study |
| Costs | Naturalistic prospective cost study |

the best primary study design varies, where 'best' is interpreted as 'least likely to give misleading answers to the question'.

In all cases, however, a well-conducted systematic review of the appropriate type of study is likely to yield a better answer than a single study.

Deciding on the best design type to answer a specific clinical or public health question does not mean that studies of different design types addressing the same question were discarded.

## 3.5    SYSTEMATIC CLINICAL LITERATURE REVIEW

The aim of the clinical literature review was to identify and synthesise relevant evidence from the literature systematically in order to answer the specific clinical questions developed by the GDG. Thus, clinical practice recommendations are evidence-based, where possible, and if evidence was not available, informal consensus methods were used (see Section 3.5.7) and the need for future research was specified.

### 3.5.1    Methodology

A stepwise, hierarchical approach was taken to locating and presenting evidence to the GDG. The NCCMH developed this process based on methods set out in *The Guidelines Manual*[3] (NICE, 2006c) and after considering recommendations from a range of other sources. These included:

● Clinical Policy and Practice Program of the New South Wales Department of Health (Australia)
● Clinical Evidence Online
● The Cochrane Collaboration
● Grading of Recommendations: Assessment, Development, and Evaluation (GRADE) Working Group
● New Zealand Guidelines Group
● NHS Centre for Reviews and Dissemination
● Oxford Centre for Evidence-Based Medicine
● Oxford Systematic Review Development Programme
● Scottish Intercollegiate Guidelines Network (SIGN)
● United States Agency for Healthcare Research and Quality.

### 3.5.2    The review process

After the scope was finalised, a more extensive search for systematic reviews and published guidelines was undertaken. Existing NICE guidelines were updated where necessary.

---

[3]Available from: www.nice.org.uk

At this point, the review team, in conjunction with the GDG, developed an evidence map that detailed all comparisons necessary to answer the clinical questions. The initial approach taken to locating primary-level studies depended on the type of clinical question and availability of evidence.

The GDG decided which questions were best addressed by good practice based on expert opinion, which questions were likely to have a good evidence base and which questions were likely to have little or no directly relevant evidence. Recommendations based on good practice were developed by informal consensus of the GDG. For questions with a good evidence base, the review process depended on the type of clinical question (see below). For questions that were unlikely to have a good evidence base, a brief descriptive review was initially undertaken by a member of the GDG (see Section 3.5.7).

Searches for evidence were updated between 6 and 8 weeks before the stakeholder consultation. After this point, studies were included only if they were judged by the GDG to be exceptional (for example, the evidence was likely to change a recommendation).

### The search process for questions concerning interventions
For questions related to interventions, the initial evidence base was formed from well-conducted RCTs that addressed at least one of the clinical questions (the review process is illustrated in Flowchart 1). Although there are a number of difficulties with the use of RCTs in the evaluation of interventions in mental health, the RCT remains the most important method for establishing treatment efficacy. For other clinical questions, searches were for the appropriate study design (see above).

All searches were based on the standard mental health related bibliographic databases (EMBASE, MEDLINE, PsycINFO, Cochrane Library, ERIC) for all trials potentially relevant to the guideline. If the number of citations generated from this search was large (more than 5000), existing systematic reviews and question-specific search filters were developed to restrict the search while minimising loss of sensitivity.

Where the evidence base was large, recent high-quality English-language systematic reviews were used primarily as a source of RCTs (see Appendix 10 for quality criteria used to assess systematic reviews). In some circumstances, however, existing data sets were utilised. Where this was the case, data were cross-checked for accuracy before use. New RCTs meeting inclusion criteria set by the GDG were incorporated into the existing reviews and fresh analyses performed.

After the initial search results had been scanned liberally to exclude irrelevant papers, the review team used a purpose built 'study information' database to manage both the included and the excluded studies (eligibility criteria were developed after consultation with the GDG). For questions without good-quality evidence (after the initial search), a decision was made by the GDG about whether to (a) repeat the search using subject-specific databases (for example, CINAHL, AMED, SIGLE or PILOTS), (b) conduct a new search for lower levels of evidence, or (c) adopt a consensus process (see Section 3.5.7). Future guidelines will be able to update and

## Flowchart 1: Guideline review process

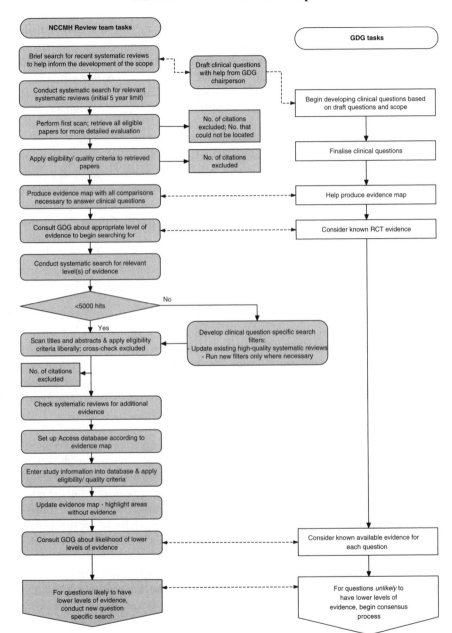

extend the usable evidence base starting from the evidence collected, synthesised and analysed for this guideline.

In addition, searches were made of the reference lists of all eligible systematic reviews and included studies, as well as the list of evidence submitted by stakeholders. Known experts in the field (see Appendix 5), based both on the references identified in early steps and on advice from GDG members, were sent letters requesting relevant studies that were in the process of being published.[4] In addition, the tables of contents of appropriate journals were periodically checked for relevant studies.

### *The search process for questions of diagnosis and prognosis*

For questions related to diagnosis and prognosis, the search process was the same as described above, except that the initial evidence base was formed from studies with the most appropriate and reliable design to answer the particular question. That is, for questions about diagnosis, the initial search was for systematic reviews and meta-analyses as well as cross-sectional, factor analytic, genetic and diagnostic studies; for questions about prognosis, it was for cohort studies of representative patients. In situations where it was not possible to identify a substantial body of appropriately designed studies that directly addressed each clinical question, a consensus process was adopted (see Section 3.5.7).

### *Search filters*

Search filters developed by the review team consisted of a combination of subject heading and free-text phrases. Specific filters were developed for the guideline topic, and where necessary, for each clinical question. In addition, the review team used filters developed for systematic reviews, RCTs and other appropriate research designs (see Appendix 8).

### *Study selection*

All primary-level studies included after the first scan of citations were acquired in full and re-evaluated for eligibility at the time they were being entered into the study information database (see Appendix 9 for screen shots of the database). Specific eligibility criteria were developed for each clinical question and are described in the relevant clinical evidence chapters. Eligible systematic reviews and primary-level studies were critically appraised for methodological quality (see Appendix 10 for the quality checklists). The eligibility of each study was confirmed by at least one member of the appropriate topic group.

For some clinical questions, it was necessary to prioritise the evidence with respect to the UK context (that is, external validity). To make this process explicit, the topic groups took into account the following factors when assessing the evidence:

● participant factors (for example, gender, age, ethnicity)

---

[4]Unpublished full trial reports were also accepted where sufficient information was available to judge eligibility and quality (see section on unpublished evidence).

- provider factors (for example, model fidelity, the conditions under which the intervention was performed and the availability of experienced staff to undertake the procedure)
- cultural factors (for example, differences in standard care and differences in the welfare system).

It was the responsibility of each topic group to decide which prioritisation factors were relevant to each clinical question in light of the UK context and then decide how they should modify their recommendations.

*Unpublished evidence*

The GDG used a number of criteria when deciding whether or not to accept unpublished data. First, the evidence must have been accompanied by a trial report containing sufficient detail to assess the quality of the data properly. Second, the evidence must be submitted with the understanding that data from the study and a summary of the study's characteristics would be published in the full guideline. Therefore, the GDG did not accept evidence submitted as commercial in confidence. Having said that, the GDG recognised that unpublished evidence submitted by investigators might later be retracted by those investigators if the inclusion of such data would jeopardise publication of their research.

### 3.5.3    Data extraction

Outcome data were extracted from all eligible studies, which met the quality criteria, into RevMan 4.2.10 (Review Manager, The Cochrane Centre, 2003) or Word tables. Studies with factor analysis were quality assessed using a checklist elaborated and agreed by the GDG members (see Chapter 5).

For each outcome, a hierarchy of most suitable outcome measures was agreed upon by the GDG members. If a study reported more than one relevant outcome measure for a given outcome, only the measure with the highest hierarchy was included in the meta-analysis.

For a given outcome (continuous and dichotomous), where more than 50% of the number randomised to any group were not accounted for by trial authors, the data were excluded from the review because of the risk of bias.[5] Where possible, however, dichotomous efficacy outcomes were calculated on an intention-to-treat basis (that is, a 'once-randomised-always-analyse' basis). This assumes that those participants who ceased to engage in the study – from whatever group – had an unfavourable outcome. This meant that the 50% rule was not applied to dichotomous outcomes where there was good evidence that those participants who ceased to engage in the study were likely to have an unfavourable outcome (in this case, early withdrawals were included in both the numerator and denominator). Adverse effects were entered into Review Manager as reported by the study authors because it was usually not

---

[5]'Accounted for' in this context means using an appropriate method for dealing with missing data (for example, last observation carried forward [LOCF] or a regression technique).

possible to determine whether early withdrawals had an unfavourable outcome. For the outcome 'leaving the study early for any reason', the denominator was the number randomised.

Where some of the studies failed to report standard deviations (for a continuous outcome), and where an estimate of the variance could not be computed from other reported data or obtained from the study author, the following approach was taken:[6]

1.  When the number of studies with missing standard deviations was small and when the total number of studies was large, the pooled standard deviation from all the other available studies in the same meta-analysis was used. In this case, the appropriateness of the imputation was made by comparing the standardised mean differences (SMDs) of those trials that had reported standard deviations against the hypothetical SMDs of the same trials based on the imputed standard deviations. If they converged, the meta-analytical results were considered to be reliable.

2.  When the number of studies with missing standard deviations was large or when the total number of studies was small, standard deviations were taken from a previous systematic review (where available), because the small sample size may allow unexpected deviation due to chance. In this case, the results were considered to be less reliable.

The meta-analysis of survival data, such as time to any mood episode, was based on log hazard ratios and standard errors. Since individual patient data were not available in included studies, hazard ratios and standard errors calculated from a Cox proportional hazard model were extracted. Where necessary, standard errors were calculated from confidence intervals (CIs) or p-value according to standard formulae (for example, Cochrane Reviewers' Handbook 4.2.2.). Data were summarised using the generic inverse variance method using Review Manager.

Consultation was used to overcome difficulties with coding. Data from studies included in existing systematic reviews were extracted independently by one reviewer and cross-checked with the existing data set. Where possible, two independent reviewers extracted data from new studies. Where double data extraction was not possible, data extracted by one reviewer was checked by the second reviewer. Disagreements were resolved with discussion. Where consensus could not be reached, a third reviewer resolved the disagreement. Masked assessment (that is, blind to the journal from which the article comes, the authors, the institution and the magnitude of the effect) was not used since it is unclear that doing so reduces bias (Jadad *et al.*, 1996; Berlin, 2001).

### 3.5.4 Synthesising the evidence

Where possible, meta-analysis was used to synthesise the evidence using Review Manager. If necessary, reanalyses of the data or sub-analyses were used to answer clinical questions not addressed in the original studies or reviews.

---

[6]Based on the approach suggested by Furukawa and colleagues (2006).

Dichotomous outcomes were analysed as relative risks (RR) with the associated 95% CI (for an example, see Figure 1). A relative risk (also called a risk ratio) is the ratio of the treatment event rate to the control event rate. An RR of 1 indicates no difference between treatment and control. In Figure 1, the overall RR of 0.73 indicates that the event rate (that is, non-remission rate) associated with intervention A is about three quarters of that with the control intervention or, in other words, the RR reduction is 27%.

**Figure 1: Example of a forest plot displaying dichotomous data**

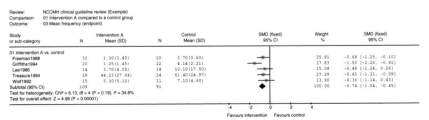

The CI shows with 95% certainty the range within which the true treatment effect should lie and can be used to determine statistical significance. If the CI does not cross the 'line of no effect', the effect is statistically significant.

Continuous outcomes were analysed as weighted mean differences (WMD), or as an SMD when different measures were used in different studies to estimate the same underlying effect (for an example, see Figure 2). If provided, intention-to-treat data, using a method such as 'last observation carried forward', were preferred over data from completers.

To check for consistency between studies, both the $I^2$ test of heterogeneity and a visual inspection of the forest plots were used. The $I^2$ statistic describes the proportion of total variation in study estimates that is due to heterogeneity (Higgins & Thompson, 2002). The $I^2$ statistic was interpreted in the follow way:

● Greater than 50%: notable heterogeneity (an attempt was made to explain the variation, for example outliers were removed from the analysis or sub-analyses were conducted to examine the possibility of moderators. If studies with heterogeneous results were found to be comparable, a random-effects model was used to summarise the results [DerSimonian & Laird, 1986]. In the random-effects analysis, heterogeneity is accounted for both in the width of CIs and in the

**Figure 2: Example of a forest plot displaying continuous data**

estimate of the treatment effect. With decreasing heterogeneity the random-effects approach moves asymptotically towards a fixed-effects model).

● 30 to 50%: moderate heterogeneity (both the chi-squared test of heterogeneity and a visual inspection of the forest plot were used to decide between a fixed and random-effects model)

● Less than 30%: mild heterogeneity (a fixed-effects model was used to synthesise the results).

To explore the possibility that the results entered into each meta-analysis suffered from publication bias, data from included studies were entered, where there was sufficient data, into a funnel plot. Asymmetry of the plot was taken to indicate possible publication bias and investigated further.

An estimate of the proportion of eligible data that were missing (because some studies did not include all relevant outcomes) was calculated for each analysis.

The Number Needed to Treat–Benefit (NNTB) or the Number Needed to Treat–Harm (NNTH) was reported for each outcome where the baseline risk (that is, control group event rate) was similar across studies. In addition, NNTs calculated at follow-up were only reported where the length of follow-up was similar across studies. When the length of follow-up or baseline risk varies (especially with low risk), the NNT is a poor summary of the treatment effect (Deeks, 2002).

Study characteristics tables, generated automatically from the study database, were used to summarise general information about each study (see Appendix 17). Where meta-analysis was not appropriate and/or possible, the reported results from each primary-level study were also presented in the included studies table (and included, where appropriate, in a narrative review).

### 3.5.5    Presenting the data to the GDG

Study characteristics tables and, where appropriate, forest plots generated with Review Manager were presented to the GDG in order to prepare a GRADE evidence profile table for each review and to develop recommendations.

*GRADE evidence profile tables*
A GRADE evidence profile was used to summarise both the quality of the evidence and the results of the evidence synthesis (see Table 4 for an example of an evidence profile). For each outcome, quality may be reduced depending on the study design, limitations (based on the quality of individual studies; see Appendix 10 for the quality checklists), inconsistency (see Section 3.5.4 for how consistency was measured), indirectness (that is, how closely the outcome measures, interventions and participants match those of interest), and imprecision (based on the CI around the effect size). For observational studies, the quality may be increased if there is a large effect, plausible confounding would have changed the effect, or there is evidence of a dose-response gradient (details would be provided under the other considerations column). Each evidence profile also included a summary of the findings: number of patients included in each group, an estimate of the magnitude of the effect, and the overall quality of the evidence for each outcome. The quality of the evidence was

## Table 4: Example of GRADE evidence profile

| No. of studies | Design | Quality assessment | | | | | Summary of findings | | | | Quality |
|---|---|---|---|---|---|---|---|---|---|---|---|
| | | Limitations | Inconsistency | Indirectness | Imprecision | Other considerations | No. of patients | | Effect | | |
| | | | | | | | Intervention | Control | Relative (95% CI) | Absolute | |
| **Outcome 1** | | | | | | | | | | | |
| 6 | randomised trial | no serious limitations | no serious inconsistency | no serious indirectness | serious[1] | none | 8/191 | 7/150 | RR 0.94 (0.39 to 2.23) | 0 fewer per 100 (from 3 fewer to 6 more) | ⊕⊕⊕◯ MODERATE |
| **Outcome 2** | | | | | | | | | | | |
| 6 | randomised trial | no serious limitations | no serious inconsistency | no serious indirectness | serious[2] | none | 55/236 | 63/196 | RR 0.44 (0.21 to 0.94)[3] | 18 fewer per 100 (from 2 fewer to 25 more) | ⊕⊕⊕◯ MODERATE |
| **Outcome 3** | | | | | | | | | | | |
| 3 | randomised trial | no serious limitations | no serious inconsistency | no serious indirectness | no serious imprecision | none | 83 | 81 | – | MD −1.51 (−3.81 to 0.8) | ⊕⊕⊕⊕ HIGH |

*Continued*

53

**Table 4:** (*Continued*)

| No. of studies | Design | Limitations | Inconsistency | Indirectness | Imprecision | Other considerations | No. of patients | | Effect | | Quality |
|---|---|---|---|---|---|---|---|---|---|---|---|
| | | | | | | | Intervention | Control | Relative (95% CI) | Absolute | |
| **Outcome 4** | | | | | | | | | | | |
| 3 | randomised trial | no serious limitations | no serious inconsistency | no serious indirectness | serious[4] | none | 88 | 93 | – | SMD −0.26 (−0.56 to 0.03) | ⊕⊕⊕◯ MODERATE |
| **Outcome 5** | | | | | | | | | | | |
| 4 | randomised trial | no serious limitations | no serious inconsistency | no serious indirectness | serious[4] | none | 109 | 114 | – | SMD −0.13 (−0.6 to 0.34) | ⊕⊕⊕◯ MODERATE |

[1]The upper confidence limit includes an effect that, if it were real, would represent a benefit that, given the downsides, would still be worth it.
[2]The lower confidence limit crosses a threshold below which, given the downsides of the intervention, one would not recommend the intervention.
[3]Random-effects model.
[4]95% CI crosses the minimal importance difference threshold.

54

based on the quality assessment components (study design, limitations to study quality, consistency, directness and any other considerations) and graded using the following definitions:

- **High** = Further research is very unlikely to change our confidence in the estimate of the effect.
- **Moderate** = Further research is likely to have an important impact on our confidence in the estimate of the effect and may change the estimate.
- **Low** = Further research is very likely to have an important impact on our confidence in the estimate of the effect and is likely to change the estimate.
- **Very low** = Any estimate of effect is very uncertain.

For further information about the process and the rationale of producing an evidence profile table, see GRADE (2004).

*Forest plots*
Each forest plot displayed the effect size and CI for each study as well as the overall summary statistic. The graphs were organised so that the display of data in the area to the left of the 'line of no effect' indicated a 'favourable' outcome for the treatment in question.

### 3.5.6    Forming the clinical summaries and recommendations

Once the GRADE profile tables relating to a particular clinical question were completed, summary tables incorporating important information from the GRADE profiles were developed (these tables are presented in the evidence chapters where used). Finally, the systematic reviewer in conjunction with the topic group lead produced a clinical evidence summary.

Once the GRADE profiles and clinical summaries were finalised and agreed by the GDG, the associated recommendations were drafted, taking into account the trade-off between the benefits and downsides of treatment as well as other important factors. These included economic considerations, values of the GDG and society, and the group's awareness of practical issues (Eccles *et al.*, 1998).

### 3.5.7    Method used to answer a clinical question in the absence of appropriately designed, high-quality research

In the absence of level-I evidence (or a level that is appropriate to the question), or where the GDG were of the opinion (on the basis of previous searches or their knowledge of the literature) that there was unlikely to be such evidence in this guideline, an informal consensus process was adopted. This process focused on those questions that the GDG considered a priority.

*Informal consensus*
The starting point for the process of informal consensus was that a member of the topic group identified, with help from the systematic reviewer, a narrative review that most directly addressed the clinical question. Where this was not possible, a brief review of the recent literature was initiated.

This existing narrative review or new review was used as a basis for beginning an iterative process to identify lower levels of evidence relevant to the clinical question and to lead to written statements for the guideline. The process involved a number of steps:

1. A description of what is known about the issues concerning the clinical question was written by one of the topic group members.
2. Evidence from the existing review or new review was then presented in narrative form to the GDG and further comments were sought about the evidence and its perceived relevance to the clinical question.
3. Based on the feedback from the GDG, additional information was sought and added to the information collected. This may include studies that did not directly address the clinical question but were thought to contain relevant data.
4. If, during the course of preparing the report, a significant body of primary-level studies (of appropriate design to answer the question) were identified, a full systematic review was conducted.
5. At this time, subject possibly to further reviews of the evidence, a series of statements that directly addressed the clinical question were developed.
6. Following this, on occasions and as deemed appropriate by the GDG, the report was then sent to appointed experts outside the GDG for peer review and comment. The information from this process was then fed back to the GDG for further discussion of the statements.
7. Recommendations were then developed and could also be sent for further external peer review.
8. After this final stage of comment, the statements and recommendations were again reviewed and agreed upon by the GDG.

## 3.6    HEALTH ECONOMICS METHODS

The aim of the health economics was to contribute to the guideline's development by providing evidence on the cost effectiveness of interventions for children, young people and adults with ADHD covered in the guideline, in areas with likely major resource implications. This was achieved by:

- systematic literature review of existing economic evidence
- economic modelling, in areas where economic evidence was lacking or was considered inadequate to inform decisions.

### 3.6.1    Key economic issues

The following economic issues relating to diagnosis and management of children, young people and adults with ADHD were identified by the GDG in collaboration with the health economist as primary key issues that should be considered in the guideline:

- the cost effectiveness of parent training for pre-school age children and CBT for older children and young people

- the cost effectiveness of CBT for adults with ADHD
- the relative cost effectiveness of different pharmacological interventions for children and adults with ADHD
- the cost effectiveness of intensive medication management for children
- the relative cost effectiveness of psychological, pharmacological and combination therapies for children.

In addition, literature on health related quality of life (HRQoL) of children and adults with ADHD was systematically searched to identify studies reporting appropriate utility weights that could be utilised in a cost-utility analysis.

The rest of this section describes the methods adopted in the systematic literature review of economic studies. Methods employed in economic modelling are described in the respective sections of the guideline.

### 3.6.2    Search strategy

For the systematic review of economic evidence on treatments for ADHD the standard mental-health-related bibliographic databases (EMBASE, MEDLINE, CINAHL and PsycINFO) were searched. For these databases, a health economics search filter adapted from the Centre for Reviews and Dissemination at the University of York was used in combination with a general filter for ADHD. Additional searches were performed in specific health economics databases (NHS EED, OHE HEED), as well as in the HTA database. For the HTA and NHS EED databases, the general filter for ADHD was used. OHE HEED was searched using a shorter, database-specific strategy. Initial searches were performed in June 2006. The searches were updated regularly, with the final search conducted 5 weeks before the consultation period.

In parallel to searches of electronic databases, reference lists of eligible studies and relevant reviews were searched by hand. Studies included in the clinical evidence review were also screened for economic evidence.

The systematic search for economic evidence resulted in 47 potentially relevant studies. Full texts of all potentially eligible studies (including those for which relevance/eligibility was not clear from the abstract) were obtained. These publications were then assessed against a set of standard inclusion criteria by the health economists, and papers eligible for inclusion were subsequently assessed for internal validity. The quality assessment was based on the checklists used by the *British Medical Journal* to assist referees in appraising full and partial economic analyses (Drummond & Jefferson, 1996) (see Appendix 12).

### 3.6.3    Selection criteria

The following inclusion criteria were applied to select studies identified by the economic searches for further analysis:

- No restriction was placed on language or publication status of the papers.

- Studies published from 1990 onwards were included. This date restriction was imposed in order to obtain data relevant to current healthcare settings and costs.
- Only studies from Organisation for Economic Co-operation and Development countries were included, as the aim of the review was to identify economic and HRQoL information transferable to the UK context.
- Selection criteria based on types of clinical conditions and patients were identical to the clinical literature review.
- Studies were included provided that sufficient details regarding methods and results were available to enable the methodological quality of the study to be assessed, and provided that the study's data and results were extractable. Poster presentations or abstracts were in principle excluded; however, they were included if they reported additional data from studies which had already been published elsewhere and met the inclusion criteria, or if they contained appropriate input data required for economic modelling that were not otherwise available.
- Full economic evaluations that compared two or more relevant options and considered both costs and consequences (that is, cost-effectiveness analysis, cost-utility analysis, cost-consequences analysis or cost-benefit analysis) were included in the review. HRQoL studies were included if they reported utility weights appropriate to use in a cost-utility analysis.

### 3.6.4    Data extraction

Data were extracted by the health economist using a standard economic data extraction form (see Appendix 13).

### 3.6.5    Presentation of economic evidence

The economic evidence identified by the health economics systematic review is summarised in the respective chapters of the guideline, following presentation of the clinical evidence. The characteristics and results of all economic studies included in the review are provided in the form of evidence tables in Appendix 14. Results of additional economic modelling undertaken alongside the guideline development process are also presented in the relevant chapters.

### 3.7    FOCUS GROUP METHODOLOGY

Besides making recommendations based on the clinical and cost effectiveness of interventions for ADHD, an important function of developing this guideline was understanding the experience of ADHD from the service user's point of view.

In order to provide sufficient breadth of context and depth of understanding of children's views on taking stimulant medicine, the NCCMH commissioned the London School of Economics to undertake a qualitative focus group study with children and young people on their perceptions of their use of stimulant medication, together with a review of the available literature on young people's experiences. The full version of this report, including the extensive bibliography, can be found in Appendix 15, and a summary of the findings in Chapter 4.

Besides being reviewed by the GDG, the focus group proposal was also reviewed by a nationally sanctioned ethics committee and local research and development committees. The research team undertaking the focus group interviews and analyses were experienced both in qualitative methodologies and working with young people. Before data collection, they carefully researched the issues on the extra care required both in the design and execution of data collection methods in order to ensure that the information gathered was robust and usable, and that all ethical considerations relating to the vulnerable participant group were met.

### 3.7.1    Focus group participants

Participants in the study had all been diagnosed with ADHD and all were taking stimulant medication. They were recruited from clinics at three hospitals: Richmond Royal Hospital, London; the Maudsley Hospital, London; and Queen's Medical Centre, Nottingham.

The sample consisted of 16 children (14 boys and two girls) ranging in age from 9 to 15 years old. All were attending state schools and all were white, with the exception of one child who was of mixed race. Fifty per cent of the children were living in two-parent homes, and 37% lived in single-mother homes. Two children lived with their fathers; and one child lived with his grandmother. Educational achievement and type of employment were used as indicators of socioeconomic status.[7] A majority of parents had completed O levels or GCSEs; one parent had attended university. Seventy-two percent of parents' job types ranged from semi-skilled to skilled work. A majority of mothers did not report having employment.

### 3.7.2    Data collection

Semi-structured focus groups were used to collect data about how children and young people experience stimulant medication. Allowing children to describe their experiences through qualitative interviews has been found to be both reliable and valid (Deatrick & Faux, 1991; Sorensen, 1992), and there is compelling evidence to suggest that children are competent research participants (Singh, 2007). Children's competence as research participants is supported by the literature on children's capacity and competence as patients. Children have been found to be capable of understanding the complexities of their condition; they have the capacity to give informed

---

[7]Data were only available on mothers. Fathers' educational achievement and job types would be more reliable indicators of socioeconomic status.

consent to invasive treatments, to contribute to deliberations over treatment strategies, and, in the case of diabetic children, to take responsibility for administering their own treatment (Alderson *et al.*, 2006; Bluebond-Langner *et al.*, 2005).

Thirteen children were interviewed as part of a series of focus groups. Three children were interviewed one-to-one, either because they were unable to attend the focus groups or because they preferred to be interviewed individually. The interviews took place in a room based at the hospital clinic and lasted approximately 1 hour. Written informed consent was obtained from one parent and also from the participant. Parents were also asked to complete a basic demographic questionnaire.

### 3.7.3    Methodology of focus groups

Focus groups are a widely used method in qualitative health research, and are often used when the research aim is to gather information in a little-understood or under-researched area. Focus groups elicit a range of experiences, opinions and feelings about a topic (Krueger & Casey, 2000), and the interaction in focus groups can result in enhanced disclosure, as participants challenge each other's perceptions and opinions.

The collective nature of focus group discussion is often said to provide 'more than the sum of its parts' (Wilkinson, 1998). Interactive data result in enhanced disclosure, better understanding of participants' own agendas, the production of more elaborated accounts, and the opportunity to observe the co-construction of meaning in action. Focus groups are, then, an ideal method for exploring people's own meanings and understandings of health and illness.

Although focus groups with children are less commonly used in social science health research, market research with children (including market research around health and well-being) more commonly uses a focus group approach (for example, Caruana & Vassallo, 2003). Focus groups with children provide access to children's own language and concepts and encourage elaboration of children's own concerns and agendas.

### 3.7.4    Interviews

Interviews were conducted in a conversational style and included a standard set of open-ended questions (see Appendix 15 for the complete topic guide).

The first half of the interview involved posing broad questions that were followed by more specific probe questions. Principle areas of investigation included children's understanding of ADHD diagnosis and behaviours, perceptions of how tablets helped them (or not), experiences of stigma, experiences of non-drug interventions for ADHD behaviours, impact of tablets on children's perceptions of personal agency, and experiences of psychiatric services.

The second half of the interview involved a set of games and a vignette which provided children with the opportunity to elaborate their experiences and perceptions of medication in more creative and imaginative ways. The primary aims in this section of the interview were to contextualise children's perceptions of tablets within their perceptions, understandings and/or experiences of other means of improving behaviour, and to elicit their ideas about resources that could help them have more positive experiences of an ADHD diagnosis and of medication.

The following methods were used in the second half of the interview (see Appendix 15 for further elaboration):

a.  Children were asked to compare how the experience of taking tablets was similar to, or different from, doing other things that were commonly considered good for them.
b.  Children were asked to respond to a vignette that elicited their ideas about what sorts to things can help a child's behaviour.
c.  Children were asked to think up and discuss an invention that could help children with ADHD.
d.  Children were asked to rank in order a list of items that described common concerns voiced by school-age children. Each item was written on a separate card, and children were asked to put the cards in order of what they worried about most, to what they worried about least. The list included global warming, having ADHD, taking tablets, exams, homework and friendships. Global warming and exams were included on the list because these concerns were found to be significant sources of anxiety in a recent large cohort study of UK school-age children (Alexander & Hargreaves, 2007)

### 3.7.5    Data analysis

All interviews were digitally recorded, transcribed and analysed using rigorous qualitative coding practices that meet established criteria of validity and relevance to qualitative health research (Mays & Pope, 2000). Focus groups were coded using content analysis. The coding process captured the data on two analytic levels: individual concepts were coded first, and then these concepts were grouped together under higher order themes. Systematic coding meant that it was possible to code at both the individual level and at the group level. Group-level data were represented in the frequency with which concepts and themes were expressed by group members. Transcript excerpts elucidated the meaning of codes.

A coding frame was drawn up by the lead author of the study, Ilina Singh, and validated within a coding team. The coding team applied the same codes to a transcript in order to discuss their definition and validity. This discussion resulted in refinements to the structure of categories and sub-categories, as well as refinements to individual codes. The coding team was able to reach agreement on the validity of a majority of codes.

### 3.8    STAKEHOLDER CONTRIBUTIONS

Professionals, service users, and companies have contributed to and commented on the guideline at key stages in its development. Stakeholders for this guideline include:
●  service user/carer stakeholders: the national service user and carer organisations that represent people whose care is described in this guideline

- professional stakeholders: the national organisations that represent healthcare professionals who are providing services to service users
- commercial stakeholders: the companies that manufacture medicines used in the treatment of ADHD
- Primary Care Trusts
- Department of Health and Welsh Assembly Government.

Stakeholders have been involved in the guideline's development at the following points:

- commenting on the initial scope of the guideline and attended a briefing meeting held by NICE
- commenting on the draft of the guideline.


## 3.9    VALIDATION OF THIS GUIDELINE

Registered stakeholders had an opportunity to comment on the draft guideline, which was posted on the NICE website during the consultation period. The GRP also reviewed the guideline and checked that stakeholders' comments had been addressed.

Following the consultation period, the GDG finalised the recommendations and the NCCMH produced the final documents. These were then submitted to NICE. NICE then formally approved the guideline and issued its guidance to the NHS in England and Wales.

# 4. THE EXPERIENCE OF TREATMENT AND CARE FOR ADHD

## 4.1 INTRODUCTION

This chapter aims to provide a service user and carer context for the chapters on interventions and services for ADHD. The first section summarises the results of a qualitative focus group study with children and young people, which set out to ascertain how they felt about the diagnosis and having treatment (particularly taking stimulant medication for ADHD). The second section comprises a review of the available literature on diagnosis in adult life. The third part contains personal accounts from people with ADHD and their families and carers and the fourth part provides a summary of the accounts.

## 4.2 THE EXPERIENCES OF CHILDREN AND YOUNG PEOPLE OF ADHD AND STIMULANT MEDICATION

### 4.2.1 Background

As there is little published research on the views and experiences of children taking stimulant medication for the symptoms of ADHD, researchers at the London School of Economics were commissioned to undertake a qualitative focus group study with children and young people, together with a review of the available literature on young people's experiences. The study identified children and young people's experience of the diagnosis of ADHD and treatments for it in general.

A summary of the findings of this study follows. The full version of the report by Singh and colleagues, including the extensive bibliography, can be found in Appendix 15.

### 4.2.2 Previous research

Qualitative studies of the experience of children with ADHD suggest a 'trade-off' between the positive and negative experience of stimulant medications (Efron *et al.*, 1998; Kendall *et al.*, 2003; Meaux *et al.*, 2006).

While these studies report that medication helped to control hyperactivity, increased concentration, improved grades and helped behaviour (Kendall *et al.*, 2003; Meaux *et al.*, 2006) negative physiological aspects such as the taste of the medication and side effects of stomach aches and headaches (Kendall *et al.*, 2003) were also mentioned, along with psychological side effects of feeling less sociable and a sense of not feeling authentically themselves (Meaux *et al.*, 2006).

Stigma associated with taking medication to manage behaviour was the source of considerable concern for interviewees in these studies. They did not want others to know about their taking medication for fear of being laughed at and a number did not want to take medication because they did not like the changes they experienced in themselves (Kendall *et al.*, 2003). A similar source of concern involved frustration, anger, sadness, and embarrassment at having to leave the classroom to be given medication (Meaux *et al.*, 2006).

As there is little research on children's experiences of taking medication for ADHD, the commissioned study's literature review included the experience of young people taking medication for other conditions. It was felt that the issues of stigma, labelling and difference would be common or at least similar to that experienced by children prescribed stimulants for ADHD. However, when compared with epilepsy, the stigma of taking medication was more apparent for children taking medicine for ADHD. Similarly, more children with ADHD (40% versus 32.5%) categorised themselves as non-compliant, and they reported being less likely to tell their friends about their medication than those with epilepsy (32.5% versus 55%) (McElearney *et al.*, 2005), suggesting that the experience of stigma is more acute with ADHD than with epilepsy.

### 4.2.3    Principal areas of investigation

In the current study, the researchers looked principally at children's:
- understanding of ADHD
- perceptions of how tablets helped them (or not)
- experiences of stigma
- experiences of non-drug interventions for ADHD
- impact of tablets on the children's perceptions of personal agency
- experiences of psychiatric services.

In addition, the study aimed to contextualise children's perceptions of their ADHD medication within the perceptions, understanding and experiences of other means of improving their behaviour. The study also elicited ideas from children about resources that could help them to have more positive experiences of their diagnosis and medication.

The investigations were conducted through a combination of broad open-ended questions, games and vignettes.

### 4.2.4    Participants

The participants were 16 children (14 boys, two girls) with an age range of 9–15 years. Fifteen children were white and one was mixed race. Fifty percent of the children were living in two-parent homes, 37% in single-mother homes (the others with single fathers or grandparents). They were recruited from three major hospital clinics: Richmond Royal Hospital, London; the Maudsley Hospital, London; and Queen's

Medical Centre, Nottingham. All of the children had a primary diagnosis of ADHD, with approximately 30% having a secondary comorbid diagnosis such as conduct disorder or dyslexia. A fuller discussion of the methods employed can be found in Chapter 3.

### 4.2.5    Main findings

*Understanding of ADHD*
- Children in this study identified a range of behaviours similar to those listed as symptoms indicated in DSM-IV and ICD-10. The most frequently discussed types of behaviours were impulsiveness, physical aggression and hyperactivity. Children felt that these types of behaviours were particularly annoying to others.
- Behaviours identified as symptomatic of ADHD were frequently discussed in terms of their positive dimensions by children in the study. Their peers were thought to fear how out-of-control and overwhelming children with ADHD could be. Participants were able to perceive the tension between their experiences of the more negative and more positive aspects of their ADHD-symptomatic behaviours but the majority were not disturbed by this tension.

*Medication*
- The children in this study had generally positive experiences of stimulant medica-tion. This does not mean they liked being on medication, but rather that they were willing to put up with the 'annoying' aspects of taking medication in return for the perceived benefits. Rather than seeing medication as a panacea, children had reasonable understandings of the benefits and limitations of the medication.
- The children associated their tablets primarily with helping to improve their social and disruptive behaviour and, consequently, relationships with peers (as opposed to improving their school work and academic functioning).
- Although side effects of the medication such as problems sleeping and reduction in appetite were commonly experienced, this did not make up a major theme of their discussions.
- All children interviewed felt they needed to be on their tablets; older children were more likely to be looking ahead to a time when they could manage without tablets.
- All children in the study believed medication to be the most effective available treatment for their ADHD symptoms, but they also understood that a diagnosis of ADHD and effective drug treatment did not mean that they were absolved of responsibility or of agency for their behaviours.

*Experience of stigma*
- One of the most strongly stated desires communicated by this group of children was for better public understanding of ADHD. Children felt this would create empathy for their situation and relieve them of some of the stigma of negative assumptions attached to a diagnosis of ADHD.

- Children reported experiences of stigma as a direct result of taking tablets; however, experiences of stigma as a result of ADHD diagnosis and symptomatic behaviours were far more frequently expressed. Feelings of being different and alienated were also stronger around diagnosis and ADHD behaviours, than around the need for medication.
- Stigma associated with a diagnosis of ADHD and the attendant behaviours was experienced through:
  - bullying and name-calling by peers
  - negative assumptions made by peers, peers' families, teachers and relatives
  - being treated differently by peers, peers' families, teachers and relatives.
- Close friendships were mentioned as an important protective factor against the initiation and/or continuation of fights that arose as a result of bullying. These friendships were mentioned as frequently as, or more often than, medication, as factors that helped children to restrain their impulse to fight and/or to continue fighting.
- The children in this study reported that their experiences of stigma resulted in a lack of self-esteem and low self-confidence. They reported less frequently the experience of stigma associated with their medication.

*Perceptions of effective non-drug interventions*
Interviewees were less likely to identify spontaneously effective formal non-drug interventions for their ADHD behaviours (such as CBT or parent training) but they did identify some key aspects that helped them or they thought might help them. These included:

- participation in sport
- better public understanding of ADHD (the children reported that this would be likely to result in less bullying and less fighting)
- close friendships
- better understanding from teachers of the needs of children with ADHD.

*Impact of tablets on the children's perceptions of personal agency*
The children in this study did not appear to be ethically compromised by their experience of taking stimulant medication. They were able to express personal agency and a willingness to take responsibility for behaviour associated with their ADHD. The children were also able to express appropriate moral evaluations of difficult social situations.

*Experience of services*
In view of the distress many children experienced in relation to an ADHD diagnosis, ADHD behaviours and tablets, only one child in this study viewed their clinical encounters within child psychiatry services as having a therapeutic component. While no child had any strong complaints about services, several children reported not being able to get in to see a clinician and feeling that they would like more time with a psychiatrist. Some children felt that clinicians didn't really care about them. A majority of children felt appointments were routine and boring, and that appointments were primarily for medication checks and for getting prescriptions.

*ADHD diagnosis and medication in the context of other life stressors*

● Although ADHD and medication were important in the lives of this group of children, with various daily reminders of the burden of mental disorder and the need to take medication, when compared with a list of other stressors, 'ADHD diagnosis' and 'taking tablets' were not listed as the most important worries. Younger children worried the most about friendships and global warming, while older children were most concerned about exams and friendships. While friendships and academic performance are often difficult for children with ADHD, these concerns are similarly shared by other children, as demonstrated in a study of a large cohort of UK children who identified them as their primary sources of anxiety (Alexander & Hargreaves, 2007).

● In the current study, a diagnosis of ADHD was ranked as more worrying than taking tablets for ADHD by almost all children. Results from this study suggest that children have relatively more positive experiences of medication, as compared with more negative experiences of ADHD diagnosis and behavioural symptoms.

## 4.3    THE EXPERIENCE OF DIAGNOSIS IN ADULT LIFE

### 4.3.1    Introduction

Many of the issues raised by the young people in Singh and colleagues' study (see Section 4.2) can also be found in studies of those who received a diagnosis of ADHD in adulthood, and of their partners. Young and colleagues' (2008a) qualitative research into the impact of receiving a diagnosis of ADHD in adulthood revealed a six-stage model of psychological acceptance of the diagnosis:

● relief and elation
● confusion and emotional turmoil
● anger
● sadness and grief
● anxiety
● accommodation and acceptance.

The study asked participants to review the past, to discuss the emotional impact of the diagnosis and to give consideration to the future.

Partners of people with ADHD expressed a sense of inadequacy; they identified the emotional impact of the diagnosis on both them and their affected partners, and raised the issue that medication, however helpful, was not a panacea (Young *et al.*, 2008b).

### 4.3.2    Reviewing the past

In reviewing the past participants described feeling 'different' from others and experiencing negative judgements from others, including family members, friends and teachers. Participants responded to these judgements by either accepting that what others said was true, or by ignoring them.

### 4.3.3　Emotional impact of a diagnosis of ADHD

Participants expressed an initial sense of relief at the diagnosis, finally learning that there was an external cause and explanation for their behaviour. This also gave them a sense of optimism for the future. This initial elation was quickly followed by a sense of turmoil and anger that they could have been helped earlier. Some expressed sadness at the past wasted years and felt that their life experiences could have been more positive and more successful with an earlier diagnosis.

The next stage of the process was an adjustment to living with a chronic condition and the potential negative impact on their future lives. Ultimately this adjustment led to acceptance of ADHD as part of their lives and of who they are.

Partners also described the emotional impact of the diagnosis and their own need to come to terms with its implications. They stated that they felt emotionally ill equipped to provide appropriate support and to cope with the situation. Having the diagnosis, however, allowed partners a framework in which to better understand the person with ADHD, shifting their perspective from the patient 'being' the problem to them 'having' a problem.

Partners identified an initial increase in self-esteem in the people with ADHD following the diagnosis. Partners also described a process leading towards acceptance of the diagnosis and the status of the person with ADHD.

### 4.3.4　Consideration of the future

Participants expressed concern about the stigma attached to ADHD and hoped for this stigma to diminish in the future. Parallels with the acceptance of dyslexia were drawn.

Participants reported the positive influence of stimulant medication which they said allowed them to function as 'normal' people and improved their social interactions, motivation and focus. Importantly the medication allowed people to be optimistic about the future. Partners also expressed relief at the initiation of medical treatment and reported general improvements, particular in the ability to focus.

Despite the positive impact of the medication, participants noticed a rapid reoccurrence of symptoms, revealing that there was no 'miracle cure' for their condition. Nevertheless this experience allowed people to distinguish between problems strongly associated with their symptoms and those less influenced by symptoms, allowing them to take greater personal responsibility for their behaviours.

Similarly, partners expressed disappointment that medication was not a 'cure all', and that symptoms rapidly returned once the effects wore off. Patients' self-esteem remained a cause for concern, reflecting a lifetime of repeated failures and under achievement.

Partners identified that the patients could be better supported by mental health professionals and believed that they would benefit from non-pharmacological therapy.

### 4.3.5    Conclusions

The study by Young and colleagues (2008a) indicates that adults receiving a diagnosis of ADHD tend to engage in a psychological process that involves a review of the past, an emotional journey towards acceptance of the diagnosis and a consideration of a future with ADHD. The lack of a diagnosis in childhood seems to have led to an internalisation of blame for their behaviours and a negative impact on their hopes for the future. In the long term, this may increase the risk of depression and low self-esteem.

Partners of adults diagnosed with ADHD also went through an emotional journey towards acceptance. They expressed uncertainty about the future of the relationship and how to provide support. Medication was seen as helpful initially but was not a cure, and many problems remained, particularly low self-esteem.

Partners seem to report a better appreciation of functional improvements following treatment with medication than did the patients, particularly in respect to interpersonal relationships.

The research by Young and colleagues (2008a) reveals a need for psychological treatment (in particular cognitive behavioural techniques) for adults diagnosed with ADHD, and their partners, at the point of diagnosis to help them cope with the adjustment process. Psychological therapy can also have a role in helping adults diagnosed with ADHD to reframe their experiences through an encouragement to learn from the past.

Anxiety about the future could be alleviated by emphasising the positive aspects of the disorder and/or the individual's particular strengths, and to capitalise on them.

Adults with a diagnosis of ADHD should be taught skills to help them anticipate future hurdles and challenges and to apply appropriate coping strategies.

Work with partners also indicates that it would be beneficial for adult patients with ADHD to be helped to develop realistic expectations for the future, and to develop skills to overcome 'learned helplessness'.

Partners also believed that psychological treatments would be helpful for people with ADHD, enabling them to anticipate future challenges and hurdles, to apply appropriate coping strategies and to manage ongoing difficulties with low self-esteem.

Information leaflets for partners of newly-diagnosed adults with ADHD, and/or directing them to local support groups would do much to support partners in dealing with the process.


## 4.4    PERSONAL ACCOUNTS FROM PEOPLE WITH ADHD AND THEIR CARERS

### 4.4.1    Introduction

This section presents personal accounts from people with ADHD and their families and carers. The views represented here are illustrative only and are not intended to be representative of the experience of people with ADHD and their families and carers.

The writers of the accounts were contacted primarily through the service user and carer representatives on the GDG. The people who were approached to write the accounts were asked to consider a number of questions when composing their narratives. These included:

- What is the nature of your experience of living with ADHD?
- When were you diagnosed and how old were you? How did you feel about the diagnosis or 'label'?
- Do you think that any life experiences led to the onset of the condition? If so, please describe if you feel able to do so.
- When did you seek help from the NHS and whom did you contact? (Please describe this first contact.)
- What possible treatments were discussed with you?
- What treatment(s) did you receive?
- Was the treatment(s) helpful? (Please describe what worked for you and what didn't work for you.)
- How would you describe your relationship with your practitioner(s)? (GP/community psychiatric nurse/psychiatrist, and so on)
- Did you attend a support group and was this helpful? Did any people close to you help and support you?
- How has the nature of the condition changed over time?
- How do you feel now?
- If your condition has improved, do you use any strategies to help you to stay well? If so, please describe these strategies.
- In what ways has ADHD affected your everyday life (such as schooling, employment and making relationships) and the lives of those close to you?

The questions for carers were based on the above.

The first two accounts from people with ADHD (A and B) are written by adults reflecting on their experience. The third account (C) is by a young person (male) still at school. In the accounts from parents, one is written by the mother (parent E) of the child in personal account C. Two of the accounts (B and D) are written by the same person; account D was written from the perspective of a mother of a child with ADHD and account B was written with hindsight, reflecting on how her son's behaviour mirrored her own behaviour as a child and young person.

### 4.4.2    Personal accounts from people with ADHD

*Personal account (A)*

My mother comments that she immediately saw many differences between me as a baby and my three older sisters; however she ascribed this to me being a boy. As a baby I used to bite my mum so much that she had bruises all down her arm. I was obsessed with things involving movement, especially cars. Apparently I used to look at the main road watching the cars for hours at a time, murmuring my first words – 'car' or 'bus'. When I first went to nursery I refused to interact or even share a room with the other children, instead playing with cars in another room, and reacting aggressively to anyone who tried to interfere. I frequently had tantrums and made no friends. My mother, who is a paediatrician, feared I may have obsessive-compulsive disorder, but at this time did not follow it up. My main other problem was sleep; as a child it would regularly take me a long time to switch off and get to sleep, and this has stayed with me my whole life. (I now find I can function well on only about 5 hours a night, possibly due to my hyperactivity, and I regularly use a herbal mix to help me get to sleep.)

Starting at my first primary school was a mixed experience. I did not make friends easily and although I was fairly bright I did not apply myself to my work with any commitment or enthusiasm. The older I got the more trouble I got into: answering back to teachers, lying to other children and performing stupid pranks to try and gain credibility. When my parents moved away from the area and I started a new school I had even more problems. I did not like the school or my teachers. I was rude, lazy and aggressive and I lied constantly; as a result I was very lonely. I struggled to make any friends in the new village and it was left up to my mum to try and fulfil my constant demands outside school.

When I was 7 years old and had only been in the new school for less than two terms, my parents took me to see an educational psychologist. I completed a few tests and had a short interview with him. He concluded that I had some obsessive tendencies, anxiety and esteem problems. He recommended to my parents that I move to a smaller school with smaller classes. This meant going to a private school, where I was relatively happy for 2 years; I enjoyed boarding and found myself able to build good relationships with other children. I also really enjoyed sport, and eventually captained the cricket and rugby teams. I still got into trouble a fair amount, but the headmaster was very patient and not punitive.

My fortunes changed when a new headmaster came to the school. He and I did not see eye to eye from the start. He was a military-styled bully who suspended me on the second day he was there for getting into a fight with his son (who received no punishment). From then on he assumed that I was an idle, lying bully, and in time this is what I became. Driving him mad became a source of great enjoyment to me; I was suspended on numerous occasions, though he never carried through the expulsion which he constantly threatened. His punishments were severe and eventually he took away any self-respect I had left when he forced a confession out of me for something I hadn't done, in the process helping me to lose a good friend. At the age of 12 my behaviour had become enough of a concern for a visit to a private paediatrician, which my mum arranged. She had been fairly sure for some time that I had ADHD and contacted a paediatrician in London. He immediately diagnosed me with ADHD, and wanted to prescribe me methylphenidate; however my family history of epilepsy was thought at this time to be a risk, so I was not given it. I was not offered any other treatment either medical or behavioural, and my mum, who by this time ran a paediatric ADHD clinic, didn't feel like she needed any support at home.

My senior year was perhaps one of my best. We were a very small group (only ten in the class), and my teacher made a huge difference to my experience of school when he realised that a lot of the time I did not ignore people but in fact did not hear them. I had small plastic drainage tubes (to treat glue ear) inserted into my ears, and this had an immediate and positive impact. When I got to the end of my senior year I passed my exams and went off to public school.

My headmaster, who described me as his 'hair shirt', had one last punishment in store for me however, ensuring that an absolutely terrible reference would get to my new school before I did. The effect was so obvious it was as if everyone had been told that I was someone to watch out for. I made no friends, did not apply myself to either study or sport, and hated the other activities we had to do. The place was like a prison and the routine suffocating. After 6 weeks I walked out of school and into a local shop where I shoplifted an item in obvious view of the camera. When I was called before the headmaster the following day I hoped I was going to be expelled. However I got put on 'headmaster's jankers' instead, a dehumanising experience involving complete and highly visible exclusion from normal school activities and about 4 hours of manual labour per day. After half-term I refused to go back.

I then went to the local comprehensive, where I started with quite high hopes (I knew some people from my time in the two local primary schools). However, I was teased relentlessly as a 'poof' or 'posh boy' for my time at private school, and my teachers thought that my ADHD was an excuse for needless bad behaviour and laziness, and as such I wasn't offered any treatment or intervention for it. Once again this became a mould I fitted into: I ignored my studies completely, was often in trouble, bullied other children, stopped participating in the sport I had previously enjoyed, and on several occasions I took flasks of alcohol into school and would drink during lessons. I still lied compulsively, and stole frequently from other children and from my parents. I had also started smoking when I was 11 and this became heavier; I regularly skived off school to smoke, drink or get high. I quickly put on weight, and the bigger I became the more I ate and drank, until at 16, despite being below average height, I was almost 16 stone. I barely passed my GCSE exams, and though I was admitted on to an A level course, I stuck it for less than a term before I decided to leave school.

When I left home and got my own place, there were many times when I felt much more content. I started to make some good friends, with whom I still remain very close today. However, drugs and alcohol were still an increasing problem. I worked in pubs and clubs and would get drunk most days; I experimented with many drugs – mostly pills and LSD. I frequently drove while in a dangerous state, and although I had many friends, lying was still a problem. I got bored with the jobs I did very quickly – one lasted only a single day, and the most I managed was 6 months. Eventually things fell apart completely following a disastrous relationship. I returned home depressed and feeling like I had failed. My father and I did not really see eye to eye at this point; he could not understand that I had no interest in going to university, we argued and I ended up leaving again.

For the next 3 or 4 months I lived a nomadic existence; I wandered round the town with a friend who was in a similar position, and we stopped at various places to buy, sell or take drugs, and slept on sofas or in the park. Though this experience was cathartic in some ways, and I built some very strong relationships, after some time it became clear that I would have to do something with my life. My mum, who had stayed in regular contact with me, told me that my dad had managed to get an interview for me in London. I was afraid of leaving the life I had created for myself, and London seemed like a very frightening prospect; however, a close friend managed to talk me round and I went for the interview and got the job. My sister in London offered me a room in her house.

I had not thought about my ADHD for a long time, and I had not made the connection between it and dropping out of school, not committing to a job and my extensive drug and alcohol abuse. (Only later did I discover that the disorder was also associated with my frequent trips to casualty: I have broken both my funny bones, have cracked ribs and have fractured my skull, as well as having many injuries from cycling accidents. I also had five car accidents in my first 2 years of driving.) However, signs of my ADHD came back to me in my new job, which was very repetitive laboratory work. After about 2 months my careless mistakes – due to inattention – were causing a problem, and I moved departments and left a month later. I fell back on my pub and club experience, which left me short of money and exhausted. I started drinking and using drugs heavily again.

Eventually I went to see a psychiatrist in London, a very compassionate and patient man, whom I spoke to for about an hour, and who I really opened up to. He described me as an underachiever and said he thought I was depressed, for which he offered me drugs, but I refused them. Instead I made the decision to go back to college to try and complete my A-levels. I had a fantastic experience on the course and excelled in my studies, managing to get into a top university. I found disciplining myself at university very difficult due to the lack of structure and availability of drugs and alcohol. In my first year, after another painful relationship ended, I found myself drinking alone most days and neglecting my studies. I barely passed the end of year exams, and this was sufficient to scare me into working harder. Towards the end of my second year I met my current girlfriend, who helped me cut down on my drinking and knuckle down to my studies. We are now considering marriage – she has made a massive difference to my life and I have great faith in our future.

My educational re-birth has taken me through a degree and masters and I am now in the final year of a PhD. This most recent experience has been a great challenge requiring long-term commitment, organisation, concentration, and a huge amount of reading, research and analysis. However, since giving up alcohol over 2 months ago, I have a renewed enthusiasm for the project and am confident of a successful conclusion.

I have never taken drugs for my ADHD, though I have no doubt they would help me. At times the symptoms have impaired me greatly, and they remain a challenge, as does my depression. However I have managed to overcome these challenges through other means. There are many things that I do which help greatly: regular exercise is a must, and without it I get restless and depressed. I also ensure that I reserve plenty of time for creative activities – I have played the guitar for many years and love composing, performing and recording music. I also love writing, something my current work lends itself very well to, and I have already had three papers published. I had a very difficult experience at school and there are many things I would do differently if I could. However, I am currently happier than I have ever been and enjoying a very demanding new world of work, in which I use my difficult experiences at school to try and effect change in the systems and structures of our institutions, particularly with those children who are marked out as difficult and suffer as a consequence.

It is only in the last 5 years, since I have been working on ADHD academically as part of my graduate studies, that I have started to consider the role it may have played in my life. Previously I had never acknowledged that there was a causal or explanatory role for the disorder. I did not use it as a means to explain my behaviour at school, and I felt as indifferent to my diagnosis as I did to the demands of teachers. My perspective now, which is a combination of personal experience and research, is that ADHD represents a complex bio-cultural construct, which is contingent on the influence of medicine and genetics in explaining life problems, on the examination of individuals in terms of deficit and dysfunction, on limiting and competitive academic environments, and, in my case, on my mum's knowledge of the disorder. Although it offends my sense of personal agency to do so, I can acknowledge that the symptoms associated with ADHD can be very impairing; even harder to acknowledge is that the effects frequently bypass my conscious control. I still take offence when anyone uses the disorder to explain any of my actions; even though I am limited by the symptoms, I do not think they explain my behaviour, and my academic work now can be read partly as an attempt to push the boundaries of what 'someone with ADHD' may or may not be capable of. As such, I have, whether passively or actively, always resisted the label. I do recognise, however, that the principal factor that has kept me from some of the more extreme outcomes of the disorder has been good fortune, which many people with ADHD will not share with me.

I am very fortunate in having a supportive family and friends. As well as my girlfriend, I have a very loving family around me – my mum, in particular, worked tirelessly to make me happy as a child, and I would love to be able to give her back her sleepless nights and tears of concern. I was fortunate in my parents both being doctors, because they could afford to send me to fee-paying schools, and could help me out when I was working in crappy jobs; and if it hadn't been for my sister putting a roof over my head when I moved back to London then I may never have gone, and may never have started the ball rolling back to a happy and fulfilling life.

*Personal account (B)*

I realised that I was different from other kids when I was at primary school. I remember having both the desire to do really bad things and then acting them out, like poking my mum in the eye with a pencil or ripping up the book she was reading. I really struggled at school with reading (because of my impulsiveness and also because of dyslexia which was only diagnosed when I was an adult) and used to steal money from my parents to pay other children to read the books I was supposed to so that I was able to tell the teacher the story. I thought I was evil inside and took an overdose when I was about 8 years old because I thought my whole life would be bad and nobody seemed to take my concerns seriously. I was not treated for the after-effects of the overdose – my parents seemed to be in denial about it. I tried to run away from home on several occasions.

By the time I entered secondary school I had a reputation as being one of those 'bright but naughty' kids, which is what I guess most kids with ADHD were called then. I gravitated towards similar kids and started experimenting with soft drugs and alcohol at around 11 years old. My only love in life was sport, and I swam, cycled, did athletics and surfed. I enjoyed high-risk activities, and rode around on older boys' motorbikes, started taking hard drugs and had regular sex by the time I was 13. I didn't listen to my teachers' cautions and stopped attending school because I found it too difficult and either went to the beach to surf and have sex, or hung around town shoplifting and drinking. I got cautioned by the police several times. I often got into physical fights both in and out of school and started carrying a knife. I never really remember being satisfied with what I was doing. I got pregnant but didn't follow it through, and chronically under-achieved at school.

My parents complained that I was too difficult to control, and they now say that they nearly separated because of my bad behaviour. My father had a terrific temper and we often got into verbal and physical fights. When I finished school I left home and drifted through a number of manual jobs, not ever being able to complete the tasks required of me. I met up with some travellers and bought a bus in which I travelled around the country financed by selling drugs. I developed a serious heroin addiction and had to steal a great deal to pay for my habit. I took lots of different types of drugs: LSD, opium, tranquillizers – just about anything I could get my hands on. I made quick and silly decisions; for example, I often stole cars and drove while drunk or drug-impaired. I got involved with credit card fraud and worked in a topless bar when I was sober. I spent a brief time in prison on drugs-related charges too. I had a problem with authority and was consistently defiant in my attitude to life. My self-esteem was very low and I took stimulants to control my weight after quitting heroin in a rehabilitation centre. I also tried to take my life again and had to be resuscitated, which led to short-term seizures. At no point during this period was it suggested that I should see a psychiatrist.

It was not until I was in my 20s that I received professional and personal help. I can put my success as an adult down to a few influential people in my life. They saw my potential and put in place the appropriate help and support to enable me to succeed. One of them helped me through a period of depression in my 20s, when I was institutionalised and given electroconvulsive therapy. I went into counselling and saw psychiatrists for 4 years which helped me sort out many issues. The other saw the potential in the poetry I wrote and convinced me to go to university to study English literature as a mature student with extra support for my dyslexia. I graduated with a first class degree and went on to study for a masters degree. Eventually I met someone at university who also saw my potential and only seemed to bring out the best in me. He is now my husband.

When our son Isaac was diagnosed with ADHD I realised that I had displayed many of his behaviours as a child myself (see personal account D below). I continued to have an issue controlling the amount of alcohol I drank, and had a problem with my temper, especially during premenstrual times. I was frightened I was going to physically hurt my child when I lost my temper, so my GP suggested I try SSRIs for pre-menstrual tension. These worked really well, and I still take medication daily. I did however continue to indulge in high-risk behaviour, which led to a serious motorbike accident that has left me disabled. A few years ago I stopped drinking alcohol because I finally realised I only drank to get drunk; but I almost immediately developed problems with anxiety and mild obsessive-compulsive disorder. My GP doubled my dose of SSRIs, which has helped a lot. I have also recently stopped smoking cannabis on a daily basis – something I had done for nearly 25 years.

I realise now, from the stories my father has told me about his behaviour (being in trouble with the law, under-achieving at school, oppositional defiance, alcohol abuse, and so on), that he also probably would have had a diagnosis of ADHD if he was a child today.

With all the support I have received from counsellors, psychiatrists, friends and my husband I now have a successful professional career and have been married for 10 years. I believe my own insight into ADHD helps me to be a better mother to my own child, and is helping him achieve his potential without the struggles I faced.

*Personal account (C)*

When I was diagnosed with ADHD I was about 8 years old and when I was told I had ADHD I didn't have a clue what it was or what it stood for. All I knew was that it was called 'ADHD'. I do not think any life experiences I had before I was diagnosed led to the onset of the condition, I just believe that it is DNA-based – someone else in the family has or may have had ADHD.

I go to a private clinic for help with my ADHD; they originally diagnosed me and I go there every 6 to 8 months to see a consultant. From what I can remember not a lot of treatments were discussed with me, except different types of medication. I found that to start with the medication I was given, which was Ritalin, was not effective in controlling my bad habits and behaviour. We had to go back to the clinic more often over the years to try and get my medication sorted and get the right balance and also the right type of medication. After going through all of this process the clinic finally managed to get the medication right when I was about 14; I know I have to take a mixture of different types and strengths of medication. But now I am on the right medication my ADHD has got better in my mind. I have stopped all the tics that I used to do and I find that I am a lot calmer than I was. However, the only problem I have with taking my medication, Concerta XL, is that my body has built up a large tolerance to it because I have been on it for so long, so I have to have come off the tablet every weekend and have medication called Dexedrine.

Due to my medication being an expensive drug and a dangerous one if it is misused, my parents and I had many problems with my GPs. One of the problems was that they were not willing to pay for the drug and also some of them did not know what the drug is like so they did not want to administer it in case anything went wrong and they lost their job because of it. The other main problem was that most of the time GPs did not have a clue about ADHD. Because of this me and my parents got to have a better understanding of what ADHD is, and most of the time I just think that the GPs need to know more and also have a better general knowledge of what ADHD is.

I found that my ADHD had a big effect on my education in many ways. When I was just diagnosed and for a long period of time after, until I managed to get the medication balanced, I used to be aggressive at school. I also used to get in a lot of fights because when I got wound up I became aggressive because of my ADHD and I found it hard to control my aggression. I was also very disruptive in the classroom as I used to call out in class often and I was easily distracted. However, as I managed to get the medication right and as I moved into upper school and progressed through year 9 and year 10 I found that all of the disruptive behaviour in the classroom slowly went away. Since then I have had little problems in the classroom.

Now I have a full understanding of ADHD but there are still some things I have questions about, like will I always have ADHD, will I be able to drive and will I be able to have certain types of jobs? I know for a fact that my ADHD will have an effect on my future life.

### 4.4.3    Personal accounts from carers of people with ADHD

*Personal account: parent (D)*

My son Isaac is now 7 years old. When he was born I breastfed him on demand. He shook his head and threw his arms around continuously which made feeding him difficult. My breastfeeding counsellor described him as 'fussy' and demonstrated how to swaddle him to prevent his arms from moving. This helped to control his writhing both when feeding and when he slept in bed with my husband and me at night. At 6 months old he attended a crèche on a part-time basis. When he was 18 months old the crèche began asking if there were any issues at home they should know about because he had become increasingly aggressive towards other children, displaying biting, punching and other violent behaviours.

Within a few weeks of this conversation my husband and I moved to the Philippines to begin new jobs. Looking back now I realise that Isaac never took well to changes in routine, and the move overseas was probably quite disruptive for him. He continued being aggressive and bit relentlessly any people who cared for him. He attended a Montessori pre-school, and the teachers often said how different he was from other children. His head teacher said that he showed no signs of socialisation, as if he'd never been exposed to other children, even though he'd attended a crèche in the UK for over a year. Other children did not want to play with him outside of school because they would often become injured or hurt from his robust play.

My husband and I made many trips to our Australian GP in the Philippines for minor family health problems. When I finally mentioned that I had concerns about Isaac's behaviour, he said he'd been waiting for me to say something for a long time. He immediately told us that he thought Isaac had ADHD and could refer us to a specialist paediatrician in Australia for an assessment. I had suspected that Isaac had ADHD from all the reading and research I had done on the internet, so I felt relieved that I was not imagining things.

During this time my marriage began to take the strain of a child who would want to be played with continually and was often violent. Isaac did not like it when my husband and I talked to one other, and would physically try to separate us. He constantly moved from one activity to another, and displayed increasingly impulsive and reckless behaviour. He climbed at every available opportunity and would not respond to discipline. His impulsivity presented as punching a dog, running after cars, eating dog faeces or head butting me when I read stories to him.

I took him to Australia when he was 3 years and 3 months old for an assessment. My husband and myself, and Isaac's teachers, completed a test before the consultation. (I later learned this was the Conners' rating.) Travelling to Australia on my own was very hard with a hyperactive and impulsive child. His behaviour was often exacerbated by environments with a lot of stimuli. I lost him several times at the airport, and he even disappeared off the end of the baggage carousel. Isaac's assessment by the Australian paediatrician resulted in a diagnosis of ADHD; he was described as being at the 'extreme end of the ADHD spectrum'. It was recommended that he take medication, but we resisted. We spent another year attempting to modify his behaviour, trying as many alternatives as possible to medication. During this year he continued to be impulsive, lacked attention and was violent – he punched a child's teeth out at school and was aggressive to his teachers.

When Isaac was 4 years and 4 months, a clinical psychologist assessed him and described him as having a range of problematic behaviours: fidgeting, climbing, being always on the move and easily distracted, having difficulty sustaining attention, being talkative, violent, aggressive and defiant. He averaged one accident a week. He liked routine and found transitions (for example, returning to school after the weekend) difficult. My marriage was becoming increasingly strained, so we decided to try medication and Isaac started taking methylphenidate. It seemed like a 'miracle'. He was able to focus, remain calm, play without being aggressive and make friends for the first time. He displayed slightly more anxiety immediately after taking the medication, but was able to tolerate it. He started on a low dose that was increased after 6 months. He now takes a modified-release preparation.

We returned to the UK in 2005. Since Isaac started the medication we have never looked back. Isaac does continue to be very challenging, and is clearly a very complex child. He has learning difficulties, finding it very difficult to produce legible writing and is significantly below the national average for reading. In addition to ADHD, Isaac also displays some autistic spectrum behaviours, though not enough for a formal diagnosis. We all regularly attend our local CAMHS, and Isaac has assessments from an educational psychologist who visits his school. I am not very impressed by the support we get from CAMHS. The psychiatrist weighs and measures Isaac, but cannot engage with him very well. I also had to ask about parent-training courses, rather than be offered them. When I asked about behavioural management strategies, no concrete examples were given, so I bought myself a copy of *1-2-3 Magic*, which has helped a huge amount.

Isaac is a really intelligent child, who is humorous and quirky. Adults think he is really interesting, but his peers find him strange, and he is constantly bullied at school. He recently started talking about killing himself and ways he may do this. Again our local CAHMS service were not very helpful with ways in which to address these issues, instead we got help with writing a 'social story book' from other professionals in the field whom we have met.

Isaac channels a lot of his excess energy into sport and enjoys rugby, karate, rock climbing, gymnastics and skateboarding. He wants to be a stunt man when he grows up! For us parents he is excellent company and constantly asks questions and spends time thinking carefully about the answers. He shows a natural aptitude for science and constructive activities. Isaac still needs a lot of routine, continuous behavioural moni-toring and moderation, a reward system for good behaviour and incentives to keep him on track. We learned all of these skills by reading lots of books on the subject and doing online research. We joined a few email support groups for parents of children with ADHD which have again provided lots of resources. There are no local support groups for parents of kids with ADHD in our area. Our biggest challenge now is to maintain Isaac's interest in school and keep his self-esteem as high as possible as he struggles with formal literacy skills and bullying in a mainstream school.

*Personal account: parent (E)*
I am the mother of a 15-year-old boy with ADHD (see personal account C above), who also has oppositional defiant disorder, a sleep disorder and vocal tics. From early infancy he was very active, never settling well to feed, and would only sleep for short periods. As soon as he could crawl he was into everything; we bought a playpen to put him in so we knew where he was, but he started to stand on his toys to climb over the top. Once he was walking we were unable to leave him unsupervised; he would climb over the stair gate and out of his cot, and would run everywhere. By the time he went to nursery school we had had many trips to casualty with our son for various injuries.

At nursery school he was very disruptive, constantly on the go, never wanting to share anything, playing in an 'over-the-top' way, not knowing when to stop, and alienating the other children so no one would play with him. This carried on into reception and years 1, 2, and 3, where he was also very disruptive in class, would not settle to work and was constantly fidgeting with anything he could get his hands on. By this time he was constantly being physically bullied, coming home with cuts and bruises. He was never invited to parties or out to play, and he became socially isolated. He had developed very low self-esteem, anxiety, poor social skills, vocal and physical tics, and learning difficulties. He would have panic attacks if put in a strange environ-ment, and he self-harmed. His sleep pattern was totally out of the window – he would be up 15 and more times a night, running round the house barking like a dog. He was physically aggressive to me, kicking, punching and lashing out. He would fly into a rage that would last sometimes 2 hours or more; on some of these occasions we would have to physically restrain him, even resorting to sitting on him, just to try to stop him from harming himself or trashing the house. He would frequently destroy his toys, clothes and his room, even tearing curtains from the wall and pulling the fitted carpet up. We learnt not to take him to the supermarket, which resulted in one of us going late at night on our own. We gave up clothes shopping in town, and would only take him in for shoes or a haircut. He once threw a huge tantrum in a department store; I walked out and left him lying on the floor under some clothes, and a security guard stopped me and asked if I had forgotten something! He became the child of night-mares, the child that you thought you could not possibly have, because we were 'sensible' parents!

We had great difficulty disciplining him, not because we did not want to, but because we had tried everything and anything that our friends suggested: sitting on the stairs, no toys, no telly, bed early, no playing outside, no treats. Nothing worked, he just shrugged his shoulders at us. We had reached breaking point, our marriage was suffering, and our other younger son was upset; he started to have night terrors and began pulling his hair out, resorting to hiding in a cupboard when his older brother was in one of his 'rages'.

By the time our son had reached the age of 7 and a half we had become increasingly concerned by his uncontrollable behaviour at home and at school. I raised my concerns with his teacher about his behaviour and his inability to concentrate, and also about the constant bullying he was receiving at school. We agreed that he may have a learning/behavioural disorder. I did some research into childhood disorders, contacting NHS Direct for information. They sent me literature on ADHD, and I read the book that it recommended (*Understanding ADHD* by Christopher Green); I thought, 'this could have been written about my son'. I was actually relieved that there could be a reason for all of his 'problems', and it was not us being bad parents. I showed the book to my son's teacher and she offered to write to my GP supporting my concerns. I took this letter, together with a diary I had started to keep of my son's behaviour, to the GP. He listened and agreed to refer my son to the local Child, Adolescent and Family Consultation Service (my son had just turned 8). However, they refused to see him because he did not meet their admission criteria; they were only taking 'emergencies' at the time, and because he was not displaying suicidal tendencies, he was not considered an emergency. They suggested that I should attend a 'child behaviour management' course instead, which when I contacted them had no spaces. My GP then referred our son to the same service 'out of area', but they too were unable to see him.

I was given details of a private clinic that specialised in ADHD and also took NHS referrals from GPs if funding was in place. My GP agreed to refer my son, and applied for funding from the local health authority. After 6 weeks of not hearing anything I contacted them directly myself. After describing the great distress that our son's behaviour was causing him and everyone around him, they agreed to fund him, as they were unable to provide a service for him locally. During this period the school had requested an educational psychologist to assess him; she agreed that he required further 'specialist' assessment, and she supported his referral to the private clinic.

The clinic diagnosed our son with ADHD, oppositional defiant disorder and other comorbid conditions. We were offered various strategies to help cope with his behaviour, some very useful. The consultant suggested that our son should have a trial of methylphenidate. We decided that we would like to research the medication route before agreeing to follow this course of action. After much discussion, my husband and I decided this was the best way to offer our son some sort of 'normal' childhood. Our son was started on Equasym (5 mg every 4 hours), and there was an improvement in his concentration levels almost immediately, and he was also much calmer. The dosage had to be slowly increased and we found that it was effective for 3 to 3 and a half hours; he was therefore experiencing 'peaks and troughs'. We had difficulties with the school as they refused to give our son his medication, insisting that I went and gave it to him. He got to the stage where he had to take medication before he went to school, at first break, lunchtime and then after school. Our GP at this time was fairly supportive, although he admitted that he had no knowledge of the condition, and was happy to be led by the guidance of the clinic, and my experience as a mother. It was suggested by the consultant that we try Ritalin SR, which my son took early morning and at lunchtime, followed by regular Ritalin in the early evening. This combination proved effective for approximately 6 months, during which time his sleep pattern was constantly disturbed. We also had problems with his appetite – it took him about 2 hours to eat a meal. The consultant suggested that we try melatonin to help get him to sleep. Our GP (we had moved house by this time and changed GPs) refused to prescribe this medication, saying, in front of our son, that the drugs were very expensive and he had his budget to think of. We moved to a different surgery where all the GPs were very supportive, and happy to prescribe under the guidance of our son's consultant. They remained supportive for 5 years, until we moved house, and had to change surgeries again.

Ritalin SR became less and less effective. The consultant felt that he had become tolerant to this form of medication, so it was decided to change him to Concerta XL, which would provide him with a sustained dose for approximately 12 hours. It was also decided at this time to introduce him to clonidine to help with his oppositional defiant disorder, tics and also to help him sleep; he had a small dose before school, and then a larger one an hour before bed. This medication regime proved very effective for a considerable time, but as my son grew, so did his tolerance to Concerta XL (at this stage he was taking 108 mg, plus 10 mg of Ritalin at lunchtime and 20 mg of Ritalin after school). By the time he was 13 and due to start upper school his medication was not as effective as it had been. The consultant suggested that we 'wash out' his medication every school holiday (every 4 months), and this worked well for a year and a half.

Our son is now 15 and 6 feet tall and we have had to change the medication regime again. He is currently on the following on weekdays: 50 mcg of clonidine and 108 mg of Concerta XL on rising; 20 mg of Ritalin after school and 125 mcg of clonidine 1 hour before bed. At weekends he takes 50 mcg of clonidine and 15 mg Dexedrine on rising; 15 mg of Dexedrine at lunchtime, 10 mg of Dexedrine at teatime and 125 mcg of clonidine 1 hour before bed. This regime is proving extremely effective at present, and he displays no signs of sleepiness, and is doing well at school – far better than we ever thought possible. He takes reduced dosages when he does any sport, as the adrenaline helps him to self-medicate.

My son has remained at the private clinic, where the staff are extremely supportive; the provision of telephone support, offering the opportunity to speak to a consultant when needed, and even adjusting medication over the phone have proved really valuable. There is an educational psychologist who is able to offer advice, and he recently went through our son's GCSE options with him; they also have a school liaison officer who is able to offer advice to teachers.

We have always encouraged our son to take a very active part in sports because we found that he was able to expend some of his energies that way. He has been a member of a swimming club since he was 4, and is now county standard, training for approximately 8 hours a week. He has been coaching the younger children at the pool and is really good with them. He also had karate lessons for 4 years and has done very well; we found that karate benefited his coordination and self-discipline tremendously.

We also found that by encouraging our son to take part in these sports, and also by being able to achieve in them, it has helped his self-esteem greatly.

We learned not to put him into situations that he was not able to cope with, like going to the supermarket or into town. We also learned to try and focus on the good behaviour, to give praise, and to try and ignore as much of the bad/annoying behaviour as possible. By doing this, and also by virtue of the fact that he could concentrate at school, and was not constantly in trouble, we found that his self-esteem slowly increased, the self-harming stopped, and the panic attacks and anxiety abated, only occasionally appearing when he was extremely stressed.

Our son is at his worst and most oppositional in the early morning and late evening, which is before and after the medication is at its most effective. His vocal tics are also at their highest volume. He is quite happy to take his medication; he says he can 'turn his brain off'. He actually went to school a few weeks ago having forgotten to take his medication – he said it was awful; he was unable to concentrate, he constantly fidgeted and was very disruptive. He only escaped being excluded from school because the teacher recognised he was not his usual self, and when he explained that he had forgotten his medication, she let him off. Without the medication I am certain that our family would not have survived and that my son would have been permanently excluded from school, and worse, be in a young offender's institution. Instead he has just achieved the highest grade for his GCSE IT coursework and exam.

Our son does not have fizzy drinks, rarely eats chocolate or sweets, and we try to avoid packet/processed food and 'E' numbers. He has also taken pure fish oil for several years, and this seems to help with his mood levels; he says that he feels he concentrates better when he is taking it.

However our son is still socially isolated. He does not get invited to parties and he never goes to school discos because crowds and noise are too much for him. He has many acquaintances at school but there is no one close and no one comes to our house to see him.

We have never received, or been offered, support from local NHS child development services, CAMHS or community psychiatric nurses. There are no local support groups and our wider family has not been understanding of our son's condition and subsequent needs. Our close friends tried to offer us support, but they have children of their own.

The family environment has become easier in the last couple of years, and my relationship with my son has improved – I don't 'hate' him any more for being a horrible child! Instead I am proud of what he has achieved and how far he has come.

*Personal account: parent (F)*

Before our son was born I believed that we were 'good' parents and I was proud of the way we parented our children and met their individual needs; however this soon changed as the youngest of our three children entered the world. We discovered that we had a baby who hated to sleep, constantly required attention and, as he began toddling, managed to destroy everything that got in his way. His tantrums, head butting, fear of enclosed and crowded areas made it impossible to take him shopping.

He hated bright lights and loud noises; he was obsessed with his toy cars and lining them up in a certain way and by colour; and he was cruel to the family cat.

Our son's behaviour concerned us, so much so that he was referred to child and family guidance at the age of 2 and a half. He was excluded from almost every nursery he attended due to his behaviour, and he was admitted into hospital on several occasions for drinking any liquids in sight (he was constantly thirsty). He was the only child on the children's ward who required his parents to be there constantly because the staff were not able to deal with his behaviour and tantrums.

By the time our son was 7 he had more fixed-term exclusions from school than I care to remember and by age 12 there were services involved that I never knew existed. We sat in meeting after meeting with many professionals including a paediatrician, GPs, psychologists, educational psychologists, a child psychiatrist, staff from early years provision, education welfare officers, social workers, behaviour support workers, special educational needs case workers, a youth offending team, the police, and heads of schools and teaching staff. He was cautioned for arson, charged with theft and would constantly run away from school and not return home until he was found by the police or us.

A child psychiatrist was involved for almost 10 of the first 12 years of our son's life but failed to assess and address our son's needs. At no time during this period were the needs of our two older children considered; for example how the abuse, threats and behaviour inflicted on them by their younger brother may be impacting on their young lives, and also how our spending so much time in dealing with our youngest child denied them the quality time they should have had from us.

When our son went to high school we thought it would be a 'fresh start' and that the move would provide him with the much needed support he required. However, in the first 6 months we received numerous calls and letters from the school about our son's behaviour. He was seen by an educational psychologist for special educational needs, and was assessed as having emotional and behavioural difficulties; during this assessment our son was permanently excluded from the school.

For almost 15 months our son was tutored at home but received little if any education because he would abscond before the tutors arrived. It was at this time that we were mistakenly sent a copy of a letter from the child psychiatrist who had written to the school's educational psychologist and family GP providing his account of our son's needs. The letter stated that our son's behaviour was due to 'parental inconsistency' and 'poor parenting' and that he would benefit from local authority care, that is, removal from the family home.

I had always been taught to respect those in authority as professional people educated in their line of work. But seeing that our son was being failed by so many of these professionals, my respect for them was rapidly decreasing. Outraged by the letter, I wrote a strong response and requested that our son receive a second opinion from another child and adolescent psychiatrist. Within 4 months of making the request, our son was finally diagnosed with severe ADHD, sleep disorder, conduct disorder and moderate learning needs.

I had never heard of ADHD so how could I support my son and how would others support his needs? I learned what I could about the disorder; I undertook training on special educational needs and the law and fought for my son to be educated and treated appropriate to his needs. Because of this he was placed at a residential school outside the county, which was fully funded by the local authority. We demanded that he be allowed home at weekends as we did not want our son thinking that we were rejecting him – he had received enough rejection in his young life.

Over the summer, during the weeks prior to starting his new school, he was prescribed Ritalin for the ADHD and melatonin for his sleep disorder. The changes in our son were remarkable – we now had a child who sat around the table for family chats, took part in family outings and, most importantly, could sit and concentrate for more than a few minutes at a time. We had a happy child with so much love to give and receive.

Things were now going relatively well; our son settled into his new school and I continued to learn more about ADHD in order to support the school in meeting our son's needs. His medication was administered by the school nurse on clear instructions from me. However, neither the teaching staff nor the school's in-house educational psychologist had any knowledge or understanding of ADHD. This contributed towards major conflicts; they stated that ADHD was just an excuse for 'bad behaviour' and excluded our son from taking part in after-school activities. When he was at home at weekends we began to notice that he was rather withdrawn; he would not communicate and would not show the same love and affection he had done over the summer. When he went back to school I enquired as to the cause and found that the staff were continually changing, which seemed to affect our son's routine; also, the school nurse was not always on the premises to administer the medication, therefore our son was receiving his Ritalin as and when it suited the school.

Other students learned of our son being on medication prescribed by a psychiatrist and he was called names such as 'psycho', 'crazy man', 'nutcase' and so on, which led to our son refusing to take the medication to treat his ADHD symptoms because he thought it was for 'psychos'. Things soon reverted back to the old ways; his behaviour was out of control, he was smoking cannabis, drinking, stealing and running away, all of which contributed towards his being permanently excluded from the school. He refused to take any medication apart from the melatonin and we were now left to pick up the pieces and fight for his education.

Feeling somewhat battered and bruised and totally exhausted, I approached my GP who handed me a prescription for Prozac and told me I was just depressed. This was the day on which I finally snapped and told a professional exactly what I thought of his prescription and lack of support for our son. From that day to this I have continued to fight for justice for our son and others like him and their families. I joined several other parents who had a child diagnosed with ADHD to meet for coffee and share our stories. Meeting other parents in a similar situation was like having a release valve to let off steam.

Another placement was found at a school nearer to home with boarding during the week; but this too was short lived as none of the teaching staff knew about ADHD. Once again our son was permanently excluded. (Several months later it was announced on local radio that the head and deputy head of the school had been suspended under investigation due to their disciplinary procedures.)

For children with a special educational needs provision, like our son, it is the duty of the local education authority to draw up a transition plan for ongoing school provision and review it when the child turns 14. All the local services and agencies involved in that child's care should be invited to the transition review meeting. The local authority must also notify social care, who then decide whether the young person is defined as having a disability. Social care notified us that under the 1948 National Assistance Act our son was not defined as being disabled. We challenged this decision using both the National Assistance Act and the 1989 Children Act and we were successful in our appeal. We then requested that our son be placed on the 'Children with Disabilities Register'; when this was denied we took the matter up with the local government ombudsman and it was found that our authority did not have such a register. Due to our actions we were delighted that children and young people with ADHD can now be entered on to the 'Children with Disabilities Register'. We have never received any letters of apology from the local authority and our son received no education from the date of his exclusion at 14 plus.

When our son turned 16 we were told that he was no longer a child and that he was responsible for his own actions. But he was a 16 year old who acted like a 12 year old, who had little education and no knowledge of NHS services, how to claim state benefits, and how to pay bills, shop or clean. Yet he was expected to manage these affairs on his own. The understanding was that I would be copied in to any appointment letters – this way I could assure his attendance. All was fine until a new psychiatrist became involved; the letters stopped arriving, our son failed to turn up one day and due to this the community mental health team (CMHT) decided to close his case file.

It would seem that our adult CMHT had very little knowledge of ADHD or understanding of the needs of those with the disorder and of the impact it was having on our son's day-to-day life. (We educated our son as much as we possibly could about ADHD; we felt this was necessary to help him understand the disorder, as well as to help him explain his difficulties to others, in particular service providers.) After letters were sent to the CMHT chief executive, the services were reinstated and I was included in correspondence. I believe that this was initiated after we requested that our son be seen by experts who understood ADHD and related disorders. However there has been no continuity with the psychiatrists my son sees and this seems to have had a knock-on effect on him and his willingness to trust new people involved in his care.

My son's psychiatrist prescribed him antidepressants with no other form of support strategies being delivered. I challenged this and asked why he was not being offered anger management, behaviour management, counselling, therapy and so on, or appropriate medication to treat his ADHD symptoms, since the alternatives he was taking on a daily basis were clearly not working. We felt that our son was still a child by rights, and therefore should have had access to the same treatments and therapies as other children under the care of children's services. After this our son was prescribed Concerta XL, and the transformation was the same as when he first took Ritalin. Once again we had a son who seemed more compliant, and he started reducing the amount of cannabis he had been using. (When asked why he used cannabis our son explained that he felt 'normal', that he could socialise and communicate better with his peers, and that it took away all the anger inside him.) Once again, however, due to changes in psychiatrists, our son's appointments became few and far between and he stopped receiving his medication.

When our son was almost 17 he decided to leave home, which was a concern as we wondered how long he would survive. We registered him for social housing with the council but in the meantime we paid a deposit to a private landlord for a room in shared accommodation and made an application for appropriate housing and council tax benefits. He now considered himself a responsible adult so we let him do things his way, but this was short lived when he found himself without money or food, his flat was raided and while he lay drunk in his bed his belongings were stolen by individuals he thought were his friends. After contacting the local council regarding our son's social housing needs and writing numerous letters, we involved the Shelter organisation. We continued to fight for his accommodation as well as the appropriate state benefits, thinking that if these were in place it would assist us as well as our son to live within the community as an adult.

Within 4 months our son received a one bedroom housing association flat. To this day, 8 years on, we have managed to keep this roof over our son's head (as well as keeping him out of prison) by being guarantors for his rent, making applications and becoming appointees for this state benefits, making use of other services for grants, such as the Soldiers, Sailors, Airmen and Families Association (SSAFA) Forces help, decorating and furnishing the flat, undertaking regular cleaning, shopping and laundry, replacing furniture damaged or destroyed during outbursts of anger, and intervening with the housing association when they threatened eviction. We bailed him out of debt for credit cards and mobile phone bills, made sure he was 'red flagged' on the police system as requiring an appropriate adult in attendance when in custody (which we were at all hours of day and night), communicated with and educated the solicitors acting for our son on ADHD, wrote to the courts in order to put our son's case across, acted as expert witnesses when our son when to court and advised the solicitor to seek an appropriate expert witness with knowledge of ADHD. When our son attempted suicide while detained in custody we referred the case to the Police Complaints Commission.

By the age of 22, our son underwent a private psychiatric assessment ordered by the courts; it was this assessment that initiated further assessments through the CMHT and at the Maudsley, and how we learned that our son not only had severe ADHD but also Asperger's syndrome as well as other mental health and learning needs. Later, at yet another court hearing, further medical evidence was needed, which required an expert in ADHD and Asperger's. The expert provided the much needed evidence that prison would have a severely detrimental effect on our son and on his safety.

This made us wonder how services and agencies could have misunderstood our son for over 20 years. It took the assessment and report of the expert witness involved in our son's case, and ourselves as parents and carers, to highlight the areas of concern in relation to our son's diagnosis and the impact the disorder has on his day-to-day life. It is crucial that professionals with great knowledge and understanding of ADHD are instructed by the legal bodies representing people like our son in order to provide the necessary evidence with which to demonstrate that a prison sentence would have serious outcomes.

Our son is now 25 and we still provide the support he needs. We have stood by him no matter what has been thrown at us throughout the years and to this day we believe that our parenting was our road to success in managing and dealing with our son, rather than his being another statistic within our penal system. He is now on a medication known as Strattera and is doing remarkably well. For the first time he has remained in a relationship for over a year, he has become engaged and is slowly dealing with matters relating to his own finances and household management.

It has certainly not been an easy task to access the appropriate healthcare, and social and educational services for our son; it has felt as though we have lived through a nightmare, and in a way we are still going through the tail end of one as we continue to support and care for our son. It angers and frustrates us that professionals see parents like us, who have gained the knowledge and experience of living with and managing ADHD within our family unit, as a threat. They should be working with us and using our knowledge in order to provide the best possible care and support package for their patients.

It would seem that there has been very little improvement in services for people with ADHD and their families in recent years. As parents and carers we have never been offered or directed to any support services relating to ADHD by health or social care professionals; we have managed to access advice and support through family members and the internet. Our experiences as a family have helped us to support other families facing similar situations. I am the chair of a local ADHD support group, which was set up in 1994. The group has received an award for community endeavour as well as local community volunteer awards. We are represented on various local working groups and boards and are also involved in local prisons and young offender institutions. The group has assisted other service providers and authorities set up parent support for ADHD as well as presenting at many conferences on the subject.

## 4.5    LIVING WITH ADHD

This section is written from the perspective of people with ADHD and their families and carers. It also draws out some of the main themes from the personal accounts above and summarises the primary points of concern.

### 4.5.1    Children with ADHD

ADHD is a full-time disorder, extending beyond bad behaviour and problems at school, and has an impact on all aspects of a person's life. Children with ADHD are not problem children, but children with a genuine problem. They have a medical condition that is difficult for them and for those around them, and they stand out as different from peers and siblings at all stages of development (personal information, Dr Geoffrey Kewley, Learning Assessment and Neurocare Centre, UK, 2007).

Little social research has been undertaken about how children feel and behave with ADHD. Some children may be aware that they are different from others (see account B), but some may not have a highly developed self-concept of what it means to act differently from other children. Research indicates that children have dichotomous experiences when taking or not taking medication, which is reinforced by parents and teachers, for example feeling good/bad, happy/sad, playing nicely/fighting, and so on (Singh, 2006). This is also borne out by the accounts above (see accounts D and F). As the young man in account A explained, because some of his teachers treated him as if he were 'bad' then this became the 'mould' he would fit himself into. Children with ADHD have different social skills from those without ADHD; they may have tantrums and be aggressive towards others, and they find it harder to make and keep friends (Green *et al.*, 2005). As a consequence the parents may attempt to fill the void, which can add to the pressures they face (see accounts A and F above). This is where teachers and other adults in positions of responsibility can alleviate some of the pressure at home, by being patient, attentive and supportive to the child at school, and understanding how ADHD manifests. The accounts above suggest that routine and a stable environment is very important in managing ADHD symptoms, as is continuity with the healthcare professionals that the child sees.

As children grow up their symptoms will probably change and may extend into other areas (Farrington, 1995; Barkley *et al.,* 1990). For example, between the ages of 11 and 16 children with ADHD are more likely to be regular smokers and drinkers and are more likely to have taken drugs (Green *et al.*, 2005). As the child in account F remarks to his parents, he used cannabis to feel 'normal', so that he could socialise and communicate better with his peers, and to take away 'all the anger inside him'. In terms of treatment, children may decide by themselves to stop taking medication at a particular time in their lives, or may continue into adulthood. As the mother in account F points out, it is important to recognise that delineations in the health service based on age may need to be more flexible when it comes to young people with ADHD; she cites the example of her own son who, when aged 16, had the outlook of a 12 year old.

### 4.5.2    Adults with ADHD

The professional discourse surrounding ADHD and adulthood is much less developed than with children; indeed most information regarding aetiology, symptoms or treatment comes from observations or studies of children (Weiss *et al.*, 1999). Subsequently, adults with ADHD may encounter greater obstacles in terms of having the condition identified and recognised and being supported. It is claimed that between 30 and 50% of children with ADHD will carry the disorder through into adulthood (Wender, 1998). Adult experiences of the disorder may be characterised by similar feelings of restlessness and disinhibition as in childhood. In adulthood there is also a strong association with both depression and substance misuse.

Developmental changes may mean that sometimes levels of self-awareness or motivation towards a certain task may make the symptoms easier to manage – though this is not always the case. Living with ADHD as an adult can present daily challenges at work and at home and can impede the building of habits and routines upon which 'normal' lives are often grounded. Problem areas often centre on organisation, motivation and commitment. Organising a busy work and social schedule can present a constant challenge; any opportunity to habituate some practice or impose some routine structure may have a positive impact. While new projects and directions may be sought with some vigour, retaining this initial motivation may prove more of a challenge, and frequently taking the long view of events may cause some disillusionment. Strong relationships at home can be hugely empowering, though these too need commitment and hard work, and will frequently prove frustrating for both parties.

### 4.5.3    Labelling and stigma

In addition to coping with a medical problem, an additional consideration for a child or adult diagnosed with ADHD, is adjusting to the experience of being labelled with a psychiatric diagnosis and the negative consequences this may have. Labelling theory in the social sciences (Goffman, 1968a; Rosenhan, 1973; Scheff, 1975) suggests that psychiatric labels can have effects on the bearer in terms of their own identity construction, that is, how they see themselves, and in terms of the social reaction to them.

The symptoms of ADHD describe a child who finds peer interactions difficult and is disruptive or inattentive at home and school. As such, the child is likely to feel a sense of difference or alienation in social situations. Interventions at school, such as special needs provision or disciplinary procedures, may work to reinforce this difference. The child becomes a member of different groups of children who are known as 'different', 'special' or 'difficult'. Such changes in group membership alter the way the child thinks about themselves as well as the way others think about them.

A label such as ADHD reinforces this difference by medicalising and highlighting certain characteristics that are perceived to have a negative social impact. The introduction of a medical label also institutes the concept of stigma and research suggests that stigma is one of the most keenly felt consequences of being labelled (Bauman, 2007; Fennell & Liberato, 2007; Hinshaw, 2005; Muthukrishna, 2006; Read, 2007; Stier & Hinshaw, 2007). Once a label has been introduced the bearer is obliged, regardless of what they may think of the label, to consider themselves in relation to it. Likewise, those around them will think about and react to that person differently as a result of the label. This process will necessarily effect changes in the bearer's choices and actions, one consequence of which may be that they produce more of the behaviours associated with the label. As such, labels are thought to accrue self-fulfilling prophecies for the bearer.

Many of the aspects of school, both in terms of curriculum and pedagogy, work to differentiate children from one another (Armstrong, 2003; Benjamin *et al.*, 2003; Meo & Parker, 2004). One criticism that can be made of diagnoses such as ADHD is that they may 'medicalise' the child who for one reason or another finds themselves on the wrong side of these mechanisms. Once such a label is applied the bearer will be obliged to consider themselves in relation to it. Whether they accept the descriptions as fitting or reject the label and offer further resistance, their individual differences have now been fixed and medicalised, and they are now obliged to live with what has been termed a 'spoiled identity' (Goffman, 1968b). As such it is important to exercise caution in the application of such labels, and to make a full investigation into the child's social situation, bearing in mind the forces that may have worked to mark them as different in the first place.

### 4.5.4 Impact of ADHD on family life and relationships

ADHD can have a significant impact upon family life and relationships with friends (World Federation for Mental Health, 2005). Parents of children with ADHD need a great deal of support to help them manage their child's problems. It is not only a case of having to manage the day-to-day challenges of living with a child with ADHD; parents also have to deal with school problems which are so common in these children, with many requiring a statement of special educational needs. Children with ADHD require much more support and guidance than their peers in most of their everyday lives. This is a full-time disorder, requiring full-time care. Professionals need to understand the stress and exhaustion that many parents experience.

Parents (as demonstrated by the mothers who have given accounts above) are concerned about the impact that the lack of understanding of ADHD from health and social care professionals, staff in schools and the wider society can have on their child's life:

- 91% of parents were shown to be often stressed or worried about their child's life
- 68% stated that their ADHD child had been excluded from social activities because of their ADHD symptoms
- 61% said their family activities were disrupted
- 51% said the diagnosis took too long
- 63% said their primary care doctor did not know much about ADHD.

According to a survey conducted by the World Federation for Mental Health, the average length of time to receive an assessment and subsequent diagnosis is 2.44 years, with 17% waiting for more than 5 years (World Federation for Mental Health, 2005). As the accounts above suggest, parents and carers can provide a wealth of information to healthcare professionals about their child's ADHD symptoms and behaviours, which can enable the professional not only to reach an accurate diagnosis, but also to deliver treatment and care that is tailored to the child's individual needs.

There are a number of public misconceptions about ADHD that need to be addressed in the best interests of children and their families. In order to address these misconceptions, it is important to understand more about the impact of the disorder on families and specifically how *well* families' needs are being addressed. For example, the impact on brothers and sisters living with siblings with ADHD cannot be underestimated (see parents E and F above), and professionals must always consider and be mindful of the disruption that can be caused to their lives.

As the mothers in the accounts above make clear, parents often feel that they are being judged and/or criticised by friends, family and other people. Professionals may also attribute the child's 'bad' behaviour to the parents (see account F). This can significantly undermine parents; they can become overwhelmed and feel like failures, wondering why the behaviour regime that seems to work so well for others does not work with their child. If they have other children who do not have ADHD, they may begin to question their own parenting skills (see accounts A and F) when their other child begins to show signs of ADHD. Parents may see no easy answers, and wonder what happened to the joys of parenting.

Families affected by ADHD will benefit from support from all agencies, such as education, social services, their GP, mental health services and in some cases the youth justice system and police. These agencies can best help families and those with ADHD by working together to offer a package of support for the child/young person *and* the family. Medication alone is not the answer; they still require a great deal of support to manage the disorder. Behavioural monitoring and moderation, structured activities and a reward system with incentives may also be beneficial, as the mother in account D suggests.

One or both parents of a child with ADHD may suspect the child is different from other children and actively seek professional support[8]. Teachers are often the first to recognise signs of ADHD, seek referral and support both the parents and child alike. As the personal accounts from parents relate, and as the *Mental Health of Children and Young People in Great Britain, 2004* report states, teachers 'are likely to have complained about [the child's] overactivity, impulsiveness and poor attention' (Green *et al.*, 2005), which can lead to difficulties with learning basic skills at school: 'Almost three-quarters (71%) of children with hyperkinetic disorders had officially recognised special educational needs (compared with 16% of other children)' (Green *et al.*, 2005). The accounts above all speak of the difficulties in finding the right educational environment where the child can be supported and flourish and where his or her individual needs can be met.

Parents may also seek support from mental health services, primary care or specialist educational services. There are still questions about whether ADHD exists (or whether the child is just naughty) and at what age a diagnosis can be made, which may explain why some parents find it hard to get a referral to a healthcare professional. Parents may seek informal advice from family, friends, self-help groups or the internet (Green *et al.*, 2005), although as the mother in account F states, this may be the only support available to them.

Parents will inevitably face the dilemma over whether to embark on treatment for ADHD symptoms, or whether to use alternative therapies or change their child's diet. If parents choose medication, they may feel guilty, and in turn decide to have 'medication holidays' to allow the 'real child' to emerge (Singh, 2005). Parents may receive mixed messages from the media about medication for ADHD, and believe that too many children take medication. According to the *Mental Health of Children and*

---

[8]'Almost all (95%) parents of children with hyperkinetic disorder had sought some form of help in the previous 12 months because of concerns about their child's mental health. Most (93%) had accessed some professional service. The most commonly used source of professional help were teachers (70%) but parents also sought help from, or were referred to, other professional sources such as mental health services (52%), primary health care (46%) and specialist education services, such as educational psychologists (37%)' (Green *et al.*, 2005).

*Young People in Great Britain* report 'about 2 in 5 (43%) children with a hyperkinetic disorder are taking some kind of medication' (Green *et al.*, 2005).

ADHD often goes hand-in-hand with other conditions, such as conduct disorder (Green *et al.*, 2005), making behavioural and emotional challenges even more complex (see accounts A and F above). These complications have ramifications for other areas of the lives of children and young people; for example, it is reported that almost one third of children with hyperkinetic disorders have been excluded from school (Green *et al.*, 2005). Such children may also go on have problems with the law.

Given this set of circumstances, parents and carers of children with ADHD can find being a mother or a father challenging. They are more likely to separate if they are a couple, have emotional disorders and function less well as a family, when compared with parents without children with ADHD (Green *et al.*, 2005).

Parent and carers therefore require support from healthcare professionals, who should consider:

- ensuring parents/carers have good support networks, for example access to a self-help group, and are aware of local and national organisations
- recommending useful resources (books, leaflets, websites, and so on)
- helping parents/carers find outlets for their child to boost their self-esteem (for example, sports or creative activities)
- keeping dialogue as open as possible with the parents and the child (social story books may be used for self-esteem issues)
- recognising that ADHD is a complex disorder, and rarely without coexisting conditions
- recognising that transition and change may be hard
- helping parents/families to obtain support for relationship/marriage problems and for any siblings
- encouraging parents to keep a diary of behaviours to feed back to CAHMS meetings and other healthcare professionals
- asking the parents to complete a questionnaire before medication is started so that they can compare differences.


## 4.6 RECOMMENDATIONS

4.6.1.1 Healthcare professionals should develop a trusting relationship with people with ADHD and their families or carers by:
- respecting the person and their family's knowledge and experience of ADHD
- being sensitive to stigma in relation to mental illness.

4.6.1.2 Healthcare professionals should provide people with ADHD and their families or carers with relevant, age-appropriate information (including written information) about ADHD at every stage of their care. The information should cover diagnosis and assessment, support and self-help, psychological treatment, and the use and possible side effects of drug treatment.

4.6.1.3    When assessing a child or young person with ADHD, and throughout their
care, healthcare professionals should:
- allow the child or young person to give their own account of how they
feel, and record this in the notes
- involve the child or young person and the family or carer in treatment
decisions
- take into account expectations of treatment, so that informed consent
can be obtained from the child's parent or carer or the young person
before treatment is started.

4.6.1.4    Healthcare professionals working with children and young people with
ADHD should be:
- familiar with local and national guidelines on confidentiality and the
rights of the child
- able to assess the young person's understanding of issues related to
ADHD and its treatment (including Gillick competence)
- familiar with parental consent and responsibilities, child protection
issues, the Mental Health Act (2007) and the Children Act (1989).

4.6.1.5    Adults with ADHD should be given written information about local and
national support groups and voluntary organisations.

4.6.1.6    Healthcare professionals should ask families or carers about the impact of
ADHD on themselves and other family members, and discuss any
concerns they may have. Healthcare professionals should:
- offer family members or carers an assessment of their personal, social
and mental health needs
- encourage participation in self-help and support groups where appropriate
- offer general advice to parents and carers about positive parent– and
carer–child contact, clear and appropriate rules about behaviour, and
the importance of structure in the child or young person's day
- explain that parent-training/education programmes do not necessarily
imply bad parenting, and that their aim is to optimise parenting skills
to meet the above-average parenting needs of children and young
people with ADHD.

# 5.   DIAGNOSIS

## 5.1   INTRODUCTION

This guideline is applicable to people above the age of 3 and of all levels of intellectual ability, who show symptoms of hyperactivity, impulsivity or inattention to a degree that severely impairs their mental or social development causing failure to make expected progress in the domains of intellectual development, personal relationships, physical or mental health or academic function. This includes people with ADHD whether or not they have other coexisting developmental or mental health disorders or whether the ADHD behaviours and symptoms result from genetic, physical environmental or social-environmental causes. This chapter sets out to look at the issue of diagnostic categorisation and assessment that should trigger the use of this guideline. Sections 5.3 to 5.14 address the validity of the diagnostic construct of DSM-IV-TR ADHD and ICD-10 hyperkinetic disorder as diagnostic categories that give rise to significant impairments. Sections 5.15 to 5.17 provide guidance for clinical practice.

For ADHD the question is whether a diagnostic category associated with clear evidence of impairment, that most people would consider requires some form of medical, social or educational intervention, can be reliably defined. To provide guidance for clinicians involved in the medical component of such intervention, the validity of the diagnostic concept of ADHD is addressed using the definition of a clinical disorder or illness as any condition that causes discomfort, dysfunction, distress or social problems to the person concerned. This part of the guideline addresses the question of validity of the diagnostic construct of ADHD and provides practice guidelines for the diagnostic process.

## 5.2   DEFINITIONS OF TERMS

The terminology applied to ADHD and related problems has been used in different ways at different times and by different groups of people. This section clarifies some of the major terms used in this chapter. A description of the diagnostic terms is provided in Chapter 2.

*ADHD and hyperkinetic disorder*
The terms *ADHD (DSM-IV-TR)* and *hyperkinetic disorder (ICD-10)* are used when talking about the specific diagnostic categories of ADHD as defined by DSM-IV-TR and hyperkinetic disorder as defined by ICD-10 respectively. The criteria for hyperkinetic disorder are more stringent that those for ADHD with hyperkinetic disorder forming a subgroup of the DSM-IV-TR ADHD combined type diagnosis (see Chapter 2). When discussing the disorder more broadly 'ADHD' is used as an umbrella term. Some of the earlier literature used the term 'hyperactivity' for the cluster of hyperactive, impulsive and inattentive symptoms. In this guideline the term 'hyperactivity' will be

restricted to mean the combination of symptoms that define overactive behaviour and the term 'ADHD symptoms' used to refer to the combination of hyperactive, impulsive and inattentive symptoms.

*Symptoms*
The behavioural phenomena that describe ADHD will be referred to as *symptoms* of ADHD throughout this chapter. This choice of wording is intended to reflect the fact that the behavioural phenomena that characterise ADHD may not always be reported as observed behaviours, but may also be reported as subjective changes in mental state. For simplicity the term *ADHD symptoms* will be used whether the guideline is discussing impairing levels of behaviour or mental phenomena, or referring to the normal range of behaviour of these phenomena. For example, many people have low to moderate levels of ADHD symptoms, which do not reflect an impairing condition or mental health disorder.

Having said that, the GDG recognises that behaviours that describe ADHD are not strictly symptoms, as this term is usually used to refer to changes in physical or mental state associated with significant morbidity that is a change from a premorbid state: for example, symptoms experienced during an episode of depression or attack of anxiety. The behavioural and mental phenomena that characterise ADHD are in contrast trait-like, in the sense that they are non-episodic and may have been present from early childhood. Furthermore, in children the criteria are usually applied on the basis of parent and teacher reports of behaviour, rather than subjective reports of mental state phenomena. Older children and adults are usually able to provide detailed descriptions of their subjective experiences of inattention, hyperactivity and impulsivity.

*Oppositional defiant disorder and conduct disorder*
The use of these terms is restricted to mean the definitions of oppositional defiant disorder and conduct disorder as described in DSM-IV-TR. The GDG recognises, however, that the terms oppositional defiant disorder and conduct disorder are widely used outside of these narrow diagnostic definitions. Many studies cited in this review have used rating scale measures for aspects of oppositional defiant disorder and conduct disorder and people often use the term conduct disorder when they are talking about oppositional behaviour. We will therefore use the terms *conduct problems* or *oppositional defiant problems* when referring to these classes of behaviour where the DSM-IV-TR definitions have not been strictly applied.

## 5.3    THE VALIDITY OF ADHD AS A DIAGNOSTIC CATEGORY

The use of the diagnosis of ADHD has been the subject of considerable controversy and debate and the diagnosis itself has varied across time and place as diagnostic systems have evolved (Rhodes *et al.*, 2006). Points of controversy identified by the GDG included both specific issues, such as the wide variation in prevalence rates reported for ADHD and the possible reasons for these differences, and the nature of the aetiological factors that increase the risk for ADHD, as well as more complex broader sociological and philosophical issues.

The GDG wished to evaluate evidence for the validity of the diagnostic category of ADHD and formulate a position statement on the use of the diagnosis. It is recognised that defining neurodevelopmental and mental health disorders is a difficult process because of the overlapping nature of syndromes, the complexity of the aetiological processes and the lack of a 'gold standard' such as a biological test. In this regard ADHD is similar to other common psychiatric disorders that rely on the identification of abnormal mental phenomena. Although biological tests for ADHD do not exist, the diagnosis can be reliably applied when data capture tools such as standardised clinical interviews used by trained individuals and operational diagnostic criteria are employed (for example, Taylor *et al.*, 1986; Schwab-Stone *et al.*, 1993; Schwab-Stone *et al.*, 1994; Epstein *et al.*, 2005).

In keeping with most common mental health disorders, the distinction between the clinical condition and normal variation in the general population is difficult to define on the basis of symptom counts alone. This is because there is continuity in the level of ADHD symptoms between those with an impairing mental health disorder and those who are unimpaired. The distinction between ADHD and normal variation in the general population requires the association of a characteristic cluster of symptoms and significant levels of impairment. This is comparable to normal variation for medical traits such as hypertension and type II diabetes, as well as psychological problems such as anxiety or depression. Controversial issues surround changing thresholds applied to the definition of illness as new knowledge and treatments are developed (Kessler *et al.*, 2003) and the extent to which it is acknowledged that clinical thresholds are socially and culturally influenced and determine how an individual's level of functioning within the 'normal cultural environment' is assessed (Sonuga-Barke, 1998). In considering these issues, a key question is to define the level of ADHD symptoms and associated impairments required to trigger the use of this guideline.

Undertaking a systematic review of diagnostic categories is not a straightforward exercise for behavioural and mental health disorders because in most cases definitive diagnostic tests for the presence or absence of disorder do not exist. The relative lack of a validated reference standard (indicated by SIGN diagnostic study quality assessment, see Appendix 16) means that the question of validity for the diagnosis of ADHD needs to draw on evidence from a wide range of sources. There is also potential for ascertainment bias, particularly in clinic-referred populations, and considerable variability resulting from the use of different clinical and demographic subgroups, differences in disease prevalence and severity among various populations sampled for research, and the use of different behavioural and symptom measures (Whiting *et al.*, 2004). The GDG wishes to emphasise that psychiatric nosology is a dynamic and developing field and changes are to be expected as more data are accrued over time.

## 5.4    METHODOLOGY

To ensure that a transparent, structured approach was taken, the GDG agreed to use one similar to the Washington University Diagnostic Criteria (Feighner *et al.*, 1972). The methodology used to create the Washington University Diagnostic Criteria has been widely accepted for this purpose, and similar approaches have been taken to validate diagnostic categories for the Research Diagnostic Criteria, the DSM and the ICD. The approach involves setting out criteria for validating a particular disorder and seeing how far a particular set of phenomena are consistent with those criteria. Using these criteria as a framework this chapter sets out to answer the following questions:

A: To what extent do the phenomena of hyperactivity, impulsivity and inattention, which define the current DSM-IV-TR and ICD-10 criteria for ADHD and hyperkinetic disorder, cluster together in the general population and into a particular disorder that can be distinguished from other disorders and from normal variation?

B: Is the cluster of symptoms that defines ADHD associated with significant clinical and psychosocial impairments?

C: Is there evidence for a characteristic pattern of developmental changes, or outcomes associated with the symptoms, that define ADHD?

D: Is there consistent evidence of genetic, environmental or neurobiological risk factors associated with ADHD?

Studies were selected for inclusion in this review if they met the SIGN quality assessment criteria for systematic reviews and cohort studies. For diagnostic and factor analytic studies the GDG established a set of criteria approved by NICE: (1) the study addresses an appropriate and clearly focused question (or hypothesis) and (2) the sample population being studied are selected either as a consecutive series or randomly, from a clearly defined study population.

A literature search was conducted for existing systematic reviews and meta-analyses on CINAHL, EMBASE, MEDLINE, PsycINFO, which were considered to be the best level of evidence. The initial search found 5,516 reviews of which nine were relevant to the questions about ADHD and application of the Washington University Diagnostic Criteria. Where insufficient evidence was found from previous systematic reviews, a search for primary studies was carried out (see Appendix 16).

In addition to the review of the literature, a consensus conference was held to bring together experts in the field who held a range of views and could address the concept of ADHD from different perspectives. This provided an opportunity to debate the key issues surrounding the use of the diagnostic category and thereby to assist the GDG with the task of deciding what should trigger the use of the guideline and for whom the guideline is intended. A summary of the consensus conference is provided in Section 5.14.

## 5.5   REVIEWING THE VALIDITY OF THE DIAGNOSIS: SUMMARY OF THE EVIDENCE

The first issue to be addressed is: To what extent do the phenomena of hyperactivity, impulsivity and inattention, which define the current DSM-IV-TR and ICD-10 criteria for ADHD and hyperkinetic disorder, cluster together in the general population and into a particular disorder that can be distinguished from other disorders and from normal variation?

The evidence addressing this issue is divided into three main questions:

5.5.1:  Do the phenomena of hyperactivity, inattention and impulsivity cluster together?

5.5.2:  Are ADHD symptoms distinguishable from other conditions?

5.5.3:  Are the phenomena of hyperactivity, inattention and impulsivity distinguishable from the normal spectrum?

## 5.5.1  Do the phenomena of hyperactivity, inattention and impulsivity cluster together?

No evidence was found from the systematic search of reviews that was of direct relevance to this question. This is because, despite a large primary literature, no systematic reviews in this area have been undertaken. Therefore a systematic search of factor-analytic and cluster-analytic studies was carried out. Additional factor-analytic and cross-sectional studies were identified by the GDG (Appendix 17.1). None of these studies met the SIGN inclusion criteria that require an appropriate reference standard for diagnostic measures, but most did meet the extension to the SIGN criteria approved for this review, since the aim of the question was to evaluate whether the phenomena of hyperactivity, inattention and impulsivity cluster together in the population, rather than to assess the accuracy of diagnostic tests.

The inclusion criteria for factor- and cluster-analytic studies were defined as follows: (i) that the study addresses an appropriate and clearly focused question (ii) that the sample being studied was selected either as a consecutive series or randomly, from a clearly defined study population.

*Evidence*

Many factor analyses indicate a two-factor model: 'hyperactivity-impulsivity' and 'inattention'. This has been replicated in population-based studies (Lahey *et al.*, 1994; Leviton *et al.*, 1993; Wolraich *et al.*, 1996) and clinical samples (Bauermeister *et al.*, 1992; Lahey *et al.*, 1988; Pelham *et al.*, 1992).

In an early study, 'hyperactivity-impulsivity' was reported as a single factor, where the factor 'hyperactivity' was defined as 'impulsive, excitable hyperactivity' (Dreger *et al.*, 1964).

More recent factor-analytic studies based on DSM-IV criteria support previous findings that the phenomena of inattention and hyperactivity-impulsivity form distinct symptom clusters in children (Molina *et al.*, 2001; Amador-Campus *et al.*, 2005; Zuddas *et al.*, 2006) and young people (Hudziak *et al.*, 1998).

Looking specifically at children identified as having a behavioural problem, Conners (1969) found 'hyperactivity' and 'inattention' as separate and distinct factors. The factor structure of adolescent self-report behavioural data was investigated by Conners and colleagues (1997): six factors were identified, including 'hyperactivity' and 'cognitive problems'. The 'hyperactivity' factor included characteristics such as being unable to sit still for very long, squirming and fidgeting and feeling restless inside when sitting still. The 'cognitive problems' factor consisted of having trouble keeping focused attention, having problems organising tasks and forgetting things that were learnt. In a further study by Conners and colleagues (1998) similar findings were reported. An attentional problem factor was found that overlapped with the DSM-IV criteria for the inattentive subtype of ADHD, with a similar overlap between the factor items for hyperactivity and the DSM-IV criteria for hyperactivity-impulsivity.

Some studies have identified three factors, with 'hyperactivity' and 'impulsivity' as two distinct factors in addition to 'inattention', in both population (Gomez *et al.*, 1999; Glutting *et al.*, 2005) and clinical samples (Pillow *et al.*, 1998). However, Gomez and colleagues (1999) showed that the model fit for the three-factor solution was only marginally better than the two-factor model. In the study of Pillow and colleagues (1998) of boys with ADHD, the impulsive and hyperactive symptoms formed a single factor when oppositional-defiant and conduct disorder items were also included in the factor analysis.

Werry and colleagues (1975), however, found that hyperactivity, impulsivity and inattention formed a single factor using both population control and 'hyperactive' samples.

Latent class analysis (LCA) identifies clusters of symptoms that group together. Using this approach, Hudziak and colleagues (1998) found that hyperactivity-impulsivity and inattentive symptoms cluster together as a 'combined' type latent class, as well as separate hyperactive-impulsive and inattentive latent classes. The latent classes map closely to the DSM-IV criteria, with DSM-IV combined type ADHD falling entirely within the severe combined type latent class, whereas individuals with the DSM-IV inattentive subtype fell either within the severe inattentive or the severe combined type latent classes.

The clustering of hyperactivity, impulsivity and inattention appear to be stable across a number of countries. Ho and colleagues (1996) found separate robust dimensions for ADHD symptoms, antisocial and neurotic behaviour in a sample of 3,069 Chinese schoolboys. Correlations among different dimensions were similar to those reported in European and US samples. Taylor and Sandberg (1984) compared data from 437 English schoolchildren with published data from the US and New Zealand. They identified a factor of hyperactivity-inattention that was distinct from conduct disorder. The comparisons supported the view that English schoolchildren were similar to their contemporaries in the US and New Zealand with differences in prevalence rates between different countries accounted for by discrepancies in diagnostic practice.

In adult population samples a two-factor model has been identified (DuPaul *et al.*, 2001; Smith & Johnson, 2000) as well as a three-factor model (Kooij *et al.*, 2005). Glutting and colleagues (2005) assessed university students aged 17 to 22 using parent-rated information in addition to self-rated data. They reported slightly contrasting findings within each set of data: exploratory and confirmatory analysis showed that DSM-IV ADHD symptoms generated a three-factor model in the self-report data and a two-factor model in the parent-informant data.

Although most studies show separate factors for inattention and hyperactivity-impulsivity, these are highly correlated in children (Gomez *et al.*, 1999) and adult samples (Kooij *et al.*, 2005).

There may be age-dependent changes in the factor structure. Bauermeister and colleagues (1992) found that there was a single attention/impulsivity-hyperactivity factor in pre-school children, and separation into two factors in school-age children. Nearly all the studies of school-age children reported two factors. In contrast, the study from Glutting (2005) using college students aged 17 to 22 found three factors, with the separation of hyperactive and impulsive symptoms. Similarly Kooij and colleagues (2005) using adult samples identified three separate factors.

*Summary*

There was strong evidence for clustering of inattentive and hyperactive-impulsive symptoms in both population and clinical samples. Evidence for one-, two- and three-factor models was found, with most studies supporting a two-factor model. Most studies found two correlated factors for hyperactivity-impulsivity and inattention, while others were able to distinguish between hyperactivity and impulsivity and a few found one combined factor for all three domains. There is some evidence that the number of factors identified depends on the age of the sample, with nearly all studies of school-age children reporting two factors. These findings have been observed in both population and clinical samples and in a number of different cultural settings. LCA in population samples detects clustering of symptoms into groups that are similar but not identical to DSM-IV subtypes for ADHD.


### 5.5.2    Are ADHD symptoms distinguishable from other conditions?

No systematic reviews were identified in the literature that addresses this question. The GDG considered that the most important and controversial distinction to be made was between ADHD and oppositional-defiant and conduct disorders. These are also the most commonly reported coexisting conditions in children and young people diagnosed with ADHD and define a set of behaviours that might be difficult to distinguish from ADHD. It was therefore decided to restrict a formal literature search to identify studies that indicate whether a distinction can be made between ADHD, oppositional-defiant and conduct problems. Additional references were identified by the GDG members (see Appendix 17.1).

*Evidence*

*ADHD and oppositional-defiant and conduct problems* Most of the studies using factor-analytic approaches for the analysis of ADHD symptoms report separate factors for hyperactivity-impulsivity, inattention and oppositional-defiant or conduct problems. These include most of the studies reviewed in the previous section on the factor structure of ADHD symptoms (for example, Bauermeister *et al.*, 1992; Conners, 1969; Conners, 1997; Ho *et al.*, 1996; Pelham *et al.*, 1992; Taylor & Sandberg, 1984; Werry *et al.*, 1975; Wolraich *et al.*, 1996). These studies are highly consistent in being able to separate the items that describe oppositional-defiant and conduct problems from hyperactivity-impulsivity and inattention. Although the behavioural items fall into separate dimensions there are significant correlations between the various behavioural factors.

Two studies using LCA came to different conclusions. Frouke and colleagues (2005) conducted a diagnostic study of 2,230 Dutch pre-adolescents from the general population. LCA revealed that ADHD symptoms clustered together with symptoms of oppositional defiant disorder and conduct disorder. A further study from the Netherlands of disruptive behaviour in 636 7-year-old children (van Lier *et al.*, 2003) came to similar conclusions. LCA identified three main classes of children with: (i) high levels of oppositional defiant disorder and ADHD; (ii) intermediate levels of oppositional defiant disorder and ADHD with low levels of conduct problems; and (iii) low levels of all disruptive problems. No classes were identified with only ADHD, oppositional defiant disorder or conduct problems.

In contrast, King and colleagues (2005a) identified five distinct groups using a cluster analysis, which like LCA identifies discrete groups of symptoms clusters: ADHD with inattention (ADHD-I), ADHD with hyperactivity-impulsivity (ADHD-H/I), ADHD with both hyperactivity/impulsivity and inattention (ADHD-C), ADHD-C with oppositional defiant disorder, and ADHD-I with oppositional defiant disorder. For both the inattentive symptoms and combined inattentive/hyperactive-impulsive symptoms they found clustering either with or without symptoms of oppositional defiant disorder.

Latent dimension modelling by Ferguson and colleagues (1991) looking at children with ADHD and conduct disorder suggested that these could be seen as independent dimensions, although they are highly inter-correlated. Having said that, the two often occurred independently of each other and only partially shared aetiological factors.

ADHD can be a precursor of other problems. When ADHD and disruptive behavioural problems coexist, the history usually suggests that symptoms of ADHD appear first before the development of disruptive behavioural problems. A follow-up of a community sample of children with ADHD symptoms but no oppositional behaviour between the ages of 7 and 17 found that children with ADHD symptoms could develop oppositional behaviour at a later stage, but that the reverse pathway from oppositional behaviour to ADHD was uncommon (Taylor *et al.*, 1996).

Population twin studies find that symptoms of ADHD are distinct from but share overlapping genetic influences with conduct problems (Thapar *et al.*, 2001; Silberg *et al.*, 1996; Nadder *et al.*, 2002). Multivariate twin modelling suggests that while the genetic influences on conduct disorder are largely shared with those that influence ADHD, there are in addition important environmental factors shared equally that influence the risk for conduct problems but not ADHD (Thapar *et al.*, 2001). In nearly all twin studies of ADHD there is evidence for the influence of unique environmental factors but not shared (familial) environment; whereas for conduct problems, twin studies find evidence of shared environmental influences. Nadder and colleagues (2002) conclude that the co-variation of ADHD and oppositional defiant disorder/conduct disorder is the result of shared genetic influences with little influence from environmental factors. There are, however, substantial additional influences from shared environmental factors on oppositional defiant disorder/conduct disorder, especially when they are not accompanied by ADHD (Silberg *et al.*, 1996; Eaves *et al.*, 1997).

*ADHD and other coexisting conditions* Population twin studies find that symptoms of ADHD are distinct from but share overlapping familial and genetic influences with other neurodevelopmental traits including reading ability (Gilger *et al.*, 1992; Willcutt *et al.*, 2000; Willcutt *et al.*, 2007), general cognitive ability (Kuntsi *et al.*, 2004), symptoms of developmental coordination disorder (Martin *et al.*, 2006) and symptoms of pervasive developmental disorders (Ronald *et al.*, 2008).

ADHD is reported to coexist with personality disorder in young offenders (Young *et al.*, 2003). A prison survey found that 45% of incarcerated young adults had a previous history and persistence of ADHD symptoms (Rosler *et al.*, 2004). The distinction between ADHD and personality disorder in adults raises important nosological questions and remains poorly investigated.

Dysthymia, depression and anxiety symptoms and disorders are frequently associated with ADHD in adults. In the US National Comorbidity Survey, adults with ADHD had increased rates of mood disorders, anxiety disorders, substance misuse disorders and impulse control disorders (Kessler *et al.*, 2006). The causal links between ADHD and these coexisting symptoms, syndromes and disorders remains poorly investigated.

*Summary*

In the majority of factor-analytic studies, ADHD symptoms (inattention, hyperactivity and impulsivity) are found to represent separate but correlated factors from oppositional behaviour and conduct problems. This suggests that they exist as separate dimensions or traits.

When symptom clusters were considered using statistical approaches that aim to identify symptoms that group together, ADHD symptoms were found to group with oppositional behaviour in two studies that used LCA; but in another study using a cluster-analytic approach, two groups of children with ADHD symptoms were identified, one group where ADHD symptoms occurred with oppositional behaviour and a separate group where ADHD symptoms were not accompanied by oppositional behaviour. The GDG concluded that on the basis of these findings, symptoms of ADHD and oppositional and conduct problems represent distinct but correlated sets of behaviours that often coexist. The relationship of ADHD symptoms and oppositional and conduct problems cannot be clearly defined on the basis of statistical analysis of child behaviour that makes use of cross-sectional data alone.

One study using longitudinal data suggested that ADHD represents a separate condition that is a risk factor for the development of oppositional and conduct problems, since ADHD came first and was associated with the future development of oppositional/conduct problems, whereas the reverse situation of oppositional/conduct problems leading to ADHD did not occur. There was, however, no other similar study with which to compare this result.

Twin studies suggest overlapping genetic influences on ADHD and conduct problems, but there are also shared environmental influences on oppositional defiant disorder/conduct disorder that do not act on ADHD. Twin studies of ADHD and oppositional defiant disorder/conduct disorder show different patterns of twin correlations suggesting the existence of shared environmental influences on oppositional defiant disorder/conduct disorder but not on ADHD. This suggests that some aspect of the environment shared by children in the same family increases the risk for oppositional defiant disorder/conduct disorder but not the risk for ADHD; this indicates a separation between the two at the level of aetiological risk factors.

The correlation between ADHD and several neurodevelopmental traits (cognitive ability, reading ability, developmental coordination and pervasive developmental disorders) is due largely to the effects of shared genetic influences. For this reason ADHD may be viewed as one component of a general propensity to neurodevelopmental problems that arises from shared aetiological influences.

In adults, coexisting symptoms, syndromes and disorders are frequently found to exist alongside the core ADHD syndrome, but their distinction from ADHD and the reasons for high rates of coexistence are not well addressed in the current literature.

### 5.5.3    Are the phenomena of hyperactivity, inattention and impulsivity distinguishable from the normal spectrum?

No systematic reviews were identified that were of direct relevance to this question. The previous search for primary studies revealed two factor-analytic studies relevant to this question. The GDG identified further factor-analytic and quantitative genetic studies that addressed this question (see Appendix 17).

*Evidence*
Many studies have found a strong correspondence between quantitative measures of ADHD symptoms and the categorical diagnosis (Biederman *et al.*, 1993; Biederman *et al.*, 1996; Boyle *et al.*, 1997; Chen *et al.*, 1994; Edelbrock *et al.*, 1986). These studies show that children with ADHD appear to be at one extreme of a quantitative dimension of ADHD symptoms in the population and that on this quantitative dimension of symptoms there is no obvious bi-modality that separates children with ADHD from children who do not have ADHD.

Twin studies using individual differences approaches (reviewed in Thapar *et al.*, 1999; Faraone *et al.*, 2005) and De Fries-Fulker (DF) extremes analysis (Gjone *et al.*, 1996; Levy *et al.*, 1997; Willcutt *et al.*, 2000; Price *et al.*, 2001) estimate similar magnitudes for the proportion of genetic, shared environmental and non-shared environmental influences on ADHD symptoms in general population twin samples. These studies indicate that aetiological influences on ADHD symptoms are distributed throughout the population and there is no obvious threshold or cut-off between people with high levels of ADHD symptoms and the continuous distribution of symptoms throughout the population. These studies do not take impairment into account, but only investigate the proportion of genetic and environmental influences on ADHD symptom counts.

Using LCA, ADHD symptoms can be divided into multiple groups, distinguished on the basis of three symptom groupings: inattention, hyperactivity-impulsivity and the combination of these two symptom domains. In addition, the symptom groups are separated on the basis of low, medium and high levels into distinct severity groups.

Twin data from female adolescents in Missouri and children in Australia both found a similar pattern of familial segregation for the latent classes suggesting that familial influences can distinguish between ADHD and the normal range of behaviour (Rasmussen *et al.*, 2004). These data provide evidence for the distinction of ADHD into inattentive, hyperactive-impulsive and combined subtypes and suggest that ADHD might be distinguishable from the normal range on the basis of familial risks for the observed symptom clusters.

*Summary*

Most analytic approaches are unable to make a clear distinction between the diagnosis of ADHD and the continuous distribution of ADHD symptoms in the general population. Twin studies suggest that the genetic and environmental influences on groups with high levels of ADHD symptoms are of the same magnitude as those that influence ADHD symptom levels in the normal range. It is not yet known whether the same specific factors are involved, but the studies using DF analysis suggest that there are at least some overlapping genetic influences on ADHD symptoms and the continuity of ADHD symptoms throughout the population.

Twin studies have in most cases defined ADHD on the basis of symptom criteria alone. It is not yet known whether the results would be different if full diagnostic criteria, including impairment, were to be applied. In contrast, LCA can distinguish groups with high, moderate and low levels of ADHD symptoms and suggests that these groups can be distinguished on the basis of familial risks. The current literature does not address the difference in interpretation of the latent class and quantitative approaches.

The GDG concluded that on the basis of current evidence, ADHD was similar to other common medical and psychiatric conditions that represent the extreme of dimensional traits, such as hypertension, obesity, anxiety and depression. The disorder can therefore only be defined on the basis of high levels of symptoms and their association with significant clinical impairments and risk for development of future impairments.

## 5.6 IS THE CLUSTER OF SYMPTOMS THAT DEFINES ADHD ASSOCIATED WITH SIGNIFICANT CLINICAL AND PSYCHOSOCIAL IMPAIRMENTS?

There were no systematic reviews that addressed this question. A search for cohort studies was carried out and additional primary studies were identified by the GDG members (see Appendix 17).

### 5.6.1 Evidence

*Academic difficulties*

Follow-up studies of people diagnosed with ADHD in childhood have consistently indicated impairment in their academic functioning. Children and young people with

ADHD have been shown to have greater impaired attention, less impulse control, and greater off-task, restless and vocal behaviour (Fischer *et al.*, 1990). They also have higher rates of both specific and generalised learning disabilities, poor reading skills (McGee *et al.*, 1992) and speech and language problems (Hinshaw, 2002) when compared with healthy controls. These impairments often lead to grade retention (Hinshaw, 2002), to a lower probability of completing schooling when compared with children who do not have ADHD (Mannuzza *et al.*, 1993), suggesting potential long-term ramifications for vocational, social and psychological functioning into adulthood (Biederman *et al.*, 1996; Young *et al.*, 2005a & b; Wilson & Marcotte, 1996).

An important question about educational impairment of children with ADHD is whether, given an appropriate educational environment, this is determined primarily by the presence of high levels of ADHD symptoms or the association with coexisting behavioural conditions such as conduct disorder or learning disabilities. Wilson and Marcotte (1996) found that the presence of ADHD in young people increased the risk for lower academic performance and poorer social, emotional and adaptive functioning, but that the additional presence of conduct disorder further increased the risk for maladaptive outcomes. In another study the association of conduct disorder with academic underachievement was found to be because of its comorbidity with ADHD (Frick *et al.*, 1991).

*Family difficulties*

Impaired family relationships have been reported in families of children with ADHD. Follow-up studies indicate that mothers of children and young people with ADHD have more difficulty in child behaviour management practices and in coping with their child's behaviour (August *et al.*, 1998), and display higher rates of conflict behaviours, such as negative comments, social irritability, hostility and maladaptive levels of communication and involvement (August *et al.*, 1998; Fletcher *et al.*, 1996).

Family impairment also permeates the parents' lives. Parents of children with ADHD report having less time to meet their own needs, fewer close friendships, greater peer rejection, less time for family activities, factors which together might lead to less family cohesion and a significant effect on the parents' emotional health (Bagwell *et al.*, 2001).

Coexisting conduct and emotional problems may drive the association between maternal expressed emotion (negativity, resentment and emotional over-involvement) and ADHD (Psychogiou *et al.*, 2007).

*Social difficulties*

Girls with ADHD tend to have fewer friends (Blachman & Hinshaw, 2002) and more problems with peers and the opposite sex (Young *et al.*, 2005a & b). Hyperactive children with or without conduct problems have higher rates of problems with peers and higher rates of social problems because of lack of constructive social activities (Taylor *et al.*, 1996). In a study by Ernhardt and Hinshaw (1994) it was reported that a diagnosis of ADHD significantly predicted peer rejection; having said that, aggressive and non-compliant disruptive behaviours were important and accounted for 32% of the variance in peer rejection.

### Antisocial behaviour

Antisocial behaviour is more prevalent in children and young people with ADHD than non-ADHD groups. Some studies show increased rates of antisocial acts (for example, drug misuse) in comparison with children who do not have ADHD (Barkley *et al.*, 2004; Mannuzza *et al.*, 1998).

Follow-up studies have also shown that people with high levels of ADHD symptoms had significantly higher juvenile and adult arrest rates than normal control boys (Satterfield & Schell, 1997). Young adults with a diagnosis of 'hyperactivity' in childhood were more likely to have a diagnosis of antisocial disorder (32% versus 8%) and drug misuse (10% versus 1%) than were healthy controls at follow-up (Mannuzza *et al.*, 1991).

ADHD is also a risk factor for psychiatric problems including persistent hyperactivity, violence and antisocial behaviours (Biederman *et al.*, 1996; Taylor *et al.*, 1996) and antisocial personality disorder (Mannuzza *et al.*, 1998).

In a prospective follow-up of 103 males diagnosed with ADHD, the presence of an antisocial or conduct disorder almost completely accounted for the increased risk for criminal activities. Mannuzza and colleagues (2002) reported that antisocial disorder was more prevalent in children with pervasive and school-only ADHD. Lee and Hinshaw (2004), however, reported that the predictive power of ADHD status to adolescent delinquency diminishes when key indices of childhood externalising behaviour related to ADHD are taken into account.

Boys with ADHD and high defiance ratings show significantly higher felony rates than healthy controls (Satterfield *et al.*, 1994). However, ADHD diagnosed in childhood increases the risk of later antisocial behaviour even in the absence of oppositional defiant disorder or conduct disorder (Mannuzza, 2004).

### Adolescent and adult problems

A 10-year prospective study of young people with ADHD found that the lifetime prevalence for all categories of psychopathology were significantly greater in young adults with ADHD compared with controls. This included markedly elevated rates of antisocial, addictive, mood and anxiety disorders (Biederman *et al.*, 2006b).

In adolescence and adult life, symptoms of ADHD begin to associate with other diagnoses that are seldom made in childhood. Adolescent substance misuse, in particular, seems to be more common in people with the diagnosis of ADHD (Wilens *et al.*, 2003), though it is not yet clear whether it is the ADHD *per se* that generates the risk or the coexisting presence of antisocial activities and peer groups.

Both cross-sectional epidemiological studies and follow-up studies of children with ADHD show increased rates of unemployment compared with controls (Biederman *et al.*, 2006b; Kessler *et al.*, 2006; Barkley *et al.*, 2006). Adults with ADHD were found to have significantly lower educational performance and attainment, with 32% failing to complete high school; they had been fired from more jobs and were rated by employers as showing a lower job performance (Barkley *et al.*,

2006). The survey from Biederman and colleagues (2006b) showed that 33.9% of people with ADHD were employed full time versus 59% of controls.

An increased rate of road traffic violations and driving accidents in adults with ADHD has been documented by several authors (Reimer *et al.*, 2007; Barkley and Cox, 2007; Thompson *et al.*, 2007; Jerome *et al.*, 2006; Fischer *et al.*, 2007).

### 5.6.2    Summary

ADHD symptoms are associated with a range of impairments in social, academic, family, mental health and employment outcomes. Longitudinal studies indicate that ADHD symptoms are predictive of both current and future impairments. Impairments also result from the presence of coexisting problems including conduct problems, emotional problems and overlapping neurodevelopmental disorders. Adults with ADHD are found to have lower paid jobs and lower socioeconomic status and have more car accidents. Impairment is an essential criterion when considering the diagnosis of ADHD. The presence of high levels of ADHD symptoms is associated with impairment in multiple domains; it is not possible, however, to delineate clearly a specific number of ADHD symptoms at which significant impairment arises.

### 5.7    IS THERE EVIDENCE FOR A CHARACTERISTIC PATTERN OF DEVELOPMENTAL CHANGES, OR OUTCOMES ASSOCIATED WITH THE SYMPTOMS, THAT DEFINE ADHD?

The search for systematic reviews and meta-analyses identified one review that was of relevance to this question. Additional reviews and primary studies were identified by the GDG members (see Appendix 17).

### 5.7.1    Evidence

There is evidence for continuity of ADHD symptoms over the lifespan. Faraone and colleagues (2006) analysed data from 32 follow-up studies of children with ADHD into adulthood. Where full criteria for ADHD were used approximately 15% of children were still diagnosed with ADHD at age 25. In addition, the meta-analysis found that approximately 65% of children by age 25 fulfilled the broader definition of DSM-IV ADHD 'in partial remission', indicating persistence of some symptoms of ADHD associated with continued clinically meaningful impairments.

Relative to controls, levels of overactivity and inattention are developmentally stable (Taylor *et al.*, 1996). Longitudinal studies of children with ADHD show similar rates of ADHD in adolescence (Biederman *et al.*, 1996; Faraone *et al.*, 2002; Molina & Pelham, 2003).

Population twin studies have also addressed the stability of ADHD symptoms throughout childhood and adolescence. Rietveld and colleagues (2004) reported that parent ratings of attentional problems were moderately stable from age 3 to 7, and greater stability from age 7 to 10. They further showed that such stability appeared to be mediated largely by overlapping genetic influences such that most, but not all, genetic influences at one age influenced ADHD at another age. Price and colleagues (2005) reported similar findings with correlations around 0.5 between ADHD symptoms at ages 2, 3 and 4. This stability was estimated to be mediated 91% by genetic influences. Kuntsi and colleagues (2004) extended these data to age 8, and found similar moderate stability between the data for ages 2, 3 and 4 and the data for age 8. Larsson and colleagues (2004) completed a similar longitudinal twin study of 8 to 13 year olds and found fairly high stability between the two ages. They further concluded that this stability was the result of shared genetic effects. Change in symptoms between childhood and adolescence was thought to be because of new genetic and environmental effects that become important during adolescence.

### 5.7.2     Summary

There is evidence for the persistence of ADHD symptoms from early childhood through to adulthood. Longitudinal studies confirm that ADHD persists into adulthood but developmentally appropriate criteria have yet to be developed for ADHD in adults. Using child criteria, approximately 15% of children with ADHD retain the diagnosis by age 25 but a much larger proportion (65%) are in partial remission, with persistence of some symptoms associated with continued impairments. The profile of symptoms may alter with a relative persistence of inattentive symptoms compared with hyperactive-impulsive symptoms. The evidence base for this conclusion is poor, however; it is based on the analysis of developmentally inappropriate measures of hyperactivity-impulsivity in adults.

The GDG concluded that there is currently insufficient evidence to warrant a different diagnostic concept in childhood and in adulthood. Having said that, it is envisaged that improved definitions that take into account developmental changes will develop as further evidence is accrued. Familial and genetic influences in ADHD symptoms appear to be stable through childhood and early adolescence, but there is a lack of data on the factors that modify the course of ADHD into adulthood.

### 5.8     IS THERE CONSISTENT EVIDENCE OF GENETIC, ENVIRONMENTAL OR NEUROBIOLOGICAL RISK FACTORS ASSOCIATED WITH ADHD?

The literature search identified eight systematic reviews and meta-analyses. GDG members identified additional reviews and primary studies (see Appendix 17). When interpreting this section it is important to note that associations do not imply causal associations and may represent epiphenomena of ADHD rather than causal processes.

### 5.8.1    Evidence

*Cognitive experimental studies*

Willcutt and colleagues (2005) reviewed 83 studies that had administered executive functioning measures and found significant differences between ADHD and non-ADHD groups where the former showed executive function deficits. The size of the difference between children with ADHD and unaffected controls, while significant, was moderate rather than large. The term *executive function* refers to a set of higher cognitive and emotional mental functions involved in the control and regulation of behaviour and performance. This includes concepts such as cognitive inhibition and initiation, self-regulation and motor output. The neural mechanisms by which the executive functions are implemented is a topic of ongoing debate in the field of cognitive neuroscience. It is not yet clear whether impairments in the performance of executive tasks is because of primary deficits in the brain processes underlying executive functions, or whether the performance deficits are secondary to more general processes.

Differences in executive functioning between ADHD and non-ADHD groups have also been reported in adults (Hervey *et al.*, 2004; Boonstra *et al.*, 2005; Schoechlin & Engel, 2005; Woods *et al.*, 2002). The results of studies of ADHD in adults suggest a wide variety of general and specific performance on cognitive-experimental tasks that are similar to those seen in children with ADHD. The review from Hervey and colleagues (2004) did not point to impairments in one area of cognitive performance, but rather impairments across a range of cognitive functions.

The interpretation of cognitive-experimental studies in ADHD remains controversial, but most authorities agree that both executive and non-executive processes are disrupted in people with ADHD. Although work has largely focused on the executive functions, there is an interest in non-executive processes (Rhodes *et al.*, 2006; Berwid *et al.*, 2005). A recent meta-analysis of the stop-signal paradigm concluded that there are significantly slower mean reaction times, greater reaction time variability and slower stop signal reaction times in children with ADHD relative to controls (Alderson *et al.*, 2007). The pattern of findings suggested a more generalised impairment of attentional and cognitive processing rather than a primary deficit of behavioural inhibition alone. Recently it has emerged that intra-individual variability is one of the more consistent associations with ADHD in both children and adults (Klein *et al.*, 2006).

In an adoptive study conducted by Sprich and colleagues (2000), higher rates of hyperactivity were found in the biological parents of children with ADHD compared with their adoptive parents.

*Neuroimaging studies*

In an attempt to provide a robust summary of available functional magnetic resonance imaging (fMRI) studies, Dickstein and colleagues (2006) performed a quantitative meta-analysis of task-based imaging studies using 13 fMRI studies and four positron emission tomography (PET)/single-photon emission computed tomography (SPECT) studies that had published stereotactic space coordinates. The meta-analytic data showed reduced activation in regions in the left pre-frontal cortex, the anterior cingulate cortex, the right parietal lobe, the occipital cortex and in the thalamus and claustrum. When only response inhibition studies were included in the analysis, a more restricted network was identified, which included the right caudate (part of the striatum). The analysis also identified certain regions where the ADHD groups tended to show hyperactivation: these included parts of the left pre-frontal cortex, the left thalamus and the right paracentral lobule. The extent of neural networks remains uncertain since the available data were limited by the narrow selection of tasks. A major limitation was the small number of suitable datasets and the unavoidable inclusion of studies that differed in the specific aspects of design and quality.

A systematic review of available fMRI studies in ADHD reached several conclusions (Paloyelis *et al.*, 2007). First, in tasks that examined brain activation during successful inhibitory control, there were large inconsistencies among studies in the direction of group differences. Group differences were also spread across many different brain regions, but the frontal lobes were predominantly involved. For this reason no firm conclusions can be drawn on the association of brain activation changes during response inhibition tasks in ADHD. Second, in analyses that examined inhibition errors, as well as in tasks that tapped attention processes, motor function and working memory, the ADHD group almost exclusively showed lower brain activity; in the attentional tasks this was mostly over temporal and parietal areas; in motor function tasks mostly over frontal areas. Third, among the different brain regions, the most consistent findings as regards direction of activation were observed in the striatum. In all but one study significant group differences were observed in which the ADHD group showed lower activity in the striatum. The only study where increased activation was observed had used a sample of young people of whom only half met full criteria for ADHD at the time of testing. Fourth, the review included a summary of findings from people with ADHD who had not used stimulant or other medication. These studies suggest that altered brain activation patterns in children with ADHD are not due to the effects of long-term stimulant treatment. Pliszka and colleagues (2006) was the only study to compare individuals with ADHD on long-term medication with those that were drug naïve as well as healthy controls. The study found no differences between the treated and untreated ADHD groups on most comparisons. Where some differences were found the treated group was more similar to controls than the untreated group.

A systematic meta-analytic study of brain structural changes in ADHD analysed all brain regions reported by all the studies found (Valera *et al.*, 2007). The study found global reductions in brain volume in ADHD cases compared with controls. Regions most commonly assessed and showing the largest differences included cerebellar regions, the splenium of the corpus callosum, total and right cerebral volume and right caudate. Several frontal regions examined in only two studies also showed significant differences. It was not possible to include or exclude the role of medication in the observed changes to brain volume and structure.

*Molecular genetic studies*

A systematic meta-analysis of molecular genetic association for associated markers in or near to the dopamine D4 (DRD4), dopamine D5 (DRD5) and dopamine transporter (DAT1) genes, found strong evidence for the association of DRD4 and DRD5 but not DAT1 (Li *et al.*, 2006). Although there are many other individual and meta-analytic studies of genetic findings in ADHD, Li and colleagues (2006) compiled most of the available data for three of the best-studied findings to date, and found significant levels that were in excess of that expected from scanning the entire human genome: $8 \times 10^{-8}$ for DRD5 and $2 \times 10^{-12}$ for DRD4. A significance level close to $5 \times 10^{-8}$ is widely accepted to indicate a true association after adjusting for the number of potential false positive findings in a scan of the entire human genome (for example, Risch & Merikangas, 1996). Other reported genetic associations with ADHD, including DAT1, do not reach this level of significance in the literature and cannot be confirmed or refuted at this time. The level of risk associated with DRD4 and DRD5 is small with odds ratios in the order of 1.2 to 1.4. This level of risk is similar to that seen for genetic influences in common medical conditions such as diabetes (Altshuler & Daly, 2007). As with all other types of risk factor associated with ADHD, the individual genetic variants associated with the disorder are neither sufficient nor necessary to cause it, but contribute a small increase to the overall risk for ADHD.

*Quantitative genetic studies*
A systematic review of 20 population twin studies found an average heritability estimate of 76%. In most cases, heritability in these studies is estimated from the difference in the correlations for ADHD symptoms between identical and non-identical twin pairs, as reported by parents and teachers: with the correlation for identical twin pairs in the region of 60 to 90% and for non-identical twin pairs being half or less than half of this figure in most studies (Faraone, 2005). Under the equal environment assumption for the two types of twin pairs, heritability can be estimated as twice the difference in the two sets of correlations.

The assumption of 'equal environment' for identical and non-identical twins can be questioned. If it were not valid, then the estimated effect of genetic influences would decrease and that of shared environmental influences would increase. Even if this were to be the case, however, it would not argue against the validity of the disorder. It is not in doubt that twins' scores are highly correlated – the level of ADHD symptoms in one child predicts that in the other. This tendency to run in families supports the idea that it is a coherent syndrome, whether the reasons are genetic or environmental.

Sibling correlations (the similarity between two siblings) can arise from either shared environmental or shared genetic influences. The equal environment assumption impacts on the estimate of the proportion of the familial risk that is due to genes or shared environment (for example, Horwitz *et al.*, 2003). Because the estimated heritability of ADHD is less than 100% we know that environmental influences are likely to cause differences in siblings and contribute to why one child in a family might have ADHD while another child does not (so-called unique environmental effects). High heritability and low shared environmental factors estimated by twin studies do not exclude an important additional contribution of the environment, acting through mechanisms of gene-environment interaction (Moffitt *et al.*, 2005) or gene-environment correlation (Jaffee & Price, 2007). Much more work is needed to understand the complex interplay of genetic and environmental influences on the risk for ADHD.

Evidence for genetic influences also comes from adoption research. One study showed increased rates of ADHD among the biological parents of non-adopted children with ADHD when compared to adoptive parents of children with ADHD and biological parents of non-adopted children who did not have ADHD (Sprich *et al.*, 2000). To date there are no published studies that compare the adoptive and biological parents of adopted children.

*Physical environmental risk studies*

Schab and Trinh (2004) completed a systematic meta-analysis of the effect of exposure to food additives on ADHD symptoms. They identified 15 studies that met initial inclusion criteria and estimated an effect size of around 0.2, but many of the studies were either of a non-ADHD sample or sample sizes were very small (n < 10) and/or were not properly randomised. The authors report associations between the use of food additives and ADHD, but given the limitations of the studies included it is difficult to establish a clear conclusion.

More recently in the UK, Stevenson and colleagues (McCann *et al.*, 2007) completed a double-blinded placebo-controlled crossover trial of food additives in 3-year-old and 8/9-year-old children. This study confirmed the association between food additives (artificial colours, sodium benzoate, or both) on increased levels of ADHD symptoms in the child populations studied. These studies indicate short-term toxic effects of food additives on the level of ADHD symptoms in children whether they have ADHD or not and might contribute towards significant impairment in some cases. There is no indication that food additives cause long-term effects on child development.

Linnet and colleagues (2003) completed a systematic review of the evidence for association between prenatal exposure to nicotine, alcohol, caffeine and psychosocial stress. They concluded that exposure in utero to the consequences of tobacco smoking is associated with an increased risk for ADHD. In contrast contradictory findings were found for the risk from prenatal maternal use of alcohol and no conclusions could be drawn from the use of caffeine. Studies of psychosocial stress indicated possible but inconsistent evidence for an association with ADHD.

Talge and colleagues (2007) completed a systematic review of studies that indicate the association of antenatal maternal stress on aspects of child development including ADHD symptoms, emotional and cognitive problems, anxiety and language delay. These effects appear to be independent of postnatal depression and anxiety. Two studies identified an increase in ADHD symptoms in children between the ages of 4 and 15 (O'Connor *et al.*, 2002; van den Bergh and Marcoen, 2004). The effect size of the association was marked. Van den Bergh and Marcoen estimated that 22% of the variance in symptoms of ADHD was accounted for by maternal anxiety during pregnancy. O'Connor and colleagues (2002, 2003) found that women in the top 15% for symptoms of anxiety at 32 weeks' gestation increased the risk of symptoms of ADHD, conduct disorder, anxiety or depression by 5 to 10%. Prenatal maternal stress is therefore associated with an increase in ADHD symptoms but is not specific to ADHD. The mechanisms involved in this association are poorly understood.

*Non-physical environmental risk studies*

As stated in the section on associated impairments, impaired family relationships have been reported in families of children with ADHD. Follow-up studies indicate that mothers of children and young people with ADHD have more difficulty in child behaviour management practices and coping with their child's behaviour (August *et al.*, 1998), and display higher rates of conflict behaviours, such as negative comments, social irritability, hostility and maladaptive levels of communication and involvement (August *et al.*, 1998; Fletcher *et al.*, 1996).

Persistent problems with inattention and overactivity have been documented in a sample of institution-reared children adopted from Romania before the age of 43 months. The syndrome of inattention and overactivity was strongly associated with early institutional deprivation lasting 6-months or more, with higher rates in boys than girls, and was strongly associated with conduct problems, disinhibited attachment and executive function impairments (Stevens *et al.*, 2008; Rutter & O'Connor, 2004).

In general, the diagnosis of ADHD is distributed unequally across different levels of deprivation and is mediated by social class and ethnicity (Bauermeister *et al.*, 2005; Cunningham & Boyle, 2002). Maltreatment has been associated with higher rates of ADHD in addition to oppositional behaviour and post-traumatic stress disorder (Famularo *et al.*, 1992). McLeer and colleagues (1994) found very high rates of ADHD (46%) among children with a history of sexual abuse.

Adversity in the form of familial risk factors has also been shown to be associated with ADHD (Biederman *et al.*, 1995). In a sample of clinical cases of ADHD, exposure to parental psychopathology and exposure to parental conflict were used as indicators of adversity, and their impact on ADHD and ADHD-related psychopathology and dysfunction in children was assessed. The analyses showed significant associations between the index of parental conflict and several of the measures of psychopathology and psychosocial functioning in the children confirming the role of adversity on the risk for ADHD and its associated impairments.

Work by Rutter and colleagues (1975) revealed that it was the aggregate of adversity factors (severe marital discord, low social class, large family size, paternal criminality, maternal mental disorder and foster care placement) rather than the presence of any single factor that led to impaired child development (Rutter *et al.*, 1975). Based on this work, Biederman and colleagues (1995), using a sample of 140 ADHD and 120 normal control probands and using Rutter's indicators of adversity, investigated whether family-environment risk factors were associated with ADHD. A positive association was found to exist between adversity indicators and the risk for ADHD as well as for its associated psychiatric, cognitive, and psychosocial impairments, supporting the importance of adverse family-environment variables as risk factors for children with ADHD.

### 5.8.2 Summary

There is consistent evidence from family, twin and adoption studies of both genetic and environmental influences on ADHD symptoms throughout the population. Under the equal environment assumption, twin studies indicate that sibling similarity for ADHD symptoms results mainly from genetic influences. Some supportive evidence is given by adoptive research. Unique environmental influences play a role in bringing about differences in ADHD symptoms within families. Environment may also play an important role in ADHD acting through mechanisms of gene-environment interaction and correlation. Environmental measures associated with ADHD have been identified, including maternal use of tobacco during pregnancy and prenatal maternal stress. Other associated environmental measures include early deprivation, maltreatment and sexual abuse, family factors including severe marital discord, low social class, large family size, paternal criminality, maternal mental disorder and foster care placement. Some dietary components have been shown to increase the level of ADHD symptoms in children and are expected to contribute to increased levels of ADHD symptoms in all children. These may give rise to increased symptoms and impairments in a sub-group of individuals who go on to develop ADHD, although this has yet to be clearly demonstrated.

The causal relationships between environmental measures and ADHD are not well understood. In most cases it is not known whether specific associated environmental variables represent direct risks for ADHD, or indirect risks acting through correlated environmental or genetic factors, or are passively correlated with the ADHD symptoms themselves.

The GDG concluded that specific genetic variants associated with small increases in the risk for ADHD have been identified within the dopamine D4 receptor gene and close to the dopamine D5 receptor gene. These are the only two genetic findings where convincing levels of evidence have accrued as demonstrated by the recent meta-analytic study from Li and colleagues (2006). Other genetic findings require further data before they can be included or refuted as true associations with ADHD.

Analysis of ADHD versus non-ADHD groups has identified consistent changes in brain structure, function and performance on neurocognitive tests; however differences from controls are not universal, do not characterise all children and adults with a clinical diagnosis of ADHD, and do not usually establish causality in individual cases. The degree to which the observed heterogeneity in the associations with neurobiological and psychological measures represent multiple aetiological contributions to a common causal pathway, or independent contributions to multiple causal pathways, is not yet understood. It may also be the case that these associations represent epiphenomena of the ADHD syndrome and play no direct causal role.

## 5.9    LIMITATIONS

In line with methodology agreed with NICE, the approach adopted initially was to identify all available systematic reviews and meta-analytic studies that related to the questions on validity of the diagnosis. While this was possible for much of the neurobiological, genetic and environmental data, there were few systematic reviews in other areas such as the factor- or cluster-analytic studies. Where systematic reviews were not available for the studies of ADHD symptoms and studies that investigated the differentiation of ADHD from oppositional-defiant and conduct problems, a systematic review of the primary literature was conducted. For the interpretation of factor and cluster analytical approaches it is important to recognise the limitations that arise from the high variability in quality of these types of exploratory statistical analyses papers. Factor- and cluster-analytic methods require a certain degree of unstructured judgments to be made by researchers, rarely produce reproducible results and in the majority of cases were underpowered. Despite this, as outlined in the evidence, a reasonable level of reproducibility in the findings was observed.

For other sub-questions addressed in this section, the systematic evidence was supplemented with expert opinion, drawing on evidence known to members of the GDG. Additional evidence was obtained following a review of the initial draft of this chapter by independent experts (see Appendix 16 for their commentary). The lack of specific reference standards for the diagnosis of ADHD led to an adaptation of the SIGN criteria to ensure sufficient quality of the data used to derive recommendations for this guideline. The revised criteria agreed by the GDG members were as follows: (1) the study addresses an appropriate and clearly focused question (or hypothesis); (2) the sample population being studied is selected either as a consecutive series or randomly, from a clearly defined population.

When considering the Washington University Diagnostic Criteria (Feighner *et al.*, 1972) for validity of a psychiatric disorder, the question of whether there are characteristic responses to pharmacological, psychological, educational and other interventions for ADHD was excluded from this section, because the response of ADHD to these interventions is considered in detail elsewhere in this guideline. The related question of the specificity of the response to therapeutic interventions for ADHD was surprisingly difficult to determine on the basis of available published evidence. For example, behavioural, educational and pharmacological treatments can all alter the behaviour of children whether they have ADHD or not.

In relation to the use of stimulants we were unable to identify studies that investigated their effects on mental health disorders other than ADHD. The GDG identified a literature on the misuse potential of stimulants, indicating that methylphenidate and dexamfetamine increase ratings of subjective activity, alertness (wakefulness) and energetic and high feelings (for example, Stoops *et al.*, 2004), but there were no direct comparisons with the effects of people fulfilling diagnostic criteria for ADHD. One paper was identified that addressed the effects in a normal population; it did not meet the quality control criteria for the evidence sections of this chapter, but it is mentioned here because of its potential importance. The authors reported the response to dexamfetamine and placebo in a group of 14 pre-pubertal boys who did not fulfil criteria for ADHD (Rapoport, 1978). When amphetamine was given, the group showed a decrease in motor activity and reaction time and improved performance on cognitive tests that was similar to that seen in other studies of children with ADHD. The very small numbers used in this study and lack of further similar studies means that caution must be taken in drawing firm conclusions from this one study. Nevertheless, the similarity of the response observed in children without ADHD to that reported in children with the disorder provides further evidence that the aetiological processes in ADHD are similar to those that influence levels of ADHD symptoms throughout the population.

The question of a paradoxical effect of stimulants on people with ADHD has been raised but is not well studied. For example, do stimulants have an impact on the same processes and in the same way in all people, whether they have ADHD or not? Or is there a different pattern of effects in people with high levels of ADHD symptoms compared with people with low levels? The GDG concluded that the critical question for these guidelines is whether stimulants and other non-pharmacological interventions effectively treat the impairments associated with high levels of ADHD symptoms. The effectiveness and cost benefits of these interventions are addressed in other sections of this guideline.

## 5.10     SUMMARY OF VALIDATION OF THE DIAGNOSIS OF ADHD

The diagnosis of ADHD is difficult and somewhat controversial for a number of reasons. Of particular concern has been the rapid increase in the recognition and treatment of children with ADHD and the very high prevalence rates reported in some studies, leading some people to question the validity of the disorder. In common with most mental health conditions there is no definitive biological test for ADHD; diagnosis depends on the observation of clusters of symptoms in three main behavioural domains according to the DSM-IV and ICD-10 criteria. In order to examine the validity of the diagnosis, the Washington University Diagnostic Criteria (Feighner *et al.*, 1972) were applied to demonstrate whether there are well-defined clinical correlates, characteristic course and outcome, neurobiological underpinnings and associations with genetic and environmental factors. The review above identified clinical, genetic, environmental and neurobiological factors associated with ADHD or correlated with levels of ADHD symptoms in the general population that were sufficient to validate the diagnostic construct of ADHD.

One of the key issues addressed in the review was the question of whether ADHD represents a discrete clinical entity or the extreme end of a continuum of normal behaviour. Indeed, the debate between a categorical diagnostic view and a dimensional approach is longstanding in psychological and sociological research. The diagnosis of many common psychological conditions, such as anxiety and depression represents a line drawn at one end of a continuum of a population characteristic that is continuously distributed throughout the population; the threshold for diagnosis being drawn at a point where significant impairment arises.

The review concluded that on the basis of current evidence, ADHD is best conceptualised as the extreme of a continuous trait that is distributed throughout the population; the distinction from normality being made by the presence of high levels of ADHD symptoms when they are accompanied by significant impairments. This highlighted the importance of defining what amounts to a significant impairment and ensuring that impairment is fully evaluated when applying the diagnostic criteria.

## 5.11     DEFINING SIGNIFICANT IMPAIRMENT

The GDG wished to define more precisely the level of impairment indicating when the guidelines should be triggered. The GDG recognised the breadth of views on what amounts to a significant impairment. The existence of polarised views in this debate, and the implication for both under-and over-diagnosis, means that a balanced and pragmatic view is required that takes into account concerns on both sides. For example the GDG recognised that people with hyperkinetic disorder (ICD-10) do not always receive a diagnosis and treatment despite the presence of marked impairments, while on the other hand in some cases stimulants have been used to boost academic performance in the absence of more pervasive and enduring impairments. The following criteria were discussed and agreed by a consensus within the group:

1. The GDG wishes to emphasise the importance of significant impairment in defining the difference between a set of mental health problems and a mental health disorder. An appreciation of this difference is helpful in preventing over-diagnosis. In addition, the diagnosis of ADHD should not be applied to justify the use of stimulant medication for the sole purpose of increasing academic performance, in the absence of a wider range of significant impairments indicating a mental health disorder.

2. Many mental health problems, including those with ADHD features, are transitory and related to psychosocial stresses. They often clear up spontaneously or do so after a basic-level intervention by, for example, parents and teachers. In contrast, a mental health disorder implies something far more serious. Without a specialist professional or a higher level of intervention by others to ameliorate the problems, there are likely to be long-term adverse implications for the person affected as well as problems in the short and medium term. It is therefore important that the assessing clinician considers whether the clinical presentation is indicating a threat to *general development and psychosocial adjustment* that would be more likely than not to occur if expert help or some other significant intervention was not to take place. This would apply to the current presentation and also the longer-term outlook.

3. The GDG concluded that impairment should be pervasive, occur in multiple settings and be at least of moderate severity. Significant impairment should not be considered where the impact of ADHD symptoms are restricted to academic performance alone, unless there is a moderate to severe impact in other domains: these would include self-esteem, personal distress from the symptoms, social interactions and relationships, behavioural problems, and the development of coexisting psychiatric syndromes.

## 5.12    POSITION STATEMENT ON THE VALIDITY OF ADHD

On the basis of the evidence reviewed above the GDG drew the following conclusions:

● Symptoms that define hyperactive, impulsive and inattentive behaviours are found to cluster together.

● Hyperactivity, inattention and impulsivity cluster together both in children and in adults and can be recognised as distinct from other symptom clusters, although they frequently coexist alongside other symptom clusters.

● Symptoms of ADHD appear to be on a continuum in the general population.

- ADHD is distinguished from the normal range by the number and severity of symptoms and their association with significant levels of impairment.
- The importance of evaluating impairment and the difficulty in establishing thresholds on the basis of symptom counts alone needs to be addressed. It is not possible to determine a specific number of symptoms at which impairment arises.
- There is evidence for psychological, social and educational impairments in both children and adults with ADHD.
- ADHD symptoms persist from childhood through to adulthood in the majority of cases. In a significant minority the diagnosis persists and in the majority, sub-clinical symptoms continue to be detectable and are associated with significant impairments.
- In adults the profile of symptoms may alter with a relative persistence of inattentive symptoms compared with hyperactive-impulsive symptoms.
- There is evidence of both genetic and environmental influences in the aetiology of ADHD. The extent to which there is diversity in the aetiology of the disorder is not known. Current evidence indicates the presence of multiple risk factors of minor effect.
- The complex interplay between genes and environment is not well understood. Environmental risks may interact with genetic factors, be correlated with genetic factors or have main effects. Similarly genetic factors may interact or correlate with environment or have main effects. There will be a different balance of factors in individual cases.
- There is evidence of genetic associations with specific genes, environmental risks and neurobiological changes in groups of children with ADHD. However, no neurobiological, genetic or environmental measure is sufficiently predictive to be used as a diagnostic test.
- The diagnosis remains a descriptive behavioural presentation and can only rarely be linked to specific neurobiological or environmental causes in individual cases.
- Hyperkinetic disorder (ICD-10) is a narrower and more severe subtype of DSM-IV-TR combined type ADHD. It defines a more pervasive and generally more impairing form of the disorder. Both concepts are useful (Santosh *et al.*, 2005).
- There was limited evidence to support a different concept of ADHD in children and adults. Age-related changes in the presentation are recognised, however. Theses changes are not yet reflected in the current diagnostic criteria.
- All current assessment methods have their limitations. There is evidence of the need for flexibility and for a consideration of levels of impairment in assessments and when deriving appropriate diagnoses.

## 5.13    CONSENSUS CONFERENCE

In addition to a review of published evidence on the question of validity, a consensus conference was held to bring together experts in the field with a range of views, in order to debate the key issues of the use of ADHD as a diagnostic category. The aim was to provide a range of contemporary perspectives that would assist the GDG with the task of deciding what should trigger the use of the guideline and for whom the guideline is intended (see Chapter 3). The speakers delivered a 15-minute presentation addressing the key questions relating to the validity of the ADHD diagnosis set out by the GDG, followed by questioning from the GDG members and a subsequent discussion of the presentation among members of the GDG. Each presenter was subsequently asked to provide a summary of their presentation and these are presented in Appendix 16.

The consensus conference involved presentations from professionals who came from a range of backgrounds and with differing perspectives on the validity and aetiology of ADHD. The range of views contributed to highlight the importance of an interdisciplinary approach to the diagnosis and treatment of children and young people with ADHD. The conference did not consider diagnosis and treatment of adults with ADHD.

Here some of the issues that were raised, and the areas of controversy arising from differences in the perceptions of the speakers at the consensus conference, are discussed. Some of the complex areas of controversy relate to broader sociological and philosophical issues representing two conceptual paradigms, broadly characterised as medical–scientific and social–scientific. The latter perspective casts doubts on the utility and legitimacy of ADHD as a diagnostic category by emphasis on: the problematic nature of the meaning of ADHD, the social determinants of the behaviours that come to be labelled as ADHD, and the spectrum of human behaviour that results in indistinct boundaries of many medical diagnostic categories. While it is important to acknowledge the validity of the social scientific paradigm and its body of literature, in the context of the development of practical clinical guidelines, it is not possible to offer alternative processes for clinical assessment or treatment. It is accepted that the research literature reflects the dominant medical scientific paradigm and hence the nature of the evidence base.

The evidence presented at the consensus conference indicated that there was a high degree of unanimity about there being a group of people who could be seen as having distinct and impairing difficulties and who should trigger the use of this guideline. While recognition of a particular group was agreed upon, uncertainty about the breadth of diagnosis was discussed, namely, whether the use of a narrow (ICD-10 hyperkinetic disorder) versus a broad (DSM-IV ADHD) diagnosis should be used. The problems of using a narrow diagnosis are: (i) the under-recognition of people that are in need of help and (ii) the lack of connection with the research literature, which is based mainly on the broader definition of DSM-IV ADHD. It was established that the main differences between people falling into narrow or broad diagnoses are the breadth of symptoms (requirement for both inattentive and impulsive-hyperactive behaviour versus only one domain being sufficient), more or less stringent criteria for situational pervasiveness and the requirement for no major comorbidity (apart from oppositional defiant disorder or conduct disorder) under ICD-10. Both groups present similar problems of impairment. Overall there was general agreement that both the use of broad DSM-IV ADHD diagnosis and narrow ICD-10 hyperkinetic disorder criteria were useful.

It should be emphasised that the current definitions of ADHD are descriptions of a behavioural syndrome with associated mental phenomena, and do not implicate specific causal pathways. Validation of the cluster of symptoms that contribute to the diagnosis of ADHD occur at the level of their association with impairments, familial risks, genetic risks, environmental risks and the association with measures of changes in cognitive function and brain structure and function. Few direct causal inferences have yet been established, however. For example the associations with changes in cognitive and brain function may represent epiphenomena of ADHD rather than imply a causal process. Environmental measures associated with ADHD may not themselves represent direct risk factors, but may be correlated with more proximal environmental or genetic risks. A common conceptualisation is that both intrinsic and extrinsic processes are involved in generating the cluster of behavioural symptoms that we call ADHD. Extrinsic factors, such as parental coping and consistency, might exacerbate problems of behavioural control in a child with intrinsic difficulties in regulating core processes such as attention and activity level. The child's difficult behaviour may further exacerbate the difficulties in providing consistent parenting. Parental behaviour itself will also be influenced by both genetic and environmental factors, further increasing the complexity of the aetiological relationships involved. Given the complexity of this question, the GDG does not seek here to put forward a particular causal model, but wishes to emphasise the role that both genes and environment play on both intrinsic and extrinsic factors in generating the clinical syndrome of ADHD.

One of the major issues of controversy in the UK setting is the very high and variable prevalence rates reported in the literature. For example, recent prevalence figures range from 6.8 to 15.8% for DSM-IV ADHD (Faraone *et al.*, 2003) while the British Child and Mental Health Survey reported a prevalence of 3.6% in male children and less than 1% in females (Ford *et al.*, 2003). Reasons for this are discussed in Faraone and colleagues (2003) who conclude that prevalence rates derived from symptom counts alone, or from ratings in one setting, were higher than those that took into account functional impairment and pervasiveness. For example Wolraich and colleagues (1998) estimated prevalence to be 16.1% on the basis of symptom counts, but 6.8% when functional impairment was taken into account. A study in the UK that specifically addressed the role of impairment found that among 7 to 8 year olds, 11.1% had the ADHD syndrome based on symptom count alone (McArdle *et al.*, 2004). In contrast, 6.7% had ADHD with Children's Global Assessment Scale (C-GAS: measuring impairment) scores of less than 71; 4.2% had C-GAS scores of less than 61. When pervasiveness included both parent- and teacher-reported ADHD and the presence of psychosocial impairment, prevalence fell lower to 1.4%. The literature on prevalence therefore indicates that the rate of ADHD is sensitive to the degree of impairment associated with the symptom criteria and the degree to which the disorder shows situational pervasiveness.

All the speakers acknowledged the importance of functional impairments in relation to diagnosis. In other words, the diagnostic threshold should be based on pragmatic grounds such as impairment and the need for treatment. There was also agreement that defining suitable thresholds for impairment is difficult, since different people hold a range of views on what amounts to significant impairment. The fear was expressed that too broad a definition would lead to the over-diagnosis of children as a way of justifying the use of stimulant medication to enhance academic performance, in the absence of a wider range of pervasive and enduring impairments. Given the sensitivity of the prevalence rates of ADHD to definitions of impairment, this could potentially lead to very high numbers of children being treated when educational or psychological interventions might be sufficient, or where the level of impairment does not warrant a therapeutic intervention at all. The GDG concurred with this view, but were equally concerned to ensure that the thresholds for the diagnosis were not so restricted as to leave children with ADHD (who by definition have significant impairment) undiagnosed and therefore untreated.

The level and types of behaviour that define impairment remain a contentious issue and are to some extent dependent on the cultural and environmental context. For this reason expert clinical advice is required to evaluate the level of impairment to ensure that: the child's view is taken into consideration and not just that of the child's parents and teachers; that everyone's perspective is taken into account; and that cultural factors are considered.

Considering when use of this guideline should be triggered, the GDG concluded that it would be difficult to be prescriptive for any individual case, but that measurement of impairment linked to the symptoms of ADHD is a key component of the decision. Significant problems can arise at various levels, including personal distress from symptoms of the disorder, difficulties in forming stable social relationships and emotional bonds, difficulties with education and long-term risk for negative outcomes such as emotional problems, antisocial behaviour and addiction disorders. The GDG concluded that those responsible for initiating diagnosis and treatment must take into account the severity of the disorder in terms of clinical and psychosocial impairments. When monitoring treatment response, evidence of improvement in such impairment is critical and should be monitored in addition to the narrow focus on changes in reported levels of ADHD symptoms.

One of the areas of controversy highlighted in the consensus conference was the degree of impairment and severity of ADHD needed to trigger the diagnosis and, related to this, treatment with medication. Concern was expressed that the diagnosis automatically leads to treatment with medication and this is not always desirable when the breadth of the definition includes people who might gain substantial benefit from education or psychosocial interventions alone. Having said that, even the most ardent supporters of non-pharmacological interventions in ADHD recognised the importance of pharmacological treatment in the most severe cases. In this context the participants in the consensus conference made an important contribution by raising the important question of suitable thresholds for 'significant impairments associated with ADHD symptoms' and hence the proportion of children fulfilling criteria for the disorder and triggering use of the guideline. The related issue is the importance of considering the full breadth of effective interventions (including educational, social and psychological support and pharmacological treatment), depending on the severity of the disorder, the extent of impairment and needs of each individual case.

One conclusion is that the acceptable thresholds for impairment are partly driven by the contemporary societal view of what is an acceptable level of deviation from the norm. Impairment in ADHD should not be based only on the views of others because people with ADHD, particularly older adolescents and adults, have strong subjective experience of the impact of their condition on their functioning.

The GDG did not consider that the diagnosis should be reserved only for the most serious cases, however, since the broader concept of ADHD is important in triggering educational and behavioural support in addition to pharmacological approaches. The GDG concluded that defining appropriate thresholds of impairment associated with the disorder was important, but that treatment implications might be different for individuals falling above or below particular thresholds.

Confirmatory factor-analytic studies clarify that ADHD symptoms represent a distinct set of symptoms and behaviours that co-vary together in both clinical and control populations. However, these cross-sectional studies are far less informative than longitudinal studies, which can clarify the predictive outcomes of early ADHD. Having said that, there are a few studies that provide suitable data on the relative outcomes of ADHD and other disruptive disorders such as oppositional defiant disorder, which are important in delineating specificity in the outcomes related to ADHD. The available evidence suggests that when considering the link between ADHD and conduct problems, ADHD comes first and conduct problems develop later. In contrast there is no evidence that conduct problems in the absence of ADHD lead to the later development of ADHD. The small number of suitable longitudinal outcome studies highlights an important area for future research.

The aetiology of ADHD remains another area of controversy. In the view of the GDG this largely stems from the complex nature of ADHD and the many factors involved in aetiology. Major identified risk factors associated with the disorder include having a first-degree relative with ADHD and prenatal maternal stress. These are likely to be proxy markers of processes that are themselves expected to be highly complex, however. At the level of specific factors such as individual genes or direct environmental stresses, the increased risk of ADHD is expected to be small. There is an ongoing debate about the degree to which ADHD represents a homogeneous disorder, with multiple risk factors of small effect contributing to the disorder, or whether ADHD represents the syndromic end-point of multiple different processes. Further research is required to provide a full understanding of the complex aetiology involved.

One important question raised by the consensus conference was the interpretation of family, twin and adoption studies and the relative contributions between genetic and environmental influences indicated by these studies. The argument against important genetic influences is not strong unless one questions the conventional interpretation of twin and adoption data. The findings from twin studies are not, however, controversial because they have been replicated many times. The main finding is that parent and teacher reports of ADHD symptoms show high correlations of around 70 to 80% in monozygotic (identical) twins, and around 20 to 40% in dizygotic (non-identical) twins (Thapar *et al.*, 1999). The usual interpretation of these findings is that the large difference in monozygotic and dizygotic correlations results from genetic influences. The alternative argument that the equal environment assumption is incorrect would not alter the basic conclusion that ADHD tends to run in families and is therefore a familial disorder, since the level of ADHD symptoms in one child is highly predictive of the level of ADHD symptoms in their siblings. It is therefore non-controversial that ADHD is familial and this in itself is strong evidence that the construct is sufficiently delineated to show clear familial effects.

Interestingly there are limited data from twin studies using ADHD cases (for example, concordance rates for the clinical disorder), so the literature mainly uses extremes analysis of rating scale data for ADHD symptoms and does not take into account other important aspects of the clinical disorder such as pervasiveness and impairment. Similarly there is a lack of twin data in adult populations.

Adoption studies also indicate that genetic as well as environmental influences increase the risk for ADHD. All adoption studies show that adopted children with ADHD are more similar to their biological parents than to their adoptive parents. These studies, except for one (Sprich *et al.*, 2000) are, however, limited by small sample size and in most cases the interviewers were not blind to psychiatric or adoptive status; the studies have therefore not been used as evidence of validity in this chapter.

There was broad agreement that environmental influences play an important role in the aetiology of ADHD. However, the nature of the specific risk factors and the mechanisms involved are poorly understood and remain an area of controversy. Twin studies indicate that unique environmental effects are expected to cause differences between siblings and would explain in part why one child in a family has ADHD while another child from the same family does not. Environmental risks may be the sole or main cause of ADHD in some cases, for example, where there is extreme deprivation in early childhood (Rutter & O'Connor, 2004; Rutter *et al.*, 2007). One important question is whether the evidence of genetic influences in ADHD can be reconciled with the view that environmental influences play a critical role in development of the disorder. In fact, high heritability is consistent with the existence of environmental risks for ADHD that are very common, and for this reason explain little of the observed variance in ADHD symptoms in the population. Environmental risks may also be modified by genetic risks (gene-environment interactions) or correlated with genetic risks (gene-environment correlation). The complexity of the interplay between genes and environment in the risk for ADHD is not well understood and for this reason is one of the main focuses for contemporary research. The GDG considered that polarised positions in this debate are not helpful since the contemporary understanding of complex behavioural disorders emphasises the interplay between nature and nurture.

The GDG wishes to stress that the role of genetic influences in ADHD does not exclude an important role for environmental influences for several reasons. Individual differences in genetic risk factors are likely to alter the sensitivity of an individual to environmental risks. Either genetic or environmental risks alone may play a prominent role in individual cases. Reducing environmental risks would be expected to reduce the risk for ADHD under most models of gene-environment interplay in the contemporary literature.

The GDG also wishes to emphasise that the extent to which the disorder results from genetic influences has no direct bearing on the choice of treatment and in particular, does not provide sufficient justification alone for the use of pharmacological interventions. For example, traits such as obesity or diabetes are influenced by both genetic and environmental factors, yet individual changes in lifestyle as well as the use of medication in some (but not all) cases is indicated. In ADHD, educational, social, psychological, and pharmacological treatments all need to be considered and could be important in improving levels of impairment and preventing the development of negative long-term outcomes. The evidence base for treatment of ADHD is dealt with in other sections of this guideline.


## 5.14    SUMMARY FROM REVIEW OF THE DIAGNOSIS

On the basis of this review, the GDG summarised the evidence for the diagnosis of ADHD upon which the guideline recommendations are made:

● ADHD is a valid clinical condition that can be distinguished from coexisting conditions and the normal spectrum.

● ADHD is distinguished from the normal spectrum by the co-occurrence of high levels of ADHD symptoms when they are associated with significant clinical, psychosocial and educational impairments. These impairments should be enduring and occur across multiple settings.

● There is no specific biological test for ADHD, so the diagnosis must be made on the basis of a full developmental and psychiatric history, observer reports and examination of the mental state.

● In the absence of a biological test for the diagnosis of ADHD or hyperkinetic disorder, validity is based on the association of ADHD symptoms with genetic, environmental, neurobiological and demographic factors; and the association of high levels of ADHD symptoms with impairments in multiple domains.

● Hyperkinetic disorder (ICD-10) identifies a sub-group of people with ADHD with severe impairment in multiple domains.

● ADHD commonly persists throughout childhood and into adult life, either as the full diagnostic criteria or in partial remission, where it continues to cause significant clinical and psychosocial morbidity.


## 5.15    IMPLICATIONS FOR PRACTICE

### 5.15.1    General principles for the diagnostic process

The aim of this section of the guideline is to provide a commentary and further recommendations on the implementation of the diagnostic process. As reviewed above there is sufficient evidence that ADHD is a valid diagnostic category to apply to relevant children, young people and adults. The GDG concluded that on the basis of current evidence ADHD is a complex disorder resulting from multiple genetic and environmental risk factors, representing the extreme and impaired tail of a normally distributed trait in the population. The disorder is recognised by the presence of a high level of pervasive and enduring problems with attention, overactivity and impulsiveness when they lead to a significant degree of clinical, psychosocial and/or academic impairments.

The current operational criteria for ADHD (DSM-IV-TR) and hyperkinetic disorder (ICD-10) are highly reliable when they are applied by trained individuals following the careful evaluation of reported behaviours and symptoms, and when the criteria define a group with clear clinical implications. The diagnosis depends on the evaluation of two necessary components, both of which are required to trigger the use of this guideline. The first is the presence of the symptom cluster of age-inappropriate levels of inattentive, hyperactive and impulsive behaviours; and the second is the presence of significant clinical and psychosocial impairments. Other key criteria include onset during childhood and situational pervasiveness. Behaviours and symptoms that are restricted narrowly to one environmental setting only (for example, school), or one set of impairments (for example, educational attainment alone) would not be considered sufficient grounds to make the diagnosis.

The implementation of the diagnostic and treatment process should be within the framework of a structured *stepped pathway* as described in Chapter 6. Within this framework a flexible approach to assessment should be adopted that enables an evaluation of individual and family needs, drawing on the experience and expertise of the individual clinician and other professionals involved, and taking into account different perspectives using an interdisciplinary approach.

### 5.15.2    Implementation of the diagnostic criteria

Diagnostic criteria are constantly evolving in the light of new information. The GDG reviewed the current diagnostic criteria and made recommendations that reflect the current state of knowledge and clinical practice. Below is a list of common questions with the summary statements upon which the recommendations are based.

*(A) Should ADHD be recognised in the presence of pervasive developmental disorders/autism spectrum disorders?*
ICD-10 unequivocally says this is not permitted and DSM-IV-TR states that, 'symptoms should not occur exclusively in the course of a pervasive developmental disorder' (APA, 2000); yet pervasive developmental disorders once established are in most cases always present.

The evidence that core symptoms of ADHD occur together with those of pervasive developmental disorders/autism spectrum disorders is strong and therefore the GDG recommends that for effective practice ADHD should be recognised on the basis of core symptoms of ADHD, even when pervasive developmental disorders/autism spectrum disorders are present.

**Summary statement:** ADHD can be diagnosed in the presence of pervasive developmental disorders.

*(B) Should ADHD be recognised in the presence of general learning disability?*
Both DSM-IV-TR and ICD-10 state that symptoms of ADHD must be developmentally inappropriate. This means that the levels of ADHD symptoms should be inappropriate and impairing in comparison with other people at the same developmental

stage taking into account both age and general cognitive ability. DSM-IV-TR states that symptoms should be 'excessive for mental age'. The GDG recognised the importance of an appropriate developmental comparison group and recommends that adjustment is made for mental age.

For example a mental age of 5 in a 10 year old should have the same standard of what is expected for impulsiveness and inattention as a mental age of 5 in a 5 year old. However, derivation of 'mental age' through standardised cognitive assessment does not always correlate with emotional and behavioural age. Professionals undertaking clinical evaluation should have expertise in both ADHD and learning disability, and awareness of the normal range of behaviour in the equivalent peer group of comparable age and general cognitive ability.

**Summary statement:** ADHD can be recognised in the presence of a general learning disability, with behavioural symptoms compared to a group of similar mental age.

### (C) How should impairment be judged?

The GDG agreed that the presence of impairment associated with the core behavioural symptoms of ADHD is critical to recognising the disorder; but difficulties arise since impairment is itself a continuum.

Moderate impairment is a requirement for the diagnosis of ADHD. Moderate ADHD in children and young people is taken to be present when the symptoms of hyperactivity/impulsivity and/or inattention, or all three, occur together, and are associated with at least moderate impairment, which should be present in multiple settings (for example, home and school or a healthcare setting) and in multiple domains where the level appropriate to the child's chronological and mental age has not been reached: self-care (in eating, hygiene, and so on); travelling independently; making and keeping friends; achieving in school; forming positive relationships with other family members; developing a positive self-image; avoiding criminal activity; avoiding substance misuse; maintaining emotional states free of excessive anxiety and unhappiness; and understanding and avoiding common hazards. The level of impairment could also be estimated by using a predetermined level on a global adjustment scale (for example, a score of less than 60 on the C-GAS). In later adolescence and adult life, the range of possible impairments extends to occupational underachievement, dangerous driving, difficulties in carrying out daily activities such as shopping and organising household tasks, in making and keeping friends, in intimate relationships (for example, excessive disagreement) and with child care.

Severe ADHD corresponds approximately to the ICD-10 diagnosis of hyperkinetic disorder and the GDG took this to be present when hyperactivity, impulsivity and inattention are all present in multiple settings and when impairment is severe (that is, it affects multiple domains in multiple settings).

The GDG considered that impairment needs to be considered relative to a comparable peer group since this represents the potential of each individual. For example, relative academic impairment would include a child with a chronological age of 7, a mental age of 10, but an academic achievement age only of 7. Importantly, impairment should be pervasive and enduring, affecting several aspects of an individual life. This would mean that impaired academic achievement alone would not be sufficient to trigger the diagnosis, but would be sufficient where this were accompanied by significant impairments in other areas such as emotional or social development (see Section 5.6).

**Summary statement:** Impairment should be pervasive and enduring, affecting several aspects of an individual life.

*(D) Should the age of onset before 7 years be strictly applied?*

The GDG recognised the inadequacy of the current age of onset criteria, which would exclude individuals with typical ADHD with an apparent onset after the age of 6 years. Symptoms may not be recognised in young children and impairments may not be pronounced. This is likely to be particularly true where the predominant symptoms are those of inattention rather than impulsive or overactive behaviour and because it can be the later development of coexisting problems that draws attention to the difficulties that a particular child is having. Recent evidence indicates that the level of impairments are similar for individuals with onset before and after age 7 years leading the GDG to consider that ADHD should be diagnosed in some cases where onset is dated between the ages of 7 and 12 years (Applegate *et al.*, 1997).

**Summary statement:** ADHD should be diagnosed in some cases where onset is dated between the ages of 7 and 12 years.

*(E) Should some kinds of aetiology be excluded?*

The GDG recognised that ADHD is a complex heterogeneous disorder with a range of different aetiologies, including environmental, genetic and non-genetic neurobiological factors. The DSM urges the distinction of ADHD from 'children from inadequate, disorganised or chaotic environments' (APA, 2000).

The GDG considered that there is not yet sufficient data to include or exclude individual cases on the basis of aetiology. For example exposure to chaotic environments might be one potential cause of ADHD, and prenatal exposure to alcohol another. The GDG therefore recommends that the diagnosis of ADHD should be distinguished from other behavioural disorders on the basis of the pattern and type of behaviours, rather than on the basis of specific aetiologies. This is an important point since the diagnosis might be excluded in the presence of a severe environmental risk such as child abuse. The view that child abuse is the cause of behavioural problems, while likely to be important in an individual case, should not lead to the exclusion of the individual from these guidelines if they fulfil the diagnostic criteria for ADHD.

**Summary statement:** In the current state of knowledge, ADHD should be considered whenever diagnostic criteria are fulfilled, regardless of the presence of any specific aetiological factors.

*(F) Should the same definitions be used for both genders?*

Epidemiological studies typically apply the same definitions to boys and girls, and typically find a male preponderance – most commonly about 3 to 1 (Schachar & Tannock, 2002). The gender ratio for children attending ADHD clinics is typically higher than in community surveys, raising the possibility of under-recognition in females. The outcome in adolescence seems to be no better for girls than has been reported for boys (Young *et al.*, 2005a & b).

In adult life, the male-female ratio for ADHD appears to be approximately equal (Kooij *et al.*, 2005), again raising the possibility that the high gender ratios in childhood may be partly a result of under-identifying the problem in girls, or of a different presentation of symptoms in girls.

The evidence does not allow for a clear scientific consensus, so the practice is still to apply diagnostic criteria regardless of gender. Research is needed, however, to clarify the nature and prognostic implications of different presentations in boys and girls.

**Summary statement:** In current knowledge, the same diagnostic criteria should be applied to males and females.

*(G) Can the diagnosis be made from rating scales only?*
Despite reasonably high sensitivity and specificity from rating scales, the GDG took the view that diagnosis of ADHD should not rely on rating scale measures alone. Rather, it is important to complete a full evaluation including diagnostic clinical interviews with parents, children (especially older children and adolescents) and other corroborative evidence such as school reports. The use of rating scale data alone will generate both false positive and negative diagnoses and would remove the critical element of an in-depth appraisal of the entire clinical picture including onset, cause, associated developmental and mental health exacerbating and causal factors.

**Summary statement:** The diagnosis of ADHD should only be made after a full clinical and psychosocial evaluation, and never on the basis of rating scale data alone.

*(H) Can the diagnosis be made on the basis of observation alone?*
Direct observation of an individual with ADHD, particularly older adolescents and adults, for short periods of time during assessment sessions may not demonstrate any obvious features of the condition. This should not exclude the diagnosis where there is a clear account of inattentive, impulsive or hyperactive behaviours in usual situations. The reason is that some people with ADHD can regulate their behaviour for short periods of time and because ADHD behaviours are typically reduced in situations where a person is engaged in an important task. The GDG advises that diagnosis should only be made on the basis of a full assessment.

**Summary statement:** The diagnosis of ADHD should not be made on the basis of observational data alone.

*(I) How should social, cultural and economic circumstances and factors be taken into account in making the diagnosis of ADHD?*
At a general level, diagnoses of ADHD are distributed unequally by relative level of deprivation, mediated by social class and ethnicity (Bauermeister *et al.*, 2005; Cunningham & Boyle, 2002; Dahl *et al.*, 1991; Timimi, 2006). While these factors are not thought to cause the behavioural symptoms of ADHD, such immediate environmental circumstances may have a role to play in mediating the experience of symptoms and impairment (Isaacs, 2006). Relative deprivation increases the likelihood that a child will be subject to various environmental risk factors, potentially increasing the risk of ADHD and associated disorders (Hartl *et al.*, 2005; Lahti *et al.*, 2006; Neuman *et al.*, 2007; Rodriguez & Bohlin, 2005). Additionally the ethics and

beliefs of those responsible for the daily care of children have a role to play in their perception of symptoms and impairment (Couture *et al.*, 2003; Curtis *et al.*, 2006; Epstein *et al.*, 2005; Rey *et al.*, 2000; Singh, 2003; Wolraich *et al.*, 2003). This being so, some attempt should be made to investigate and if possible either discount or take account of the immediate environmental circumstances of the child.

If existing evaluations of the social, cultural and economic circumstances have already been made through multi-agency collaboration then this information may be readily available at the time of referral (Burgess, 2002; San Roman, 2007). However, if these investigations have not been carried out by the relevant services (for example, social services, health visiting services or school health services), or if for some reason this information has not been made available, then they should be made part of the medical assessment.

There is a growing literature on the measures that can be taken to help the child with ADHD in the school and at home and as a minimum it should be ensured that such measures have been taken (Hughes & Cooper, 2006; Lloyd *et al.*, 2006; Merrell & Tymms, 2002; Prosser, 2006). Regardless of socio-cultural circumstances, psychiatric diagnosis and treatment will have a significant impact on these circumstances, and this needs to be acknowledged by the individual and family concerned (Singh, 2004, 2005). The active participation of the child or young person should be sought at all stages of the diagnostic process (Wright *et al.*, 2006).

**Summary statement:** Social, cultural and economic circumstances should always be evaluated by an expert and whenever possible by a multidisciplinary team.

## 5.16 DIFFERENTIATING ADHD IN ADULTS FROM OTHER COEXISTING CONDITIONS

### 5.16.1 Personality disorders

There is currently considerable nosological confusion that stems from the early onset and persistence of ADHD behavioural symptoms that therefore appear as stable traits or personality characteristics rather than symptoms. The difference in definition between a trait and a symptom is that symptoms represent a change from a normal pre-morbid state, such as the onset of adult depression or psychosis, whereas traits are considered to be enduring characteristics. Current psychiatric training in adult mental health tends to focus on the distinction between symptoms and traits and gives rise to a nosology that does not fit well with the concept of ADHD. First, because of the trait-like quality of ADHD phenomena, significant psychopathology often goes unnoticed or is regarded as a personality characteristic, resulting in a different set of treatments and expectations for the clinical course and outcome compared with ADHD. Second, because ADHD phenomena are sometimes associated with persistent disruptive and oppositional behaviour or development of poor interpersonal skills, it is often assumed that this represents an ingrained and therapeutically resistant set of behavioural traits. Further confusion stems from the definition of cluster B personality disorders, like antisocial, borderline and emotionally unstable personality disorder, which include symptoms such as mood instability, impulsivity and anger outbursts that are commonly seen to coexist in adults with ADHD.

The diagnostic issue is to recognise when there is evidence for ADHD, that is whether the operational criteria were fulfilled in childhood and whether ADHD symptoms that started in childhood have persisted and continue to bring about significant impairments. While the diagnostic focus should be on the main symptoms that define inattention, hyperactivity and impulsivity it is also important to remember that mood instability and impulsivity are commonly seen in adults with ADHD. Care must be taken to distinguish between uncontrolled, impulsive, oppositional and anti-social behaviours that arise in the context of a specific ADHD syndrome from those that do not. For this reason it is often useful to make particular enquiries about symptoms that are more specific to ADHD such as short attention span, variable performance, distractibility, forgetfulness, disorganisation, physical restlessness and over-talkativeness rather than focus only on the occurrence of maladjusted and disruptive behaviours.

### 5.16.2    Mood disorders

*Depression*

A volatile and irritable mood is frequently seen in adult ADHD and is not usually the consequence of coexisting depression or bipolar disorder. The overlap of mood symptoms does mean that care must be taken to exclude the possibility of a major affective disorder and that mood lability does not occur solely within the context of such disorders. Attending to the time-course of the symptoms and psychopathology can help to distinguish the two. Early onset, chronic trait-like course, frequent mood swings throughout the day, no recent deterioration or severe exacerbation frequently accompany ADHD, whereas extreme low or high moods, sustained mood change for long periods of time and recent onset are more indicative of a primary affective disorder. Some individuals previously diagnosed with atypical depression, cyclothymia or unstable emotional personality disorder will have a primary diagnosis of ADHD.

*Bipolar disorder*

Traditionally, the distinction between ADHD and bipolar disorder has been fairly easy to make. Bipolar disorder has been associated with euphoria, grandiosity and a cycling course, with each episode lasting for several days at least. ADHD, by contrast, has been regarded as a persisting disability in which euphoria is not particularly a feature. The goal-directed over-activity of mania is usually seen to be in contrast with the disorganised and off-task activity of ADHD. Individuals with ADHD often have difficulty sleeping but unlike mania or hypomania they complain about their lack of sleep and often feel exhausted during the day. In general individuals with ADHD report that they cannot function effectively and this is often associated with chronic low self-esteem, very different from the feelings of heightened efficiency seen in mania. In ADHD thoughts are often described as 'on the go' all the time, but unlike mania or hypomania, these are experienced as unfocused, muddled and inefficient and there is no subjective sense of improved efficiency of thought processes.

There has, however, been a broadening of the concept of bipolar disorder, to include cases where the mood change is not euphoria but irritability or chronic mixed affective states, and where the cyclical nature consists of many changes within a single day (indistinguishable from a volatile, labile mood). This leads to a very considerable similarity in formal definitions between this so-called ultradian version of bipolar disorder and ADHD. An unstable and over-reactive mood is very commonly seen in ADHD, even though it is not part of the diagnostic definitions, and the development of an oppositional disorder, in which frequent tantrums are common, can be described as an 'irritable' state and therefore contributes to a bipolar diagnosis.

One of the main questions relates to the validity of a diagnostic concept broadly-defined as bipolar disorder, or whether mood instability/irritability in the presence of ADHD may be more adequately described by a new dimension, such as mood dysregulation. Until the relevant empirical data become available, the classic definition of mania should be maintained: a diagnosis of bipolar disorder requires euphoria, grandiosity and episodicity, and the differential between ADHD and bipolar disorder remains explicit.

### 5.16.3    Anxiety disorders

Individuals with ADHD commonly report high levels of anxiety on rating scales. However, a more detailed enquiry about the psychopathology shows that in some cases the ADHD syndrome mimics some aspects of anxiety. Individuals with ADHD may have difficulty coping with social situations because they are unable to focus on conversations; difficulty travelling because they are unable to organise the journey; and difficulty shopping because they may become irritable waiting in queues and because they may forget things and be highly disorganised. Problems with simple everyday tasks that most people take for granted are a source of considerable concern and are often accompanied by avoidance of stressful tasks and poor self-esteem. In combination with ceaseless mental activity, these legitimate concerns and responses may take on the appearance of a mild to moderate anxiety state, although lacking the systemic manifestations of anxiety disorders. An important distinction is to consider whether the symptoms have a similar onset and time course to ADHD or whether they arise episodically and in response to stressors, which is characteristic of anxiety.

### 5.16.4    Psychotic disorders

Severe inattention may rarely mimic the thought disorder symptoms seen in some psychoses, such as derailment, tangential thought processes, circumstantiality and flight of ideas. Careful monitoring of both psychotic symptoms and ADHD symptoms is advised but it may be difficult to distinguish residual symptoms of a major mental illness from persistence of ADHD symptoms.


## 5.17    RECOMMENDATIONS

### 5.17.1    Diagnosis

5.17.1.1    A diagnosis of ADHD should only be made by a specialist psychiatrist, paediatrician or other appropriately qualified healthcare professional with training and expertise in the diagnosis of ADHD, on the basis of:
- a full clinical and psychosocial assessment of the person; this should include discussion about behaviour and symptoms in the different domains and settings of the person's everyday life, and
- a full developmental and psychiatric history, and
- observer reports and assessment of the person's mental state.

5.17.1.2    A diagnosis of ADHD should not be made solely on the basis of rating scale or observational data. However rating scales such as the Conners' rating scales and the Strengths and Difficulties questionnaire are valuable adjuncts, and observations (for example, at school) are useful when there is doubt about symptoms.

5.17.1.3    For a diagnosis of ADHD, symptoms of hyperactivity/impulsivity and/or inattention should:
- meet the diagnostic criteria in DSM-IV or ICD-10 (hyperkinetic disorder),[9] **and**
- be associated with at least moderate psychological, social and/or educational or occupational impairment based on interview and/or direct observation in multiple settings, **and**
- be pervasive, occurring in two or more important settings including social, familial, educational and/or occupational settings.

    As part of the diagnostic process, include an assessment of the person's needs, coexisting conditions, social, familial and educational or occupational circumstances and physical health. For children and young people, there should also be an assessment of their parents' or carers' mental health. (Key priority)

5.17.1.4    ADHD should be considered in all age groups, with symptom criteria adjusted for age-appropriate changes in behaviour.

5.17.1.5    In determining the clinical significance of impairment resulting from the symptoms of ADHD in children and young people, their views should be taken into account wherever possible.

---

[9]The ICD-10 exclusion on the basis of a pervasive developmental disorder being present, or the time of onset being uncertain, is not recommended.

**5.17.2    Post-diagnostic advice for parents**

5.17.2.1    Following a diagnosis of ADHD, healthcare professionals should consider providing all parents or carers of all children and young people with ADHD self-instruction manuals, and other materials such as videos, based on positive parenting and behavioural techniques.

**5.18    RESEARCH RECOMMENDATIONS**

5.18.1.1    Grounds for diagnosis of ADHD in adults
- What is the prevalence of inattention, impulsivity, and hyperactivity/restlessness in males and females in the adult population? How far do the core symptoms of inattention, impulsivity and hyperactivity/restlessness cluster together? To what extent are the core symptoms comorbid with other forms of mental disturbance? To what extent are the core symptoms associated with neuropsychological and social impairment? This would be best conducted as an epidemiological survey.
- Why this is important: There is evidence that ADHD symptoms can persist into adulthood and cause impairment, but there are no clear conclusions about the level of ADHD symptoms in adults that should be considered as grounds for intervention, or whether the symptoms take a different form in adulthood. The costs to society and to the affected people and their families make it pressing to know whether, and how far, services should be expanded to meet the needs of this group.

5.18.1.2    Influences determining the impact of symptoms on impairment and on the risk of later disorder
- For people of all ages and both genders with ADHD, what are the influences determining the impact of symptoms on their functioning ('impairment') and on the risk of later disorder? Symptomatology and its impact should be based on reliable assessments from several sources, and the outcomes should be specific to the effect caused in major social and developmental domains. The possible influences to be measured as moderators of the relationships between symptoms and impairment should include: gender and developmental level (in case different symptom criteria should be applied for different groups), the timing of any recognition and intervention (to estimate benefits and risks of early diagnosis and treatment) and potentially modifiable environmental circumstances (such as family atmosphere, peer group, and socioeconomic adversity). Additional research should examine the same relationships in short-term longitudinal designs to include a predictive element.
- Why this is important: The research is needed in view of currently varying practice in the application of diagnostic criteria and unsatisfactory knowledge about the levels of symptoms and impairment that

should indicate whether treatment is required. Such research is also needed to guide practitioners on the clinical features to target as part of comprehensive management.

5.18.1.3 The extent to which neuropsychological tests can be used to guide psychological interventions

- For children and young people with ADHD, what is the extent to which neuropsychological tests can effectively be used to guide psychological interventions? Standardised tests should be developed, normed and applied to functions such as response inhibition, delay-of-reward gradients and aversion to delay. Educational recommendations based on individual profiles of these and established executive function tests should be compared with standard advice for their acceptability to teachers, their implementation in practice, and the effects on child behaviour and learning in the classroom.

- Why this is important: Scientific investigation has established robust associations between the behaviours of ADHD and deviations in performance on neuropsychological tests. These results however remain in the research arena only, partly because of a shortage of norms for the tests (required for diagnosing individuals) and partly because of uncertainty about the benefits to be obtained from prescriptions for remedial intervention based upon them.

5.18.1.4 The prevalence of ADHD in young people and adults in substance misuse and/or forensic populations; and how individuals in these specific populations might best be treated

- It has been claimed that there are much higher rates in these populations compared with the normal population, but this is not based on good evidence because many of the studies are methodologically flawed, for example by being based on rating scale screens only, and not controlling for a history of conduct disorder. Surveys should be mounted, using not only rating scales, but also clinical identification with interviews and source informants. There should also be an assessment of the efficacy, in these groups, of the ADHD treatments already recommended for ADHD in the community. Randomised controlled trial design is recommended with outcome measures including not only those of ADHD itself but also those relevant to the target populations (for example, offending and substance misuse).

- Why this is important: It is important that individuals with ADHD are identified and receive treatment in these settings as this may have a positive impact on their quality of life, increase the effectiveness of other forensic rehabilitation activities and treatments provided to them, contribute to a reduction in antisocial behaviour and offending and increase public safety. Treatment of ADHD symptoms may improve treatment engagement and readiness more generally and provide service benefits by shortening length of stay within forensic secure services.

# 6.   THE ORGANISATION OF CARE FOR ADHD

## 6.1    INTRODUCTION

This chapter describes a stepped care model of service delivery for ADHD. A chronic disease management model similar to approaches employed for conditions such as depression, asthma or diabetes may be useful. Such a population-based model involves several components including: the identification of children with high levels of hyperactivity, impulsivity and/or inattention; encouraging self-help approaches (in this case, management approaches by parents and teachers); training and support of primary care and school professionals; the development of care pathways that enable access to treatment; and services for adults with ADHD.

## 6.2    STEPPED CARE MODEL FOR ADHD: SCHOOL-AGE CHILDREN AND YOUNG PEOPLE

### 6.2.1    Introduction

Stepped care traditionally reflects the primary–secondary care interface for chronic conditions. Child mental health and paediatric services are organised in somewhat different ways. CAMHS tier 1 refers to primary care workers; tier 2 to specialist professionals working in a single-handed way; tier 3 to multidisciplinary teams; and tier 4 to tertiary services. Most community paediatric services, therefore, correspond to a combination of tiers 2 and 3, which this guideline refers to as secondary care.

In a stepped care model, children and families move up (or down) a step in the care pathway according to their particular needs and outcomes as well as what has already been tried.

### 6.2.2    Self-help approaches

Parents may have noticed hyperactivity, impulsivity and/or inattention in their child, or these features may have been brought to their attention by other family members, friends or a professional who is in contact with the child. At this stage, self-help approaches (for example, national and local parent organisations, parenting books, manuals, video or DVD and materials from the internet) are available, but were not evaluated as part of this guideline.

### 6.2.3    Tiered model of care

For illustrative purposes, a modified tiered model that reflects the key specialist role of both paediatric and mental health professionals in diagnosing and treating ADHD is described here. An assessment could be carried out by either CAMHS or paediatric services, depending on local availability, resources and skills. Nationally, there is huge variation in models of service provision. Ideally, there should be a locally agreed multidisciplinary and multi-agency integrated care pathway, management guidelines between the different tiers and shared care protocols.

Children with suspected ADHD will usually present initially via tier 1 services, either via general practice or through school or nursery services. In those children presenting via primary care, parental concern is often the most important trigger for referral (Sayal, 2002). It has been suggested that there may be significant delays between a parent seeking help and the actual diagnosis of ADHD (Coghill, 2006), so a robust referral pathway from tier 1 is essential.

*Tier 1*

The parent has an initial discussion with a tier 1 professional (for example, a teacher, health visitor, GP, school or practice nurse, any other healthcare professional who may be seeing the child for any reason or someone in the voluntary sector). These professionals should have a basic understanding of ADHD and be able to ask key questions to ascertain possible symptoms and level of impairment. This can be backed up by the use of rating scales (broad-band rating scales such as the Strengths and Difficulties questionnaire or narrow-band rating scales such as the Conners' rating scales). For this to be feasible, and to enhance awareness and accurate knowledge about ADHD and associated conditions, tier 1 professionals will require access to appropriate training or materials.

At this point, the parent and the professional can agree to a period of watchful waiting (encouraging self-help and simple behaviour management) or, if there are more severe problems, a referral to a CAMHS professional or specialist paediatrician. Management within the pre-school or school would be at the level of 'School Action', that is the child should be registered as having special educational needs involving the special educational needs coordinator (SENCO), and an Individual Education Plan developed. If indicated, an external referral (increasing the level to 'School Action Plus') might be made to an educational psychologist, to outreach specialist teaching services through Behaviour and Learning Support or to a CAMHS professional or paediatrician.

Tier 1 professionals (including healthcare professionals and teachers) working in settings where children at high risk of ADHD might present should consider the possibility of ADHD. Early case identification might be appropriate in high-risk groups such as children born pre-term and those who have behaviour or developmental problems (such as cerebral palsy, epilepsy and coordination difficulties) and poorer reading ability (Ford *et al.*, 2004).

Who can refer depends on local circumstances: it could include the SENCO, educational psychologist, health visitor, GP, school or practice nurse, or any other healthcare professional that may be seeing the child for any reason. If someone has been diagnosed with ADHD and/or is taking medication but has not been seen by secondary care, or if they have pervasive high scores on appropriate rating scales, such as the Strengths and Difficulties questionnaire or Conners' rating scales, they should be referred. As part of the collection of information for this, the referrer should liaise with the GP and the school. Similarly, if the GP or school professional is the referrer, then they should liaise with each other.

Where appropriate, tier 1 professionals should consider the possibility of referring a child for an ADHD assessment. Access to parent-training programmes (such as the Webster-Stratton parenting intervention) should be available at tier 1 where there is associated oppositional defiant disorder and conduct disorder. Referral criteria here should be in keeping with the NICE technology appraisal (TA) *Parent-training/ education programmes in the management of children with conduct disorders* (NICE, 2006a). This means that there are two options for a referral: either referring for an ADHD assessment or referral to a parent-training/ education programme. At the end of the parent-training/education programme, the referrer should carry out a review and assess what problems still remain. If the ADHD symptoms remain prominent, then the child should be referred for assessment.

Standard 9 of the Children's NSF (Department of Health, 2004) emphasises that tier 3 CAMHS and/or specialist paediatricians have a remit for training tier 1 professionals. At a local level, service commissioning should take this into account and provide funding for this remit to be met.

### Tier 2

Following a referral, depending on local service configuration, further assessment regarding the possibility of ADHD can be carried out by a CAMHS primary care mental health worker (who obtains further information from the family, school, and primary care), another uni-disciplinary CAMHS professional (that is, tier 2 CAMHS) or a community paediatrician (if appropriate, to identify a general developmental level or any specific learning disorders). Ideally, this should be a single assessment to avoid any additional delay. The key competencies of this professional are to carry out a generic assessment in order to consider the possibility of ADHD and to know whether to refer to tier 3.

### Tier 3

If ADHD seems likely following the initial wider mental health and developmental assessment, there should be a multi-disciplinary assessment involving a specialist paediatrician, child and adolescent psychiatrist, learning disability psychiatrist, specialist nurse or clinical psychologist. Depending on the findings of the initial assessment and information from other sources (especially educational), other professionals may be involved such as speech and language and/or occupational therapists.

Following a diagnosis of ADHD, a healthcare professional could be allocated to the role of case manager or care coordinator. Their roles might include providing feedback, education and information for the family and child, guidance for basic behavioural management, identifying multi-agency needs, organising follow-up and liaising with the child's school as well as any other appropriate agencies. The care coordinator will also ensure that local shared care protocols with primary care are followed.

### Tier 4

Where there is a high level of uncertainty about a diagnosis, marked severity or complexity, or complex issues around psychopharmacology, there should be access to a regional ADHD service that supports tier 3 CAMHS or a paediatrician. There is a need for tier 4 capacity building nationally, particularly for treatments going beyond these guidelines.

### 6.2.4 Transitional arrangements from child to adult mental health services

The services required for the treatment of ADHD in adults are described in detail in Section 6.4. A key issue for people diagnosed with ADHD in childhood and adolescence who require continued treatment into adulthood, is the transition of care from CAMHS or paediatric services to AMHS. At a local level, tier 3 CAMHS professionals or paediatricians should collaborate with adult services to develop a transitional service and, where required, to ensure the adequate training of psychiatrists and other adult mental health workers.

### 6.3 STEPPED-CARE MODEL FOR ADHD: PRE-SCHOOL CHILDREN

*Tier 1*

In many parts of the country, there are specialist health visitor services for assessing and managing behavioural disorders in the pre-school population. Health visitors should be able to suggest basic behavioural and other strategies to be used in the home to address overactive, impulsive and non-compliant behaviour. In some areas, special programmes, either managed or staffed by health visitors, are also available, such as within SureStart, the Child Behaviour Intervention Initiative and the Positive Behaviour Intervention Service. These programmes are designed to help parents of pre-school children in a more systematic way and will often involve group-based parent-effectiveness training programmes. Staff in kindergarten and nursery settings may also have basic skills to address similar difficulties in these pre-school settings although this will be variable depending upon initial and in-service training, and the fact that attendance at pre-school settings is not a legal requirement.

*Tiers 2/3*

Children aged 2 to 5 with ADHD symptoms or behavioural problems unresponsive to initial tier-1 intervention could be referred to paediatric services or CAMHS if the ADHD symptoms are causing significant impairment to the child's development and to social and family functioning. The choice may be determined by local care pathways but it may be appropriate for a referral to be made to a developmental paediatric service for a general developmental paediatric assessment where it is suspected that there are associated developmental disorders, such as global developmental delay, learning disabilities or autistic spectrum problems.

When a firm or provisional diagnosis of ADHD is made by professionals within a tier 2/3 service, a parent-training/education programme could be provided if it has not been provided in tier 1. This should be accompanied with information about

ADHD and perhaps dietary advice if food intolerance or reactions to food additives or preservatives are suspected. Where group-based parent-effectiveness interventions have been provided at tier 1 a more individualised approach using behavioural therapy principles could be offered in tier 2/3 services. If such interventions are effective it would be appropriate to monitor the child until starting school because at such times of transition symptoms may re-emerge. If the interventions prove ineffective, and the child is 6 years or older, medication (methylphenidate in the first instance) could be considered.

## 6.4    SERVICES FOR ADULTS WITH ADHD

Currently there are few established adult mental health or psychological services for adults with ADHD in the UK. This poses considerable problems for individuals who require diagnostic evaluations and treatment programmes for ADHD beyond the school years. In a few areas excellent services have been established and this guideline draws on their experience. In this section we provide guidance on the healthcare services that are required for this group of people and indicate how such services might be established.

In considering the care pathway needs for adults with ADHD there are several categories of need that can be distinguished:

1. **Currently treated group:** Diagnosed and treated for ADHD in childhood (or adulthood) and still requiring treatment. This group can be further sub-divided into:
    (a)  stably maintained on medication, no need for psychological treatment
    (b)  stably maintained on medication, need for psychological treatment
    (c)  not stably maintained on medication, requires further titration of pharmacological treatments and/or psychological treatment.
2. **Currently untreated group:** diagnosed with ADHD in childhood and currently untreated.
3. **Never diagnosed:** diagnosis of ADHD not made in childhood.

For people in each of these groups, a psychiatric evaluation is required by a specialist in adult mental health with the training to diagnose and advise on treatment for ADHD. Full psychiatric evaluations are required for all groups apart from those that are previously diagnosed and stably maintained on treatment (group 1a) and require no further intervention apart from a follow-up service for drug monitoring. The other groups require follow-up services to monitor the current and future needs for medical and psychological interventions. The benefits and disadvantages of both pharmacological and psychological treatments for each individual case need to be considered and both should be available.

The following services need to be available:

1. **Drug monitoring service:** For patients taking stimulant or other medication there needs to be a drug monitoring service. Any suitable trained specialist including adult psychiatrists, nurse practitioners and primary care physicians can provide this. In most cases shared-care protocols should be established in which primary care takes responsibility for routine prescribing and health checks (pulse, blood

pressure, weight), and specialist services monitor the dose and continued need for treatment.

2. **Psychological treatment services:** Psychological support should be available, targeted at the particular problems related to ADHD. This includes a wide range of treatments and could include psychoeducation, anger management, daily living skills and treatment of comorbid anxiety and depression. Counselling may be required particularly with emotional problems related to chronic impairment from early childhood. Adults starting on pharmacological treatment for the first time will often need advice on how best to take advantage of potential improvements in their mental state and level of functioning. ADHD coaching or long-term support will be important in some cases where short-term psychological interventions are insufficient. For those with a high level of impairment, community healthcare provision may be required on a longer-term basis. Occupational therapy will be important in some cases.

   Advice and support about the following should be considered: workplace and career, college and educational matters, time management and organisation, family and relationship concerns and support groups. Specific advice may be given to partners and relatives of adults with ADHD and to people with ADHD concerning gender-specific issues.

3. **Diagnostic services:** Specialist services for the diagnosis of ADHD in adults should be available. This includes the diagnosis of adults who were and were not initially diagnosed with ADHD in childhood. Since the recognition of ADHD in children was rare before the mid-1990s, there is a large population of people who went undiagnosed and untreated in childhood and present for the first time as adults.

   The diagnosis of ADHD should be made by a specialist with training in general adult psychiatry, who can take account of the full range of mental health problems (usually a consultant or other trained psychiatrist, or child and adolescent psychiatrist working within an adult mental health team). Where medication is indicated, diagnostic services should initiate and monitor treatment during the titration phase. Prescribing during this initial phase can, however, be devolved to the primary care physician where a shared care protocol is established.

## 6.5   MODELS OF CARE FOR ADULTS WITH ADHD IN ESTABLISHED SERVICES

At the time of publication, mental healthcare provision for adults with ADHD is very poor in the UK. Having said that, services in several regions are developing and in a few are highly developed:

1. **Transitional care:** In several regions transition services from child and adolescent to adult mental health services have been established and these provide the treatment and monitoring of adults who started treatment in childhood and need to continue treatment as young adults. In some cases this service is provided by child and adolescent psychiatrists, and in others by adult psychiatrists.

Arrangements for the transition of care from child and adolescent to adult mental health services should be available in all regions.

2. **Diagnostic services:** In addition to managing the transition from child to adult mental health services, a service is also needed for the first-time diagnosis of adults with ADHD and those who were treated as children but 'fell out' of treatment during their adolescent years and seek help later on as young adults. It is very important that people who stop treatment during adolescence, but still require (and request) treatment as adults, have access to diagnostic and treatment services.

There are two broad models for healthcare provision, both of which have been successfully adopted in different regions:

1. **Generic services:** Trained psychiatrists and adult mental health teams have included the diagnosis and treatment of ADHD within their general adult psychiatric practice. This model is recommended since the symptoms of adult ADHD overlap with a range of other common psychiatric disorders, and the specialist should be aware of the full range of adult psychopathology when evaluating adults with ADHD. Common disorders that need to be differentiated from ADHD include dysthymia and atypical depression, personality disorder (particularly borderline), anxiety, cyclothymia and type II bipolar disorder.

2. **Specialist neurodevelopmental services:** An alternative model is to establish a specialist service for common neurodevelopmental disorder in adulthood that could incorporate overlapping conditions such as autism and mild learning disability. The advantage of this model is that an expert team can be developed to optimise sensitivity to the diagnosis and care pathways, including both pharmacological and psychological treatments. Where such services have been successfully established, they have usually incorporated transitional services in addition to the evaluation of new patients.

## 6.6 COMPETENCIES FOR EVALUATION OF ADHD IN CHILDREN AND YOUNG PEOPLE

A central problem confronted when drawing up guidance in this area is the difficulty of providing a standardised national guideline that addresses the importance of diagnosing the individual in their family and sociocultural context, while retaining the clinical independence of the individual clinician. Another factor that has an impact on local care pathways is the wide national variation in the organisation of services for individuals with ADHD. To overcome these difficulties, this section focuses on the competencies and skills required by individuals involved at various stages of the care pathway, rather than stating which specific professionals should be involved. This approach, however, places greater responsibility upon the individual professionals and their experience and expertise. The GDG also wishes to emphasise the importance of different perspectives and the benefits of a multidisciplinary approach in providing a complete picture of the individual within various environmental settings.

### 6.6.1    Skills required by those involved in detection of ADHD in tier 1

*Specific areas of competence for tier 1 should include the following:*
1.  Recognition of the three core symptoms of ADHD: inattention, hyperactivity and impulsivity. Core symptoms need to have been present since childhood or early adolescence. It is worth noting that direct observation of a child for a short time in a primary care setting may not demonstrate any obvious features of the condition and is not necessarily a helpful diagnostic approach. Children with predominant symptoms of inattention are less likely to be diagnosed.
2.  An awareness that symptoms should occur in all environments (although may not be impairing in all settings). If a child presents via primary care then some form of feedback from the school or nursery is very helpful.
3.  Consideration of the use of symptom checklists for parents, child or teacher may be helpful in determining which children need further referral (for example, Conners' rating scales, Strengths and Difficulties questionnaire or standardised DSM-IV checklists) if used in association with clinical assessment.
4.  An awareness of the conditions that may coexist with ADHD, such as oppositional defiant disorder, conduct disorder, autistic spectrum, and so on.
5.  An awareness of family circumstances. In particular recent changes in behaviour which may be linked to life events are far less likely to be because of ADHD.
6.  An awareness of the child's developmental and medical history; issues such as hearing problems or inadequate sleep may be particularly relevant.

### 6.6.2    Skills required for assessment in tier 2/3

Services providing facilities for the diagnostic assessment of ADHD need to be competent in a number of related areas. The skills required will in most cases be acquired during the training of consultant paediatricians (those specialising in mental health, community child health or neurodisability) and child and adolescent psychiatrists, but can usefully be extended to training of GPs in primary care, as well as specialist nurses, psychologists and occupational therapists. The required skills are not specific to any class of professional healthcare worker and can be acquired by people from a range of backgrounds as listed in Section 6.2.2. Assessments by an interdisciplinary team will in many cases increase the range of expertise and the quality of the assessments. These competencies are therefore those expected of the service rather than of individual clinicians.

*Specific areas of competence should include the following:*
1.  A sound understanding of the normal patterns of infant, child and adolescent development.
2.  An ability to differentiate behaviours/symptoms of ADHD from the normal patterns of cognitive function and behavioural features, appropriate for the developmental age.

3. An ability to differentiate the behaviours/symptoms of ADHD from the patterns of cognitive function and behavioural features of other developmental disorders (such as global or specific learning disabilities, including specific reading difficulties, developmental coordination disorder, autism and related spectrum disorders, and Tourette's syndrome).
4. An ability to identify and assess the contribution of mental health disorders, such as anxiety (including obsessive-compulsive disorder), mood disorders (including depression and bipolar disorder) and schizophrenia.
5. An ability to identify and assess the contribution of medical predisposing factors (such as fetal alcohol conditions, extreme prematurity) and coexisting conditions (such as epilepsy).
6. An ability to identify and assess the contribution of family and social adversity, including neglect and abuse.
7. An ability to identify and assess the contribution of the above coexisting disorders and risk factors to the behavioural/symptom profile and level of impairment.

## 6.7 ASSESSMENT FRAMEWORK AND COMPETENCIES FOR EVALUATION OF ADHD IN ADULTS

Adults with ADHD are usually identified in several ways:
1. People with a previous history of childhood ADHD referred from paediatric services, CAMHS or primary care.
2. People with a previous history of treatment for childhood ADHD, but no longer being monitored or treated for it.
3. People who were not diagnosed with ADHD in childhood and where ADHD is recognised by a primary care or secondary care physician.

Adults would usually be referred to specialist diagnostic services for ADHD (general adult psychiatry or a specialist service within adult mental health) by child and adolescent psychiatrists (transitional service) or by non-specialist doctors in primary care and/or psychiatrists with no training in the diagnosis and treatment of ADHD and psychologists in mental health. ADHD in adults is more likely to present within certain specialist clinics including addiction services, personality disorder and affective disorder clinics.

To enable the recognition of ADHD non-specialists should be aware that ADHD persists into adulthood as the full disorder in around 15% of cases or in partial remission with persistence of some symptoms associated with significant clinical impairments in a further 50%. ADHD in adults should be considered for all adult mental health problems that appear to start in early childhood and where the specific problems associated with the disorder (hyperactivity/impulsivity and/or inattention) persisted into adult life. Awareness of the typical early onset and persistent (non-fluctuating) course of the symptoms are important for recognition of potential cases. Mood symptoms such as chronic low self-esteem, volatile mood (irritable and unstable mood, easily frustrated) are commonly seen in adults with ADHD and should not exclude the possibility of the diagnosis. People with ADHD may not show marked symptoms of ADHD (fidgety restlessness, poor attention span) during brief clinical assessments – but they may report such problems in their daily lives. Absence of other major psychiatric conditions – such as bipolar disorder, major depression or somatic anxiety states that explain the disorder – can usually be excluded as a cause of ADHD because they are typically episodic. People with personality disorder should be referred for assessment of ADHD if they present with significant levels of hyperactivity/impulsivity accompanied by inattention.

Family history of ADHD or other neurodevelopmental problems in close family relatives is common. Screening tools can be used to assist in recognition of the disorder, such as the Adult ADHD Self Report Scale or the Barkley scales based on the DSM-IV checklist for ADHD symptoms. Services providing facilities for the diagnostic assessment of ADHD need to be competent in a number of related areas. The skills required will in most cases be acquired during the training of consultant psychiatrists and other professional groups dealing with common adult mental health problems. Training in this area of mental health is very poorly developed in the UK, however, and this, combined with a lack of service provision, is currently a major impediment to implementation of this guideline in the adult population. Professional groups who require this training include psychiatrists, psychiatric nurses, psychologists, occupational therapists and primary care physicians involved in the treatment of common psychiatric disorders. Assessments by an interdisciplinary team will in many cases increase the range of expertise and the quality of the assessments. The GDG recognises the need for the following services: (1) routine monitoring and follow-up of people with ADHD stably maintained on drug treatments for ADHD; (2) provision of social and psychological support services for people with ADHD; and (3) diagnostic services for people with ADHD who were not diagnosed during childhood or adolescence. It is recommended that the formal diagnosis and initiation of treatment for ADHD be carried out in secondary care. For the adult population this will usually mean general adult psychiatrists who have received training in the diagnosis and treatment of ADHD. This might also include child psychiatrists working with colleagues in AMHS.

*Specific areas of competence should include the following:*
1. An understanding of the normal patterns of infant, child, adolescent and adult development.
2. An ability to differentiate behaviours/symptoms of ADHD from the normal patterns of cognitive function and behavioural features, appropriate for the developmental age, recognise the three core symptom domains of hyperactivity, impulsivity and inattention and understand the way that these behaviours/symptoms present in adults.
3. An ability to differentiate the behaviours/symptoms of ADHD from the patterns of cognitive function and behavioural features of other developmental disorders (such as global or specific learning disabilities, including specific reading difficulties, autism and related spectrum disorders).
4. An ability to identify and assess the contribution of mental health disorders, such as anxiety, depression, bipolar disorder and schizophrenia.

5. An ability to identify and assess the contribution of coexisting conditions (such as epilepsy).
6. An ability to identify and assess the contribution of family and social factors.
7. An ability to identify and assess the contribution of the coexisting conditions and risk factors to the behavioural/symptom profile and level of impairment.

## 6.8    RECOMMENDATIONS

### 6.8.1    The organisation and planning of services

6.8.1.1    Mental health trusts, and children's trusts that provide mental health/child development services, should form multidisciplinary specialist ADHD teams and/or clinics for children and young people and separate teams and/or clinics for adults. These teams and clinics should have expertise in the diagnosis and management of ADHD, and should:

- provide diagnostic, treatment and consultation services for people with ADHD who have complex needs, or where general psychiatric services are in doubt about the diagnosis and/or management of ADHD
- put in place systems of communication and protocols for information sharing among paediatric, child and adolescent, forensic, and adult mental health services for people with ADHD, including arrangements for transition between child and adult services
- produce local protocols for shared care arrangements with primary care providers, and ensure that clear lines of communication between primary and secondary care are maintained
- ensure age-appropriate psychological services are available for children, young people and adults with ADHD, and for parents or carers.

The size and time commitment of these teams should depend on local circumstances (for example, the size of the trust, the population covered and the estimated referral rate for people with ADHD).

6.8.1.2    Every locality should develop a multi-agency group, with representatives from multidisciplinary specialist ADHD teams, paediatrics, mental health and learning disability trusts, forensic services, child and adolescent mental health services, the Children and Young People's Directorate (CYPD) (including services for education and social services), parent support groups and others with a significant local involvement in ADHD services. The group should:

- oversee the implementation of this guideline
- start and coordinate local training initiatives, including the provision of training and information for teachers about the characteristics of ADHD and its basic behavioural management
- oversee the development and coordination of parent-training/education programmes

● consider compiling a comprehensive directory of information and services for ADHD including advice on how to contact relevant services and assist in the development of specialist teams.

### 6.8.2     Training

6.8.2.1    Trusts should ensure that specialist ADHD teams for children, young people and adults jointly develop age-appropriate training programmes for the diagnosis and management of ADHD for mental health, paediatric, social care, education, forensic and primary care providers and other professionals who have contact with people with ADHD. (Key priority)

6.8.2.2    Child and adult psychiatrists, paediatricians, and other child and adult mental health professionals (including those working in forensic services) should undertake training so that they are able to diagnose ADHD and provide treatment and management in accordance with this guideline.

### 6.8.3     Care pathway: identification, pre-diagnostic intervention in the community and referral to secondary services

6.8.3.1    Referral from the community to secondary care may involve health, education and social care professionals (for example, GPs, paediatricians, educational psychologists, SENCOs, social workers) and care pathways can vary locally. The person making the referral to secondary care should inform the child or young person's GP.

6.8.3.2    When a child or young person presents in primary care with behavioural and/or attention problems suggestive of ADHD, primary care practitioners should determine the severity of the problems, how these affect the child or young person and the parents or carers and the extent to which they pervade different domains and settings.

6.8.3.3    If the child or young person's behavioural and/or attention problems suggestive of ADHD are having an adverse impact on their development or family life, healthcare professionals should consider:
● a period of watchful waiting of up to 10 weeks
● offering parents or carers a referral to a parent-training/education programme (this should not wait for a formal diagnosis of ADHD).
If the behavioural and/or attention problems persist with at least moderate impairment, the child or young person should be referred to secondary care (that is, a child psychiatrist, paediatrician, or specialist ADHD CAMHS) for assessment.

6.8.3.4    If the child or young person's behavioural and/or attention problems are associated with severe impairment, referral should be made directly to secondary care (that is, a child psychiatrist, paediatrician, or specialist ADHD CAMHS) for assessment.

6.8.3.5    Primary care practitioners should not make the initial diagnosis or start drug treatment in children or young people with suspected ADHD.

6.8.3.6    A child or young person who is currently treated in primary care with methylphenidate, atomoxetine, dexamfetamine, or any other psychotropic drug for a presumptive diagnosis of ADHD, but has not yet been assessed by a specialist in ADHD in secondary care, should be referred for assessment to a child psychiatrist, paediatrician, or specialist ADHD CAMHS as a matter of clinical priority.

6.8.3.7    Adults presenting with symptoms of ADHD in primary care or general adult psychiatric services, who do not have a childhood diagnosis of ADHD, should be referred for assessment by a mental health specialist trained in the diagnosis and treatment of ADHD, where there is evidence of typical manifestations of ADHD (hyperactivity/impulsivity and/or inattention) that:
● began during childhood and have persisted throughout life
● are not explained by other psychiatric diagnoses (although there may be other coexisting psychiatric conditions)
● have resulted in or are associated with moderate or severe psychological, social and/or educational or occupational impairment.

6.8.3.8    Adults who have previously been treated for ADHD as children or young people and present with symptoms suggestive of continuing ADHD should be referred to general adult psychiatric services for assessment. The symptoms should be associated with at least moderate or severe psychological and/or social or educational or occupational impairment.

### 6.8.4    Transition to adult services

6.8.4.1    A young person with ADHD receiving treatment and care from CAMHS or paediatric services should be reassessed at school-leaving age to establish the need for continuing treatment into adulthood. If treatment is necessary, arrangements should be made for a smooth transition to adult services with details of the anticipated treatment and services that the young person will require. Precise timing of arrangements may vary locally but should usually be completed by the time the young person is 18 years.

6.8.4.2    During the transition to adult services, a formal meeting involving CAMHS and/or paediatrics and adult psychiatric services should be considered, and full information provided to the young person about adult services. For young people aged 16 years and older, the care programme approach (CPA) should be used as an aid to transfer between services. The young person, and when appropriate the parent or carer, should be involved in the planning.

6.8.4.3    After transition to adult services, adult healthcare professionals should carry out a comprehensive assessment of the person with ADHD that includes personal, educational, occupational and social functioning, and assessment of any coexisting conditions, especially drug misuse, personality disorders, emotional problems and learning difficulties.

# 7. PSYCHOLOGICAL INTERVENTIONS AND PARENT TRAINING

## 7.1 INTRODUCTION

This chapter reviews the evidence on non-pharmacological interventions for ADHD. Psychological interventions for ADHD include a range of cognitive behavioural approaches, including behavioural interventions and parent training, cognitive training and social skills training. Throughout this guideline, when the terms 'parent training' or 'parent-training/education programme' are used 'parent' also refers to carers and guardians. Interventions with parents or carers of children with ADHD that do not fall into the category of parent training are also addressed, for example psychoeducation in the form of written material for parents. For younger children with ADHD (up to 6 years) behavioural approaches, primarily parent-training interventions, are the main focus of research, while for older children other approaches such as CBT, social skills training and self-instructional training coupled with parent training predominate. Psychological interventions for adults with ADHD are less developed, with the focus of research to date being on CBT, whether delivered as an individual intervention or in a brief workshop-style intervention. There is also some research on the use of other types of therapy for ADHD, such as biofeedback and relaxation training, and these are also discussed along with the use of environmental manipulation and management (see Section 7.4).

Despite the predominance of pharmacological management of ADHD symptoms psychological interventions for ADHD have attracted the interests of clinicians and researchers for a number of reasons as set out below.

*Short-term effects of medication*
Despite the effectiveness of stimulants in achieving a reduction in core symptoms, there have been questions over their long-term effectiveness, with some studies indicating that improvements may not be maintained over the longer term and into adolescence (Swanson *et al.*, 1993). Similarly, some studies have indicated that many of the benefits of stimulant medication may be state-dependent – effects may only last for as long as the person is receiving the medication and may not generalise to situations in which treatment is absent (Whalen & Henker, 1991). Therefore other forms of intervention have been considered as a way perhaps of prolonging drug effects.

*Narrow clinical benefits of medication*
Children and adults with ADHD typically have secondary problems which are not resolved with medication. For example, Pelham and Gnagy (1999) point out that although stimulants may improve parent-child interactions in analogue settings (that is, settings where measures may be taken, such as a clinic), families of children with

ADHD are dysfunctional in multiple domains with problems that may include maternal stress and depression, paternal alcohol misuse and inappropriate parenting skills. Furthermore, problems of low self-esteem, poor peer relationships and other secondary or coexisting problems may exacerbate ADHD symptoms and may not be improved by medication alone. Equally, studies have not demonstrated clear effects of stimulants on academic performance or learning (Swanson *et al.*, 1993).

*Non-responsiveness to medication*
A significant number of children and adults with ADHD fail to respond to stimulant medication (Safren *et al.*, 2005; Swanson *et al.*, 1995). These significant sub-groups of those with ADHD have legitimate interventional needs.

*Weak responsiveness of ADHD symptoms to medication*
Of those children who do respond to medication, the improvement may not necessarily bring them within the clinically normal range (Pelham & Murphy, 1986) and so, even if medication has some beneficial effects, there may be a need to enhance them.

*Intolerance to medication*
A significant number of children and adults with ADHD may be intolerant to stimulant medication. Side effects of stimulants can be significant and interfere with treatment adherence or cause treatment discontinuation (see Chapter 10 for a review of the side effects of stimulants). Side effects sometimes occur only in the early stages of treatment as they may be removed by adjustments to dosage. Nevertheless, the issue has been important for the development of alternative or complementary psychological approaches given that Schachar and colleagues (1997) found that 15% of children treated with methylphenidate terminated treatment at 4 months because of side effects.

*Clinical needs of younger children*
ADHD may present and require intervention before age 6, yet except for dexamfetamine (which is approved in the UK for the treatment of ADHD in children of 3 years and older) manufacturers of stimulant medications for ADHD do not recommend their use for the treatment of children under 6 years. Other types of therapy, particularly behavioural, have therefore proved attractive to clinicians and researchers for this age group.

*Ethical and other objections to medication*
Even if medication has proved to be a complete solution, some professionals, parents or carers and children and adults with ADHD have objections and ethical concerns about the use of medication (Perring, 1997). The reasons are varied and include a general unhappiness about using any type of psychotropic medication in children, concerns about possible side effects and long-term harms, concerns that medication may take away individual responsibility for problems, and an unease that the focus of treatment should be solely on the child instead of the interface between them and the social and educational systems of which they are a part.

### 7.1.1    The aims of psychological interventions for ADHD

In addition to the limitations and objections to medication discussed above, there are other reasons why psychological interventions may be chosen. Most presentations of ADHD in children and adults are associated with behavioural problems and coexisting mental disorders, commonly depression, anxiety, defiant and oppositional behaviour, poor self-esteem, relationship difficulties and learning problems. A complete and comprehensive therapeutic intervention devised for a given individual might therefore include non-pharmacological therapies of proven benefit. A further objective might be to use psychological interventions to reduce the dosage of stimulant medication that might be required to achieve a positive clinical outcome.

The main aim of all psychological interventions for ADHD is to improve the daily functioning of the child or young person by improving their behaviour and family and peer relationships. Interventions for parents are designed to help parents develop optimum strategies to cope with the difficult behaviour secondary to, or coexisting with, ADHD rather than addressing the core symptoms of inattention, hyperactivity and impulsivity.

### 7.1.2    Outcome measures for the review of the effectiveness of psychological interventions for ADHD

Most studies tend to include a wide range of outcome measures from different sources (parents, teachers, clinicians and self) to explore the wider clinical benefits of interventions for ADHD. In addition to being of research interest, this wider approach to outcomes probably mirrors general clinical practice and as such is of particular value to the evaluation of psychological interventions for ADHD.

When undertaking the meta-analysis evaluating the effectiveness of psychological interventions for ADHD, in addition to looking at the impact of interventions on measures of the core symptoms of ADHD the GDG looked at measures of other outcome categories reflecting aspects of behaviour and functioning that ADHD may have an impact upon: conduct problems, social skills, emotional outcomes and self-efficacy. For each of the included studies the GDG considered whether any of the reported outcomes were acceptable measures of any of these additional outcome categories. Where studies reported useable outcomes they were used in the meta-analysis for the additional outcome categories.

For each outcome category, a hierarchy of the most suitable outcome measures was agreed upon by the GDG members. If a study reported more than one relevant measure (or subscales) for a given outcome category, only the measure highest in the agreed outcome hierarchy was included in the analysis. For each outcome category separate analysis was undertaken for parent-, teacher-, other observer- or self-reported outcomes. Generally studies reported outcome measures for only some of the outcome categories. Only outcome measures that were judged to be established and valid were used in the analysis; outcome measures that were developed for a study and behavioural observations were therefore not used.

In addition, analysis was undertaken to look at the effects of interventions on measures of reading and writing as these were agreed as the key educational outcome categories.

### 7.1.3 Definitions of psychological interventions for children and young people

Although there are many types of psychological therapies the three main types used to treat ADHD are CBT, social skills training and family therapy. CBT approaches that are relevant to the treatment of children with ADHD include behavioural therapy, parent training and cognitive therapy. CBT techniques have been extensively used with the aim of helping to improve motor behaviour, inattention and impulsivity. CBT helps clients understand links between thoughts, feelings and behaviours and how these may result in unhelpful, inappropriate or maladaptive consequences. A second component of the therapy is learning to change these thoughts, feelings and behaviours to produce more desirable outcomes. Essential to the therapeutic process is putting any identified changes into practice. CBT approaches often combine behavioural and cognitive aspects, but in work with children CBT therapies have often had either a behavioural or cognitive emphasis. The main psychological interventions for ADHD are described below.

*Behaviour therapy*
The chief technique involves the use of rewards or reinforcers that are judged likely to encourage the young person to implement targeted changes in motor, impulse or attentional control. This may involve tangible rewards such as extra time for recreational and leisure activities or the means to obtain items that the young person values. Schemes using 'tokens' (such as stars, chips, marbles, and so on) may for younger children be rewarding in their own right, whereas for older children tokens may be exchanged for items of value to them. Another type of reward is social approval such as praise or achievement certificates and this may also include self-praise. Care is required in the choice of rewards because they may be specific to an individual – what is of value to one child is not necessarily of value to another. There are also practical, financial, cultural and moral issues that make some rewards more suitable for some parents than others.

A further set of techniques involves negative consequences. Although less frequently used than rewards, this approach may have a valuable function, especially where a particular behaviour is disruptive or offensive to others and needs to be stopped immediately – impulsive behaviour frequently falls into this category. Verbal reprimands, which have the merit of being simple and effective, may be delivered by parents, other carers and teaching staff. Response cost techniques involve the loss of a potential reinforcer. These can take the form of deductions either from rewards already earned or from an agreed set of rewards given in advance but from which deductions can be made for inappropriate behaviour.

The third most common technique is 'time out' (short for 'time out from social reinforcement'), which involves the young person being placed away from the attention of others for a set period during which time they are expected to be quiet and co-operative, otherwise the procedure is implemented again. This particular approach is helpful where it is felt that inappropriate, overactive or impulsive behaviour is being maintained by the attention of others such as parents, siblings or peers.

*Parent training*

Parent training (or parent-effectiveness training) is, to all intents and purposes, a behaviour therapy intervention in that it teaches the parents to use behaviour therapy techniques with their child. Parent training originated in the 1960s and was based on behavioural learning theory and play therapy, although play therapy was not acknowledged as being as important. The intervention has developed further into addressing issues such as beliefs, emotions and wider social issues along with issues that hinder the effectiveness of parents such as poor self-confidence, depression, social isolation and marital difficulties (Scott, 2002).

The main goals of parent-training programmes are to teach the principles of child behaviour management, increase parental competence and confidence in raising children and to improve the parent/carer-child relationship by using good communication and positive attention to aid the child's development. These programmes are structured and follow a set curriculum over several weeks; they are mainly conducted in groups, but can be modified for individual treatments. Examples of recognised programmes are the Triple P (Sanders *et al.*, 2004) and Webster-Stratton (Webster–Stratton, 1981). The focus is primarily with the child or young person's main caregiver although some programmes add a child-directed component based on the principles of social skills training.

*Cognitive therapy*

Self-instructional training is probably the most commonly used cognitive therapeutic approach in the psychological treatment of ADHD. It comprises several different techniques, including cognitive modelling, self-evaluation, self-reinforcement and response cost.

The therapy involves helping the young person develop a more planned and reflective way of thinking and behaving by learning how to adopt a more reflective, systematic and goal-directed approach to tasks and problem solving. The learning strategies typically involve abstract self-instructional schemas along with more concrete step-by-step approaches and perhaps physical cues and reminders.

An early example of teaching an abstract strategy was the 'Think Aloud' programme by Camp and Bash (1981) based on ideas by Meichenbaum (1977) and Meichenbaum and Goodman (1971). Children are encouraged to adopt a four-point schema when faced with a problem or task:

1. What is the problem?
2. What is my plan?
3. Do I use my plan?
4. How did I do?

The strategy is taught initially using cognitive modelling involving an adult verbalising their response to a problem-solving task. The young person then emulates this first by talking out aloud, then whispering and finally using covert (inner) self-talk. Self-evaluation is then encouraged.

More task-specific strategies can also be taught and may be related to particular situations such as school work, relationship issues and recreational and leisure pursuits (for example, Kendall & Wilcox, 1980; Kendall & Braswell, 1982). Programmes may also feature other techniques, such as teaching self-reinforcement (for example, 'I did well!') and response cost techniques in which the young person pays penalties for making mistakes or alternatively earns rewards for success in implementing the strategies taught (Kendall & Finch, 1978).

### Social skills training
Social skills training was developed in the early 1970s and according to Jacobs (2002) its aim is to teach the micro skills of social interaction such as eye contact, smiling and body posture. Children and young people who have ADHD often present with difficult family relationships and may have poor social skills and peer relationships. Social skills are described as the behaviours and skills necessary to engage in developing and maintaining constructive social relationships. Social skills training uses techniques from cognitive and behavioural approaches and is conducted within groups.

In addition to social skills training, problem-solving approaches have been developed and are concerned with the child and young person's ability to self-regulate (the capacity of the child and young person to initiate, delay, modify or modulate the amount or intensity of a thought, emotion, behaviour or psychological response) and cope with stress (the ability to self-regulate responses to perceived stressful events) (Compas *et al.*, 2002).

### Family therapy
The practice of family therapy varies widely and is based on the recognition of interpersonal relationships within families. Family therapy aims to produce changes in the ways that families function. There are different models of family therapy:
- Structural family therapy is based on the assumption that all well-functioning families have an intergenerational hierarchy with demarcated roles and boundaries. The role of the therapist is to challenge family functioning and difficult interpersonal relationships, and thereby enable family disorganisation to be resolved.
- Strategic family therapy is based on the view that difficulties stem from repeated patterns of dysfunctional family communications.
- Brief solution-focused therapy focuses on when the problems are not evident or less problematic in order to examine what is different about these interactions to prove that the family already possess the solution.

### 7.1.4    Support for parents of children with ADHD

Relationship and family issues are well documented for children and families with a diagnosis of ADHD (Johnston & Mash, 2001). Parents often feel that they are unable to manage the complexity of their child's difficulties and this places a strain on the parents themselves as well as the family and siblings who do not have ADHD. Parents/carers of children with ADHD therefore often need support, including information about ADHD and the disorders that occur with it, and information and support to help them to cope. Local parental support groups can provide peer support and an opportunity for parents to exchange experiences and advice about caring for a child or young person with ADHD on a day-to-day basis; they may also be helpful in providing a source of advocacy.

### 7.1.5    Psychological therapies for adults with ADHD

CBT interventions may be used with adults to help them to develop strategies and learn practical techniques to reduce the impact of their ADHD symptoms on their functioning, for example by teaching problem-solving skills, techniques to reduce distractibility and stress management skills. These interventions, which may be offered on a group or individual basis, vary in duration and may be provided only as brief intensive treatments, for example in the form of brief solution-focused therapy. The development of CBT for adults with ADHD has lagged behind its development for children (Ramsey & Rostain, 2003), partly as a consequence of the under recognition of ADHD in adults.

Other approaches with adults are brief solution-focused therapy and coaching. Coaching is an intervention that aims to help people with ADHD identify and draw on their personal strengths as well as to negotiate their problems and cope with life on a daily basis. The coaching relationship has a collaborative focus with the coach and client working together in partnership. The aim is to change old behaviour patterns by developing new ones, as well as to identify personal goals and generate strategies to counter potential obstacles to achievement and success. The coaching or mentoring role is not prescribed in terms of there being a recommended level of contact or number of sessions as it operates along the lines of a 'buddy system' whereby the coach is an ally who provides encouragement and support, especially when the client must face and manage difficult situations. The process of the intervention and level of commitment varies immensely. Much depends upon the quality of the coach/client relationship as personal coaching involves an individualised approach that focuses on the client's goals and needs.

### 7.1.6    Current practice

Little is known about the extent and quality of non-pharmacological treatment patterns of children, young people and adults with ADHD in the UK. There are very few adult clinics specialising in ADHD and services for children are variable and provided by community health services, CAMHS and education services.

Current practice in the use of psychological interventions for ADHD is, in all probability, variable. It is likely that the pattern of the availability of psychological interventions will vary according to locality and the resources within that locality.

Much will also depend on the individual diagnosis, with a care plan being tailored to each individual's needs rather than a universal intervention package being offered within each setting. Furthermore, the accessibility of services for children and families may vary. Services may not be accessible to all children and families unless they are delivered in a venue that is local and accessible to children and families, has flexible delivery hours (including evenings and weekends), and provides crèche facilities for families with younger children.

*Children*

Nationally, the responsibility for providing services for children with ADHD is shared between paediatric services and CAMHS, with the former probably seeing the majority of cases. The exact configuration of services at the local level is highly variable – services for children with ADHD may either be shared between these services, or primarily the remit of either one or the other service.

The most common initial intervention is the provision of parental advice and guidance on an individual basis. This may be delivered informally, for example by nurse specialists. Where indicated, this may be combined with a parent-training/education programme using behaviour therapy principles on an individual or group basis. Such programmes are offered by CAMHS and some paediatric services, primary health services or by voluntary organisations, but the provision of such interventions is patchy with marked geographical variations. In addition it is common for CAMHS professionals to offer additional psychological and other therapies to children and their families to address coexisting or secondary mental health problems that may present with ADHD. It is recognised that in some paediatric settings local psychological interventions may not always be available and therefore not routinely offered.

It is less usual for individual or group work to be undertaken with children – the most widely used interventions are those that aim to improve social skills or 'self-control', with the latter focusing on anger management or problem-solving skills. The provision of these types of intervention is again variable, but of the two, social skills training is probably the most frequently offered.

The provision of help in primary schools is very limited and rarely specific to the needs of children with ADHD. However, some schools offer group training for anger management and social skills, and while such programmes are often related to anti-bullying initiatives they may be of some help to children with ADHD.

An informal intervention is assisting children to engage in a variety of leisure and recreational pursuits, usually to meet their need for stimulation and also as a release for physical energy. This is often arranged on an intuitive basis by parents, but some therapists may address such needs as part of a wider intervention package.

*Young people*

With young people there is much more of a focus on individual work to reduce identified impairments in functioning which may be continuing to threaten general development and psychosocial adjustment. In CAMHS settings individual therapy using cognitive-behavioural principles is commonly employed to target social skills, self-esteem, behaviour and emotional adjustment. In more complex presentations approaches that may be employed include family therapy and individual work with parents on behavioural management techniques for younger adolescents.

As with primary schools, secondary schools are unlikely to offer interventions specifically for ADHD. Nevertheless, they may offer individual support and coun-selling as well as group programmes for social skills difficulties and reducing aggres-sive and bullying behaviours, which may be a consequence of, or associated with, ADHD. In addition to the core ADHD problem of inattention many children with ADHD also have learning difficulties, including literacy problems. These young people may have help individually or in small groups, which are often overseen or run by SENCOs in each school. Self-instructional training using cognitive therapy prin-ciples is often employed in such contexts but the provision is probably quite limited and variable nationally.

*Adults*

When treating adults with ADHD, current practice in the UK does not routinely include the provision of psychological treatment. There are, however, many reasons why psychological treatment might be appropriate for people who often do not achieve their personal potential by young adulthood because they have been hampered by their symptoms and/or coexisting conditions. When psychological ther-apies are used with adults with ADHD they are generally considered as additional to treatment with medication. However, as young adults mature and their symptoms remit, and treatment with medication may no longer be recommended, a need for psychological treatment may continue, if not arise, to address feelings of helplessness and low self-esteem.

Individuals who have not received their diagnosis until adulthood will require psychological support as they often appear to undergo a process of acceptance and understanding associated with their late diagnosis (Young *et al.*, 2008a). Often these adults have a history of multiple presentations to child and adult services in an attempt to access help (Dalsgaard *et al.*, 2002; Young *et al.*, 2003), with their need for psychological treatment being recognised by both themselves and their partners (Young *et al.*, 2008a; Young *et al.*, 2008b).


## 7.2 PSYCHOLOGICAL INTERVENTIONS FOR CHILDREN WITH ADHD

### 7.2.1 Introduction

This section reviews the evidence on the clinical effectiveness of psychological inter-ventions for children with ADHD. Evidence on the types of psychological interventions for children and young people discussed in the section on definitions in the introduction (see Section 7.1.3) is included, but evidence on other non-pharmacological interven-tions and interventions for carers is not reviewed here.

The GDG took the decision to analyse data from studies of parent-training programmes for ADHD together with data from studies of child-directed interventions on the grounds that parent training is in effect a behavioural intervention with the child because parents are taught to implement behaviour management techniques. This decision was further justified by the available evidence because, in general, interventions were not discretely parent or child focused (see Section 7.2.2).

The GDG also considered the issue of the medication status of participants in studies of psychological interventions for ADHD and concluded that trials should be included as long as the medication status of the participants in the intervention group and control group was similar. Included trials therefore fall into three groups: those with no participants on medication, those in which some or all of the participants in both intervention and control groups continued to receive medication for ADHD as part of their usual care, and those where no information on the medication status of participants was given. In trials where participants received medication as part of usual care, individual participants might receive a variety of types and doses of medication. Where no information was given on the medication status of the participants in a trial they were assumed to be receiving usual care and possibly on medication for ADHD.

At the outset the GDG proposed that separate analyses should be undertaken for studies where participants were not medicated and studies where some or all participants were on medication for ADHD. However, because of the relatively small number of trials the data were all included in one analysis for any medication status. The analysis thus represents a naturalistic population as it includes both medicated and unmedicated children with ADHD.

Trials of the combined use of medication and psychological interventions for ADHD (that is, where the medication regimen and psychological interventions were both determined by the trial protocol) were excluded and analysed separately (see Chapter 11). Trials were also excluded if the medication status of the group receiving the psychological intervention differed from that of the control group. For example, trial data was not included where the intervention group did not receive medication for ADHD but some or all of the control group were on medication as part of their usual care.

## 7.2.2    Limitations and rationale

The nature of the experimental psychological interventions for ADHD that have been evaluated and reported in the literature is such that it is difficult to identify which specific attributes of an intervention are key to any beneficial effects of treatment. In general the interventions evaluated by studies investigating the effectiveness of psychological therapies for ADHD do not involve only the child with ADHD or only their parents. Where the focus of an intervention is on the child there is often some additional parental involvement, such as sessions for parents that relate the content of the intervention and aim to encourage parental reinforcement of what the child is learning in the intervention. In some cases teachers are also involved with a similar aim. Likewise, parent-training interventions may include some work with the child. It is also the case that the experimental interventions generally consist of a number of sessions with a therapist or trainer and might cover a number of approaches and techniques that are potentially of therapeutic value, including cognitive approaches and problem solving, social skills training, and behavioural techniques. Furthermore, while most experimental interventions involve a broadly comparable number of sessions and are spread over a comparable duration, some are longer lasting and more intense.

### 7.2.3    Databases searched and inclusion/exclusion criteria

Information about the databases searched and the inclusion/exclusion criteria used for this section of the guideline can be found in Table 5.

**Table 5:  Databases searched and inclusion/exclusion criteria
for clinical evidence**

| | |
|---|---|
| Electronic databases | CENTRAL, MEDLINE, EMBASE, CINAHL, PsycINFO |
| Date searched | Database inception to 18.12.07 |
| Study design | RCT |
| Patient population | Children diagnosed with ADHD |
| Interventions | Any non-pharmacological intervention used to treat ADHD symptoms and/or associated behavioural problems |
| Outcomes | ADHD symptoms*; conduct problems*; social skills*; emotional outcomes*; self-efficacy*; reading; mathematics; leaving study early due to any reason; non-response to treatment. |

*Separate outcomes for teacher, parent, self, and independent ratings.

### 7.2.4    Studies considered[10]

From the primary RCT search, the review team identified trials comparing a psychological intervention with a control group. Acceptable control conditions included no treatment, assignment to a waiting list, treatment as usual and benign interventions

---

[10]Here and elsewhere in the guideline, each study considered for review is referred to by a study ID in capital letters (primary author and date of study publication, except where a study is in press or only submitted for publication, then a date is not used).

with comparable contact times but lacking the active therapeutic components of the experimental intervention. Studies were excluded if the comparison group received an active and potentially therapeutic intervention. The included studies varied in relation to two key characteristics of the sample populations that might impact on the effectiveness of a psychological intervention – the medication status and age of the children with ADHD.

Ten trials met the eligibility criteria set by the GDG, providing data on 549 participants. All were published in peer-reviewed journals between 1997 and 2007. In addition, 71 studies were excluded from the analysis. The most common reasons for exclusion were related to study design or because there was no appropriate intervention. One study of a parent-training intervention was excluded from the analysis as the level of attendance was poor to the extent that any difference between the intervention and control groups might not be attributable to the intervention (BARKLEY2000). In this trial only 13% of parents assigned to parent training attended a minimum of nine out of 14 sessions, and while the majority did attend at least one session (67%) under half (42%) attended a minimum of five sessions. The children in this study also differed somewhat from others as they were younger (mean age 4.8 years) and were included on the basis of a parent measure of disruptive behaviour (14 symptom items for ADHD and eight symptom items for oppositional defiant disorder). Further information about both included and excluded studies can be found in Appendix 17.

In trials where participants continued to receive usual care medication for ADHD, the type and dose of medication participants received might vary. This contrasts with trials of combination treatment for ADHD, where both the pharmacological and psychological interventions are determined by the study protocol. As discussed above, the GDG concluded that trials of combination treatment for ADHD should be excluded from the analysis of the effectiveness of psychological interventions for children with ADHD, even where they had a group on medication only that could be compared with a group receiving medication plus a psychological intervention (studies of combination treatment for ADHD are reviewed in Chapter 11). Studies were also excluded if the intervention and comparison groups differed in terms of their receipt of medication for ADHD. The Multimodal Treatment Study of Children with ADHD (MTA) (MTA Co-operative Group, 1999a) was therefore excluded as two-thirds of the community care comparison group received medication for ADHD whereas the group receiving the intensive MTA behavioural intervention did not receive medication.

In all included studies, the psychological interventions were broadly based on CBT principles, with the different approaches used reflecting clinical practice for the age range of the study population. The studies involving only pre-school children with ADHD looked at parent-training interventions (BOR2002; SONUGA-BARKE2001), as did the studies involving school-age children with ADHD where the mean age of participants was under 8 years (HOATH2002; HOOFDAKKER2007). Studies involving participants with a mean age of 8 or 9 looked at the effects of work with both the child and the parents or family (BLOOMQUIST1991; FEHLINGS1991; PFIFFNER1997; TUTTY2003) or just the child (ANTSHEL2003; GONZALEZ2002).

Five of the included studies were three-arm trials. For the purposes of this review, only two arms of each trial were included in the analysis. For BLOOMQUIST1991 and PFIFFNER1997, Group 1 and 3 were included; for BOR2002 and GONZALEZ 2002, Group 2 and 3 were included; for SONUGA-BARKE2001, Group 1 and 2 were included (further information about each group can be found in Appendix 17).

No RCTs of family therapy interventions for ADHD were identified that allowed a comparison between the family therapy intervention and a control condition.

### 7.2.5    Clinical evidence for psychological interventions for children with ADHD

Important study population characteristics and a summary of the evidence are presented in Table 6. The associated forest plots can be found in Appendix 18.

**Table 6:  Study information and evidence summary table for trials of psychological interventions**

|  | **Psychological intervention versus control** |
|---|---|
| Total number of studies (number of participants) | 10 (549) |
| Study ID | ANTSHEL2003 BLOOMQUIST1991 BOR2002 FEHLINGS1991 GONZALEZ2002 HOATH2002 HOOFDAKKER2007 PFIFFNER1997 SONUGA-BARKE2001 TUTTY2003 |
| *Study population characteristics* | |
| Pre-school children with ADHD | BOR2002 SONUGA-BARKE2001 |
| School-age children with ADHD | ANTSHEL2003 BLOOMQUIST1991 FEHLINGS1991 GONZALEZ2002 |

**Table 6:** (*Continued*)

| | Psychological intervention versus control |
|---|---|
| | HOATH2002<br>HOOFDAKKER2007<br>PFIFFNER1997<br>TUTTY2003 |
| Not on medication for ADHD | BOR2002<br>FEHLINGS1991<br>SONUGA-BARKE2001 |
| Some on treatment-as-usual medication for ADHD | HOATH2002<br>HOOFDAKKER2007<br>PFIFFNER1997 |
| All on treatment-as-usual medication for ADHD | ANTSHEL2003<br>GONZALEZ2002<br>TUTTY2003 |
| Medication status unclear | BLOOMQUIST1991 |
| ***Benefits (end of treatment)*** | |
| Core ADHD symptoms at end of treatment (teacher-rated) | SMD $-0.25$ ($-0.56$ to $0.07$)<br>Quality: High<br>K = 4, N = 163 |
| Core ADHD symptoms at end of treatment (parent-rated) | SMD $-0.57$ ($-1.00$ to $-0.14$)<br>Quality: Moderate<br>K = 5, N = 288 |
| Conduct at end of treatment (teacher-rated) | SMD $-0.12$ ($-0.61$ to $0.38$)<br>Quality: Moderate<br>K = 3, N = 63 |
| Conduct at end of treatment (parent-rated) | SMD $-0.54$ ($-1.05$ to $-0.04$)<br>Quality: Moderate<br>K = 5, N = 231 |
| Social skills at end of treatment (teacher-rated) | SMD $-0.40$ ($-1.33$ to $0.54$)<br>Quality: Moderate<br>K = 1, N = 18 |
| Social skills at end of treatment (parent-rated) | SMD $-0.59$ ($-1.80$ to $0.61$)<br>Quality: Low<br>K = 2, N = 138 |
| Social skills at end of treatment (child-rated) | SMD $-0.23$ ($-0.61$ to $0.15$)<br>Quality: High<br>K = 1, N = 120 |

*Continued*

**Table 6:** (*Continued*)

| | Psychological intervention versus control |
|---|---|
| Emotional outcomes at end of treatment (teacher-rated) | SMD −0.20 (−1.12 to 0.73)<br>Quality: Moderate<br>K = 1, N = 18 |
| Emotional outcomes end of treatment (parent-rated) | SMD −0.36 (−0.73 to 0.01)<br>Quality: High<br>K = 2, N = 112 |
| Self-efficacy at end of treatment (child-rated) | SMD −0.03 (−0.48 to 0.42)<br>Quality: High<br>K = 3, N = 78 |
| *Benefits (3–6 months post-treatment)* | |
| Core ADHD symptoms at 5–6 months post-treatment (teacher-rated) | SMD −0.05 (−0.44 to 0.35)<br>Quality: High<br>K = 2, N = 101 |
| Core ADHD symptoms at 5–6 months post-treatment (parent-rated) | SMD −0.91 (−1.23 to −0.59)<br>Quality: High<br>K = 3, N = 174 |
| Conduct at 3–4 months post-treatment (teacher-rated) | SMD −0.13 (−1.05 to 0.80)<br>Quality: Moderate<br>K = 1, N = 18 |
| Conduct at 3–5 months post-treatment (parent-rated) | SMD −0.51 (−1.01 to −0.01)<br>Quality: High<br>K = 2, N = 68 |
| Social skills at 3–4 months post-treatment (teacher-rated) | SMD −0.06 (−0.98 to 0.86)<br>Quality: Moderate<br>K = 1, N = 18 |
| Social skills at 3–4 months post-treatment (parent-rated) | SMD 0.06 (−0.29 to 0.42)<br>Quality: High<br>K = 2, N = 138 |
| Social skills at 3 months post-treatment (child-rated) | SMD 0.04 (−0.34 to 0.42)<br>Quality: High<br>K = 1, N = 120 |
| Emotional outcomes at 3–4 months post-treatment (teacher-rated) | SMD −0.19 (−1.11 to 0.74)<br>Quality: Moderate<br>K = 1, N = 18 |

**Table 6:** (*Continued*)

| | Psychological intervention versus control |
|---|---|
| Emotional outcomes at 3–4 months post-treatment (parent-rated) | SMD 0.04 (−0.89 to 0.96) Quality: Moderate K = 1, N = 18 |
| Self-efficacy at 5 months post-treatment (child-rated) | SMD −0.89 (−1.70 to −0.08) Quality: Moderate K = 1, N = 26 |
| *Dichotomous outcomes* | |
| Leaving study for any reason | Data not pooled ANTSHEL2003: 0% (psychological inter-view) versus 0% (control) BLOOMQUIST1991: 31% versus 0% BOR2002: 31% versus 16% FEHLINGS1991: 0% versus 0% GONZALEZ2002: not reported HOATH2002: 10% versus 0% HOOFDAKKER2007: 2% versus 2% PFIFFNER1997: 0% versus 0% SONUGA-BARKE2001: 7% total TUTTY2003: 9% versus 0% |
| Non-responders | RR 0.49 (0.27 to 0.88) Quality: High K = 1, N = 48 |

### 7.2.6 Clinical evidence summary for psychological interventions for children with ADHD

For individual outcomes, the quality of the evidence was generally moderate to high. Overall, the evidence shows that compared with control conditions psychological interventions for children with ADHD have moderate beneficial effects on parent ratings of ADHD symptoms and conduct problems at the end of treatment. These beneficial effects are sustained at follow-up 3 to 6 months after the end of treatment. If the small study by Pfiffner and McBurnett (PFIFFNER1997) is excluded from the analysis the effect of psychological interventions on conduct problems at the end of treatment remains positive, but beneficial effects do not reach statistical significance at the later follow-up. The meta-analysis therefore cannot be regarded as establishing that psychological interventions have sustained effects on conduct problems in children with ADHD. There is no evidence that psychological interventions for children with ADHD have positive effects on teacher ratings of either ADHD symptoms or conduct-related behaviours. Beneficial effects of psychological interventions for ADHD therefore do not appear to transfer to the classroom environment.

In the absence of evidence that psychological interventions have a positive effect on teacher ratings of ADHD symptoms and conduct behaviour, the evidence of beneficial effects based on ratings by parents should be interpreted with some caution. Parent ratings may be potentially subject to bias because in trials of psychological interventions for children with ADHD that do not use a control intervention, parents will know whether they and/or their child has received the intervention. Even where teachers are also aware which children are receiving the intervention it is possible that there is a greater risk of bias in parents' ratings as they have more invested in the child and may therefore be less objective. However, it is impossible to determine whether bias has contributed to the findings on parent outcomes; indeed an alternative explanation for the discrepancy between parent and teacher ratings is that behavioural symptoms are less severe in the more structured classroom environment. There is therefore less scope for a psychological intervention to deliver measurable benefits. A further consideration is that the primary focus of psychological interventions, particularly parent-training interventions and other interventions that involve the parents or family as a whole, may be to improve behaviour in the home environment, in which case greater improvements might be expected in parent ratings of behaviour.

With respect to the other outcomes that it was considered might be targeted by psychological interventions, or on which psychological interventions might have a greater impact (social skills, emotional state as represented by internalising symptoms and anxiety, self-efficacy and academic performance), beneficial effects were not generally in evidence. Positive effects were detected for self-efficacy at follow-up 3 to 6 months after the end of treatment, but this finding comes from only one small study that reported a self-efficacy outcome at this follow-up time point (FEHLINGS1991). At the end of treatment neither this trial nor the overall meta-analysis pointed to positive effects of psychological interventions on self-efficacy, and the one finding at follow-up therefore cannot be taken as establishing an effect of psychological interventions on self-efficacy in children with ADHD.

Unfortunately, owing to the limited number of RCTs meeting inclusion criteria, there was insufficient data to allow robust sub-analyses to be performed to look at the circumstances in which psychological interventions might be effective for children with ADHD. Questions of particular interest are whether:

- psychological interventions are effective in the subgroup of children with ADHD not on medication for ADHD
- psychological interventions are effective in the subgroup of children with ADHD continuing to receive medication for ADHD as part of their usual care
- psychological interventions are effective in pre-school children with ADHD
- psychological interventions are effective in school-age children with ADHD
- psychological interventions targeting parents are effective for children with ADHD
- psychological interventions targeting children with ADHD are effective
- psychological interventions targeting both children and parents, and family interventions, are effective for children with ADHD
- psychological interventions delivered to groups are effective for children with ADHD

● psychological interventions delivered individually are effective for children with ADHD.

However, it is notable that when separate analyses were undertaken for trials where participants were not on medication (BOR2002; FEHLINGS1991; SONUGA-BARKE2001) and for trials where some or all of the participants were on continuing medication for ADHD or where no details of the medication status of participants were given (ANTSHEL2003; BLOOMQUIST1991; GONZALEZ2002; HOATH2002; HOOFDAKKER2007; PFIFFNER1997; TUTTY2003), similar effects or trends were found to those reported in the overall analysis. While only tentative inferences can be drawn from these sub-analyses, they tend to support the validity of analysing trials with participants not on medication and trials with participants on usual care medication together. The analysis conducted here therefore suggests that CBT interventions for ADHD can have beneficial effects whether delivered in the absence of medication or as an adjunct to continued routine medication for ADHD.

The evidence for the benefits of CBT for children with ADHD is based on studies including children between 3 and 13 years. In all the studies that included children up to 12 or 13 years the mean age was 9 or under and children aged 12 or over were more than one standard deviation above the mean age for the sample (ANTSHEL2003; FEHLINGS1991; GONZALEZ2002; HOOFDAKKER2007; TUTTY2003). One other study of CBT for school-age children with ADHD did not specify the age range, but participants were drawn from a US 'elementary school' population (BLOOMQUIST1991). The RCT evidence on the effects of CBT for children therefore does not apply to adolescent populations with ADHD.

### 7.2.7 Clinical evidence for other interventions with parents/carers for children with ADHD

For the review of other interventions with parents/carers for children with ADHD, important study characteristics and a summary of the evidence are presented in Table 7. The forest plots can be found in Appendix 18.

Parent training is included in the review of the effectiveness of psychological interventions for ADHD (see 7.2.5) because it is to all intents and purposes a behavioural intervention in that the parents are taught to use behavioural training techniques with their child. Other types of intervention targeting the parents or main carer may also aim to address the child's ADHD symptoms. Studies were included where they were RCTs that compared a group receiving an intervention for parents or carers of children with ADHD (other than parent training) with a control group not receiving the intervention. Only studies giving outcome data for the child with ADHD were included (outcomes for parents were not included in the analysis). Studies were only included if the medication status of the children in the intervention and control groups was comparable.

### 7.2.8 Clinical evidence summary for other interventions with parents/carers for children with ADHD

One small trial (32 families) of psychoeducation for parents of children with ADHD (LONG1993) met the inclusion criteria for this review. In this study, parents were

**Table 7:  Study information and evidence summary table for trials of other interventions with parents or carers for children with ADHD**

| | Psychological intervention versus control |
|---|---|
| Total number of studies (number of participants) | 1 (32) |
| Study ID | LONG1993 |
| ***Benefits*** | |
| Core ADHD symptoms (parent-rated) | SMD −0.69 (−1.41 to 0.03) Quality: Moderate K = 1, N = 32 |
| Conduct (parent-rated) | SMD −0.71 (−1.43 to 0.01) Quality: Moderate K = 1, N = 32 |
| Conduct (teacher-rated) | SMD −1.01 (−1.75 to −0.27) Quality: Moderate K = 1, N = 32 |

given a manual outlining various behavioural techniques for managing oppositional child behaviour. The findings suggest that children with ADHD may benefit from their parents being given written material on behavioural management techniques (see Table 7). Outcomes measured around 2 months after the material was given to parents point to a significant benefit of the intervention on teacher ratings of conduct problems. While parent ratings of ADHD symptoms and conduct problems favoured the intervention, neither reached significance (teacher ratings of ADHD symptoms were not reported). Given the focus of the intervention on the management of oppositional behaviour an effect on conduct problems might be expected. These findings indicate that a larger-scale RCT of a similar psychoeducation intervention might be of value to clarify whether written materials on behavioural management are an effective intervention for ADHD symptoms and other behavioural problems associated with ADHD.

While there are other interventions for parents and carers of children with ADHD, including counselling, CBT and peer support groups, these are more directed at improving the parents' or carers' well-being and helping them cope, for example by teaching stress management techniques or providing mutual support. Such interventions would have been included in the review if there were RCTs that reported outcomes for the child with ADHD. Studies of support for parents and/or carers that only reported outcomes for the parents were excluded, however, because they were outside the scope of the guideline.

RCTs of approaches currently used to support parents and carers of children with ADHD would be valuable. In order to determine whether those interventions are effective for ADHD, study protocols would need to include measures of outcomes for the child, particularly measures of ADHD symptoms and conduct problems.

### 7.2.9 NICE guidance on parent-training/education programmes in the management of children with conduct disorders

NICE, in collaboration with the Social Care Institute for Excellence (SCIE), recently published a technology appraisal (TA) on the use of parent-training/education programmes for the management of children with conduct disorders (NICE, 2006a). In the context of this TA the term 'conduct disorders' is used to refer to conduct disorder and oppositional defiant disorder and the term 'parent' applies to the main carer of the child. Conduct disorders are characterised by a repetitive and persistent pattern of antisocial, aggressive or defiant conduct and are often seen in association with ADHD. The high prevalence of comorbid conduct disorders in children with ADHD – estimates suggest that somewhere between 43% and 93% of children with ADHD will have a comorbid conduct disorder (Jensen *et al.*, 1997) – supports the generalisation of this TA to children with ADHD, and in particular those who have conduct problems in addition to core ADHD symptoms.

For children with ADHD, the relevance of the TA is further supported by the relatively inclusive population sample and by the inclusion of populations with comorbidities including ADHD. The evidence on which the guidance is based comes from studies that include a wider population than just those with diagnosed conduct disorders. Studies were included where children were defined as having behavioural problems either by scales that measure aspects of child behaviour or by descriptive criteria without any attempt to classify or grade behaviour.

In seven of the included studies some or all children had ADHD – indeed while only 24% of the total sample had diagnosed conduct disorders, over 12% either had a diagnosis of ADHD or were on stimulant medication (some of those with ADHD had comorbid conduct disorders). Furthermore, though the actual level of ADHD in the sample population on which the guidance is based is impossible to determine, it is likely to be substantially higher than 12%. First, this estimate does not include studies where some participants with ADHD are included in the sample but there are no details of the number of participants with coexisting conditions. Second, in studies where participants have diagnosed conduct disorders, and in the absence of the exclusion of comorbid populations or details on comorbidity, it might be assumed that the proportion of participants who have comorbid ADHD would be consistent with the estimates of the prevalence of ADHD in children with conduct disorders in the general population. Third, studies that include children with behaviour problems, whether defined by behavioural scales or descriptively, are likely to include children with ADHD unless coexisting conditions are explicitly excluded. Conversely, it should be noted that a number of the studies included in the analysis for the TA excluded children receiving treatment – a criterion which would exclude some children with ADHD but which might not necessarily exclude children with ADHD who were not receiving treatment at the time of recruitment for the trial.

The TA along with a summary of the supporting background information in the guidance document is given below (for more detailed information see www.nice.org.uk/TA102/NICE, 2006).

### Guidance from the NICE TA102

The TA guidance on parent-training/education programmes in the management of children with conduct disorders only applies to the management of children aged 12 years or younger or with a developmental age of 12 years or younger. The guidance states:

1. Group-based parent-training/education programmes are recommended in the management of children with conduct disorders.
2. Individual-based parent-training/education programmes are recommended in the management of children with conduct disorders only in situations where there are particular difficulties in engaging with the parents or a family's needs are too complex to be met by group-based parent-training/education programmes.
3. It is recommended that all parent-training/education programmes, whether group- or individual-based, should:
   - be structured and have a curriculum informed by principles of social-learning theory
   - include relationship-enhancing strategies
   - offer a sufficient number of sessions, with an optimum of 8–12, to maximise the possible benefits for participants
   - enable parents to identify their own parenting objectives
   - incorporate role-play during sessions, as well as homework to be undertaken between sessions, to achieve generalisation of newly rehearsed behaviours to the home situation
   - be delivered by appropriately trained and skilled facilitators who are supervised, have access to necessary ongoing professional development, and are able to engage in a productive therapeutic alliance with parents
   - adhere to the programme developer's manual and employ all of the necessary materials to ensure consistent implementation of the programme.
4. Programmes should demonstrate proven effectiveness. This should be based on evidence from randomised controlled trials or other suitable rigorous evaluation methods undertaken independently.
5. Programme providers should also ensure that support is available to enable the participation of parents who might otherwise find it difficult to access these programmes.

### Parent-training/education programmes for conduct disorders

The main goals of parent-training/education programmes for conduct disorders are to enable parents to improve their relationship with their child and to improve their child's behaviour. Interventions are structured, with the key components documented so that programmes can be reliably applied by different workers with appropriate training. Many programmes are conducted primarily with the parents and involve no direct intervention with the child, although in some individual programmes both parent and child will be observed in order to see how the parents are relating to their child with a view to individualising the intervention.

Most programmes combine elements of the two main approaches: behavioural programmes, which focus on teaching the parenting skills needed to address the causes of problem behaviour; and relationship programmes, which aim to help parents understand both their own and their child's emotions and behaviour and to improve their communication with the child. Programmes tend to be focused and short term (around 1 and a half to 2 hours every week for 8 to 12 weeks), and can be conducted in small groups of 6 to 12 or individually. Settings, which may include the hospital, clinic, community or home, should be congenial and accessible to parents, and have crèche facilities.

Programmes can be run by psychologists, therapists/counsellors, social workers or community workers, but in some cases voluntary agencies or parents who have been through programmes themselves can be involved. Self-administered programmes in the home use printed or audiovisual training materials. Some programmes combine parent training with other interventions such as child training or have additional elements to address factors interfering with effective parenting, such as marital problems, depression and lack of adult social skills.

*Population characteristics*
The scope for the TA defined the population as children diagnosed with conduct disorders (including oppositional defiant disorder), aged up to 12 years or with a developmental age of 12 years or younger. Forty-one RCTs were included in the analysis, giving a total sample population of 2,436 children. However, only 14 studies used the DSM-III, DSM-III-R or DSM-IV diagnoses of conduct disorder and/or oppositional defiant disorder for the inclusion of their population. In the majority of studies children were included if they were above a set cut-off point on scales measuring child behaviour problems or were described as having behaviour problems, and it is therefore likely that many of the children in the included studies would not meet diagnostic criteria for conduct disorders. Studies were not excluded if children had coexisting conditions, providing that more than 50% of children had a behavioural disorder.

The majority of studies involved only pre-adolescent children (12 years or under) and boys made up around two-thirds of the total population included in the analysis (based on those included studies that provided information). In terms of the family characteristics, parents involved in the studies were from a wide range of socioeconomic backgrounds; there were similar proportions of one- and two-parent families but a large proportion of the parents were white. Recruitment to studies was commonly by media advertisements or fliers in community centres, medical practices, kindergartens, schools or similar, where parents would respond by referring their children.

*Intervention characteristics and settings*
Only interventions that focused solely on the parents were included in the review for the TA. Included parent-training/education programmes had to have content that was documented and repeatable, and be run over a defined time period, but there were no

restrictions regarding the theoretical basis of a programme, the length, setting or mode of delivery. Where programmes also involved children and/or teachers they were excluded because it was judged likely that their effectiveness might differ from that of programmes targeting parents only. Interventions where children attended sessions to give parents an opportunity to rehearse skills under therapist guidance, and non-structured parent-focused interventions such as a support groups or informal home visits, were also excluded.

The interventions included group-based therapist-led training, self- (parent-) administered programmes and individual one-to-one sessions. The person delivering the interventions varied between studies and included people educated to graduate, masters or PhD level as well as nurses and school counsellors. Mothers were the primary focus of the trials, with only a small proportion of fathers also participating. The majority of included studies were conducted in the US but studies conducted in Australia, the UK, Canada and Ireland were also included.

*Evidence and interpretation*

Meta-analyses were undertaken for child behaviour outcome measures reported consistently across a high proportion of the included RCTs – the Child Behaviour Checklist (CBCL), the Eyberg Child Behaviour Inventory (ECBI), and the Dyadic Parent–Child Interaction Coding System (DPICS) child deviance total score. There was a consistent trend across studies for an improvement in all measures for parent-training/education compared with no-treatment controls. Meta-analysis of the CBCL and ECBI outcome measures established that parent-training programmes were more effective than a waitlist control. For the DPICS there was a trend in favour of parent-training/education programmes. Longer-term follow-up data suggested that parent-training/education programmes had sustained effects up to 3 years later. The meta-analysis did not find a difference in the effects of group compared with individual interventions.

The results were regarded as clinically meaningful and it is suggested that the effect of the intervention on child behaviour might have been underestimated because the meta-analysis was conducted on the CBCL total score rather than the externalising score. Though the majority of trials were conducted outside the UK, the findings of the meta-analysis were considered to be generalisable to UK practice.

Parent participants who did not complete the studies were more likely to be significantly younger, come from a lower socioeconomic group, have less social support, have higher levels of life stress, be significantly less educated, be a mother with higher ratings on the Depression Anxiety Stress Scales (DASS) or have higher levels of parental dysfunction.

Qualitative work conducted by the SCIE and NICE project teams identified characteristics that appear to be essential components of effective programmes. Based on this work, the appraisal committee proposed that parent-training/education programmes should have the elements as stated in recommendation 3 of TA102 (see above).

The TA concluded that parent-training/education programmes that contained these essential elements were clinically effective. Group-based programmes containing these elements were recommended for the management of children with conduct disorders as they offered best value for money. Individual programmes containing the same elements were recommended only where there are particular difficulties in engaging with the parents and/or the complexities of the family's needs cannot be met by group programmes. Examples of programmes that demonstrated the essential characteristics listed above included the Webster-Stratton Incredible Years Programme and the Triple P – Positive Parenting Programme.

As parents who might have the greatest needs could find it difficult to access these programmes it was considered important that programme providers should enable participation by providing accessible venues, helping with transport and providing support for any caring responsibilities that might hinder participation.

## 7.2.10   Characteristics of effective psychological interventions for ADHD

In the review of psychological interventions for ADHD, six studies were identified that demonstrated that psychological interventions improved outcomes for children with ADHD (BOR2002; FEHLINGS1991; LONG1993; PFIFFNER1997; SONUGA-BARKE2001; TUTTY2003). Further information about each study can be found in Appendix 17. The studies suggest that slightly different approaches are necessary for pre-school children and for older children. None of the studies showing effectiveness involves significant numbers of young people but some inferences about suitable interventions can be obtained from those designed for younger age groups.

*Psychological interventions for pre-school children*
Parent training was found to be an effective intervention in two studies (BOR2002; SONUGA-BARKE2001), both of which involved parents with 3-year-old children. These studies add weight to the inference that the NICE TA for children with conduct disorders is relevant to children with ADHD. The parent-training intervention in one of the studies (BOR2002) was a generic programme (Triple P) that includes the essential components identified by the NICE TA (see above). In this study an enhanced version of the parent-training intervention that included adjunctive interventions on partner support and coping skills was also investigated, but data from the group receiving the standard intervention were used in the analysis as the standard intervention had a larger effect on child outcomes.

The studies of Bor and colleagues (BOR2002) and Sonuga-Barke and colleagues (SONUGA-BARKE2001) suggest that parent training is effective when structured interventions are delivered on an individual participant basis. Equally, the findings of the NICE TA for parent training in conduct disordered populations for this age group show that both group and individual programmes are effective for children with conduct disorders and problem behaviours. Given the overlap between the population included in the TA and the ADHD population it is reasonable to extrapolate from the TA that group parent-training programmes would also be effective for children with ADHD.

The interventions in both studies (BOR2002; SONUGA-BARKE2001) employed structured interventions based on social learning and behavioural learning principles. Both approaches involved giving information on ADHD and involved active learning strategies such as role play, modelling and active feedback, individualised homework assignments, diaries and observation.

The study conducted by Bor and colleagues (BOR2002) suggests that involving fathers and partners may be an important element, at least for some families. Sessions were primarily clinic-based, although some home-based sessions were incorporated to allow for observation and feedback. The study conducted by Sonuga-Barke and colleagues (SONUGA-BARKE2001) predominantly involved mothers, but children were also involved in the sessions, which were delivered in the home.

*Psychological interventions for older children – parent-effectiveness training*
On the basis of the NICE TA (NICE, 2006a) it appears that parent training is likely to be an effective intervention for older children and young adolescents (up to 12 to 13 years) with ADHD. No studies were found that used group parent training alone as an intervention for this age group. A small RCT study by Long and colleagues (1993) demonstrated the value of providing parents of children aged 6 to 11 with a manual on behavioural techniques as an adjunct to stimulant medication and there were positive improvements in child behaviour in the children whose parents received the manual.

*Psychological interventions for school-age children – CBT and social skills training*
Four studies were found that demonstrated positive effects of psychological interventions on core ADHD symptoms together with ratings of conduct, social skills or self-efficacy (FEHLINGS1991; LONG1993; PFIFFNER1997; TUTTY2003). The interventions studied were either mixed CBT/social skills interventions delivered to groups (PFIFFNER1997; TUTTY2003) or predominantly CBT interventions (FEHLINGS1991; LONG1993).

In PFIFFNER1997, social skills training was the main intervention but also had an element of parent training to support the skills acquisition of the child participants. Similarly, in Tutty and colleagues' (TUTTY2003) study, children were engaged in a course of social skills training but parents, in separate group sessions, learned about parenting skills and behavioural management principles. It is difficult to ascertain if all, or just some, of these elements are effective but whether the target is social skills or behaviour generally, psychological intervention seems to have a positive effect on core ADHD symptoms.

FEHLINGS1991 involved teaching children CBT techniques to improve behaviour in home settings. Time was taken to teach problem-solving techniques, which included identifying the problem, goal setting, generating problem-solving strategies, choosing a solution and evaluating the outcome. Active learning methods were used including modelling and role play. Homework assignments were set and related to individual problem situations at home. Learning gains were reinforced with reward strategies such as tokens and so on. As in TUTTY2003 and PFIFFNER1997, separate parent sessions were also held. Parents received education about ADHD and training in CBT techniques that they were then encouraged to use to reinforce target behaviours in individual homework tasks given to each child participant.

The mixed social skills/CBT interventions (PFIFFNER1997; TUTTY2003) were delivered in group sessions whereas the CBT intervention (FEHLINGS1991) was delivered in individual sessions. Conceptually, there is no reason why either group or individual approaches should not be considered but cost issues may be the determining factor.

It is noteworthy that in all three studies, separate child and parent groups were involved which may have contributed to outcome effectiveness. Perhaps supportive of this, are findings from three studies which met the guideline's methodological criteria and were included in our analyses, but for which statistically positive results were not found. In the HOOFDAKKER2007 and HOATH2002 studies involving behavioural parent training, no child groups were incorporated. In the study of social skills training (ANTSHEL2003), there was a parent-training element but this comprised only three sessions including giving information about the programme and explaining how to monitor homework assignments given to the child.

LONG1993 studied the effects of a CBT intervention that simply involved providing parents with a 4,200-word manual on CBT strategies to use at home while children were receiving medication for ADHD. Significant improvements in child behaviour were achieved as a result of the addition of the manual. The manual comprised behavioural strategies including attending, rewarding, time out and behavioural charts, and so on. This intervention probably represents the simplest type of CBT but is a useful indicator of what is needed, especially since basic CBT principles are widely available as manuals, books and in visual media.

*Psychological interventions for young people*
None of the included studies yielded evidence on what might constitute an effective intervention for young people of 13 years and older; however it is likely that CBT/social skills therapy as described for older children above would be applicable to young people with ADHD.

*Adapting parent-training/education programmes for children with ADHD*
The available evidence indicates that the essential elements for working with children who have ADHD are likely to be included in established parent-training programmes that are effective where children have disordered conduct. It is important to add a component to provide information about ADHD and the behavioural and emotional sequelae that arise from the condition. There is no indication that existing programmes such as Triple P have to be significantly extended to achieve this, nor do they need to incorporate add-on elements such as partner support, communication between partners and other family functioning issues. This means that existing parent-effectiveness training programmes need only a modest adaptation for working with parents who have children with ADHD.

### 7.2.11 Initiation and optimum duration of psychological interventions for children with ADHD

*Initiation of therapy*
There is no reliable evidence on the relationship between waiting time and outcome. It is likely, however, that for most parents this will be a key issue. It takes several

weeks from referral to the child receiving a diagnosis of ADHD and parents will be naturally keen to have their child's difficulties addressed in the shortest possible time. Drug treatment has the perceived advantage of providing symptomatic relief rapidly and optimum dosage can be achieved within 6 weeks. Psychological therapy, whether parent training, CBT or social skills training, takes a minimum of 8–10 weeks if delivered on consecutive weeks. Clearly this may be a disincentive for some parents to agree to psychological therapy. The disincentive is even greater if there is a significant waiting time before psychological treatment starts and may result in an adverse effect on recruitment, adherence and skills acquisition.

*Optimum duration*

There is a surprising consistency across all successful psychological intervention studies on the duration of treatment and this allows helpful inferences to be drawn. For pre-school children, programmes in the BOR2002 and SONUGA-BARKE2001 parent-training intervention studies were delivered by specifically trained facilitators or therapists and involved between eight and ten sessions lasting 1 to 1 and a half hours. For school-age children, CBT/social skills training interventions consisted of between eight and 12 sessions lasting 50 to 90 minutes for children and eight sessions lasting 50 to 120 minutes for parents, and were delivered by specifically trained facilitators. Where there is a large age range (for example, TUTTY2003) there may be value in breaking participants into more homogeneous age groups.

### 7.2.12 Promoting adherence to psychological interventions for children with ADHD

The studies demonstrating the effectiveness of psychological interventions for pre-school and older children up to early adolescence suggest that issues of adherence may be important elements in intervention effectiveness. This is true of most interventions but with group treatments it is more so. If programmes are not appealing or seen as relevant, it can take several weeks for sufficient numbers to be recruited to enable the programme to get under way. During this time, the young person with ADHD may be deprived of much needed help. Equally, if there are significant drop-outs during the course of a programme, there may be adverse effects on the functioning of the remaining group through, for example, loss of group cohesion, support and friendships.

Participants are likely to have to be strongly convinced of the need for involvement particularly in view of the time commitment and inconvenience involved. Typically parents, and also children, may have to commit themselves for between 1 and 1 and a half hours each week over a 2- to 3-month period. Child care arrangements may pose problems for many parents who have other children. Involving fathers/partners, although desirable, may again pose problems for many families. Travel to treatment centres may also be difficult for some families, especially in rural areas. Some studies report holding out-of-hours sessions and/or running them in local health or community centres. The SONUGA-BARKE2001 parent-training intervention with the parents of pre-school children held individual sessions at home.

Theoretically, it would be possible to run interventions over the long summer school holiday. There might, however, be interruptions when families and/or staff go on holiday and this might not leave enough time for learning tasks to be put into practice at home during the intervention programme.

Successful programmes tend to use active learning methods such as role play, modelling, observation and feedback. They also involve individualised elements often with homework assignments and diary keeping. These methods contribute to effective learning but they may have the added advantage of improving adherence through maintaining interest and offering relevance.

A further characteristic of both studies of parent-training interventions that demonstrated beneficial effects (BOR2002; SONUGA-BARKE2001) is that efforts were made to hold sessions at times and/or locations convenient for participants. The BOR2002 intervention was delivered at centres in local neighbourhoods and the SONUGA-BARKE2001 intervention was delivered in participants' own homes. One study of a parent-training intervention with the parents of pre-school children was not included in the analysis because of an unusually high subject attrition and other methodological issues (BARKLEY2000). The study illustrates the need for a careful approach to the design of interventions which maximise compliance.

### 7.2.13    Health economic evidence

*Systematic literature review*
No evidence on the cost effectiveness of psychological interventions versus a control condition (no intervention, waitlist control, standard care or a control intervention) for children with ADHD was identified by the systematic search of the economic literature. Details on the methods used for the systematic search of the economic literature are described in Chapter 3.

*Economic analysis in the NICE guidance on parent-training/education programmes for children with conduct disorders*
The NICE TA on parent-training/education programmes in the management of children with conduct disorders (NICE, 2006a) incorporated economic evidence from two *de novo* economic models assessing the cost effectiveness of parent-training/ education programmes relative to no active intervention for this population. The initial economic analysis (Dretzke *et al.*, 2005) assessed the cost effectiveness of three parent-training/education programmes differing in the mode of delivery and the setting: a group community-based programme, a group clinic-based programme and an individually delivered, home-based programme. Costs included intervention costs only; no potential cost savings to the NHS following reduction of antisocial behaviour in treated children were considered. Total costs of these three types of interventions were estimated based on a 'bottom-up' approach, using expert opinion alongside information from the literature in order to determine the healthcare resources required for providing such programmes. Meta-analysis of clinical data had demonstrated that there was no difference in clinical effectiveness between

group-based and individually delivered programmes. According to the findings of the economic analysis, the group clinic-based programme was the dominant option among the three parent-training/education programmes, as it provided the same health benefits (same clinical effectiveness) at the lowest cost (total intervention cost per family was £629 for the group clinic-based programme, £899 for the group community-based programme, and £3,839 for the individual home-based programme).

Further analyses were undertaken to estimate the cost effectiveness of parent-training/education programmes assuming various levels of response to treatment and various levels of improvement in children's HRQoL. According to this analysis, and after assuming an 80% uptake of such programmes, the group clinic-based programme resulted in a cost per responder of £10,060 and £1,006 at a 5% and 50% success (response) rate, respectively; and a cost per quality adjusted life year (QALY) of £12,575 and £3,144 at a 5% and 20% improvement in HRQoL, respectively.

In contrast, provision of an individual home-based programme was demonstrated to incur a rather high cost of £19,196 per QALY gained, assuming it provided a 20% improvement in HRQoL. At lower levels of improvement in HRQoL, this figure became well above the £20,000 per QALY threshold of cost effectiveness set by NICE (NICE, 2006c), rising at approximately £77,000 per QALY when a 5% improvement in HRQoL was assumed. This means that, for families where individual parent training is the preferred option, for example in cases where parents are difficult to engage with, or the complexities of the family's needs cannot be met by group-based programmes, the improvement in HRQoL of the child needs to reach at least 20%, for the intervention to meet the cost-effectiveness criteria set by NICE.

The initial economic analysis was based on hypothetical rates of response and percentages of improvement in HRQoL following provision of parent-training/education programmes, as well as on a number of assumptions. Therefore, the results should be interpreted with caution, as acknowledged by its authors. On the other hand, it should be noted that estimated figures were conservative, as they did not include any potential cost savings resulting from reduction in antisocial behaviour in treated children and associated costs of its management. Despite its limitations, the analysis demonstrated that group-based parent-training/education programmes for children with conduct disorders were, as expected, substantially more cost effective than individually delivered ones, because the two modes of delivery did not differ in terms of clinical effectiveness, while the intervention costs of group-based programmes were spread to a large number of treated families.

The additional economic analysis undertaken to support NICE guidance evaluated the cost effectiveness of the three parent-training/education programmes described above, plus an individually delivered clinic-based programme, over a time horizon of 1 year. Costs included intervention costs as the initial analysis, but they also incorporated cost savings to the NHS, education and social services following provision of parent-training/education programmes to children with conduct disorders. The analysis modelled three different health states, that is, normal behaviour, conduct problems and conduct disorders. It was found that the mean net cost of a parent-training/education programme in improving a child's behaviour from conduct disorders to a better state (either conduct problems or normal behaviour) was £90, £1,380, and £2,400 for a group community-based programme, an individually delivered clinic-based programme, and an individually delivered home-based programme, respectively; the group clinic-based programme proved to be overall cost saving. These results further support the argument that group-delivered parent-training/education programmes for children with conduct disorders are most likely to be cost effective, especially when long-term benefits, such as the sustained effects of therapy and a reduction in the rates of future offending behaviour, as well as future cost savings to healthcare, education and social services, are considered.

*Economic modelling*

*Objective*    The objective of the analysis was to assess the cost effectiveness of parent training for children diagnosed with ADHD, since no economic evidence on this area was identified in the systematic search of the economic literature.

*Interventions examined*    The economic analysis compared parent training with no treatment. Parent training consisted of 10 hourly sessions provided by clinical psychologists to groups of parents of children with ADHD over a 10-week period.

*Methods*

*Model structure*    An economic model in the form of a decision tree was developed to estimate costs and benefits associated with parent training for children with ADHD. According to the model structure, hypothetical cohorts of children with ADHD received therapy in the form of parent training or no treatment. The time horizon of the analysis was 1 year. Parents of children responding to parent training over 10 weeks attended three further booster sessions until the end of the year. Children responding to parent training or showing clinically significant improvement with no treatment were assumed to retain improved symptoms (that is, to remain responsive) for the remaining time of the analysis. A schematic diagram of the decision tree is provided in Figure 3.

**Figure 3.  Schematic diagram of the structure of the economic model**

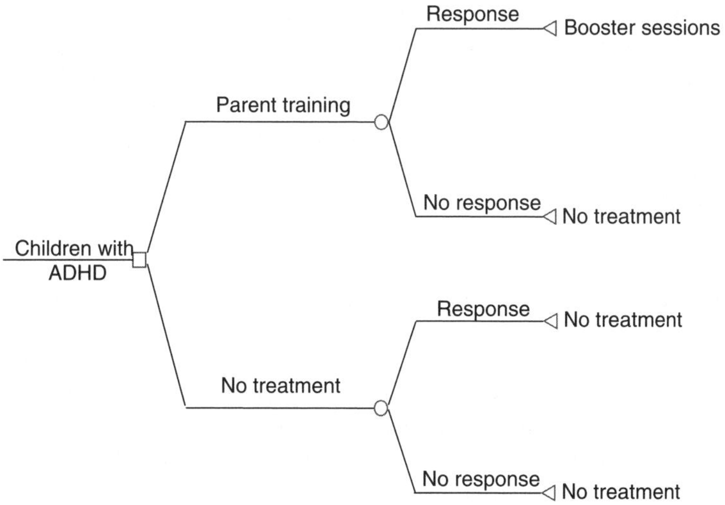

*Costs and health benefit measures included in the analysis*　The analysis adopted the perspective of the NHS. Health service costs consisted of intervention costs of parent training. Costs of personal social services and education services were not included in the analysis owing to lack of relevant data. Other societal costs, such as social benefit payments and productivity losses of carers of children with ADHD, were not considered as they were beyond the scope of this analysis.

The measure of benefits was the number of QALYs gained. QALYs are considered to be the most appropriate generic measure of health benefit that incorporates both gains from reduced mortality and improvements in HRQoL.

Total costs and health benefits over 1 year associated with each arm of the model were estimated and combined in an incremental cost-effectiveness ratio (ICER) expressing the additional cost required in order to achieve an additional unit of health benefit provided by parent training versus no treatment to children with ADHD.

*Effectiveness data*　Clinical-effectiveness data used in the economic model were derived from the meta-analysis of studies included in the guideline systematic literature review of clinical evidence. There was a considerable variation in the methods used to measure clinical effectiveness. Generally, the clinical studies can be divided into two main categories: those who reported outcomes as changes in scores on scales developed to measure ADHD symptoms, and those who reported outcomes as rates of clinically significant response to treatment, with response defined as a percentage improvement or a final score beyond/below a cut-off point on one of the scales measuring ADHD symptoms. Although outcomes expressed as changes in scores are useful in evaluating clinical effectiveness, they cannot be easily translated into a measure of change in HRQoL (that is, a utility score), which is required in order to estimate QALYs gained by treatment. This is because the change in HRQoL depends not only on the overall change in a score (effect size), but also on the point on a scale where this change occurs. Moreover, no evidence exists to link changes in scores on scales measuring ADHD symptoms with utility scores. On the other hand, it is possible to convert response or no response to treatment into a utility score expressing HRQoL for responders and non-responders respectively. In fact, there is published literature linking response or no response to treatment for children with ADHD with respective utility scores. Therefore, for all economic analyses undertaken for this guideline, it was decided to utilise data only from clinical studies reporting outcomes as response rates, with response defined in a way that the GDG found both clinically meaningful and significant.

The guideline systematic review identified four studies evaluating parent-based psychological therapies versus no active treatment for children with ADHD that reported outcomes as response rates (BOR2002; HOATH2002; PFIFFNER1997; SONUGA-BARKE2001). Three of the studies examined enhanced and/or standard parent training (BOR2002; HOATH2002; SONUGA-BARKE2001), while PFIFFNER 1997 evaluated a social skills training programme with parent-mediated generalisation. Therapies were provided individually or in groups. In two studies (HOATH2002; PFIFFNER1997) some children had been receiving medication during the intervention period. Response was determined in all studies by use of the Reliable Change

Index, which was considered appropriate by the GDG. For the base-case analysis, it was decided to synthesise data from BOR2002, HOATH2002, SONUGA-BARKE2001; inclusion of data from PFIFFNER1997 in the meta-analysis of clinical studies was considered in a sensitivity analysis. Analysis of efficacy data was based on intention-to-treat. Details of the studies in terms of interventions examined, mode of delivery, medication status of children, and definition of response are presented in Table 8. Full details of the studies are provided in Appendix 17.

*Utility data and estimation of QALYs*    In order to express clinical outcomes in the form of QALYs, utility scores for health states of children with ADHD were required. Utility scores represent the HRQoL associated with specific health states; they are estimated using preference-based measures capturing people's preferences and perceptions on HRQoL characterising the health states under consideration. The systematic review of the literature identified four studies providing utility scores for health states of children with ADHD (Coghill *et al.*, 2004; Gilmore & Milne, 2001; Matza *et al.*, 2005; Secnik *et al.*, 2005b).

Gilmore and Milne (2001) estimated utility scores for children with ADHD before and after treatment, using the Index of Health Related Quality of Life (IHRQL). This index measures three dimensions of HRQoL: pain, social or physical disability and emotional distress. The authors estimated that, before treatment, children with ADHD experienced no pain, slight social disability and moderate emotional distress; after treatment, responders experienced no pain, no physical or social disability, and slight emotional distress. These health states of the IHRQL translated into utility scores of 0.884 (before treatment) and 0.970 (after treatment – responders).

The study by Coghill and colleagues (2004) was available as a poster presentation; it reported utility scores for children with ADHD that either responded or did not respond to treatment, generated from Euro-Qol 5-Dimension (EQ-5D) scores. The study asked parents of 151 children with ADHD in the UK to fill in EQ-5D

**Table 8:  Characteristics of the studies examining parent-based therapies for children with ADHD included in the guideline systematic literature review**

| Study | Intervention examined | Mode of delivery | Medication status |
|-------|----------------------|------------------|-------------------|
| BOR2002 | Enhanced and standard positive parenting programme | Individual | None |
| HOATH2002 | Enhanced positive parenting programme | Group | Some |
| PFIFFNER1997 | Social skills training with parent generalisation | Group | Some |
| SONUGA-BARKE2001 | Parent training | Individual | None |

questionnaires, and then linked the responses with symptom severity or symptom improvement following treatment, as determined by physicians. EQ-5D is a generic measure of HRQoL, covering five dimensions of health: mobility, self-care, usual activities, pain/discomfort and anxiety/depression. Health states defined by the five-dimensional descriptive system can be converted into utility scores by using existing value sets for EQ-5D health states, elicited from general population samples. Such value sets for the general UK population have been developed using the Visual Analogue Scale (Gudex *et al.*, 1996) and the Time Trade-Off (TTO) method (Dolan, 1997). The utility values generated for children with ADHD as reported by Coghill and colleagues (2004) were 0.837 for responders (symptom improvement) and 0.773 for non-responders (no symptom improvement). Since the methodology used to obtain these values was not described in detail, it is not known whether the authors made use of any of the existing value sets produced from the general UK population, or followed a different methodology in order to convert EQ-5D scores into utility scores.

Matza and colleagues (2005) evaluated parent preferences for health states of children with ADHD in the US. Using the Standard Gamble (SG) technique, the authors asked 43 parents to value their child's current health and 11 hypothetical health states, presented to parents as vignettes describing untreated ADHD, as well as ADHD treated with a stimulant or non-stimulant, covering aspects such as response to treatment and presence of intolerable side effects. The health states were defined according to parent and clinical opinion, supported by a literature review. The resulting utility scores, adjusted on a scale from 0 (death) to 1 (perfect health), ranged from 0.90 (severe untreated ADHD) to 0.98 (treatment with non-stimulant, response to treatment, tolerable side effects).

Secnik and colleagues (2005b), using a similar methodology to Matza and colleagues (2005), produced utility scores by interviewing 83 parents of children with ADHD in England. Parents were asked to value their child's current health plus 14 hypothetical health states, also using the SG technique. The 14 health states were comparable with those described in Matza and colleagues (2005), but distinguished between IR and MR stimulants. The utility scores resulting from this exercise, adjusted on a scale from 0 (death) to 1 (perfect health), ranged from 0.88 (treatment with IR or MR stimulant, no response, presence of side effects) to 0.95 (no medication, symptom improvement).

NICE recommends a standardised and validated generic instrument for the measurement of HRQoL in cost-utility analyses, with utility scores generated according to public preferences using a choice-based method, that is, TTO or SG technique. EQ-5D is suggested as the most appropriate choice in the UK; at the same time, it is acknowledged that under certain circumstances EQ-5D may not be suitable to use in the estimation of QALYs (NICE, 2004). Following NICE guidance, the utility scores reported in Coghill and colleagues (2004), which were generated from EQ-5D, were used in the base-case analysis of all economic evaluations of interventions for children with ADHD in this guideline, also taking into account that they were used in the recent NICE TA on the use of pharmacological treatments for the management of children and adolescents with ADHD (NICE, 2006b). The GDG expressed concern that the EQ-5D, as a generic measure, was not sensitive enough to capture all aspects of HRQoL in children with ADHD. As an alternative option, the utility values reported by Secnik and colleagues (2005b), which were produced by SG technique using vignettes describing health states of children with ADHD in the UK, were tested in a sensitivity analysis; for the current analysis of parent training versus no treatment, utility scores for health states characterised by no medication/untreated ADHD described in Secnik and colleagues (2005b) were assumed to describe the HRQoL of all children in the model, despite the fact that in the clinical studies a number of children were reported to receive some medication during the intervention period. This was necessary as no details on the type of medication and the rate of side effects were reported for those children; however, this is unlikely to have affected the results of the analysis, as the overall use of medication was similar between the two arms of the model.

It was assumed that HRQoL in children initially responding to treatment improved linearly over 10 weeks starting from the utility score of non-responders and reaching the utility score for responders (10 weeks was the average duration of interventions in the clinical trials considered in the economic analysis), and remained at this value for the remaining time of the analysis.

*Resource utilisation and cost data*   Owing to lack of patient-level cost data, deterministic costing of the treatment options assessed was undertaken. Relevant healthcare resource use was estimated and subsequently combined with unit prices to provide total costs associated with parent training or no treatment. Costs of children receiving medication, as described in some clinical studies that provided the effectiveness data, were not estimated, but these were likely to be similar in the two arms of the model. Resource use estimates associated with parent training were based on average resource use reported in the clinical studies that provided effectiveness data. The GDG confirmed that these estimates reflected optimal resource use and were consistent with clinical practice in the UK. In addition, booster sessions for responders were modelled according to optimal practice required to retain a positive outcome (GDG expert opinion).

Two of the trials of parent-based psychological therapies versus no treatment described group-based interventions (HOATH2002 and PFIFFNER1997), while the remaining two trials examined individually-delivered programmes (BOR2002 and SONUGA-BARKE2001). The results of the meta-analysis showed that there was no heterogeneity between group-based or individual programmes regarding clinical effect size. Therefore, it was estimated that the clinical effectiveness of parent-training/education programmes for children with ADHD did not depend on the mode of delivery and was similar in individual and group-based interventions. Given that the intervention costs of group-based therapies are spread over a number of families, group-based parent training dominates individually delivered parent training, as it produces the same clinical outcome at a lower cost. For this reason, group-based parent training has been modelled in the base-case analysis; the cost effectiveness of individual parent training, indicated under certain circumstances, has been explored in a sensitivity analysis.

Group-based parent training consisted of ten meetings (lasting 1 hour each) of clinical psychologists with groups of parents of children with ADHD. Every group comprised ten families. Clinical psychologists were assumed to spend an extra hour for training and preparation. Following completion of the intervention, parents of children responding to parent training attended three further individual booster sessions with psychologists, lasting 30 minutes each, in order to maintain children's response for the remaining time of the analysis.

The unit cost of clinical psychologists was taken from the Unit Costs for Health and Social Care 2006 (Curtis & Netten, 2006). This cost does not include qualification costs, as the latter are not available for clinical psychologists. Discounting was not applied, as costs and benefits were measured over a period of 1 year.

All input parameters, including effectiveness data, utility scores and cost data utilised in the base-case economic analysis of parent training versus no treatment are presented in Table 9.

**Table 9: Input parameters utilised in the base-case economic analysis of parent training versus no treatment for children with ADHD**

| Input parameter | Base-case value | Source/comments |
|---|---|---|
| Response rates<br>Parent training<br>No treatment | 0.522<br>0.206 | Meta-analysis of BOR2002, HOATH2002 and SONUGA-BARKE2001; analysis based on intention-to-treat |
| Utility scores<br>Responder<br>Non-responder | 0.837<br>0.773 | Coghill *et al.*, 2004; scores based on EQ-5D; questionnaires filled in by parents of children with ADHD in the UK |
| Parent training cost<br>10 × 1 hour group sessions with clinical psychologist<br>1 extra hour training and preparation<br>Total intervention cost<br>Total cost per family, assuming 10 families in each group | £660<br><br>£29<br><br>£689<br>£69 | Curtis & Netten, 2006; clinical psychologist cost per hour: £29; cost per hour of client contact: £66; qualification costs excluded |
| 3 × 0.5 hour individual booster sessions for responders | £99 | |
| **Total cost for responders over 1 year** | **£168** | |

*Sensitivity analysis* Sensitivity analysis was undertaken to investigate the robustness of the results under the uncertainty characterising input parameters of the model. The following scenarios were tested in one-way sensitivity analyses:

1. Changes in response rates to treatment
   - Use of the upper and lower 95% CIs of the RR of parent training to no treatment (mean RR = 2.48; 95% CIs = 1.46 to 4.23)
   - Inclusion of data from PFIFFNER1997 in the meta-analysis of clinical studies.
2. Utility scores obtained from Secnik and colleagues (2005b) for the health state of no medication/untreated ADHD. The scores for responders and no responders were 0.95 and 0.90 respectively.
3. Changes in resource use estimates for parent training
   - Group-based CBT, appropriate for school-age children, provided by clinical psychologists, consisting of ten 1-hour sessions with parents and ten 1-hour sessions with children (ten parents and ten children in each group, respectively), plus 2 extra hours for training and preparation. In addition, three individual booster sessions, lasting 30 minutes each, were offered to parents of children responding to treatment, in order to maintain children's response for the remaining time of the analysis. The cost of this intervention was £237 per family.
   - In addition to the above intervention, provision of two extra individual sessions of clinical psychologists with the children's teachers at school, lasting 30 minutes each. The additional cost of these extra sessions was £69, including clinical psychologists' travel costs.
   - Individual parent training, consisting of ten weekly sessions with a clinical psychologist, lasting 1 hour each, in cases where group-based programmes are not a suitable option. This scenario explored the cost effectiveness of individual parent training under a number of alternative hypotheses, such as use of the upper and lower 95% CIs of the RR of parent training to no treatment, inclusion of data from PFIFFNER1997 in the meta-analysis of clinical studies, use of utility scores obtained from Secnik and colleagues (2005b), as well as provision of parent training by health visitors instead of clinical psychologists (at a unit cost of £61 per clinic hour excluding qualification costs, according to Curtis and Netten, 2006).

*Results*

*Base-case analysis* Group-based parent training incurred an incremental cost of £6,608 per QALY compared with no treatment. This value is well below the cost-effectiveness threshold of £20,000 per QALY set by NICE (NICE, 2006c); therefore, this finding indicates that group-based parent training is a cost-effective option for children with ADHD. Full results of the base-case analysis are presented in Table 10.

*Sensitivity analysis* The ICER of group-based parent training versus no treatment remained below the cost-effectiveness threshold set by NICE (NICE, 2006c) under any scenario tested in sensitivity analysis. In contrast, individual parent training was clearly not a cost-effective option: its ICER versus no treatment was £39,007 per QALY gained in the basic sensitivity analysis, and remained above £20,000 per QALY in the vast majority of the alternative hypotheses examined. The only case

**Table 10: Cost effectiveness of parent training versus no treatment
in children with ADHD: results of the base-case analysis over 1 year**

| Intervention | Total QALYs/ child | Total cost/ child | ICER |
|---|---|---|---|
| Parent training | 0.803 | £168 | **Parent training versus no treatment: £6,608/QALY** |
| No treatment | 0.785 | 0 | |

where the ICER of individual parent training versus no treatment fell below the cost-effectiveness threshold of £20,000 per QALY was when the upper 95% CI of the RR of parent training versus no treatment was used (that is, when effect size was maximised); in this case the ICER fell to £19,360 per QALY.

Full results of the one-way sensitivity analyses for group-based and individual parent training are shown in Table 11 and Table 12.

Threshold analysis showed that individual parent training was cost effective (with an ICER reaching £17,302/QALY) when it consisted of four 1-hour sessions only (instead of ten, as modelled in the base-case analysis). It is unlikely, however, that parent training can be as effective as demonstrated in the meta-analysis of clinical studies with only 4 hours of contact.

*Limitations of the economic analysis*
The results of the economic analysis were based on a simple decision-analytic model developed to estimate costs and health benefits associated with provision of parent training in children with ADHD over the period of 1 year. Clinical evidence was derived

**Table 11: Results of one-way sensitivity analysis for group-based parent
training versus no treatment in children with ADHD**

| Scenario | ICER |
|---|---|
| Upper 95% CI of RR of parent training to no treatment | £4,028/QALY |
| Lower 95% CI of RR of parent training to no treatment | £17,980/QALY |
| Inclusion of PFIFFNER1997 | £5,567/QALY |
| Utility scores from Secnik *et al.* (2005b) | £8,458/QALY |
| Group-based CBT for school-age children – no extra sessions with teachers | £10,384/QALY |
| Group-based CBT for school-age children – including extra sessions with teachers | £14,144/QALY |

**Table 12: Results of one-way sensitivity analysis for individual parent training versus no treatment in children with ADHD**

| Scenario | ICER |
|---|---|
| Main scenario of individual parent training | £39,007/QALY |
| Upper 95% CI of RR of parent training to no treatment | £19,360/QALY |
| Lower 95% CI of RR of parent training to no treatment | £125,663/QALY |
| Inclusion of PFIFFNER1997 | £31,831/QALY |
| Utility scores from Secnik *et al.* (2005b) | £49,929/QALY |
| Individual parent training delivered by health visitor | £36,052/QALY |

from three trials that reported outcomes in the form of response to treatment. The total number of participants in these trials was small (N = 132). Additional evidence coming from studies reporting outcomes in the form of changes on scales measuring ADHD symptoms that were included in the guideline systematic review and meta-analysis suggested a moderate beneficial effect of parent training in children with ADHD.

Costs consisted of intervention costs only; potential cost savings to the healthcare, social and education services resulting from improvement in ADHD symptoms of children were not considered owing to lack of relevant data. It is therefore likely that the cost effectiveness of parent-training/education programmes for children with ADHD is greater than that suggested by the results of the analysis.

Estimates on healthcare resource use were based on descriptions of resource use in the clinical studies utilised in the economic analysis. According to the GDG expert opinion, these estimates reflected optimal resource use, and were consistent with clinical practice in the UK. Nevertheless, the clinical studies described only vaguely some aspects of resource use, and obviously they did not provide any relevant data for resource use beyond the duration of the trials (that is, beyond 10 weeks of treatment). It is unknown whether three booster sessions with parents are sufficient to retain a positive outcome in children with ADHD over 1 year (as assumed in the economic model), as no relevant follow-up data are available. Likewise, the long-term effectiveness of parent-training/education programmes in children with ADHD is unknown. Therefore, it is not possible to estimate the cost effectiveness of parent-training/education programmes in the long-term.

Utility scores used in the base-case analysis were based on EQ-5D questionnaires filled in by parents of children with ADHD in England. EQ-5D is a generic measure of HRQoL and, as such, it has been recommended by NICE for use in economic evaluation. However, the full methods used to convert EQ-5D scores into utility scores were not reported in the study that provided the utility data for this economic analysis. Furthermore, the GDG expressed concerns about the appropriateness of using a generic measure to capture aspects of quality of life in children with ADHD.

For this reason, utility scores developed using vignettes describing health states specific to ADHD were used in the sensitivity analysis. Utility scores used both in the base-case and sensitivity analysis were generated using parents of children with ADHD as proxy reporters of their children's perceptions of their own HRQoL. There are concerns about using parents' ratings as proxies to children's experience; however, for some groups of children who are unable to report their own perceptions and preferences reliably, parent proxies may be appropriate (Wallander *et al.*, 2001; De Civita *et al.*, 2005). In the area of ADHD, no data on HRQoL preferences directly reported by children rather than by their parents are currently available.

The findings of the base-case analysis regarding the cost effectiveness of group-based programmes rely on the hypothesis of equivalent efficacy between group-based and individually delivered programmes; such equivalence has not been established in head-to-head comparisons, but existing indirect clinical evidence suggests that the mode of delivery does not affect the clinical effectiveness of parent-training/ education programmes. In fact, HOATH2002, which described group-based parent training, reported a larger effect size than that reported in BOR2002 and SONUGA-BARKE2001, both examining individually delivered interventions. The ICER of £6,608 per QALY, characterising parent training delivered in groups, was based on intension-to-treat analysis. This means that estimated clinical effectiveness took into account the fact that some children/families might drop out of treatment. On the other hand, full intervention costs were estimated, assuming that all children completed treatment. This assumption has probably overestimated the total cost of parent training.

*Overall conclusions from the economic analysis*
The results of the economic analysis indicate that group-based parent-training/ education programmes (or CBT for school-age children) are likely to be cost effective for children with ADHD, if the mode of delivery of such programmes does not affect their clinical effectiveness. Individual parent training is unlikely to be a cost-effective option. Further research is needed to explore the long-term benefits and cost savings associated with parent-training/education programmes for children with ADHD, as well as to investigate in depth the perceptions of children and their carers on aspects of HRQoL associated with ADHD. Moreover, future head-to-head comparisons need to confirm the equivalence of efficacy between group-based and individually delivered parent-training/education programmes, so that the cost effectiveness of group-based parent training can be effectively established.

### 7.2.14 From evidence to recommendations: psychological interventions for children and young people with ADHD

Overall, the evidence indicates that psychological interventions for children with ADHD have moderate beneficial effects on parent ratings of ADHD symptoms and conduct problems, both for children not on medication and as an adjunct to continued routine medication for ADHD. However, the evidence suggests that slightly different approaches are necessary for pre-school and older children.

For the pre-school group there is good evidence that individual parent training is helpful for core ADHD symptoms and conduct problems. The characteristics of effective interventions are that they: are structured, are based on social learning and behavioural learning principles, include provision of information on ADHD and involve active learning strategies such as role play, modelling and active feedback, individualised homework assignments, diaries and observation.

Further evidence on the use of parent-training/education programmes as an intervention for ADHD comes from the findings of the NICE TA of parent training as an intervention for children up to 12 with conduct disorders (NICE, 2006a). The GDG concluded that the TA was broadly generalisable to children with ADHD given the overlap between the population included in the TA and the population with ADHD. The TA indicates that both group and individual programmes are likely to be effective.

Taken as a whole the available clinical evidence indicates that referring parents of children with ADHD to established parent-training programmes, such as Triple P, is likely to result in beneficial effects for the child. However, it may be important to incorporate information about ADHD and the behavioural and emotional sequelae that arise from the condition into a generic programme attended by parents of children with ADHD.

For school-age children the available clinical evidence indicates that interventions offering mixed CBT and social skills training group sessions for children along with parallel group sessions for parents are beneficial. Effective interventions all followed a structured curriculum. Areas that effective interventions addressed include: challenging and oppositional behaviour in the home; problem solving; listening skills; recognising, dealing with and expressing feelings; anger management, self-control and ignoring provocation; accepting consequences; assertiveness and conflict resolution; friendship skills; self-esteem and good sportsmanship. Successful programmes tended to use active learning methods such as role play, modelling, observation and feedback along with reward systems such as star boards and token rewards, with similar rewards for home-based objectives. They also involved individualised elements, often with homework assignments and diary keeping. The evidence indicates that parent sessions should be designed to reinforce and support child learning while also incorporating training in parenting skills and behavioural management principles.

There is also some evidence that providing parents of school-age children with written manuals on behavioural strategies to use at home may result in positive improvements in child behaviour. While not a substitute for parent training this is an intervention that can be delivered immediately.

No RCT evidence on interventions for young people of 13 years and older was identified but it is likely that CBT/social skills therapy interventions as described for older children would be applicable to young people with ADHD.

With respect to the delivery of interventions, the evidence indicates that psychological interventions may be beneficial for children with ADHD whether delivered in group or individual contexts. For parent training the included studies involved structured interventions delivered on an individual basis to parents of pre-school children with ADHD. However, TA102 (NICE, 2006a) found that both group and individual programmes were effective interventions for children with problem behaviours. Given the overlap between the population included in the TA and the ADHD population, it is reasonable to extrapolate from the TA and conclude that group parent-training programmes would also be effective for children with ADHD. For school-age children with ADHD the evidence of benefits from psychological interventions comes from both group and individual approaches to delivering social skills training and/or CBT for the child together with a parallel parental intervention.

The economic analysis undertaken for this guideline indicates that both group-based parent-training programmes and group CBT for school-age children are likely to be cost-effective interventions for children with ADHD. In contrast, individually delivered parent training is probably not cost effective. These findings are supported by economic evidence reported in the NICE TA. It must be noted that long-term benefits of parent training and potential cost savings to the healthcare, social and education services resulting from improvement in ADHD symptoms of children were not considered in the analysis, owing to lack of relevant data. Therefore, the reported cost effectiveness of parent training for children with ADHD is likely to be a conservative estimate.

In some special circumstances it may be necessary to deliver parent training and other psychological interventions for ADHD on an individual basis. Such circumstances include situations where there are particular difficulties in engaging with the parents or when a family's needs are too complex to be met by group-based programmes. On occasion factors such as parental ill health and diversity, disability and accessibility issues may also necessitate intervention on an individual basis. For older adolescents with ADHD and moderate impairment, individual psychological interventions (such as CBT or social skills training) may be more acceptable than group interventions. Additionally, in some services it may be necessary to deliver interventions on an individual basis because participant numbers are low with the result that viable group interventions are difficult to achieve or the need to recruit a group would result in undue delays in commencing therapy.

In summary, the psychological interventions for ADHD that were evaluated are well established and constitute a repertoire of interventions in current clinical practice that are based on CBT principles and have beneficial effects for children with ADHD: parent training, cognitive and behavioural therapy approaches, social skills training, and self-instructional manuals. Generally therapist-led psychological interventions were delivered in courses of between eight and 12 sessions lasting 1 to 2 hours. Individual parent training that involves working with the child and parent together may be favoured for pre-school children. However, the NICE TA of parent training as an intervention for children with conduct disorders indicates that group interventions are also likely to be effective for both pre-school and school-age children with ADHD. For school-age children interventions that involve separate group sessions for parents and children appear favoured. Given the concerns about the use of medication for ADHD, psychological interventions therefore appear to present a deliverable and potentially effective alternative therapeutic approach for children and young people with ADHD.

## 7.3    PSYCHOLOGICAL INTERVENTIONS FOR ADULTS WITH ADHD

### 7.3.1    Databases searched and inclusion/exclusion criteria

Information about the databases searched and the inclusion/exclusion criteria used for this section of the guideline can be found in Table 13.

### 7.3.2    Studies considered[11]

From the primary RCT search, the review team identified trials of psychological interventions in adults with ADHD.

One trial met the eligibility criteria set by the GDG, providing data on 31 participants (further information about the included study can be found in Appendix 17).

### 7.3.3    Clinical evidence for psychological interventions for adults with ADHD versus control

Important study characteristics and a summary of the evidence are presented in Table 14. The associated forest plots can be found in Appendix 18.

**Table 13:  Databases searched and inclusion/exclusion criteria for clinical effectiveness of psychological interventions**

| | |
|---|---|
| Electronic databases | MEDLINE, EMBASE, PsycINFO, Cochrane Library |
| Date searched | Database inception to 18.12.07 |
| Study design | RCT |
| Patient population | Adults diagnosed with ADHD |
| Interventions | Any non-pharmacological intervention used to treat ADHD symptoms and/or associated behavioural problems |
| Outcomes | ADHD symptoms*; conduct problems*; social skills*; emotional outcomes*; self-efficacy*; reading; mathematics; leaving study early due to any reason; non-response to treatment. |

*Separate outcomes for teacher, parent, self, and independent ratings.

---

[11]Here and elsewhere in the guideline, each study considered for review is referred to by a study ID in capital letters (primary author and date of study publication, except where a study is in press or only submitted for publication, then a date is not used).

**Table 14: Evidence summary table for trials of psychological interventions for adults with ADHD**

|  | CBT versus control |
|---|---|
| Total number of studies (number of participants) | 1 (31) |
| Study ID | SAFREN2005 |
| *Benefits (end of treatment)* | |
| Core ADHD symptoms at end of treatment (independent evaluator) | ADHD-RS SMD $-0.60$ ($-1.32$ to $0.12$) Quality: Moderate K = 1, N = 31 |
| Emotional outcomes at end of treatment (independent evaluator) | Hamilton Anxiety Scale SMD $-0.85$ ($-1.59$ to $-0.11$) Quality: High K = 1, N = 31 |
| Emotional outcomes at end of treatment (self-rated) | Hamilton Anxiety Scale SMD $-0.81$ ($-1.54$ to $-0.07$) Quality: High K = 1, N = 31 |
| *Dichotomous outcomes* | |
| Non-responders | Less than 2 point change on CGI RR 0.50 (0.28 to 0.91) Quality: High K = 1, N = 31 |

### 7.3.4 Review of clinical evidence for psychological interventions for adults with ADHD

Psychological treatment may be required at different points in time and/or stages in youth and adult development. This may begin with *de novo* diagnosis in adulthood in order to help the individual undergo a process of understanding and acceptance of their diagnosis and to cognitively reframe their past (Young *et al.*, 2008a; Young *et al.*, 2008b). The few studies that have investigated the psychological treatment of adults with ADHD have all used a cognitive-behavioural paradigm, either applied on an individual or group basis. This reflects the broad consensus that individual needs will be best met by this approach (Young, 2007a; Young & Bramham, 2007). Furthermore, CBT has a strong evidence base for many of the coexisting problems associated with ADHD.

Evidence on psychological interventions to treat ADHD in adults is very sparse. Nevertheless there is consensus from clinicians working with these populations that psychological interventions adapted for ADHD may have a therapeutic role in its treatment (Ramsay & Rostain, 2003; Weiss & Murray, 2003; Wilens *et al.*, 1999; Young & Bramham, 2007). Only one small RCT of a psychological intervention for adults with ADHD met inclusion criteria (SAFREN2005).

While the search identified two other trials of psychological interventions for adults with ADHD (Stevenson *et al.*, 2002; Stevenson *et al.*, 2003), these were excluded because although they appear to report two different studies (one of a modified version of the intervention used in the other) and appear to have different sample sizes, the main outcome data tables report identical means and standard deviations. These two studies were by the same authors and efforts were made to seek clarification from them regarding what data could be included, but no response was received and it was concluded that the data as published could not be cited.

The one RCT of a psychological intervention for adults with ADHD was a small study comparing 16 participants receiving CBT plus continued medication for ADHD with 15 participants receiving continued medication for ADHD alone (Safren *et al.*, 2005). Analysis of the data conducted for this guideline indicates that for adults with ADHD on continuing medication CBT delivers a positive impact on anxiety as rated by both the individual and an independent evaluator blind to treatment assignment. The analysis also indicates that there is a trend for beneficial effects of CBT on ADHD symptoms. Although not statistically significant, the effect size for ADHD symptoms rated at end of treatment by an independent evaluator was moderate. The intervention was provided on an individual basis and seems to have varied in duration according the participants' needs up to a maximum of 15 weeks. The CBT intervention comprised three core modules: providing psychoeducation; developing skills to attend, organise and plan; and cognitive restructuring and learning adaptive thinking skills. There were also three optional modules for participants showing clinically significant difficulties in procrastination, anger/frustration and/or communication.

While the available RCT evidence therefore suggests that CBT interventions might provide some benefits for adults with ADHD, the findings from only one small study should be only be regarded as tentative. RCTs of CBT, coaching and other approaches currently used with adults with ADHD are needed in order to clarify whether psychological interventions are effective for adults with ADHD.

Given the lack of RCT evidence, consideration of the potential value of psychological therapies for adults with ADHD may also be informed by a recent non-randomised controlled study of a group CBT workshop-style brief intervention for adults with ADHD (Bramham *et al.*, 2008). Forty-one completers receiving CBT plus treatment as usual were compared with 37 participants receiving treatment-as-usual who were on a waiting list for CBT (the majority of participants were taking medication for ADHD). The objectives of the brief intervention were to provide psychoeducation and to teach techniques and develop psychological skills with the aim of improving the confidence, self-esteem and self-efficacy of participants. The workshops included sessions about inattention and memory, impulsivity, frustration and anger, anxiety, depression, social relationships, time management, problem solving and preparing for the future. Compared with baseline there were significant improvements in measures of anxiety and depression for both groups, but the CBT plus usual care group had significantly greater improvements in measures of knowledge about ADHD, self-efficacy and self-esteem than the usual care group. Participants' evaluations of the sessions suggested that sharing personal experiences with other adults with ADHD was an important aspect of the intervention. These findings suggest that CBT group treatments, even when delivered in a brief intense design, may be an acceptable and beneficial intervention for adults with ADHD.

The studies by Safren and colleagues (2005) and Bramham and colleagues (2008) both provided treatment based on a CBT paradigm. There are, however, some key differences between the two. Bramham and colleagues (2008) provided a group treatment delivered as three 1-day workshops using a non-randomised waitlist control design while Safren and colleagues (2005) evaluated a randomly allocated course of individual CBT sessions. Furthermore, Safren and colleagues (2005) titrated the treatment according to the clients' needs and thus evaluated specific changes in interpersonal functioning while Bramham and colleagues (2008) provided a more generalised treatment and evaluated more global change. Nevertheless, taken together these two studies indicate that psychological interventions may have a beneficial impact for adults with ADHD, whether provided on an individual or group basis.

The use of coaching interventions for people with ADHD is growing. These are supportive interventions that have strong parallels with brief solution-focused therapies, but in practice what is provided varies greatly and no studies investigating the effectiveness of coaching interventions were identified.

The addition of psychological interventions may be especially important in the treatment of older adolescents and adults with ADHD and comorbid antisocial behaviour. Along with interventions to treat the symptoms and problems associated with ADHD, this subgroup of ADHD individuals may benefit from interventions that aim to develop specific skills in prosocial competence, emotional control, problem solving and conflict resolution. Longer and more intensive treatment programmes may be required to address these issues, and while the overall cost of treatment is therefore likely to be relatively high, this has to be balanced against the financial burden these individuals place on social, health, educational and criminal justice services, as well as wider potential costs to society.

### 7.3.5    Clinical evidence summary

Psychological treatment may be required at different points in time and/or stages in youth and adult development. There is some evidence from both service users and carers to support the need for psychological treatment to be provided following *de novo* diagnosis of ADHD in adulthood. While there is little research evidence about the psychological treatment of adults with ADHD, strong clinical consensus exists that cognitive behavioural treatments are the most appropriate. Two studies, drawing on different methodologies, indicate that both group and individual CBT interventions may have beneficial effects for adults with ADHD. However, the inference that CBT might be a useful intervention for adults with ADHD should only be regarded as tentative as it is based on one small RCT and a non-randomised controlled trial. Group treatments that provide the opportunity to meet others and share experiences may be the preferred approach to the psychological treatment of ADHD for adults.

### 7.3.6    Health economic evidence

*Systematic literature review*
No evidence on the cost effectiveness of psychological interventions versus a control condition (no intervention, waitlist control, standard care or a control intervention) for adults with ADHD was identified by the systematic search of the economic literature. Details on the methods used for the systematic search of the economic literature are described in Chapter 3.

*Economic modelling*
*Objective*    The objective of the analysis was to assess the cost effectiveness of psychological treatments for adults with ADHD, given that no economic evidence relating to this issue was identified in the systematic search of the economic literature. *Interventions examined*    The treatment options examined were CBT added to standard medication versus standard medication alone. CBT was defined as 1-day sessions with a clinical psychologist, addressing different issues such as psychoeducation about ADHD, learning skills to reduce distractibility, cognitive restructuring and so on, lasting in total 15 hours over a 15-week period. Standard medication was defined as provision of a variety of pharmacological treatments for adults with ADHD. The treatment options examined in the analysis were determined by the availability of clinical data.

*Methods*
*Model structure*    An economic model in the form of a decision tree was developed to estimate costs and benefits associated with provision of CBT on top of standard medication in adults with ADHD. According to the model structure, hypothetical cohorts of adults with ADHD received CBT in addition to their usual medication or were given their usual medication alone. The time horizon of the analysis was 1 year. Adults responding to CBT over 15 weeks received two further booster sessions until the end of the year. All adults in both arms continued their usual medication for the whole duration of the analysis. Adults showing response to either treatment option retained improved symptoms (that is, remained responsive) for the remaining time of the analysis. A schematic diagram of the decision tree is provided in Figure 4.
*Costs and health benefit measures included in the analysis*    The analysis adopted the perspective of the NHS. Health service costs consisted solely of intervention costs. The cost of CBT was the only intervention cost estimated, since standard medication costs were assumed to be equal in the two groups. These included drug acquisition costs, costs of visits to healthcare professionals and other monitoring

**Figure 4:  Schematic diagram of the structure of the economic model**

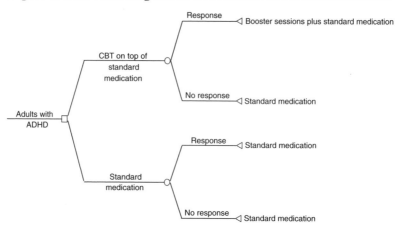

costs, as well as costs of treating side effects. Costs of personal social services were not included in the analysis owing to lack of relevant data. Other societal costs, such as social benefit payments and productivity losses, were not considered, as they were beyond the scope of this analysis. The measure of benefit was the number of QALYs gained. Results are reported in the form of ICERs.

*Effectiveness data*   Only one study providing evidence on the effectiveness of psychological interventions in adults with ADHD was identified by the systematic literature search for clinical evidence (SAFREN2005). The study compared individual CBT added to usual medication versus usual medication alone. The study population consisted of 31 adults stabilised on medication for a minimum of 2 months, who continued to show clinically significant symptoms. Medication involved mainly use of stimulants and/or bupropion or velanfaxine. Outcomes were reported as response rates, as well as changes in scores on the ADHD-RS. No discontinuations from treatment were reported. Response was defined as a 2-point change in the Clinical Global Impression (CGI) instrument, which was considered clinically meaningful and significant by the GDG. Therefore, response rates reported in this study were used to inform an economic analysis. More details on the study characteristics can be found in Appendix 17.

*Utility data and estimation of QALYs*   The systematic review of the literature identified one poster presentation providing utility weights for health states in adults with ADHD (Laing & Aristides, 2005). The study was based on an RCT comparing atomoxetine 40 mg versus atomoxetine 80 mg in 218 adults with ADHD. The original study measured the HRQoL in the study population at baseline and endpoint of the trial using the Short Form-36 (SF-36), and then linked these outcomes with response or no response to treatment, determined by severity of ADHD symptoms as measured on the Conners' Adult ADHD Rating Scale (CAARS) (Adler *et al.*, 2006). SF-36 is a generic measure of HRQoL, consisting of eight health domains: physical functioning, bodily pain, role limitations because of physical problems, role limitations because of emotional problems, general health perceptions, mental health, social functioning and vitality. SF-36 scores for responders and non-responders were converted into SF-6D scores (SF-6D is a shorter version of SF-36), and subsequently into utility scores reflecting preferences of the UK population, using published algorithms based on the SG technique (Brazier *et al.*, 1998; Brazier & Roberts, 2004). The resulting utility weights are in accordance with NICE recommendations on methods for measuring HRQoL in cost-utility analysis (NICE, 2004) and were therefore utilised in this economic model.

The utility scores reported by Laing and Aristides (2005) were 0.678 for adults with ADHD responding to treatment, 0.634 for non-responders at beginning of observation, and 0.630 for non-responders at end of observation. For this analysis, it was decided to use the score for non-responders at beginning of observation, as the utility score for non-responders at the end of observation in Laing and Aristides (2005) probably reflected decrement in HRQoL coming from the presence of newly developed side effects. However, the study population in this analysis consisted of adults that were already on drugs for at least 2 months, and continued drugs over the whole time of the analysis, and therefore side effects were likely to be already present at the beginning of the analysis.

It was assumed that HRQoL in adults responding to treatment improved linearly over 15 weeks, starting from the utility score of non-responders and reaching the utility score for responders (15 weeks was the duration of the trial in SAFREN2005), and remained at this value for the remaining time of the analysis. Decrement in quality of life owing to presence of side effects was assumed to be the same in both groups and therefore was not considered in the analysis.

*Resource utilisation and cost data* Owing to lack of patient-level cost data, deterministic costing of the treatment options assessed was undertaken. Relevant healthcare resource use was estimated and subsequently combined with unit prices to provide total costs associated with CBT. Costs of medication were not estimated, as these were assumed to be equal in the two treatment arms. Resource use estimates associated with CBT reflected resource use described in SAFREN2005, which was the only study that provided clinical data for the economic model. The GDG confirmed that these estimates represented optimal resource use and were consistent with clinical practice in the UK. In addition, booster sessions for responders were modelled according to optimal practice required to retain a positive outcome (GDG expert opinion).

CBT consisted of 1-day individual sessions with a clinical psychologist lasting in total 15 hours over a 15-week period. Following completion of the intervention, responders attended two more booster sessions lasting 1 hour each, in order to remain responsive to treatment for the remaining time of the analysis.

The unit cost of clinical psychologists was taken from the Unit Costs for Health and Social Care 2006 (Curtis & Netten, 2006). This cost does not include qualification costs, as the latter are not available for clinical psychologists. Discounting was not applied, as costs and benefits were measured over a period of 1 year.

All input parameters, including effectiveness data, utility scores and cost data utilised in the base-case economic analysis of psychological interventions for adults with ADHD are presented in Table 15.

**Table 15: Input parameters utilised in the economic model of psychological interventions for adults with ADHD**

| Input parameter | Base-case value | Source-comments |
|---|---|---|
| Response rates<br>CBT added to standard medication<br>Standard medication alone | 0.563<br>0.133 | SAFREN2005 |
| Utility scores<br>Responder<br><br>Non-responder | 0.678<br><br>0.634 | Laing & Aristides, 2005; scores based on SF-36 |
| Individual CBT cost<br>15 hours with clinical psychologist<br><br><br><br>2 × 1-hour booster sessions for responders | £990<br><br><br><br>£132 | Curtis & Netten, 2006; cost of clinical psychologist per hour of client contact: £66; qualification costs excluded |
| **Total cost for responders over one year** | **£1,122** | |

*Sensitivity analysis* Sensitivity analysis was undertaken to investigate the robustness of the results under the uncertainty characterising input parameters of the model. The following scenarios were tested in one-way sensitivity analysis:

1. Use of the upper and lower 95% CIs of the RR of CBT on top of standard medication to standard medication alone (mean RR = 4.22; 95% CIs = 1.08 to 16.45).
2. Use of utility scores generated for disease-specific health states for children with ADHD (Secnik *et al.*, 2005b), given the lack of any other utility data for adults with ADHD. Utility scores for the health states characterised by use of MR stimulants were used. The scores for responders and non-responders were 0.93 and 0.90 respectively, when no side effects occurred; and 0.91 and 0.88 respectively, when side effects were present. In both cases the difference in utility between responders and non-responders was 0.03, which meant that use of any pair of scores (referring to presence or absence of side effects) would give the same results.
3. Replacing individually delivered CBT resource-use estimates by group-based CBT, consisting of 15 hours in total, delivered to groups of 10 adults by two clinical psychologists (reflecting optimal routine practice for adults with ADHD – GDG expert opinion). The cost of 15 hours of CBT under this scenario was £198 per adult (excluding booster sessions, which were assumed to be provided individually, as in the base-case analysis). This scenario explored the cost effectiveness of

group CBT under further hypotheses, such as use of the upper and lower 95% CIs of the RR of CBT on top of standard medication to standard medication alone, as well as the use of utility scores obtained from Secnik and colleagues (2005b).

In addition to the above scenarios, threshold analyses were carried out to identify the values of selected parameters at which the conclusions of the cost-effectiveness analysis would be reversed. The following parameters were tested:

● total number of hours of (individual) sessions of CBT

● minimum difference in utility between responders and non-responders.

*Results*

*Base-case analysis*    CBT added to standard medication was more effective and more expensive than standard medication alone, at an additional cost of £65,279/QALY. This value is well beyond the cost-effectiveness threshold of £20,000/QALY set by NICE (NICE, 2006c). This means that, according to the base-case results, CBT is not cost effective when it is added to standard medication in adults with ADHD. Full results of the base-case analysis are presented in Table 16.

**Table 16:  Cost effectiveness of CBT added to standard medication versus standard medication alone in adults with ADHD: results of the base-case analysis over 1 year**

| Treatment option | Total QALYs/ adult | Total additional cost/adult | ICER |
|---|---|---|---|
| CBT on top of standard medication | 0.655 | £1,122 | **CBT on top of standard medication versus standard medication: £65,279/QALY** |
| Standard medication alone | 0.639 | 0 | |

*Sensitivity analysis*    The ICER of individual CBT on top of standard medication versus standard medication alone remained above the cost-effectiveness threshold set by NICE (NICE, 2006c) under any scenario tested in sensitivity analysis. In contrast, group-based CBT was shown to be a potentially cost-effective option, with an ICER of £16,699 per QALY in the main sensitivity analysis, although this ratio ranged widely from £13,566 to £535,556 per QALY in the various alternative hypotheses tested. It must be noted, however, that the estimated cost effectiveness of group-based CBT relies greatly on the hypothesis that group-based CBT is as effective as individually delivered CBT.

Full results of one-way sensitivity analysis are shown in Table 17 and Table 18.

As shown in threshold analysis, individual CBT was cost effective (with an ICER reaching £16,699/QALY), when it lasted 3 hours in total (instead of 15, as modelled in the base-case analysis). It is extremely unlikely, however, that CBT can be as

**Table 17: Results of one-way sensitivity analysis for individual CBT added to standard medication versus standard medication alone in adults with ADHD**

| Scenario | ICER |
|---|---|
| Upper 95% CIs of RR of CBT on top of medication to medication | £53,029/QALY |
| Lower 95% CIs of RR of CBT on top of medication to medication | £672,397/QALY |
| Utility scores from Secnik *et al.* (2005b) | £96,592/QALY |

**Table 18: Results of one-way sensitivity analysis for group-based CBT added to standard medication versus standard medication alone in adults with ADHD**

| Scenario | ICER |
|---|---|
| Main scenario of group-based CBT | £16,699/QALY |
| Upper 95% CIs of RR of CBT on top of medication to medication | £13,566/QALY |
| Lower 95% CIs of RR of CBT on top of medication to medication | £535,556/QALY |
| Utility scores from Secnik *et al.* (2005) | £24,710/QALY |

effective as described in SAFREN2005 with 3 hours of contact only. Another threshold analysis showed that a minimum improvement of 0.15 in the utility score (from the health state of no response to that of response) was required in order for individually provided CBT to become cost effective. A respective analysis showed that the minimum improvement in utility score required in order for group-based CBT to be cost effective was only 0.037.

*Limitations of the economic analysis*
The results of the economic analysis were based on a simple decision-analytic model developed to estimate additional costs and health benefits associated with provision of CBT in adults with ADHD already taking medication, over the period of 1 year. Clinical evidence was derived from the only available trial evaluating the effectiveness of psychological therapies in adults with ADHD. The total number of participants in this trial was very small (N = 31). CBT was shown to have a significant effect when response rates were used as the measure of outcome. Changes in score on the ADHD-RS, while favouring CBT, were nevertheless not significantly different between the two arms of the trial. The study population consisted of adults who continued to show clinically significant ADHD symptoms, despite having received

medication for at least 2 months before CBT was started. It is uncertain whether the results of the clinical study (and, subsequently, of the economic analysis) would be the same on a population of adults less resistant to medication.

Costs consisted of intervention costs only; potential cost savings to the healthcare and social services resulting from improvement in ADHD symptoms of adults were not considered owing to lack of relevant data. It is therefore likely that the cost effectiveness of CBT added to standard medication in adults with ADHD is greater than that suggested by the results of the analysis.

Estimates on healthcare resource use were based on description of resource use in SAFREN2005, which was the only source of clinical-effectiveness data for this economic analysis. According to GDG expert opinion, these estimates reflected optimal resource use, and were consistent with clinical practice in the UK. Nevertheless, SAFREN2005 only roughly described some aspects of resource use relating to CBT, and did not provide any data on resource use beyond the duration of the trial. It is unknown whether two booster sessions are sufficient to retain a positive outcome in adults with ADHD (as assumed in the economic model), as no relevant follow-up studies are available. Likewise, the long-term effectiveness of CBT if added to standard medication in this population is unknown. Therefore, it is not possible to estimate the cost effectiveness of CBT in the longer term.

Utility scores used in the economic model, taken from a poster presentation, were based on SF-36 scores obtained from an RCT comparing two different doses of atomoxetine in adults with ADHD (Laing & Aristides, 2005). These were the only utility scores available for adults with ADHD. The study population in this trial consisted of adults taking medication, mainly stimulants. It is possible that the resulting utility scores are not fully representative of the HRQoL of the study population in the economic analysis. Nevertheless, they were derived from a generic, validated instrument, which is in accordance with NICE recommendations (NICE, 2004). Use of alternative utility scores taken from paediatric populations with ADHD showed that neither individual nor group-based CBT was cost effective. However, these scores were generated by parents of children with ADHD who are likely to represent perceptions of adults with ADHD at an even lower degree than that characterising utility data reported in Laing and Aristides (2005), used in the base-case analysis.

A key assumption used in the sensitivity analysis was that individual and group-based CBT are equally effective. Group-based CBT was shown to be potentially cost effective in sensitivity analysis, assuming that its effectiveness was equal to that of individual CBT. The clinical effectiveness data used in the economic analysis were taken from SAFREN2005, which examined individually delivered CBT. According to GDG expert opinion, it is likely that group-based CBT has similar effectiveness with individually delivered CBT. The clinical effectiveness of group-based CBT is supported by evidence from a non-randomised controlled study of a group CBT workshop-style brief intervention for adults with ADHD (Bramham *et al.*, 2008). At the time of publication existing evidence supporting equivalence in clinical effectiveness between individual and group-based CBT programmes is very limited. The ICER of £16,699 per QALY, characterising group-based CBT, was based on intention-to-treat analysis. This means that estimated clinical effectiveness took into account the fact that some individuals might drop out of treatment. On the other hand, full intervention costs were estimated, assuming that all individuals completed treatment. This assumption has probably overestimated the total cost of CBT.

*Overall conclusions from the economic analysis*
The results of the economic analysis indicate that individually delivered CBT is not a cost-effective option for adults with ADHD who have already taken stimulants but still have clinically significant ADHD symptoms. However, if group-based CBT has similar effectiveness to individual CBT in this population, then group-based CBT is potentially a cost-effective option from the perspective of the NHS.

Further research is needed to explore the long-term benefits and potential cost savings associated with provision of CBT to adults with ADHD, and to further investigate the HRQoL of this population. More importantly, future research is required to examine the effectiveness of group-based CBT versus individually delivered CBT, so that the cost effectiveness of group-based CBT can be determined.

### 7.3.7 From evidence to recommendations: psychological interventions for adults with ADHD

Psychological treatment may be required at different points in time and/or stages in youth and adult development, including when there is a *de novo* diagnosis in adulthood, and may help the adult with ADHD to undergo a process of understanding and acceptance of their diagnosis and to cognitively reframe their past. The sparse evidence available indicates that CBT interventions deliver therapeutic benefits for adults with ADHD, whether provided on an individual or group basis. CBT may be particularly relevant to adults on medication who have persisting functional impairments associated with ADHD.

Areas that it may be important for CBT interventions to address include: psychoeducation; developing skills to attend, organise and plan; and cognitive restructuring and learning adaptive thinking skills. Where there are clinically significant difficulties in procrastination, anger/frustration and/or communication it may also be useful to address these areas.

Brief workshop-style group CBT interventions that aim to improve confidence, self-esteem and self-efficacy may deliver therapeutic benefits for adults with ADHD and appear to be an acceptable way of providing CBT to this population. Such interventions can provide psychoeducation and teach techniques and psychological skills to address inattention and memory, impulsivity, frustration and anger, anxiety, depression, social relationships, time management, problem solving and preparing for the future. In group interventions participants may value the opportunity to share personal experiences with other adults with ADHD.

Economic analysis indicates that group-based CBT for adults with ADHD is potentially a cost-effective option, if it has similar effectiveness to individual CBT in this population. On the other hand, individually delivered CBT is probably not cost effective. In some cases, however, individual CBT may be more appropriate for adults than group CBT sessions. For example, severe symptoms may prevent some individuals from concentrating in a group setting which provides greater opportunity for distraction. Individuals who additionally experience social anxiety may also benefit more from individual sessions. Group sessions will prioritise core problems and associated difficulties in general, but some adults may require idiosyncratic treatment and support for specific settings or problems (for example, in the workplace).

It must be noted that potential cost savings to the healthcare and social services resulting from improvement in symptoms experienced by adults with ADHD were not considered in the analysis, owing to lack of relevant data. Therefore, the reported cost effectiveness of CBT for adults with ADHD is likely to be a conservative estimate. Future research is required so that the effectiveness and cost effectiveness of group-based CBT can be confirmed.

## 7.4    OTHER NON-PHARMACOLOGICAL APPROACHES

A number of non-pharmacological approaches have been used as therapies for ADHD, including biofeedback, relaxation training and environmental manipulation and management.

### 7.4.1    Environmental manipulation and recreational interventions

It is not unusual to find suggestions in the therapy literature of interventions that involve making changes to the environment to address core ADHD symptoms. Keeping distracting stimuli to a minimum in home and school settings is supported by research showing that distractions in the environment result in decreases in time on task (Whalen *et al.*, 1979) and that ADHD may be associated with neuropsychological impairments characterised by deficits in executive functioning and/or an aversion to waiting for rewards (Thorell, 2007; Sonuga-Barke, 2003). Children with ADHD seem to seek stimulation when low levels of it are present (Antrop *et al.*, 2000), and this finding would support strategies that ensure that sufficient stimulation is available. This may mean keeping 'idle' time to a minimum while at other times making it possible for children to engage in a psychologically stimulating activity.

It is difficult to judge how important the concept of environmental manipulation is in practice. It is likely that teachers in employing usual classroom management techniques will tend to reduce the amount of distracting stimulation a child with ADHD is exposed to, for example by seating them at the front of the class. Parents too may naturally ensure that their children have sufficient appropriate recreational and leisure activities so as to reduce the likelihood of inappropriate behaviour occurring. It is not known whether this type of intervention is employed in a systematic way by clinicians and teachers, despite the possible theoretical underpinnings.

Related to environmental manipulation are strategies designed to stimulate through recreation parts of the brain that may confer some control over disinhibition, executive functioning and inattentiveness (Rabinowitz, 2004). It is not known how extensively such approaches are used and the evidence base is poor. Nevertheless, it is likely that at least on an intuitive level some parents and therapists develop and use such techniques.

Somewhat more widespread, but again with a weak evidence base, are recreational and leisure strategies designed to appeal to the needs of children for stimulus and activity but to do so through engaging in socially acceptable activities. There is no systematic research on the efficacy of this approach, but anecdotally it seems that it may be in widespread informal use. Parents and therapists may see such recreational and leisure pursuits not only as an opportunity for youngsters to 'let off steam', but also a way of providing opportunities for them to develop social skills and self-control.

### 7.4.2    Biofeedback

Biofeedback has been employed as a non-invasive treatment for children with ADHD since the 1970s but is probably not used as a significant intervention in UK clinical practice. A wide range of feedback presentations that are suitable for children are available and its rationale lies in theories of brain plasticity and cortical self-regulation that suggest it may be possible to countermand deficits of cortical activation (see Heinrich *et al.*, 2006). The use of electro-encephalography (EEG) biofeedback derived from the initial hypothesis of Satterfield and colleagues (Satterfield & Dawson, 1971; Satterfield *et al.*, 1973) that attentional deficits result from dysfunction of the central nervous system and that children with ADHD exhibit behaviours consistent with 'low arousal'. It is assumed that variations in alertness and behavioural control are directly related to specific thalamocortical generator mechanisms and that such variations are evident in distinctive EEG frequency rhythms that emerge over specific topographic regions of the brain (Sterman, 1996). It is proposed that ADHD neuropathology could alter these rhythms and that EEG biofeedback training directed at normalising these rhythms might therefore yield sustained clinical benefits.

Biofeedback techniques thus involve training individuals to exercise a certain amount of control over their brainwaves (as recorded by EEG) through bioelectrical neuroregulation. The mechanism by which it is proposed that this can be achieved is based on the assumption that the central nervous system can regulate a series of physiological functions in addition to its own activity. Intentional modulation of cortical self-regulation is achieved through a process of operant learning through the provision of training aimed to decrease excessive theta or slow wave activity (which is associated with feeling drowsy) and increase beta activity (which is associated with 'alertness' and attentional and memory processes). Biofeedback training involves the clinician setting desired thresholds on the biofeedback equipment. These thresholds are based on treatment goals, for example to decrease theta rhythm and increase beta rhythm. As the individual's physiological changes approach and surpass the set thresholds, the equipment provides either auditory or visual feedback, which serves as positive reinforcement for the desired changes. Thus, as an individual decreases theta and increases beta waves during EEG biofeedback, reinforcement is provided to encourage them to become more aware of what they are doing to achieve this desired state and to continue in the same manner. In children a focus has been on the training of slow cortical potentials as well as theta and beta waves, and the use of a computer-based delivery seems to assist with the acceptability of the method.

### 7.4.3    Relaxation training and other physical therapies

Relaxation training involves the systematic tensing and relaxing of specific muscle groups. These techniques can be used to help children, young people and adults in situations where they feel anxious and tense and to gain a sense of self-control. Other physical therapies that have similar aims include yoga and massage.

### 7.5    RECOMMENDATIONS

### 7.5.1    Identification, pre-diagnostic intervention and referral in children and young people

7.5.1.1    Group-based parent-training/education programmes are recommended in the management of children with conduct disorders.[12] (NICE, 2006c).

### 7.5.2    Treatment for pre-school children

7.5.2.1    Healthcare professionals should offer parents or carers of pre-school children with ADHD a referral to a parent-training/education programme as the first-line treatment if the parents or carers have not already attended such a programme or the programme has had a limited effect. (Key priority)

7.5.2.2    Group-based parent-training/education programmes, developed for the treatment and management of children with conduct disorders[13], should be fully accessible to parents or carers of children with ADHD whether or not the child also has a formal diagnosis of conduct disorder.

7.5.2.3    Individual-based parent-training/education programmes[14] are recommended in the management of children with ADHD when:
- a group programme is not possible because of low participant numbers
- there are particular difficulties for families in attending group sessions (for example, because of disability, needs related to diversity such as language differences, parental ill-health, problems with transport, or where other factors suggest poor prospects for therapeutic engagement)

---

[12]This recommendation is taken from TA102 (NICE, 2006c). See recommendation 7.5.2.2 for the extended use of these programmes to include children with ADHD.
[13]As recommended in TA102 (NICE, 2006c).
[14]Ibid.

- a family's needs are too complex to be met by group-based parent-training/education programmes.

7.5.2.4  When individual-based parent-training/education programmes for pre-school children with ADHD are undertaken, the skills training stages should involve both the parents or carers and the child.

7.5.2.5  It is recommended that all parent-training/education programmes, whether group- or individual-based, should:

- be structured and have a curriculum informed by principles of social-learning theory
- include relationship-enhancing strategies
- offer a sufficient number of sessions, with an optimum of 8–12, to maximise the possible benefits for participants
- enable parents to identify their own parenting objectives
- incorporate role-play during sessions, as well as homework to be under-taken between sessions, to achieve generalisation of newly rehearsed behaviours to the home situation
- be delivered by appropriately trained and skilled facilitators who are supervised, have access to necessary ongoing professional development, and are able to engage in a productive therapeutic alliance with parents
- adhere to the programme developer's manual and employ all of the neces-sary materials to ensure consistent implementation of the programme[15].

7.5.2.6  Consideration should be given to involving both of the parents or all carers of children or young people with ADHD in parent-training/education programmes wherever this is feasible.

7.5.2.7  Programmes should demonstrate proven effectiveness. This should be based on evidence from randomised controlled trials or other suitable rigorous evaluation methods undertaken independently[16].

7.5.2.8  Programme providers should also ensure that support is available to enable the participation of parents who might otherwise find it difficult to access these programmes[17].

7.5.2.9  If overall treatment, including parent-training/education programmes, has been effective in managing ADHD symptoms and any associated impair-ment in pre-school children, before considering discharge from secondary care healthcare professionals should:

- review the child, with their parents or carers and siblings, for any resid-ual coexisting conditions and develop a treatment plan for these if needed
- monitor for the recurrence of ADHD symptoms and any associated impairment that may occur after the child starts school.

7.5.2.10  If overall treatment, including parent-training/education programmes, has not been effective in managing ADHD symptoms and any associated

---

[15]This recommendation is taken from TA102 (NICE, 2006c).
[16]Ibid.
[17]Ibid.

impairment in pre-school children, healthcare professionals should consider referral to tertiary services for further care.

### 7.5.3 Treatment for school-age children with ADHD and moderate impairment

7.5.3.1    If the child or young person with ADHD has moderate levels of impairment, the parents or carers should be offered referral to a group parent-training/education programme, either on its own or together with a group treatment programme (CBT and/or social skills training) for the child or young person. (Key priority)

7.5.3.2    When using group treatment (CBT and/or social skills training) for the child or young person in conjunction with a parent-training/education programme, particular emphasis should be given to targeting a range of areas, including social skills with peers, problem solving, self-control, listening skills and dealing with and expressing feelings. Active learning strategies should be used, and rewards given for achieving key elements of learning.

7.5.3.3    For older adolescents with ADHD and moderate impairment, individual psychological interventions (such as CBT or social skills training) may be considered as they may be more effective and acceptable than group parent-training/education programmes or group CBT and/or social skills training.

7.5.3.4    For children and young people (including older age groups) with ADHD and a learning disability, a parent-training/education programme should be offered on either a group or individual basis, whichever is preferred following discussion with the parents or carers and the child or young person.

7.5.3.5    When parents or carers of children or young people with ADHD undertake parent-training/education programmes, the professional delivering the sessions should consider contacting the school and providing the child or young person's teacher with written information on the areas of behavioural management covered in these sessions. This should only be done with parental consent.

7.5.3.6    Following successful treatment with a parent-training/education programme and before considering discharge from secondary care, the child or young person should be reviewed, with their parents or carers and siblings, for any residual problems such as anxiety, aggression or learning difficulties. Treatment plans should be developed for any coexisting conditions.

### 7.5.4 Treatment for school-age children with severe ADHD (hyperkinetic disorder)

7.5.4.1    If a group parent-training/education programme is effective in children and young people with severe ADHD who have refused drug treatment, healthcare professionals should assess the child or young person for possible coexisting conditions and develop a longer-term care plan.

### 7.5.5 Treatment for all children with ADHD

7.5.5.1 Healthcare professionals should work with children and young people with ADHD and their parents or carers to anticipate major life changes (such as puberty, starting or changing schools, the birth of a sibling) and make appropriate arrangements for adequate personal and social support during times of increased need. The need for psychological treatment at these times should be considered.

### 7.5.6 Treatment of adults with ADHD

7.5.6.1 For adults with ADHD stabilised on medication but with persisting functional impairment associated with the disorder, or where there has been no response to drug treatment, a course of either group or individual CBT to address the person's functional impairment should be considered. Group therapy is recommended as the first-line psychological treatment because it is the most cost effective.

7.5.6.2 For adults with ADHD, CBT may be considered when:
- the person has made an informed choice not to have drug treatment
- drug treatment has proved to be only partially effective or ineffective or the person is intolerant to it
- people have difficulty accepting the diagnosis of ADHD and accepting and adhering to drug treatment
- symptoms are remitting and psychological treatment is considered sufficient to target residual (mild to moderate) functional impairment.

### 7.6 RESEARCH RECOMMENDATIONS

7.6.1.1 Effectiveness of group-based parent training
- Are group-based behavioural parent-training/education methods more effective than drug treatment in school-age children and young people with ADHD in terms of symptoms, quality of life and cost effectiveness? This would be best evaluated by a head-to-head randomised controlled trial.
- Why this is important: The evidence for the effect of group-based parent-training/education programmes is largely based on studies of younger children. These programmes are an important part of the management of ADHD although their cost effectiveness is not clear for older children and adolescents.

7.6.1.2    Effectiveness of non-drug treatments for adults with ADHD

- Are non-drug treatments (including focused psychological treatments and supportive approaches such as coaching) more effective than drug treatment (methylphenidate) in terms of symptoms, quality of life, cost effectiveness, drug misuse and other coexisting conditions, and the cost of health, forensic and criminal justice services, in the treatments of adults with ADHD? This would be best conducted as a randomised controlled trial.
- Why this is important: Currently there is good evidence supporting the effectiveness of methylphenidate in people with ADHD symptoms and associated impairment. However, there is insufficient evidence on whether non-drug treatments could have specific advantages in some important aspects of the life of a person with ADHD. Given the strong association of ADHD in adults with substance misuse, personality disorder and involvement in the criminal justice system, a health economic approach would be essential.

7.6.1.3    Effectiveness of environmental manipulation and recreational activity

- Are there any benefits in making changes to home, school or work environments to reduce ADHD core symptoms? Some recent laboratory studies indicate the importance of stimulation seeking and delay aversion in the maintenance of ADHD symptomatology. Related to this, do recreational activities assist in symptom reduction for both young people and adults? Such activities are undertaken, often on an intuitive basis, but those with ADHD, on an anecdotal level, report finding value in such activities.
- Why this is important: Such approaches are used in current practice without a significant evidence base. If environmental manipulation and/or recreation interventions are not effective they may involve a diversion of valuable professional time. If they are effective they could represent very cost effective interventions that could be implemented by a wide range of professionals, carers and those with ADHD themselves.

# 8. INTERVENTIONS FOR CHILDREN WITH ADHD IN EDUCATIONAL SETTINGS

## 8.1 INTRODUCTION

This chapter reviews the literature and makes recommendations for interventions for children with ADHD within educational settings, while recognising that such interventions need to be considered as one component within the overall service provision.

Children with ADHD fall behind their peers academically (Barbaresi *et al.*, 2007; Barkley *et al.*, 1990; Frazier *et al.*, 2007; Lahey *et al.*, 1994; Marshall *et al.*, 1999; Nussbaum *et al.*, 1990; Willcutt *et al.*, 2000; Zentall, 1993). It has been shown that this trend extends to children who are severely inattentive, hyperactive and impulsive in the classroom, even if they do not have a formal diagnosis of ADHD (Barry *et al.*, 2002; Gaub & Carlson, 1997; McGee *et al.*, 2002; Merrell & Tymms, 2001; Merrell & Tymms, 2005a). The studies by Merrell and Tymms, which are based upon a large sample of English school children aged between 5 and 7 years, showed that the inattentive factor was particularly related to academic underachievement, and that the greater the number of symptoms, the greater the impairment (Merrell & Tymms, 2005b). Further, children who had been identified by their teachers in the first (reception) year of school as having severe ADHD symptoms were shown to fall behind their peers academically at least until the end of primary schooling at age 11 years.

There can be little doubt that when a child has symptoms of ADHD his or her behaviour varies across different situations. Rutter and colleagues (1979) showed clear differences in behaviour across secondary schools using observation and self-report. Similar differences were noted by Mortimore and colleagues (1988) across primary schools, although they relied on teachers' questionnaires. In reviewing the evidence, Galloway and colleagues (1995) proposed that 'differences between teachers are substantially greater than differences between schools', suggesting that the teacher was the dominant influence on behaviour in the classroom. Gray and Sime (1988) suggested that 60% of the variance in behaviour lay within schools. In the Elton report (HMSO, 1989) it is stated that 'a teacher's general competence has a strong influence on his or her pupils' behaviour'.

Although the ordinary experience of teachers and anecdotal evidence suggests that the behaviour of children with ADHD is influenced by school and teachers, there is no formal evidence to support this. Clearly, there would be many advantages if the behaviour of children with ADHD could be modified with school-based interventions. Although evidence is lacking, the desired outcomes for children with ADHD are, nevertheless, improvements in their behaviour within the school setting, academic achievement, attitude to school, self-esteem, peer relationships, social inclusion and post-education opportunities. Another desired outcome, which extends beyond the clinical question (see Appendix 6) but is important to bear in mind, is an improvement in the quality of life for teachers of children with ADHD (Barbaresi & Olson, 1998).

## 8.2    DATABASES SEARCHED AND INCLUSION CRITERIA

Information about the databases searched and the inclusion/exclusion criteria used for this section of the guideline can be found in Table 19.

## 8.3    STUDIES CONSIDERED[18]

The review team conducted a new systematic search for RCTs that assessed the efficacy and/or safety of interventions delivered by teachers in educational settings for children and young people with ADHD.

Six trials met the eligibility criteria set by the GDG, providing data on 26,117 children. Three of the trials were cluster RCTs. All trials were published in peer-reviewed journals between 1989 and 2006. In addition, four studies were excluded from the analysis. The most common reason for exclusion was that they were not RCTs (further information about both included and excluded studies can be found in Appendix 17).

**Table 19:  Databases searched and inclusion/exclusion
criteria for clinical evidence**

| Electronic databases | CENTRAL, MEDLINE, EMBASE, CINAHL, PsycINFO, ERIC |
|---|---|
| Date searched | Database inception to April 2006; table of content October 2007 March 2006 |
| Study design | RCT (efficacy) |
| Patient population | Participants (children) diagnosed with ADHD |
| Interventions | Screening; teacher advice; teacher advice + screening; teacher-led interventions; teacher training; multicomponent teacher training |
| Outcomes | Improvement on ADHD symptoms (teacher-rated and parent-rated); improvement on conduct problems (teacher-rated and parent-rated); improvement on reading; improvement on mathematics |

---

[18]Here and elsewhere in the guideline, each study considered for review is referred to by a study ID in capital letters (primary author and date of study publication, except where a study is *in press* or only submitted for publication, then a date is not used).

## 8.4     CLINICAL EVIDENCE FOR SCREENING FOR ADHD IN EDUCATIONAL SETTINGS

### 8.4.1     Introduction

Key behaviours related to ADHD are readily observable in children at school and it might be advantageous for teachers to be able to recognise those pupils who may have ADHD. In the US, clinical practice guidelines recommend that teachers should be involved in the process of diagnosing ADHD by completing rating scales and providing information about possible symptoms and impairment in the school setting (American Academy of Child and Adolescent Psychiatry, 2007). Teachers thus have a crucial role in assisting with accurate clinical case identification.

A screening programme for ADHD has attractions: the early identification of problems; early intervention; and, if repeated regularly throughout primary and secondary school, recognising cases that 'slipped through the net' or have a late onset. The potential downsides of screening are the identification of false positive or false negative cases, as well as the economic costs involved.

*Current practice*
To the best of the knowledge of the GDG and the review team, no screening interventions for children with ADHD are carried out in schools in the UK.

*Definitions*
Two types of screening have been defined. One, a 'case identification' approach, may be seen as screening, but it is distinct from a universal programme of screening which collects data across all children in schools and selects possible cases of ADHD for further assessment or referral. This section considers the latter possibility.

### 8.4.2     Clinical evidence for screening versus no intervention

There was only one study from the six included trials that involved a comparison of screening of children with ADHD as an intervention compared with no intervention in a school setting (TYMMS2006) (see Table 20 for further details). This study also involved advice to teachers in a factorial design and that is dealt with in the next section (TYMMS2006). The class teachers of 2,040 participating English primary schools completed a rating scale at the end of the children's first year at school. The rating scale was based on the DSM-IV diagnostic criteria. The intervention involved identifying children who, at the end of the first year of school, exhibited severe ADHD symptoms, based on the cut-off points for the number of criteria deemed to represent severe ADHD symptoms as suggested in DSM-IV. The names of these pupils in half of the schools in the sample were forwarded to the new class teachers. The schools were randomly selected. Outcome measures were collected 18 months later, half-way through school year 2 when pupils were aged 6 to 7 years. The identification of children with severe ADHD symptoms had no detectable impact on ADHD symptoms, reading or mathematics.

Study information and evidence from the important outcomes and overall quality of evidence are presented in Table 20. The full evidence profiles and associated forest plots can be found in Appendix 19 and Appendix 18, respectively.

**Table 20: Study information and evidence summary table
for trials of screening**

|  | **Screening versus no intervention** |
|---|---|
| Total no. of trials (total no. of participants) | 1 (25,482) |
| Study ID | TYMMS2006 |
| Diagnosis | Pupils in school |
| Baseline severity | PIPS On-entry: 2.23 (3.53) |
| Treatment length | 2 years |
| Age of subjects | 4 years at initial visit |
| *Benefits* |  |
| ADHD core symptoms (teacher-rated) | Y2 Behaviour scale: SMD 0.04 (−0.16 to 0.24) Quality: Moderate K = 1, N = 25482 |
| Mathematics | KS1: SMD −0.05 (−0.18 to 0.09) Quality: Moderate K = 1, N = 25482 PIPS: SMD 0.09 (−0.07 to 0.26) Quality: Moderate K = 1, N = 25482 |
| Reading | KS1: SMD −0.10 (−0.24 to 0.05) Quality: Moderate K = 1, N = 25482 PIPS: SMD −0.11 (−0.28 to 0.05) Quality: Moderate K = 1, N = 25482 |

### 8.4.3    Clinical evidence summary

From the original search only one study (TYMMS2006) was identified that assessed the efficacy of screening in educational settings. The quality of the evidence was moderate given that only one study was included. Evidence suggests that there is little to no effect in introducing a screening programme on children's ADHD symptoms or academic achievement.

## 8.5 CLINICAL EVIDENCE FOR ADVICE TO TEACHERS ABOUT ADHD, EFFECTIVE CLASSROOM INTERVENTIONS AND TEACHER TRAINING

### 8.5.1 Introduction

This section reviews the effect of advising teachers about ADHD in general and of providing classroom management techniques for children with ADHD. It then considers the issue of teacher training.

### 8.5.2 Advice to teachers about classroom strategies for children with ADHD

*Introduction*

Some parents conceptualise ADHD as more of an educational than a health problem and request educational input and services (Poduska, 2000). In the UK two-thirds of parents of children with ADHD have consulted and discussed their concerns with teachers (Sayal *et al.*, 2006a). Therefore, improving teachers' knowledge of ADHD alongside providing advice on how to work with children who might have ADHD may improve outcomes. To achieve this, teachers need to be equipped with information about the behavioural problems that children with ADHD are likely to exhibit in the classroom, possible reasons for that behaviour, suggestions for its management and information about seeking further help with particular children.

*Current practice*

The review team was unable to find any recent UK-based surveys of teachers' knowledge of ADHD. At the present time, it is highly likely that teachers' knowledge of the disorder varies according to the training that they have received and whether they have direct experience of children with ADHD. A recent study set in one Local Education Authority (LEA) found that over half the teachers had experience of teaching a child with a clinical diagnosis of ADHD (Sayal *et al.*, 2006b), and the provision of a brief educational intervention for teachers has been found to raise awareness and improve recognition of children with possible ADHD (Barbaresi & Olson, 1998; Sayal *et al.*, 2006b). Beyond the recognition of children with ADHD, providing advice to teachers about ADHD and how to help children with the disorder within mainstream classrooms has, in some studies, also been combined with other related approaches such as screening and parent training.

*Definition and aim of intervention*

In the context of this section, the advice for teachers is not part of their pre- or in-service training, delivered in person. The kind of advice that is considered is communicated in the form of written information about the underlying causes of ADHD, and strategies for helping children with the disorder in the classroom setting. The strategies generally involve making adjustments to the classroom environment, groupings with other pupils and interactions with the teacher. Advice can also be more specific; for example, updating a teacher on the treatment of a particular child given by other professionals with suggestions about how the teacher might build upon that work.

### 8.5.3    Clinical evidence for advice given to teachers as an education intervention

Of the six included trials, three involved advice given to teachers as an intervention (see Table 21 for further details).

**Table 21:  Study information and evidence summary table for trials of teacher advice**

| | Teacher advice versus no intervention | Teacher advice + screening versus no intervention | Teacher advice (TA) + parent training (PT) versus parent training |
|---|---|---|---|
| Total no. of trials (total no. of participants) | 1 (25,482) | 1 (25,482) | 1 (30) |
| Study ID | TYMMS2006 | TYMMS2006 | CORKUM2005 |
| Diagnosis | Pupils in school | Pupils in school | ADHD |
| Baseline severity | PIPS On-entry: 2.23 (3.53) | PIPS On-entry: 2.23 (3.53) | CPRS-R (short): PT: 71.94(9.42) PT + TA: 73.07(8.38) CTRS-R (short): PT: 71.40(17.57) PT + TA: 64.75(12.18) |
| Treatment length | 2 years | 2 years | 10 weeks |
| Age of subjects | 4 years at initial visit | 4 years at initial visit | 9 years |

*Continued*

**Table 21:** (*Continued*)

|  | Teacher advice versus no intervention | Teacher advice + screening versus no intervention | Teacher advice (TA) + parent training (PT) versus parent training |
|---|---|---|---|
| **Benefits** | | | |
| ADHD core symptoms (combined teacher/ parent-rated) | – | – | ADHD Index: SMD −1.15 (−2.03 to −0.28) Quality: Moderate K = 1, N = 30 |
| ADHD core symptoms (teacher-rated) | Y2 Behaviour: SMD −0.19 (−0.39 to 0.01) Quality: Moderate K = 1, N = 25,482 | Y2 Behaviour: SMD −0.13 (−0.32 to 0.07) Quality: Moderate K = 1, N = 25,482 | – |
| Conduct problems (combined teacher/ parent-rated) | – | – | CPRS/CTRS (oppositional): SMD 0.08 (−0.88 to 0.72) Quality: Moderate K = 1, N = 30 |
| Mathematics | KS1: SMD −0.05 (−0.18 to 0.09) Quality: Moderate K = 1, N = 25,482 PIPS: SMD 0.05 (−0.12 to 0.21) Quality: Moderate K = 1, N = 25,482 | KS1: SMD 0.15 (0.01 to 0.28) Quality: Moderate K = 1, N = 25,482 PIPS: SMD −0.01 (−0.17 to 0.15) Quality: Moderate K = 1, N = 25,482 | – |
| Reading | KS1: SMD −0.02 (−0.17 to 0.12) Quality: Moderate K = 1, N = 25,482 PIPS: SMD −0.09 (−0.26 to 0.08) K = 1, N = 25,482 | KS1: SMD 0.19 (0.04 to 0.34) Quality: Moderate K = 1, N = 25,482 PIPS: SMD 0.17 (0.01 to 0.33) K = 1, N = 25,482 | – |

In one study (TYMMS2006), the intervention consisted of sending an advice booklet to half of the schools (randomly selected). This booklet contained general information about ADHD as well as teaching and classroom management strategies that had been previously shown to help children with ADHD, such as those evaluated in the meta-analyses published by DuPaul and Eckert (1997) and Purdie and colleagues (2002). In this same study (TYMMS2006) the effectiveness of this advice booklet was assessed in conjunction with screening (mentioned previously in Section 8.4). The third teacher advice intervention (CORKUM2005) consisted of providing teachers with a general information package about ADHD including the CHADD Educators' Manual (Fowler & the National Education Committee, 1992) at the start of the intervention period and then sending them weekly brief updates about what the parents had learned that week in a concurrent parent-training programme, and suggestions on how to use similar strategies in the classroom.

Study information and evidence from critical outcomes and overall quality of evidence are presented in Table 21. Full evidence profiles and associated forest plots can be found in Appendix 19 and Appendix 18, respectively.

*Clinical evidence summary*
*Advice given to teachers versus no intervention*  The quality of the evidence was moderate given that only one study (TYMMS2006) addressed the comparison of advice given to teachers and no intervention. The evidence suggests that there is little to no effect in providing advice to teachers in relation to children's ADHD symptoms or academic achievement. The authors of the study, however, state that the advice booklet was read by a small percentage of the teachers, which could account for the lack of positive results.
*Advice given to teachers + screening versus no intervention*  There is limited evidence from one study (TYMMS2006) of the combined effect of advice given to teachers and screening. The results indicate little to no effect in children's ADHD symptoms or academic achievement. The intervention had a negative effect on some of the academic outcome measures.
*Advice given to teachers as an added intervention to parent training*  A further study (CORKUM2005) examined the efficacy of giving advice to teachers in addition to a parent-training programme in improving the behaviour of children with ADHD. The general quality of the evidence was moderate reflecting the paucity of the data in this area.

The effectiveness of giving advice to teachers in addition a parent-training programme was large (SMD 1.15) in reducing children's ADHD core symptoms as rated by both parents and teachers. However, there was little to no effect (SMD 0.08) of this intervention when added to parent training in improving children's conduct problems.

In summary, there is some evidence that advice to teachers as an added intervention to a parent-training programme is effective in reducing children's ADHD core symptoms.

### 8.5.4    Clinical evidence for teacher-led educational interventions for children with ADHD

*Introduction*
As discussed in the introduction to the guideline and to this chapter, children with ADHD are at risk academically and socially, and they can be difficult to manage in

the classroom. Interventions to improve those difficulties are desirable and since teachers work with these children for several hours each day, they are in a position to be able to implement strategies in the context of the school environment. Additionally, all children and young people, including those with ADHD, have the right to a school experience that provides a broad, balanced and relevant curriculum, including the National Curriculum, which is appropriately differentiated according to their needs (DfES, 2001). The Special Educational Needs Code of Practice (DfES, 2001) further describes the kind of assistance which may be required by particular children, including those who demonstrate the symptoms of ADHD.

Teacher-led educational interventions mainly consist of managing academic activities or adapting the physical environment. A description of a wide range of strategies for use with children with ADHD is given by Cooper and Ideus (1996). They suggest techniques such as:

- seating the child in a place that is relatively free from distraction (for example, doors and windows) in a position where the teacher can easily intervene if the child is not attending
- having a designated quiet area for a child to work in
- providing stimulating activities
- giving concise, clear instructions
- following a defined, regular timetable
- avoiding repetitive tasks
- breaking down tasks into a series of small steps
- giving frequent positive feedback
- working in a pair rather than a group
- isolating the child from the class for a short time when they are misbehaving
- giving points or tokens as rewards to be exchanged at a later time for a favourite activity or treat
- taking away points or tokens if the child misbehaves.

*Current practice*
According to the Special Needs Code of Practice, the LEA will need to consider, on an individual basis, whether these interventions can be provided through *School Action Plus* or whether the LEA needs to undertake a statutory assessment. Although there is a statutory requirement to provide appropriate education to all children, including those with ADHD, local practice varies.

*Definition and aims of interventions*
Teacher-led interventions are defined as programmes and/or techniques delivered by teachers within the classroom such as those described in the introduction above.

*Teacher-led interventions versus no intervention*
From the six included trials, there was one comparison involving a teacher-led intervention named 'giving effective commands' (Barkley, 1997), which consists of the teacher giving the child a command once and, if necessary, proceeding to a warning where the child is informed of the consequences of not carrying out the command;

in cases where the child does not comply, the threat is carried out (KAPALKA2005) (see Table 22 for further details). Children's behaviour was assessed using the School Situation Questionnaire as rated by their teachers.

Study information and evidence from critical outcomes and overall quality of evidence are presented in Table 22. Full evidence profiles and associated forest plots can be found in Appendix 19 and Appendix 18, respectively.

*Clinical evidence summary*

The only reported relevant outcome was conduct problems (teacher-rated) and the quality of the evidence was moderate, reflecting the paucity of the data.

There is evidence from KAPALKA2005 indicating a large effect (SMD $-1.47$) of teacher-led behaviour interventions compared with a control group in reducing conduct problems as rated by teachers.

**Table 22: Study information and evidence summary table for trials of teacher-led interventions**

|  | **Teacher-led intervention versus no intervention** |
|---|---|
| Total no. of trials (total no. of participants) | 1 (86) |
| Study ID | KAPALKA2005 |
| Diagnosis | ADHD |
| Baseline severity | School Situations Questionnaire: Treatment: 5.6 (1) Control: 5.5 (1.05) |
| Treatment length | 2 weeks |
| Age of subjects | 7.4 years |
| ***Benefits*** | |
| Conduct problems (teacher-rated) | School Situations Questionnaire: SMD $-1.47$ ($-1.94$ to $-0.99$) Quality: Moderate K $=$ 1, N $=$ 86 |

### 8.5.5 Clinical evidence for teacher training on the identification of ADHD and school-based interventions

*Introduction*

The Special Educational Needs Code of Practice published by the DfES (2001) states that for mainstream schools:

> *Provision for pupils with special educational needs is a matter for the school as a whole. In addition to the governing body, the school's head teacher, the SENCO*

> *or SEN team and all other members of staff have important responsibilities. In practice the division of day-to-day responsibilities is a matter for individual schools, to be decided in the light of a school's circumstances and size, priorities and ethos.*

The NSF for Children (2004) highlights the need for support and training of front-line professionals who have daily contact with children. Despite this, teachers receive limited training about child mental health problems (Gowers *et al.*, 2004) or special needs in general (Aubrey *et al.*, 2007).

As discussed earlier, in England teachers' knowledge about ADHD and experience of teaching a child with a diagnosis of ADHD is variable. In the US, where over 90% of teachers have reported experience of teaching a child with ADHD (Bussing *et al.*, 2002; Power *et al.*, 1995), the following topics have been highlighted as important for in-service education: ADHD; adapting lessons for pupils with ADHD; managing stress caused by children with ADHD in the classroom; behavioural management; and implementation of behaviour plans (Barbaresi & Olson, 1998; Bussing *et al.*, 2002; Walter *et al.*, 2006).

The provision of in-service training, peer observation and coaching by professionals can be effective (Adey *et al.*, 2004; Dreyfus & Dreyfus, 1986; Dall'Alba & Sandberg, 2006; Joyce & Showers, 1980; Sparks, 1986), but the process takes time, and Adey and colleagues (2004) suggested that 30 hours of in-service provision are required for sustained changes to teachers' classroom practice.

Since, first, teachers have to deal with children with ADHD on a daily basis, second, schools and their staff have responsibilities for such children and third, the knowledge basis is variable, it makes sense to consider enhancing the training of teachers in the area at the pre-service and in-service stages.

*Current practice*
Anecdotally, parents report that they need to be proactive in terms of educating teachers about ADHD and that consistent teacher education approaches (for example, in-service education or training for SENCOs) are desirable.

*Teacher-training versus no intervention* From the six included trials only two involved a comparison of teacher training with control. One study (BLOOMQUIST 1991) consisted of one 2-hour in-service and six 45- to 60-minute consultation sessions over a 10-week period. Teachers were given educative and restructuring exercises to help modify potential dysfunctional opinions they might have held toward pupils with ADHD in mainstream classes. Teachers were trained in behavioural child management methods and encouraged to actively participate with their students in 'collaborative problem-solving'. A second study (BARKLEY2000) consisted of a teacher-training programme where teachers were trained by a master teacher and child psychologist in behavioural treatments. During the training, teachers were given information about defiant behaviour and behavioural interventions such as rewarding children for nondisruptive behaviour, setting up a home token system, time out, response cost and managing children in public places with 'think aloud-think ahead' strategies. Teachers implemented these behavioural treatments in special treatment classes.

*Multicomponent teacher training versus no intervention*  Three studies were identified that compared multicomponent teacher training with control. The former consisted of teacher training much like that described above together with other components such as parent interventions and, at times, child interventions.

In the multicomponent intervention in BARKLEY2000, teachers participated in a teacher-training programme described previously (BARKLEY2000). As a second component of the intervention, parents were trained in the same way as teachers by a child psychologist.

In BLOOMQUIST1991, teachers were trained as described above (see BLOOMQUIST1991). In addition, parents were given seven 90-minute sessions by a therapist, the aim of which was to provide a comprehensive educational programme of ADHD, establish a supportive atmosphere among parents, and present parents with an intensive cognitive behavioural training programme similar to the one imparted to teachers. Children were also trained by school psychologists in a step-by-step framework to guide problem-solving efforts, which included: problem recognition; generation of alternative solutions; thinking of consequences for potential solutions; anticipation of obstacles; and execution of specific behaviours to solve problems.

In BRASWELL1997, the teacher-training component involved a 2-hour in-service session and five 45-minute in-building sessions. Teachers were trained via didactic instruction, live and videotaped modelling and role play. Teachers were given information regarding ADHD, methods of increasing compliance and the use of problem-solving methods and self-monitoring techniques. The multicomponent intervention also consisted of giving parents information about ADHD in fifteen group sessions of 2 hours' duration each. Each session involved didactic presentation, modelling, role-play exercises and videotaped examples. Parents received a manual with information and were given homework assignments for using the trained skills with their children. The child element of this multicomponent intervention consisted in children participating in eighteen 45- to 60-minute peer training group sessions with co-leaders (school psychologists trained for this specific role). Children were also taught skills via didactic instruction, modelling and role-play exercises.

*Multicomponent teacher training versus teacher training*  Two studies were identified that compared the effectiveness of a multicomponent teacher training with teacher training only. BLOOMQUIST1991 compared multicomponent teacher training involving teacher training, parent and child involvement (see description of BLOOMQUIST1991) with teacher training only (see description of BLOOMQUIST 1991). BARKLEY2000 compared the multicomponent teacher training described previously (see description of BARKLEY2000) with teacher training alone (see description of BARKLEY2000).

Study information and evidence from critical outcomes and overall quality of evidence are presented in Table 23. Full evidence profiles and associated forest plots can be found in Appendix 19 and Appendix 18, respectively.

Table 23: Study information and evidence summary table for trials of teacher-training interventions

| | Teacher training versus no intervention | | Multicomponent teacher training (MTT) versus no intervention | | Multicomponent teacher training (MTT) versus teacher training (TT) | |
|---|---|---|---|---|---|---|
| | Mainstream classes | Outside mainstream | Mainstream classes | Outside mainstream | Mainstream classes | Outside mainstream |
| Total no. of trials (total no. of participants) | 1 (52) | 1 (158) | 2 (361) | 1 (158) | 1 (52) | 1 (158) |
| Study ID | BLOOMQUIST 1991 | BARKLEY2000 | BLOOMQUIST1991 BRASWELL1997 | BARKLEY2000 | BLOOMQUIST 1991 | BARKLEY2000 |
| Diagnosis | ADHD (mild to moderate) 35% comorbid with oppositional defiant disorder | Children with ADHD symptoms | ADHD (mild to moderate) 35% comorbid with oppositional defiant disorder Children with hyperactivity | Children with ADHD symptoms | ADHD (mild to moderate) 35% comorbid with oppositional defiant disorder | Children with ADHD symptoms |
| Baseline severity | Conners' Hyperactivity Index: Treatment (TT): 1.57 (0.54) Control: 1.75 (0.47) | CBCL (attention): Treatment (TT): 62.7 (7.4) Control: 58.1 (7.8) | Conners' Hyperactivity Index: Treatment (MTT): 1.70 (0.7) to 1.82 (0.51) Control: 1.70 (0.7) to 1.75 (0.47) | CBCL (attention): Treatment (MTT): 65 (9.7) Control: 58.1(7.8) | Conners' Hyperactivity Index: Treatment (MTT): 1.82 (0.51) Treatment (TT): 1.57 (0.54) | CBCL (attention): Treatment (TT): 62.7 (7.4) Treatment (MTT): 65 (9.7) |

| | 10 weeks | 5 years | 10 weeks to 2 years | 5 years | 10 weeks | 5 years |
|---|---|---|---|---|---|---|
| Treatment length | 10 weeks | 5 years | 10 weeks to 2 years | 5 years | 10 weeks | 5 years |
| Age of subjects | 8.74 years | 4.8 years | 8.74 years 4th grade (mean age not reported) | 4.8 years | 8.74 years | 4.8 years |
| Benefits | | | | | | |
| ADHD core symptoms (teacher-rated) | CTRS (HI): SMD −0.13 (−0.82 to 0.57) Quality: Moderate K = 1, N = 52 | CBCL (attention): SMD −0.30 (−0.75 to 0.15) Quality: Moderate K = 1, N = 158 | CTRS (HI): SMD −0.13 (−0.80 to 0.53) Quality: Low K = 2, N = 361 | CBCL (attention): SMD −0.27 (−0.71 to 0.16) Quality: Moderate K = 1, N = 158 | CTRS (HI): SMD −0.51 (−1.18 to 0.16) Quality: Moderate K = 1, N = 52 | CBCL-Teacher (attention): SMD 0.05 (−0.39 to 0.50) Quality: Moderate K = 1, N = 158 |
| ADHD core symptoms (parent-rated) | – | CBCL (attention): SMD −0.24 (−0.69 to 0.21) Quality: Moderate K = 1, N = 158 | – | CBCL (attention): SMD 0.10 (−0.33 to 0.54) Quality: Moderate K = 1, N = 158 | – | CBCL-Parent (attention): SMD 0.31 (−0.14 to 0.76) Quality: Moderate K = 1, N = 158 |

*Continued*

221

**Table 23:** (*Continued*)

| | Teacher training versus no intervention | | Multicomponent teacher training (MTT) versus no intervention | | Multicomponent teacher training (MTT) versus teacher training (TT) | |
|---|---|---|---|---|---|---|
| | Mainstream classes | Outside mainstream | Mainstream classes | Outside mainstream | Mainstream classes | Outside mainstream |
| Conduct problems (teacher-rated) | Conners (conduct problems): SMD −0.33 (−1.03 to 0.37) Quality: Moderate K = 1, N = 52 | CBCL (aggression): SMD −0.34 (−0.79 to 0.11) Quality: Moderate K = 1, N = 158 | Conners (conduct problems): SMD −0.49 (−1.16 to 0.18) Quality: Moderate K = 1, N = 52 | CBCL (aggression): SMD −0.34 (−0.77 to 0.10) Quality: Moderate K = 1, N = 158 | Conners (conduct problems): SMD −0.09 (−0.75 to 0.56) Quality: Moderate K = 1, N = 52 | CBCL-T (aggression): SMD −0.02 (−0.46 to 0.43) Quality: Moderate K = 1, N = 158 |
| Conduct problems (parent-rated) | – | CBCL (aggression): SMD −0.20 (−0.65 to 0.25) Quality: Moderate K = 1, N = 158 | – | CBCL (aggression): SMD 0.03 (−0.40 to 0.47) Quality: Moderate K = 1, N = 158 | – | CBCL-P (aggression): SMD 0.22 (−0.23 to 0.66) Quality: Moderate N = 1, N = 158 |

*Clinical evidence summary*

*Teacher-training versus no intervention* There were two studies that compared teacher-training with no intervention: BLOOMQUIST1991 was conducted in mainstream classes while BARKLEY2000 was carried out in two special treatment classrooms. The quality of the evidence was moderate. There was a small but not statistically significant effect (SMD −0.33; −1.03 to 0.37) of teacher training in mainstream classes on improving children's conduct problems as rated by teachers. There was little to no effect of teacher training in mainstream classes on children's ADHD core symptoms when compared with no intervention. However, when looking at teacher training in special treatment classrooms there was a small yet not statistically significant effect in reducing both children's ADHD symptoms and conduct problems (SMD range −0.20 to −0.34).

*Multicomponent teacher training versus no intervention* The quality of the evidence of multicomponent teacher training versus no intervention was low to moderate. The effectiveness of multicomponent teacher training in mainstream classes compared with no intervention in improving children's conduct problems (teacher-rated) was small to medium (SMD −0.49; −1.16 to 0.18) but not statistically significant. There was little to no effect of this intervention on reducing children's ADHD core symptoms when compared with no intervention. Multicomponent teacher training carried out in special treatment classes had a small but not statistically significant effect in reducing teacher's reports of children's ADHD core symptoms (SMD −0.27; −0.71 to 0.16) and conduct problems (SMD −0.34; −0.77 to 0.10). There was little to no effect of this intervention on improving parents' ratings of their children's ADHD symptoms or conduct problems. As mentioned previously, the authors of BARKLEY2000 point out that parents' attendance at the training programme was poor and this might explain the lack of effectiveness in their ratings.

*Multicomponent teacher training versus teacher training* The overall quality of the evidence of multicomponent teacher training versus teacher training alone was moderate. This is mainly due to only one study being found that addressed this comparison in mainstream classes and only one study in special treatment classes. There is evidence of a medium but not statistically significant effect of multicomponent teacher training in mainstream classes over teacher training alone in reducing children's ADHD core symptoms as rated by teachers (SMD −0.51; −1.18 to 0.16). There was little to no effect of this comparison in relation to conduct problems. However, when comparing multicomponent teacher training in special treatment classes versus teacher training alone the evidence favoured teacher training alone in improving children's ADHD symptoms and conduct problems as rated by parents (SMD 0.31, 0.22, respectively). Poor attendance by parents at parent-training programmes was reported by authors and could account for the results.

To summarise, there is some evidence that teacher-training and multicomponent teacher-training involving parent training and child interventions have a small effect in improving the behaviour of children with ADHD. Because of the lack of statistical significance of all these results, the findings are inconclusive.

### 8.5.6    Children with suspected ADHD in the context of disordered conduct

TA102 (NICE, 2006a) examined the impact of parent training on children with various conduct problems. Given the large percentage of children with ADHD symptoms and hyperactivity in conduct disordered populations, the GDG decided it would be appropriate that, for children suspected of ADHD in the context of conduct disorder in the educational setting, their parents should have access to parent-training/education programmes.

## 8.6    FROM EVIDENCE TO RECOMMENDATIONS

There is no evidence to indicate that universal screening or teacher advice for children with ADHD have beneficial effects on ADHD core symptoms and conduct problems.

The evidence indicates that teacher-led interventions, such as giving effective commands, have large beneficial effects on conduct problems of children with ADHD.

The beneficial effects of teacher training on children with ADHD remain inconclusive.

## 8.7    RECOMMENDATIONS

8.7.1.1    Universal screening for ADHD should not be undertaken in nursery, primary and secondary schools.

8.7.1.2    The Department for Children, Schools and Families should consider providing more education to trainee teachers about ADHD by working with the Training and Development Agency for Schools (TDA) and relevant health service organisations to produce training programmes and guidance for supporting children with ADHD.

8.7.1.3    When a child or young person with disordered conduct and suspected ADHD is referred to a school's special educational needs coordinator (SENCO), the SENCO, in addition to helping the child with their behaviour, should inform the parents about local parent-training/education programmes.

8.7.1.4    Following a diagnosis of ADHD in a child of pre-school age, healthcare professionals should, with the parent or carer's consent, contact the child's nursery or pre-school teacher to explain:
● the diagnosis and severity of symptoms and impairment
● the care plan
● any special educational needs.

8.7.1.5    Following a diagnosis of ADHD in a school-age child or young person healthcare professionals should, with the parents' or carers' consent, contact the child or young person's teacher to explain:
● the diagnosis and severity of symptoms and impairment
● the care plan
● any special educational needs.

8.7.1.6    Following a diagnosis of severe ADHD in a school-age child or young
           person healthcare professionals should, with the parents' or carers'
           consent, contact the child or young person's teacher to explain:
           ● the diagnosis and severity of symptoms and impairment
           ● the care plan
           ● any special educational needs.
8.7.1.7    Teachers who have received training about ADHD and its management
           should provide behavioural interventions in the classroom to help children
           and young people with ADHD. (Key priority)


## 8.8       RESEARCH RECOMMENDATIONS

8.8.1.1    Effect of providing training in behavioural management of ADHD for
           teachers
           ● Does the training of teachers in behavioural management of children
             with ADHD in primary and secondary schools improve ADHD symp-
             toms and academic attainment, the teacher's experience of stress in the
             classroom and the impact of ADHD on other pupils when compared
             with current education methods? This would be best conducted as a
             randomised trial.
           ● Why this is important: Secondary school is typically a different envi-
             ronment from primary school, particularly in terms of organisation of
             the daily timetable and expectations of the increasing independence of
             pupils. These factors may have an adverse impact on young people
             with ADHD, but the effect of understanding and modifying the impact
             has not yet been researched. The potential for teachers to take a more
             active role in the behavioural management of primary and secondary
             school children with ADHD shows some significant promise in at least
             one trial. The benefits of examining primary and secondary education,
             compared with education as usual, and examining the broader impact
             on the child, the teacher and the wider classroom, would significantly
             improve future versions of this guideline.
8.8.1.2    The effectiveness of interventions for each subtype of ADHD
           ● Do educational interventions delivered in primary and secondary
             schools differ in their effectiveness for each subtype of ADHD? Could
             interventions intended to improve behavioural, academic and attitudi-
             nal outcomes be more effectively tailored to each subtype?
           ● Why this is important: Inattention is particularly associated with
             academic underachievement. Hyperactivity and impulsivity have less
             of a negative impact but impulsivity can be a problem in the classroom.
             Children with predominantly inattentive behaviour may respond
             differently to interventions from children who are diagnosed with the
             predominantly hyperactive/impulsive or combined subtypes of ADHD.

There is a dearth of randomised trials into the effectiveness of interventions to help children with ADHD succeed in the classroom, particularly in England, and the effectiveness of those that are available is not reported by subtype.

8.8.1.3 The identification in schools of children with problems related to ADHD and referral for assessment

- Does raising teachers' awareness of identifying children with ADHD symptoms in the classroom lead to quicker referral, diagnosis and implementation of support packages, and ultimately improve behavioural, academic and attitudinal outcomes?

- Why this is important: Children spend a significant proportion of their time in school and their teachers are well placed to identify individuals with ADHD symptoms. While universal screening of the school population is not recommended, teachers may benefit from receiving some training to help them spot children who are suspected of having ADHD in order to initiate referrals and to implement support packages at the earliest possible stage. This has been researched on a modest scale in England and outcomes have been positive, therefore it is suggested that further work is carried out.

# 9.    DIETARY INTERVENTIONS

## 9.1    INTRODUCTION

Dietary interventions in the treatment of ADHD have been widely used and take the form of supplementation with substances thought to be deficient or exclusion of substances thought to be harmful. Research, however, has encountered many difficulties of methodology and feasibility: changes in food and drink are subject to many confounding influences, are difficult to disguise in controlled trials and may be hard to comply with. Trials often fail to meet the usual criteria of quality for these reasons, or because of poor reporting of methodological details, because of very small numbers, or because most of the studies are based on non-ADHD samples. Furthermore, most of the trial evidence is based on crossover studies that do not lend themselves to a quantitative methodology, especially when pre-crossover scores are not provided. Therefore a narrative, rather than a systematic, approach has been taken for this topic, and any conclusions are correspondingly tentative.

## 9.2    ELIMINATION DIETS

Elimination diets were introduced with the 'Feingold theory' that implicated artificial colourings, preservatives and cross-reacting natural salicylates in a variety of illnesses including ADHD (Feingold, 1985). Public concern led to several trials being conducted. At present the Feingold diet is not part of conventional management of ADHD.

Multiple idiosyncratic reactions to food and drink have been alleged to lead to hyperactive behaviour (McCann *et al.*, 2007). The notion is that susceptible children can each be affected by one or more substances triggering adverse reactions. Therefore the intervention aims to discover and eliminate from the diet the substances individually implicated for each child.

### 9.2.1    Elimination of tartrazine and other artificial colourants
and preservatives

Several trials have addressed multiple idiosyncratic reactions to food, focusing either on tartrazine, or on mixed additives, or on a range of potentially harmful substances that can vary from child to child. Conners and colleagues (1976) found a significant difference between a 'Feingold diet' (excluding artificial additives and natural salicylates) and a 'placebo' diet; but the generalisability was limited by unexplained order effects and by doubts over whether there was adequate disguise of the treatment allocation. Harley and colleagues (1978) reported a similar comparison, with enhanced measures to preserve the disguise, and found no consistent effects. Williams and colleagues (1978) used a crossover design to compare the elimination of additives, methylphenidate, and placebo in a group of 26 children who were known to be responders to stimulant medication. They found that the diet was superior to 'placebo' but inferior to medication. By contrast, Levy and colleagues (1978) and Mattes and Gittelman (1981) found no differences between additives and placebo in double-blind crossover designs in small groups of hyperactive children.

### 9.2.2 Elimination of individually identified food substances

Four published studies have used randomised trial designs to examine the possibility that individual children with ADHD may be adversely affected by foodstuffs that would not influence the behaviour of most children with ADHD.

Two studies (Egger *et al.*, 1985; Carter *et al.*, 1993) have used open trials to identify the foods that affected individual children, and then introduce those identified substances in double-blind crossover design. The incriminated foods varied substantially between children, and included natural foods (for example, cows' milk, wheat flour, citrus fruit, eggs) as well as artificial colourings and preservatives. Both studies indicated that the results of the open trial could be replicated in a double-blind design: some children were helped by individually designed elimination diets, at least in the short term. One of the studies suggested that children's responsiveness to incriminated foods was predicted by parents' informal observations (Carter *et al.*, 1993).

Two studies (Kaplan *et al.*, 1989; Schmidt *et al.*, 1997) have randomly allocated young people to a diet excluding the commonest provoking substances or a 'normal' diet. Both are limited by small numbers, and one (Schmidt *et al.*, 1997) by an inpatient sample; but both have reported the superiority of the elimination diet.

There are also potential adverse effects to consider in elimination regimes. They are potentially difficult for families to manage, and might lead to unbalanced diets and nutritional problems; the issue has not been satisfactorily addressed by trials. Good clinical practice suggests that such diets should be embarked on with professional advice and subject to clinical assessment of the child's needs.

### 9.3 SUPPLEMENTATION DIETS

After a preliminary review of studies on supplementation diets, those using fatty acids were selected as the most promising.

### 9.3.1 Fatty acids

Long-chain polyunsaturated fatty acids (PUFA) are used for many purposes, including the development of nerve cells and their membranes (see Chapter 2). A deficiency could result either from a restricted diet or from an increased metabolic need. Omega-3 and omega-6 PUFA differ in their chemical structure and potentially in their physiological effects. Different commercial preparations have different proportions of PUFAs.

A few comparisons of fatty acid supplementation have been reported, but for the most part have not met the quality criteria for systematic review. One exception comes from Stevens and colleagues (2003) who randomised 47 children to receive either a proprietary preparation of PUFA or an olive oil placebo. The analysis suggested a small or absent effect: out of ten primary outcome measures, just one (teacher-rated attention) showed a statistically significant difference between PUFA and placebo, and the finding would not have reached significance had allowance not been made for the number of comparisons.

Earlier RCTs did not find benefit from evening primrose oil (providing omega-6 rather than omega-3 PUFA) (Aman *et al.*, 1987). Their generalisability, however, was limited by the short treatment period (1 month only), which might not have allowed time for the effects of the supplement on brain function.

More recent investigations have considered omega-3 PUFA more specifically. Randomised trials in the US (Voigt *et al.*, 2001) and Japan (Hirayama *et al.*, 2004) have found, respectively, no difference compared with placebo, or differences only in a small number of a wide variety of outcome measures.

Some trials have described behavioural improvements with PUFA supplements in children with other learning difficulties (Richardson & Puri, 2002) or developmental coordination disorder (Richardson & Montgomery, 2005), but are not considered further here as they were not carried out on children with diagnosed ADHD. Other trials on ADHD have not yet reported their results.

### 9.3.2    Clinical evidence summary

The quality of the evidence for dietary interventions is generally poor, reflecting the paucity of the data.

The evidence that elimination or supplementation diets when compared with placebo may reduce ADHD symptoms is inconclusive.

### 9.4    RECOMMENDATIONS

9.4.1.1    Healthcare professionals should stress the value of a balanced diet, good nutrition and regular exercise for children, young people and adults with ADHD.

9.4.1.2    The elimination of artificial colouring and additives from the diet is not recommended as a generally applicable treatment for children and young people with ADHD.

9.4.1.3    Clinical assessment of ADHD in children and young people should include asking about foods or drinks that appear to influence their hyperactive behaviour. If there is a clear link, healthcare professionals should advise parents or carers to keep a diary of food and drinks taken and ADHD behaviour. If the diary supports a relationship between specific foods and drinks and behaviour, then referral to a dietitian should be offered. Further management (for example, specific dietary elimination) should be jointly undertaken by the dietitian, mental health specialist or paediatrician, and the parent or carer and child or young person.

9.4.1.4    Dietary fatty acid supplementation is not recommended for the treatment of ADHD in children and young people.

# 10. PHARMACOLOGICAL TREATMENT

## 10.1 INTRODUCTION

The aim of this chapter is to produce evidence-based recommendations to guide the pharmacological management of children, young people and adults with ADHD.

It is over 70 years since the serendipitous observation that stimulant drugs can improve hyperactive behaviour in children (Bradley, 1937). The IR stimulant medications methylphenidate and dexamfetamine have been available since 1955 in the US. From the mid-1990s the level of drug prescribing for ADHD has increased markedly in the UK, coinciding initially with changes in the regulatory framework and more recently with the introduction of MR (once-daily) methylphenidate preparations (Concerta XL®, Equasym XL®, Medikinet XL®) and the non-stimulant atomoxetine (Strattera®). Other drugs used less commonly to treat ADHD and which are not approved for the treatment of ADHD include clonidine, bupropion, modafinil, imipramine, risperidone and nicotine patches.

Despite a large literature supporting the short-term benefits of stimulant medication in children with ADHD (Spencer *et al.*, 1996), uncertainty still surrounds the balance of risks and benefits of long-term drug treatment (Poulton, 2006). Little empirical evidence is available to guide clinicians on questions such as the optimum duration of treatment, when it is appropriate to consider drug discontinuation and how and when to combine pharmacological and psychological treatments. Furthermore, the increasing use of stimulants in clinical practice has raised concerns about the potential for stimulant drug misuse and diversion. Finally, important clinical questions also relate to the balance of risks and benefits of ADHD drug treatment in less well-studied groups including pre-school children, adults and those with coexisting mental health problems or learning disabilities.

This chapter incorporates the recommendations produced by the TA on *Methylphenidate, atomoxetine and dexamfetamine for the treatment of attention deficit hyperactivity disorder in children and adolescents* (NICE, 2006b). The GDG did not undertake any fresh analyses examining the data supporting the TA. Recommendations derived from the TA have therefore been incorporated in their entirety. The GDG has undertaken all other analyses relating to the use of these and other drugs and have, therefore, extended and contextualised the recommendations in the TA to produce a more detailed and focused guidance. The full set of integrated recommendations can be found in Section 10.18.

## 10.2 PRESCRIBING FOR CHILDREN, YOUNG PEOPLE AND ADULTS

In the UK, methylphenidate and atomoxetine are licensed for the treatment of ADHD (hyperkinetic disorders) in children aged 6 years and older while dexamfetamine is licensed for children from age 3 years. Methylphenidate and dexamfetamine are not currently licensed for the treatment of ADHD in adults, although dexamfetamine is licensed for the treatment of narcolepsy. Atomoxetine is licensed for the continued treatment of ADHD in adults when treatment was initiated in childhood.

Other less frequently used drugs such as clonidine, bupropion, modafinil, imipramine, risperidone and nicotine patches are not licensed for the treatment of ADHD. However there is some clinical experience of their use in young people with ADHD, particularly those with coexisting conditions.

In 2000, the Royal College of Paediatrics and Child Health issued a policy statement on the use of unlicensed medicines, or the use of licensed medicines for unlicensed applications, in children and young people. This stated clearly that such use is necessary in paediatric practice and that doctors are legally allowed to prescribe unlicensed medicines where there are no suitable alternatives and where the use is justified by a responsible body of professional opinion (Joint Royal College of Paediatrics and Child Health/Neonatal and Paediatric Pharmacists Group Standing Committee on Medicines, 2000). Similar considerations apply in licensed use of medicines in adults.

## 10.3    THE REGULATORY FRAMEWORK

Methylphenidate has been used for over 50 years for the treatment of ADHD. Ritalin® (Novartis Pharmaceuticals UK), an IR form of methylphenidate was only available in the UK on a named-patient basis until April 1995 when it was licensed under the trade name Ritalin as a Class B Schedule 2 Prescription-Only Medicine. Subsequently, other IR preparations such as Equasym and generic methylphenidate have been made available. These immediate-release preparations are licensed as part of a comprehensive treatment programme for ADHD in children aged 6 years and older.

In 1999, the Committee on Safety of Medicines (CSM) were informed that concern had been raised about a recent rise in prescribing of methylphenidate, which may increase the potential for misuse of this drug. The committee noted the rise in prescribing but were informed that there had been an increase in the diagnosis of ADHD and so a corresponding increase in prescribing was to be expected. The CSM's Subcommittee on Pharmacovigilance proposed that the patient information leaflet might also include the advice that methylphenidate should only be used under the supervision of a specialist.

In 2005 the US Food and Drug Administration (FDA) reviewed data from the FDA's Adverse Event Reporting System (AERS) database and identified 12 cases of sudden death in paediatric patients who were being treated with Adderall and Adderall XR (mixed amphetamine salts). Of these cases, five occurred in patients with undiagnosed underlying structural heart defects (abnormal arteries or valves, abnormally thickened walls, and so on), which are all conditions that increase the risk for sudden death. Several of the remaining cases presented problems of interpretation, including: a family history of ventricular arrhythmia; association of death with heat exhaustion; dehydration and near-drowning; very rigorous exercise; fatty liver;

heart attack; and type 1 diabetes mellitus. One case was reported 3 to 4 years after the event and another had above-toxic blood levels of amphetamine. The duration of treatment varied from 1 day to 8 years (http://www.fda.gov/cder/drug/InfoSheets/ HCP/AdderallHCPSheet.pdf).

Subsequently, the FDA reviewed reports of serious cardiovascular adverse events in patients taking usual doses of ADHD products (stimulants plus atomoxetine) that revealed 17 sudden death cases (16 with Adderall, one with dexamfetamine) including some patients with underlying serious heart problems or defects, and reports of stroke and heart attack in adults with certain risk factors. Furthermore, the FDA review of ADHD medicines revealed a slight increased risk (about 1 per 1000) for drug-related psychiatric adverse events, such as hearing voices, becoming suspicious for no reason, or becoming manic, even in patients who did not have previous psychiatric problems. In February 2007, the FDA directed the manufacturers of all drug products approved for the treatment of ADHD to develop 'Patient Medication Guides'[19] to alert patients to possible cardiovascular risks and risks of adverse psychiatric symptoms associated with the medicines, and to advise them of precautions that can be taken (http://www.fda.gov/cder/drug/infopage/ADHD/default.htm). Adderall is not licensed in the UK.

Subsequent analysis did not suggest that the sudden death rate associated with stimulants was higher than the base rate in the population; however, the FDA was unable to draw firm conclusions because of the deficiency of the spontaneous reporting system data and inaccurate estimation of the exposure data. Consequently, the FDA has initiated a large-scale study to investigate the association of sudden death and ADHD treatment, which was still on-going when this guideline was being prepared in 2007.

*Atomoxetine*
On 15 September 2005 the Medicines and Healthcare Products Regulatory Agency (MHRA) was informed by the marketing authorisation holder for atomoxetine (Eli Lilly) that clinical trial data had identified a statistically significant increased risk of suicidal thoughts with atomoxetine compared with placebo in children with ADHD. On discussion with the CSM it was agreed that these new data warranted a full risk–benefit evaluation of atomoxetine in its licensed indications, particularly in light of previous concerns about its safety profile including serious hepatic reactions and seizures.

The Pharmacovigilance Working Party of the Committee for Medicinal Products for Human Use (CHMP) considered safety of atomoxetine in January 2006 and advised that the overall balance of risks and benefits of atomoxetine remained positive in its licensed indication but recommended that the amendments to the product information included the potential risk of seizures and QT prolongation.

---

[19]Patient Medication Guides are handouts given to patients, families and caregivers when a medicine is dispensed. The guides contain FDA-approved patient information that could help prevent serious adverse events.

## 10.4 DATABASES SEARCHED AND INCLUSION/EXCLUSION CRITERIA FOR CLINICAL EVIDENCE

Information about the databases searched and the inclusion/exclusion criteria used for this section of the guideline can be found in Table 24.

## 10.5 STUDIES CONSIDERED IN THE SYSTEMATIC REVIEW OF CLINICAL EVIDENCE[20]

The review team conducted a new systematic search for RCTs that assessed the efficacy and/or safety of pharmacological treatments for children, young people and adults with ADHD.

A total of 49 trials relating to clinical evidence met the eligibility criteria set by the GDG, providing data on 7500 participants. All trials were published in peer-reviewed journals between 1976 and 2007. In addition, 537 studies were excluded from the analysis, the most common reason for exclusion was the lack of validated outcome measures (as agreed to by the GDG) (further information about both included and excluded studies can be found in Appendix 17).

**Table 24: Databases searched and inclusion/exclusion criteria for clinical evidence**

| Electronic databases | CENTRAL, MEDLINE, EMBASE, CINAHL, PsycINFO |
|---|---|
| Date searched | Database inception to April 2006; table of contents December 2007 |
| Study design | RCT (efficacy, acceptability, tolerability, adverse events) Observational study (long-term adverse events) |
| Patient population | Participants (all ages) diagnosed with ADHD |
| Interventions | Methylphenidate (including MR preparations); dexamfetamine; atomoxetine; tricyclic antidepressants (TCAs); bupropion; nicotine (as skin patches); atypical antipsychotics; modafinil; clonidine |
| Outcomes | Improvement on ADHD symptoms (teacher-rated and parent-rated); improvement on conduct problems (teacher-rated and parent-rated); clinical improvement (clinician-rated); adverse events; leaving study early due to adverse events; leaving study early due to any reason |

---

[20]Here and elsewhere in the guideline, each study considered for review is referred to by a study ID (primary author and date of study publication, except where a study is *in press* or only submitted for publication, then a date is not used).

234

## 10.6     METHYLPHENIDATE (STIMULANT)

### 10.6.1     Pharmacology and prescribing

Methylphenidate is a CNS stimulant. While the mechanism by which it reduces symptoms in ADHD is not completely clear, it is believed that it increases intrasynaptic concentrations of dopamine and noradrenaline in the frontal cortex as well as subcortical brain regions associated with motivation and reward (Volkow *et al.*, 2004). Methylphenidate blocks the presynaptic membrane dopamine transporter (DAT) and thereby inhibits the reuptake of dopamine and noradrenaline into the presynaptic neuron.

Methylphenidate is rapidly and almost completely absorbed. Owing to its pronounced first-pass metabolism the absolute bioavailability is low at only 30% (11–51%) of the dose. Maximum plasma concentrations are reached on average 1–2 hours after administration of 10 mg of IR preparation. The maximum plasma concentrations vary considerably between individuals. The relatively short half-life correlates well with the duration of action of 1 to 4 hours for IR preparations. Therefore a twice or three times daily dose is needed. MR preparations have been developed to give longer duration of action following a single dose: Concerta XL (approximately 12 hours), Medikinet XL and Equasym XL (approximately 8 hours). The IR formulation is normally started at a dose of 5 mg twice, or three times, daily (every 4 hours) at breakfast, lunchtime and late afternoon/early evening. Dosage and frequency can be titrated according to symptom response to a maximum recommended daily dose of 60 mg.

With a short duration of action of approximately 4 hours, some patients find the effects of the dose diminish in the evening requiring an additional smaller dose, although a balance needs to be achieved as methylphenidate can cause insomnia.

This multiple dosage regimen also brings with it other difficulties such as the administration of medication at school, which causes problems such as storage of a controlled drug, timing of doses and stigmatisation of the child having to take medication in front of peers. These considerations led to the development of sustained or modified-release preparations of methylphenidate: Concerta XL, Equasym XL and Medikinet XL. These medications are taken once daily in the morning (although clinical need may require twice-daily dosing) resulting in an initial release of medication similar to the IR formulation followed by a gradual release over 8 to 12 hours.

### 10.6.2     Safety and adverse effects

The common adverse effects of methylphenidate include decreased appetite, sleep disturbance, headaches, stomach aches, drowsiness, irritability, tearfulness, mildly increased blood pressure and pulse (Wolraich *et al.*, 2007). Rare but more severe adverse events can include psychotic symptoms and sensitivity reactions requiring discontinuation of the medication.

*Pharmacological treatment*

*Weight and growth*
While there remains some conflicting evidence regarding weight and growth in children receiving methylphenidate (Bereket *et al.*, 2005; Poulton, 2006), a significant decrease in appetite can lead to a decrease in expected growth during the active period of drug treatment (MTA Co-operative Group, 2004b; Swanson *et al.*, 2007). Suppression of growth and height may be dose related (Barkley, 1990b). It is unclear whether final adult height is affected (Poulton, 2006).

*Tics*
There remains controversy regarding the association of methylphenidate and tics. In a study of children with Tourette's syndrome, tics increased only with high doses of stimulant medication and were observed to diminish over time in some of those treated with methylphenidate (Castellanos *et al.*, 1997). Other studies have found no association between methylphenidate and exacerbations of tics (Gadow *et al.*, 1999).

*Pulse and blood pressure*
Research regarding the effect of methylphenidate on blood pressure has indicated a small but clinically non-significant effect (average increase <5 mmHg) from methylphenidate on blood pressure in short-term use (Findling *et al.*, 2001) with a slight increase in pulse rate (average <5 bpm) (Brown *et al.*, 1984). The research on ambulatory blood pressure monitoring of boys who had been receiving the medication for at least 2 months (Stowe *et al.*, 2002) indicated statistically significant increases in systolic and diastolic blood pressure when the child was awake and a decrease in sleep.

*Seizures*
The possibility of methylphenidate lowering the seizure threshold for those with epilepsy has been investigated in recent studies in those patients whose seizures were under control. These studies did not find an increase in seizures (Feldman *et al.*, 1989; Gross-Tsur *et al.*, 1997). It is noted in the literature that patients with seizures are generally excluded from the majority of studies regarding treatment for ADHD (Hemmer *et al.*, 2001).

### 10.6.3    Clinical evidence for methylphenidate

Of the 49 included trials, there were 18 involving a comparison of methylphenidate with placebo or waitlist control. Of these, one trial involved pre-school children, 14 involved school-age children, and three were of an adult population. In all trials, the participants had been diagnosed with ADHD (common coexisting conditions included conduct disorder and oppositional defiant disorder in the population of school-age children and mood, anxiety and psychiatric disorders in the adult population; see Table 25 for the full list of coexisting conditions). One trial (KUPIETZ1998) recruited children with ADHD and comorbid developmental reading disorder. One study of school-age children (BROWN1985) compared methylphenidate with a waitlist control while the other trials used placebo as a comparator (see Table 25).

236

Table 25: Study information and evidence summary table for trials of methylphenidate

| | In pre-school children | In school-age children | | | In adults |
|---|---|---|---|---|---|
| | | Methylphenidate versus placebo | | Methylphenidate versus waitlist | Methylphenidate versus placebo |
| | Mixed comorbidity | Mixed comorbidity | Specific comorbidity (developmental reading disorder) | Mixed comorbidity | Mixed comorbidity |
| Total no. of trials (total no. of participants) | 1 (114) | 12 (1582) | 1 (58) | 1 (20) | 3 (340) |
| Study ID | KOLLINS2006 | BUTTER1983 CONNERS1980 FINDLING2006 GITTELMANKLEIN1976A GREENHILL2002 GREENHILL2006 IALONGO1994 KOLLINS2006 KURLAN2002 LERER1977 PLISZKA2000 WILENS2006 | KUPIETZ1988 | BROWN1985 | BIEDERMAN2006A KOOIJ2004 SPENCER2005 |
| Diagnosis | ADHD | ADD with hyperkinesis, ADHD, hyperkinetic | ADD with hyperactivity and | ADHD symptoms | ADHD (common coexisting conditions: mood, |

*Continued*

237

Table 25: (*Continued*)

| | In pre-school children | In school-age children | | | In adults |
| --- | --- | --- | --- | --- | --- |
| | | Methylphenidate versus placebo | | Methylphenidate versus waitlist | Methylphenidate versus placebo |
| | Mixed comorbidity | Mixed comorbidity | Specific comorbidity (developmental reading disorder) | Mixed comorbidity | Mixed comorbidity |
| | | disorder, hyperkinetic reaction of childhood, MBD (common coexisting conditions: oppositional defiant disorder and/or conduct disorder) | developmental reading disorder | | anxiety and psychiatric disorders [treated] |
| Baseline severity (mean range) | CPRS: 35.48 (8.85) | CRS range: 35.48 to 42.05 | CPRS: 20.55 (4.69) | CTRS (Abbrev): 18.55 (4.30) | ADHD-RS: 69.7 |
| Dose | 14.2 (8.1) mg/day | Low: ≤0.4 mg/kg/day Medium: > 0.4 > 0.8 mg/ kg/day High: ≥0.8 mg/kg/day | Low: 0.3 mg/kg Medium: 0.5 mg/kg High: 0.7 mg/kg | 0.3 mg/kg/day | Medium: 0.5 to 0.75 mg/kg/day High: 80.9 mg/kg/day |
| Treatment length (mean range) | 28 days | 7–112 days | 196 days | 84 days | 21–42 days |

*Continued*

| *Benefits* | | | | | |
|---|---|---|---|---|---|
| ADHD core symptoms (mean at endpoint) (teacher-rated) | – | Various measures: Low dose: SMD –0.40 (–0.95 to 0.15) Quality: High K = 2, N = 78 High dose: SMD –0.84 (–1.06 to –0.62) Quality: High K = 5, N = 806 | CTRS (hyperactivity): Low dose: SMD –1.61 (–2.69 to –0.53) Quality: High K = 1, N = 58 Medium dose: SMD –1.35 (–2.29 to –0.40) Quality: High K = 1, N = 58 High dose: SMD –2.37 (–3.54 to –1.20) Quality: High K = 1, N = 58 | CTRS: SMD –111 (–2.07 to –0.15) Quality: High K = 1, N = 20 | – |
| ADHD core symptoms (mean change) (teacher-rated) | – | CATQ: Medium dose: SMD –1.69 (–2.24 to –1.14) Quality: High K = 1, N = 136 | – | – | – |
| ADHD core symptoms (mean at | – | CPRS: Low dose: SMD 0.66 (–0.06 to 1.37) | – | CPRS: SMD –1.29 (–2.27 to –0.3) | – |

**Table 25:** (*Continued*)

| | In pre-school children | In school-age children | | | | In adults |
|---|---|---|---|---|---|---|
| | | Methylphenidate versus placebo | | | Methylphenidate versus waitlist | Methylphenidate versus placebo |
| | Mixed comorbidity | Mixed comorbidity | Specific comorbidity (developmental reading disorder) | | Mixed comorbidity | Mixed comorbidity |
| endpoint) (parent-rated) | | Quality: high K = 1, N = 48 High dose: SMD −0.79 (−1.14 to −0.45) Quality: High K = 4, N = 747 | | | Quality: Moderate K = 1, N = 20 | |
| ADHD core symptoms (mean change) (parent-rated) | – | Various measures: Medium dose: SMD −1.34 (−3.26 to 0.58) Quality: High K = 2, N = 186 | – | | – | – |
| ADHD core symptoms (mean at endpoint) (investigator-rated) | – | – | – | | – | AISRS: High dose: SMD −1.40 (−1.80 to −1.01) Quality: Moderate K = 1, N = 146 |

| | | | | | ADHD-RS (total): Medium dose: SMD −0.29 (−0.88 to 0.30) Quality: Moderate K = 1, N = 45 |
|---|---|---|---|---|---|
| ADHD core symptoms (mean at endpoint) (self-report) | — | — | — | — | — |
| Conduct problems (mean at endpoint) (teacher-rated) | — | Various measures: Low dose: SMD −0.43 (−1.13 to 0.27) Quality: Moderate K = 1, N = 48 High dose: SMD −0.58 (−0.84 to −0.31) Quality: High K = 4, N = 485 | — | — | — |
| Conduct problems (mean change) (teacher-rated) | — | IOWA (oppositional/defiant): Medium dose: SMD −1.21 (−1.72 to −0.71) Quality: High K = 1, N = 136 | — | — | — |
| Conduct problems (mean at endpoint) (parent-rated) | — | Various measures: High dose: SMD −0.73 (−1.06 to −0.41) Quality: High K = 2, N = 378 | — | — | — |

Continued

**Table 25:** (*Continued*)

| | In pre-school children | In school-age children | | In adults | |
| | | Methylphenidate versus placebo | | Methylphenidate versus waitlist | Methylphenidate versus placebo |
|---|---|---|---|---|---|
| | Mixed comorbidity | Mixed comorbidity | Specific comorbidity (developmental reading disorder) | Mixed comorbidity | Mixed comorbidity |
| Clinical improvement (clinician-rated) | – | Various measures: Medium dose: RR 3.08 (1.40 to 6.78) Quality: High K = 2, N = 186 High dose: RR 1.81 (1.46 to 2.24) Quality: High K = 5, N = 823 | – | – | AISRS 50% decrease: High dose: RR 2.16 (1.46 to 3.20) Quality: High K = 1, N = 149 |
| Clinical improvement (parent and teacher) | SNAP: RR 1.61 (0.70 to 3.74) Quality: Moderate K = 1, N = 114 | – | – | – | – |

Continued

| Harms | | | | | |
|---|---|---|---|---|---|
| Insomnia | – | High dose: NNTH 12 (7 to 33) Quality: High K = 3, N = 318 | | – | High dose: NNTH 7 (4 to 50) Quality: High K = 1, K = 149 |
| Anorexia | – | High dose: NNTH 16 (11 to 50) Quality: High K = 4, N = 634 | | – | – |
| Increased crying | – | High dose: NNTH 3 (NNTH 1 to ∞ to NNTB 50) Quality: Moderate K = 1, N = 1 | | – | – |
| Increased irritability | – | High dose: NNTH 14 (NNTH 4 to ∞ to NNTB 16) Quality: Moderate K = 2, N = 119 | | – | – |
| Moodiness | – | High dose: NNTH 16 (NNTH 8 to ∞ to NNTB 100) Quality: High K = 2, N = 141 | | – | High dose: NNTH 100 (NNTH 20 to ∞ to NNTB 50) Quality: Moderate K = 1, N = 149 |
| Thirst | – | High dose: NNTH 20 (NNTH 5 to ∞ to NNTB 13) | | – | High dose: NNTH 3 (2 to 6) |

**Table 25:** (*Continued*)

| | In pre-school children | In school-age children | | | In adults |
| --- | --- | --- | --- | --- | --- |
| | | Methylphenidate versus placebo | | Methylphenidate versus waitlist | Methylphenidate versus placebo |
| | Mixed comorbidity | Mixed comorbidity | Specific comorbidity (developmental reading disorder) | Mixed comorbidity | Mixed comorbidity |
| | | Quality: Moderate K = 1, N = 41 | | | Quality: High K = 1, N = 149 |
| Itching | – | High dose: NNTH 10 (NNTH 4 to ∞ to NNTB 20) Quality: Moderate K = 1, N = 41 | – | – | – |
| Diarrhoea | – | High dose: NNTH 50 (NNTH 20 to ∞ to NNTB 100) Quality: High K = 3, N = 318 | – | – | – |
| Palpitations | – | High dose: NNTH 20 (NNTH 5 to ∞ to NNTB 13) Quality: Moderate K = 1, N = 41 | – | – | – |

| | | | | |
|---|---|---|---|---|
| Stuttering | High dose: NNTH 20 (NNTH 5 to ∞ to NNTB 13) Quality: Moderate K = 1, N = 41 | – | – | – |
| Negativism | High dose: NNTH 20 (NNTH 5 to ∞ to NNTB 13) Quality: Moderate K = 1, N = 41 | – | – | – |
| Reddened eyes | High dose: NNTH 20 (NNTH 5 to ∞ to NNTB 13) Quality: Moderate K = 1, N = 41 | – | – | – |
| Incoherent speech | High dose: NNTH 20 (NNTH 5 to ∞ to NNTB 13) Quality: Moderate K = 1, N = 41 | – | – | – |
| 7% decrease in bodyweight | High dose: NNTH 9 (5 to 50) Quality: Moderate K = 1, N = 100 | – | – | – |
| Decreased appetite | High dose: NNTH 9 (5 to 50) Quality: Moderate K = 1, N = 59 | – | – | High dose: NNTH 3 (2 to 5) Quality: High K = 1, N = 149 |

*Continued*

**Table 25:** (*Continued*)

| | In pre-school children | In school-age children | | | In adults |
|---|---|---|---|---|---|
| | | Methylphenidate versus placebo | | Methylphenidate versus waitlist | Methylphenidate versus placebo |
| | Mixed comorbidity | Mixed comorbidity | Specific comorbidity (developmental reading disorder) | Mixed comorbidity | Mixed comorbidity |
| Gastrointestinal problems | – | – | – | – | High dose: NNTH 6 (2 to 6) Quality: High K = 1, N = 149 |
| Tension | – | – | – | – | High dose: NNTH 5 (3 to 11) Quality: High K = 1, N = 149 |
| Cardiovascular complaints | – | – | – | – | High dose: NNTH 12 (6 to ∞) Quality: Moderate K = 1, N = 149 |
| Depression | – | – | – | – | High dose: NNTH 14 (7 to 100) |

| | | | | |
|---|---|---|---|---|
| Dizziness | – | – | – | High dose: NNTH 14 (7 to 100) Quality: Moderate K = 1, N = 149 |
| Anxiety | – | – | – | High dose: NNTH 16 (8 to ∞) Quality: Moderate K = 1, N = 149 |
| Autonomic symptoms | – | – | – | High dose: NNTH 33 (NNTH 11 to ∞ to NNTB 50) Quality: Moderate K = 1, N = 149 |
| Increased energy | – | – | – | High dose: NNTH 33 (NNTH 11 to ∞ to NNTB 50) Quality: Moderate K = 1, N = 149 |
| Tics | – | – | – | High dose: NNTH 33 (NNTH 12 to ∞ to NNTB 50) Quality: Moderate K = 1, N = 149 |
| | | | | Quality: Moderate K = 1, N = 149 |

*Continued*

**Table 25:** (*Continued*)

| | In pre-school children | In school-age children | | | In adults |
| --- | --- | --- | --- | --- | --- |
| | Mixed comorbidity | Methylphenidate versus placebo | | Methylphenidate versus waitlist | Methylphenidate versus placebo |
| | | Mixed comorbidity | Specific comorbidity (developmental reading disorder) | Mixed comorbidity | Mixed comorbidity |
| Skin problems | – | – | – | – | High dose: NNTH 100 (NNTH 20 to ∞ to NNTB 50) Quality: Moderate K = 1, N = 149 |
| Easy bruising | – | – | – | – | High dose: NNTH 100 (NNTH 20 to ∞ to NNTB 50) Quality: Moderate K = 1, N = 149 |
| Sexual problems | – | – | – | – | High dose: NNTH 100 (NNTH 20 to ∞ to NNTB 50) |

248

| | | | | | |
|---|---|---|---|---|---|
| | | | | | Quality: Moderate<br>K = 1, N = 149 |
| Leaving study early due to adverse events | – | Low dose: not estimable<br>Quality: High<br>K = 1, N = 30<br>Medium dose: NNTB 100 (NNTB 25 to ∞ to NNTH 50)<br>Quality: High<br>K = 2, N = 186<br>High dose: ∞ (∞ to NNTH 33)<br>Quality: High<br>K = 2, N = 424 | – | – | High dose: NNTH 11 (5 to ∞)<br>Quality: Moderate<br>K = 1, N = 149 |
| Leaving study early due to any reason | – | Low dose: NNTB 25 (NNTB 4 to ∞ to NNTH 6)<br>Quality: High<br>K = 2, N = 78<br>Medium dose: NNTB 8 (4 to 50)<br>Quality: High<br>K = 2, N = 186<br>High dose: NNTB 11 (6 to 25)<br>Quality: High<br>K = 5, N = 767 | NNTB 14 (NNTH 9 to ∞ to NNTB 4)<br>Quality: Moderate<br>K = 1, N = 58 | – | High dose: NNTH 16 (NNTH 6 to ∞ to NNTB 33)<br>Quality: high<br>K = 2, N = 295 |

For methylphenidate statistically significant adverse events and/or with an RR greater than 5% are displayed in Table 25. For a full list of adverse events refer to Appendix 18 (forest plot).

Study information and evidence from the important outcomes and overall quality of evidence are presented in Table 25. The full evidence profiles and associated forest plots can be found in Appendix 19 and Appendix 18, respectively.


### 10.6.4    Long-term evidence review – efficacy

*Evidence included*
The MTA study (MTA Co-operative Group 1999a, 2004a, 2004b; Jensen *et al.,* 2007) began as a large (n = 579) randomised trial where children were assigned to one of the following groups: medication management, intensive behavioural treatment, combination treatment or community care (which included medication for approximately two-thirds of the sample). Medication management began with a 28-day, double-blind, daily-switch titration of methylphenidate using five randomly ordered repeats each of placebo or different doses of methylphenidate (5 mg, 10 mg, 15 mg or 20 mg). Experienced (blinded) clinicians agreed the child's initial dose after reviewing parent/teacher responses to each of the four doses. For those not responding adequately to methylphenidate during titration, alternative medications were titrated openly until a satisfactory one was found. Of the 289 subjects assigned to medication management (n = 144) and combined treatment (n = 145), 256 successfully completed titration. Of these, 198 (68.5%) were assigned to methylphenidate. The remaining titration completers were either openly titrated to dextroamphetamine (n = 26) or to no medication (n = 32) because of robust placebo response. The children were followed up and results of the MTA study have been reported at 14, 24 and 36 months.

*Key findings*
At 14 months (MTA Co-operative Group, 1999a) the outcome strongly favoured careful medication (whether or not in combination with behaviour therapy); at that point the randomisation ended, families were free to choose treatment or not, and the intensive interventions (medication monitoring and behavioural work) were discontinued.

Subsequent reports have provided details of naturalistic follow-up of the groups at 24 (Jensen *et al.*, 2007) and 36 months after randomisation, and conference presentations have outlined preliminary findings at the 8-year point. By the 3-year mark, the outcome was similar for all four groups.

These results have been widely interpreted as showing no long-term impact of medication or behaviour therapy. While this is one possible reading, it is not demonstrated by the study and other explanations need to be considered.

First, the end of randomisation entails that patients and families select which intervention is best for them. This may lead to a situation in which each individual gets whatever combination suits them best, so all interventions would have reasonably good outcomes.

Second, the end of intensive therapy could mean that any effects additional to those of usual good treatment wane when the intensity is reduced: therefore all treatment arms become similar to community treatment.

Third, the absence of an untreated control group makes it impossible to know whether the treatments were better than not intervening. Outcome scores at 36 months remained considerably better than the levels before treatment; the conclusion may be that all treatments work rather than that none do.

Fourth, the MTA investigators did not report that the treatments had no effect. They agreed that there was some evidence of medication benefit when the results were analysed by growth mixture modelling, which divides the sample into latent classes based on their trajectory over time. The best fit was three classes. One of the classes (34% of the sample) showed gradual improvement with continuing benefit from medication over the entire 3 years. The second class (52% of the sample) had an initial large response, maintained for 3 years; in another 14% a large initial response was followed by deterioration. In the second group who responded well, there was a significant preponderance of children who had been assigned to the intense MTA medication algorithm in the first 14 months, whether or not they continued medication.

Adverse events at the 24- and 36-month points after randomisation included influences on growth in height and weight – an effect of 0.75 inches at the 2-year mark, with no further loss at the 3-year point and (in conference reports) catch-up growth by the 8-year point, suggesting no growth suppression in that time scale.

It would therefore not be correct to regard behaviour therapy or stimulant medication as short-term treatments only.

### 10.6.5    Long-term evidence review – harm

*Evidence included*
The safety of the use of methylphenidate was further assessed by examining long-term data. The review team conducted a search for long-term RCTs (more than 2 months in duration) and observational studies (also more than 2 months) that assessed the safety of methylphenidate for children, young people and adults with ADHD. Nine sources of long-term use of methylphenidate met the eligibility criteria set by the GDG: a cross-sectional study involving hyperactive children receiving the drug for at least 4 months but not longer than 18 months and where data was obtained after 5 years of initial assessment (Weiss *et al.*, 1975); a 4-year follow-up study of children with ADHD receiving methylphenidate (Spencer *et al.*, 1996); a 3-year follow-up of the MTA study of 370 children with ADHD of which 70 had received consistent medication management, 88 were newly medicated and 147 had been inconsistently medicated (Swanson *et al.*, 2007); a 2-year RCT observational follow-up of 34 children with ADHD and either chronic motor tic disorder or Tourette's syndrome taking methylphenidate (Gadow *et al.*, 1999); a 2-year cohort study of 61 young adults who were treated with methylphenidate hydrochloride in childhood for at least 6 months (Gittelman-Klein *et al.*, 1988); a review of three short-term RCTs (1 to 4 weeks) and two open-label studies lasting 2 years (only the two long-term

studies are reported on within this section; the short-term data is summarised in the following section) (Palumbo *et al.*, 2004); a 4-month RCT of children with ADHD assigned to either methylphenidate or placebo (Schachar *et al.*, 1997); a safety review assessing sudden deaths associated with the use of CNS stimulants (Villalba, 2006); and a safety review by the FDA (FDA, 2004).

*Key findings*

It was not possible to pool the data of these studies given the different outcome measures used and, in some, the lack of variability measures reported. There is some indication that children's height (Swanson *et al.*, 2007) and weight (Swanson *et al.*, 2007; Schachar *et al.*, 1997) is affected by the use of methylphenidate, but, in some studies this difference failed to reach statistical significance (Spencer *et al.*, 1996; Gadow *et al.*, 1999; Gittelman-Klein, 1988) or the growth curve increased after methylphenidate was discontinued (Weiss *et al.*, 1975).

There is evidence of tics in children taking methylphenidate (Gadow *et al.*, 1999; Palumbo *et al.*, 2004). In terms of emotional factors, one study (Weiss *et al.*, 1975) found no significant differences between children taking methylphenidate and those taking placebo with respect to emotional adjustment, delinquency or the mother-child relationship. In a follow-up study of children with ADHD treated with methylphenidate (Gadow *et al.*, 1999) condition effects were evident for systolic blood pressure and heart rate, but not diastolic blood pressure.

In 2006 the US FDA conducted a review[21] on reports of sudden death in patients treated with ADHD medications using data from the AERS. The review identified 14 paediatric and four adult sudden death cases reported with methylphenidate between January 1992 and February 2005. The review reported that none of them appears solely or directly related to methylphenidate. Six of the 14 paediatric sudden deaths occurred in children with structural cardiovascular abnormalities that likely preceded the use of methylphenidate.

The review concluded that the rate of sudden death with methylphenidate and atomoxetine was below background rates available. However, no definitive conclusions can be drawn from the analyses of AERS cases because of the inherent limitations of the AERS and uncertainty regarding information on drug utilisation and background incidence of sudden death. Further studies were being conducted by the FDA (2008a) at the time this guideline was being prepared (January, 2008).

### 10.6.6    Drug misuse and diversion

Stimulants are controlled drugs and have the potential for misuse and diversion, either for subjective effects or for effects on performance. Oral use carries very little risk of inducing euphoria: the time course of the action on receptors is slower than that of drugs maintaining dependence. Intravenous administration or inhalation, however, can

---

[21]The review also investigated Adderall and Adderall XR (amphetamine/dextroamphetamine) which were not marketed in the UK at the time that this guideline was being prepared.

produce a 'high'. Extended-release preparations of stimulants are probably less easy to misuse in this way than are IR tablets. Atomoxetine is considered not to carry potential for euphoria or for inducing dependence. More commonly, oral stimulants can be misused to enhance performance in sports or some kinds of cognitive tasks and examinations (Wilens *et al.*, 2008).

People with ADHD have a higher risk than the ordinary population of taking illegal drugs, smoking and/or drinking excessively. The risk may be associated with the presence of conduct disorder and social adversity. In UK clinical experience, however, the misuse of prescribed drugs by people with ADHD is very uncommon. The use of illicit drugs, such as cannabis and cocaine, is probably not increased by receiving stimulants, at least in the short term. It may even be reduced; for example, a meta-analysis suggested that treatment with stimulants for ADHD was associated with a substantial reduction (approximately two-fold) in drug misuse (Wilens *et al.*, 2003). One epidemiological study has suggested the contrary: that young people who have been prescribed psychostimulants are more likely to misuse amphetamines later in life (Lambert, 2005).

The issue of long-term risk is not yet settled. A systematic review by McDonagh and colleagues (2007) found somewhat contradictory evidence: two other longer-term studies had found no sign that stimulant medication in childhood contributed to illicit drug use in adulthood, and no conclusion was possible. More recently, two studies conducted by researchers at New York University School of Medicine have concluded that early stimulant treatment for ADHD does not contribute to substance misuse later in life (Mannuzza *et al.*, 2008; Biederman *et al.*, 2008). Furthermore, observational follow-up of the MTA trial has suggested that medication does not contribute significantly to the risk for substance misuse in adolescence and behaviour therapy is associated with reduction of risk (Molina *et al.*, 2007). Reasons for a reduced risk of substance misuse with treatment may include reduced impulsivity and conduct disorder symptoms and improved academic performance and family relations.

The use of stimulants in people who are already known to misuse substances is not necessarily contraindicated (Bukstein, 2008). The available research is based primarily on open trials, with few RCTs to indicate the most efficacious treatment approaches in this group. The evidence so far has been reviewed, which indicated that stimulants, when given to people with the dual problem of ADHD and drug misuse, lead to improvement in ADHD symptoms and no worsening of substance misuse (Wilens *et al.*, 2005a). The presence of alcohol or cannabis consumption is not a contraindication to stimulant prescribing. While there is no evidence to guide practice in those misusing cocaine, the similarity of the mechanism of action of the two drugs (inhibition of the dopamine transporter, albeit with different time courses) suggests that there could be particular dangers in the combination. Concomitant cannabis and stimulant use should be closely monitored in those with a family history or past history of psychosis.

Drug diversion refers to the potential, for people who have been given prescribed stimulants, to sell or give them to other people. A systematic review by Wilens and colleagues (2008) indicates that the practice is rife in North America, and, while the extent of diversion in England, Wales and Northern Ireland is not known, practitioners should be aware of the possibility. Clinicians will be alert to pointers such as the presence of drug-misusing relatives, the patient being in a drug-misusing peer group, the combination of absence of effect with ongoing requests for prescriptions and prescription records suggesting over-frequent prescription requests.

The possibilities of stimulant drug diversion and misuse in people with ADHD who are already involved in drug misuse, together with the psychiatric comorbidity and adherence issues in this group, require detailed assessment and consideration of treatment options prior to decisions being made regarding treatment for their ADHD.

### 10.6.7    Clinical evidence summary

For individual outcomes, the quality of the evidence was generally moderate to high.

*Methylphenidate in pre-school children*
Only one study (KOLLINS2006) evaluated the effect of methylphenidate in pre-school children. There is small clinical improvement (RR 1.61) in pre-school children taking methylphenidate when compared with placebo. However, this result is not statistically significant and therefore the evidence is inconclusive.

*Methylphenidate in school-age children*
In school-age children, there is evidence that methylphenidate when compared with placebo or waitlist control produced a medium to large effect in reducing children's ADHD symptoms and conduct problems.

There is some indication that there is improvement in outcomes when increasing the dose.

Methylphenidate (high dose) is more likely than placebo to cause the following side effects: insomnia, anorexia, increased irritability, moodiness, thirst, itching, diarrhoea, palpitations, stuttering, negativism, reddened eyes, incoherent speech and decrease in bodyweight.

The long-term studies of methylphenidate indicate an increased risk of side effects, increase in systolic blood pressure and heart rate problems. Given the lack of background rates, the association between the use of methylphenidate and sudden death is not clear.

*Special circumstances – ADHD comorbid with developmental reading disorder*
Only one study, KUPIETZ1988, compared methylphenidate with placebo in an ADHD population comorbid with developmental reading disorder. Methylphenidate in low, medium and high doses is effective in reducing children's ADHD core symptoms. The evidence suggests that methylphenidate when compared with placebo may reduce the risk of discontinuation.

*Conclusion (methylphenidate in children)*
Methylphenidate is effective in reducing ADHD core symptoms and conduct problems in children with ADHD. There is evidence suggesting that methylphenidate may increase side effects.

*Methylphenidate in adults*

In adults with ADHD, methylphenidate (high dose) showed evidence of a reduction in ADHD symptoms as rated by an investigator but a small effect of improvement in medium doses as measured from self-reports. There was also evidence of global clinical improvement when compared with placebo.

Only one RCT (BIEDERMAN2006A) assessed side effects and indicated that methylphenidate (high dose) is more likely than placebo to cause the following side effects: decreased appetite, gastrointestinal problems, tension, cardiovascular complaints, depression, dizziness, anxiety, autonomic symptoms, increased energy, tics, skin problems, bruising and sexual problems. Methylphenidate may reduce the risk of discontinuation when compared with placebo.

Long-term studies of side effects in adults are scarce but the safety reviews indicated an association between the use of methylphenidate and sudden death. Given the lack of background rates, however, the evidence is inconclusive.

*Conclusion (methylphenidate in adults)*

Methylphenidate is effective in reducing ADHD core symptoms and in producing clinical improvement as rated by investigators in adults with ADHD. There is evidence suggesting that methylphenidate (high dose) may increase side effects.


## 10.7 DEXAMFETAMINE (STIMULANT)

### 10.7.1 Pharmacology and prescribing

Dexamfetamine is a more potent stimulant than methylphenidate. In addition to blocking the reuptake of dopamine and noradrenaline via the dopamine transporter (DAT) it also releases dopamine and noradrenaline into the extraneuronal space by blocking the intraneuronal vesicular monoamine transporter (VMAT).

Dexamfetamine is readily absorbed from the gastrointestinal tract. It is resistant to metabolism by monoamine oxidase. It is excreted in the urine as an unchanged parent drug together with some hydroxylated metabolites. Elimination is increased in acidic urine. After high doses, elimination in the urine may take several days. The apparent elimination half-life of dexamfetamine in children is 6.8 hours, which suggests that once or twice daily dosing is sufficient (Brown *et al.*, 1979).

For the treatment of hyperkinetic states in children, the usual starting dosage for 3 to 5 year olds is 2.5 mg a day, increased if necessary by 2.5 mg a day at weekly intervals; for 6 year olds and over, the usual starting dose is 5–10 mg a day increasing if necessary by 5 mg at weekly intervals. While the usual upper limit is 20 mg a day, some older children have needed 40 mg or more for optimal response (UCB Pharma Limited, 2005).

### 10.7.2 Clinical evidence for dexamfetamine

There was only one study that compared dexamfetamine with placebo in adults with ADHD (PATERSON1999), which involved 45 adults.

*Pharmacological treatment*

Study information and evidence from the important outcomes and overall quality of evidence are presented in Table 26. The full evidence profiles and associated forest plots can be found in Appendix 19 and Appendix 18, respectively.

### 10.7.3 Evidence from the TA: Methylphenidate, atomoxetine and dexamfetamine for the treatment of attention deficit hyperactivity disorder in children and adolescents (NICE, 2006b)

No efficacy studies were available for meta-analysis meeting basic quality criteria. In children, adverse effects are unknown (mixed amphetamine salts were not included in the analysis).

### 10.7.4 Long-term clinical evidence review

*Evidence included*
Long-term data on the use of dexamfetamine was also assessed. The review team conducted a search for long-term RCTs (more than 2 months' duration) and observational studies (also more than 2 months) that assessed the safety of dexamfetamine for children, young people and adults with ADHD. There was only one study found that met the criteria set by the GDG: an 8-week RCT of 61 hyperactive boys (Greenberg *et al.*, 1972).

*Key findings*
Children receiving dexamfetamine complained of decreased appetite and had stomach aches more often than the control groups (hydroxyzine and placebo). Of the dexamfetamine group, two manifested marked regressive, dependent behaviour, and one became overtly psychotic. The intensity of all side effects subsided with a decrease in dosage.

### 10.7.5 Clinical evidence summary

For individual outcomes, the quality of the evidence was moderate reflecting the paucity of the data. For children, we found no trials that met the quality criteria and therefore had no evidence on its efficacy.

*Dexamfetamine in adults*
There is some evidence of global clinical improvement in adults taking dexamfetamine when compared with placebo.

There is evidence that dexamfetamine when compared with placebo increases the risk of the following side effects: sleep disturbance, dry mouth, thirst and weight loss. The long-term study indicates the risk of side effects such as decreased appetite, stomach aches and the risk of regressive, dependent behaviour and psychosis.

**Table 26: Study information and evidence summary table**
**for trials of dexamfetamine**

| | **In adults**<br>**Dexamfetamine versus placebo**<br>**Mixed comorbidity** |
|---|---|
| Total no. of trials (total no. of participants) | 1 (45) |
| Study ID | PATERSON1999 |
| Baseline severity (mean range) | CGI (severity): 4.05 |
| Dose | Mean:<br>4.77 tablets<br>Range:<br>1–7 tablets per day |
| Treatment length (mean range) | 42 days |
| *Benefits* | |
| Clinical improvement (clinician-rated) | CGI:<br>RR 4.38<br>(1.08 to 17.75)<br>Quality: High<br>K = 1, N = 45 |
| *Harms* | |
| Sleep disturbance | NNTH 2<br>(1 to 5)<br>Quality: High<br>K = 1, N = 45 |
| Dry mouth | NNTH 9<br>(2 to 9)<br>Quality: Moderate<br>K = 1, N = 45 |
| Thirst | NNTH 7<br>(NNTH 3 to ∞ to NNTB 50)<br>Quality: Moderate<br>K = 1, N = 45 |
| Weight loss | NNTH 2<br>(1 to 4)<br>Quality: Moderate<br>K = 1, N = 45 |

*Conclusion from clinical evidence*
There is some evidence of the effectiveness of dexamfetamine in producing global improvement in adults with ADHD. Dexamfetamine may increase the risk of side effects and regressive, dependent behaviour as well as psychosis.

## 10.8 ATOMOXETINE

### 10.8.1 Pharmacology and prescribing

Atomoxetine is a non-stimulant drug licensed for use in children of 6 years and over and young people for the treatment of ADHD. Its precise mechanism of action in the treatment of ADHD is not clear but it is thought that it works by selectively inhibiting the pre-synaptic noradrenaline transporter thus inhibiting noradrenaline reuptake. While both atomoxetine and stimulants both increase intrasynaptic concentrations of dopamine and noradrenaline in the cortex, it is thought that atomoxetine differs from a stimulant in having less effect on subcortical brain regions associated with motivation and reward.

As it is neither a stimulant medication nor a controlled substance, atomoxetine has less potential for misuse and does not require the same strict prescribing and storage conditions as methylphenidate and dexamfetamine. Atomoxetine is taken as a once-daily dose in the morning, though some patients may benefit from dividing the daily dose and taking it twice daily, once in the morning and again late afternoon or early evening. Atomoxetine is rapidly and almost completely absorbed after oral administration, reaching mean maximal observed plasma concentration (Cmax) approximately 1 to 2 hours after dosing. The absolute bioavailability of atomoxetine following oral administration ranges from 63 to 94%, depending upon inter-individual differences in the modest first pass metabolism. The mean elimination half-life of atomoxetine after oral administration is 3.6 hours in extensive metabolisers and 21 hours in poor metabolisers. Approximately 7% of Caucasians have a genotype corresponding to a non-functional CYP2D6 enzyme (CYP2D6 poor metabolisers). Patients with this genotype have a several-fold higher exposure to atomoxetine when compared with patients with a functional enzyme. Poor metabolisers may be at higher risk of adverse events. For patients with a known poor metaboliser genotype, a lower starting dose and slower titration of the dose may be considered. Given that 2D6 status is rarely known for an individual patient, a low starting dose and slow titration will reduce the risk of adverse events.

### 10.8.2 Safety and adverse effects

Common adverse effects associated with atomoxetine include abdominal pain, nausea and vomiting, decreased appetite with associated weight loss, dizziness and slight increases in heart rate and blood pressure (Wolraich *et al.*, 2007). These effects are normally transient and may not require discontinuation of treatment. Very rarely, liver toxicity, manifested by elevated hepatic enzymes and bilirubin with jaundice, has been reported. Seizures are a potential risk for atomoxetine (Eli Lilly and Company Ltd, 2008). Suicide-related behaviour (suicide attempts and suicidal ideation) has been reported in patients treated with atomoxetine. In double-blind clinical trials, suicide-related behaviours occurred at a frequency of 0.44% in atomoxetine-treated patients (6 out of 1,357 patients treated, one case of attempted suicide and five of suicidal ideation). The age range of children experiencing these events was 7 to 12 years. There were no events in the placebo group (n = 851). It should be noted that the number of adolescent patients included in the clinical trials was low (Eli Lilly and Company Ltd, 2008).

### 10.8.3    Clinical evidence for atomoxetine

Of the 49 included trials 14 included a comparison of atomoxetine with placebo. Of these, 11 were of school-age children and three were of adults. In all trials, participants had been diagnosed with ADHD (common coexisting conditions included oppositional defiant disorder and conduct disorder). One study (ALLEN2005) recruited school-age children with ADHD and comorbid tic disorders. Two studies (NEWCORN2008; WANG2007) involved a comparison of atomoxetine with methylphenidate.

One trial (NEWCORN2006) included a comparison of atomoxetine low dose (0.5 mg/kg/day) with atomoxetine high dose (1.8 mg/kg/day) in children with ADHD. Another trial (ADLER2006), included a comparison of atomoxetine once daily with atomoxetine twice daily in adults with ADHD.

For atomoxetine statistically significant adverse events and/or with an RR greater than 5% are displayed in Table 27. For a full list of adverse events refer to Appendix 18 (forest plot).

Study information and evidence from the important outcomes and overall quality of evidence are presented in Table 27. The full evidence profiles and associated forest plots can be found in Appendix 19 and Appendix 18, respectively.

### 10.8.4    Long-term clinical evidence review

*Evidence included*
Long-term data of the use of atomoxetine was examined. The review team conducted a search for long-term RCTs (more than 2 months' duration) and observational studies (also more than 2 months) that assessed the safety of atomoxetine for children, young people and adults with ADHD. There was only one study (a review of three 1-year follow-up studies of children and young people with ADHD taking atomoxetine; Wernicke *et al.*, 2003) that met the criteria set by the GDG as well as one safety review mentioned previously (Villalba *et al.*, 2006).

*Key findings*
The evidence is inconclusive regarding the increase of heart rate and blood pressure with the use of atomoxetine.

259

**Table 27: Study information and evidence summary table for trials of atomoxetine**

| | In school-age children | | | | In adults | |
| --- | --- | --- | --- | --- | --- | --- |
| | Mixed comorbidity | Specific comorbidity (tic disorder) | Mixed comorbidity | Mixed comorbidity | Mixed comorbidity | |
| | Atomoxetine versus placebo | Atomoxetine versus placebo | Atomoxetine (low dose) versus atomoxetine (high dose) | Methylphenidate versus atomoxetine | Atomoxetine versus placebo | Atomoxetine (once daily) versus atomoxetine (twice daily) |
| Total no. of trials (total no. of participants) | 10 (1850) | 2 (189) | 1 (229) | 2 (772) | 3 (820) | 1 (218) |
| Study ID | BOHNSTEDT2005 BROWN2006 KELSEY2004 MICHELSON2001 MICHELSON2002 MICHELSON2004 SPENCER2002A SPENCER2002B WEISS2005 WERNICKE2004A | ALLEN2005 SPENCER2002C | NEWCORN2006 | NEWCORN2008 WANG2007 | MICHELSON 2003A MICHELSON 2003B WERNICKE 2004B | ADLER2006 |
| Diagnosis | ADHD (coexisting conditions: oppositional defiant disorder and/or conduct disorder) | ADHD and tic disorders | ADHD | ADHD | ADHD, hyperkinetic disorder | ADHD |

| | | | | | | |
|---|---|---|---|---|---|---|
| Baseline severity (mean range) | ADHD-RS (total) range: Atomoxetine: 37.8 (7.9) to 42.1 (9.2) Placebo: 37.6 (8.0) to 42.3 (7.1) | ADHD-RS (total): Atomoxetine: 38.9 (9.1) Placebo: 35.0 (9.5) | ADHD-RS (total): Low dose: 15.1(7.7) High dose: 14.0 (7.2) | CGI-ADHD-S: Methylphenidate: 5.3 (0.9) Atomoxetine: 5.3 (0.8) | CAARS-Inv (total) range: Atomoxetine: 33.6 (7.2) to 34.9 (6.9) Placebo: 33.2 (7.8) to 34.2 (7.5) | CAARS-Inv (total): Once daily: 38.4 Twice daily: 37.2 |
| Dose | Low: ≤0.8 mg/kg/day Medium: > 0.8 > 1.6 mg/kg/day High: ≥1.6 mg/kg/day | Medium: 1.33 mg/kg/day | Low: 0.5 mg/kg/day High: max 1.8 mg/kg/day | Methylphenidate: 0.2 to 0.6 mg/kg/day Osmotically released methylphenidate: 18 to 54 mg/day Atomoxetine: 0.8 to 1.8 mg/kg/day | Medium: 60 mg/day (max) High: 90 mg/day (max) | 80 mg/day |
| Treatment length (mean range) | 49–238 days | 102 days | 240 days | 42–56 days | 70 days | 42 days |

*Continued*

**Table 27:** (*Continued*)

| | In school-age children | | | | In adults | |
| | Mixed comorbidity | Specific comorbidity (tic disorder) | Mixed comorbidity | Mixed comorbidity | Mixed comorbidity | |
| | Atomoxetine versus placebo | Atomoxetine versus placebo | Atomoxetine (low dose) versus atomoxetine (high dose) | Methylphenidate versus atomoxetine | Atomoxetine versus placebo | Atomoxetine (once daily) versus atomoxetine (twice daily) |
|---|---|---|---|---|---|---|
| *Benefits* | | | | | | |
| ADHD core symptoms (mean change) (teacher-rated) | Medium dose: SMD −0.43 (−0.73 to −0.12) Quality: High K = 1, N = 171 High dose: SMD −0.37 (−0.54 to −0.21) Quality: High K = 4, N = 738 | – | – | – | – | – |
| ADHD core symptoms (mean at endpoint) (parent-rated) | High dose: SMD −0.86 (−1.16 to −0.57) Quality: High K = 1, N = 194 | – | – | – | – | – |

| | | | | | |
|---|---|---|---|---|---|
| ADHD core symptoms (mean change) (parent-rated) | Low dose: SMD −0.33 (−0.70 to 0.04) Quality: Moderate K = 1, N = 297 Medium dose: SMD −0.65 (−0.87 to −0.43) Quality: High K = 2, N = 468 High dose: SMD −0.59 (−0.71 to −0.47) Quality: High K = 7, N = 916 | ADHD-RS-P: SMD −0.56 (−0.89 to −0.23) Quality: High K = 1, N = 148 | — | ADHD-RS-IV-P: SMD −0.05 (−0.27 to 0.17) Quality: Moderate K = 1, N = 330 | — |
| ADHD core symptoms (mean change) (investigator-rated) | — | ADHD-RS: SMD 0.19 (−0.07 to 0.45) Quality: Moderate K = 1, N = 229 | — | Medium dose: CAARS: SMD −0.44 (−0.62 to −0.26) Quality: High K = 2, N = 572 High dose: CAARS: SMD −0.37 (−0.54 to −0.19) Quality: High K = 2, N = 515 | — |

Continued

**Table 27: (Continued)**

| | In school-age children | | | | In adults | |
| --- | --- | --- | --- | --- | --- | --- |
| | Mixed comorbidity | Specific comorbidity (tic disorder) | Mixed comorbidity | Mixed comorbidity | Mixed comorbidity | |
| | Atomoxetine versus placebo | Atomoxetine versus placebo | Atomoxetine (low dose) versus atomoxetine (high dose) | Methylphenidate versus atomoxetine | Atomoxetine versus placebo | Atomoxetine (once daily) versus atomoxetine (twice daily) |
| ADHD core symptoms (mean change) (self-report) | – | – | – | – | High dose: CAARS: SMD –0.39 (–0.57 to 0.22) Quality: High K = 2, N = 536 | – |
| Conduct problems (mean change) (teacher-rated) | Medium dose: SMD 0.0 (–0.24 to 0.24) Quality: Moderate K = 1, N = 416 | – | – | – | – | – |
| Conduct problems (mean change) (parent-rated) | Low dose: SMD –0.46 (–0.83 to –0.08) Quality: High K = 1, N = 297 Medium dose: SMD | – | – | – | – | – |

| | | | | | | |
|---|---|---|---|---|---|---|
| | −0.31<br>(−0.49 to −0.14)<br>Quality: High<br>K = 2, N = 713<br>High dose: SMD −0.23<br>(−0.54 to 0.07)<br>Quality: Moderate<br>K = 1, N = 297 | — | — | ADHD-RS:<br>RR 0.80<br>(0.66 to 0.97)<br>Quality: High<br>K = 1, N = 442<br>CGI-ADHD-S:<br>SMD −0.15<br>(−0.37 to 0.07)<br>Quality: Moderate<br>K = 1, N = 330 | — | — | NNTB 6<br>(3 to 20)<br>Quality:<br>Moderate<br>K = 1, N = 218 |
| Clinical improvement (clinician-rated) | Various measures:<br>High dose: RR 1.46<br>(0.92 to 2.31)<br>Quality: High<br>K = 3, N = 669 | — | — | — | | |
| *Harms* | | | | | | |
| Nausea | Medium dose: NNTH 20<br>(9 to ∞)<br>Quality: High<br>K = 2, N = 468<br>≥10% population:<br>NNTH 10 (5 to 33)<br>Quality: Moderate<br>K = 2, N = 275 | NNTH 10<br>(5 to 33)<br>Quality: High<br>K = 1,<br>N = 148 | — | — | High dose:<br>NNTH 14<br>(8 to 33)<br>Quality: High<br>K = 1,<br>N = 280 | |

*Continued*

**Table 27:** (*Continued*)

| | In school-age children | | | | In adults | |
| --- | --- | --- | --- | --- | --- | --- |
| | Mixed comorbidity | Specific comorbidity (tic disorder) | Mixed comorbidity | Mixed comorbidity | Mixed comorbidity | |
| | Atomoxetine versus placebo | Atomoxetine versus placebo | Atomoxetine (low dose) versus atomoxetine (high dose) | Methylphenidate versus atomoxetine | Atomoxetine versus placebo | Atomoxetine (once daily) versus atomoxetine (twice daily) |
| Cough | Low dose: NNTH 11 (NNTH 5 to ∞ to NNTB 50) Quality: Moderate K = 1, N = 297 | – | – | – | – | – |
| Decreased appetite | Medium dose: NNTH 9 (5 to 25) Quality: High K = 2, N = 468 High dose: NNTH 11 (6 to 33) Quality: High K = 2, N = 494 ≥10% population: NNTH 7 (4 to 14) Quality: High K = 2, N = 275 | NNTH 7 (4 to 14) Quality: High K = 1, N = 148 | – | – | High dose: NNTH 12 (7 to 25) Quality: High K = 1, N = 280 | – |

| | | | | | |
|---|---|---|---|---|---|
| Dyspepsia | Medium dose: NNTH 11 (6 to 33)<br>Quality: High<br>K = 1, N = 171<br>High dose: NNTH 20 (NNTH 10 to ∞ to NNTB 100)<br>Quality: Moderate<br>K = 1, N = 197 | — | — | Medium dose: NNTH 50 (NNTH 25 to ∞ to NNTB 100)<br>Quality: Moderate<br>K = 1, N = 284 | — |
| Vomiting | Medium dose: NNTH 12 (7 to 50)<br>Quality: High<br>K = 2, N = 468<br>High dose: NNTH 20 (10 to ∞)<br>Quality: High<br>K = 2, N = 494 | — | — | — | — |
| Asthenia | Medium dose: NNTH 25 (NNTH 12 to ∞ to 100)<br>Quality: Moderate<br>K = 2, N = 468 | — | — | — | — |
| Dizziness | Medium dose: NNTH 25 (14 to ∞)<br>Quality: High<br>K = 2, N = 468<br>High dose: NNTH 25 (NNTH 11 to ∞ to NNTB 50) | — | — | High dose: NNTH 25 (12 to 100)<br>Quality: Moderate<br>K = 1, N = 280 | — |

*Continued*

**Table 27:** (*Continued*)

| | In school-age children | | | | In adults | |
| | Mixed comorbidity | Specific comorbidity (tic disorder) | Mixed comorbidity | Mixed comorbidity | Mixed comorbidity | |
| | Atomoxetine versus placebo | Atomoxetine versus placebo | Atomoxetine (low dose) versus atomoxetine (high dose) | Methylphenidate versus atomoxetine | Atomoxetine versus placebo | Atomoxetine (once daily) versus atomoxetine (twice daily) |
|---|---|---|---|---|---|---|
| | Quality: Moderate K = 1, N = 297 | — | — | — | — | — |
| Pruritus | Medium dose: NNTH 100 (NNTH 25 to ∞ to NNTB 50) Quality: Moderate K = 1, N = 297 High dose: NNTH 16 (8 to ∞) Quality: Moderate K = 1, N = 297 | | | | | |
| Somnolence | High dose: NNTH 10 (6 to 20) Quality: High K = 2, N = 494 | — | — | — | — | — |
| Fatigue | High dose: NNTH 12 (7 to 50) Quality: Moderate K = 1, N = 197 | | | | — | — |

| | A | B | C | D | E | F |
|---|---|---|---|---|---|---|
| Rash | High dose: NNTH 20 (NNTB 8 to ∞ to NNTB 50) Quality: Moderate K = 1, N = 297 | – | – | – | – | – |
| Infection | High dose: NNTH 16 (8 to ∞) Quality: Moderate K = 1, N = 297 | – | – | – | – | – |
| Nervousness (≥10% population) | NNTH 12 (NNTB 4 to ∞ to NNTB 25) Quality: Moderate K = 1, N = 127 | – | – | – | – | – |
| Emotional lability | ≥10% population: NNTH 9 (4 to 50) Quality: Moderate K = 1, N = 127 | – | NNTH 25 (11 to ∞) Quality: Moderate K = 1, N = 229 | – | – | – |
| Pain in limb | – | – | – | – | Medium dose: NNTH 50 (20 to ∞) Quality: Moderate K = 1, N = 284 | – |

*Continued*

**Table 27:** (*Continued*)

| | In school-age children | | | | In adults | |
| | Mixed comorbidity | Specific comorbidity (tic disorder) | Mixed comorbidity | Mixed comorbidity | Mixed comorbidity | |
| | Atomoxetine versus placebo | Atomoxetine versus placebo | Atomoxetine (low dose) versus atomoxetine (high dose) | Methylphenidate versus atomoxetine | Atomoxetine versus placebo | Atomoxetine (once daily) versus atomoxetine (twice daily) |
|---|---|---|---|---|---|---|
| Sinusitis | – | – | – | – | Medium dose: NNTH 33 (16 to ∞) Quality: Moderate K = 1, N = 284 | – |
| Insomnia | – | – | – | – | High dose: NNTH 14 (9 to 33) Quality: High K = 2, N = 564 | – |
| Irritability | – | – | – | – | Medium dose: NNTH 50 (20 to ∞) Quality: Moderate K = 1, N = 284 | – |

| | | | | High dose: | |
|---|---|---|---|---|---|
| Dry mouth | – | – | – | – | NNTH 7 (5 to 11) Quality: Moderate K = 1, N = 280 | – |
| Constipation | – | – | – | – | High dose: NNTH 14 (9 to 33) Quality: Moderate K = 1, N = 280 | – |
| Libido decreased | – | – | – | – | High dose: NNTH 20 (11 to 50) Quality: High K = 1, N = 280 | – |
| Difficulty getting/ maintaining an erection | – | – | – | – | High dose: NNTH 16 (11 to 50) Quality: High K = 1, N = 280 | – |
| Sweating | – | – | – | – | High dose: NNTH 25 (14 to 50) Quality: High K = 1, N = 280 | – |

*Continued*

271

**Table 27:** (*Continued*)

| | In school-age children | | | | In adults | |
| --- | --- | --- | --- | --- | --- | --- |
| | Mixed comorbidity | Specific comorbidity (tic disorder) | Mixed comorbidity | Mixed comorbidity | Mixed comorbidity | |
| | Atomoxetine versus placebo | Atomoxetine versus placebo | Atomoxetine (low dose) versus atomoxetine (high dose) | Methylphenidate versus atomoxetine | Atomoxetine versus placebo | Atomoxetine (once daily) versus atomoxetine (twice daily) |
| Leaving study early due to adverse events | Low dose: NNTH 50 (NNTH 12 to ∞ to NNTB 33) Quality: Moderate K = 1, N = 297 Medium dose: NNTH 50 (NNTH 20 to ∞ to NNTB 100) Quality: High K = 2, N = 468 High dose: NNTH 33 (20 to 100) Quality: High K = 5, N = 1189 | NNTH 100 (NNTH 16 to ∞ to NNTB 33) Quality: Moderate K = 1, N = 148 | NNTB 100 (NNTB 20 to ∞ to NNTH 25) Quality: Moderate K = 1, N = 229 | NNTB 33 (0 to 16) Quality: High K = 2, N = 442 | High dose: NNTH 33 (25 to 100) Quality: High K = 2, N = 536 | NNTH 12 (NNTH 5 to ∞ to NNTB 100) Quality: Moderate K = 1, N = 218 |

| Leaving study early due to any reason | Low dose: NNTH 12 (NNTH 4 to ∞ to NNTB 16) Quality: High K = 1, N = 297 Medium dose: NNTH 50 (NNTH 10 to ∞ to NNTB 20) Quality: High K = 2, N = 468 High dose: NNTB 25 (NNTB 12 to ∞ to NNTH 100) Quality: High K = 8, N = 1485 | NNTH 100 (NNTH 16 to ∞ to NNTB 33) Quality: Moderate K = 1, N = 148 | NNTH 14 (NNTH 5 to ∞ to NNTB 20) Quality: Moderate K = 1, N = 229 | — | High dose: NNTB 100 (NNTB 20 to ∞ to NNTH 50) Quality: High K = 2, N = 536 | NNTH 25 (NNTH 6 to ∞ to NNTB 12) Quality: Moderate K = 1, N = 218 |
|---|---|---|---|---|---|---|

*Pharmacological treatment*

The safety review found seven cases of sudden death (three children and four adults) of which one had lymphocytic myocarditis and two had toxic levels of olanzapine or a possible seizure preceding death; none of these patients had prior history of cardiovascular problems or cardiovascular structural abnormalities. The review reported that none of the cases appears solely or directly attributable to atomoxetine at therapeutic doses. The cases were highly confounded. None of the patients had structural cardiovascular abnormalities. However, the extent of the role of atomoxetine in these deaths is difficult to establish. Further studies were being conducted by the FDA (2008b) at the time this guideline was being prepared (January, 2008).

### 10.8.5    Clinical evidence summary: atomoxetine

For individual outcomes, the quality of the evidence was generally moderate to high.

*Atomoxetine in school-age children*
There is evidence that atomoxetine has a small to medium effect in reducing ADHD core symptoms in children with ADHD, as rated by both parents and teachers. In one outcome measure (ADHD core symptoms as rated by teachers) the effect was large when children were given a high dose of atomoxetine. Regarding conduct problems, there was a small effect in the reduction of these as reported by parents and no effect when reported by teachers, although this data was only from one study (MICHELSON2004). There is some evidence of global clinical improvement (RR 1.46) in children taking a high dose of atomoxetine when compared with placebo groups.

The evidence suggests there is a slight improvement in reducing children's conduct problems when the dose of atomoxetine is reduced.

There is evidence that atomoxetine in children with ADHD causes the following side effects: nausea, cough, decreased appetite, dyspepsia, vomiting, asthenia, dizziness, pruritus, somnolence, fatigue, rash, infection, nervousness and emotional lability. There is also an increased risk of decreased appetite, dyspepsia and vomiting when dosage is augmented. The evidence suggests there is an increase of risk of discontinuation of atomoxetine when compared with placebo but this risk is not present when children are given high doses of atomoxetine. The safety reviews report sudden deaths in children taking atomoxetine, but given the lack of background rates, no conclusions can be drawn from this data.

*Atomoxetine versus methylphenidate*
One study (WANG2007) indicated that there is little to no difference in efficacy between methylphenidate and atomoxetine in reducing ADHD core symptoms or general clinical improvement. Another study (NEWCORN2008) showed that osmotically released methylphenidate was more effective than atomoxetine in children's clinical improvement. In terms of leaving the study early due to adverse events, the evidence from the two studies suggests that there is an increased risk in adverse events in children taking atomoxetine when compared with methylphenidate.

The effect sizes of the studies comparing methylphenidate with placebo ranged from SMD −1.40 (−1.80 to −1.01) to −0.29 (−0.88 to 0.33). The effect sizes for atomoxetine when compared with placebo were lower, ranging from SMD −0.44 (−0.62 to −0.26) to −0.37 (−0.54 to −0.19).

*Conclusion (school-age children)*
Atomoxetine is effective in reducing ADHD core symptoms and clinical improvement in children with ADHD. There is no effect of atomoxetine on children's conduct problems as rated by teachers. There is evidence suggesting that atomoxetine may increase side effects when compared with placebo and when compared with methylphenidate.

*Special circumstances – ADHD comorbid with tic disorder*
Only one study (ALLEN2005) compared the effect of atomoxetine with placebo in a population of children with ADHD comorbid with tic disorder. The results indicate that there is a medium effect (SMD −0.56) in the reduction of ADHD core symptoms as rated by parents.

The ALLEN2005 study also suggests that there is increased nausea, decreased appetite and risk of discontinuation in children taking atomoxetine.

*Atomoxetine in adults*
There is evidence of the effectiveness of atomoxetine in reducing ADHD core symptoms in adults with ADHD (mixed comorbidities) when compared with placebo.

There is evidence that atomoxetine increases the risk of side effects in adults with comorbid and non-comorbid ADHD when compared with placebo. Atomoxetine is more likely than placebo to increase the risk of discontinuation. The safety reviews report cases of sudden death in adults taking atomoxetine. Once again, because of the lack of background rates the evidence is inconclusive.

*Conclusion (adults)*
Atomoxetine is effective in reducing ADHD core symptoms in adults with ADHD. The association between sudden death and the use of atomoxetine in adults is difficult to establish.

## 10.9 CLONIDINE

### 10.9.1 Pharmacology and prescribing

Clonidine is an alpha$_2$ noradrenergic agonist which is thought to work in ADHD by affecting noradrenaline transmission in the frontal cortex. Clonidine is licensed for the treatment of hypertension, migraine (from age 12) and menopausal flushing. Unlicensed uses of clonidine include the treatment of tics, Tourette's syndrome and ADHD.

### 10.9.2    Safety and adverse effects

Common adverse effects of clonidine include sedation and reduction in heart rate.

### 10.9.3    Clinical evidence for clonidine

Two trials were found that included a comparison of clonidine with placebo. One trial (HAZELL2003) was done with a sample of school-age children with ADHD (common coexisting conditions included oppositional defiant disorder and/or conduct disorder). The second study (KURLAN2002) involved adults with ADHD and comorbid Tourette's syndrome, chronic motor tic disorder or chronic vocal tic disorder. This same study (KURLAN2002) also included a comparison of clonidine with methylphenidate.

For clonidine, statistically significant adverse events and/or with an RR greater than 5% are displayed in Appendix 19. For a full list of adverse events refer to Appendix 18 (forest plot).

Study information and evidence from the important outcomes and overall quality of evidence are presented in Table 28. The full evidence profiles and associated forest plots can be found in Appendix 19 and Appendix 18, respectively.

### 10.9.4    Clinical evidence summary: clonidine

For individual outcomes, the quality of the evidence was moderate reflecting the paucity of the data.

*Clonidine in school-age children*
There is evidence that clonidine reduces children's ADHD core symptoms and conduct problems as well as producing general clinical improvement. When outcomes were measured by teachers the effect sizes were medium; when measured by parents, they were small to no effect.

Clonidine is more likely than placebo to decrease the risk of discontinuation.

*Special circumstances – ADHD comorbid with Tourette's syndrome, chronic motor tic or chronic vocal tic disorder*
In children with ADHD and comorbid Tourette's syndrome, chronic motor tic or chronic vocal tic disorder, clonidine produced a large effect in reducing ADHD core symptoms and conduct problems. These results are based on only one study (KURLAN2002).

As in the mixed comorbid ADHD population, clonidine is more likely than placebo to decrease the risk of discontinuation.

**Table 28: Study information and evidence summary table for trials of clonidine**

**In school-age children**

| | Clonidine versus placebo | | Methylphenidate versus clonidine |
|---|---|---|---|
| | **Mixed comorbidity** | **Specific comorbidity (Tourette's syndrome, chronic motor tic disorder or chronic vocal tic disorder)** | **Specific comorbidity (Tourette's syndrome, chronic motor tic disorder or chronic vocal tic disorder)** |
| Total no. of trials (total no. of participants) | 1 (67) | 1 (136) | 1 (136) |
| Study ID | HAZELL2003 | KURLAN2002 | KURLAN2002 |
| Diagnosis | ADHD with oppositional defiant disorder or conduct disorder | ADHD with Tourette's syndrome, chronic motor tic disorder or chronic vocal tic disorder | ADHD with Tourette's syndrome, chronic motor tic disorder or chronic vocal tic disorder |
| Baseline severity (mean range) | Number of inattentive symptoms: Clonidine: 7.16 (1.54) Placebo: 7.32 (1.54) | Conners' ASQ-T: Clonidine: 18.4 (5.9) Placebo: 16.0 (6.2) | Conners' ASQ-T: Methylphenidate: 18.9 (6.3) Clonidine: 18.4 (5.9) |
| Dose | 0.18 mg/day | 0.6 mg/day (max) | 0.6 mg/day (max) |
| Treatment length (mean range) | 42 days | 112 days | 112 days |

*Continued*

277

**Table 28:** (*Continued*)

| | In school-age children | | |
|---|---|---|---|
| | Clonidine versus placebo | | Methylphenidate versus clonidine |
| | Mixed comorbidity | Specific comorbidity (Tourette's syndrome, chronic motor tic disorder or chronic vocal tic disorder) | Specific comorbidity (Tourette's syndrome, chronic motor tic disorder or chronic vocal tic disorder) |
| *Benefits* | | | |
| ADHD core symptoms (teacher-rated) | CTRS: SMD −0.57 (−1.06 to −0.08) Quality: High K = 1, N = 67 | ASQ-T: SMD −2.42 (−3.07 to −1.76) Quality: High K = 1, N = 136 | ASQ-T: SMD −2.18 (−2.81 to −1.56) Quality: High K = 1, N = 136 |
| ADHD core symptoms (parent-rated) | CPRS: SMD −0.16 (−0.64 to 0.32) Quality: Moderate K = 1, N = 67 | ASQ-P: SMD −2.41 (−3.07 to −1.75) Quality: High K = 1, N = 136 | ASQ-P: SMD −2.41 (−3.09 to −1.73) Quality: High K = 1, N = 136 |

| | | | |
|---|---|---|---|
| Conduct problems (teacher-rated) | CTRS: SMD −0.68 (−1.18 to −0.18) Quality: High K = 1, N = 67 | IOWA: SMD −1.11 (−1.64 to −0.58) Quality: High K = 1, N = 136 | IOWA: SMD −1.10 (−1.62 to −0.57) Quality: High K = 1, N = 136 |
| Conduct problems (parent-rated) | CPRS: SMD −0.31 (−0.8 to 0.17) Quality: Moderate K = 1, N = 67 | — | — |
| Clinical improvement (clinician-rated) | — | CGI: RR 1.98 (1.11 to 3.52) Quality: High K = 1, N = 136 | CGI: RR 0.28 (0.14 to 0.56) Quality: High K = 1, N = 136 |
| *Harms* | | | |
| Leaving study early due to any reason | NNTB 16 (NNTB 4 to ∞ to NNTH 11) Quality: Moderate K = 1, N = 67 | NNTB 10 (NNTB 3 to ∞ to NNTH 12) Quality: High K = 1, N = 136 | NNTB 100 (NNTB 6 3 to ∞ to NNTH 7) Quality: Moderate K = 1, N = 136 |

### 10.9.5    Clinical evidence summary: clonidine versus methylphenidate

In one study of ADHD with comorbid tics (KURLAN2002) there was a small preference for methylphenidate over clonidine in reducing ADHD symptoms and conduct
problems.

## 10.10    BUPROPION

### 10.10.1    Pharmacology and prescribing

Bupropion is a selective inhibitor of the neuronal reuptake of noradrenaline and
dopamine. It is licensed as an aid to smoking cessation in combination with motivational support in nicotine-dependent patients; it is currently not licensed for patients
under 18 years or for the treatment of ADHD (GlaxoSmithKline UK, 2008). The
mechanism by which bupropion enhances the ability of patients to abstain from
smoking is unknown. It is presumed that this action is mediated by noradrenergic
and/or dopaminergic mechanisms (GlaxoSmithKline UK, 2008).

### 10.10.2    Safety and adverse effects

Many adverse events have been reported: dry mouth, gastro-intestinal disturbances,
taste disturbance; insomnia (reduced by avoiding dose at bedtime), tremor, impaired
concentration, headache, dizziness, depression, agitation, anxiety; fever; rash, pruritus, sweating; less commonly, chest pain, tachycardia, hypertension, flushing, confusion, tinnitus, asthenia, and visual disturbances; rarely jaundice, hepatitis, palpitation,
postural hypotension, hallucinations, depersonalisation dystonia, ataxia, abnormal
dreams, memory impairment, paraesthesia, blood-glucose disturbances, urinary
retention, urinary frequency, Stevens-Johnson syndrome, and exacerbation of psoria-
sis; very rarely delusions and aggression (British Medical Association & the Royal
Pharmaceutical Society of Great Britain, 2007; GlaxoSmithKline UK, 2008). Many
of these adverse events could also be caused by stopping smoking (GlaxoSmithKline
UK, 2008).

   Bupropion is associated with a dose-related risk of seizure with an estimated incidence of approximately 0.1%. There have been 184 reports in the UK of seizures
suspected of being associated with the use of bupropion (MHRA, 2002). In approximately one half of the reports, patients had either a past history of seizure(s) and/or
risk factors for their occurrence. To reduce the risk of seizures, bupropion is
contraindicated in patients with a current seizure disorder or any history of seizures,
with current or previous diagnosis of bulimia or anorexia nervosa, with a known
CNS tumour, and those experiencing abrupt withdrawal from alcohol or benzodiazepines (MHRA, 2002).

## 10.10.3  Clinical evidence for bupropion

Of the 49 trials, five included a comparison of bupropion with placebo. Two of these studies recruited school-age children with ADHD (a common coexisting condition was conduct disorder). Three trials involved adults with ADHD (common coexisting conditions included major depression, anxiety disorders and antisocial personality disorder).

Study information and evidence from the important outcomes and overall quality of evidence are presented in Table 29. The full evidence profiles and associated forest plots can be found in Appendix 19 and Appendix 18, respectively.

### Table 29:  Study information and evidence summary table for trials of bupropion

|  | In school-age children Bupropion versus placebo Mixed comorbidity | In adults Bupropion versus placebo Mixed comorbidity |
|---|---|---|
| Total no. of trials (total no. of participants) | 2 (139) | 3 (261) |
| Study ID | CASAT1987 CONNERS1996B | REIMHERR2005A WILENS2001A WILENS2005B |
| Diagnosis | ADD with hyperactivity (common coexisting conditions: conduct disorder) | ADHD (common coexisting conditions: major depression, anxiety disorders, antisocial personality disorders) |
| Baseline severity (mean range) | Conners' TQ Abbrev: Bupropion: 19.93 (4.62) to 20.35 (5.21) Placebo: 20.67 (7.87) to 21.50 (4.08) | Global Assessment of Functioning: Bupropion: 53.3 (4.6) to 57.1 (10.0) Placebo: 54.6 (3.1) to 58.1 (10.9) |
| Dose | 6 mg/kg (max) | 298 to 393 mg/kg |
| Treatment length (mean range) | 28 days | 42–56 days |

*Continued*

**Table 29:** (*Continued*)

|  | In school-age children<br>Bupropion versus placebo<br>Mixed comorbidity | In adults<br>Bupropion versus placebo<br>Mixed comorbidity |
|---|---|---|
| *Benefits* | | |
| ADHD core symptoms (teacher-rated) | CPTQ-T:<br>SMD −0.70<br>(−1.11 to 0.29)<br>Quality: High<br>K = 2, N = 139 | − |
| ADHD core symptoms (parent-rated) | CPTQ-P:<br>SMD −0.88<br>(−1.89 to 0.13)<br>Quality: High<br>K = 2, N = 139 | − |
| ADHD core symptoms (mean at endpoint) (investigator-rated) | − | Various measures:<br>SMD −0.36<br>(−0.79 to 0.07)<br>Quality: High<br>K = 2, N = 99 |
| ADHD core symptoms (mean change) (investigator-rated) | − | ADHD-RS:<br>SMD −0.42<br>(−0.73 to −0.11)<br>Quality: High<br>K = 1, N = 162 |
| Conduct problems (teacher-rated) | CTQ (conduct):<br>SMD −0.44<br>(−1.21 to 0.32)<br>Quality: Moderate<br>K = 1, N = 30 | − |
| Conduct problems (parent-rated) | CPQ:<br>SMD 0.0<br>(−0.76 to 0.76)<br>Quality: Moderate<br>K = 1, N = 30 | − |

**Table 29:** (*Continued*)

| | In school-age children Bupropion versus placebo Mixed comorbidity | In adults Bupropion versus placebo Mixed comorbidity |
|---|---|---|
| Clinical improvement (clinician-rated) | – | Various measures: RR 2.01 (1.36 to 2.95) Quality: High K = 3, N = 261 |
| *Harms* | | |
| Rash | NNTH 10 (NNTH 4 to ∞ to NNTB 34) Quality: Moderate K = 1, N = 109 | – |
| Dry mouth | – | NNTH 25 (NNTH 7 to ∞ to NNTB 16) Quality: High K = 2, N = 202 |
| Nausea | – | NNTH 20 (NNTH 8 to ∞ to NNTB 100) Quality: Moderate K = 1, N = 162 |
| Nasopharyngitis | – | NNTH 16 (NNTH 7 to ∞ to NNTB 100) Quality: Moderate K = 1, N = 162 |
| Dizziness | – | NNTH 20 (NNTH 9 to ∞ to NNTB 100) Quality: Moderate K = 1, N = 162 |
| Constipation | – | NNTH 25 (NNTH 10 to ∞ to NNTB 34) Quality: Moderate K = 1, N = 162 |
| Irritability | – | NNTH 25 (NNTH 10 to ∞ to NNTB 34) |

*Continued*

**Table 29: (*Continued*)**

|  | In school-age children Bupropion versus placebo Mixed comorbidity | In adults Bupropion versus placebo Mixed comorbidity |
|---|---|---|
|  |  | Quality: Moderate K = 1, N = 162 |
| Tinnitus | – | NNTH 16 (8 to 100) Quality: Moderate K = 1, N = 162 |
| Chest pain | – | NNTH 10 (NNTH 4 to ∞ to NNTB 20) Quality: Moderate K = 1, N = 40 |
| Leaving study early due to adverse events | NNTH 20 (NNTH 8 to ∞ to NNTB 100) Quality: High K = 2, N = 139 | – |
| Leaving study early due to any reason | NNTH 33 (NNTH 7 to ∞ to NNTB 16) Quality: Moderate K = 2, N = 139 | NNTH 20 (NNTH 6 to ∞ to NNTB 20) Quality: High K = 2, N = 202 |

### 10.10.4    Clinical evidence summary

For individual outcomes, the quality of the evidence was generally moderate to high.

*Bupropion in school-age children*
There is no statistically significant evidence that bupropion reduces ADHD core symptoms or behaviour in children with ADHD.

One study reports an increase of rash in children taking bupropion when compared with placebo. When compared with placebo, bupropion may increase the risk of discontinuation.

*Conclusion (school-age children)*
There is no evidence that bupropion is effective in reducing ADHD core symptoms or conduct problems in children with ADHD. There is limited evidence that bupropion may increase the risk of rash.

*Bupropion in adults*

There is some evidence that bupropion when compared with placebo reduces ADHD core symptoms and produces clinical improvement in adults with ADHD (mixed comorbidities).

Bupropion is more likely than placebo to produce the following side effects: dry mouth, insomnia and chest pain as well as increasing the risk of discontinuation.

*Conclusion (adults)*

There is some evidence that bupropion is effective in reducing ADHD core symptoms and producing clinical improvement in adults with ADHD. There is also evidence that bupropion may increase the risk of side effects.

## 10.11    MODAFINIL

### 10.11.1    Pharmacology and prescribing

Modafinil is an antinarcoleptic and mood-enhancing drug; the pharmacological mechanism by which it acts as both is still under investigation. It has been proposed that modafinil acts on the GABAergic inhibitory network of the thamalocortical system, in agreement with the previously described effect on GABAergic networks in sleep and non-sleep-related areas (Urbano *et al.*, 2007).

Modafinil is licensed for the symptomatic relief of excessive sleepiness associated with narcolepsy, obstructive sleep apnoea/hypopnoea syndrome and moderate to severe chronic shift work sleep disorder (Cephalon UK Limited, 2008).

### 10.11.2    Safety and adverse effects

Reported side effects are: dry mouth, appetite changes, gastro-intestinal disturbances (including nausea, diarrhoea, constipation and dyspepsia), abdominal pain; tachycardia, vasodilation, chest pain, palpitation; headache (uncommonly migraine), anxiety, sleep disturbances, dizziness, depression, confusion, abnormal thinking, paraesthesia, agitation, asthenia; visual disturbances; less commonly mouth ulcers, glossitis, pharyngitis, dysphagia, taste disturbance, hypertension, hypotension, brady-cardia, arrhythmia, peripheral oedema, hypercholesterolaemia, rhinitis, dyspnoea, dyskinesia, amnesia, emotional lability, abnormal dreams, tremor, decreased libido, weight changes, hyperglycaemia, urinary frequency, menstrual disturbances, eosinophilia, leucopenia, myasthenia, muscle cramps, dry eye, sinusitis, epistaxis, myalgia, arthralgia, acne, sweating, rash, and pruritus (British Medical Association & the Royal Pharmaceutical Society of Great Britain, 2007; Cephalon UK Limited, 2008).

For modafinil, statistically significant adverse events and/or with an RR greater than 5% are displayed in Table 30. For a full list of adverse events see Appendix 18 (forest plot).

**Table 30: Study information and evidence summary table
for trials of modafinil**

| | In school-age children<br>Modafinil versus placebo<br>Mixed comorbidity |
|---|---|
| Total no. of trials (total no. of participants) | 5 (910) |
| Study ID | BIEDERMAN2005<br>BIEDERMAN2006B<br>GREENHILL2006<br>RUGINO2003<br>SWANSON2006 |
| Diagnosis | ADHD (common coexisting conditions: oppositional defiant disorder, conduct disorder, learning disorder, phobias, separation anxiety) |
| Baseline severity (mean range) | ADHD-RS (total):<br>Modafinil: 27.3 (14.1) to 38.8 (8.9)<br>Placebo: 24.5 (13.8) to 37.9 (9.0) |
| Dose | 264 to 425 mg/day |
| Treatment length (mean range) | 28 to 63 days |
| *Benefits* | |
| ADHD core symptoms (mean at endpoint) (teacher-rated) | ADHD-RS:<br>SMD $-0.52$<br>($-0.82$ to 0.22)<br>Quality: High<br>K = 1, N = 200 |
| ADHD core symptoms (mean change) (teacher-rated) | ADHD-RS:<br>SMD $-0.63$<br>($-0.84$ to $-0.43$)<br>Quality: High<br>K = 2, N = 438 |
| ADHD core symptoms (mean at endpoint) (parent-rated) | ADHD-RS:<br>SMD $-0.57$<br>($-0.87$ to $-0.26$) |

**Table 30:** (*Continued*)

| | In school-age children<br>Modafinil versus placebo<br>Mixed comorbidity |
|---|---|
| | Quality: High<br>K = 1, N = 200 |
| ADHD core symptoms<br>(mean change)<br>(parent-rated) | ADHD-RS:<br>SMD −0.54<br>(−0.74 to −0.33)<br>Quality: High<br>K = 2, N = 438 |
| Conduct problems<br>(mean change)<br>(parent-rated) | CPRS-R-S:<br>SMD −0.31<br>(−0.57 to −0.04)<br>Quality: High<br>K = 1, N = 248 |
| Clinical improvement<br>(clinician-rated) | CGI:<br>RR 2.79<br>(2.02 to 3.86)<br>Quality: High<br>K = 3, N = 686 |
| *Harms* | |
| Insomnia | NNTH 4<br>(3 to 5)<br>Quality: High<br>K = 2, N = 438 |
| Decreased appetite | NNTH 8<br>(5 to 12)<br>Quality: Moderate<br>K = 1, N = 24 |
| Pain | NNTH 25<br>(12 to ∞)<br>Quality: Moderate<br>K = 1, N = 248 |
| Vomiting | NNTH 11<br>(NNTH 3 to ∞ to NNTB 8)<br>Quality: Moderate<br>K = 1, N = 24 |

*Continued*

**Table 30: (*Continued*)**

| | In school-age children<br>Modafinil versus placebo<br>Mixed comorbidity |
|---|---|
| Stomach ache | NNTH 5<br>(NNTH 2 to ∞ to NNTB 15)<br>Quality: Moderate<br>K = 1, N = 24 |
| Headache | NNTH 11<br>(NNTH 3 to ∞ to NNTB 8)<br>Quality: Moderate<br>K = 1, N = 24 |
| Tearfulness | NNTH 11<br>(NNTH 3 to ∞ to NNTB 8)<br>Quality: Moderate<br>K = 1, N = 24 |
| Irritability | NNTH 11<br>(NNTH 3 to ∞ to NNTB 8)<br>Quality: Moderate<br>K = 1, N = 24 |
| Tonsillitis | NNTH 11<br>(NNTH 3 to ∞ to NNTB 8)<br>Quality: Moderate<br>K = 1, N = 24 |
| Pharyngitis | NNTH 11<br>(NNTH 3 to ∞ to NNTB 8)<br>Quality: Moderate<br>K = 1, N = 24 |
| Leaving study early due to adverse events | NNTH ∞<br>(NNTH 25 to ∞ to NNTB 33)<br>Quality:<br>K = 4, N = 720 |
| Leaving study early due to any reason | NNTB 25<br>(NNTB 8 to ∞ to NNTH 25)<br>Quality:<br>K = 4, N = 662 |

### 10.11.3    Clinical evidence for modafinil

Of the 49 studies included only five involved a comparison of modafinil with placebo. All trials were of school-age children with ADHD (common coexisting conditions included oppositional defiant disorder, conduct disorder, learning disorder, phobias and separation anxiety).

Study information and evidence from the important outcomes and overall quality of evidence are presented in Table 30. The full evidence profiles and associated forest plots can be found in Appendix 19 and Appendix 18, respectively.

### 10.11.4    Clinical evidence summary

For individual outcomes, the quality of the evidence was generally moderate to high.

Overall, the evidence shows that modafinil when compared with placebo has a medium effect in reducing ADHD symptoms and conduct problems as well as producing general clinical improvement. Adverse effects include an increased risk of insomnia, decreased appetite, pain, vomiting, stomach ache, headache, tearfulness, irritability, tonsillitis and pharyngitis.

Modafinil reduced the risk of discontinuation in children with ADHD.

No data were available for modafinil in adults.

### 10.12    ANTIDEPRESSANTS

### 10.12.1    Pharmacology and prescribing

Tricyclic antidepressants (TCAs) are thought to block the synaptic reuptake of monoamines including 5-hydroxytryptamine (5HT or serotonin), noradrenaline and dopamine. TCAs have gradually been replaced in clinical practice by selective serotonin reuptake inhibitors (SSRIs) and serotonin and noradrenaline reuptake inhibitors (SNRIs) which block the uptake of 5HT and noradrenaline respectively.

### 10.12.2    Safety and adverse effects

TCAs have significant side effects and high toxicity in overdose. Concerns regarding potential cardiotoxicity of desipramine have led to its withdrawal in the UK. There is limited evidence that SSRIs and SNRIs may increase the risk of suicidal ideation and/or behaviour.

### 10.12.3    Clinical evidence summary

There is no evidence that TCAs, SSRIs or SNRIs are of value in the treatment of the symptoms of ADHD.

## 10.13    ATYPICAL ANTIPSYCHOTICS

### 10.13.1    Pharmacology and prescribing

Atypical antipsychotic drugs such as risperidone are most often used to treat psychoses (including schizophrenia). Atypical antipsychotics are also used to treat some forms of bipolar disorder, psychotic depression, obsessive-compulsive disorder, Tourette's syndrome and autistic spectrum disorders. The atypical antipsychotics have found favour among clinicians and are gradually replacing the typical antipsychotics. The mechanism of action of these agents is unclear but it is thought that these drugs are D2 receptor antagonists and 5-HT2A receptor antagonists. The receptor binding profile of the atypical antipsychotics varies substantially, and this variability may be responsible for clinical differences.

### 10.13.2    Safety and adverse effects

The side effect profile of atypical antipsychotics includes increased appetite, weight gain and metabolic disturbances.

### 10.13.3    Clinical evidence summary

There is no evidence that atypical antipsychotics are of value in treatment of the symptoms of ADHD.

## 10.14    EFFICACY/HARMS IN SPECIAL CIRCUMSTANCES

Pharmacological treatment may need to be more cautious in special circumstances, such as specific coexisting conditions, because of the possible increase of risk of medical issues.

The search for RCTs identified studies of pharmacological treatment of children with ADHD and comorbid developmental reading disorder (see Section 10.6.6), tic disorder (see Section 10.8.5), Tourette's syndrome, chronic motor tic or chronic vocal tic disorder (see Section 10.9.4). No studies were identified that met the quality assessment criteria for children with ADHD and comorbid learning disability and/or developmental disorders.

The GDG identified and discussed the relevant literature and consensus agreement was reached about possible risks and/or benefits of drug treatment.

Treatment of ADHD in individuals with autism or learning disabilities should follow the guidelines as described. There needs to be careful assessment prior to the decision to use medication, however, because of the increased risk of medical issues. Treatment may need to be more cautious if there are significant neurological problems because of the increased risk of side effects. In those individuals who have difficulty communicating, careful consideration needs to be given to enable them to take part in discussions about their medication and to monitor the effects of the medication. Carers will also have a pivotal role in carefully monitoring and looking for any evidence of side effects in those patients who are unable to discuss their medication fully.

While the pharmacological treatment of ADHD in the context of autism can be effective in reducing the core features of ADHD, the possibility of exacerbating the ritualistic behaviours and stereotypies means that careful monitoring is required.

### 10.14.1    Quality of evidence reviewed

The quality of the evidence reviewed was generally moderate to low. Efficacy studies were typically of short duration only (range: 21 to 238 days) and authors were usually not explicit about the inclusion or exclusion of conditions coexisting with ADHD. Most studies compared a single active drug with placebo. There are few direct 'head-to-head' comparisons of active drugs.

Interpretation of harm-related outcomes was limited to a small number of short-term clinical trials that reported harm data. Overall, adverse events have been reported infrequently and poorly, and further research is recommended.

## 10.15    CONCLUSION FROM CLINICAL EVIDENCE

Methylphenidate and atomoxetine are the only drugs where clear RCT evidence exists for clinical effectiveness in reducing ADHD symptoms in school-age children, young people and adults. When compared with placebo, the size of clinical effect is largest for methylphenidate. Two studies were found that involved head-to-head comparison between the two drugs and the result from one study indicated that there are no significant differences in terms of its effectiveness in children with ADHD. However, in this study the administered dose for methylphenidate was relatively 'small' (0.2 to 0.6 mg/kg/day) compared with a 'larger' atomoxetine dose administered (0.8 to 1.8 mg/kg/day). The second study showed that methylphenidate was more effective in children's clinical improvement.

Methylphenidate and atomoxetine have a similar adverse event profile with respect to effects on appetite, growth, pulse and blood pressure requiring similar monitoring. Rarer harm events associated with atomoxetine include increased risk of suicidal behaviour and hepatic damage. There is no evidence from high-quality RCTs for the efficacy of dexamfetamine in children, although there are crossover trials that show efficacy. It is based on these that the TA (NICE, 2006b) recommends dexamfetamine. In addition, there is one trial supporting improvement in adults.

There is some limited evidence that the off-label use of modafinil, clonidine and bupropion reduces symptoms of ADHD in children (and adults for bupropion) while these drugs all produce more adverse effects than placebo.

## 10.16    HEALTH ECONOMICS EVIDENCE

### 10.16.1    Pharmacological treatment in children and young people with ADHD

The systematic literature search identified five economic studies that assessed the cost effectiveness of specific pharmacological treatments compared with placebo or other pharmacological treatments for children with ADHD, including the economic analysis undertaken to support NICE guidance on the use of methylphenidate, atomoxetine and dexamfetamine in this population (Donnelly *et al.*, 2004; Gilmore & Milne, 2001; King *et al.*, 2006; Narayan & Hay, 2004; Zupancic *et al.*, 1998). Of the identified studies, one was conducted in the US, one in Canada, one in Australia and two in the UK. Details on the methods used for the systematic search of the economic literature are described in Chapter 3. Information on the methods used and the results reported in all economic studies included in the systematic literature review are presented in the form of evidence tables in Appendix 14.

Gilmore and Milne (2001) performed a cost-utility analysis to assess the cost effectiveness of methylphenidate compared with no treatment, in children aged 6 to 12 years with hyperkinetic disorder in the UK. The study was based on decision-analytic modelling, using a time horizon of 1 year. The perspective of the analysis was that of the NHS; costs included drug acquisition costs and outpatient clinic costs. The measure of outcome was the number of QALYs gained by use of methylphenidate compared with no treatment. Clinical effectiveness was based on a systematic review of the literature; no meta-analysis of the clinical studies was undertaken. QALYs were generated using the IHRQL and a number of assumptions regarding the HRQoL of children with hyperkinetic disorder responding or not responding to treatment. Resource use data were based on expert opinion. The ICER of methylphenidate compared with no treatment was found to be £9,177 per QALY gained (1997 prices). In sensitivity analysis, this ratio ranged from £5,782 to £29,049 per QALY gained. The authors concluded that short-term treatment of hyperkinetic children with methylphenidate was a cost-effective option from the point of view of the NHS. The major limitations of the analysis were the lack of systematic search of the literature for evidence on the clinical effectiveness of methylphenidate, the use of IHRQL for the measurement of HRQoL in the study population, which was considered quite insensitive by the authors, and the further assumptions made in order to estimate the number of QALYs gained with therapy.

Donnelly and colleagues (2004) evaluated the use of methylphenidate and dexamfetamine compared with standard care, which included contacts with healthcare professionals but no medication, in children with ADHD in Australia. The study was based on decision-analytic modelling. Clinical effectiveness data were derived from meta-analysis of studies identified in a systematic literature review. Data on the severity of ADHD in Australia and the usage of health services by the study population were taken from a national survey. The study adopted the Australian health services' perspective, including costs to the healthcare sector and to the children's families. The measure of outcome was the number of Disability Adjusted Life Years (DALYs) averted by use of medication compared with standard care. The time horizon of the analysis was 1 year. The ICER of methylphenidate versus standard care was found to equal approximately Aus\$15,000 per DALY averted (95% CI: Aus\$9,100 to Aus\$22,000 per DALY averted), while the ICER of dexamfetamine versus standard care was Aus\$4,100 per DALY averted (95% CI: dexamfetamine dominant to \$14,000 per DALY averted). The cost year was 2000. In the comparison between the two medications, dexamfetamine was the dominant option, as its effectiveness was similar to that of methylphenidate but its cost was significantly lower. The authors concluded that both medications were cost effective compared with standard care; given that dexamfetamine, but not methylphenidate, was partially subsidised by the government, methylphenidate might be more attractive financially for the government while dexamfetamine was more cost-effective from the perspective of the family. Potential limitations of the study, as acknowledged by the authors, were the difficulty in determining the change in disability weights resulting from pharmacological treatment, as well as possible publication bias affecting the clinical effectiveness data used in the analysis. In addition, the study did not consider the treatment of frequently coexisting conditions, the long-term side effects of medication, the long-term educational, occupational, criminal and social outcomes and the resulting cost savings associated with provision of medication in children with ADHD. The authors estimated that had they considered all the above factors, medications might prove to be overall more cost effective than demonstrated.

Narayan and Hay (2004) assessed the cost effectiveness of methylphenidate, amphetamine/dexamfetamine mixed salts, and no treatment in children with ADHD in the US. The study was based on decision-analytic modelling. Clinical and cost data were derived from a literature review. The perspective of analysis was stated to be societal, but indirect costs (that is, productivity losses) were not taken into account at the estimation of costs. Costs included healthcare costs (costs of drugs, outpatient visits and laboratory tests), school administration costs as well as out-of-pocket expenses. Outcome was expressed in QALYs, generated using the IHRQL. The time horizon of the analysis was 1 year. The study demonstrated that methylphenidate was dominated by amphetamine/dexamfetamine mixed salts (meaning that methylphenidate was more expensive and less effective than amphetamine/dexamfetamine mixed salts). The ICER of amphetamine/dexamfetamine mixed salts versus no treatment was US\$21,957 per QALY gained in 2003 prices (the ICER of methylphenidate versus no treatment was roughly US\$50,000 per QALY gained). Results were robust under most scenarios examined in sensitivity analysis. The major driver of cost-effectiveness results was the relative compliance of the two medications; utility weights were also important factors affecting the cost effectiveness of medications compared with no treatment. The authors' conclusion was that both medications were cost effective compared with no treatment and that it was difficult to make strong conclusions about the relative cost effectiveness between medications given their essentially equal efficacy and similar side-effect profiles. The limitations of the analysis were the lack of systematic review and meta-analysis of clinical studies of the assessed interventions, and the short time horizon that did not allow long-term benefits and harms of medication to be considered.

Zupancic and colleagues (1998) assessed the cost effectiveness of methylphenidate, dexamfetamine, pemoline, psychological/behavioural therapy and combination therapy (consisting of psychological/behavioural therapy and methylphenidate) in comparison with no treatment from the perspective of a third-party payer in Canada. A decision-analytic model with a time horizon of 1 year was developed for this purpose. The clinical effectiveness data were derived from meta-analysis of studies included in a systematic literature review. Resource estimates were based on expert opinion and a published survey. Costs of medications included acquisition costs, costs of contacts with healthcare professionals and laboratory testing costs, as well as hospitalisation costs regarding management of toxic hepatitis associated with use of pemoline. Costs of psychological/behavioural therapy included contacts with psychologists alongside parent- and teacher-training. The outcome of the analysis was the change in the Conners' Teacher Rating Scales (CTRS) score. The meta-analysis of the clinical studies concluded that the efficacy of methyl-phenidate, dexamfetamine and pemoline was comparable. In the economic analysis, methyl-phenidate was found to dominate dexamfetamine. This result was robust under the majority of scenarios explored in sensitivity analysis. The ICER of methylphenidate versus no treatment was Can$64 per point change in the CTRS score, or Can$384 per 6-point change in the CTRS score, which was considered as a clinically significant difference. The ICER of pemoline versus methylphenidate was Can$246 per point change, or Can$1,476 per 6-point change in the CTRS score (1997 prices). However, there were concerns about the drug's safety because pemoline is associated with potentially fatal hepatic failure. The results of the analysis relating to other treatments (psychological/behavioural and combination therapy) are provided in Chapter 11. The authors reported as a general limitation of the analysis the heterogeneity characterising the treatments assessed and the outcome measures across published trials, which did not allow for a comprehensive synthesis of data and a robust comparison across the treatment options evaluated. More specifically, the number of trials for each treatment strategy was small, resulting in wide 95% CIs of the efficacy data. Moreover, the meta-analysis was limited to effects of treatment measured by changes in CTRS score, as no dichotomous measures, indicating a clinically significant improvement, were available for all options. Subsequently, in order to interpret the results of the economic analysis, it was assumed that treatment efficacy was constant across different levels of ADHD severity. Additional concerns were expressed regarding the harms of pemoline, and the fact that mortality from hepatic failure was not captured in the measure of outcome used. Taking the last point into consideration, methylphenidate was probably the most cost effective among the medications assessed in the analysis.

### 10.16.2 NICE TA on the use of methylphenidate, atomoxetine and dexamfetamine for children and adolescents with ADHD

King and colleagues (2006) conducted an economic analysis to assess the cost effectiveness of methylphenidate, atomoxetine and dexamfetamine in children and adolescents with ADHD. As this evidence was used to support the recent NICE TA on this area (NICE, 2006b), it is discussed in more detail.

The analysis was based on decision-analytic modelling. The medications assessed were IR methylphenidate, two forms of MR methylphenidate with 8 and 12 hours action respectively, atomoxetine, and dexamfetamine. The analysis evaluated the use of these medications alone, as well as in combination with behavioural therapy. The economic model considered alternative sequences of treatments in a hypothetical cohort of children with ADHD aged 6 years. The time horizon of the analysis was 1 year. Children not responding to one treatment or withdrawing from treatment owing to the presence of intolerable side effects were assumed to move to the next treatment in line, until they reached no treatment at the end of the sequence. Children responding to treatment remained on therapy and continued being responsive for the remainder of the year. It was assumed that no intolerable side effects developed after the titration period, and, therefore, any side effects experienced after titration were relatively minor and tolerable and did not lead to discontinuation of treatment. A secondary analysis extended the time horizon of the analysis until children reached 18 years of age.

Preliminary analysis showed that strategies consisting of three lines of active treatment were cost effective compared with strategies containing only one or two lines of treatment. For this reason, the results presented for the base-case and sensitivity analyses included strategies consisting of three lines of active treatment plus no treatment at the end of the sequence. In total, the analysis examined 18 strategies consisting of all possible three-line sequences of the medications assessed, and a strategy of no treatment. A secondary analysis considered another 18 strategies of three-line sequences of combined treatment, making the total number of strategies assessed 37.

The analysis adopted the perspective of the NHS and personal social services. Costs included medications, contacts with healthcare professionals (GPs, psychiatrists, paediatricians) and laboratory testing. Resource use estimates were based on expert opinion. The price year was 2003. The measure of outcome was expressed in QALYs. Clinical effectiveness data were taken from a systematic review of the literature and meta-analysis of RCTs. Only studies reporting outcomes as response rates to treatment were considered; first because this type of outcome expressed a clinically meaningful change on a rating scale, and second because such data would allow a cost-utility analysis to be conducted (that is, an economic analysis where the outcome is expressed in QALYs), given that the literature review had identified studies providing utility data for children with ADHD responding or not to treatment. The base-case analysis included only clinical studies that defined response as a score of 0–2 (from completely well to improved) on the Clinical Global Impression Improvement subscale (CGI-I). Sensitivity analyses relaxed the criteria of definition of response, and incorporated trials that used other definitions, such as a 25% or greater reduction in the ADHD-RS score, a score 0 or 1 on the SNAP-IV scale, and so on. It needs to be noted, however, that studies defining response using scales other than the CGI-I were not available for all interventions under assessment. In order to pool clinical data from all trials considered in the economic analysis, a mixed treatment comparison model was developed. Utility weights were based on Coghill and colleagues (2004); the study generated utility weights for children with ADHD by asking parents of 142

295

children with ADHD in the UK to fill in EQ-5D questionnaires (more details of this study are provided in the economic sections of Chapter 7).

The base-case analysis demonstrated that all treatment strategies consisting of drug monotherapies followed by no treatment were similar in terms of QALYs gained. This was expected given the uncertainty surrounding the relative clinical effectiveness of all pharmacological interventions examined. Nevertheless, one dominant strategy was identified, which was associated with the lowest costs and the highest QALYs gained compared with the other 18 strategies. This strategy was a sequence of first-line dexamfetamine, second-line IR methylphenidate and third-line atomoxetine, followed by no treatment. Table 31 shows the total costs and benefits associated with the 18 strategies of three-line drug sequences plus the strategy of no treatment. It can be seen that strategy 13 incurs the lowest costs and results in maximum health benefits.

Probabilistic analysis showed that strategy 13 had the highest expected net benefit for willingness-to-pay (WTP) between 0 and £60,000 per QALY. Sensitivity analysis showed that this strategy remained optimal when additional costs of coexisting conditions were included, when the model was extrapolated until children reached 18 years of age and when alternative estimates on resource use were tested. In contrast, this result was sensitive to utility weights used. When alternative utility weights were employed (taken from a manufacturer's submission), then strategy 11 was the optimal strategy. However, the authors acknowledged that because of limitations characterising the alternative utility data tested, this result should be interpreted with caution. They concluded that strategy 13 was clearly an optimal treatment strategy, but acknowledged the limitations of the analysis. The limitations included using a subset of the clinical evidence available because of the need to utilise outcomes reported as response rates; the assumptions required in the model structure because of lack of data; and the lack of evidence on long-term outcomes associated with the evaluated treatments. Therefore the authors highlighted the possibility of a significant change in the results as new data on long-term outcomes emerge. Results of the sub-analysis that incorporated combination strategies are reported in Chapter 11.

Overall, the review of the economic evidence demonstrated that pharmacological treatments are cost effective compared with no treatment in children with ADHD. The relative cost effectiveness of different medications cannot be established with confidence according to this literature, because of the uncertainty characterising their relative clinical effectiveness, the heterogeneity of outcome measures used in the clinical literature that makes synthesis of available evidence problematic and the lack of evidence on long-term benefits and harms of medication, alongside the lack of comprehensive data on the HRQoL of children with ADHD.

### 10.16.3    Medication management – economic analysis of the MTA study

The MTA study (MTA Co-operative Group 1999a, 2004a, 2007), undertaken on children aged 7 to 9.9 years with ADHD combined type in the US, incorporated an economic analysis that aimed to determine the cost effectiveness of the interventions

**Table 31: Results of the base-case analysis of the economic model developed to support NICE guidance on the use of methylphenidate (MPH), atomoxetine (ATX) and dexamfetamine (DEX) for children and adolescents with ADHD (taken from the NICE assessment report[22])**

| Strategy | Order of treatments | Cost | QALYs |
|---|---|---|---|
| 1 | IR-MPH – ATX – DEX – No treatment | £1233 | 0.8279 |
| 2 | MR-MPH8 – ATX – DEX – No treatment | £1470 | 0.8273 |
| 3 | MR-MPH12 – ATX – DEX – No treatment | £1479 | 0.8278 |
| 4 | ATX – IR-MPH – DEX – No treatment | £1480 | 0.8278 |
| 5 | ATX – MR-MPH8 – DEX – No treatment | £1550 | 0.8277 |
| 6 | ATX – IR-MPH12 – DEX – No treatment | £1563 | 0.8274 |
| 7 | IR-MPH – DEX – ATX – No treatment | £1140 | 0.8283 |
| 8 | MR-MPH8 – DEX – ATX – No treatment | £1336 | 0.8277 |
| 9 | MR-MPH12 – DEX – ATX – No treatment | £1410 | 0.8284 |
| 10 | ATX – DEX – IR-MPH – No treatment | £1466 | 0.8281 |
| 11 | ATX – DEX – MR-MPH8 – No treatment | £1485 | 0.8281 |
| 12 | ATX – DEX – MR-MPH12 – No treatment | £1488 | 0.8278 |
| 13 | DEX – IR-MPH – ATX – No treatment | £1098 | 0.8289 |
| 14 | DEX – MR-MPH8 – ATX – No treatment | £1157 | 0.8287 |
| 15 | DEX – MR-MPH12 – ATX – No treatment | £1159 | 0.8287 |
| 16 | DEX – ATX – IR-MPH – No treatment | £1158 | 0.8288 |
| 17 | DEX – ATX – MR-MPH8 – No treatment | £1177 | 0.8288 |
| 18 | DEX – ATX – MR-MPH12 – No treatment | £1180 | 0.8285 |
| 19 | No treatment | £1223 | 0.7727 |

assessed in the trial, that is, medication management, intensive behavioural treatment, a combination of the two and routine community care. The economic assessment referred to a follow-up period of 14 months. Two publications provided results of this economic analysis (Jensen *et al.*, 2005; Foster *et al.*, 2007). Details of these studies

---

[22]Available at http://www.nice.org.uk/guidance/index.jsp?action=download&o=33226

are presented in the form of evidence tables in Appendix 14. The two studies selected a different measure of outcome as the primary outcome of the economic analysis. Jensen and colleagues (2005) chose the proportion of 'normalised' children, with normalisation defined by a score 0 or 1 on the SNAP scale; Foster and colleagues (2007) chose the change on Columbia Impairment Scale Effect Size (CIS ES). The perspective adopted by both studies was that of a third-party payer, including any costs paid by a patient, an insurer, or other third parties. Estimated costs included all real treatment costs of the MTA study, such as drug acquisition costs, costs associated with healthcare professional contacts (psychiatrists, psychologists, paediatricians, and so on), teachers and teacher aides' costs, but excluded any costs associated with the research component of the study. Prices referred to year 2000. Results were reported for four sub-groups of children according to their comorbidity status: children with ADHD only (32%), children with ADHD and internalising coexisting conditions, that is, anxiety or depression (14%), children with ADHD and externalising coexisting conditions, that is, conduct or oppositional defiant disorder (30%), and children with ADHD and both coexisting conditions (24%). This section describes the results from the comparison between medication management and routine community care. Full results of the MTA economic analysis are provided in Chapter 11.

Jensen and colleagues (2005) reported that medication management was more effective than routine community care in terms of the proportion of children normalised in the total population of children with ADHD as well as in any of the sub-groups with/without coexisting conditions. The costs associated with medication management were higher than the costs of routine community care in all sub-populations, with the exception of children with pure ADHD, in which medication management was slightly cheaper than routine community care (US$1,079 versus US$1,131 per child with pure ADHD treated, respectively). Therefore, in children with pure ADHD, medication management was dominant over routine community care (more effective and less costly). The ICER of medication management versus routine community care for the total population of children with ADHD combined was US$360 per child normalised. The respective ICERs for the sub-groups of children with coexisting conditions ranged from US$140 (ADHD plus internalising disorder) to US$988 (ADHD plus both internalising and externalising disorders) per child normalised. It was reported that, for the total population of children with ADHD combined type, the difference in costs and outcomes between medication management and routine community care were statistically significant. The authors estimated that the additional costs of medication strategy over routine community care were modest compared with the large respective gains in the number of children effectively treated, and therefore concluded that, compared with routine community care available in the US, medication management was a cost-effective intervention for children with ADHD, with or without coexisting conditions.

Foster and colleagues (2007) reported that medication management was also more effective than routine community care when the outcome was measured as a change in functioning, expressed in CIS ES, in all sub-groups of children examined. The authors presented their findings in the form of cost-effectiveness acceptability curves (CEACs), which demonstrate the probability of an intervention being the most cost effective among all the interventions assessed at different levels of WTP for one unit of outcome gained (in this case one standard deviation of the CIS). CEACs showed that medication management had a higher probability of being cost effective compared with routine community care at any level of WTP.

The results of the above studies indicate that medication management is likely to be a cost-effective intervention from the perspective of a third-party payer in the US. The authors acknowledged as a limitation of their analyses the fact that they did not address potential longer-term costs and benefits associated with treatment, as well as broader societal costs, such as parental absence from work and related productivity losses, costs of special education services, and costs of other social services, including the juvenile justice system. Another limitation of the analysis, as stated in Foster and colleagues (2007), was the inability to generalise the results in other settings, as routine community care may vary considerably across different sites. It must be noted that routine community care described in the study included quite intensive psychosocial therapy (as indicated by high respective costs associated with routine community care), as well as provision of medication, mainly stimulants, in two-thirds of the study population; hence the intervention described in the MTA study may have been more intensive than community care received routinely in the UK.

Schlander and colleagues (2006a, 2006b, 2006c) evaluated the relative cost effectiveness of the interventions examined in the MTA study in the context of four European countries, including the UK. Resource use estimates still reflected US practice (taken from the MTA trial), but country-specific unit costs were employed. The perspective of the analysis referring to the UK was that of the NHS (direct medical expenditures). Costs for all countries were calculated in local currencies and then converted to 2005 Euros (€). In addition to previous sub-group distinctions, the authors provided results for children with ADHD combined type (according to DSM-IV), hyperkinetic/ conduct disorder (according to ICD-10), pure ADHD (without coexisting conditions), and pure hyperkinetic disorder (without coexisting conditions). The outcome measures used in the economic analyses were the number of children with ADHD normalised, the CIS ES, and also the QALYs gained by treatment. This section provides the results from the comparison between medication management and routine community care. Results from the comparisons across medication management, intensive behavioural therapy and combination therapy are presented in Chapter 11.

The ICER of medication management versus routine community care per normalised child in the UK was found to be approximately €3,720 for ADHD combined type, €3,540 for pure ADHD, €4,000 for hyperkinetic/conduct disorder, and €1,520 for pure hyperkinetic disorder (or £2,565, £2,440, £2,760, and £1,050 respectively, using a conversion rate of 1UK£ = 1.45€). When the measure of outcome was the CIS ES, then the ICER of medication management versus routine community care was estimated at roughly €3,000 for ADHD combined type, €2,775 for pure ADHD, €6,730 for hyperkinetic/conduct disorder, and €160 for pure hyperkinetic disorder (or £2,070, £1,915, £4,655, and £110 respectively, at a conversion rate of 1UK£ = 1.45€). CEACs demonstrated that for the majority of sub-populations examined, medication management had a higher probability of being cost effective compared with routine community care at any level of WTP. For children with hyperkinetic/conduct disorder, routine community care was likely to be more cost effective than medication management for low levels of WTP, that is, for up to roughly €6,000 (£4,100) per CIS ES. It was also found that for children with externalising coexisting conditions routine community care was likely to be more cost effective than medication management up to a WTP of approximately €4,000 (£2,700) per child normalised.

Schlander and colleagues (2006a) also provided a range of ICERs across the four European countries considered, with outcomes expressed in QALYs. However, no outcomes specific to the UK were available in the poster presentation. Using the reported costs per child treated in the UK context, the proportions of children normalised in the MTA study in the various sub-populations, and utility weights reported by Coghill and colleagues (2004), it was possible to estimate the incremental cost per QALY of medication management versus routine community care in the UK context. The estimated ICERs were £33,490 per QALY for ADHD combined type, £32,150 per QALY for pure ADHD, £36,590 per QALY for hyperkinetic/conduct disorder, and £13,990 per QALY for pure hyperkinetic disorder. In order to estimate QALYs associated with any treatment option it was assumed that improvement in HRQoL occurred at time zero for responders. It must be noted that decrement in HRQoL from medication was not considered.

The above results suggest that medication management may actually not be a cost-effective option for children with ADHD in the UK, according to the cost-effectiveness threshold set by NICE (2006c), apart from the sub-population of children with pure hyperkinetic disorder. However, this analysis is characterised by important limitations, as resource use estimates in both medication management and routine community care arms reflect clinical practice in the US setting, and may not be representative of UK practice. Therefore, the results of all economic analyses related to the MTA study, even those referring to the UK context in terms of unit costs used, need to be interpreted with caution.

### 10.16.4  Pharmacological treatment in adults with ADHD

The systematic search of the economic literature identified no studies evaluating the cost effectiveness of pharmacological interventions for adults with ADHD. Therefore, it was decided to develop an economic model in order to assess the relative cost effectiveness of potential first-line medications in this population. Clinical evidence was available for four medications: methylphenidate, atomoxetine, dexamfetamine and bupropion. Given that dexamfetamine and bupropion are not licensed for the treatment of adults with ADHD and after taking into account the lack of experience in using these two medications routinely for this purpose, the GDG deemed that the most appropriate comparison would be between methylphenidate, atomoxetine[23] and

---

[23]In adolescents whose symptoms persist into adulthood and who have shown clear benefit from treatment, it may be appropriate to continue treatment into adulthood. However, start of treatment with atomoxetine in adults is not appropriate.

no treatment. As discussed in Chapter 7, clinical effectiveness data in the form of dichotomous outcomes, such as response rates to treatment, are the most suitable to utilise in a cost-utility analysis, where the measure of outcome is expressed in QALYs. However, no clinical studies of atomoxetine reporting dichotomous outcomes were identified in the systematic search of the literature for adults with ADHD. Subsequently, an attempt was made to undertake an economic analysis based on studies reporting outcomes as changes in scores on scales measuring ADHD symptoms. Again, the clinical data were sparse and heterogeneous, and did not permit the development of a decision-analytic model that would allow for a comparison between methylphenidate and atomoxetine. More specifically, there were no head-to-head comparisons between methylphenidate and atomoxetine for adults with ADHD. The economic analysis would need to be based on indirect comparisons between the two drugs, with placebo being the common comparator in the available clinical studies. Two studies assessed the clinical effectiveness of methylphenidate versus placebo. SPENCER2005 expressed outcome as a mean score of Adult ADHD Investigator System Report Scale (AISRS) at endpoint of analysis; KOOIJ2004 expressed outcome as mean score of the ADHD-RS at endpoint of analysis. On the other hand, the three trials comparing atomoxetine to placebo in adults with ADHD (MICHELSON2003a, MICHELSON2003b, and WERNICKE 2004b) measured the mean change in CAARS from baseline to endpoint of analysis. It is evident that the scales used and the time points of measuring outcomes were different between the studies of methylphenidate and those of atomoxetine. Using these studies in an economic analysis would introduce bias, would require a number of assumptions and would, consequently, result in conclusions with high uncertainty.

Bearing in mind the comments above, economic considerations are important in the formulation of clinical practice recommendations. Medication has been shown to be cost effective in children with ADHD when compared with no treatment. The economic analysis undertaken to support the NICE TA on the use of methylphenidate, atomoxetine and dexamfetamine in children and adolescents with ADHD (NICE, 2006b) concluded that all sequences of drug monotherapies examined were more cost effective than no treatment (King *et al.*, 2006). The results from this analysis, presented in Table 31, showed that some strategies dominated no treatment, and the rest were more effective than no treatment at a cost below £6,500 per QALY in all cases. The effect sizes of drugs in adults with ADHD are overall somewhat lower than the respective effect sizes in children with the same condition, although comparison between the two populations is in some cases difficult, given the variety characterising outcome measurement in the trials included in the systematic review of clinical evidence. Nevertheless, it was considered that the relative magnitude of effect size of medication in adults (compared with children) was such that the ICER of medication as a whole versus no treatment was unlikely to exceed the cost-effectiveness threshold of £20,000 per QALY set by NICE (NICE, 2006c), and therefore provision of medication in adults with ADHD was estimated to be a cost-effective intervention.

In order to compare methylphenidate and atomoxetine, a rough cost analysis was attempted to measure the costs associated with provision of these two drugs in adults with ADHD. Assuming that the healthcare professional costs for titration and monitoring are similar, the drug acquisition costs over a year were estimated for the two medications. Provision of generic, IR methylphenidate at a daily dose of 60 mg costs £30 per month or £360 per year (Joint Formulary Committee, 2008). MR methylphenidate at a daily dose of 72 mg costs £81 per month or £972 per year (British Medical Association & the Royal Pharmaceutical Society of Great Britain [2007], Concerta XL®). Atomoxetine at a dose of 80 mg daily costs £129 per month or £1,548 per year (British Medical Association & the Royal Pharmaceutical Society of Great Britain [2007], Strattera®). Atomoxetine is therefore more expensive than methylphenidate in terms of drug acquisition costs.

The interpretation of all available clinical evidence indicated that methylphenidate is likely to be more effective than atomoxetine in adults with ADHD. Consequently, methylphenidate is possibly a dominant option over atomoxetine as a first-line pharmacological treatment in adults with ADHD. However, other factors need to be assessed, such as the presence of intolerable side effects that lead to discontinuation of treatment and initiation of second-line therapy; the management of other side effects; the acceptability of a drug that affects continuation rates; and compliance. These additional factors may affect the relative cost effectiveness of methylphenidate and atomoxetine.

## 10.17　FROM EVIDENCE TO RECOMMENDATIONS

On the whole, the evidence indicates that methylphenidate in the treatment of children and adults with ADHD has moderate to high beneficial effects on ADHD core symptoms and conduct problems. The evidence for atomoxetine as a treatment of ADHD in children and adults suggests a moderate beneficial effect on ADHD core symptoms and conduct problems. Two studies involved a head-to-head comparison between methylphenidate and atomoxetine and the results indicated that methylphenidate had more beneficial effects in children with ADHD.

Only lower-level evidence was found for the use of dexamfetamine in children with ADHD. For adults with ADHD, one study showed high beneficial effect of dexamfetamine on clinical improvement. However, the use of dexamfetamine in clinical practice is marginal and is not licensed for adults with ADHD.

For pre-school children there is no evidence that drug treatment is effective in the treatment of ADHD.

The review of the economic evidence demonstrated that drug treatments are cost effective compared with no treatment in children with ADHD. The relative cost effectiveness of different medications cannot be established owing mainly to the uncertainty characterising clinical-effectiveness data and the difficulty in synthesising available evidence. It must also be noted that long-term benefits and harms from medication have not been taken into account in the assessment of cost effectiveness as relevant data were not available or not suitable for a modelling exercise. Medication in adults is likely to be cost effective too, considering that the effect size of medication in adults with ADHD is significant and only moderately lower than that in children. Medication management was shown to be a cost-effective intervention in the US. However, the cost effectiveness results of the MTA study cannot be extrapolated to the UK context without caution, as the interventions assessed and the clinical practice in the US are likely to differ substantially from respective interventions and clinical practice in the UK.

As presented in Chapter 11, an economic analysis undertaken for this guideline comparing psychological, pharmacological and combined treatments for children with ADHD indicated that group behavioural therapy or group CBT for school-age children were more cost effective than medication. Combined therapies were not cost effective, as they incurred very high costs for a rather low additional effect. Again in this case, long-term benefits and harms from medication and psychological therapy were not considered in the economic analysis, as data appropriate to inform the economic model did not exist. A similar assessment of the cost effectiveness of psychological versus pharmacological interventions in adults with ADHD was not possible because of a complete lack of relevant clinical data.

## 10.18    RECOMMENDATIONS

### 10.18.1    Treatment for pre-school children

10.18.1.1    Drug treatment is not recommended for pre-school children with ADHD.

### 10.18.2    Treatment for school-age children with moderate ADHD

10.18.2.1    Drug treatment is not indicated as the first-line treatment for all school-age children and young people with ADHD. It should be reserved for those with severe symptoms and impairment or for those with moderate levels of impairment who have refused non-drug interventions, or whose symptoms have not responded sufficiently to parent-training/education programmes or group psychological treatment.

10.18.2.2    Following treatment with a parent-training/education programme, children and young people with ADHD and persisting significant impairment should be offered drug treatment.

### 10.18.3    Treatment for school-age children with severe ADHD (hyperkinetic disorder) and severe impairment

10.18.3.1    In school-age children and young people with severe ADHD, drug treatment should be offered as the first-line treatment. Parents should also be offered a group-based parent-training/education programme. (Key priority)

10.18.3.2    Drug treatment should only be initiated by an appropriately qualified healthcare professional with expertise in ADHD and should be based on a comprehensive assessment and diagnosis. Continued prescribing

and monitoring of drug therapy may be performed by general practitioners, under shared care arrangements[24].

10.18.3.3   If drug treatment is not accepted by the child or young person with severe
ADHD, or their parents or carers, healthcare professionals should advise
parents or carers and the child or young person about the benefits and superiority of drug treatment in this group. If drug treatment is still not
accepted, a group parent-training/education programme should be offered.

10.18.3.4   If a group parent-training/education programme is not effective for a
child or young person with severe ADHD, and if drug treatment has not
been accepted, discuss the possibility of drug treatment again or other
psychological treatment (group CBT and/or social skills training), highlighting the clear benefits and superiority of drug treatment in children
or young people with severe ADHD.

### 10.18.4   Pre-drug treatment assessment

10.18.4.1   Before starting drug treatment, children and young people with ADHD
should have a full pre-treatment assessment, which should include:
- full mental health and social assessment
- full history and physical examination, including:
  - assessment of history of exercise syncope, undue breathlessness
    and other cardiovascular symptoms
  - heart rate and blood pressure (plotted on a centile chart)
  - height and weight (plotted on a growth chart)
  - family history of cardiac disease and examination of the cardio-
    vascular system
- an electrocardiogram (ECG) if there is past medical or family history
  of serious cardiac disease, a history of sudden death in young family
  members or abnormal findings on cardiac examination
- risk assessment for substance misuse and drug diversion (where the
  drug is passed on to others for non-prescription use).

10.18.4.2   Drug treatment for children and young people with ADHD should always
form part of a comprehensive treatment plan that includes psychological,
behavioural and educational advice and interventions. (Key priority)

### 10.18.5   Choice of drug for children and young people with ADHD

10.18.5.1   Where drug treatment is considered appropriate, methylphenidate,
atomoxetine and dexamfetamine are recommended, within their licensed

---

[24]This recommendation is taken from TA98 (NICE, 2006b). At the time of publication, methylphenidate
and atomoxetine did not have UK marketing authorisation for use in children younger than 6 years.
Informed consent should be obtained and documented.

indications, as options for the management of ADHD in children and adolescents[25].

10.18.5.2  The decision regarding which product to use should be based on the following:
- the presence of comorbid conditions (for example, tic disorders, Tourette's syndrome, epilepsy)
- the different adverse effects of the drugs
- specific issues regarding compliance identified for the individual child or adolescent, for example problems created by the need to administer a mid-day treatment dose at school
- the potential for drug diversion (where the medication is forwarded on to others for non-prescription uses) and/or misuse
- the preferences of the child/adolescent and/or his or her parent or guardian[26].

10.18.5.3  When a decision has been made to treat children or young people with ADHD with drugs, healthcare professionals should consider:
- methylphenidate for ADHD without significant comorbidity
- methylphenidate for ADHD with comorbid conduct disorder
- methylphenidate or atomoxetine when tics, Tourette's syndrome, anxiety disorder, stimulant misuse or risk of stimulant diversion are present
- atomoxetine if methylphenidate has been tried and has been ineffective at the maximum tolerated dose, or if the child or young person is intolerant to low or moderate doses of methylphenidate. (Key priority)

10.18.5.4  When prescribing methylphenidate for the treatment of children or young people, modified-release preparations should be considered for the following reasons:
- convenience
- improving adherence
- reducing stigma (because the child or young person does not need to take medication at school)
- reducing problems schools have in storing and administering controlled drugs
- their pharmacokinetic profiles.

Alternatively, immediate-release preparations may be considered if more flexible dosing regimens are required, or during initial titration to determine correct dosing levels.

---

[25]This recommendation is taken from TA98 (NICE, 2006b). At the time of publication, methylphenidate and atomoxetine did not have UK marketing authorisation for use in children younger than 6 years. Informed consent should be obtained and documented.
[26]Ibid.

10.18.5.5     When starting drug treatment children and young people should be monitored for side effects. In particular, those treated with atomoxetine should be closely observed for agitation, irritability, suicidal thinking and self-harming behaviour, and unusual changes in behaviour, particularly during the initial months of treatment, or after a change in dose. Parents and/or carers should be warned about the potential for suicidal thinking and self-harming behaviour with atomoxetine and asked to report these to their healthcare professionals. Parents or carers should also be warned about the potential for liver damage in rare cases with atomoxetine (usually presenting as abdominal pain, unexplained nausea, malaise, darkening of the urine or jaundice).

10.18.5.6     If there is a choice of more than one appropriate drug, the product with the lowest cost (taking into account the cost per dose and number of daily doses) should be prescribed[27].

10.18.5.7     Antipsychotics are not recommended for the treatment of ADHD in children and young people.

### 10.18.6     Poor response to treatment

10.18.6.1     If there has been a poor response following parent-training/education programmes and/or psychological treatment and treatment with methylphenidate and atomoxetine in a child or young person with ADHD, there should be a further review of:

- the diagnosis
- any coexisting conditions
- response to drug treatment, occurrence of side effects and treatment adherence
- uptake and use of psychological interventions for the child or young person and their parents or carers
- effects of stigma on treatment acceptability
- concerns related to school and/or family
- motivation of the child or young person and the parents or carers
- the child or young person's diet.

10.18.6.2     Following review of poor response to treatment, a dose higher than that licensed for methylphenidate or atomoxetine should be considered following consultation with a tertiary or regional centre. This may exceed 'British national formulary' (BNF) recommendations: methylphenidate can be increased to 0.7 mg/kg per dose up to three times a day or a total daily dose of 2.1 mg/kg/day (up to a total maximum dose of 90 mg/day for immediate release; or an equivalent dose of modified-release

---

[27]Ibid.

methylphenidate[28]); atomoxetine may be increased to 1.8 mg/kg/day (up to a total maximum dose of 120 mg/day). The prescriber should closely monitor the child or young person for side effects.

10.18.6.3   Dexamfetamine should be considered in children and young people whose ADHD is unresponsive to a maximum tolerated dose of methylphenidate or atomoxetine.

10.18.6.4   In children and young people whose ADHD is unresponsive to methylphenidate, atomoxetine and dexamfetamine, further treatment should only follow after referral to tertiary services. Further treatment may include the use of medication unlicensed for the treatment of ADHD (such as bupropion, clonidine, modafinil and imipramine[29]) or combination treatments (including psychological treatments for the parent or carer and the child or young person). The use of medication unlicensed for ADHD should only be considered in the context of tertiary services.

10.18.6.5   A cardiovascular examination and ECG should be carried out before starting treatment with clonidine in children or young people with ADHD.

### 10.18.7   Treatment of adults with ADHD

10.18.7.1   For adults with ADHD, drug treatment[30] should be the first-line treatment unless the person would prefer a psychological approach.

---

[28]Stimulant dose equivalents (mg)

| IR-MPH | Concerta XL | Equasym XL | Medikinet XL |
|--------|-------------|------------|--------------|
| 10 | – | 10 | 10 |
| 15 | 18 | – | – |
| 20 | – | 20 | 20 |
| 30 | 36 | 30 | 30 |
| – | – | – | 40 |
| 45 | 54 | – | – |
| 60 | 72* | 60 | – |

IR-MPH: immediate-release methylphenidate; Concerta XL, Equasym XL and Medikinet XL: brands of modified-release methylphenidate.

*licensed up to 54 mg.

[29]At the time of publication, bupropion, clonidine, modafinil and imipramine did not have UK marketing authorisation for use in children and young people with ADHD. Informed consent should be obtained and documented.

[30]At the time of publication, methylphenidate, dexamfetamine and atomoxetine did not have UK marketing authorisation for use in adults with ADHD. However, atomoxetine is licensed for adults with ADHD when the drug has been started in childhood. Informed consent should be obtained and documented.

10.18.7.2    Drug treatment for adults with ADHD should be started only under the guidance of a psychiatrist, nurse prescriber specialising in ADHD, or other clinical prescriber with training in the diagnosis and management of ADHD.

10.18.7.3    Before starting drug treatment for adults with ADHD a full assessment should be completed, which should include:
- full mental health and social assessment
- full history and physical examination, including:
  - assessment of history of exercise syncope, undue breathlessness and other cardiovascular symptoms
  - heart rate and blood pressure (plotted on a centile chart)
  - weight
  - family history of cardiac disease and examination of the cardiovascular system.
- an ECG if there is past medical or family history of serious cardiac disease, a history of sudden death in young family members or abnormal findings on cardiac examination
- risk assessment for substance misuse and drug diversion.

10.18.7.4    Drug treatment for adults with ADHD should always form part of a comprehensive treatment programme that addresses psychological, behavioural and occupational needs. (Key priority)

10.18.7.5    Following a decision to start drug treatment in adults with ADHD, methylphenidate should normally be tried first. (Key priority)

10.18.7.6    Atomoxetine or dexamfetamine should be considered in adults unresponsive or intolerant to an adequate trial of methylphenidate (this should usually be about 6 weeks)[31]. Caution should be exercised when prescribing dexamfetamine to those likely to be at risk of stimulant misuse or diversion.

10.18.7.7    When starting drug treatment, adults should be monitored for side effects. In particular, people treated with atomoxetine should be observed for agitation, irritability, suicidal thinking and self-harming behaviour, and unusual changes in behaviour, particularly during the initial months of treatment, or after a change in dose. They should also be warned of potential liver damage in rare cases (usually presenting as abdominal pain, unexplained nausea, malaise, darkening of the urine or jaundice). Younger adults aged 30 years or younger should also be warned of the potential of atomoxetine to increase agitation, anxiety, suicidal thinking and self-harming behaviour in some people, especially during the first few weeks of treatment.

10.18.7.8    Where there may be concern about the potential for drug misuse and diversion (for example in prison services), atomoxetine may be considered as the first-line drug treatment for ADHD in adults[32].

---

[31]At the time of publication, methylphenidate, dexamfetamine and atomoxetine did not have UK marketing authorisation for use in adults with ADHD. However, atomoxetine is licensed for adults with ADHD when the drug has been started in childhood. Informed consent should be obtained and documented.
[32]Ibid.

10.18.7.9   Drug treatment for adults with ADHD who also misuse substances should only be prescribed by an appropriately qualified healthcare professional with expertise in managing both ADHD and substance misuse. For adults with ADHD and drug or alcohol addiction disorders there should be close liaison between the professional treating the person's ADHD and an addiction specialist.

10.18.7.10   Antipsychotics are not recommended for the treatment of ADHD in adults.

## 10.18.8   General principles on the use of medication

10.18.8.1   Prescribers should be familiar with the pharmacokinetic profiles of all the modified-release and immediate-release preparations available for ADHD to ensure that treatment is tailored effectively to the individual needs of the child, young person or adult.

10.18.8.2   Prescribers should be familiar with the requirements of controlled drug legislation governing the prescription and supply of stimulants.

10.18.8.3   During the titration phase, doses should be gradually increased until there is no further clinical improvement in ADHD (that is, symptom reduction, behaviour change, improvements in education and/or relationships) and side effects are tolerable.

10.18.8.4   Following titration and dose stabilisation, prescribing and monitoring should be carried out under locally agreed shared care arrangements with primary care.

10.18.8.5   Side effects resulting from drug treatment for ADHD should be routinely monitored and documented in the person's notes.

10.18.8.6   If side effects become troublesome in people receiving drug treatment for ADHD, a reduction in dose should be considered.

10.18.8.7   Healthcare professionals should be aware that dose titration should be slower if tics or seizures are present in people with ADHD.

## 10.18.9   Initiation and titration of methylphenidate, atomoxetine and dexamfetamine in children and young people

10.18.9.1   During the titration phase, symptoms and side effects should be recorded at each dose change on standard scales (for example, Conners' 10-item scale) by parents and teachers, and progress reviewed regularly (for example, by weekly telephone contact and at each dose change) with a specialist clinician.

10.18.9.2   If using methylphenidate in children and young people with ADHD aged 6 years and older:
- initial treatment should begin with low doses of immediate-release or modified-release preparations consistent with starting doses in the BNF

- the dose should be titrated against symptoms and side effects over 4–6 weeks until dose optimisation is achieved
- modified-release preparations should be given as a single dose in the morning
- immediate-release preparations should be given in two or three divided doses.

10.18.9.3　If using atomoxetine in children and young people with ADHD aged 6 years and older:

- for those weighing up to 70 kg, the initial total daily dose should be approximately 0.5 mg/kg; the dose should be increased after 7 days to approximately 1.2 mg/kg/day
- for those weighing more than 70 kg, the initial total daily dose should be 40 mg; the dose should be increased after 7 days up to a maintenance dose of 80 mg/day
- a single daily dose can be given; two divided doses may be prescribed to minimise side effects.

10.18.9.4　If using dexamfetamine in children and young people with ADHD:

- initial treatment should begin with low doses consistent with starting doses in the BNF
- the dose should be titrated against symptoms and side effects over 4–6 weeks
- treatment should be given in divided doses increasing to a maximum of 20 mg/day
- for children aged 6–18 years, doses up to 40 mg/day may occasionally be required.

## 10.18.10　Initiation and titration of methylphenidate, atomoxetine and dexamfetamine in adults

10.18.10.1　In order to optimise drug treatment, the initial dose should be titrated against symptoms and side effects over 4–6 weeks.

10.18.10.2　During the titration phase, symptoms and side effects should be recorded at each dose change by the prescriber after discussion with the person with ADHD and, wherever possible a carer (for example, a spouse, parent or close friend). Progress should be reviewed (for example, by weekly telephone contact and at each dose change) with a specialist clinician.

10.18.10.3　If using methylphenidate in adults with ADHD:

- initial treatment should begin with low doses (5 mg three times daily for immediate-release preparations; the equivalent dose for modified-release preparations)
- the dose should be titrated against symptoms and side effects over 4–6 weeks
- the dose should be increased according to response up to a maximum of 100 mg/day

- modified-release preparations should usually be given once daily and no more than twice daily
- modified-release preparations may be preferred to increase adherence and in circumstances where there are concerns about substance misuse or diversion
- immediate-release preparations should be given up to four times daily.

10.18.10.4  If using atomoxetine in adults with ADHD:
- for people with ADHD weighing up to 70 kg, the initial total daily dose should be approximately 0.5 mg/kg; the dose should be increased after 7 days to approximately 1.2 mg/kg/day
- for people with ADHD weighing more than 70 kg, the initial total daily dose should be 40 mg; the dose should be increased after 7 days up to a maintenance dose of 100 mg/day
- the usual maintenance dose is either 80 or 100 mg, which may be taken in divided doses
- a trial of 6 weeks on a maintenance dose should be allowed to evaluate the full effectiveness of atomoxetine.

10.18.10.5  If using dexamfetamine in adults with ADHD:
- initial treatment should begin with low doses (5 mg twice daily)
- the dose should be titrated against symptoms and side effects over 4–6 weeks
- treatment should be given in divided doses
- the dose should be increased according to response up to a maximum of 60 mg per day
- the dose should usually be given between two and four times daily.

## 10.18.11    Monitoring side effects and the potential for misuse in children, young people and adults

10.18.11.1  Healthcare professionals should consider using standard symptom and side effect rating scales throughout the course of treatment as an adjunct to clinical assessment for people with ADHD.

10.18.11.2  In people taking methylphenidate, atomoxetine, or dexamfetamine:
- height should be measured every 6 months in children and young people
- weight should be measured 3 and 6 months after drug treatment has started and every 6 months thereafter in children, young people and adults
- height and weight in children and young people should be plotted on a growth chart and reviewed by the healthcare professional responsible for treatment.

10.18.11.3  If there is evidence of weight loss associated with drug treatment in adults with ADHD, healthcare professionals should consider monitoring body mass index and changing the drug if weight loss persists.

10.18.11.4    Strategies to reduce weight loss in people with ADHD, or manage decreased weight gain in children, include:

- taking medication either with or after food, rather than before meals
- taking additional meals/snacks early in the morning or late in the evening when the stimulant effects of the drug have worn off
- obtaining dietary advice
- consuming high-calorie foods of good nutritional value.

10.18.11.5    If growth is significantly affected by drug treatment (that is, the child or young person has not met the height expected for their age), the option of a planned break in treatment over school holidays should be considered to allow 'catch-up' growth to occur.

10.18.11.6    In people with ADHD, heart rate and blood pressure should be monitored and recorded on a centile chart before and after each dose change and routinely every 3 months.

10.18.11.7    For people taking methylphenidate, dexamfetamine and atomoxetine, routine blood tests and ECGs are not recommended unless there is a clinical indication.

10.18.11.8    Liver damage is a rare and idiosyncratic adverse effect of atomoxetine and routine liver function tests are not recommended.

10.18.11.9    For children and young people taking methylphenidate and dexamfetamine, healthcare professionals and parents or carers should monitor changes in the potential for drug misuse and diversion, which may come with changes in circumstances and age. In these situations, modified-release methylphenidate or atomoxetine may be preferred.

10.18.11.10   In young people and adults, sexual dysfunction (that is, erectile and ejaculatory dysfunction) and dysmenorrhoea should be monitored as potential side effects of atomoxetine.

10.18.11.11   For people taking methylphenidate, dexamfetamine or atomoxetine who have sustained resting tachycardia, arrhythmia or systolic blood pressure greater than the 95th percentile (or a clinically significant increase) measured on two occasions should have their dose reduced and be referred to a paediatrician or adult physician.

10.18.11.12   If psychotic symptoms (for example, delusions and hallucinations) emerge in children, young people and adults after starting methylphenidate or dexamfetamine, the drug should be withdrawn and a full psychiatric assessment carried out. Atomoxetine should be considered as an alternative.

10.18.11.13   If seizures are exacerbated in a child or young person with epilepsy, or *de novo* seizures emerge following the introduction of methylphenidate or atomoxetine, the drug should be discontinued immediately. Dexamfetamine may be considered as an alternative in consultation with a regional tertiary specialist treatment centre.

10.18.11.14 If tics emerge in people taking methylphenidate or dexamfetamine, healthcare professionals should consider whether:
- the tics are stimulant-related (tics naturally wax and wane)
- tic-related impairment outweighs the benefits of ADHD treatment.

If tics are stimulant-related, reduce the dose of methylphenidate or dexamfetamine, consider changing to atomoxetine, or stop drug treatment.

10.18.11.15 Anxiety symptoms, including panic, may be precipitated by stimulants, particularly in adults with a history of coexisting anxiety. Where this is an issue, lower doses of the stimulant and/or combined treatment with an antidepressant used to treat anxiety can be used; switching to atomoxetine may be effective.

### 10.18.12    Improving adherence to drug treatment

10.18.12.1 Communication between the prescriber and the child or young person should be improved by educating parents or carers and ensuring there are regular three-way conversations between prescriber, parent or carer and the child or young person. For adults with ADHD, and with their permission, a spouse, partner, parent, close friend or carer wherever possible should be part of these conversations. Clear instructions about how to take the drug should be offered in picture or written format, which may include information on dose, duration, side effects, dosage schedule, the need for supervision and how this should be done.

10.18.12.2 Healthcare professionals should consider suggesting peer-support groups for the child or young person with ADHD and their parents or carers if adherence to drug treatment is difficult or uncertain.

10.18.12.3 Simple drug regimens (for example, once-daily modified-release doses) are recommended for people with ADHD.

10.18.12.4 Healthcare professionals should encourage children and young people with ADHD to be responsible for their own health, including taking their medication as required, and support parents and carers in this endeavour.

10.18.12.5 Healthcare professionals should advise parents or carers to provide the child or young person with visual reminders to take medication regularly (for example, alarms, clocks, pill boxes, or notes on calendars or fridges).

10.18.12.6 Healthcare professionals should advise children and young people and their parents or carers that taking medication should be incorporated into daily routines (for example, before meals or after brushing teeth).

10.18.12.7 Where necessary, healthcare professionals should help parents or carers develop a positive attitude and approach in the management of medication, which might include praise and positive reinforcement for the child or young person with ADHD.

### 10.18.13 Duration, discontinuation and continuity of treatment in children and young people

10.18.13.1 Following an adequate treatment response, drug treatment for ADHD should be continued for as long as it remains clinically effective. This should be reviewed at least annually. The review should include a comprehensive assessment of clinical need, benefits and side effects, taking into account the views of the child or young person, as well as those of parents, carers and teachers, and how these views may differ. The effect of missed doses, planned dose reductions and brief periods of no treatment should be taken into account and the preferred pattern of use should also be reviewed. Coexisting conditions should be reviewed, and the child or young person treated or referred if necessary. The need for psychological and social support for the child or young person and for the parents or other carers should be assessed.

10.18.13.2 Drug holidays are not routinely recommended; however, consideration should be given to the parent or carer and child or young person with ADHD working with their healthcare professional to find the best pattern of use, which may include periods without drug treatment.

### 10.18.14 Duration, discontinuation and continuity of treatment in adults

10.18.14.1 Following an adequate response, drug treatment for ADHD should be continued for as long as it is clinically effective. This should be reviewed annually. The review should include a comprehensive assessment of clinical need, benefits and side effects, taking into account the views of the person and those of a spouse, partner, parent, close friends or carers wherever possible, and how these accounts may differ. The effect of missed doses, planned dose reductions, brief periods of no treatment should be taken into account and the preferred pattern of use should also be reviewed. Coexisting conditions should be reviewed, and the person treated or referred if necessary. The need for psychological, social and occupational support for the person and their carers should be assessed.

10.18.14.2 An individual treatment approach is important for adults, and healthcare professionals should regularly review (at least annually) the need to adapt patterns of use, including the effect of drug treatment on coexisting conditions and mood changes.

## 10.19 RESEARCH RECOMMENDATIONS

10.19.1.1 Discontinuation of drug treatment
   - Are there any benefits or disadvantages to the extended/long-term use of methylphenidate compared with its discontinuation at least

18 months after starting treatment? To what extent does continuing drug treatment beyond 18 months alter quality of life, core ADHD symptoms, associated symptoms including emotional lability, potential adverse effects of continued drug treatment and neuropsychological function? This would be best conducted as a drug discontinuation randomised controlled trial.

● Why this is important: Methylphenidate is often given for periods of years without good evidence of whether prolonged therapy is effective or safe. Methylphenidate is also typically discontinued in late adolescence; evidence is required of the benefit of continued prescribing in this age group.

# 11. COMBINING AND COMPARING PSYCHOLOGICAL AND PHARMACOLOGICAL INTERVENTIONS

## 11.1 INTRODUCTION

This chapter reviews the evidence on the use of combined interventions where medication and psychological therapies are used together to treat ADHD. As well as the possibility of increasing treatment effects through the use of the two modalities of intervention together, the potential value of combined treatment for ADHD is an area of interest because it might lead to beneficial effects in different domains – with medication targeting core ADHD symptoms such as inattention and psychological interventions targeting secondary problems and coexisting conditions associated with ADHD. Combining pharmacological and psychological approaches may also have the potential to deliver both immediate effects on ADHD symptoms through medication along with more long-lasting effects through the development of behavioural and cognitive skills and strategies. Another area of interest in relation to combined treatment is the potential to minimise the risks of adverse effects of medication if combined treatment can achieve treatment effects comparable with medication treatment alone but with a lower dose of medication.

This chapter also reviews the evidence from trials that allow direct comparisons to be made between the effectiveness of psychological therapies and pharmacological interventions for the treatment of ADHD.

*Evidence on combined treatment for adults with ADHD*
None of the included studies investigated the effectiveness of combined interventions for adults with a diagnosis of ADHD or compared the effectiveness of psychological therapies delivered to a group not receiving medication for ADHD with those receiving stimulant medication in an adult population.

## 11.2 COMBINED INTERVENTIONS FOR CHILDREN WITH ADHD

### 11.2.1 Introduction

There are several reasons why non-pharmacological treatment, usually psychological, might be combined with pharmacological treatment. These are listed below.
- In severe presentations of ADHD, the impairment is such that medication when combined with psychological therapy might offer the prospect of a more rapid improvement than with psychological interventions alone, which are likely to take

longer to work. This may be particularly necessary if there is marked social dysfunction present, if there is severe pressure on family or marital relationships or if the child is faced with imminent exclusion from school.

- Even if a psychological intervention is the preferred option, some young people have such severe clinical presentations that they and/or their parents may not be in a position to make use of psychological techniques. The potential for medication to deliver an initial rapid improvement in the early weeks of a combined intervention might enable them to benefit from psychological techniques.
- It has been argued that stimulants may enhance conditionability, a key element of behavioural learning (Eysenck & Rachman, 1971; Sprague & Werry, 1971). In other words, stimulants may enhance the effectiveness of psychological interventions that employ behavioural and social learning principles.
- Combining stimulants with a psychological intervention may be a way of reducing the dosage and duration of medication treatment, and thus may address concerns about the use of medication.
- It has been suggested that there may be complementary benefits in combining approaches (Gitteleman-Klein *et al.*, 1976a) in that stimulants may enhance attentional processes and reduce impulsive responding, whereas social reinforcement may help the child to internalise the value of appropriate behaviours.
- There is little evidence that stimulant medication alters the relatively poor long-term outcome for many of those with ADHD (Weiss & Hechtman, 1993). Adding psychological and other therapies might therefore yield better long-term outcomes.
- There are concerns that stimulants alone may not bring symptoms within the normal clinical range and have limited effects on other problems associated with ADHD such as prosocial behaviour (Buhrmester *et al.*, 1992) and cognition (Pelham, 1986). Linked to this it is recognised that ADHD rarely presents with just the core symptoms of ADHD. A range of additional problems across multiple domains are usually present, which are likely to require a range of interventions (Wells *et al.*, 2000).

*Current practice*
Current practice in the treatment of ADHD varies. Psychological, educational and pharmacological interventions may all be used; the decision is driven by the symptoms presented, the needs of the child and family and the local availability of services.

### 11.2.2   Databases searched and inclusion/exclusion criteria

Information about the databases searched and the inclusion/exclusion criteria used for this section of the guideline can be found in Table 32 (further information about the search for health economic evidence can be found in Section 11.5). Studies were included if they were RCTs that compared combined treatment for ADHD (where medication and psychological interventions are determined by the study protocol) with medication only delivered according to the same protocol as used as for the combined intervention.

**Table 32: Databases searched and inclusion/exclusion criteria for clinical effectiveness of psychological interventions**

| Electronic databases | MEDLINE, EMBASE, PsycINFO, Cochrane Library |
|---|---|
| Date searched | Database inception to December 2007 |
| Study design | RCT |
| Patient population | Participants (all ages) diagnosed with ADHD |
| Interventions | Combined treatment for ADHD (where medication and psychological interventions are determined by the study protocol); medication only delivered according to the same protocol as used as for the combined intervention |
| Outcomes | Core ADHD symptoms; conduct problems; social skills; emotional outcomes; self-efficacy; reading; mathematics; leaving the study early; non-response to treatment |

### 11.2.3    Studies considered[33]

From the primary RCT search, the review team identified trials comparing combined treatment with medication only. Only trials that compared groups receiving true combined interventions (that is, medication for ADHD and a concurrent psychological intervention, with both interventions determined by the study protocol) with groups receiving medication alone (according to the same protocol as for the combined treatment group) were included in the review. Analyses comparing combined treatments with psychological therapies alone or with no treatment control conditions were not undertaken. The reason for this was that the analysis that directly compared pharmacological and psychological interventions (see 11.3 below) clearly favoured medication. If combined treatments were compared with psychological therapies alone or no treatment control conditions, findings favouring combination treatment might therefore only provide evidence of the effects of medication, rather than providing support for combined treatment *per se.*

Trials where participants received a psychological intervention as an adjunct to medication that they were receiving as part of their ongoing usual care were considered separately (see Chapter 7). This approach to the analysis was adopted because

---

[33]Here and elsewhere in the guideline, each study considered for review is referred to by a study ID in capital letters (primary author and date of study publication, except where a study is in press or only submitted for publication, then a date is not used).

where participants in a trial continue to receive medication as usual the medication and/or protocol determining the medication regimen may not be uniform for all participants, and if that is the case the trial could not be considered to be a true test of a combined treatment strategy. It is also likely that adherence to medication would be higher in a clinical trial context, with the consequence that the effects of medication received as part of a clinical trial might be greater than the effects of continuing to receive medication as usual. Hence, if medication modifies the response to psychological therapies it is possible that findings from true trials of combined treatment might differ from findings from trials that include participants continuing with their usual medication.

An additional analysis is reported that compares an intensive and comprehensive combined intervention for ADHD with standard care that may include medication. This analysis, based on data from the MTA study (MTA1999), was performed in order to provide a comparison of what might currently be considered the best possible care for ADHD with the more standard level of care provided in routine clinical practice.

Seven trials met the eligibility criteria set by the GDG, providing data on 544 participants. All were published in peer-reviewed journals between 1981 and 2004. In addition, 20 studies were excluded from the analysis. The most common reasons for exclusion were that the paper reported no appropriate data or the intervention was inappropriate (further information about both included and excluded studies can be found in Appendix 17).

### 11.2.4 Clinical evidence for combined treatment for ADHD versus medication only

Evidence from important outcomes and overall quality of evidence are presented in Table 33. The full evidence profiles and associated forest plots can be found in Appendix 19 and Appendix 18, respectively.

Evidence from included trials of treatment for children with ADHD that compare a combined intervention with receipt of the medication component of the intervention alone indicates that there is little or no advantage of any type of combined intervention over medication alone. Compared with medication there is no evidence of an added effect of combined treatment on measures of core ADHD symptoms, emotional state or self-efficacy.

The only evidence of a benefit of combined treatment over medication alone is for parent ratings of conduct problems at the end of treatment, however, the benefits of combined treatment on this outcome are only weak because the effect size is at the lower end of the small effect size range and no benefit of combined treatment was detected at later follow-up times.

The MTA study (MTA1999) is the largest trial of combination treatment for ADHD and although the MTA data suggests that there was a small benefit from combined treatment over medication management alone on parent ratings of conduct problems at the end of treatment, the effect did not reach the magnitude of a small effect size.

**Table 33:  Study information and evidence summary table for trials
of combined interventions versus stimulant medication**

| | **Combined intervention versus stimulant medication** |
|---|---|
| Total number of studies (number of participants) | 7 (544) |
| Study ID | ABIKOFF2004A<br>BROWN1985<br>FIRESTONE1981<br>FIRESTONE1986<br>GITTELMAN-KLEIN1976<br>KLEIN1997<br>MTA1999 |
| *Age* | 5–12 years |
| ***Benefits (end of treatment)*** | |
| Core ADHD symptoms at end of treatment (teacher-rated) | SMD −0.06 (−0.24 to 0.12)<br>Quality: High<br>K = 6, N = 482 |
| Core ADHD symptoms at end of treatment (parent-rated) | SMD −0.12 (−0.31 to 0.07)<br>Quality: High<br>K = 5, N = 428 |
| Conduct at end of treatment (teacher-rated) | SMD −0.07 (−0.26 to 0.11)<br>Quality: High<br>K = 5, N = 461 |
| Conduct at end of treatment (parent-rated) | SMD −0.21 (−0.41 to −0.01)<br>Quality: High<br>K = 3, N = 378 |
| Social skills at end of treatment (teacher-rated) | SMD −0.03 (−0.11 to 0.05)<br>Quality: High<br>K = 3, N = 333 |
| Social skills at end of treatment (parent-rated) | SMD −0.14 (−0.36 to 0.09)<br>Quality: High<br>K = 2, N = 315 |
| Social skills at end of treatment (child-rated) | SMD −0.07 (−0.54 to 0.41)<br>Quality: Moderate<br>K = 1, N = 68 |

**Table 33:** (*Continued*)

| | **Combined intervention versus stimulant medication** |
|---|---|
| Emotional outcomes at end of treatment (teacher-rated) | SMD 0.15 ($-0.09$ to 0.39)<br>Quality: High<br>K = 2, N = 265 |
| Emotional outcomes at end of treatment (parent-rated) | SMD $-0.03$ ($-0.25$ to 0.19)<br>Quality: High<br>K = 3, N = 327 |
| Emotional outcomes at end of treatment (child-rated) | SMD 0.28 ($-0.20$ to 0.76)<br>Quality: High<br>K = 1, N = 68 |
| Self-efficacy at end of treatment (child-rated) | SMD $-0.02$ ($-0.50$ to 0.45)<br>Quality: Moderate<br>K = 1, N = 68 |
| *Benefits (3–6 months post-treatment)* | |
| Core ADHD symptoms at 3 months post-treatment (teacher-rated) | SMD $-0.05$ ($-0.93$ to 0.82)<br>Quality: Moderate<br>K = 1, N = 20 |
| Core ADHD symptoms at 3 months post-treatment (parent-rated) | SMD 0.25 ($-0.63$ to 1.13)<br>Quality: Moderate<br>K = 1, N = 20 |
| *Benefits (7–12 months post-treatment)* | |
| Core ADHD symptoms at 7–9 months post-treatment (teacher-rated) | SMD 0.00 ($-0.59$ to 0.59)<br>Quality: Moderate<br>K = 1, N = 44 |
| Core ADHD symptoms at 10 months post-treatment (parent- and teacher-rated composite score) | SMD $-0.06$ ($-0.30$ to 0.18)<br>Quality: High<br>K = 1, N = 264 |
| Conduct at 7–9 months post-treatment (teacher-rated) | SMD 0.00 ($-0.65$ to 0.65)<br>Quality: Moderate<br>K = 1, N = 37 |
| Conduct at 10 months post-treatment (parent- and teacher-rated composite score) | SMD $-0.18$ ($-0.42$ to 0.06)<br>Quality: High<br>K = 1, N = 264 |

*Continued*

**Table 33:** (*Continued*)

| | Combined intervention versus stimulant medication |
|---|---|
| Social skills at 10 months post-treatment (parent- and teacher-rated composite score) | SMD −0.21 (−0.45 to 0.03)<br>Quality: High<br>K = 1, N = 264 |
| ***Benefits (13–24 months post-treatment)*** | |
| Core ADHD symptoms at 19–21 months post-treatment (teacher-rated) | SMD −0.05 (−0.90 to 0.81)<br>Quality: Moderate<br>K = 1, N = 21 |
| Core ADHD symptoms at 22 months post-treatment (parent- and teacher-rated composite score) | SMD −0.02 (−0.27 to 0.23)<br>Quality: High<br>K = 1, N = 242 |
| Conduct at 19–21 months post-treatment (teacher-rated) | SMD −0.23 (−1.09 to 0.63)<br>Quality: Moderate<br>K = 1, N = 21 |
| Conduct at 22 months post-treatment (parent- and teacher-rated composite score) | SMD −0.03 (−0.27 to 0.20)<br>Quality: High<br>K = 1, N = 282 |
| Social skills at 22 months post-treatment (parent- and teacher-rated composite score) | SMD 0.04 (−0.21 to 0.29)<br>Quality: High<br>K = 1, N = 242 |
| ***Education outcomes at end of treatment*** | |
| Reading at end of treatment | SMD 0.04 (−0.14 to 0.22)<br>Quality: High<br>K = 6, N = 478 |
| Mathematics at end of treatment | SMD −0.03 (−0.22 to 0.15)<br>Quality: High<br>K = 5, N = 437 |
| ***Education outcomes at 3–6 months post-treatment*** | |
| Reading at 3 months post-treatment | SMD 0.19 (−0.69 to 1.07)<br>Quality: Moderate<br>K = 1, N = 20 |
| Mathematics at 3 months post-treatment | SMD −0.52 (−1.42 to 0.37)<br>Quality: Moderate<br>K = 1, N = 20 |

**Table 33:** (*Continued*)

| | Combined intervention versus stimulant medication |
|---|---|
| *Education outcomes at 7–12 months post-treatment* | |
| Reading at 10 months post-treatment | SMD −0.02 (−0.25 to 0.20)<br>Quality: High<br>K = 2, N = 303 |
| *Education outcomes at 13–24 months post-treatment* | |
| Reading at 19–22 months post-treatment | SMD −0.02 (−0.26 to 0.23)<br>Quality: High<br>K = 2, N = 261 |
| *Dichotomous outcomes* | |
| Leaving study for any reason | Data not pooled:<br>ABIKOFF2004A: 18% (combination) versus 29% (medication only)<br>BROWN1985: 0% versus 0%<br>FIRESTONE1986: 0% versus 0%<br>MTA1999: 2% versus 6%<br>K = 1, N = 429 |
| Non-responders | RR 0.63 (0.47 to 0.84)<br>Quality: High<br>K = 4, N = 426 |

### 11.2.5 Clinical evidence for intensive combined treatment versus usual care for children with ADHD

Comparison of the MTA combined intervention (medication management plus an intensive multimodal psychological intervention for ADHD that involved interventions with the child and parent, and a classroom intervention) with the MTA community care group allows comparison of an intensive and comprehensive approach to care with standard care (MTA1999) (see Table 34).

The MTA study of combined intervention provides an example of what might be considered fully comprehensive care for ADHD; this is ongoing protocol-led management of stimulant medication coupled with a complex psychological intervention, that is, a multicomponent psychological intervention that continues for a year or more, includes components directed at the child, the parent and the teacher/classroom, and has intensive components (the summer camp in the case of the MTA psychological intervention). The MTA trial participants in the community care group received routine clinical care for ADHD; two-thirds of this group received medication for

**Table 34: Study information and evidence summary table for the MTA trial of combined interventions versus community care**

| | Combined intervention versus community care |
|---|---|
| Total number of studies (number of participants) | 1 (291) |
| Study ID | MTA1999 |
| *Age* | 7–9.9 years |
| ***Benefits (end of treatment)*** | |
| Core ADHD symptoms at end of treatment (teacher-rated) | SMD −0.64 (−0.89 to −0.39) Quality: High K = 1, N = 263 |
| Core ADHD symptoms at end of treatment (parent-rated) | SMD −0.74 (−0.99 to −0.49) Quality: High K = 1, N = 263 |
| Conduct at end of treatment (teacher-rated) | SMD −0.51 (−0.76 to −0.26) Quality: High K = 1, N = 262 |
| Conduct at end of treatment (parent-rated) | SMD −0.53 (−0.78 to −0.29) Quality: High K = 1, N = 263 |
| Social skills at end of treatment (teacher-rated) | SMD −0.14 (−0.22 to −0.06) Quality: High K = 1, N = 213 |
| Social skills at end of treatment (parent-rated) | SMD −0.27 (−0.52 to −0.02) Quality: High K = 1, N = 252 |
| Emotional outcomes at end of treatment (teacher-rated) | SMD −0.02 (−0.29 to 0.25) Quality: Moderate K = 1, N = 213 |
| Emotional outcomes at end of treatment (parent-rated) | SMD 0.27 (0.02 to 0.52) Quality: High K = 1, N = 252 |

**Table 34:** (*Continued*)

| | Combined intervention versus community care |
|---|---|
| ***Benefits (7–12 months post-treatment)*** | |
| Core ADHD symptoms at 10 months post-treatment (parent- and teacher-rated composite score) | SMD −0.34 (−0.58 to −0.10)<br>Quality: High<br>K = 1, N = 273 |
| Conduct at 10 months post-treatment (parent- and teacher-rated composite score) | SMD −0.31 (−0.55 to −0.07)<br>Quality: High<br>K = 1, N = 273 |
| Social skills at 10 months post-treatment (parent- and teacher-rated composite score) | SMD −0.17 (−0.41 to 0.06)<br>Quality: Moderate<br>K = 1, N = 273 |
| ***Benefits (13–24 months post treatment)*** | |
| Core ADHD symptoms at 22 months post-treatment (parent- and teacher-rated composite score) | SMD −0.11 (−0.36 to 0.15)<br>Quality: Moderate<br>K = 1, N = 243 |
| Conduct at 22 months post-treatment (parent- and teacher-rated composite score) | SMD −0.82 (−1.08 to −0.56)<br>Quality: High<br>K = 1, N = 243 |
| Social skills at 22 months post-treatment (parent- and teacher-rated composite score) | SMD 0.04 (−0.21 to 0.29)<br>Quality: High<br>K = 1, N = 243 |
| ***Education outcomes at end of treatment*** | |
| Reading at end of treatment | SMD −0.27 (−0.51 to −0.03)<br>Quality: High<br>K = 1, N = 267 |
| Mathematics at end of treatment | SMD −0.01 (−0.25 to 0.23)<br>Quality: High<br>K = 1, N = 267 |
| ***Education outcomes at 7–12 months post-treatment*** | |
| Reading at 10 months post-treatment | SMD −0.19 (−0.43 to 0.05)<br>Quality: Moderate<br>K = 1, N = 273 |

*Continued*

**Table 34:** *(Continued)*

| | Combined intervention versus community care |
|---|---|
| ***Education outcomes at 7–12 months post-treatment*** | |
| Reading 10 months post-treatment | SMD −0.12 (−0.37 to 0.13)<br>Quality: Moderate<br>K = 1, N = 243 |
| ***Dichotomous outcomes*** | |
| Leaving study for any reason | RR 0.50 (0.13 to 1.97)<br>Quality: High<br>K = 1, N = 291 |
| Non-responders at end of treatment | RR 0.43 (0.33 to 0.55)<br>Quality: High<br>K = 1, N = 290 |
| Non-responders at 10 months post-treatment | RR 0.72 (0.60 to 0.87)<br>Quality: High<br>K = 1, N = 291 |

ADHD and community care participants might also have received non-pharmacological interventions. It is also important to note that the MTA study was US based. Standard care for ADHD in the US may differ from routine care in the UK, with the potential that a higher proportion of the children with ADHD in the community care group received medication than would be the case in a similar UK sample.

The MTA combined intervention was generally favoured over usual care on parent and teacher ratings of ADHD symptoms and conduct problems. According to the composite measure of teacher and parent ratings of core ADHD symptoms that is reported for later follow-up assessments, comprehensive care continues to be favoured over routine care 10 months after the end of the intervention, but the effect is only small. Twenty-two months after the end of the intervention neither comprehensive care nor routine care is favoured according to the composite measure of core ADHD symptoms. However, measures of conduct problems point to an unequivocal advantage of comprehensive care over routine care. At the end of the intervention both parent and teacher ratings of conduct behaviour favour comprehensive care over routine care, with a moderate effect size. The composite score for parent and teacher ratings of conduct behaviour reported for the later follow-up assessments indicates that the beneficial effect of comprehensive care over routine care reduced to a small effect 10 months after the end of treatment but increased to a large effect 22 months after the end of treatment.

Parent and teacher ratings of social skills at the end of the intervention also point to small gains from comprehensive care over routine care, but these weak effects disappear at the later follow-up assessments according to a composite measure that combines parent and teacher ratings of social skills. In contrast, parent ratings of their child's emotional state point to a weak advantage of routine care over comprehensive treatment at the end of the intervention, but teacher ratings at the end of the intervention do not favour comprehensive treatment or routine care.

Taking all these findings into consideration there appears to be some benefit of a comprehensive intervention for ADHD over routine care. Measures of core ADHD symptoms at the end of the intervention indicate that comprehensive care is moderately more effective for core ADHD symptoms than community care, and comprehensive care may be particularly beneficial for conduct problems. It may be that the main factor generating the positive effects of the combined intervention is the medication management component. In any event, the comparison between outcomes for the MTA combined intervention 'comprehensive care' group and the community care group does not provide a consistent indication that comprehensive care is more effective than routine care that may include medication for ADHD. The advantage of comprehensive treatment over routine care should also be considered in the context of the lack of evidence of benefit from combined treatment approaches over active protocol-determined medication regimens (see Section 11.2.4).

## 11.2.6 Clinical evidence summary

Evidence from trials comparing combined treatment with medication interventions alone does not point to any added benefit of adding a psychological intervention to a protocol determined medication regimen. The data therefore suggests that if medication treatment for ADHD has already been instigated and the child has responded positively to treatment, then the addition of a psychological intervention to treat ADHD (whether a parent training programme or child-directed therapy) is unlikely to provide any added benefit in terms of reduced ADHD symptoms or improved behaviour, emotional state or self-esteem.

The findings on the effects of combined treatment therefore indicate that beneficial effects of psychological interventions for ADHD are not dependent on effective pharmacological treatment that allows the child with ADHD to be able to reap the benefits of a psychological intervention. It may be the case that in combined treatment trials the study-determined medication regimen has a large beneficial impact on outcomes such that any additional beneficial effects of a psychological intervention cannot be detected as there is no potential for any further improvement.

However, it should be noted that psychological interventions are effective as an adjunct to usual care medication (see Chapter 7). This may be because medication is less effective in routine clinical practice than in the context of a clinical trial. It is also the case that the MTA study (MTA1999) suggests that combinations of interventions may be helpful in targeting different problems and promoting some outcomes. Offering combination interventions may therefore allow children and parents to participate in treatment decisions and make choices about their own health outcomes (Taylor *et al.*, 2004).

## 11.3 COMPARING PSYCHOLOGICAL AND PHARMACOLOGICAL INTERVENTIONS FOR CHILDREN WITH ADHD

### 11.3.1 Introduction

Direct comparison of the effectiveness of psychological and pharmacological interventions for ADHD is possible where RCTs include a group receiving a psychological intervention without medication and a group receiving medication only. Studies that allow this comparison are potentially informative as they allow a direct head-to-head comparison of effectiveness between psychological and pharmacological interventions.

### 11.3.2 Databases searched and inclusion/exclusion criteria

Information about the databases searched and the inclusion/exclusion criteria used for this section of the guideline can be found in Table 35 (further information about the search for health economic evidence can be found in Section 11.5). Studies were only included where both the medication and psychological interventions were determined as part of the study protocol.

### 11.3.3 Studies considered[34]

From the primary RCT search, the review team identified trials comparing medication for ADHD with a psychological intervention.

**Table 35: Databases searched and inclusion/exclusion criteria for clinical effectiveness of psychological interventions**

| Electronic databases | MEDLINE, EMBASE, PsycINFO, Cochrane Library |
|---|---|
| Date searched | Database inception to December 2007 |
| Study design | RCT |
| Patient population | Participants (all ages) diagnosed with ADHD |
| Interventions | Medication for ADHD; psychological intervention |
| Outcomes | Core ADHD symptoms; conduct problems; social skills; emotional outcomes; self-efficacy; reading; mathematics; leaving the study early; non-response to treatment |

---

[34]Here and elsewhere in the guideline, each study considered for review is referred to by a study ID in capital letters (primary author and date of study publication, except where a study is in press or only submitted for publication, then a date is not used).

Six trials met the eligibility criteria set by the GDG, providing data on 462 participants. All studies were published in peer-reviewed journals between 1976 and 1999. In addition, four studies were excluded from the analysis; two because they were case studies, one because of insufficient data, and one because of methodological problems (further information about both included and excluded studies can be found in Appendix 17).

### 11.3.4 Clinical evidence for psychological interventions versus protocol-managed medication for children with ADHD

There is only sparse clinical trial evidence allowing direct comparison of the clinical effectiveness of psychological and pharmacological interventions for ADHD. Of the six trials that meet inclusion criteria, five are relatively small, with the medication or psychological intervention group sizes ranging from nine to 30. The MTA study (MTA1999) was relatively large, having 120 participants in the medication group and 119 in the psychological intervention group.

For individual outcomes, the quality of the evidence was generally moderate to high. Overall, for children with ADHD the evidence from trials that compare stimulant medication (predominantly methylphenidate) with a psychological intervention delivered to a group not receiving medication for ADHD generally favours stimulant medication, although where they reach statistical significance the effects are not large (see Table 36).

For both teacher and parent ratings of core ADHD symptoms and conduct problems at the end of treatment, stimulant medication delivers better outcomes than psychological interventions, with effect sizes in the small to moderate range. However, the benefits of stimulant medication over psychological therapies for core ADHD symptoms and conduct problems in general do not appear to be sustained at later follow-up assessments (3–6 months, 7–12 months and 13–24 months after the end of treatment). The MTA study (MTA1999) found a benefit of medication over the complex MTA psychological intervention on the composite parent- and teacher-rated measure of core ADHD symptoms at 10 months after the end of the intervention, but the effect did not reach the magnitude of a small effect size.

Stimulant medication also appears to be more effective than psychological interventions at improving social skills as rated by teachers, but this effect was small at the end of treatment, was not sustained at later follow-up assessments, and was not reflected in parent ratings of social skills, which does not point to any benefit of stimulant medication over psychological therapies at the end of treatment or any time thereafter. For emotional state (as represented by depression, anxiety, emotional adjustment and internalising symptoms) there was also a benefit of stimulant medication over psychological interventions at the end of treatment, but the effect size was small and for this outcome limited to parent ratings, with no effect on teacher ratings detected.

**Table 36: Study information and evidence summary table for trials
of stimulant medication versus psychological interventions**

|  | Stimulant medication versus psychological intervention |
|---|---|
| Total number of studies (number of participants) | 6 (462) |
| Study ID | BROWN1985<br>FIRESTONE1981<br>FIRESTONE1986<br>GITTELMAN-KLEIN1976<br>KLEIN1997<br>MTA1999 |
| *Age* | 5–12 years |
| ***Benefits (end of treatment)*** | |
| Core ADHD symptoms at end of treatment (teacher-rated) | SMD −0.72 (−1.12 to −0.32)<br>Quality: High<br>K = 5, N = 392 |
| Core ADHD symptoms at end of treatment (parent-rated) | SMD −0.45 (−0.66 to −0.23)<br>Quality: High<br>K = 4, N = 350 |
| Conduct at end of treatment (teacher-rated) | SMD −0.48 (−0.70 to −0.25)<br>Quality: High<br>K = 3, N = 321 |
| Conduct at end of treatment (parent-rated) | SMD −0.22 (−0.43 to −0.01)<br>Quality: High<br>K = 3, N = 355 |
| Social skills at end of treatment (teacher-rated) | SMD −0.33 (−0.57 to −0.08)<br>Quality: High<br>K = 2, N = 258 |
| Social skills at end of treatment (parent-rated) | SMD −0.08 (−0.33 to 0.17)<br>Quality: High<br>K = 1, N = 151 |
| Emotional outcomes at end of treatment (teacher-rated) | SMD 0.14 (−0.10 to 0.39)<br>Quality: High<br>K = 2, N = 158 |

**Table 36:** (*Continued*)

| | Stimulant medication versus psychological intervention |
|---|---|
| Emotional outcomes end of treatment (parent-rated) | SMD −0.23 (−0.45 to −0.01)<br>Quality: High<br>K = 3, N = 331 |
| *Benefits (3–6 months post treatment)* | |
| Core ADHD symptoms at 3 months post-treatment (teacher-rated) | SMD −0.20 (−1.08 to 0.68)<br>Quality: Moderate<br>K = 1, N = 20 |
| Core ADHD symptoms at 3 months post-treatment (parent-rated) | SMD −0.82 (−1.74 to 0.11)<br>Quality: Moderate<br>K = 1, N = 20 |
| *Benefits (7–12 months post-treatment)* | |
| Core ADHD symptoms at 7–9 months post-treatment (teacher-rated) | SMD −0.53 (−1.23 to 0.17)<br>Quality: Moderate<br>K = 1, N = 35 |
| Core ADHD symptoms at 10 months post-treatment (parent- and teacher-rated composite score) | SMD −0.25 (−0.49 to −0.01)<br>Quality: High<br>K = 1, N = 267 |
| Conduct at 7–9 months post-treatment (parent-rated) | SMD −0.32 (−1.02 to 0.38)<br>Quality: Moderate<br>K = 1, N = 34 |
| Conduct at 10 months post-treatment (parent- and teacher-rated composite score) | SMD −0.10 (−0.34 to 0.14)<br>Quality: High<br>K = 1, N = 267 |
| Social skills at 10 months post-treatment (parent- and teacher-rated composite score) | SMD −0.07 (−0.31 to 0.17)<br>Quality: High<br>K = 1, N = 267 |
| *Benefits (13–24 months post-treatment)* | |
| Core ADHD symptoms at 19–21 months post-treatment (teacher-rated) | SMD 0.00 (−0.88 to 0.88)<br>Quality: Moderate<br>K = 1, N = 20 |
| Core ADHD symptoms at 19–21 months post-treatment (parent-rated) | SMD 0.58 (−0.32 to 1.48)<br>Quality: Moderate<br>K = 1, N = 20 |

*Continued*

**Table 36:** (*Continued*)

| | Stimulant medication versus psychological intervention |
|---|---|
| Core ADHD symptoms at 13–24 months post-treatment (parent- and teacher-rated composite score) | SMD −0.06 (−0.21 to 0.09) Quality: High K = 1, N = 242 |
| Conduct at 22 months post-treatment (parent- and teacher-rated composite score) | SMD 0.00 (−0.25 to 0.25) Quality: High K = 1, N = 243 |
| Social skills at 22 months post-treatment (parent- and teacher-rated composite score) | SMD −0.04 (−0.29 to 0.21) Quality: High K = 1, N = 243 |
| *Education outcomes at end of treatment* | |
| Reading at end of treatment | SMD −0.10 (−0.30 to 0.09) Quality: High K = 5, N = 397 |
| Mathematics at end of treatment | SMD 0.01 (−0.20 to 0.22) Quality: High K = 4, N = 358 |
| *Education outcomes at 3–6 months post-treatment* | |
| Reading at 3 months post-treatment | SMD 0.11 (−0.77 to 0.99) Quality: Moderate K = 1, N = 20 |
| Mathematics at 3 months post-treatment | SMD 0.57 (−0.32 to 1.47) Quality: Moderate K = 1, N = 20 |
| *Education outcomes at 7–12 months post-treatment* | |
| Reading at 7–10 months post-treatment | SMD −0.05 (−0.27 to 0.18) Quality: High K = 2, N = 301 |
| *Education outcomes at 13–24 months post-treatment* | |
| Reading 19–22 months post-treatment | SMD 0.03 (−0.22 to 0.27) Quality: High K = 2, N = 260 |
| *Dichotomous outcomes* | |
| Leaving study for any reason | Data not pooled |

**Table 36: (*Continued*)**

|  | **Stimulant medication versus psychological intervention** |
|---|---|
|  | BROWN1985: 0% (medication) versus 0% (psychological) FIRESTONE1986: 0% versus 0% MTA1999: 6% versus 2% |
| Non-responders at end of treatment | RR 0.61 (0.50 to 0.76) Quality: High K = 4, N = 366 |
| Non-responders at 10 months post-treatment | RR 0.91 (0.77 to 1.07) Quality: High K = 4, N = 288 |

The lack of evidence for the sustained superiority of medication over psychological interventions for ADHD is, however, difficult to interpret. At longer follow-up time points outcomes may be influenced by the treatment a child has received since the end of the period of the experimental intervention. In particular, children who received a psychological intervention and were not on medication for ADHD during the period of the trial while the intervention was delivered may have subsequently begun to receive stimulant medication for ADHD. Notably, in the MTA trial, by the follow-up time point at 10 months after the end of the experimental intervention, 44% of the group that only received the MTA behavioural intervention had commenced medication. At 22 months after the end of the experimental intervention, the proportion of the MTA behavioural intervention group that was using medication at high levels was little changed at 45% (Jensen *et al.*, 2007). In contrast 71% of MTA study participants who were in the medication management and combined intervention groups were using medication at high levels 22 months after the end of the experimental intervention, a decrease from 91% at the end of the intervention.

### 11.3.5 Clinical evidence summary

While there is no evidence that psychological interventions are favoured over stimulant medication for any outcome, or at any time point, it is also the case that medication does not appear to be strongly favoured over psychological interventions.

### 11.4 THE MTA STUDY: IMPLICATIONS FOR TREATMENT DECISIONS

### 11.4.1 Further considerations with respect to the treatment of ADHD – additional evidence from the MTA study

A number of publications have reported on sub-analysis and secondary analysis of data gathered as part of the MTA study (for example, MTA Co-operative Group,

2004a; Jensen *et al.*, 2007). Only primary outcome data reported for the end of treatment and 14 and 22 months post-treatment follow-up have been used in the analysis of the effectiveness of interventions for ADHD, but some of the further analysis reported by the MTA Co-operative Group may help inform choices made in the treatment of ADHD.

*Longer term impact of MTA interventions and the relation to substance use and delinquency*

The MTA study group has reported follow-up outcome data at time points beyond the end of the MTA intervention (MTA Co-operative Group, 2004a; Jensen *et al.*, 2007). The initial primary outcome data was collected at the end of the MTA interventions (14 months after interventions were commenced), with follow-up data reported to date for 10 months after the end treatment and 22 months after the end treatment (or 24 and 36 months after the interventions were commenced). It is important to note that after the end of the MTA interventions the participants in the trial returned to usual care.

According to the outcome data collected 22 months after the end of the MTA interventions, the MTA treatment allocation groups could no longer be distinguished on any measure according to primary analysis (Jensen *et al.*, 2007). On average MTA participants maintained some of the gains made at the end of treatment time point on measures of both ADHD and oppositional defiant disorder symptoms. The behavioural treatment and community care groups maintained the gains they had made at the end of treatment. In contrast the combined treatment and medication management groups lost their end of treatment advantage over the behavioural treatment and community care groups, although they maintained gains over baseline that approximated to the sustained gains made by the behavioural and community care groups. These findings are, however, based on the comparison with baseline data for each group, not on a comparison with an untreated control group, and hence it is not possible to conclude that any of the MTA interventions have long-term beneficial effects over no treatment. Indeed, at 22 months after the end of treatment, prognostic factors for ADHD were found to have more of an impact on outcomes than treatment group allocation – girls and those of higher socioeconomic status fared better than boys.

Follow-up data gathered 10 months after the end of the experimental MTA interventions is in line with the data gathered at 22 months after the end of treatment (MTA Co-operative Group, 2004a). Ten months after the end of the MTA interventions, the combined treatment and medication management groups, which showed the greatest improvement compared with baseline at the end of the intervention, show some deterioration, whereas the behavioural treatment and community care groups maintain gains made in comparison with baseline during the period of the trial intervention.

Jensen and colleagues (2007) suggest that factors that may contribute to the convergence of outcomes for the four MTA study intervention groups at longer-term follow-up compared with outcomes at the end of treatment include: a decrease in ADHD symptoms related to age independent of treatment; changes in the intensity of medication use; and different degrees of starting and stopping medication in the different treatment allocation groups that occurred after the end of the MTA interventions. Other factors may also be involved. There is a degree of convergence across the four groups in terms of their use of medication for ADHD at follow-up. Medication use in the group allocated to behavioural treatment increased from 14% at the end of the MTA intervention to 45% 22 months later, whereas among MTA participants who received the medication management intervention (including the combined treatment group) medication use decreased from 91% to 71%. In the community care group medication use was near unchanged: 60% at end of treatment and 62% 22 months later. Further support for the inference that changes in medication use may have mediated the convergence between outcomes across the groups at follow-up is provided by analysis indicating that the subgroup that reported stopping taking medication 10 months after the end of treatment showed the greatest deterioration (MTA Co-operative Group, 2004b).

Substance use at 22 months after the end of the MTA interventions was lower in the MTA participants who received intensive behaviour therapy (members of the combined treatment and behavioural intervention groups) compared with those who did not (members of the medication management and community care groups) (Molina *et al.*, 2007). However, the data did not point to there being any associations between treatment allocation and early substance use, growth of delinquency over time and the level/seriousness of delinquency. Seriousness of offences was associated with self-selected use of prescription medication, and Molina and colleagues (2007) speculate that this could be reactive in that there may be a tendency to opt for medication in response to increased symptom severity.

The analysis by Molina and colleagues (2007) did not point to either a protective or adverse effect of medication for ADHD (whether study allocated or self-selected in community care participants) on the initiation of substance use in MTA participants. However, it should be noted that at the post-treatment follow-up at 22 months the mean age of participants was still relatively young (most were between 11 and 13 years of age).

*Factors associated with treatment effects according to data gathered at the end of the MTA interventions*
Analysis of the MTA data points to some impacts of socioeconomic status on treatment outcomes at the end of the intervention (Rieppi *et al.*, 2002). For children from better educated families, combination treatment may be more effective than medication management alone for ADHD symptoms whereas for low socioeconomic status families, combination treatment may be more effective for oppositional aggressive symptoms.

Other analysis found that response to treatment in the MTA study did not differ significantly by ethnicity after controlling for public assistance (Arnold *et al.*, 2003). However, at the end of the intervention medication doses reached a higher level for African American children receiving medication management only compared with the average for the group allocated to this intervention. As this was not the case for children from ethnic minorities receiving combination treatment, Arnold and colleagues (2003) suggest that it is possible that the behavioural intervention may have neutralised adverse effects of low socioeconomic status that might otherwise exacerbate symptoms and lead to a need for a higher medication dose. A speculative inference from the analysis is that white middle class children without comorbid anxiety or disruptive behaviour may not gain from adding behavioural treatment to medication, but children of low socioeconomic status, or with comorbid anxiety and disruptive behaviour, especially if from a minority ethnic group, may gain added benefit from combining behavioural treatment with medication.

Another analysis looking at potential moderators of the response to treatment in the MTA study found no moderators of response to behavioural treatment or community care (Owens *et al.*, 2003). However, the analysis indicated that parental depression decreased treatment effectiveness in the medication management group but not in the behavioural treatment group. This finding led Owens and colleagues (2003) to speculate that the parental components of the behavioural intervention may in effect treat the parents to some degree, thus mitigating negative impacts of parental depression on the outcomes for the child. Owens and colleagues (2003) also found that a high initial severity of ADHD symptoms decreased the treatment effects from the medication management and combined treatment interventions, but as the analysis used a measure of response to treatment it is possible that this may reflect the need for those with more severe symptoms at the outset to improve more so as to be classed as responding to treatment.

A further finding unrelated to behavioural treatment reported by Owens and colleagues (2003), was that for those on medication management (that is, participants receiving the medication management or combined treatment interventions), participants in the subgroup with parental depression and a higher severity of symptoms responded better to medication if they had a higher starting IQ compared with those in this subpopulation with lower IQ. In terms of implications for treatment, Owens and colleagues (2003) suggest that their analysis indicates that treatment of parental depression may be important in order to get a positive response to treatment of ADHD using medication. They also speculate that it might be important to intervene early with medication management or combined treatment before ADHD severity increases and a positive response to treatment becomes less likely.

Analysis looking at outcomes at the end of treatment for subgroups with comorbid anxiety and disruptive behaviour (oppositional defiant disorder or conduct disorder) pointed to some impacts on treatment effects (Jensen *et al.*, 2001). All MTA interventions including community care were found to be effective in the subgroup with ADHD and comorbid anxiety. For subgroups with ADHD only or ADHD and disruptive behaviour (oppositional defiant disorder or conduct disorder), medication was favoured – whether alone or in combination with behavioural treatment – but behavioural treatment alone may be contraindicated. For the subgroup with ADHD and both anxiety and disruptive behaviour, there was evidence of an advantage of combined treatment, particularly with respect to overall impairment and functioning.

Earlier analysis looking at the impact of comorbidity suggested that MTA participants with comorbid disruptive behaviours (oppositional defiant disorder and conduct disorder) did not benefit from the addition of behavioural treatment (that is, combined treatment) over medication management alone at the end of treatment time point

(MTA Co-operative Group, 1999b). A further tentative inference from the data gathered at the end of treatment is that the intensive MTA behavioural intervention may have had similar effects to routine medication because the majority (66%) of the community care group received medication for ADHD and the behavioural intervention group did not differ significantly from the community care group for end of treatment outcomes. It must, however, be noted that the absence of a statistical difference between the groups does not prove that there is no difference between the effects of the behavioural intervention and continued community care.

Secondary analysis looking at treatment response found that twice as many children met criteria for successful treatment at the end of treatment time point in the groups receiving medication management (medication management and combined treatment groups) compared with the behavioural intervention and community care groups (Swanson *et al.*, 2001). The authors infer that if medication management was adopted in usual care the number of cases successfully treated would effectively double from 30% to 62%. The analysis also suggests that the addition of intensive psychological treatment in combination with medication management would result in 12% more children being successfully treated as the response rate was 56% in the medication management group compared with 68% in the combined treatment group (equivalent to a 20% increase in the success rate through the addition of intensive psychological treatment).

A further analysis of the MTA study data gathered at the end of treatment time point indicates that the more severe subgroup meeting criteria for hyperkinetic disorder showed a larger decrease in symptoms with medication than with behaviour therapy, and a larger medication advantage than those not meeting criteria for hyperkinetic disorder (Santosh *et al.*, 2005). Accordingly, as they show a greater response to medication than the less severe non-hyperkinetic disorder subgroup, Santosh and colleagues suggest that for those with hyperkinetic disorder medication management is favoured as a first-line treatment. As the response of the non-hyperkinetic disorder subgroup to medication was in the same direction, albeit to a lesser degree, the data also suggest that stimulants may be indicated for some children with ADHD who do not meet criteria for hyperkinetic disorder.

## 11.5    HEALTH ECONOMICS EVIDENCE

### 11.5.1    Systematic literature review

The systematic literature search identified two economic studies that compared the cost effectiveness of pharmacological, psychological and combination therapies in children with ADHD (Lord & Paisley, 2000; Zupancic *et al.*, 1998), plus an economic analysis of the interventions assessed in the MTA study (Jensen *et al.*, 2005; Foster *et al.*, 2007). In addition, the economic modelling undertaken to support NICE guidance on the use of methylphenidate, atomoxetine and dexamfetamine in children with ADHD incorporated a sub-analysis that compared combination therapies with the evaluated medications (King *et al.*, 2006). Details on the methods used for the systematic search of the economic literature are described in Chapter 3. The economic analysis of the MTA study is described in a separate sub-section in this chapter. Information on the methods used and the results reported in all economic studies included in the systematic literature review are presented in the form of evidence tables in Appendix 14.

Lord and Paisley (2000) conducted an economic analysis to compare the cost effectiveness of combination therapy, consisting of methylphenidate plus behavioural therapy, with behavioural therapy alone for children with ADHD in the UK. The perspective of the analysis was that of the NHS. The study, based on a decision-analytic model, utilised clinical-effectiveness data from the MTA study. Resource use estimates were based on expert opinion and reflected clinical practice in the UK. Costs consisted of drug acquisition and pharmacotherapist costs. Costs of behavioural therapy were omitted from the analysis, as these were common in the two strategies assessed. The measure of outcome was the SMD in the SNAP-IV score between the two treatment options. The time horizon of the analysis was 14 months, the length of the MTA study. According to the results of the analysis, the ICER of combination therapy versus behavioural therapy alone was £1,596 per SMD in the SNAP-IV score (1999 prices). This ratio ranged in sensitivity analysis from £694 to £4,545 per SMD in the SNAP-IV score. One limitation of the analysis was the use of the change in SNAP-IV scores as the primary outcome measure, which could not capture the HRQoL of children with ADHD. In addition, the study utilised clinical data from the MTA study, which was conducted in the US and examined interventions that were more intensive than typical interventions in the UK. On the other hand, the resource use estimates by Lord and Paisley (2000) referred to UK clinical practice, and therefore the results of the economic analysis should be interpreted with caution.

Zupancic and colleagues (1998) assessed the cost effectiveness of methylphenidate, dexamfetamine, pemoline, psychological/behavioural therapy and combination therapy (consisting of psychological/behavioural therapy and methylphenidate) in comparison with no treatment from the perspective of a third-party payer in Canada. Details on the methodology of the study are reported in Chapter 10. The meta-analysis of clinical studies included in the systematic literature review indicated that psychological/behavioural therapy, either alone or as an adjunct to pharmacological therapy, was not effective. The economic analysis demonstrated that methylphenidate dominated both psychological/behavioural therapy and combination therapy. The limitations of the analysis are described in Chapter 10. Additional limitations specific to the evaluation of psychological/behavioural and combination therapies were: the rather poor quality and the insufficient power of clinical studies assessing these two strategies; the assumptions regarding duration of therapy (daily provision of drugs versus 16-hour provision of psychological/behavioural therapy), which, according to the authors, might have biased the results against psychological/behavioural and combination therapies; and, finally, the choice of the outcome measure, that is, the change in CTRS scores, which might have underestimated the efficacy of psychological/behavioural therapy alone or in combination, given that this therapy has been shown to be more effective in enhancing academic performance and improving conflicted peer relations rather than improving core ADHD symptoms.

The economic analysis of the NICE TA on the use of methylphenidate, atomoxetine and dexamfetamine for children and adolescents with ADHD (NICE, 2006b) incorporated a sub-analysis assessing the cost effectiveness of combination strategies relative to strategies involving only sequences of medications (King *et al.*, 2006). Details on the methodology adopted in the study analysis are provided in Chapter 10. The sub-analysis including combination therapies assessed 37 strategies in total: 18 strategies consisting of all possible three-line sequences of the medications reviewed, 18 respective strategies of three-line sequences of combined treatment, and a strategy of no treatment. After excluding all strategies ruled out by dominance, two options remained: a combination strategy consisting of behavioural therapy plus first-line dexamfetamine, second-line atomoxetine and third-line MR methylphenidate administered every 8 hours, and a medication strategy consisting of first-line dexamfetamine, second-line IR methylphenidate and third-line atomoxetine. The ICER of the first versus the second strategy was £1,241,570/QALY; consequently, the authors concluded that combination strategies were not cost effective from the perspective of the NHS. However, the available clinical data for this analysis were very limited (based on a single trial comparing IR methylphenidate alone versus in combination with behavioural therapy) and no firm conclusions could be drawn.

Overall, the existing evidence reported in Zupancic and colleagues (1998) and King and colleagues (2006) suggests that combination and psychological therapies may not be cost-effective treatment options compared with medication for children with ADHD. However, there were considerable limitations in the clinical-effectiveness data used in the economic analyses, as described above. The study by Lord and Paisley (2000) used resource use estimates representing UK routine clinical practice, and clinical data from the MTA study, which evaluated intensive interventions in the US. Considering also that the primary measure of outcome in the analysis was the SMD of SNAP-IV scores rather than a dichotomous outcome, it is evident that no safe conclusions can be made by this analysis either.

## 11.5.2    Economic modelling

*Objective*

The choice of treatment strategy among various types of interventions available to children with ADHD was identified by the GDG and the health economist as an area with potential major resource implications. The existing economic evidence in this field was limited and was characterised by considerable uncertainty; therefore a decision-analytic model was developed for this guideline to examine the relative cost effectiveness of pharmacological, psychological and combination therapies for children with ADHD.

*Treatment strategies examined*

The treatment strategies examined were medication versus behavioural therapy versus combined therapy (that is, behavioural therapy provided concurrently with medication). Medication was represented by use of methylphenidate in the economic model, for three reasons: methylphenidate was the only drug examined in the clinical trials comparing pharmacological with psychological and/or combined therapies that were included in the guideline systematic literature review; it is the most commonly used medication in clinical practice; finally, indirect clinical evidence suggests that it is likely the most effective drug in improving core symptoms in children with ADHD. Nevertheless, recommendations based on the results of the economic analysis refer to medication as a treatment option, and are not intended to be specific to the use of methylphenidate.

Medication was defined as use of IR methylphenidate at an average daily dose of 25 mg for 4 weeks (titration period), followed by use of MR methylphenidate at an average daily dose of 36 mg. Children taking medication had regular contacts with healthcare professionals (psychiatrists or paediatricians and nurse specialists), with higher intensity during the titration period. Behavioural therapy was defined as ten 1-hour meetings of clinical psychologists with groups of ten parents of children with ADHD. In addition, clinical psychologists provided telephone support to parents when needed, and had two meetings with children's teachers at school lasting 30 minutes each, in order to provide advice. Combined treatment consisted of both medication and behavioural therapy.

*Methods*
*Model structure*    An economic model in the form of a decision tree was developed to estimate total costs and benefits associated with provision of medication, behavioural therapy and combined treatment to children with ADHD. According to the model structure, hypothetical cohorts of children with ADHD were started on one of the three treatment options under assessment. If children receiving behavioural therapy or medication did not respond to treatment following completion of 8 weeks of therapy (in accordance with the duration of clinical trials that provided efficacy data), they were switched to medication or behavioural therapy, respectively, or to combined treatment. However, children not responding to combined therapy after 8 weeks were not then offered medication or behavioural therapy alone, as it was assumed that none of the 'monotherapy' interventions would be effective following unsuccessful combination therapy. It must be noted that the model assumed that non-response to a treatment option did not affect effectiveness (that is, response rates) of subsequent treatments; this means that response rates of any treatment option a child might have received were independent from each other. Children on medication or combined intervention who stopped treatment because of intolerable side effects were switched to behavioural therapy. Children who switched to combined treatment because of non-responsiveness after 8 weeks of medication were assumed not to experience intolerable side effects from combined treatment, given that they had not experienced intolerable side effects from medication alone. Children completing medication or combination therapy could also experience (tolerable) side effects that did not affect continuation of therapy. Children not responding after two lines of treatment (or one, if they completed 8 weeks of combined treatment and did not respond to it), were assumed to receive 'other treatment'. This consisted of further management of children with ADHD, including contacts with healthcare professionals, unlicensed medications, inpatient care or no treatment.

The time horizon of the analysis was 1 year. Children responding to any of the treatment options assessed were assumed to continue successful treatment beyond 8 weeks (with 100% compliance) and remain responsive (that is, retain improved symptoms) until the end of the analysis. Children non-responsive to treatment who moved to 'other treatment' remained on it until the end of the analysis. It is acknowledged that the time horizon of 1 year is rather limited and does not allow estimation of the overall, long-term costs and benefits associated with treatment of children with ADHD; however, there is no sufficient evidence to allow modelling for longer periods of time, as long-term harms and benefits of the examined interventions have not been adequately explored. A schematic diagram of the decision tree is provided in Figure 5.

**Figure 5: Schematic diagram of the structure of the economic model
SE = side effects; BT = behavioural therapy**

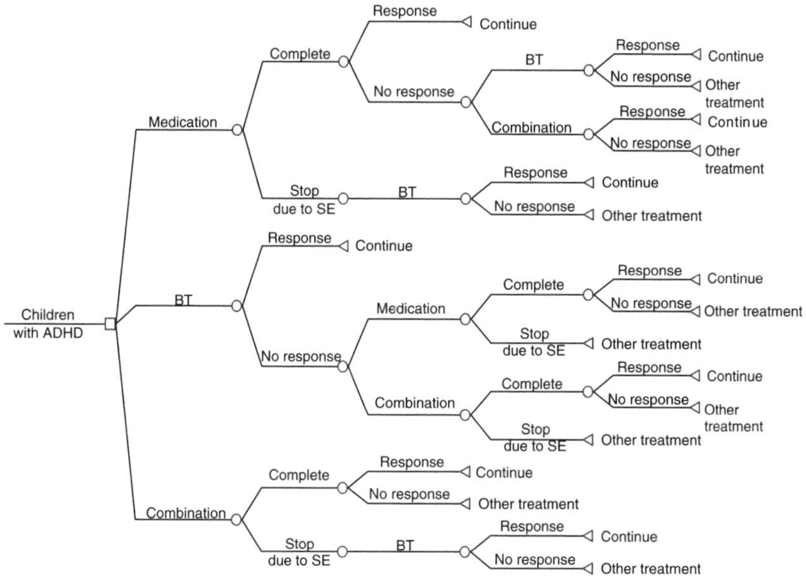

*Costs and health benefit measures included in the analysis*    The analysis adopted the perspective of the NHS. Health service costs consisted of intervention costs, costs of monitoring children who responded to treatment and therefore remained in receipt of any of the treatments assessed for the whole time horizon of the analysis, as well as costs of 'other treatment' for children not responding to the treatment options assessed.

Costs of treating side effects were not separately considered in the analysis because the majority of side effects from medication (anorexia, nausea, insomnia, headache, increased irritability, and so on) are routinely managed by healthcare professionals responsible for the monitoring of children receiving medication and were estimated not to incur extra costs.

Costs of personal social services and education services were not included in the analysis owing to lack of relevant data, but it is unlikely that these differ significantly across children receiving different types of treatment over the period of 1 year. Other societal costs, such as social benefit payments and productivity losses of carers of children with ADHD were not considered as they were beyond the scope of this analysis. Benefits were expressed in the form of QALYs. Results are reported as ICERs.

*Effectiveness data and other clinical input parameters*   As already discussed in the economic sections of Chapter 7, for the economic analyses undertaken in this guideline, it was decided to utilise data only from studies reporting outcomes as response rates, with response defined in a way that the GDG found both clinically meaningful and significant.

The guideline systematic review identified four studies that examined pharmacological versus psychological and/or combination therapies for children with ADHD and reported outcomes as response rates (ABIKOFF2004B; GITTELMAN-KLEIN1976B; KLEIN1997B; MTA1999B). GITTELMAN-KLEIN1976B and KLEIN1997B compared methylphenidate with behavioural therapy and combined treatment. ABIKOFF2004A compared methylphenidate with a combination of methylphenidate and a multimodal psychosocial treatment that included parent training and counselling, social skills training, psychotherapy and academic assistance. MTA1999B compared intensive medication management with intensive behavioural therapy and a combination of the two. The definitions of the term 'response' established by the studies were considered appropriate by the GDG. For the base-case analysis, it was decided to utilise data from GITTELMAN-KLEIN1976B and KLEIN1997B, as the studies examined the interventions of interest in this economic analysis; data from ABIKOFF2004A were considered in a sensitivity analysis; data from MTA1999B were examined separately, as the study involved interventions of high intensity.

The study population in GITTELMAN-KLEIN1976B and KLEIN1997B consisted of school-age children with pervasive symptoms of ADHD and parent reports for hyperactivity or behavioural problems at home. Both studies defined response as a final score of 1 to 3 on the CGI-I scale (that is, completely well, much improved, or improved). More details on the study characteristics can be found in Appendix 17.

Analysis of efficacy data from the above trials was based on intention-to-treat (that is, response rates were calculated taking into account the number of all children participating in each arm at the start of the trials and not completers only); other important input parameters for the economic model, such as rates of children dropping out of treatment because of intolerable side effects as well as rates of side effects in each treatment arm were not reported in these studies. For this reason, the proportions of children who stopped medication or combined treatment because of intolerable side effects were derived from the guideline meta-analysis of studies comparing methylphenidate with placebo, including comorbid and non-comorbid populations of children with ADHD. The attributable risk of stopping methylphenidate because of intolerable side effects was calculated by subtracting the overall rate of stopping placebo because of side effects from the respective rate for methylphenidate. This attributable risk estimate was applied to children who received medication or combined treatment in the analysis, while children receiving behavioural therapy were assumed not to experience intolerable side effects that would lead to discontinuation of treatment.

Rates of side effects for children under medication or combined therapy were based on the same dataset of studies (that is, placebo-controlled studies of methylphenidate in children with ADHD including comorbid and non-comorbid populations) and were estimated in a similar way. However, the existing studies did not report an overall side-effect rate, but rather provided rates of specific side effects; it was not possible to estimate an overall side-effect rate from these data as some children might have experienced more than one side effect. In order to overcome this problem, it was decided to proxy the overall rate of side effects for methylphenidate using data on the rate of appetite loss; this was selected because it is a common, statistically significant side effect of methylphenidate and also it is deemed to substantially reduce the quality of life of children with ADHD. The attributable risk of side effects for methylphenidate was therefore calculated as the difference between rate of appetite loss for methylphenidate and rate of appetite loss for placebo; this estimate was subsequently applied to children receiving medication or combined treatment; it was assumed that, for the proportion of children experiencing side effects, these persisted for the entirety of the time period when medication or combined treatment was provided. Children receiving behavioural therapy or 'other treatment' did not experience side effects from treatment.

Discontinuation of treatment for reasons other than intolerable side effects was not considered in the analysis owing to lack of data appropriate to inform the economic model: GITTELMAN-KLEIN1976B and KLEIN1997B reported very small discontinuation rates that were insignificant; moreover, it was not clearly reported from which arms of the trials children dropped out. The only other available data came from MTA1999B, which referred to intensive interventions, and therefore respective data did not reflect discontinuation of treatment options assessed in this analysis. In addition, such data could only be applied to first-line treatment, as children completing treatment without response, as well as their parents, were thought to demonstrate different attitudes towards second-line treatment, which would not be reflected in discontinuation rates characterising initiation of treatment.

The proportions of children moving to combined treatment following failure of medication or behavioural therapy was based on a trial comparing medication with behavioural therapy in which proportions of children not fully responding to the interventions assessed were subsequently switched to combined treatment (Döpfner *et al.*, 2004).

Estimation of response rate of 'other treatment' was based on a published metaanalysis of follow-up studies on children with ADHD; the study reported the annual probability of continuation of residual ADHD symptoms in the population of people with ADHD (Faraone *et al.*, 2006), which was interpreted for the purposes of this analysis as no response. From this annual rate, it was possible to estimate the response rates of children that remained under 'other treatment' for varying time periods.

Effectiveness data and other clinical input parameters utilised in the base-case economic analysis are presented in Table 37.

**Table 37: Response rates and other clinical input parameters utilised in the base-case economic analysis of pharmacological versus psychological versus combined interventions for children with ADHD**

| Input parameter | Baseline value | Source/comments |
|---|---|---|
| Response rates<br>Medication | 0.733 | Meta-analysis of GITTELMAN-KLEIN1976b and KLEIN1997b; intention-to-treat analysis |
| Behavioural therapy | 0.474 | |
| Combined treatment | 0.976 | |
| Other treatment | 0.040 | Faraone *et al.*, 2006; annual rate of elimination of residual ADHD symptoms to the population of individuals with ADHD |
| Stopping treatment because of intolerable side effects<br>Medication and combined treatment | 0.003 | Guideline meta-analysis of placebo-controlled trials of methylphenidate (including comorbid and non-comorbid populations of children with ADHD). Attributable risk (methylphenidate rate minus placebo rate) |
| Side-effect rate<br>Medication and combined treatment | 0.093 | Guideline meta-analysis of placebo-controlled trials of methylphenidate (including comorbid and non-comorbid populations of children with ADHD). Attributable risk of appetite loss (methylphenidate rate minus placebo rate) |
| Proportion of children moving to combined therapy following unsuccessful treatment<br>Medication<br>Behavioural therapy | 0.884<br>1.000 | Döpfner *et al.*, 2004 |

*Utility data and estimation of QALYs*   As already discussed in the economic section of Chapter 7, two sets of utility scores were used for the economic analyses undertaken in this guideline involving children with ADHD: base-case analyses utilised the scores reported by Coghill and colleagues (2004), generated from EQ-5D; utility scores provided by Secnik and colleagues (2005b), produced by SG technique using vignettes of health states of children with ADHD in the UK, were used in a sensitivity analysis.

One limitation of using Coghill and colleagues' (2004) utility scores in the current analysis was that they did not take into account any decrement in quality of life resulting from the presence of side effects. Nevertheless, this was an important parameter to consider in this analysis, since children under medication or combined therapy could experience side effects and a subsequent reduction in HRQoL, in contrast with children under behavioural therapy, who did not experience side effects. For this reason, a decrement in utility resulting from the presence of side effects was estimated from Secnik and colleagues (2005b) and was applied to the base-case utility scores to create additional scores for responders and non-responders experiencing side effects. Regarding the sensitivity analysis that tested the data from Secnik and colleagues (2005b), it was assumed that utility scores reflecting no medication/untreated ADHD expressed utility of children receiving behavioural therapy.

Utility scores used in the economic analysis of pharmacological versus psychological versus combined treatment for children with ADHD are provided in Table 38.

It was assumed that HRQoL in children initially responding to treatment improved linearly over 8 weeks starting from the utility score of non-responders and reaching the utility score for responders (8 weeks was the duration of interventions in the clinical trials considered in the economic analysis), and that it remained at this value for the rest of the time of the analysis. Decrement in quality of life owing to the presence of side effects was modelled from initiation of respective treatment. Once side effects occurred, they were assumed to remain over the whole period over which medication or combined therapy was provided. Children who stopped treatment because of intolerable side effects faced a decrement in quality of life for 2 weeks, after which the intolerable therapy was discontinued.

*Resource utilisation and cost data*
Owing to lack of patient-level cost data, deterministic costing of all treatment options assessed was undertaken. Relevant healthcare resource use was estimated and subsequently combined with unit prices to provide total costs associated with medication, behavioural therapy and combined treatment. Resource utilisation estimates reflected, as closely as possible, resource use described in the clinical studies utilised in the economic analysis (GITTELMAN-KLEIN1976B; KLEIN1997B). Where relevant information on resource use was lacking (for example, resource use beyond the duration of the trials) or was clearly unrepresentative of British routine practice, then estimates were produced/modified based on the expert opinion of the GDG.

For children receiving medication, the GDG estimated the average optimal daily dose of methylphenidate during titration and post-titration, which was, overall, consistent with doses reported in the clinical studies that provided efficacy data.

**Table 38: Utility scores included in the economic model of pharmacological versus psychological versus combined interventions for children with ADHD**

| Health state | Utility score | Source – comments |
|---|---|---|
| Base-case analysis | | |
| Responder – no side effects | 0.837 | Coghill *et al.*, 2004; scores based |
| Responder – side effects | 0.817 | on EQ-5D; questionnaires |
| Non-responder – no side effects | 0.773 | completed by parents of children |
| Non-responder – side effects | 0.753 | with ADHD in the UK; |
| | | decrement in HRQoL owing to |
| | | presence of side effects estimated |
| | | based on Secnik *et al.*, 2005b. |
| Sensitivity analysis | | |
| No medication – responder | 0.95 | Secnik *et al.*, 2005b; scores |
| No medication – non-responder | 0.90 | generated using SG technique, |
| IR stimulant – responder – no side effects | 0.91 | asking parents of children with ADHD in the UK to value ADHD |
| IR stimulant – responder – effects | 0.90 | health states described in side vignettes. |
| IR stimulant – non-responder – no side effects | 0.89 | |
| IR stimulant – non-responder – side effects | 0.88 | |
| MR stimulant – responder – no side effects | 0.93 | |
| MR stimulant – responder – side effects | 0.91 | |
| MR stimulant – non-responder – no side effects | 0.90 | |
| MR stimulant – non-responder – side effects | 0.88 | |

Titration was estimated to last 4 weeks, over which time children received IR methylphenidate. MR methylphenidate was administered post-titration, according to routine clinical practice in the UK. Children were attended by a psychiatrist or a paediatrician during titration. Those responding to medication were assumed to continue receiving methylphenidate until the end of the analysis, being monitored by a psychiatrist, paediatrician or a nurse at regular intervals. Children stopping medication because of intolerable side effects were assumed to receive methylphenidate for 2 weeks before discontinuing and to spend half of the total estimated time (during titration) with a psychiatrist or paediatrician.

Behavioural therapy in GITTELMAN-KLEIN1976B and KLEIN1997B was provided to parents of children with ADHD on a one-to-one basis. However, existing evidence indicated that clinical effectiveness of psychological interventions for children with ADHD did not depend on the mode of delivery and was similar in individual and group-based therapies. Given that the intervention costs of group-based therapies are spread to a number of families, group-based behavioural therapy dominates individually delivered therapy because it produces the same clinical outcome at a lower cost. For this reason, group-based behavioural therapy has been modelled in the base-case analysis; the cost effectiveness of individual behavioural therapy versus medication and combination therapy, indicated under special circumstances, has been explored in a sensitivity analysis.

According to average resource use described in clinical trials of psychological interventions for children and confirmed by GDG expert opinion, behavioural therapy was modelled as ten meetings (lasting 1 hour each) of clinical psychologists with groups of parents of children with ADHD. Every group comprised 10 families. Clinical psychologists were assumed to spend an extra hour for training and preparation. In addition, based on resource use data reported in GITTELMAN-KLEIN1976B and KLEIN1997B, these sessions were augmented by an average of 1 hour of telephone contacts with each family. Clinical psychologists also visited the teachers of the children at school and provided advice; two visits of 30 minutes each were assumed. Following completion of the intervention, parents of children responding to behavioural therapy attended three individual booster sessions with psychologists lasting 30 minutes each, in order to maintain children's response for the remaining time of the analysis.

Resource use in combined treatment was the sum of resource use of medication and behavioural therapy, given that the two interventions are led by different types of healthcare professionals and no overlap in services provided occurs.

Regarding costs of 'other treatment', no data on average annual costs associated with management of children with ADHD in the UK are available. King and colleagues (2006) gave an overall estimate of £14 million spent on follow-up care of children with ADHD by health, social and education services in England and Wales (initial specialist assessment was excluded from these costs). Using this estimate, a prevalence of ADHD equalling 3.62% in boys and 0.85% in girls (Ford *et al.*, 2003), and the population of boys and girls aged 5–18 in 2006 in England and Wales (Office for National Statistics, 2007), it was estimated that a child with diagnosed ADHD incurred on average a cost of £67 annually. This estimate may seem low, but it is likely to reflect the fact that some children with ADHD may not receive any treatment for this condition.

Unit prices were taken from the *BNF* 55 (Joint Formulary Committee, 2008), and the Unit Costs for Health and Social Care 2006 (Curtis & Netten, 2006); 2006 prices were used. The reported unit costs for clinical psychologists did not include qualification costs, owing to lack of relevant data; it was therefore decided to exclude qualification costs from the unit costs of all healthcare professions included in this analysis, for consistency purposes. Discounting was not applied, as costs and benefits were measured over a period of 1 year.

Resource use estimates and unit costs as well as total costs of interventions assessed over the 1 year of the analysis are reported in Table 39.

**Table 39: Cost data utilised in the base-case economic analysis of pharmacological versus psychological versus combined interventions for children with ADHD**

| Resource use estimate | Cost | Unit prices – sources and comments |
|---|---|---|
| Medication<br>Methylphenidate<br>Titration: 25 mg/day IR – 4 weeks<br>Post-titration: 36 mg/day<br>MR – 4 weeks<br>   – 44 weeks<br>Contacts with healthcare professionals<br>Titration: 2 hours with psychiatrist/paediatrician<br>Monitoring: 0.5 hour at months 4, 7 and 12; 50% with psychiatrist/paediatrician and 50% with nurse<br>**Total cost for 8 weeks**<br>**Total cost over 1 year for responders** | £12<br><br><br>£38<br>£415<br><br><br>£382<br><br>£191<br><br><br><br>**£432**<br>**£1,038** | *BNF 55*<br>Non-proprietary<br><br>Concerta® XL<br>Curtis & Netten, 2006; cost per hour of client contact excluding qualification costs:<br>Consultant psychiatrist: £191<br>Nurse specialist (community): £63<br>No unit costs specific to consultant paediatricians were available; the GDG judged these should be equal to unit costs of consultant psychiatrists |
| Behavioural therapy<br>10 × 1 hour group sessions with parents<br>1 extra hour training and preparation<br>Total cost of group sessions<br>Total cost of group sessions per family, assuming 10 families in each group<br>1 hour telephone calls with each family<br>2 × 0.5 hour with teachers<br>Travelling to school<br>3 × 0.5 hour individual booster sessions | £660<br><br>£29<br><br>£689<br>£69<br><br><br>£66<br><br>£66<br>£3<br>£99 | Curtis & Netten, 2006; cost per hour of client contact excluding qualification costs:<br>Clinical psychologist: £66 |

*Continued*

**Table 39: (*Continued*)**

| Resource use estimate | Cost | Unit prices – sources and comments |
|---|---|---|
| **Total cost for 8 weeks** <br> **Total cost over 1 year for responders** | **£204** <br> **£303** | |
| Combined treatment <br> **Total cost for 8 weeks** <br><br> **Total cost over 1 year for responders** | **£636** <br><br> **£1,341** | Sum of costs of medication and behavioural therapy |
| 'Other treatment' <br> **Total cost over 1 year** | **£67** | Total costs of follow-up care for children with ADHD (King *et al.*, 2006) were divided by estimated number of children with ADHD in England and Wales. |

*Sensitivity analysis*

A sensitivity analysis was undertaken to investigate the robustness of the results under the uncertainty characterising input parameters of the model. The following scenarios were tested in a one-way sensitivity analysis:

1. Changes in response rates to treatment:
   - use of the 95% CI of the RR of response rates of combined treatment to behavioural therapy (mean RR = 2.04; 95% CI, 1.46 to 2.86)
   - use of the 95% CI of the RR of response rates of medication to behavioural therapy (mean RR = 1.55; 95% CI, 1.06 to 2.27)
   - inclusion of data from ABIKOFF2004a in the meta-analysis.
2. Utility scores obtained from Secnik and colleagues (2005b).
3. Use of one line of treatment only; children responding to treatment remained on it for the rest of the time of the analysis; children not responding were switched to 'other treatment'.
4. Changes in resource use estimates for behavioural therapy (or the behavioural therapy component of combined treatment):
   - Group-based CBT, more appropriate for school-age children, provided by clinical psychologists, consisting of ten sessions lasting 1 hour each with parents and ten sessions lasting 1 hour each with children (ten parents and ten children in each group, respectively), including 1 hour of telephone calls per family, plus 2 extra hours for training and preparation and two 0.5 hour individual meetings with the children's teachers, reflecting effective, optimal routine practice for school-age children (expert opinion of the GDG). In addition, three

individual booster sessions, lasting 30 minutes each, were offered to parents of children responding to treatment, in order to maintain children's response for the remaining time of the analysis. The cost of this intervention was £371 per child.

● Individual behavioural therapy, consisting of ten weekly sessions with a clinical psychologist, lasting 1 hour each, in cases where group-based programmes are not a suitable option. The remaining components of the intervention (telephone contact with parents, visiting children's teachers at school and booster sessions for children responding to treatment) were the same as with the group intervention. The total cost of this intervention was £894 per child. This scenario explored the cost effectiveness of individual behavioural therapy under a number of alternative hypotheses, such as: use of the upper and lower 95% CIs of the RRs as described above; inclusion of data from ABIKKOF2004a in the meta-analysis of clinical studies; use of utility scores obtained from Secnik and colleagues (2005b); use of one line of treatment only; and provision of behavioural therapy by health visitors instead of clinical psychologists (at a unit cost of £61 per clinic hour excluding qualification costs, according to Curtis and Netten, 2006).

In addition to the above scenarios, threshold analyses were carried out to identify the values of selected parameters at which the conclusions of the cost-effectiveness analysis would be reversed. The following parameters were tested:

1. rate of side effects from medication (or combined therapy)
2. rate of stopping medication (or combined therapy) because of intolerable side effects
3. decrement in utility scores because of side effects
4. response to 'other treatment'
5. cost of 'other treatment'.

*Results*

*Base-case analysis*  Combined therapy resulted in greatest health benefits but at the same time it was the most expensive treatment option. Group-based behavioural therapy was the least effective and cheapest option. Medication was dominated by extended dominance. The ICER of combined therapy versus behavioural therapy was £122,682 per QALY. This value is far beyond the cost-effectiveness threshold of £20,000 per QALY set by NICE (NICE, 2006c). This means that, according to base-case results, group-based behavioural therapy is the most cost-effective treatment option among those assessed. Full results of the base-case analysis are presented in Table 40.

*Sensitivity analysis*  Group-based behavioural therapy remained the most cost-effective option under the vast majority of scenarios tested in the sensitivity analysis. The only scenario that affected conclusions of economic modelling was use of the upper 95% CIs of the RR of response rate of medication to behavioural therapy. In this case the ICER of medication versus behavioural therapy fell at £4,652 per QALY, thus medication became more cost effective than group-based behavioural therapy. In all other scenarios, either the ICERs of combined therapy and/or medication versus

**Table 40: Cost-effectiveness of pharmacological versus psychological versus combined treatment for children with ADHD – results of the base-case analysis over 1 year**

| Treatment option | Total QALYs/ child | Total cost/ child | Cost-effectiveness results |
|---|---|---|---|
| Combined therapy | 0.829 | £1,322 | **Combination versus behavioural therapy:** £122,682/QALY |
| Medication | 0.827 | £1,093 | Medication dominated by extended dominance |
| Behavioural therapy | 0.825 | £907 | |

group behavioural therapy were very high, beyond the cost-effectiveness threshold of £20,000 per QALY, or group behavioural therapy dominated the two other options.

Individual behaviour therapy was not cost effective compared with medication under any sub-analyses tested. In many scenarios it was dominated by medication (that is, it was less effective and more costly). In none of the scenarios explored was combined treatment found to be cost effective, even when it included group-based behavioural therapy. Results concerning either group or individual psychological therapies were not sensitive to any of the parameters examined in threshold analysis.

Full results of the one-way sensitivity analysis are shown in Table 41 and Table 42.

*Limitations of the economic analysis*
The results of the economic analysis were based on a simple decision-analytic model developed to estimate total costs and health benefits associated with provision of medication, behavioural therapy or combined treatment over a period of 1 year. Clinical evidence was derived from two trials that reported outcomes in the form of response to treatment. The total number of participants in these two trials was small (N = 125). Nevertheless, further evidence coming from studies reporting outcomes in the form of changes on scales measuring ADHD symptoms that were included in the guideline systematic review and meta-analysis supported clinical evidence utilised in this analysis.

Long-term harms and benefits of the treatment options assessed have not been explored in depth. Identifying potential harms of medication in the long term is likely to reduce its cost effectiveness relative to non-pharmacological interventions and in fact may raise other concerns over its use. Owing to lack of relevant data, the time horizon of the analysis was only 1 year. Despite the short duration of the analysis, a number of assumptions were still required at the development of the economic model. Children were assumed to remain improved, following initial response to treatment, over the rest of the time of the analysis up to 1 year, provided that they continued

**Table 41: Results of one-way sensitivity analysis for group-based behavioural therapy**

| Scenario | Combined treatment (combo) versus behavioural therapy (BT) | Medication (med) versus behavioural therapy (BT) |
|---|---|---|
| Upper 95% CIs of RR of combo versus BT | £92,318/QALY | Non applicable |
| Lower 95% CIs of RR of combo versus BT | BT dominates | Non applicable |
| Upper 95% CIs of RR of med versus BT | Non applicable | £4,652/QALY |
| Lower 95% CIs of RR of med versus BT | Non applicable | BT dominates |
| Inclusion of ABIKOFF2004A* | Non applicable | Non applicable |
| Utility scores from Secnik *et al.* (2005b) | BT dominates | BT dominates |
| One line of treatment only | £37,611/QALY | Med dominated by extended dominance |
| Group-based CBT[†] | £111,978/QALY | £90,471/QALY |

*ABIKOFF2004A compared combined treatment with medication; therefore, inclusion of this study does not affect results involving BT.
[†]Combo versus med £122,355/QALY.

medication under monitoring if they had responded to medication, or that they attended a number of booster sessions if they had responded to behavioural therapy. In both cases full compliance for all children was assumed, and no deterioration was modelled. Responsiveness to treatment was assumed to be independent of non-responsiveness to previous treatment provided. In reality, lack of response to one type of treatment could be related to improved or, conversely, reduced responsiveness to another type of treatment. Acceptability of the treatment to children and their carers reflected in overall continuation rates associated with pharmacological or psychological interventions for ADHD, was not considered, owing to lack of relevant data. However, this is an important factor that may significantly affect the relative cost effectiveness of an intervention.

Estimated costs consisted of intervention costs only; potential cost savings to the healthcare, social and education services resulting from improvement in ADHD

**Table 42: Results of one-way sensitivity analysis
for individual behavioural therapy**

| Scenario | Combined treatment (combo) versus behavioural therapy (BT) | Medication (med) versus behavioural therapy (BT) |
|---|---|---|
| Main scenario of individual BT | £289,821/QALY | Med dominates |
| Upper 95% CIs of RR of combo versus med | £142,016/QALY | Non applicable |
| Lower 95% CIs of RR of combo versus med | Med dominates | Non applicable |
| Upper 95% CIs of RR of med versus BT | Non applicable | Med dominates |
| Lower 95% CIs of RR of med versus BT | Non applicable | BT versus med £181,374/QALY |
| Inclusion of ABIKOFF2004A | £386,209/QALY | Non applicable |
| Utility scores from Secnik *et al.* (2005b) | Combo dominated by BT | BT versus med £60,641/QALY |
| One line of treatment only | £72,514/QALY | Med versus BT £800/QALY |
| BT delivered by health visitor | £268,181/QALY | Med dominates |

symptoms of children were not considered owing to lack of evidence. It is therefore likely that the relative cost effectiveness of the interventions assessed for children with ADHD is different from that suggested by the results of the analysis. It is expected that including potential cost savings would alter the cost-effectiveness results in favour of more effective interventions (that is, mainly combined therapy and, at a lower degree, medication).

Estimates of healthcare resource use reflected, as closely as possible, resource use described in the clinical studies utilised in the analysis; these estimates were consistent with optimal resource use in the UK, according to GDG expert opinion. Nevertheless, the clinical studies described only vaguely some aspects of resource use, and obviously they did not provide any relevant data for resource use beyond the duration of the trials (that is, beyond 8 weeks of treatment). It is unknown whether the number of booster sessions modelled for families receiving psychological interventions or the frequency and type of monitoring assumed for children taking medication are adequate to retain a positive outcome over a year, and this is a further limitation of the analysis.

Utility scores used in the base-case analysis were based on EQ-5D questionnaires completed by parents of children with ADHD in England (Coghill *et al.*, 2004). EQ-5D is a generic measure of HRQoL and as such, it has been recommended by NICE for use in economic evaluation. However, the full methods used to convert EQ-5D scores into utility scores were not reported in the study. In addition, the GDG expressed concerns about the appropriateness of using a generic measure to capture aspects of quality of life in children with ADHD. For this reason, utility scores developed using vignettes describing health states specific to ADHD (Secnik *et al.*, 2005b) were used in the sensitivity analysis. Utility scores used both in the base-case and sensitivity analysis were generated using parents of children with ADHD as proxy reporters of their children's perceptions of their own HRQoL. There are concerns about using parents' ratings as proxies to children's experience; still, for some groups of children who are unable to reliably report their own perceptions and preferences, parent proxies may be appropriate (Wallander *et al.*, 2001; de Civita *et al.*, 2005). In the area of ADHD, no data on HRQoL preferences directly reported by children, rather than by their parents, are currently available.

Behavioural therapy was assumed to be delivered in groups of parents in base-case analysis, despite the fact that both GITTELMAN-KLEIN1976B and KLEIN1997B, who provided the efficacy data for the analysis, examined individually delivered behavioural therapy. Although equivalence in efficacy between group-based and individually delivered programmes has not been established in head-to-head comparisons, existing indirect clinical evidence suggests that the mode of delivery does not affect the clinical effectiveness of psychological therapies for children with ADHD. Analysis of efficacy data was based on intention-to-treat. This means that estimated clinical effectiveness took into account the fact that some children/families might drop out of treatment. On the other hand, full intervention costs were estimated, assuming that all children completed treatment (with the exception of those children stopping treatment because of side effects, who switched to another therapy). This assumption has overestimated total costs of interventions to the disadvantage of strategies that are characterised by higher drop-out rates (and therefore lower overall costs).

### 11.5.3    Overall conclusions from the economic analysis

The results of the economic analysis indicate that group-based behavioural therapy is more cost effective than medication and combined therapy for children with ADHD. On the other hand, medication is more cost effective than individual behaviour therapy. Combination therapy was not cost effective under any scenario explored in the analysis.

The above conclusions are subject to a number of limitations, as already discussed. Further research is needed to explore fully the long-term harms and benefits associated with the treatment options assessed, as well as to investigate in depth the perceptions of children and their carers on aspects of HRQoL associated with

ADHD. Moreover, future head-to-head comparisons need to confirm the equivalence in efficacy between group-based and individually delivered behavioural therapy, so that the cost effectiveness of group-based behavioural therapy versus medication can be determined with higher certainty.

### 11.5.4 Economic analysis alongside the MTA study

Two studies (Jensen *et al.*, 2005; Foster *et al.*, 2007) assessed the cost effectiveness of the interventions examined in the MTA study (MTA Co-operative Group 1999a; 2004a; 2007) from the perspective of a third-party payer in the US. The interventions assessed in the study were medication management, intensive behavioural treatment, combination therapy and routine community care. The economic analysis of the MTA study is discussed separately from the rest of the economic literature, because it refers to intensive interventions, which are likely to differ from pharmacological, psychological and combination therapies routinely available in the UK for children with ADHD in terms of both effectiveness and associated resource use. Details on the methods adopted in the studies, their overall limitations, and results involving the comparison between medication management and routine community care are provided in Chapter 10. Characteristics and results of the studies are summarised in the form of evidence tables in Appendix 14.

According to Jensen and colleagues (2005), intensive behavioural treatment was dominated by medication management in all sub-groups of children with/without coexisting conditions examined, as well as in the total study population. Consequently it was clearly not a cost-effective option. Combined treatment was more effective than medication management in the majority of the sub-groups examined; however, the ICER of combined treatment versus medication management was rather high, ranging from US$29,840 (ADHD plus both internalising coexisting conditions, that is, anxiety and depression, and externalising coexisting conditions, that is, conduct and oppositional defiant disorders) to US$74,560 (ADHD plus externalising disorder) per normalised child, with normalisation determined by scores on the SNAP scale. For children with ADHD plus internalising disorder, medication management was more effective and cheaper than combined treatment (dominant option). The ICER of combined treatment versus medication management for the total population of children with ADHD combined was US$55,253 per child normalised (all costs expressed in 2000 prices). Based on the findings of the analysis, the authors concluded that medication management, although not as effective as combined treatment, was likely to be the most cost-effective option for children with ADHD, in particular for those without coexisting conditions. For children with ADHD and both internalising and externalising disorders they suggested that combined treatment might be relatively cost effective. Besides cost effectiveness, the authors highlighted the need to consider additional factors when making decisions on the appropriate treatment for children with ADHD, such as the presence of side effects of medication, the comfort and satisfaction of families with the treatment approach, and the family's overall feelings about the causes of ADHD.

Foster and colleagues (2007) demonstrated that, for the total population of children with ADHD, medication management was the most cost effective among the four interventions assessed at lower WTP for functioning improvement (from 0 to around US$55,000 per CIS ES). At higher levels of WTP, combined treatment became the most cost-effective strategy. These findings applied also to the population of children with ADHD and externalising disorder. For children with pure ADHD, medication management appeared to be cost effective at all levels of WTP. In contrast, for children with ADHD and internalising coexisting conditions, intensive behavioural treatment might be cost effective at high levels of WTP, while medication management appeared to be cost effective at low levels. Finally, in children with ADHD plus both internalising and externalising coexisting conditions, medication management was clearly cost effective at lower levels of WTP. At higher levels, the probabilities of medication management, intensive behavioural treatment and combined treatment being cost effective were similar and no clearly cost-effective option could be identified. Based on the results of their analysis, the authors stated that, for pure ADHD, medication management was certainly the most cost-effective option at all levels of WTP. In contrast, for coexisting conditions, WTP was crucial in determining the cost-effective treatment option: for lower WTP, medication management was the most cost-effective intervention; but for policy makers willing to pay more to avert future costs such as special education and juvenile justice costs, intensive behavioural treatment alone or combined with medication management (depending on the comorbidity) was likely to be the most cost-effective treatment.

As described previously, Schlander and colleagues (2006a, 2006b, 2006c) evaluated the relative cost effectiveness of the interventions examined in the MTA study in the context of four European countries, utilising the effectiveness data and resource use estimates reported in the MTA study, but applying country-specific unit costs. One of the analyses referred to the UK setting. The analysis adopted the perspective of the NHS (direct medical expenditures). Costs were calculated in UK£ and then converted to 2005 Euros (€). In addition to previous sub-groups identified, the authors provided results for children with ADHD combined type (according to DSM-IV), hyperkinetic/conduct disorder (according to ICD-10), pure ADHD (without coexisting conditions), and pure hyperkinetic disorder (without coexisting conditions). The measures of outcome used in the economic analyses were the number of children with ADHD normalised, the CIS ES and also the QALYs gained by treatment.

In most sub-populations of children, intensive behavioural treatment was dominated by medication management. The two exceptions were the sub-groups of children with internalising coexisting conditions and children with both internalising and externalising coexisting conditions, when the outcome was measured as CIS ES. In these cases, intensive behavioural therapy was shown to be more effective than medication at an incremental cost of €13,030 and €113,540 per CIS ES, respectively (£8,990 and £78,300, respectively, at a conversion rate of 1UK£ = 1.45€). Combined treatment achieved higher proportions of children normalised compared with medication management in all sub-groups of children examined. The ICER of combined treatment versus medication management per normalised child in the UK reached

€66,150 for ADHD combined type, €57,600 for pure ADHD, €37,320 for hyperkinetic/conduct disorder, and €26,460 for pure hyperkinetic disorder (or £45,620, £39,720, €25,740, and £18,250 respectively, at a conversion rate of 1UK£ = 1.45€). When the measure of outcome was the CIS ES, then combined treatment was less effective than medication management in children with pure ADHD, children with pure hyperkinetic disorder and children with hyperkinetic/conduct disorder. In all these cases medication management dominated combined treatment. Medication management was dominant over combined treatment also in children with internalising coexisting conditions. The ICER of combined treatment versus medication management in the total population of children with ADHD was as high as €705,115 per CIS ES.

CEACs demonstrated that, for the majority of sub-populations examined, medication management had the highest probability of being cost effective among the treatment options compared, at least for low levels of WTP. When the WTP rose up to roughly €40,000, €60,000, and €80,000 per child normalised, then combined treatment appeared to be the most cost-effective option for children with both internalising and externalising disorders, the total population of children with ADHD, and children with externalising coexisting conditions, respectively. For children with internalising coexisting conditions, medication management was the most cost-effective treatment at any level of WTP per child normalised. Regarding functional improvement, medication management was also shown to be the most cost-effective option at lower levels of WTP. However, in children with internalising coexisting conditions intensive behavioural treatment was the most likely cost-effective option at levels of WTP of around €15,000 per CIS ES and above.

Schlander and colleagues (2006a) did not provide ICERs expressing cost per QALY gained specific to the UK context. Instead, they reported ranges of such ICERs for the four European settings examined in the analysis. However, it was possible to estimate such ratios for the various sub-populations of children with ADHD, using the reported costs per child treated in the UK context, the proportions of children normalised in the MTA study and utility weights reported in Coghill and colleagues (2004). QALYs were estimated assuming that improvement in HRQoL occurred at time zero for responders. Decrement in HRQoL from medication was not considered in these estimates. Since intensive behavioural therapy was dominated by medication management when the measure of outcome was the proportions of children normalised, the appropriate comparison (apart from the comparison between medication management and routine community care, which has been reported in Chapter 10) was between combined treatment and medication management. The estimated ICERs from this comparison were £612,530 per QALY for ADHD combined type, £543,960 per QALY for pure ADHD, £351,780 per QALY for hyperkinetic/conduct disorder, and £248,060 per QALY for pure hyperkinetic disorder.

The above results indicate that intensive behavioural therapy and combined treatment are highly unlikely to be cost effective for children with ADHD from the perspective of the NHS, given also the cost-effectiveness threshold of £20,000 per QALY set by NICE (NICE, 2006c). Although these results refer to intensive interventions, they lead to the same conclusions as those reported in other published studies about the cost effectiveness of behavioural and combined therapies, and the results of the economic model described in the previous section in this chapter. Medication management was the most cost-effective option compared with intensive behavioural therapy and combined treatment, at least for modest levels of WTP. As reported in Chapter 10, routine community care reflecting US clinical practice might be more cost effective than medication management. However, no safe conclusions can be made, as routine clinical practice in the US may vary significantly from respective practice in the UK, and therefore the results of the analysis (which were based on US resource estimates) might not be representative of the UK healthcare setting.

## 11.6 FROM EVIDENCE TO RECOMMENDATIONS: TREATMENT DECISIONS AND COMBINED TREATMENT FOR CHILDREN WITH ADHD

Evidence from studies that have compared the effectiveness of stimulant medication for ADHD against the effectiveness of the use of psychological therapies for ADHD without concurrent administration of stimulant medication may help to inform the choice of first-line treatment for ADHD. Clear evidence strongly favouring one approach or another might point to an unequivocal recommendation as to which approach should always be used first, with alternatives being employed only where children do not respond to the first-line treatment.

While there is no evidence that psychological interventions are favoured for any outcome, or at any time point, it is also the case that stimulant medication for ADHD is not strongly favoured over psychological interventions, with the benefits of medication being weakest in comparison with complex psychological interventions. It also remains unclear whether the beneficial effects of stimulant medication over psychological interventions are sustained after the end of treatment. Accordingly the decision about whether to use a psychological intervention or stimulant medication for ADHD appears to be more balanced. In this context the choice of first-line intervention might be influenced by factors other than effectiveness, including possible adverse effects of medication and preferences of the child and/or parent.

Economic evidence suggests that group-based psychological interventions are likely to be more cost effective than medication (the evidential grounds for concluding that group-based psychological interventions are beneficial for children with ADHD are outlined in Chapter 7 at 7.2.14). In contrast, individually delivered psychological therapies are not cost effective compared with medication. Combined treatment is most likely not cost effective regardless of the mode of delivery of its psychological treatment component. It must be noted that because of lack of data on the long-term benefits and harms of interventions assessed, safe conclusions on the relative cost effectiveness between medication and psychological interventions in the long run cannot be drawn. Existing economic evidence indicates that intensive behavioural therapy alone or in combination with medication management is unlikely to be cost effective for children with ADHD.

## 11.7. RECOMMENDATION

11.7.1.1 Drug treatment is not indicated as the first-line treatment for all school-age children and young people with ADHD. It should be reserved for those with severe symptoms and impairment or for those with moderate levels of impairment who have refused non-drug interventions, or whose symptoms have not responded sufficiently to parent-training/education programmes or group psychological treatment[35].

---

[35]This recommendation is also included as 10.18.2.1 in Chapter 10.

# 12. SUMMARY OF RECOMMENDATIONS

## 12.1 PREREQUISITES OF TREATMENT AND CARE FOR ALL PEOPLE WITH ADHD

### 12.1.1 Organisation and planning of services

12.1.1.1 Mental health trusts, and children's trusts that provide mental health/child development services, should form multidisciplinary specialist ADHD teams and/or clinics for children and young people and separate teams and/or clinics for adults. These teams and clinics should have expertise in the diagnosis and management of ADHD, and should:

- provide diagnostic, treatment and consultation services for people with ADHD who have complex needs, or where general psychiatric services are in doubt about the diagnosis and/or management of ADHD
- put in place systems of communication and protocols for information sharing among paediatric, child and adolescent, forensic, and adult mental health services for people with ADHD, including arrangements for transition between child and adult services
- produce local protocols for shared care arrangements with primary care providers, and ensure that clear lines of communication between primary and secondary care are maintained
- ensure age-appropriate psychological services are available for children, young people and adults with ADHD, and for parents or carers.

The size and time commitment of these teams should depend on local circumstances (for example, the size of the trust, the population covered and the estimated referral rate for people with ADHD).

12.1.1.2 Every locality should develop a multi-agency group, with representatives from multidisciplinary specialist ADHD teams, paediatrics, mental health and learning disability trusts, forensic services, child and adolescent mental health services (CAMHS), the Children and Young People's Directorate (CYPD) (including services for education and social services), parent support groups and others with a significant local involvement in ADHD services. The group should:

- oversee the implementation of this guideline
- start and coordinate local training initiatives, including the provision of training and information for teachers about the characteristics of ADHD and its basic behavioural management
- oversee the development and coordination of parent-training/education programmes
- consider compiling a comprehensive directory of information and services for ADHD including advice on how to contact relevant services and assist in the development of specialist teams.

**12.1.2    Information, consent, the law and support for people with ADHD and their carers**

12.1.2.1    Healthcare professionals should develop a trusting relationship with people with ADHD and their families or carers by:
- respecting the person and their family's knowledge and experience of ADHD
- being sensitive to stigma in relation to mental illness.

12.1.2.2    Healthcare professionals should provide people with ADHD and their families or carers with relevant, age-appropriate information (including written information) about ADHD at every stage of their care. The information should cover diagnosis and assessment, support and self-help, psychological treatment, and the use and possible side effects of drug treatment.

12.1.2.3    When assessing a child or young person with ADHD, and throughout their care, healthcare professionals should:
- allow the child or young person to give their own account of how they feel, and record this in the notes
- involve the child or young person and the family or carer in treatment decisions
- take into account expectations of treatment, so that informed consent can be obtained from the child's parent or carer or the young person before treatment is started.

12.1.2.4    Healthcare professionals working with children and young people with ADHD should be:
- familiar with local and national guidelines on confidentiality and the rights of the child
- able to assess the young person's understanding of issues related to ADHD and its treatment (including Gillick competence)
- familiar with parental consent and responsibilities, child protection issues, the Mental Health Act (2007) and the Children Act (1989).

12.1.2.5    Healthcare professionals should work with children and young people with ADHD and their parents or carers to anticipate major life changes (such as puberty, starting or changing schools, the birth of a sibling) and make appropriate arrangements for adequate personal and social support during times of increased need. The need for psychological treatment at these times should be considered.

12.1.2.6    Adults with ADHD should be given written information about local and national support groups and voluntary organisations.

12.1.2.7    Healthcare professionals should ask families or carers about the impact of ADHD on themselves and other family members, and discuss any concerns they may have. Healthcare professionals should:
- offer family members or carers an assessment of their personal, social and mental health needs
- encourage participation in self-help and support groups where appropriate

361

- offer general advice to parents and carers about positive parent– and carer–child contact, clear and appropriate rules about behaviour, and the importance of structure in the child or young person's day
- explain that parent-training/education programmes do not necessarily imply bad parenting, and that their aim is to optimise parenting skills to meet the above-average parenting needs of children and young people with ADHD.

### 12.1.3  Training

12.1.3.1  Trusts should ensure that specialist ADHD teams for children, young people and adults jointly develop age-appropriate training programmes for the diagnosis and management of ADHD for mental health, paediatric, social care, education, forensic and primary care providers and other professionals who have contact with people with ADHD.

12.1.3.2  Child and adult psychiatrists, paediatricians, and other child and adult mental health professionals (including those working in forensic services) should undertake training so that they are able to diagnose ADHD and provide treatment and management in accordance with this guideline.

12.1.3.3  The Department for Children, Schools and Families should consider providing more education to trainee teachers about ADHD by working with the Training and Development Agency for Schools (TDA) and relevant health service organisations to produce training programmes and guidance for supporting children with ADHD.

## CARE PATHWAY FOR THE TREATMENT AND CARE OF PEOPLE WITH ADHD

### 12.2  IDENTIFICATION, PRE-DIAGNOSTIC INTERVENTION IN THE COMMUNITY AND REFERRAL TO SECONDARY SERVICES

### 12.2.1  Identification and referral in children and young people with ADHD

12.2.1.1  Universal screening for ADHD should not be undertaken in nursery, primary and secondary schools.

12.2.1.2  When a child or young person with disordered conduct and suspected ADHD is referred to a school's special educational needs coordinator (SENCO), the SENCO, in addition to helping the child with their behaviour, should inform the parents about local parent-training/education programmes.

12.2.1.3  Referral from the community to secondary care may involve health, education and social care professionals (for example, GPs, paediatricians, educational psychologists, SENCOs, social workers) and care pathways can vary locally. The person making the referral to secondary care should inform the child or young person's GP.

12.2.1.4    When a child or young person presents in primary care with behavioural and/or attention problems suggestive of ADHD, primary care practitioners should determine the severity of the problems, how these affect the child or young person and the parents or carers and the extent to which they pervade different domains and settings.

12.2.1.5    If the child or young person's behavioural and/or attention problems suggestive of ADHD are having an adverse impact on their development or family life, healthcare professionals should consider:
● a period of watchful waiting of up to 10 weeks
● offering parents or carers a referral to a parent-training/education programme (this should not wait for a formal diagnosis of ADHD).
If the behavioural and/or attention problems persist with at least moderate impairment, the child or young person should be referred to secondary care (that is, a child psychiatrist, paediatrician, or specialist ADHD CAMHS) for assessment.

12.2.1.6    If the child or young person's behavioural and/or attention problems are associated with severe impairment, referral should be made directly to secondary care (that is, a child psychiatrist, paediatrician, or specialist ADHD CAMHS) for assessment.

12.2.1.7    Group-based parent-training/education programmes are recommended in the management of children with conduct disorders[36].

12.2.1.8    Primary care practitioners should not make the initial diagnosis or start drug treatment in children or young people with suspected ADHD.

12.2.1.9    A child or young person who is currently treated in primary care with methylphenidate, atomoxetine, dexamfetamine, or any other psychotropic drug for a presumptive diagnosis of ADHD, but has not yet been assessed by a specialist in ADHD in secondary care, should be referred for assessment to a child psychiatrist, paediatrician, or specialist ADHD CAMHS as a matter of clinical priority.

### 12.2.2    Identification and referral in adults with ADHD

12.2.2.1    Adults presenting with symptoms of ADHD in primary care or general adult psychiatric services, who do not have a childhood diagnosis of ADHD, should be referred for assessment by a mental health specialist trained in the diagnosis and treatment of ADHD, where there is evidence of typical manifestations of ADHD (hyperactivity/impulsivity and/or inattention) that:
● began during childhood and have persisted throughout life

---

[36]This recommendation is taken from TA102 (NICE, 2006a). See recommendation 12.5.1.4 for the extended use of these programmes to include children with ADHD.

- are not explained by other psychiatric diagnoses (although there may be other coexisting psychiatric conditions)
- have resulted in or are associated with moderate or severe psychological, social and/or educational or occupational impairment.

12.2.2.2 Adults who have previously been treated for ADHD as children or young people and present with symptoms suggestive of continuing ADHD should be referred to general adult psychiatric services for assessment. The symptoms should be associated with at least moderate or severe psychological and/or social or educational or occupational impairment.

## 12.3 DIAGNOSIS OF ADHD

12.3.1.1 A diagnosis of ADHD should only be made by a specialist psychiatrist, paediatrician or other appropriately qualified healthcare professional with training and expertise in the diagnosis of ADHD, on the basis of:
- a full clinical and psychosocial assessment of the person; this should include discussion about behaviour and symptoms in the different domains and settings of the person's everyday life, and
- a full developmental and psychiatric history, and
- observer reports and assessment of the person's mental state.

12.3.1.2 A diagnosis of ADHD should not be made solely on the basis of rating scale or observational data. However rating scales such as the Conners' rating scales and the Strengths and Difficulties questionnaire are valuable adjuncts, and observations (for example, at school) are useful when there is doubt about symptoms.

12.3.1.3 For a diagnosis of ADHD, symptoms of hyperactivity/impulsivity and/or inattention should:
- meet the diagnostic criteria in DSM-IV or ICD-10 (hyperkinetic disorder)[37], **and**
- be associated with at least moderate psychological, social and/or educational or occupational impairment based on interview and/or direct observation in multiple settings, **and**
- be pervasive, occurring in two or more important settings including social, familial, educational and/or occupational settings.

As part of the diagnostic process, include an assessment of the person's needs, coexisting conditions, social, familial and educational or occupational circumstances and physical health. For children and young people, there should also be an assessment of their parents' or carers' mental health.

12.3.1.4 ADHD should be considered in all age groups, with symptom criteria adjusted for age-appropriate changes in behaviour.

---

[37]The ICD-10 exclusion on the basis of a pervasive developmental disorder being present, or the time of onset being uncertain, is not recommended.

12.3.1.5 In determining the clinical significance of impairment resulting from the symptoms of ADHD in children and young people, their views should be taken into account wherever possible.

## 12.4 POST-DIAGNOSTIC ADVICE

### 12.4.1 General advice

12.4.1.1 Following a diagnosis of ADHD, healthcare professionals should consider providing all parents or carers of all children and young people with ADHD self-instruction manuals, and other materials such as videos, based on positive parenting and behavioural techniques.

### 12.4.2 Dietary advice

12.4.2.1 Healthcare professionals should stress the value of a balanced diet, good nutrition and regular exercise for children, young people and adults with ADHD.

12.4.2.2 The elimination of artificial colouring and additives from the diet is not recommended as a generally applicable treatment for children and young people with ADHD.

12.4.2.3 Clinical assessment of ADHD in children and young people should include asking about foods or drinks that appear to influence their hyperactive behaviour. If there is a clear link, healthcare professionals should advise parents or carers to keep a diary of food and drinks taken and ADHD behaviour. If the diary supports a relationship between specific foods and drinks and behaviour, then referral to a dietitian should be offered. Further management (for example, specific dietary elimination) should be jointly undertaken by the dietitian, mental health specialist or paediatrician, and the parent or carer and child or young person.

12.4.2.4 Dietary fatty acid supplementation is not recommended for the treatment of ADHD in children and young people.

## 12.5 TREATMENT FOR CHILDREN AND YOUNG PEOPLE

### 12.5.1 Treatment for pre-school children

12.5.1.1 Drug treatment is not recommended for pre-school children with ADHD.

12.5.1.2 Following a diagnosis of ADHD in a child of pre-school age, healthcare professionals should, with the parents' or carers' consent, contact the child's nursery or pre-school teacher to explain:
● the diagnosis and severity of symptoms and impairment

- the care plan
- any special educational needs.

12.5.1.3  Healthcare professionals should offer parents or carers of pre-school children with ADHD a referral to a parent-training/education programme as the first-line treatment if the parents or carers have not already attended such a programme or the programme has had a limited effect.

12.5.1.4  Group-based parent-training/education programmes, developed for the treatment and management of children with conduct disorders,[38] should be fully accessible to parents or carers of children with ADHD whether or not the child also has a formal diagnosis of conduct disorder.

12.5.1.5  Individual-based parent-training/education programmes[39] are recommended in the management of children with ADHD when:
- a group programme is not possible because of low participant numbers
- there are particular difficulties for families in attending group sessions (for example, because of disability, needs related to diversity such as language differences, parental ill-health, problems with transport, or where other factors suggest poor prospects for therapeutic engagement)
- a family's needs are too complex to be met by group-based parent-training/education programmes.

12.5.1.6  When individual-based parent-training/education programmes for pre-school children with ADHD are undertaken, the skills training stages should involve both the parents or carers and the child.

12.5.1.7  It is recommended that all parent-training/education programmes, whether group- or individual-based, should:
- be structured and have a curriculum informed by principles of social-learning theory
- include relationship-enhancing strategies
- offer a sufficient number of sessions, with an optimum of 8–12, to maximise the possible benefits for participants
- enable parents to identify their own parenting objectives
- incorporate role-play during sessions, as well as homework to be undertaken between sessions, to achieve generalisation of newly rehearsed behaviours to the home situation
- be delivered by appropriately trained and skilled facilitators who are supervised, have access to necessary ongoing professional development, and are able to engage in a productive therapeutic alliance with parents
- adhere to the programme developer's manual and employ all of the necessary materials to ensure consistent implementation of the programme[40].

---

[38]As recommended in TA102 (NICE, 2006a).
[39]Ibid.
[40]This recommendation is taken from TA102 (NICE, 2006a).

12.5.1.8   Consideration should be given to involving both of the parents or all carers of children or young people with ADHD in parent-training/education programmes wherever this is feasible.

12.5.1.9   Programmes should demonstrate proven effectiveness. This should be based on evidence from randomised controlled trials or other suitable rigorous evaluation methods undertaken independently[41].

12.5.1.10 Programme providers should also ensure that support is available to enable the participation of parents who might otherwise find it difficult to access these programmes[42].

12.5.1.11 If overall treatment, including parent-training/education programmes, has been effective in managing ADHD symptoms and any associated impairment in pre-school children, before considering discharge from secondary care healthcare professionals should:
- review the child, with their parents or carers and siblings, for any residual coexisting conditions and develop a treatment plan for these if needed
- monitor for the recurrence of ADHD symptoms and any associated impairment that may occur after the child starts school.

12.5.1.12 If overall treatment, including parent-training/education programmes, has not been effective in managing ADHD symptoms and any associated impairment in pre-school children, healthcare professionals should consider referral to tertiary services for further care.

## 12.5.2   Treatment for school-age children and young people with ADHD and moderate impairment

12.5.2.1   Drug treatment is not indicated as the first-line treatment for all school-age children and young people with ADHD. It should be reserved for those with severe symptoms and impairment or for those with moderate levels of impairment who have refused non-drug interventions, or whose symptoms have not responded sufficiently to parent-training/education programmes or group psychological treatment.

12.5.2.2   Following a diagnosis of ADHD in a school-age child or young person healthcare professionals should, with the parents' or carers' consent, contact the child or young person's teacher to explain:
- the diagnosis and severity of symptoms and impairment
- the care plan
- any special educational needs.

12.5.2.3   Teachers who have received training about ADHD and its management should provide behavioural interventions in the classroom to help children and young people with ADHD.

---

[41]Ibid.
[42]Ibid.

12.5.2.4   If the child or young person with ADHD has moderate levels of impair-ment, the parents or carers should be offered referral to a group parent-training/education programme, either on its own or together with a group treatment programme (CBT and/or social skills training) for the child or young person.

12.5.2.5   When using group treatment (CBT and/or social skills training) for the child or young person in conjunction with a parent-training/education programme, particular emphasis should be given to targeting a range of areas, including social skills with peers, problem solving, self-control, listening skills and dealing with and expressing feelings. Active learning strategies should be used, and rewards given for achieving key elements of learning.

12.5.2.6   For older adolescents with ADHD and moderate impairment, individual psychological interventions (such as CBT or social skills training) may be considered as they may be more effective and acceptable than group parent-training/education programmes or group CBT and/or social skills training.

12.5.2.7   For children and young people (including older age groups) with ADHD and a learning disability, a parent-training/education programme should be offered on either a group or individual basis, whichever is preferred follow-ing discussion with the parents or carers and the child or young person.

12.5.2.8   When parents or carers of children or young people with ADHD undertake parent-training/education programmes, the professional delivering the sessions should consider contacting the school and providing the child or young person's teacher with written information on the areas of behav-ioural management covered in these sessions. This should only be done with parental consent.

12.5.2.9   Following successful treatment with a parent-training/education programme and before considering discharge from secondary care, the child or young person should be reviewed, with their parents or carers and siblings, for any residual problems such as anxiety, aggression or learning difficulties. Treatment plans should be developed for any coexisting conditions.

12.5.2.10  Following treatment with a parent-training/education programme, children and young people with ADHD and persisting significant impairment should be offered drug treatment.

## 12.5.3   Treatment for school-age children and young people with severe ADHD (hyperkinetic disorder) and severe impairment

12.5.3.1   In school-age children and young people with severe ADHD, drug treat-ment should be offered as the first-line treatment. Parents should also be offered a group-based parent-training/education programme.

12.5.3.2   Drug treatment should only be initiated by an appropriately qualified healthcare professional with expertise in ADHD and should be based on a comprehensive assessment and diagnosis. Continued prescribing and monitoring of drug treatment may be performed by general practitioners, under shared care arrangements[43].

12.5.3.3    If drug treatment is not accepted by the child or young person with severe ADHD, or their parents or carers, healthcare professionals should advise parents or carers and the child or young person about the benefits and superiority of drug treatment in this group. If drug treatment is still not accepted, a group parent-training/education programme should be offered.

12.5.3.4    If a group parent-training/education programme is effective in children and young people with severe ADHD who have refused drug treatment, healthcare professionals should assess the child or young person for possible coexisting conditions and develop a longer-term care plan.

12.5.3.5    If a group parent-training/education programme is not effective for a child or young person with severe ADHD, and if drug treatment has not been accepted, discuss the possibility of drug treatment again or other psychological treatment (group CBT and/or social skills training), highlighting the clear benefits and superiority of drug treatment in children or young people with severe ADHD.

12.5.3.6    Following a diagnosis of severe ADHD in a school-age child or young person healthcare professionals should, with the parents' or carers' consent, contact the child or young person's teacher to explain:

● the diagnosis and severity of symptoms and impairment
● the care plan
● any special educational needs.

12.5.3.7    Teachers who have received training about ADHD and its management should provide behavioural interventions in the classroom to help children and young people with ADHD.

### 12.5.4    Pre-drug treatment assessment

12.5.4.1    Before starting drug treatment, children and young people with ADHD should have a full pre-treatment assessment, which should include:

● full mental health and social assessment
● full history and physical examination, including:
  − assessment of history of exercise syncope, undue breathlessness and other cardiovascular symptoms
  − heart rate and blood pressure (plotted on a centile chart)
  − height and weight (plotted on a growth chart)
  − family history of cardiac disease and examination of the cardiovascular system

---

[43]This recommendation is taken from TA98 (NICE, 2006b). At the time of publication, methylphenidate and atomoxetine did not have UK marketing authorisation for use in children younger than 6 years. Informed consent should be obtained and documented.

- an electrocardiogram (ECG) if there is past medical or family history of serious cardiac disease, a history of sudden death in young family members or abnormal findings on cardiac examination
- risk assessment for substance misuse and drug diversion (where the drug is passed on to others for non-prescription use).

12.5.4.2 Drug treatment for children and young people with ADHD should always form part of a comprehensive treatment plan that includes psychological, behavioural and educational advice and interventions.

## 12.5.5 Choice of drug for children and young people with ADHD

12.5.5.1 Where drug treatment is considered appropriate, methylphenidate, atomoxetine and dexamfetamine are recommended, within their licensed indications, as options for the management of ADHD in children and adolescents[44].

12.5.5.2 The decision regarding which product to use should be based on the following:
- the presence of comorbid conditions (for example, tic disorders, Tourette's syndrome, epilepsy)
- the different adverse effects of the drugs
- specific issues regarding compliance identified for the individual child or adolescent, for example problems created by the need to administer a mid-day treatment dose at school
- the potential for drug diversion (where the medication is forwarded on to others for non-prescription uses) and/or misuse
- the preferences of the child/adolescent and/or his or her parent or guardian[45].

12.5.5.3 When a decision has been made to treat children or young people with ADHD with drugs, healthcare professionals should consider:
- methylphenidate for ADHD without significant comorbidity
- methylphenidate for ADHD with comorbid conduct disorder
- methylphenidate or atomoxetine when tics, Tourette's syndrome, anxiety disorder, stimulant misuse or risk of stimulant diversion are present
- atomoxetine if methylphenidate has been tried and has been ineffective at the maximum tolerated dose, or the child or young person is intolerant to low or moderate doses of methylphenidate.

12.5.5.4 When prescribing methylphenidate for the treatment of children or young people, modified-release preparations should be considered for the following reasons:
- convenience
- improving adherence
- reducing stigma (because the child or young person does not need to take medication at school)

---

[44]Ibid.
[45]Ibid.

- reducing problems schools have in storing and administering controlled drugs
- their pharmacokinetic profiles.

Alternatively, immediate-release preparations may be considered if more flexible dosing regimens are required, or during initial titration to determine correct dosing levels.

12.5.5.5 When starting drug treatment children and young people should be monitored for side effects. In particular, those treated with atomoxetine should be closely observed for agitation, irritability, suicidal thinking and self-harming behaviour, and unusual changes in behaviour, particularly during the initial months of treatment, or after a change in dose. Parents and/or carers should be warned about the potential for suicidal thinking and self-harming behaviour with atomoxetine and asked to report these to their healthcare professionals. Parents or carers should also be warned about the potential for liver damage in rare cases with atomoxetine (usually presenting as abdominal pain, unexplained nausea, malaise, darkening of the urine or jaundice).

12.5.5.6 If there is a choice of more than one appropriate drug, the product with the lowest cost (taking into account the cost per dose and number of daily doses) should be prescribed[46].

12.5.5.7 Antipsychotics are not recommended for the treatment of ADHD in children and young people.

## 12.5.6    Poor response to treatment

12.5.12.1 If there has been a poor response following parent-training/education programmes and/or psychological treatment and treatment with methylphenidate and atomoxetine in a child or young person with ADHD, there should be a further review of:

- the diagnosis
- any coexisting conditions
- response to drug treatment, occurrence of side effects and treatment adherence
- uptake and use of psychological interventions for the child or young person and their parents or carers
- effects of stigma on treatment acceptability
- concerns related to school and/or family
- motivation of the child or young person and the parents or carers
- the child or young person's diet.

12.5.6.2 Following review of poor response to treatment, a dose higher than that licensed for methylphenidate or atomoxetine should be considered following

---

[46]Ibid.

consultation with a tertiary or regional centre. This may exceed 'British national formulary' (BNF) recommendations: methylphenidate can be increased to 0.7 mg/kg per dose up to three times a day or a total daily dose of 2.1 mg/kg/day (up to a total maximum dose of 90 mg/day for immediate release; or an equivalent dose of modified-release methylphenidate)[47]; atomoxetine may be increased to 1.8 mg/kg/day (up to a total maximum dose of 120 mg/day). The prescriber should closely monitor the child or young person for side effects.

12.5.6.3 Dexamfetamine should be considered in children and young people whose ADHD is unresponsive to a maximum tolerated dose of methylphenidate or atomoxetine.

12.5.6.4 In children and young people whose ADHD is unresponsive to methylphenidate, atomoxetine and dexamfetamine, further treatment should only follow after referral to tertiary services. Further treatment may include the use of medication unlicensed for the treatment of ADHD (such as bupropion, clonidine, modafinil and imipramine)[48] or combination treatments (including psychological treatments for the parent or carer and the child or young person). The use of medication unlicensed for ADHD should only be considered in the context of tertiary services.

12.5.6.5 A cardiovascular examination and ECG should be carried out before starting treatment with clonidine in children or young people with ADHD.

## 12.6 TRANSITION TO ADULT SERVICES

12.6.1.1 A young person with ADHD receiving treatment and care from CAMHS or paediatric services should be reassessed at school-leaving age to establish the need for continuing treatment into adulthood. If treatment is necessary,

---

[47]Stimulant dose equivalents (mg)

| IR-MPH | Concerta XL | Equasym XL | Medikinet XL |
|--------|-------------|------------|--------------|
| 10 | – | 10 | 10 |
| 15 | 18 | – | – |
| 20 | – | 20 | 20 |
| 30 | 36 | 30 | 30 |
| – | – | – | 40 |
| 45 | 54 | – | – |
| 60 | 72* | 60 | – |

IR-MPH: immediate-release methylphenidate; Concerta XL, Equasym XL and Medikinet XL: brands of modified-release methylphenidate.

*Licensed up to 54 mg.

[48]At the time of publication, bupropion, clonidine, modafinil and imipramine did not have UK marketing authorisation for use in children and young people with ADHD. Informed consent should be obtained and documented.

arrangements should be made for a smooth transition to adult services with details of the anticipated treatment and services that the young person will require. Precise timing of arrangements may vary locally but should usually be completed by the time the young person is 18 years.

12.6.1.2 During the transition to adult services, a formal meeting involving CAMHS and/or paediatrics and adult psychiatric services should be considered, and full information provided to the young person about adult services. For young people aged 16 years and older, the care programme approach (CPA) should be used as an aid to transfer between services. The young person, and when appropriate the parent or carer, should be involved in the planning.

12.6.1.3 After transition to adult services, adult healthcare professionals should carry out a comprehensive assessment of the person with ADHD that includes personal, educational, occupational and social functioning, and assessment of any coexisting conditions, especially drug misuse, personality disorders, emotional problems and learning difficulties.

## 12.7    TREATMENT OF ADULTS WITH ADHD

12.7.1.1 For adults with ADHD, drug treatment[49] should be the first-line treatment unless the person would prefer a psychological approach.

12.7.1.2 Drug treatment for adults with ADHD should be started only under the guidance of a psychiatrist, nurse prescriber specialising in ADHD, or other clinical prescriber with training in the diagnosis and management of ADHD.

12.7.1.3 Before starting drug treatment for adults with ADHD a full assessment should be completed, which should include:
- full mental health and social assessment
- full history and physical examination, including:
  - assessment of history of exercise syncope, undue breathlessness and other cardiovascular symptoms
  - heart rate and blood pressure (plotted on a centile chart)
  - weight
  - family history of cardiac disease and examination of the cardiovascular system
- an ECG if there is past medical or family history of serious cardiac disease, a history of sudden death in young family members or abnormal findings on cardiac examination
- risk assessment for substance misuse and drug diversion.

---

[49]At the time of publication, methylphenidate, dexamfetamine and atomoxetine did not have UK marketing authorisation for use in adults with ADHD. However atomoxetine is licensed for adults with ADHD when the drug has been started in childhood. Informed consent should be obtained and documented.

12.7.1.4 Drug treatment for adults with ADHD should always form part of a comprehensive treatment programme that addresses psychological, behavioural and educational or occupational needs.

12.7.1.5 Following a decision to start drug treatment in adults with ADHD, methylphenidate should normally be tried first.

12.7.1.6 Atomoxetine or dexamfetamine should be considered in adults unresponsive or intolerant to an adequate trial of methylphenidate (this should usually be about 6 weeks)[50]. Caution should be exercised when prescribing dexamfetamine to those likely to be at risk of stimulant misuse or diversion.

12.7.1.7 When starting drug treatment, adults should be monitored for side effects. In particular, people treated with atomoxetine should be observed for agitation, irritability, suicidal thinking and self-harming behaviour, and unusual changes in behaviour, particularly during the initial months of treatment, or after a change in dose. They should also be warned of potential liver damage in rare cases (usually presenting as abdominal pain, unexplained nausea, malaise, darkening of the urine or jaundice). Younger adults aged 30 years or younger should also be warned of the potential of atomoxetine to increase agitation, anxiety, suicidal thinking and self-harming behaviour in some people, especially during the first few weeks of treatment.

12.7.1.8 For adults with ADHD stabilised on medication but with persisting functional impairment associated with the disorder, or where there has been no response to drug treatment, a course of either group or individual CBT to address the person's functional impairment should be considered. Group therapy is recommended as the first-line psychological treatment because it is the most cost effective.

12.7.1.9 For adults with ADHD, CBT may be considered when:
● the person has made an informed choice not to have drug treatment
● drug treatment has proved to be only partially effective or ineffective or the person is intolerant to it
● people have difficulty accepting the diagnosis of ADHD and accepting and adhering to drug treatment
● symptoms are remitting and psychological treatment is considered sufficient to target residual (mild to moderate) functional impairment.

12.7.1.10 Where there may be concern about the potential for drug misuse and diversion (for example, in prison services), atomoxetine may be considered as the first-line drug treatment for ADHD in adults[51].

12.7.1.11 Drug treatment for adults with ADHD who also misuse substances should only be prescribed by an appropriately qualified healthcare professional with expertise in managing both ADHD and substance misuse. For adults with ADHD and drug or alcohol addiction disorders there should be close

---

[50]Ibid.
[51]Ibid.

liaison between the professional treating the person's ADHD and an addiction specialist.

12.7.1.12 Antipsychotics are not recommended for the treatment of ADHD in adults.

## 12.8 HOW TO USE DRUGS FOR THE TREATMENT OF ADHD

### 12.8.1 General principles

12.8.1.1 Prescribers should be familiar with the pharmacokinetic profiles of all the modified-release and immediate-release preparations available for ADHD to ensure that treatment is tailored effectively to the individual needs of the child, young person or adult.

12.8.1.2 Prescribers should be familiar with the requirements of controlled drug legislation governing the prescription and supply of stimulants.

12.8.1.3 During the titration phase, doses should be gradually increased until there is no further clinical improvement in ADHD (that is, symptom reduction, behaviour change, improvements in education and/or relationships) and side effects are tolerable.

12.8.1.4 Following titration and dose stabilisation, prescribing and monitoring should be carried out under locally agreed shared care arrangements with primary care.

12.8.1.5 Side effects resulting from drug treatment for ADHD should be routinely monitored and documented in the person's notes.

12.8.1.6 If side effects become troublesome in people receiving drug treatment for ADHD, a reduction in dose should be considered.

12.8.1.7 Healthcare professionals should be aware that dose titration should be slower if tics or seizures are present in people with ADHD.

### 12.8.2 Initiation and titration of methylphenidate, atomoxetine and dexamfetamine in children and young people

12.8.2.1 During the titration phase, symptoms and side effects should be recorded at each dose change on standard scales (for example, Conners' 10-item scale) by parents and teachers, and progress reviewed regularly (for example, by weekly telephone contact and at each dose change) with a specialist clinician.

12.8.2.2 If using methylphenidate in children and young people with ADHD aged 6 years and older:
- initial treatment should begin with low doses of immediate-release or modified-release preparations consistent with starting doses in the BNF
- the dose should be titrated against symptoms and side effects over 4–6 weeks until dose optimisation is achieved

- modified-release preparations should be given as a single dose in the morning
- immediate-release preparations should be given in two or three divided doses.

12.8.2.3 If using atomoxetine in children and young people with ADHD aged 6 years and older:
- for those weighing up to 70 kg, the initial total daily dose should be approximately 0.5 mg/kg; the dose should be increased after 7 days to approximately 1.2 mg/kg/day
- for those weighing more than 70 kg, the initial total daily dose should be 40 mg; the dose should be increased after 7 days up to a maintenance dose of 80 mg/day
- a single daily dose can be given; two divided doses may be prescribed to minimise side effects.

12.8.2.4 If using dexamfetamine in children and young people with ADHD:
- initial treatment should begin with low doses consistent with starting doses in the BNF
- the dose should be titrated against symptoms and side effects over 4–6 weeks
- treatment should be given in divided doses increasing to a maximum of 20 mg/day
- for children aged 6–18 years, doses up to 40 mg/day may occasionally be required.

### 12.8.3 Initiation and titration of methylphenidate, atomoxetine and dexamfetamine in adults

12.8.3.1 In order to optimise drug treatment, the initial dose should be titrated against symptoms and side effects over 4–6 weeks.

12.8.3.2 During the titration phase, symptoms and side effects should be recorded at each dose change by the prescriber after discussion with the person with ADHD and, wherever possible, a carer (for example, a spouse, parent or close friend). Progress should be reviewed (for example, by weekly telephone contact and at each dose change) with a specialist clinician.

12.8.3.3 If using methylphenidate in adults with ADHD:
- initial treatment should begin with low doses (5 mg three times daily for immediate-release preparations; the equivalent dose for modified-release preparations)
- the dose should be titrated against symptoms and side effects over 4–6 weeks
- the dose should be increased according to response up to a maximum of 100 mg/day

- modified-release preparations should usually be given once daily and no more than twice daily
- modified-release preparations may be preferred to increase adherence and in circumstances where there are concerns about substance misuse or diversion
- immediate-release preparations should be given up to four times daily.

12.8.3.4 If using atomoxetine in adults with ADHD:
- for people with ADHD weighing up to 70 kg, the initial total daily dose should be approximately 0.5 mg/kg; the dose should be increased after 7 days to approximately 1.2 mg/kg/day
- for people with ADHD weighing more than 70 kg, the initial total daily dose should be 40 mg; the dose should be increased after 7 days up to a maintenance dose of 100 mg/day
- the usual maintenance dose is either 80 or 100 mg, which may be taken in divided doses
- a trial of 6 weeks on a maintenance dose should be allowed to evaluate the full effectiveness of atomoxetine.

12.8.3.5 If using dexamfetamine in adults with ADHD:
- initial treatment should begin with low doses (5 mg twice daily)
- the dose should be titrated against symptoms and side effects over 4–6 weeks
- treatment should be given in divided doses
- the dose should be increased according to response up to a maximum of 60 mg per day
- the dose should usually be given between two and four times daily.

## 12.8.4 Monitoring side effects and the potential for misuse in children and young people and adults

12.8.4.1 Healthcare professionals should consider using standard symptom and side effect rating scales throughout the course of treatment as an adjunct to clinical assessment for people with ADHD.

12.8.4.2 In people taking methylphenidate, atomoxetine, or dexamfetamine:
- height should be measured every 6 months in children and young people
- weight should be measured 3 and 6 months after drug treatment has started and every 6 months thereafter in children, young people and adults
- height and weight in children and young people should be plotted on a growth chart and reviewed by the healthcare professional responsible for treatment.

12.8.4.3 If there is evidence of weight loss associated with drug treatment in adults with ADHD, healthcare professionals should consider monitoring body mass index and changing the drug if weight loss persists.

12.8.4.4    Strategies to reduce weight loss in people with ADHD, or manage decreased weight gain in children, include:
- taking medication either with or after food, rather than before meals
- taking additional meals or snacks early in the morning or late in the evening when the stimulant effects of the drug have worn off
- obtaining dietary advice
- consuming high-calorie foods of good nutritional value.

12.8.4.5    If growth is significantly affected by drug treatment (that is, the child or young person has not met the height expected for their age), the option of a planned break in treatment over school holidays should be considered to allow 'catch-up' growth to occur.

12.8.4.6    In people with ADHD, heart rate and blood pressure should be monitored and recorded on a centile chart before and after each dose change and routinely every 3 months.

12.8.4.7    For people taking methylphenidate, dexamfetamine and atomoxetine, routine blood tests and ECGs are not recommended unless there is a clinical indication.

12.8.4.8    Liver damage is a rare and idiosyncratic adverse effect of atomoxetine and routine liver function tests are not recommended.

12.8.4.9    For children and young people taking methylphenidate and dexamfetamine, healthcare professionals and parents or carers should monitor changes in the potential for drug misuse and diversion, which may come with changes in circumstances and age. In these situations, modified-release methylphenidate or atomoxetine may be preferred.

12.8.4.10   In young people and adults, sexual dysfunction (that is, erectile and ejaculatory dysfunction) and dysmenorrhoea should be monito red as potential side effects of atomoxetine.

12.8.4.11   For people taking methylphenidate, dexamfetamine or atomoxetine who have sustained resting tachycardia, arrhythmia or systolic blood pressure greater than the 95th percentile (or a clinically significant increase) measured on two occasions should have their dose reduced and be referred to a paediatrician or adult physician.

12.8.4.12   If psychotic symptoms (for example, delusions and hallucinations) emerge in children, young people and adults after starting methylphenidate or dexamfetamine, the drug should be withdrawn and a full psychiatric assessment carried out. Atomoxetine should be considered as an alternative.

12.8.4.13   If seizures are exacerbated in a child or young person with epilepsy, or *de novo* seizures emerge following the introduction of methylphenidate or atomoxetine, the drug should be discontinued immediately. Dexamfetamine may be considered an alternative in consultation with a regional tertiary specialist treatment centre.

12.8.4.14   If tics emerge in people taking methylphenidate or dexamfetamine, healthcare professionals should consider whether:
- the tics are stimulant-related (tics naturally wax and wane)
- tic-related impairment outweighs the benefits of ADHD treatment.

If tics are stimulant-related, reduce the dose of methylphenidate or dexamfetamine, consider changing to atomoxetine, or stop drug treatment.

12.8.4.15 Anxiety symptoms, including panic, may be precipitated by stimulants, particularly in adults with a history of coexisting anxiety. Where this is an issue, lower doses of the stimulant and/or combined treatment with an antidepressant used to treat anxiety can be used; switching to atomoxetine may be effective.

## 12.8.5 Improving adherence to drug treatment

12.8.5.1 Communication between the prescriber and the child or young person should be improved by educating parents or carers and ensuring there are regular three-way conversations between prescriber, parent or carer and the child or young person. For adults with ADHD, and with their permission, a spouse, partner, parent, close friend or carer wherever possible should be part of these conversations. Clear instructions about how to take the drug should be offered in picture or written format, which may include information on dose, duration, side effects, dosage schedule, the need for supervision and how this should be done.

12.8.5.2 Healthcare professionals should consider suggesting peer-support groups for the child or young person with ADHD and their parents or carers if adherence to drug treatment is difficult or uncertain.

12.8.5.3 Simple drug regimens (for example, once-daily modified-release doses) are recommended for people with ADHD.

12.8.5.4 Healthcare professionals should encourage children and young people with ADHD to be responsible for their own health, including taking their medication as required, and support parents and carers in this endeavour.

12.8.5.5 Healthcare professionals should advise parents or carers to provide the child or young person with visual reminders to take medication regularly (for example, alarms, clocks, pill boxes, or notes on calendars or fridges).

12.8.5.6 Healthcare professionals should advise children and young people and their parents or carers that taking medication should be incorporated into daily routines (for example, before meals or after brushing teeth).

12.8.5.7 Where necessary, healthcare professionals should help parents or carers develop a positive attitude and approach in the management of medication, which might include praise and positive reinforcement for the child or young person with ADHD.

## 12.8.6 Duration, discontinuation and continuity of treatment in children and young people

12.8.6.1 Following an adequate treatment response, drug treatment for ADHD should be continued for as long as it remains clinically effective. This should be reviewed at least annually. The review should include a comprehensive assessment of clinical need, benefits and side effects, taking into account the views of the child or young person, as well as those of parents, carers and teachers, and how these views may differ. The effect of missed doses, planned dose reductions and brief periods of no treatment should be taken into account and the preferred pattern of use should also be reviewed. Coexisting conditions should be reviewed, and the child or young person treated or referred if necessary. The need for psychological and social support for the child or young person and for the parents or other carers should be assessed.

12.8.6.2  Drug holidays are not routinely recommended; however, consideration should be given to the parent or carer and child or young person with ADHD working with their healthcare professional to find the best pattern of use, which may include periods without drug treatment.

## 12.8.7  Duration, discontinuation and continuity of treatment of adults

12.8.7.1  Following an adequate response, drug treatment for ADHD should be continued for as long as it is clinically effective. This should be reviewed annually. The review should include a comprehensive assessment of clinical need, benefits and side effects, taking into account the views of the person and those of a spouse, partner, parent, close friends or carers wherever possible, and how these accounts may differ. The effect of missed doses, planned dose reductions and brief periods of no treatment should be taken into account and the preferred pattern of use should also be reviewed. Coexisting conditions should be reviewed, and the person treated or referred if necessary. The need for psychological, social and occupational support for the person and their carers should be assessed.

12.8.7.2  An individual treatment approach is important for adults, and healthcare professionals should regularly review (at least annually) the need to adapt patterns of use, including the effect of drug treatment on coexisting conditions and mood changes.

## 12.9  RESEARCH RECOMMENDATIONS

12.9.1.1  Grounds for diagnosis of ADHD in adults
- What is the prevalence of inattention, impulsivity and hyperactivity/ restlessness in males and females in the adult population?
- How far do the core symptoms of inattention, impulsivity and hyperactivity/restlessness cluster together?
- To what extent are the core symptoms comorbid with other forms of mental disturbance?
- To what extent are the core symptoms associated with neuropsychological and social impairment? This would be best conducted as an epidemiological survey.

- Why this is important: There is evidence that ADHD symptoms can persist into adulthood and cause impairment, but there are no clear conclusions about the level of ADHD symptoms in adults that should be considered as grounds for intervention, or whether symptoms take a different form in adulthood. The costs to society and to the affected people and their families make it pressing to know whether, and how far, services should be expanded to meet the needs of this group.

12.9.1.2 Discontinuation of drug treatment

- Are there any benefits or disadvantages to the extended/long-term use of methylphenidate compared with its discontinuation at least 18 months after starting treatment? To what extent does continuing drug treatment beyond 18 months alter quality of life, core ADHD symptoms, associated symptoms including emotional lability, potential adverse effects of continued drug treatment and neuropsychological function? This would be best conducted as a drug discontinuation randomised controlled trial.

- Why this is important: Methylphenidate is often given for periods of years without good evidence of whether prolonged therapy is effective or safe. Methylphenidate is also typically discontinued in late adolescence; evidence is required of the benefit of continued prescribing in this age group.

12.9.1.3 Effectiveness of group-based parent training

- Are group-based behavioural parent-training/education methods more effective than drug treatment in school-age children and young people with ADHD in terms of symptoms, quality of life and cost effectiveness? This would be best evaluated by a head-to-head randomised controlled trial.

- Why this is important: The evidence for the effect of group-based parent-training/education programmes is largely based on studies of younger children. These programmes are an important part of the management of ADHD although their cost effectiveness is not clear for older children and adolescents.

12.9.1.4 Effectiveness of non-drug treatments for adults with ADHD

- Are non-drug treatments (including focused psychological treatments and supportive approaches such as coaching) more effective than drug treatment (methylphenidate) in terms of symptoms, quality of life, cost effectiveness, drug misuse and other coexisting conditions, and the cost of health, forensic and criminal justice services, in the treatment of adults with ADHD? This would be best conducted as a randomised controlled trial.

- Why this is important: Currently there is good evidence supporting the effectiveness of methylphenidate in people with ADHD symptoms and associated impairment. However, there is insufficient evidence on whether non-drug treatments could have specific advantages in some important aspects of the life of a person with ADHD. Given the strong association of ADHD in adults with substance misuse, personality disorder and involvement in the criminal justice system, a health economic approach would be essential.

12.9.1.5 Effect of providing training in behavioural management of ADHD for teachers

- Does the training of teachers in the behavioural management of children with ADHD in primary and secondary schools improve ADHD symptoms and academic attainment, the teacher's experience of stress in the classroom and the impact of ADHD on other pupils when compared with current education methods? This would be best conducted as a randomised trial.

- Why this is important: Secondary school is typically a different environment from primary school, particularly in terms of organisation of the daily timetable and expectations of the increasing independence of pupils. These factors may have an adverse impact on young people with ADHD, but the effect of understanding and modifying this impact has not yet been researched. The potential for teachers to take a more active role in the behavioural management of primary and secondary school children with ADHD shows some significant promise in at least one trial. The benefits of examining primary and secondary education, compared with education as usual, and examining the broader impact on the child, the teacher and the wider classroom, would significantly improve future versions of this guideline.

# 13. APPENDICES

# APPENDIX 1:
# SCOPE FOR THE DEVELOPMENT OF THE
# CLINICAL GUIDELINE

**Final version**

8 August 2008

## GUIDELINE TITLE

Attention deficit hyperactivity disorder: diagnosis and management of ADHD in children, young people and adults

**Short title**

ADHD

## BACKGROUND

The National Institute for Health and Clinical Excellence ('NICE' or 'the Institute') has commissioned the National Collaborating Centre for Mental Health to develop a clinical guideline on attention deficit hyperactivity disorder for use in the NHS in England and Wales. This follows referral of the topic by the Department of Health and Welsh Assembly Government (see below). The guideline will provide recommendations for good practice that are based on the best available evidence of clinical and cost effectiveness.

The Institute's clinical guidelines will support the implementation of National Service Frameworks (NSFs) in those aspects of care where a Framework has been published. The statements in each NSF reflect the evidence that was used at the time the Framework was prepared. The clinical guidelines and technology appraisals published by the Institute after an NSF has been issued will have the effect of updating the Framework.

NICE clinical guidelines support the role of healthcare professionals in providing care in partnership with patients, taking account of their individual needs and preferences, and ensuring that patients (and their carers and families, where appropriate) can make informed decisions about their care and treatment.

## CLINICAL NEED FOR THE GUIDELINE

Attention deficit hyperactivity disorder (ADHD) is a heterogeneous behavioural syndrome and its diagnosis does not imply any specific cause. However various genetic and environmental risk factors have been implicated in its development. ADHD is characterised by the 'core' signs of inattention, hyperactivity and impulsiveness. There are two main sets of diagnostic criteria in current use, the International Classification of Mental and Behavioural Disorders 10th Revision (ICD-10) and the Diagnostic and Statistical Manual of Mental Disorders fourth edition (DSM-IV). The ICD-10 definition makes reference to hyperkinetic disorder, primarily evidenced by high abnormal levels of hyperactivity, and a combined subtype in which hyperactivity, impulsivity and inattention need to be present, together with stricter requirements for pervasiveness across situations, and exclusion of comorbidity. The DSM-IV criteria describes ADHD more broadly to include three subtypes: a combined subtype in which all three core signs are present; a predominantly inattentive subtype in which inattention is present but not hyperactivity or impulsiveness; and a predominantly hyperactive–impulsive subtype in which hyperactivity and impulsiveness are present but not inattention. Both ICD-10 and DSM-IV require 6 months duration of symptoms. The identification of ADHD in adults, and the diagnostic criteria that should underpin case recognition, are less clear and lead to uncertainties in practice.

ICD-10 and DSM-IV adopt a different approach to comorbidity. In ICD-10, secondary complications to hyperkinetic disorder include dissocial behaviour and low self-esteem. In DSM-IV common comorbidities include: disruptive behaviour disorders, mood disorders, anxiety disorders, learning disorders and communication disorders. ADHD is not diagnosed if symptoms of inattention and hyperactivity occur exclusively during the course of a pervasive developmental disorder or a psychotic disorder; but the problems may still need to be recognised and treated. It seems likely that a similar pattern of comorbidities pertains to adults with ADHD, although definitive research in this area is lacking.

A number of genetic and environmental risk factors for ADHD have been identified. Hereditary aspects, neuroimaging data and responses to pharmacotherapeutic agents support the suggestion that ADHD has a biological component. However, there is a continuing debate over the causes of ADHD.

ADHD affects children, young people and adults in different ways and to different degrees, but the consequences of severe ADHD can be serious for both the individual and their family and carers. Children with ADHD often have low self-esteem and can develop additional emotional and social problems. The secondary effects of ADHD can be damaging. For example, some children and young adults with ADHD are at increased risk of accidental harm and many later have an increased risk of automotive accidents. Moreover, affected children are often exposed to years of negative feedback about their behaviour and may suffer educational and social disadvantage. A sizeable proportion of children referred for hyperactivity disorders continue to have problems into adulthood, including emotional and social problems, substance misuse, unemployment and involvement in crime.

Estimates of the prevalence of hyperkinetic disorder/ADHD vary widely within and between countries. Prevalence estimates for hyperkinetic disorder in children and young people are around 1 to 2% in the UK. ADHD is estimated to affect 3 to 9% of school-aged children and young people in the UK, and about 2% of adults worldwide (using DSM IV diagnostic criteria). These differences are, at least in part, explained by differences in diagnostic criteria used in different countries.

Studies of clinic-based diagnoses suggest that ADHD is nine times more common in males, although this gender imbalance is inflated to some extent by referral bias; epidemiological studies suggest that prevalence is only two to four times greater in males.

The prescribing of stimulant drugs for ADHD reflects the increased frequency of diagnosis of this condition. In 1998 there were about 220,000 prescriptions in England for stimulant drugs (methylphenidate and dexamfetamine) at a net cost of about £5 million; in 2004 this number had almost doubled to 418,300 at a cost of almost £13 million.

The use of CNS stimulants has been controversial and there are concerns about prescribing such medication to children. Further anxieties surround the potential for their inappropriate prescription, abuse and unauthorised trading and/or illegal selling.

## THE GUIDELINE

The guideline development process is described in detail in two publications which are available from the NICE website (see 'Further information' below). *The guideline development process: an overview for stakeholders, the public and the NHS* describes how organisations can become involved in the development of a guideline. *Guideline development methods: information for National Collaborating Centres and guideline developers* provides advice on the technical aspects of guideline development.

This document is the scope. It defines exactly what this guideline will (and will not) examine, and what the guideline developers will consider. The scope is based on the referral from the Department of Health (see below).

The areas that will be addressed by the guideline are described in the following sections.

## POPULATION

The guideline will cover:
- The treatment of children aged 3 years and older, young people and adults with a diagnosis of ADHD and related diagnoses: hyperkinetic disorder (ICD-10) will be considered, along with the three DSM-IV ADHD subtypes.
- The management of common comorbidities in children, young people and adults with ADHD as far as these conditions affect the treatment of ADHD.
- The specific management of ADHD in those individuals who also have:
  - a learning disability
  - a defined neurological disorder.

The guideline will not cover:
- the separate management of comorbid conditions
- the management of children younger than 3 years

## HEALTHCARE SETTING

The guideline will cover the care provided by primary, community and secondary healthcare professionals who have direct contact with, and make decisions concerning, the care of children, young people and adults with ADHD.

This is an NHS guideline. It will comment on the interface with other services such as social services, educational services, the voluntary sector and young offender institutions, but it will not include recommendations relating to the services exclusively provided by these agencies, except insofar as the care provided in those institutional settings is provided by healthcare professionals funded by the NHS. Recommendations in the guideline will nevertheless map onto the tiered model of CAMHS services specified in the NSF for children and utilised in the NICE guideline on depression in children. Some of the recommendations will be made to staff in the education services, where this may have a positive contribution to the health of a child with ADHD, either directly (where this is appropriate) or indirectly through collaborative working with CAMHS professionals.

The guideline will include:
- care in general practice and NHS community care
- hospital outpatient and inpatient care
- primary/secondary interface of care
- transition from childhood services to adult services.


## CLINICAL MANAGEMENT

Areas that will be covered by the guideline:
- The full range of care routinely made available by the NHS.
- Validity, specificity and reliability of existing diagnostic criteria (ICD-10 and DSM-IV) in children, young people and adults, and to determine/specify the criteria that should be used to determine the circumstances in which this guideline should be used.
- Assessment both before and after diagnosis.
- Early identification of ADHD in children at risk, and identification of factors that should lead to investigation into the possibility of ADHD.
- Pathways to treatment.
- Identification and management of risk.
- The appropriate use of pharmacological interventions, for example initiation and duration of treatment, management of side effects and discontinuation. Specific pharmacological treatments considered will include:
  - methylphenidate and dexamfetamine (currently licensed for treatment of ADHD in children and young people)
  - atomoxetine (currently licensed for treatment of ADHD in children and in adults if treatment was initiated in childhood)
  - tricyclic and other antidepressants
  - bupropion

    – nicotine (as skin patches)
    – clonidine
    – atypical antipsychotics (particularly risperidone)
    – modafinil.

Note that guideline recommendations will normally fall within licensed indications; exceptionally, and only where clearly supported by evidence, use outside a licensed indication may be recommended. The guideline will assume that prescribers will use a drug's Summary of Product Characteristics to inform their decisions for individual patients.

- All common psychological interventions currently employed in the NHS for example, family interventions, cognitive-behavioural treatments, and parent training.
- Combined pharmacological and psychological treatments.
- Other physical treatments, including dietary elimination and supplementation.
- Treatment approaches for adults with ADHD (including longer-term outcomes and transitions from child to adult healthcare).
- Sensitivity to different beliefs and attitudes of different races and cultures, and issues of social exclusion.
- The role of the family or carers in the treatment and support of people with ADHD (with consideration of choice, consent and help), and support that may be needed by carers themselves.

Areas that will not be covered by the guideline
- Treatments not normally available in the NHS.


**STATUS**

**Scope**

This is the final scope.

The guideline will incorporate the following relevant technology appraisal guidance issued by the Institute:

*Methylphenidate, atomoxetine and dexamfetamine for the treatment of attention deficit hyperactivity disorder in children and adolescents (including a review of guidance no.13)* NICE Technology Appraisal (Published March 2006)

Previous recommendations made in other guidelines may be updated by this guideline, based on the most up-to-date evidence for this particular population.


**GUIDELINE**

The development of the guideline recommendations will begin in March 2006.

**FURTHER INFORMATION**

Information on the guideline development process is provided in:
- *The Guidelines Manual 2006.*

This booklet is available as PDF files from the NICE website (http://www.nice. org.uk/page.aspx?o=308639). Information on the progress of the guideline will also be available from the website.


**REFERRAL FROM THE DEPARTMENT OF HEALTH AND WELSH ASSEMBLY GOVERNMENT**

The Department of Health and Welsh Assembly Government asked the Institute:

*To prepare a guideline for the NHS in England and Wales on the diagnosis and treatment of attention deficit hyperactivity disorder in children, young people and adults, where evidence for treatment effectiveness is available. Treatment should include the effectiveness of methylphenidate and other pharmacological and psychological interventions in combination or separately.*

# APPENDIX 2:

# DECLARATIONS OF INTERESTS BY GDG MEMBERS

With a range of practical experience relevant to ADHD in the GDG, members were appointed because of their understanding and expertise in healthcare for people with ADHD and support for their families and carers, including: scientific issues; health research; the delivery and receipt of healthcare, along with the work of the healthcare industry; and the role of professional organisations and organisations for people with ADHD and their families and carers.

To minimise and manage any potential conflicts of interest, and to avoid any public concern that commercial or other financial interests have affected the work of the GDG and influenced guidance, members of the GDG must declare as a matter of public record any interests held by themselves or their families which fall under specified categories (see below). These categories include any relationships they have with the healthcare industries, professional organisations and organisations for people who misuse drugs and their families and carers.

Individuals invited to join the GDG were asked to declare their interests before being appointed. To allow the management of any potential conflicts of interest that might arise during the development of the guideline, GDG members were also asked to declare their interests at each GDG meeting throughout the guideline development process. The interests of all the members of the GDG are listed below, including interests declared prior to appointment and during the guideline development process.

## CATEGORIES OF INTEREST

- **Paid employment**
- **GDG members were asked to declare the following interests annually and at each meeting:**
  **Personal pecuniary interest:** Any financial involvement or planned financial involvement with the healthcare industry in the previous 12 months and, if so, whether it is ongoing. This includes:
  - holding a directorship, or other paid position
  - carrying out consultancy or fee-paid work
  - having shareholdings or other beneficial interests
  - receiving expenses and hospitality over and above what would be reasonably expected to attend meetings and conferences

  **Personal family interest:** A family member with any financial involvement or planned financial involvement with the healthcare industry in the previous 12 months. This could include:
  - holding a directorship, or other paid position

- carrying out consultancy or fee-paid work
- having shareholdings or other beneficial interests
- receiving expenses and hospitality over and above what would be reasonably expected to attend meetings and conferences

**Non-personal pecuniary interest**: Managerial responsibility within the past 12 months for a department or organisation that has had financial involvement with the healthcare industry or for which such financial involvement is planned. This includes:

- a grant or fellowship or other payment to sponsor a post, or contribute to the running costs of the department
- commissioning of research or other work
- contracts with, or grants from, NICE

**Personal non-pecuniary interest:** Having expressed a clear opinion on the matter under consideration which has been:

- reached as a conclusion of a research project
- and/or expressed as a public statement
- membership in a professional organisation or advocacy group with a direct interest in a matter under consideration by NICE
- any other reason why people might assume bias in the work done for NICE

| Declarations of interest: GDG members | |
|---|---|
| **Professor Eric Taylor – Chair, GDG** | |
| Employment | Professor of Child and Adolescent Psychiatry, Head of Department of Child and Adolescent Psychiatry, Institute of Psychiatry, King's College London. |
| Personal pecuniary interests | None |
| Personal family interests | None |
| Non-personal pecuniary interests | Research grants held: 2007–2008 Principal investigator (PI) for project grant: research trial of omega-3 fatty acid supplementation. Main funding (£98,000) from Mother & Child Foundation; Equazen Ltd (oil manufacturers) funded £28,000 and contributed oil, placebo and administrative assistance. 2000–2005 PI for programme grant: developmental psychopathology of hyperactivity and attention deficit (MRC); £1,026,000, 50% time. 2000–2003 PI for health services research project: assessment of child mental health needs in Croydon and |

*Continued*

| Declarations of interest: GDG members (*Continued*) | |
|---|---|
| | Lambeth (South London & Maudsley NHS Trust); £217,000, 5% time. |
| | 2002 PI (with S. Williams) for equipment and infrastructure funding: FMRI scanning for developmental research (JIF); £2,700,000. |
| | 2002–2005 Co-investigator for project grant: IMAGE – international multicentre genetic investigation of ADHD (National Institute of Mental Health, USA); (with S. Faraone [PI], P. Asherson, J. Sergeant, J. Buitelaar, A. Rothenberger); £2,400,000, 5% time. |
| Personal non-pecuniary interests | 2004-present Chair of the ADDISS charity professional board. |
| | 1968–2008 Extensive papers and reviews on ADHD including *People with Hyperactivity: Understanding and Managing Their Problems* (London: Mac Keith Press, 2007). |
| | 2005–2006 Expert for NICE TA on methylphenidate, dexamfetamine and atomoxetine. |
| | 2004 Presented to consensus conference on juvenile bipolar disorder for development of NICE bipolar disorder guideline. |
| | 2004 Senior author on European Clinical Guidelines for hyperkinetic disorder-first upgrade. |
| | 2006 Last author for European Clinical Guidelines on long-acting medications for ADHD. |
| | 2007-present Member, Psychiatry Expert Advisory Group for the MHRA. |
| | 2007-present Non-Executive Director, South London and Maudsley NHS Foundation Trust. |
| | 2007 Co-author with Nutt *et al.*, 'Evidence-based guidelines for management of attention-deficit/hyperactivity disorder in adolescents in transition to adult services and in adults: recommendations from the British Association for Psychopharmacology'. *Journal of Psychopharmacology*, 21, 10–41. |
| **Professor Philip Asherson** | |
| Employment | Professor of Molecular Psychiatry and Honorary Consultant Psychiatrist, MRC Social, Genetic and Developmental Psychiatry Centre, Institute of Psychiatry, King's College London. |

| Declarations of interest: GDG members (*Continued*) | |
| --- | --- |
| Personal pecuniary interests | 2008 Talk to Regional Division of the Royal College of Psychiatrists (special interest in psychopharmacology) in Manchester; Astra-Zeneca donated £1,000 to university research fund. |
| | 2008 Talk to child and adolescent psychiatric services on clinical management of ADHD in adults in London; UCB Pharma donated £500 to university research fund. |
| | 2008 Talk to child and adolescent psychiatric services on clinical management of ADHD in adults in Manchester; UCB Pharma donated £500 to university research fund. |
| | 2008 Talk on genetics of ADHD at the European Academy for Childhood Disability meeting in Zagreb; travel and accommodation funded. |
| | 2007 Live web broadcast on clinical diagnosis and treatment of ADHD in adults. Posted on website (http://www.flynnpharma.com/index.cfm/fuseaction/Pages.getPage/Id/34); funded by Flynn Pharma; £1,000 donated to university research fund. |
| | 2007 Talk to specialist nurses on clinical management of ADHD in adults in Sheffield; UCB Pharma donated £500 to university research fund. |
| | 2007 Talk to specialist nurses on clinical management of ADHD in adults in London; UCB Pharma donated £500 to university research fund. |
| | 2007 Talk on clinical treatment of ADHD in adults at the Andrew Sims Centre; the centre donated £500 to university research fund. |
| | 2007 Attended advisory board meetings for Shire, Janssen-Cilag; reimbursements of approximately £2,000 donated to the university research fund. |
| | 2007 Talk to nurses, psychiatrists and psychologists on clinical management of ADHD in adults, Central and North Western Mental Health Trust, sponsored by Eli Lilly; £500 donated to university research fund. |
| | 2007 Talk on clinical management of ADHD in adults to child and adult psychiatrists in Bromley; Eli Lilly donated £500 to university research fund. |

*Continued*

| Declarations of interest: GDG members (*Continued*) | |
|---|---|
| | 2007 Advisory panel meeting for Pfizer; approximately £1,000 donated to University research fund. |
| | 2007 Talk on clinical management of adult ADHD and genetics of ADHD, Istanbul, sponsor unknown; travel and £500 donated to University research fund. |
| | 2007 Talk on clinical management of adult ADHD, Manchester, funded by Janssen-Cilag; travel and £500 donated to university research fund. |
| | Roadshow on treating adults with ADHD for nurses funded by Shire; travel and £800 donated to university research fund. |
| | 2007–2008 British Association of Psychopharmacology training days, masterclass on diagnosis and treatment of ADHD in adults; travel and £350 donated to university research fund. |
| | December 2004, 2005, 2007. Member of the international ADHD genetics consortium, international meeting for investigators studying genetic influences on ADHD; accommodation and travel funded by a grant from the National Institute of Mental Health (NIMH) to Steve Faraone. |
| | 2006 Attended European Network of Hyperactivity Disorder (Eunethydis) meeting in Belgium; gave presentation of genetic association studies in ADHD; accommodation funded. |
| | Dopamine 50 conference in Sweden; talk on genetic influences on the risk for ADHD; travel and accommodation funded. |
| | 2004–2005 Janssen-Cilag sponsored talks (x2, $2000 each); payments donated to university research fund. |
| Personal family interests | None |
| Non-personal pecuniary interests | 2007-present Programme grant from National Institute of Clinical Health Research to study the longitudinal outcomes of ADHD and to quantify rates of adult ADHD within the health service; approximately £2,000,000. |
| | 2005–2008 Collaborator on MRC study of cognitive function in ADHD families; approximately £300,000. |
| | 2002–2007 US NIMH programme grant, International Multi-centre ADHD Genetic Project; approximately £2,000,000. |

| Declarations of interest: GDG members (*Continued*) | |
|---|---|
| | 2006–2007 Unrestricted grant from Janssen-Cilag for evoked response potential studies of adult ADHD; £5,000. |
| | 2003–2006 Co-investigator on Wellcome project of inattention and activity levels in a population sample of twins; approximately £350,000. |
| Personal non-pecuniary interests | 1996–2008 Lead clinician in the National Adult ADHD clinic at the Maudsley Hospital. |
| | 2008 Royal College of Psychiatrists training day. Talk on continuities between child and adult ADHD. |
| | 2007 Attended international psychiatric genetics meeting and gave talk on linkage and association studies of ADHD. |
| | 2007 Attended international conference for whole genome association studies of ADHD. |
| | Author of 64 peer reviewed papers on clinical and genetic aspects of ADHD. |
| | 2007 Talking genetics of ADHD with Robert Findlay, interview recorded and posted on the internet (no longer available). |
| | 2007 Published editorial in *British Journal of Psychiatry* on the need for clinical services for adults with ADHD. |
| | 2007 Article on ADHD in adults posted on BBC Horizon website. |
| | 2007 Live interview for BBC Radio 4 Woman's Hour on living with adult ADHD. |
| | 2007 Co-author with Nutt *et al.* 'Evidence-based guidelines for management of attention-deficit/hyperactivity disorder in adolescents in transition to adult services and in adults: recommendations from the British Association for Psychopharmacology'. *Journal of Psychopharmacology*, 21, 10–41. |
| **Mr Simon Bailey (2006–2007)** | |
| Employment | – |
| Personal pecuniary interests | None |

*Continued*

| Declarations of interest: GDG members (*Continued*) | |
|---|---|
| Personal family interests | None |
| Non-personal pecuniary interests | None |
| Personal non-pecuniary interests | PhD research, University of Nottingham: 'Disordered Performances: An Ethnography of ADHD in Young Children'.<br><br>Two published papers and one journal article, all expressing clear opinions on DSM-defined ADHD. |
| **Dr Karen Bretherton** | |
| Employment | Consultant Psychiatrist for Children with Learning Disabilities, Child and Adolescent Mental Health Services, Leicestershire Partnership NHS Trust. |
| Personal pecuniary interests | 2006 Attendance at Child and Adolescent Learning Disability Professional Network; fee reduced by UCB Pharma, Eli Lilly and Janssen-Cilag by £42 per delegate. |
| Personal family interests | None |
| Non-personal pecuniary interests | None |
| Personal non-pecuniary interests | 2005 Co-author of chapter on ADHD in *The Frith Prescribing Guidelines for Adults with Learning Disability* (eds. S. Bhaumik & D. Branford). London: Taylor & Francis. |
| **Dr Val Harpin** | |
| Employment | Consultant Paediatrician (Neurodisability), Ryegate Children's Centre, Sheffield Children's NHS Foundation Trust. |
| Personal pecuniary interests | Attended advisory meetings arranged by Pfizer (2007) Janssen-Cilag (2006) and Eli Lilly (2005, 2007, 2008). Gave non-promotional lectures at ADHD meetings sponsored by Pharmaceutical companies as listed below:<br><br>2007 Eli Lilly: invited speaker on ADHD and comorbidity; £250. |

| Declarations of interest: GDG members (*Continued*) | |
|---|---|
| | 2007 UCB Pharma: invited speaker on ADHD and autistic spectrum disorders; £400. |
| | 2007 Eli Lilly: attended European Society for Child and Adolescent Psychiatry meeting; course fee and accommodation. |
| | 2006 Janssen-Cilag: meeting on service networks for management of ADHD; accommodation and £300. |
| | 2006 Eli Lilly: invited speaker at ADHD study session; £500. |
| | 2006 Janssen-Cilag: invited speaker on ADHD and quality of life; £400. |
| | 2006 UCB Pharma: ADHD chair of South Yorkshire meeting; £300. |
| | 2006 Eli Lilly: invited speaker at Asian Society for Child and Adolescent Psychiatry and Allied Professions; £1000. |
| | 2006 Eli Lilly Invited speaker on ADHD and quality of life sponsored by; £800. |
| Personal family interests | None |
| Non-personal pecuniary interests | 2000–2007 Investigator on trial using atomoxetine in ADHD, funded by Eli Lilly. |
| | 2005–2006 Investigator on Sunbeam trial (2005/6) funded by Eli Lilly. The Ryegate Children's Centre received research funding from Eli Lilly for nursing and psychology assistant time to follow-up children with ADHD on these trials, which involved using drug treatments. Also enrolled some children in ADORE, a naturalistic study following children on all kinds of ADHD management (funded for time by Eli Lilly paid to Sheffield Children's Hospital Trust). |
| Personal non-pecuniary interests | Advocate of using quality of life measures to monitor ADHD and have written articles on the effect on the family of having a child with ADHD. |
| | 2007 Invited organiser of symposium on ADHD at Royal College of Paediatrics and Child Health annual meeting. |
| | 2006 Presented paper on quality of life in ADHD at European Academy of Childhood Disability. |

*Continued*

| Declarations of interest: GDG members (*Continued*) | |
|---|---|
| **Professor Chris Hollis** | |
| Employment | Professor of Child and Adolescent Psychiatry, Division of Psychiatry, University of Nottingham, Queens Medical Centre, Nottingham. |
| Personal pecuniary interests | 2005 Unrestricted support from Janssen-Cilag for chairing and organising an educational meeting on the implication of new European ADHD guidelines, Nottingham; £1000. |
| Personal family interests | None |
| Non-personal pecuniary interests | None |
| Personal non-pecuniary interests | None |
| **Dr Daphne Keen** | |
| Employment | Consultant Developmental Paediatrician, Developmental Paediatrics, St George's Hospital, London. |
| Personal pecuniary interests | 2008 International Association of Child and Adolescent Psychiatry annual meeting Istanbul funded by Janssen-Cilag. |
| | 2006 Advisory board meeting relating to Equasym XL funded by UCB Pharma; £400. |
| | 2005 Advisory board meeting relating to modafinil funded by Cephalon; £2000. |
| | 2005 Advisory board meeting relating to Concerta funded by Janssen-Cilag; £750. |
| | 2005 and 2002 Advisory board meetings relating to Strattera funded by Eli Lilly; £750 per meeting. |
| Personal family interests | None |
| Non-personal pecuniary interests | None |
| Personal non-pecuniary interests | Chair of Specialist Advisory Committee for mental health training for the Royal College of Paediatrics and Child Health. Treasurer and executive member of the British Paediatric Mental Health Group. |

| Declarations of interest: GDG members (*Continued*) | |
|---|---|
| | 2007–2008 Member of guideline development group commissioned by the Department of Health on psychoanalytic psychotherapies in the treatment and care of individuals who have experienced sexual abuse, violence and neglect in childhood. |
| **Ms Christine Merrell** | |
| Employment | Education Specialist, Curriculum, Evaluation and Management Centre, Durham University, Durham. |
| Personal pecuniary interests | None |
| Personal family interests | None |
| Non-personal pecuniary interests | 2007–2010 Evaluation of the impact of teaching and classroom management strategies on severely inattentive, hyperactive and impulsive young children, the Harlow Foundation; £10,150. |
| | 2005–2008 Department member of grant for 'Can school-based screening and interventions programmes for ADHD improve children's outcomes and access to services? A longitudinal study', Department of Health and Department for Education and Skills; £6,100. |
| | 2005–2007 Member of grant for 'Cost-effective smart identification of early attentional problems associated with literacy and numeracy indicators in pre-school children', Australian Research Council; £10,000. |
| Personal non-pecuniary interests | 2001–2004 Member of grant on screening and interventions for inattentive, hyperactive and impulsive children, Economic and Social Research Council award number R000223798; £45,670. |
| **Ms Diane Mulligan** | |
| Employment | Social Inclusion Advisor, Sightsavers International |
| Personal pecuniary interests | 2006–2007 Attendance at British Medical Association patient liaison group and equal opportunities committee; £250 reimbursement per day. |
| | 2007 Attendance at Commission for Equality and Human Rights Disability Committee; £250 reimbursement per day. |

*Continued*

| Declarations of interest: GDG members (*Continued*) | |
|---|---|
| Personal family interests | None |
| Non-personal pecuniary interests | None |
| Personal non-pecuniary interests | 2007 Member of AMAZE, Brighton.<br><br>2007 Member of the National Forum for Organisations of Disabled People Advisory Group.<br><br>2007 Member of the Brighton and Hove Vocational Forum, which works with the Commissioner for Mental Health.<br><br>2007 Involvement in the World Health Organization's community-based rehabilitation guidelines, specialising in education for disabled children (including children with ADHD). |
| **Ms Noreen Ryan** | |
| Employment | Nurse Consultant, Child and Adolescent Mental Health Services, Bolton NHS Hospital Trust, Bolton. |
| Personal pecuniary interests | None |
| Personal family interests | None |
| Non-personal pecuniary interests | None |
| Personal non-pecuniary interests | 2007 Co-author of a text book on ADHD; manuscript due November 2008, Routledge.<br><br>2007 'Non-medical prescribing in CAMHS in the UK', paper submitted to *Journal of American Psychiatric Nursing*.<br><br>2007 'Nurse prescribing in child and adolescent mental health services', *Mental Health Practice, 10*, 35–37.<br><br>2007 'Non-medical prescribing in a child and adolescent mental health service', *Mental Health Practice, 11*, 40–44.<br><br>2006 Chapter on 'Nursing children and young people with attention deficit hyperactivity disorder' in *Child and Adolescent Mental Health Nursing* (ed. T. McDougall). Oxford: Blackwell.<br><br>2005–2006 Expert for NICE TA on methylphenidate, dexamfetamine and atomoxetine. |

| Declarations of interest: GDG members (*Continued*) | |
|---|---|
| **Dr Nicola Salt** | |
| Employment | General Medical Practitioner, Thurleigh Road Surgery, London. |
| Personal pecuniary interests | 2007 Consultant for Nikko Healthcare; £8000. |
| Personal family interests | None |
| Non-personal pecuniary interests | Pharmaceutical company sponsorship of practice meetings, providing lunch and speaker, up to ten meetings per year. There have been no companies with an interest in ADHD. |
| Personal non-pecuniary interests | None |
| **Dr Kapil Sayal** | |
| Employment | Senior Lecturer in Child and Adolescent Psychiatry, Institute of Mental Health and University of Nottingham, Nottingham. |
| Personal pecuniary interests | 2005 Attendance at a conference funded by Janssen-Cilag; £1000. 2003 Co-author of Medscape CME Clinical Update Review, supported by Eli Lilly educational grant; £1000. |
| Personal family interests | None |
| Non-personal pecuniary interests | 2005–2008 'Can schools-based screening and intervention programmes for ADHD improve children's outcomes and access to services? A longitudinal study', Department of Health, administered by Department for Education and Skills; £106,595. 2004–2006 'Teacher recognition of hyperactivity: evaluation of a pilot intervention', South London and Maudsley NHS Trust Research and Development funding; £37,000. |
| Personal non-pecuniary interests | 2004–2006 Research study and a paper evaluating an educational session about ADHD for teachers. 2007 Chapter on 'Diagnosis and assessment' in *People with Hyperactivity: Understanding and Managing Their Problems* (ed. E. Taylor). London: Mac Keith Press. |

*Continued*

| Declarations of interest: GDG members (*Continued*) | |
|---|---|
| **Ms Linda Sheppard** | |
| Employment | – |
| Personal pecuniary interests | None |
| Personal family interests | None |
| Non-personal pecuniary interests | Unrestricted education grant from Janssen-Cilag to ADHD in Suffolk Family Support Group towards costs of National ADHD conference; £2000. |
| Personal non-pecuniary interests | None |
| **Dr Geoff Thorley** | |
| Employment | Head Clinical Child and Adolescent Psychologist, Child and Adolescent Mental Health Services, Leicestershire Partnership NHS Trust, Leicester; Private practice, Spire Hospital, Leicester. |
| Personal pecuniary interests | None |
| Personal family interests | None |
| Non-personal pecuniary interests | None |
| Personal non-pecuniary interests | 2005 Trustee of Cope Children's Charity, Leicester. 2005 Author of *Successful Parenting: The Four Step Approach*. Bloomington, Indiana: AuthorHouse. |
| **Professor Peter Tymms** | |
| Employment | Professor of Education and Director of the Curriculum, Evaluation and Management Centre, Durham University, Durham. |
| Personal pecuniary interests | None |
| Personal family interests | None |
| Non-personal pecuniary interests | 2007 Director of the Curriculum, Evaluation and Management Centre, Durham University which schools buy into. The centre offers ADHD assessments and sells books on ADHD for teachers. |

| Declarations of interest: GDG members (*Continued*) | |
|---|---|
| Personal non-pecuniary interests | None |

### Dr Miranda Wolpert (2006–2007)

| | |
|---|---|
| Employment | Director, CAMHS Evidence Based Practice Unit, University College London and Anna Freud Centre, London. Consultant Clinical Psychologist, Clinical Advisor on Child and Adolescent Mental Health – NIMH/Care Services' Improvement Partnership (England), London. |
| Personal pecuniary interests | 2007 Developed a course on outcomes-based CBT at University College London. |
| Personal family interests | None |
| Non-personal pecuniary interests | None |
| Personal non-pecuniary interests | 2006 Co-authored with P. Fuggle, D. Cottrell, P. Fonagy, *et al. Drawing on the Evidence: Advice for Mental Health Professionals Working With Children and Adolescents*. London: CAMHS Publications. <br> 2007 Author, 'Choosing what's best for you' booklet. London: CAMHS Publications. |

### Professor Ian Wong

| | |
|---|---|
| Employment | Professor of Paediatric Medicine Research, Centre for Paediatric Pharmacy Research, The School of Pharmacy, London. |
| Personal pecuniary interests | 2007–2008 Director of research at Therakind Ltd, a spin-off company of the School of Pharmacy, University of London, but work is not related to ADHD. <br> 2007–2008 Consultancy fees from Neuropharm Ltd via University of London on work not related to ADHD. <br> 2007 ADHD-related consultancy fees from Pharmaceutical Development Services; £500. |
| Personal family interests | None |
| Non-personal pecuniary interests | 2005–2007 Cessation of Attention Deficit Hyperactivity Disorder Drugs in the Young (CADDY), Department of Health, Health Technology Assessment Programme; £110,000. |

*Continued*

| | Declarations of interest: GDG members (*Continued*) |
|---|---|
| | 2003–2006 Educational grant from Pfizer to establish a research lecturer for 3 years; £150,000. |
| | 2004–2006 Tacrolimus Oral Paediatric Preparation Evaluation Research (TOPPER), Fujisawa Ltd; £100,000. |
| | 2004–2007 Disclofenac Safety and Kinetic in Children Post-Operation Study (DISKCOS), Rosemont Pharmaceutical Company; £100,000. |
| | 2005–2008 Electronic Prescribing in Children (EPIC), First Databank, JAC and Great Ormond Hospital for Children; £80,000. |
| | 2004–2005 Evaluation of concordance in children taking orphan medications, Orphan Europe Ltd; £23,000. |
| | 2002–2007 National Public Health Career Scientist Award for Children and Adolescent Psychiatric Pharmaco-therapy Evaluation research, Department of Health and NHS Research and Development Programme, £330,000. |
| | 2006–2007 Staff at the Centre for Paediatric Pharmacy Research gave lectures to psychiatrists, paediatricians and healthcare professionals on 'Clinical pharmacology and research of ADHD treatments'. These lectures were organised by Janssen-Cilag. Honoraria are sent to the School of Pharmacy and no staff received personal honoraria. |
| | The Department of Practice and Policy of the School of Pharmacy has received funding from several pharmaceutical companies for medicines research, but none related to ADHD. |
| Personal non-pecuniary interests | None |
| **Dr Susan Young** | |
| Employment | Senior Lecturer in Forensic Clinical Psychology, Institute of Psychiatry, Kings' College London, Honorary Consultant Clinical and Forensic Psychologist, Broadmoor Hospital, West London Mental Health Trust. |
| Personal pecuniary interests | Director of Psychology Services Limited, a private company providing conference presentations, legal and |

| Declarations of interest: GDG members (*Continued*) | |
|---|---|
| | clinical assessments, psychological treatment and training in these services. |
| | 2007 XII International Congress of the European Society for Child and Adolescent Psychiatry, Florence, Italy. Symposium 'ADHD: Integrating Treatment Perspectives'. Paper presented on 'Psychotherapy for patients with ADHD'; £1650 speaker fee including expenses paid to Psychology Services Limited by Eli Lilly. |
| | 2007 Leeds Mental Health Trust Conference, 'Adult ADHD – An Emerging Challenge'. Paper presented on 'Forensic perspective'; £150 including expenses paid to Psychology Services Limited. |
| | 2007 Dorset ADHD support group, Weymouth, 'Transitions: ADHD across the Lifespan'. Paper presented on 'ADHD adults'; £552 including expenses paid to Psychology Services Limited. |
| | 2007 University of Iceland Workshop on the Young-Bramham Programme for Adolescents and Adults with ADHD; £1,997.24 including expenses paid to Psychology Services Limited. |
| | 2006 'The Management of Co-morbidities and Complexities in an ADHD Population', Crawley. Paper presented on 'ADHD and offending'; expenses paid to Psychology Services Limited. |
| | 2006 Associacao de Psiquiatria Biologica Annual Meeting, Portugal. Paper presented on 'ADHD and the legal process' and 'Psychological treatment'; expenses paid to Psychology Services Limited. |
| | 2006 South West Study Day 'Criminal Youth Justice and Forensic Issues' sponsored by Janssen-Cilag. Paper presented on 'The impact of ADHD on offending'; expenses paid to Psychology Services Limited. |
| | 2006 Exeter meeting on forensic issues for people with ADHD; £104 and travel expenses funded by Janssen-Cilag paid to Psychology Services Limited. |
| Personal family interests | None |

*Continued*

| Declarations of interest: GDG members (*Continued*) | |
|---|---|
| Non-personal pecuniary interests | 2006 Prevalence of ADHD in young offenders and adult prisoners. Research grant funded by Janssen-Cilag; £45,840.<br><br>2004 Unrestricted research grant from Eli Lilly for ADHD/forensic aspects; £5000. |
| Personal non-pecuniary interests | 2007 Co-author with R. Ross, *R&R2 for ADHD Youths and Adults: A Prosocial Competence Training Program*. Ottawa: Cognitive Centre of Canada (cogcen@canada.com).<br><br>2007 Co-author with J. Bramham, *ADHD in Adults: A Psychological Guide to Practice*. Chichester: John Wiley & Sons.<br><br>2007 Co-author with Nutt *et al.*, 'British Pharmacological Guidelines', presented at ADDISS conference.<br><br>2007 Co-author with Nutt *et al.*, 'Evidence-based guidelines for management of attention-deficit/ hyperactivity disorder in adolescents in transition to adult services and in adults: recommendations from the British Association for Psychopharmacology'. *Journal of Psychopharmacology*, 21, 10–41. |

| Declarations of interest: NCCMH staff | |
|---|---|
| **Dr Tim Kendall – Facilitator, GDG** | |
| Employment | Joint Director, NCCMH; Deputy Director, Royal College of Psychiatrists' Research and Training Unit; Consultant Psychiatrist and Medical Director, Sheffield Health and Social Care Trust. |
| Personal pecuniary interests | None |
| Personal family interests | None |
| Non-personal pecuniary interests | None |
| Personal non-pecuniary interests | 2008 Co-author with A. Muñoz-Solomando & C. J. Whittington, 'Cognitive behavioural |

| Declarations of interest: NCCMH staff (*Continued*) | |
|---|---|
| | therapy for children and adolescents: a narrative synthesis of systematic reviews'. *Current Opinion in Psychiatry* (in press). |
| | 2007 Interviews on BBC1 News regarding the *Panorama* programme on ADHD. |
| | 2007 Article in the *Daily Mail* about ADHD. |
| | 2007 Appearance on BBC *Panorama* programme about ADHD. |
| | 2007 Article in the *Daily Telegraph* about ADHD. |
| | 2007 Telephone interview for BBC World Service News Hour, 'Child use of antidepressants up four-fold'. |
| | 2006 Interview for BBC News regarding prescribing antidepressants to children under 4 years. |
| | 2006 Interview for BBC Radio 4's *Woman's Hour* on children's mental health and purported rises in prescribing to children. |
| | 2006 Organised and appeared on BBC Radio 4's *All in the Mind* regarding mental health provision for children and young people and NICE guidelines produced to date. |
| | 2005 Co-author with C. J. Whittington & S. Pilling, 'Are SSRIs and atypical antidepressants safe and effective for children and adolescents?' *Current Opinion in Psychiatry, 18,* 21–25. |
| **Ms Amy Brown** | |
| Employment | Research Assistant, NCCMH (2006–2007) |
| Personal pecuniary | None |
| Personal family interests | None |
| Non-personal pecuniary interests | None |
| Personal non-pecuniary interests | None |
| **Ms Liz Costigan** | |
| Employment | Project Manager, NCCMH (2006–2007) |

*Continued*

| Declarations of interest: NCCMH staff (*Continued*) | |
|---|---|
| Personal pecuniary interests | None |
| Personal family interests | None |
| Non-personal pecuniary interests | None |
| Personal non-pecuniary interests | None |
| **Mr Alan Duncan** | |
| Employment | Systematic Reviewer, NCCMH |
| Personal pecuniary interests | None |
| Personal family interests | None |
| Non-personal pecuniary interests | None |
| Personal non-pecuniary interests | None |
| Personal family interests | None |
| Other interests related to ADHD | None |
| **Ms Angela Lewis** | |
| Employment | Research Assistant, NCCMH (2007–2008) |
| Personal pecuniary interests | None |
| Personal family interests | None |
| Non-personal pecuniary interests | None |
| Personal non-pecuniary interests | None |
| **Dr Ifigeneia Mavranezouli** | |
| Employment | Senior Health Economist, NCCMH |
| Personal pecuniary interests | None |
| Personal family interests | None |
| Non-personal pecuniary interests | None |
| Personal non-pecuniary interests | None |
| **Dr Alejandra Perez** | |
| Employment | Systematic Reviewer, NCCMH |
| Personal interests related to ADHD | None |
| Personal interests not specifically related to ADHD | None |

| Declarations of interest: NCCMH staff (*Continued*) | |
|---|---|
| Non-personal interests | None |
| Personal non-monetary interests | None |
| **Dr Catherine Pettinari** | |
| Employment | Centre Manager and Senior Project Manager NCCMH (2007–2008) |
| Personal interests related to ADHD | None |
| Personal interests not specifically related to ADHD | None |
| Non-personal interests | None |
| Personal non-monetary interests | None |
| Personal family interests | None |
| Other interests related to ADHD | None |
| **Ms Sarah Stockton** | |
| Employment | Senior Information Scientist, NCCMH |
| Personal interests related to ADHD | None |
| Personal interests not specifically related to ADHD | None |
| Non-personal interests | None |
| Personal non-monetary interests | None |
| **Dr Clare Taylor** | |
| Employment | Editor, NCCMH |
| Personal interests related to ADHD | None |
| Personal interests not specifically related to ADHD | None |
| Non-personal interests | None |
| Personal non-monetary interests | None |

*Continued*

| Declarations of interest: NCCMH staff (*Continued*) | |
|---|---|
| **Ms Jenny Turner** | |
| Employment | Research Assistant, NCCMH (2006–2007) |
| Personal interests related to ADHD | None |
| Personal interests not specifically related to ADHD | None |
| Non-personal interests | None |
| Personal non-monetary interests | None |

# APPENDIX 3:

# SPECIAL ADVISERS TO THE GDG

| | |
|---|---|
| **Ms Mary Sainsbury** | Practice Development Manager, Social Care Institute for Excellence |
| **Dr Ilina Singh** | Wellcome Trust University Lecturer in Bioethics and Society, London School of Economics |
| **Dr Miranda Wolpert (2007-2008)** | Director, CAMHS Evidence Based Practice Unit, University College London and Anna Freud Centre, London |

# APPENDIX 4:

# STAKEHOLDERS AND REVIEWERS WHO SUBMITTED COMMENTS IN RESPONSE TO THE CONSULTATION DRAFT OF THE GUIDELINE

## STAKEHOLDERS

ADDISS (Attention Deficit Disorder Information and Support Service)
Adults with Attention Deficit Disorder UK (AADD UK)
British Association for Psychopharmacology
British Association of Art Therapists
British Dietetic Association
British Psychological Society, The
Centre for Health Technology Evaluation
College of Mental Health Pharmacists
College of Occupational Therapists
Critical Psychiatry Network
Department of Health
Derbyshire Mental Health Services NHS Trust
Eli Lilly & Company
George Still Forum (National Paediatric ADHD Network Group)
GJ International Ltd
Hyperactive Children's Support Group (HACSG)
Janssen-Cilag Ltd
Learning Assessment & Neurocare Centre
Liverpool ADHD Foundation
Lundbeck Ltd
Medicines and Healthcare Products Regulatory Agency (MHRA)
National Association of EBD Schools
National Association of Schoolmasters Union of Women Teachers (NASUWT)
Neonatal & Paediatric Pharmacists Group (NPPG)
Neurodevelopmental Paediatrics
Ofsted
Oxfordshire and Buckinghamshire Mental Health NHS Trust
Royal College of Nursing
Royal College of Paediatrics and Child Health
Shire Pharmaceuticals Limited
Southampton City Primary Care Trust
Sussex Partnership NHS Trust
Trafford Primary Care Trust
UCB Pharma Ltd

UK Psychiatric Pharmacy Group (UKPPG)
West Dorset Attention and Concentration Group
West London Mental Health NHS Trust
Young Minds

## REVIEWERS

Kusay Hadi
Jonathan Leo
Michael Rutter

# APPENDIX 5:

# RESEARCHERS CONTACTED TO REQUEST INFORMATION ABOUT UNPUBLISHED OR SOON-TO-BE PUBLISHED STUDIES

Dr Albert Allen
Professor Gene Arnold
Professor Michael Schlander

# APPENDIX 6:

# CLINICAL QUESTIONS

## 1.    DIAGNOSIS

| **Diagnosis and assessment** | | |
|---|---|---|
| 1.1 | 1.1.1 | Is there a consistent pattern of signs and symptoms demarcating ADHD from other disorders? |
| | 1.1.2 | ● Is this pattern associated with clinically meaningful impairment? |
| | 1.1.3 | ● Is this pattern of signs and symptoms the same in children than in adults? |
| | 1.1.4 | ● Can the clinical features and impairments of ADHD be distinguished from another diagnosis? *To consider: (associated disorders)* <br> – conduct disorder and oppositional defiant disorder and antisocial personality disorder <br> – obsessive-compulsive disorder <br> – bipolar disorder <br> – affective disorders and anxiety disorders <br> – premorbid impairments in schizophrenia <br> – personality disorders (borderline) <br> – Tourette's syndrome <br> – global learning disorder <br> – specific learning disorder (for example, dyslexia, dyscalculia) <br> – attachment disorder <br> – autistic spectrum disorders <br> – alcohol/drug misuse |
| 1.2 | | Does ADHD have a characteristic course? |
| 1.3 | 1.3.1 <br> 1.3.2 <br><br><br><br> 1.3.3 | Is there any evidence of: <br> ● heritability of ADHD from family and genetic studies? <br> ● neurobiological underpinning of ADHD? <br> *To consider:* <br> – neurotransmitters <br> – brain structure (MRI) and function (fMRI/ERP) <br> Is the neurobiological evidence linked to core signs/symptoms? |
| 1.4 | | Is there evidence of the social context (environmental, familial [not including genetics] and/or educational factors) influencing ADHD? |

| 1.5 | | Is there evidence of over/under-diagnosis in some groups? *To consider:* <br>    – three sub-types of ADHD and hyperkinetic disorder <br>    – age groups <br>    – gender <br>    – socio-economic status <br>    – ethnicity <br>    – country <br>    – forensic settings <br>    – alcohol/drug users <br>    – looked after children <br>    – learning disabilities |
|-----|-------|---------------------------------------------------------------|
| 1.6 | 1.6.1 | What is the most reliable way of diagnosing the three sub-types of ADHD and hyperkinetic disorder? |
|     | 1.6.2 | ● Should the diagnosis be given by specialists only? |
|     | 1.6.3 | ● What is the minimum required assessment for a diagnosis to be given? |
|     | 1.6.4 | ● Should sub-typing be based on cross-sectional assessment of symptoms only (for example, last 6 months) or also consider sub-type at onset? |
|     | 1.6.5 | ● Is the diagnostic approach different in adults compared with children? |
| 1.7 | | What are the criteria that trigger the use of this guideline (that is, which children, young people and adults should be included in this guideline and which should not)? <br> ● (severity of symptoms) |

## 2.    PSYCHOLOGICAL AND COMBINED INTERVENTIONS

| **Treatment effectiveness, choice and moderating factors** | | |
|-----|-----|-----|
| 2.1 | For people with ADHD, do | |
| | a) psychological interventions:[52] <br> ● cognitive training <br> ● CBT | when compared with: <br> ● no intervention <br> ● waiting lists <br> ● 'standard care' | produce harm/benefits on the desired outcomes* and does this depend on: <br> ● ADHD subtype |

[52]The clinical questions originally listed: family therapy (systemic/psychodynamic, behavioural); CBT (individual behavioural therapy, individual cognitive therapy, environmental manipulation and management.

| | | | |
|---|---|---|---|
| | • behavioural approaches/ parent (effectiveness) training<br>  • multimodal interventions<br>b) other approaches:<br>  • biofeedback<br>  • physical therapies (relaxation and so on)<br>  • other approaches | • other psychological interventions<br>• medication for ADHD | • associated disorder<br>• social context<br>• age<br>• gender<br>• severity<br>• delivery systems (group/individual, family/group of family, manualised or not, student versus specialist, rater)?<br>\*ADHD symptoms/ associated mental health problems/peer relationships/school learning and progress/ family relationships/ quality of life/care needs, self-esteem<br>**Plus additional outcomes agreed as relevant to psychological interventions for ADHD** |
| 2.2 | Is the use of more than one type of psychological therapy more effective than single therapies (including psychological interventions with the child combined with parent interventions)?[53] | | |
| 2.3 | Is there evidence of the added value in terms of benefits/harm from combined treatment (medication for ADHD plus psychological interventions)?[54]<br>• Medication for ADHD plus psychological intervention versus medication for ADHD only.<br>• Medication for ADHD plus child psychological intervention versus medication for ADHD plus parent-training intervention.<br>• Medication for ADHD plus psychological intervention versus psychological intervention. | | |

[53]Inserted in place of question under *Interventions for carers*: 'Is there evidence on: the effectiveness of combined therapies compared with a single therapy?'

[54]Separate section for clinical questions on combined interventions deleted and combination comparisons rationalised to fit the scheme for psychological interventions (combinations of drugs are dealt with in the pharmacological interventions questions).

| | ● Parent training plus child psychological intervention (or multimodal psych intervention) versus medication for ADHD. |
|---|---|
| **Treatment decisions: initiation, duration, discontinuation and effect evaluation** ||
| 2.4 | When should psychological treatment be initiated?<br>● Does waiting for a treatment influence outcome? |
| 2.5 | What is the optimum duration of treatment?<br>● What are the long-term consequences of treatment? |
| 2.6 | What is the most effective first-line treatment and under what circum-stances (for example, epilepsy, potential for misuse, tics, Tourette's syndrome, and so on)?<br>● What is the recommended order of combined treatments? |
| **Adherence** ||
| 2.7 | What approaches can be used to optimise adherence with psychological treatment? |

## 3. INTERVENTION FOR CARERS

| 3.1 | Are there interventions that improve the well-being of parents/carers and may provide an indirect benefit for the child, but where evidence on outcomes for the child with ADHD is not available (peer support groups, counselling, advice/information and guidance)?[55] |
|---|---|

## 4. PHARMACOLOGICAL INTERVENTIONS

| **Drug effectiveness, choice and moderating factors** | | |
|---|---|---|
| 4.1 | | For people with ADHD |
| | | Does drug treatment:<br>● methylphenidate (including MR preparations)<br>● atomoxetine<br>● dexamfetamine    when compared with:<br>● waiting lists<br>● placebo<br>● other drug (head-to-head trials)    produce harm/benefits on the desired outcomes* and does this depend on:<br>● ADHD subtype |

---

[55]The clinical questions originally listed the following interventions for carers: psychoeducational interventions (advice/information, parental guidance); parent effectiveness training; counselling; and CBT. However, since parent-training interventions are behavioural interventions these are addressed in clinical question 2.1.

| | | |
|---|---|---|
| <ul><li>tricyclic and other antidepressants</li><li>bupropion</li><li>nicotine (as skin patches)</li><li>atypical antipsychotics</li><li>modafinil</li><li>clonidine</li></ul> | <ul><li>psychological interventions</li><li>parent training</li></ul> | <ul><li>associated disorder</li><li>social context</li><li>age</li><li>gender</li><li>severity</li><li>delivery systems (group/individual, family/group of families, manualised or not, student versus specialist, rater)?</li></ul> <br> *ADHD symptoms/ associated mental health problems/peer relationships/school learning and progress/family relationships/quality of life/care needs, self-esteem |

## Treatment decisions: duration, discontinuation and effect evaluation

| 4.2 | 4.2.1 | Which drugs should be used as a first-line, second-line treatment and so on? |
|---|---|---|
| | 4.2.2 | How should drug treatment be initiated, dose titrated and effectiveness evaluated? |
| | 4.2.3 | What is the optimum duration of drug treatment (continuous versus intermittent treatment) and <ul><li>when is discontinuation attempted?</li><li>what advice is given for discontinuation?</li></ul> |
| 4.3 | | Is there any evidence on: <ul><li>what is the most effective type of drug administration (to improve adherence) and</li><li>what is the dose optimisation and how is this best achieved (where outcome is optimal)?</li></ul> |

## Side effects, monitoring, precautions and misuse potential

| 4.4 | | What conditions contraindicate or caution the use of specific drug treatments? <br> What are the necessary baseline investigations and ongoing monitoring to support drug treatment? <br> What are the side effects of drug treatments (including misuse potential)? |
|---|---|---|

| | | What action should be taken in response to side effects? What action should be taken in response to lack of effectiveness? | | |
|---|---|---|---|---|
| 4.5 | | What are the risks of prescribing drug treatment in the presence of recreational drug use and/or alcohol use and <br> ● What approaches should be taken if in the presence of recreational drug use and/or alcohol use? | | |

**Education, adherence and shared-care**

| | | | | |
|---|---|---|---|---|
| 4.6 | | How is drug treatment monitored and <br> ● by whom (by specialist, GP and/or care coordinator)? | | |
| 4.7 | | What approaches to drug treatment can be used to support drug adherence? <br> ● Are there any interventions that can improve adherence when initiating drug treatment? <br> ● When there are problems regarding adherence to drug treatment in people with ADHD, are there any interventions that can improve adherence with medication? | | |

## 5.    EDUCATION

| | | | | |
|---|---|---|---|---|
| 5.1 | | Does educational intervention: <br> ● school screening <br> ● teacher training on ADHD <br> ● curriculum modification <br> ● classroom management <br> ● remedial teaching <br> ● a multi-agency partnership between schools and other agencies | when compared with: <br> ● standard education <br> ● health interventions | produce harm/benefits on the desired outcomes* and does this depend on: <br> ● ADHD subtype <br> ● associated disorder <br> ● social context <br> ● age <br> ● gender <br> ● severity <br><br> *Behaviour in classroom, academic achievement and progress, attitude to school, teachers' quality of life, self-esteem, behaviour and employment. |

# APPENDIX 7:

# REVIEW PROTOCOLS

| Relevant questions | Q1.1 – **Diagnosis** |
|---|---|
| | 1.1.1  Is there a consistent pattern of signs and symptoms demarcating ADHD from other disorders? |
| | ● 1.1.2  Is this pattern associated with clinically meaningful impairment? |
| | ● 1.1.3  Is this pattern of signs and symptoms the same in children as in adults? |
| | ● 1.1.4  Can the clinical features and impairments of ADHD be distinguished from another diagnosis? |
| **Chapter** | 5 Diagnosis |
| **Sub-section** | |
| **Topic Group (TG)** | TG1 Diagnosis |
| **Sub-section lead** | |
| **Search strategy** | **Databases:** CENTRAL, CINAHL, EMBASE, MEDLINE, PsycINFO |
| **Existing reviews** | |
| ● **Updated** | |
| ● **Not updated** | |
| **General search filter used** | 1st search: observational studies (OS), empirical reviews (high spec)<br>2nd search: Diagnosis, empirical reviews (ER), OS |
| **Question specific search filter** | |
| **Amendments to filter/search strategy** | |

| Eligibility criteria | |
|---|---|
| ● Intervention | |
| ● Comparator | |
| ● Population (including age, gender, etc) | Children, young people, and adults with ADHD, ADD, MBD, comorbid ADHD |
| ● Outcomes | Validity of ADHD category |
| ● Study design | SR, OS, cross-sectional studies, cohort studies, factor analytic studies |
| ● Publication status | Published and unpublished (if criteria met) |
| ● Year of study | Any |
| ● Dosage | Any |
| ● Minimum sample size | n > 10 |
| ● Study setting | Any |
| **Additional assessments** | |

| Relevant questions | Q1.1 – **Diagnosis** <br> 1.2 Does ADHD have a characteristic course? |
|---|---|
| **Chapter** | 5 Diagnosis |
| **Sub-section** | |
| **Topic Group** | TG1 Diagnosis |
| **Sub-section lead** | |
| **Search strategy** | **Databases:** CENTRAL, CINAHL, EMBASE, MEDLINE, PsycINFO |
| **Existing reviews** | |
| ● **Updated** | |
| ● **Not updated** | |

| General search filter used | 1st search: OS, empirical reviews [high spec] 2nd search: OS |
|---|---|
| Question specific search filter | |
| Amendments to filter/search strategy | |
| Eligibility criteria | |
| ● Intervention | |
| ● Comparator | |
| ● Population (including age, gender, etc) | Children, young people, and adults with ADHD, ADD, MBD, comorbid ADHD (oppositional defiant disorder, conduct disorder and/or disruptive behaviour). |
| ● Outcomes | Continuity of ADHD diagnosis |
| ● Study design | SR, observational studies, cross-sectional studies, cohort studies |
| ● Publication status | Published and unpublished (if criteria met) |
| ● Year of study | Any |
| ● Dosage | Any |
| ● Minimum sample size | n > 10 |
| ● Study setting | Any |
| Additional assessments | |

| Relevant questions | Q1.1 – **Diagnosis** |
|---|---|
| | Is there any evidence of: <br> ● 1.3.1 Heritability of ADHD from family and genetic studies? <br> ● 1.3.2 Neurobiological underpinning of ADHD? <br> *To consider:* <br> – Neurotransmitters <br> – Brain structure (MRI) and function (fMRI/ERP) |

| | 1.3.3 Is the neurobiological evidence linked to core signs/symptoms? |
|---|---|
| **Chapter** | 5 Diagnosis |
| **Sub-section** | |
| **Topic Group** | TG1 Diagnosis |
| **Sub-section lead** | |
| **Search strategy** | **Databases:** CENTRAL, CINAHL, EMBASE, MEDLINE, PsycINFO |
| **Existing reviews** | |
| ● **Updated** | |
| ● **Not updated** | |
| **General search filter used** | OS, empirical reviews [high spec] |
| **Question specific search filter** | |
| **Amendments to filter/search strategy** | |
| **Eligibility criteria** | |
| ● Intervention | |
| ● Comparator | |
| ● Population (including age, gender, etc) | Children, young people, and adults with ADHD, ADD, MBD, comorbid ADHD (oppositional defiant disorder, conduct disorder and/or disruptive behaviour). |
| ● Outcomes | Gene associations in people with ADHD |
| ● Study design | SR of genetic studies |
| ● Publication status | Published and unpublished (if criteria met) |
| ● Year of study | Any |
| ● Dosage | Any |
| ● Minimum sample size | n > 10 |

| | |
|---|---|
| ● Study setting | Any |
| **Additional assessments** | |

| | |
|---|---|
| **Relevant questions** | Q1.1 – **Diagnosis**<br>1.4 Is there evidence of the social context (environmental, familial [not including genetics] and/or educational factors) influencing ADHD?<br>1.5 Is there evidence of over-/under-diagnosis in some groups?<br>1.6.1 What is the most reliable way of diagnosing the three sub-types of ADHD plus hyperkinetic disorder?<br>● 1.6.2 Should the diagnosis be given by specialists only?<br>● 1.6.3 What is the minimum required assessment for a diagnosis to be given?<br>● 1.6.4 Should sub-typing be based on cross-sectional assessment of symptoms only (for example, last 6 months) or also consider sub-type at onset?<br>● 1.6.5 Is the diagnostic approach different in adults compared to children?<br>1.7 What are the criteria that trigger the use of this guideline (that is, which children, young people and adults should be included in this guideline and which should not)?<br>● and for those included, what is the severity of symptoms? |
| **Chapter** | 5 Diagnosis |
| **Sub-section** | |
| **Topic Group** | TG1 Diagnosis |
| **Sub-section lead** | |
| **Search strategy** | **Databases:** CENTRAL, CINAHL, EMBASE, MEDLINE, PsycINFO |
| **Existing reviews** | |
| ● **Updated** | |
| ● **Not updated** | |

| General search filter used | OS, empirical reviews [high spec] |
|---|---|
| **Question specific search filter** | |
| **Amendments to filter/search strategy** | |
| **Eligibility criteria** | |
| ● Intervention | |
| ● Comparator | |
| ● Population (including age, gender etc) | Children, young people, and adults with ADHD, ADD, MBD, comorbid ADHD (oppositional defiant disorder, conduct disorder and/or disruptive behaviour). |
| ● Outcomes | Validity of ADHD diagnosis |
| ● Study design | SR |
| ● Publication status | Published and unpublished (if criteria met) |
| ● Year of study | Any |
| ● Dosage | Any |
| ● Minimum sample size | n > 10 |
| ● Study setting | Any |
| **Additional assessments** | |

# Searches made for Diagnosis

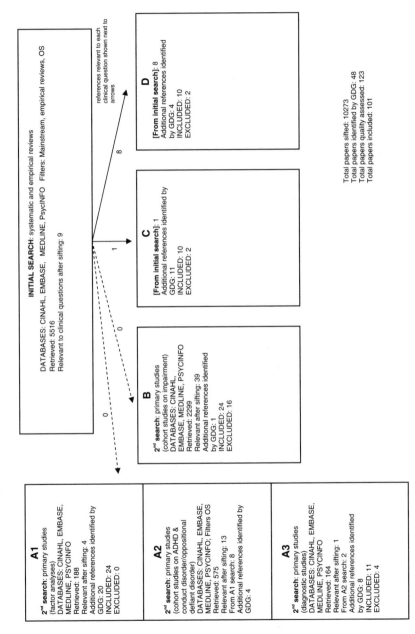

**INITIAL SEARCH:** systematic and empirical reviews

DATABASES: CINAHL, EMBASE, MEDLINE, PsycINFO  Filters: Mainstream, empirical reviews, OS
Retrieved: 5516
Relevant to clinical questions after sifting: 9

references relevant to each
clinical question shown next to
arrows

**A1**

2nd **search:** primary studies
(factor analyses)
DATABASES: CINAHL, EMBASE,
MEDLINE, PSYCINFO
Retrieved: 188
Relevant after sifting: 4
Additional references identified by
GDG: 20
INCLUDED: 24
EXCLUDED: 0

**A2**

2nd **search:** primary studies
(cohort studies on ADHD &
conduct disorder/oppositional
defiant disorder)
DATABASES: CINAHL, EMBASE,
MEDLINE, PSYCINFO; Filters OS
Retrieved: 575
Relevant after sifting: 13
From A1 search: 8
Additional references identified by
GDG: 4

**A3**

2nd **search:** primary studies
(diagnostic studies)
DATABASES: CINAHL, EMBASE,
MEDLINE, PSYCINFO
Retrieved: 164
Relevant after sifting: 1
From A2 search: 2
Additional references identified
by GDG: 8
INCLUDED: 11
EXCLUDED: 4

**B**

2nd **search:** primary studies
(cohort studies on impairment)
DATABASES: CINAHL,
EMBASE, MEDLINE, PSYCINFO
Retrieved: 2299
Relevant after sifting: 39
Additional references identified
by GDG: 1
INCLUDED: 24
EXCLUDED: 16

**C**

[From initial search]: 1
Additional references identified by
GDG: 11
INCLUDED: 10
EXCLUDED: 2

**D**

[From initial search]: 8
Additional references identified
by GDG: 4
INCLUDED: 10
EXCLUDED: 2

0

0

1

8

Total papers sifted: 10273
Total papers identified by GDG: 48
Total papers quality assessed: 123
Total papers included: 101

427

| Relevant questions | Q2.1 – **Psychological interventions** |
|---|---|
| **Chapter** | 7 Psychological interventions and parent training |
| **Sub-section** | |
| **Topic Group** | TG2 Psychology |
| **Sub-section lead** | |
| **Search strategy** | **Databases:** CENTRAL, CINAHL, EMBASE, MEDLINE, PsycINFO |
| **Existing reviews** | |
| ● **Updated** | |
| ● **Not updated** | |
| **General search filter used** | RCT |
| **Question specific search filter** | |
| **Amendments to filter/search strategy** | |
| **Eligibility criteria** | |
| ● Intervention | ● Family therapy (systemic/psychodynamic, behavioural)<br>● CBT (individual behavioural therapy, individual cognitive therapy)<br>● Environmental manipulation and management |
| ● Comparator | Waiting lists, standard care, other psychological interventions, medication |
| ● Population (including age, gender, etc) | Children, young people and adults with ADHD, ADD, MBD, comorbid ADHD |
| ● Outcomes | Improvement on score of Conners' rating scale (including all variations of this scale and subscales)<br>Improvement on score of ADHD-RS<br>Improvement on score of DuPaul Test<br>Improvement on score of SKAMP Test<br>Improvement on score of SNAP Test<br>Improvement on academic performance<br>Improvement on social skills<br>Reduction of impairment<br>Leaving study early |

| ● Study design | RCT |
|---|---|
| ● Publication status | Published and unpublished (if criteria met) |
| ● Year of study | Any |
| ● Dosage | Any |
| ● Minimum sample size | n > 10 |
| ● Study setting | Any |
| **Additional assessments** | |

| **Relevant questions** | Q2.1 – **Psychological and combined interventions** |
|---|---|
| | When should psychological treatment be initiated? does the waiting for a treatment influence outcome? What is the optimum duration of treatment? What are the long-term consequences of treatment? What approaches can be used to optimise adherence with psychological treatment? |
| **Chapter** | 7 Psychological interventions and parent training 11 Combining and comparing psychological and pharmacological interventions |
| **Sub-section** | |
| **Topic Group** | TG2 Psychology |
| **Sub-section lead** | |
| **Search strategy** | **Databases:** CINAHL, EMBASE, MEDLINE, PsycINFO, CENTRAL |
| **Existing reviews** | |
| ● **Updated** | |
| ● **Not updated** | |
| **General search filter used** | OS, empirical reviews [high spec] RCT |
| **Question specific search filter** | |

| Amendments to filter/search strategy | |
|---|---|
| **Eligibility criteria** | |
| ● Intervention | Combination of medication and psychological intervention with medication alone or psychological intervention alone |
| ● Comparator | |
| ● Population (including age, gender, etc) | Children, young people and adults with ADHD, ADD, MBD, comorbid ADHD |
| ● Outcomes (see Outcomes document for definitions) | Duration, discontinuation of psychological treatment and treatment adherence |
| ● Study design | Observational studies |
| ● Publication status | Published and unpublished (if criteria met) |
| ● Year of study | Any |
| ● Dosage | Any |
| ● Minimum sample size | n > 10 |
| ● Study setting | Any |
| **Additional assessments** | |

| | |
|---|---|
| **Relevant questions** | **Q3.1 – Intervention for carers** |
| **Chapter** | 7 Psychological interventions and parent training |
| **Sub-section** | |
| **Topic Group** | TG2 Psychology |
| **Sub-section lead** | |
| **Search strategy** | **Databases:** CENTRAL, CINAHL, EMBASE, MEDLINE, PsycINFO |
| **Existing reviews** | |

| | |
|---|---|
| ● **Updated** | |
| ● **Not updated** | |
| **General search filter used** | RCT |
| **Question specific search filter** | |
| **Amendments to filter/search strategy** | |
| **Eligibility criteria** | |
| ● Intervention | ● Psychoeducational interventions (advice/information, parental guidance) for carers<br>● Parent effectiveness training<br>● Counselling for carers<br>● CBT for carers |
| ● Comparator | |
| ● Population (including age, gender etc) | Parents of children, young people, and adults with ADHD, ADD, MBD, comorbid ADHD. |
| ● Outcomes | Improvement on score of Conners' rating scale (including all variations of this scale and subscales)<br>Improvement on score of ADHD-RS<br>Improvement on score of DuPaul Test<br>Improvement on score of SKAMP Test<br>Improvement on score of SNAP Test<br>Improvement on social skills<br>Improvement on academic performance<br>Reduction of impairment<br>Leaving study early |
| ● Study design | RCT |
| ● Publication status | Published and unpublished (if criteria met) |
| ● Year of study | Any |
| ● Dosage | Any |
| ● Minimum sample size | n > 10 |
| ● Study setting | Any |
| **Additional assessments** | |

| Relevant questions | Q4.1 – **Pharmacological treatment** (stimulants) |
|---|---|
| **Chapter** | 10 Pharmacological treatment |
| **Sub-section** | Stimulants (methylphenidate, dexamfetamine) |
| **Topic Group** | TG3 Pharma |
| **Sub-section lead** | |
| **Search strategy** | **Databases:** CENTRAL, CINAHL, EMBASE, MEDLINE, PsycINFO |
| **Existing reviews** | |
| ● **Updated** | |
| ● **Not updated** | TA (NICE, 2006b) |
| **General search filter used** | RCT |
| **Question specific search filter** | |
| **Amendments to filter/search strategy** | |
| **Eligibility criteria** | |
| ● Intervention | ● Methylphenidate (including MR preparations)<br>● Dexamfetamine |
| ● Comparator | Waiting lists, placebo; active comparator (head-to-head trials, for example, atomoxetine, TCAs, and so on) |
| ● Population (including age, gender etc) | Children, young people and adults with ADHD, ADD, MBD, comorbid ADHD |
| ● Outcomes | Improvement on score of Conners' rating scale (including all variations of this scale and subscales)<br>Improvement on score of ADHD-RS<br>Improvement on score of DuPaul Test<br>Improvement on score of SKAMP Test<br>Improvement on score of SNAP Test<br>Improvement on academic performance<br>Reduction of impairment<br>Side effects (for example, headache, insomnia, loss of appetite)<br>Leaving the study early |

| • Study design | RCT (efficacy, acceptability, tolerability, adverse events) |
|---|---|
| • Publication status | Published and unpublished (if criteria met) |
| • Year of study | Any |
| • Dosage | Any |
| • Minimum sample size | n > 10 |
| • Study setting | Any |
| **Additional assessments** | |

| **Relevant questions** | Q4.1– **Pharmacological treatment** (atomoxetine) |
|---|---|
| **Chapter** | 10 Pharmacological treatment |
| **Sub-section** | Atomoxetine |
| **Topic Group** | TG3 Pharma |
| **Sub-section lead** | |
| **Search strategy** | **Databases:** CENTRAL, CINAHL, EMBASE, MEDLINE, PsycINFO |
| **Existing reviews** | |
| • **Updated** | |
| • **Not updated** | NICE Report (2000), TA Report (2006) |
| **General search filter used** | RCT |
| **Question specific search filter** | |
| **Amendments to filter/search strategy** | |
| **Eligibility criteria** | |
| • Intervention | • Atomoxetine |
| • Comparator | • Waiting lists, placebo; active comparator (head-to-head trials, for example atomoxetine, TCAs, and so on) |

| | |
|---|---|
| ● Population (including age, gender, etc) | Children, young people and adults with ADHD, ADD, MBD, comorbid ADHD. |
| ● Outcomes | Improvement on score of Conners' rating scale (including all variations of this scale and subscales) Improvement on score of ADHD-RS Improvement on score of DuPaul Test Improvement on score of SKAMP Test Improvement on score of SNAP Test Improvement on academic performance Reduction of impairment Side effects (for example, headache, insomnia, loss of appetite) Leaving the study early |
| ● Study design | RCT (efficacy, acceptability, tolerability, side effects) |
| ● Publication status | Published and unpublished (if criteria met) |
| ● Year of study | Any |
| ● Dosage | Any |
| ● Minimum sample size | n > 10 |
| ● Study setting | Any |
| **Additional assessments** | |

| | |
|---|---|
| **Relevant questions** | Q4.1 – **Pharmacological treatment** (other medication) |
| **Chapter** | 10 Pharmacological treatment |
| **Sub-section** | Other medication |
| **Topic Group** | TG3 Pharma |
| **Sub-section lead** | |
| **Search strategy** | **Databases:** CENTRAL, CINAHL, EMBASE, MEDLINE, PsycINFO |
| **Existing reviews** | |
| ● **Updated** | |
| ● **Not updated** | |

| General search filter used | RCT |
|---|---|
| **Question specific search filter** | |
| **Amendments to filter/search strategy** | |
| **Eligibility criteria** | |
| ● Intervention | ● TCAs<br>● Bupropion<br>● Nicotine (as skin patches)<br>● Atypical antipsychotics<br>● Modafinil<br>● Clonidine |
| ● Comparator | Waiting lists, placebo; active comparator (head-to-head trials, for example atomoxetine, TCAs, and so on) |
| ● Population (including age, gender, etc) | Children, young people and adults with ADHD, ADD, MBD, comorbid ADHD |
| ● Outcomes | Improvement on score of Conners' rating scale (including all variations of this scale and subscales)<br>Improvement on score of ADHD-RS<br>Improvement on score of DuPaul Test<br>Improvement on score of SKAMP Test<br>Improvement on score of SNAP Test<br>Improvement on academic performance<br>Reduction of impairment<br>Side effects (for example, headache, insomnia, loss of appetite)<br>Leaving the study early |
| ● Study design | RCT (efficacy, acceptability, tolerability, side effects) |
| ● Publication status | Published and unpublished (if criteria met) |
| ● Year of study | Any |
| ● Dosage | Any |
| ● Minimum sample size | n > 10 |
| ● Study setting | Any |
| **Additional assessments** | |

| Relevant questions | Q4.2-**First-, second- and third-line treatment**<br>(including 4.2.1: Which drugs should be used as a first-, second- and third-line treatment?<br>How should drug treatment be initiated, dose titrated and effectiveness evaluated?<br>What is the optimum duration of drug treatment?<br>When is discontinuation attempted?<br>What advice is given for discontinuation? |
|---|---|
| **Chapter** | 10 Pharmacological treatment |
| **Sub-section** | |
| **Topic Group** | TG3 Pharma |
| **Sub-section lead** | |
| **Search strategy** | **Databases:** CENTRAL, CINAHL, EMBASE, MEDLINE, PsycINFO |
| **Existing reviews** | |
| ● **Updated** | |
| ● **Not updated** | |
| **General search filter used** | RCT |
| **Question specific search filter** | |
| **Amendments to filter/search strategy** | |
| **Eligibility criteria** | |
| ● Intervention | |
| ● Comparator | Waiting lists, placebo; active comparator (head-to-head trials, for example, atomoxetine, TCAs, and so on) |
| ● Population (including age, gender, etc) | Children, young people and adults with ADHD, ADD, MBD, comorbid ADHD |
| ● Outcomes | Improvement on score of Conners' rating scale (including all variations of this scales and subscales)<br>Improvement on score of ADHD-RS<br>Improvement on score of DuPaul Test<br>Improvement on score of SKAMP Test<br>Improvement on score of SNAP Test |

| | |
|---|---|
| | Improvement on academic performance<br>Reduction of impairment<br>Side effects (for example, headache, insomnia, loss of appetite)<br>Leaving the study early |
| ● Study design | RCTs (efficacy outcomes/acceptability/tolerability/side effects) |
| ● Publication status | Published and unpublished (if criteria met) |
| ● Year of study | Any |
| ● Dosage | Any |
| ● Minimum sample size | $n > 10$ |
| ● Study setting | Any |
| **Additional assessments** | |

| | |
|---|---|
| **Relevant questions** | Q6.1 – **Education interventions** |
| **Chapter** | 8 Interventions for children with ADHD in educational settings |
| **Sub-section** | |
| **Topic Group** | TG4 Education |
| **Sub-section lead** | |
| **Search strategy** | **Databases:** CENTRAL, CINAHL, EMBASE, MEDLINE, PsycINFO, ERIC |
| **Existing reviews** | |
| ● Updated | |
| ● Not updated | |
| **General search filter used** | OS [narrative reviews] |
| **Question specific search filter** | |
| **Amendments to filter/search strategy** | |

| **Eligibility criteria** | |
|---|---|
| ● Intervention | ● School screening<br>● Teacher training on ADHD<br>● Curriculum modification<br>● Classroom management<br>● Remedial teaching<br>● Multi-agency partnership with other schools and other agencies |
| ● Comparator | Standard education, health interventions |
| ● Population (including age, gender, etc) | Children, young people and adults with ADHD, ADD, MBD, comorbid ADHD |
| ● Outcomes | Improvement on score of Conners' rating scale (including all variations of this test and subscales)<br>Improvement on score of ADHD-RS<br>Improvement on score of DuPaul Test<br>Improvement on score of SKAMP Test<br>Improvement on score of SNAP Test<br>Improvement on academic performance<br>Reduction of impairment<br>Reading<br>Mathematics |
| ● Study design | RCT, cluster RCT (efficacy) |
| ● Publication status | Published and unpublished (if criteria met) |
| ● Year of study | Any |
| ● Dosage | Any |
| ● Minimum sample size | n > 10 |
| ● Study setting | Any |
| **Additional assessments** | |

| **Relevant questions** | Q7.1 – **Dietary Interventions** |
|---|---|
| **Chapter** | 9 Dietary interventions |
| **Sub-section** | |
| **Topic Group** | TG5 Dietary |
| **Sub-section lead** | |

| Search strategy | **Databases:** CINAHL, EMBASE, MEDLINE, OLD MEDLINE, PsycINFO |
|---|---|
| **Existing reviews** | |
| ● **Updated** | |
| ● **Not updated** | |
| **General search filter used** | RCT |
| **Question specific search filter** | |
| **Amendments to filter/search strategy** | |
| **Eligibility criteria** | |
| ● Intervention | ● Elimination diets<br>● Supplementation diets |
| ● Comparator | Waiting lists, placebo |
| ● Population (including age, gender, etc) | Children, young people and adults with ADHD, ADD, MBD, comorbid ADHD |
| ● Outcomes | Improvement on score of Conners' rating scale (including all variations of this scale and subscales)<br>Improvement on score of ADHD-RS<br>Improvement on score of DuPaul Test<br>Improvement on score of SKAMP Test<br>Improvement on score of SNAP Test<br>Improvement on academic performance<br>Reduction of impairment<br>Side effects<br>Leaving the study early |
| ● Study design | RCT (efficacy outcomes/acceptability/tolerability/side effects) |
| ● Publication status | Published and unpublished (if criteria met) |
| ● Year of study | Any |
| ● Dosage | Any |
| ● Minimum sample size | n > 10 |
| ● Study setting | Any |
| **Additional assessments** | |

# APPENDIX 8:

# SEARCH STRATEGIES FOR THE IDENTIFICATION OF DIAGNOSTIC STUDIES, CLINICAL STUDIES AND REVIEWS

| **Search:** ADHD – Diagnosis Q1.2, 1.7, 1.8 | |
|---|---|
| **Interface:** OVID | **Databases:** CINAHL, EMBASE, MEDLINE, PSYCINFO |
| **Notes: ER filter modified for more specificity** | |

| | |
|---|---|
| 1 | (attenti$ or disrupt$ or impulsiv$ or inattenti$).sh. |
| 2 | ((attenti$ or disrupt$) adj3 (adolescen$ or adult$ or behav$ or child$ or class or classes or classroom$ or condition$ or difficult$ or disorder$ or learn$ or people or person$ or poor or problem$ or process$ or youngster$)).tw. |
| 3 | disruptive$.tw,it,tm. |
| 4 | impulsiv$.tw. |
| 5 | inattentiv$.tw. |
| 6 | adhd.tw. |
| 7 | addh.tw. |
| 8 | ad hd.tw. |
| 9 | ad??hd.tw. |
| 10 | (attenti$ adj3 deficit$).tw. |
| 11 | hyperactiv$.mp. |
| 12 | (hyper adj1 activ$).tw. |
| 13 | hyperkin$.mp. |
| 14 | (hyper adj1 kin$).tw. |
| 15 | hkd.tw. |
| 16 | overactiv$.tw. not overactive bladder$.ti. |
| 17 | (over adj1 activ$).tw. not overactive bladder$.ti. |

| 18 | (minimal adj1 brain).tw. |
|----|---------------------------|
| 19 | or/1–18 |
| 20 | *"attention deficit and disruptive behavior disorders"/di or attention deficit disorder with hyperactivity/di or *attention deficit disorder/di or *attention deficit hyperactivity disorder/di |
| 21 | exp "sensitivity and specificity"/ |
| 22 | likelihood functions/or maximum likelihood/ |
| 23 | exp diagnostic error/or exp diagnostic errors/ |
| 24 | (area under curve or area under the curve).sh. |
| 25 | (reproducibility of results or reproducibility).sh. |
| 26 | (diagnos$ or differential diagnosis$ or misdiagnos$ or psychodiagnos$).sh. |
| 27 | (sensitivity$ or specificit$).tw. |
| 28 | predictive value$.tw. |
| 29 | likelihood ratio$.tw. |
| 30 | (false adj (negative$ or positive$)).tw. |
| 31 | (valid$ adj3 (adhd or attention deficit$ or hyperkin$ or diagnos$)).tw. |
| 32 | or/20–31 |
| 33 | early diagnosis.sh. |
| 34 | ((earl$ or initial or onset or preclinical or pre clinical) adj3 (detect$ or diagnos$ or distinguish$ or identif$ or intervention$ or recogni$ or therap$ or treat$)).tw. |
| 35 | or/33–34 |
| 36 | ((early or under) adj3 diagnos$).tw. |
| 37 | 19 and (or/32, 35–36) |
| 38 | (clinical study or cohort analysis or correlational studies or cross sectional studies or epidemiologic studies or family study or longitudinal study or nonconcurrent prospective studies or prospective studies or prospective study or retrospective study).sh. |
| 39 | exp case control studies/or exp case control studies/or exp cohort studies/ |
| 40 | (cohort adj (study or studies)).mp. |

| 41 | ((cohort or cross sectional or epidemiologic$ or follow? up or follow up or observational) adj (study or studies)).tw. |
|----|---|
| 42 | (case control or cohort analy$ or cross sectional or longitudinal or retrospective).tw. |
| 43 | case$.pt. |
| 44 | or/38–43 |
| 45 | and/37, 44 |
| 46 | remove duplicates from 45 |
| 47 | (empiric$ and review$).mp,pt,dt. or (data collection or health statistics or health survey$1 or psychological report$1 or report$1 or statistics).sh. |
| 48 | limit 37 to (2260 research methods & experimental design or "0400 empirical study") [Limit not valid in: CINAHL, EMBASE, Ovid MEDLINE(R); records were retained] |
| 49 | limit 37 to (2200 psychometrics & statistics & methodology or 2240 statistics & mathematics) [Limit not valid in: CINAHL, EMBASE, Ovid MEDLINE(R); records were retained] |
| 50 | limit 37 to (report or research or research instrument or research term definition or short survey) [Limit not valid in: CINAHL, EMBASE, Ovid MEDLINE(R), PsycINFO; records were retained] |
| 51 | or/48–50 |
| 52 | 37 and (47 or (51 and review$.mp,pt,dt.)) |
| 53 | remove duplicates from 52 |
| 54 | limit 37 to "0400 empirical study" [Limit not valid in: CINAHL, EMBASE, Ovid MEDLINE(R); records were retained]<br>CINAHL <1982 to September Week 3 2006> (880)<br>EMBASE <1980 to 2006 Week 37> (9543)<br>Ovid MEDLINE(R) <1966 to September Week 2 2006> (11566)<br>PsycINFO <1806 to September Week 3 2006> (2745) |
| 55 | 53 and 54 |
| 56 | from 55 keep 3625–3708 |
| 57 | 37 and (or/47, 56) |
| 58 | remove duplicates from 57 |
| 59 | from 58 keep 1–515 |

| | **Search:** ADHD – Diagnosis Q1.3, 1.4, 1.5, 1.6 | |
|---|---|---|
| **Interface:** OVID | **Databases:** CINAHL, EMBASE, MEDLINE, PSYCINFO | |
| 1 | (attention deficit$ or attention disturbance or disruptive behavior).sh. | |
| 2 | adhd.tw. | |
| 3 | addh.tw. | |
| 4 | ad hd.tw. | |
| 5 | ad??hd.tw. | |
| 6 | ((adult$ or child$) adj2 add$1).tw. | |
| 7 | (attenti$ adj3 deficit$).tw. | |
| 8 | hyperactiv$.mp. | |
| 9 | (hyper adj1 activ$).tw. | |
| 10 | hyperkin$.mp. | |
| 11 | (hyper adj1 kin$).tw. | |
| 12 | hkd.tw. | |
| 13 | (minimal adj1 brain).tw. | |
| 14 | (brain dysfunction and (ritalin or methylphenidate)).mp. | |
| 15 | ((child$ or adult$) adj3 (disrupt$ or attention$ or inattent$ or impulsiv$ or overactiv$)).tw. | |
| 16 | or/1–15 | |
| 17 | comorbid$.mp. | |
| 18 | ((dysfunction$ or function$) adj2 (change$ or executive$ or deficit$ or impair$)).tw. | |
| 19 | (neuropsychopatholog$ or psychopatholog$ or pathophysiolog$).mp. | |
| 20 | prevalen$.mp. and (diagnos$.mp. or di.fs.) | |
| 21 | ((neuropsychological test$ or psychiatric status rating scales or psycho-logical test$ or psychometrics or mental status schedule or mental test or neuropsychological assessment or psychometry or rating scale$ or scales or test$).sh. or (DSM-IV and ICD-10).tw.) and (diagnos$.mp. or di.fs.)) | |
| 22 | "Diagnostic and Statistical Manual"/or "Diagnostic and Statistical Manual of Mental Disorders"/ | |
| 23 | (affective symptoms or behavioral symptoms or clinical feature or symptom or symptoms).sh. | |

| | |
|---|---|
| 24 | attention deficit disorder/ss or attention deficit disorder with hyperactivity/ss or hyperkinesis/ss or hyperkinesia/ss |
| 25 | (attention deficit disorder/di or attention deficit disorder with hyperactivity/di or hyperkinesis/di or hyperkinesia/di) and symptom$.mp. |
| 26 | ((adhd or attention deficit$ or hyperactiv$ or hyperkin$ or detect$ or diagnos$ or identif$ or pattern$ or recogni$ or warning$) adj2 (signs or symptom$)).tw. |
| 27 | (clinical adj (feature$ or characteristic$) adj2 (adhd or attention deficit$ or hyperactiv$ or hyperkines$)).tw. |
| 28 | (symptom$ adj3 (impulsiv$ or inattenti$ or overactiv$)).tw. |
| 29 | or/17–28 |
| 30 | persistence.mp. and (age factors or age of onset or aging).sh. |
| 31 | (persist$ adj3 (adhd or attention deficit$ or hyperactiv$ or hyperkin$ or minimal brain$ or age or aging or adulthood)).tw. |
| 32 | (age$ adj3 (decline$ or less$ or reduc$)).tw. |
| 33 | or/30–32 |
| 34 | attention deficit disorder/rf or attention deficit disorder with hyperactivity/rf or hyperkinesis/rf or hyperkinesia/rf |
| 35 | (prediction or predictive$).sh. |
| 36 | ((predict$ or development$) adj3 (adhd or attention deficit or hyperactiv$ or hyperkin$ or minimal brain)).tw. |
| 37 | (trajector$ adj2 (development$ or symptom$)).tw. |
| 38 | "age of onset".sh. and (rf or di).fs. |
| 39 | or/34–38 |
| 40 | (environment or home environment or social environment or genetic$ or heredity).sh. |
| 41 | ((continuity or change$) adj3 symptom$).tw. |
| 42 | ((environment$ or gene or genes or genetics or heredit$ or heritabl$ or social environment) adj3 (symptom$ or adhd or attention deficit$ or hyperactiv$ or hyperkin$ or minimal brain$)).tw. |
| 43 | or/40–42 |
| 44 | (cognition or cognitive ability or mental performance or neuropsychology or neuropsychological test$ or psychometric$).sh. and di.fs. |

| 45 | ((neurocognitiv$ or neuropsychological$) adj2 (performance$ or measure$ or test$) adj10 diagnos$).tw. |
|----|----|
| 46 | or/44–45 |
| 47 | (familial disease or family or family characteristics or relatives).sh. |
| 48 | (famil$ adj2 (subform$ or subtype$ or antisocial$ or psychopatholog$)).tw. |
| 49 | ((subform$ or subtype$) adj2 (adhd or attention deficit or hyperactiv$ or hyperkin$ or minimal brain)).tw. |
| 50 | or/47–49 |
| 51 | ("Diagnostic and Statistical Manual"/or "Diagnostic and Statistical Manual of Mental Disorders"/) and (validity or validation$ or reproducibility or results).sh. |
| 52 | (dsm-iv adj5 valid$).tw. |
| 53 | or/51–52 |
| 54 | (disease course or genetic heterogeneity or symptom chronology).sh. |
| 55 | ((course adj2 (clinical or disease$ or disorder$ or progressive or longitudinal or naturalistic or recurrent)) or disease progression or symptom chronology).tw. |
| 56 | risk$.mp. or attention deficit disorder/rf or attention deficit disorder with hyperactivity/rf or hyperkinesis/rf or hyperkinesia/rf |
| 57 | or/54–56 |
| 58 | or/33, 39, 43, 46, 50, 53, 57 |
| 59 | (environment$ or genetic$ or genome$ or heredit$ or molecular genetic$ or social environment).sh. |
| 60 | attention deficit disorder/ge or attention deficit disorder with hyperactivity/ge or hyperkinesis/ge or hyperkinesia/ge |
| 61 | ((environment$ or gene or genes or genetic$ or genome$ or heredit$ or heritabl$ or environment$ or sibling$) adj5 (adhd or attention deficit$ or hyperactiv$ or hyperkin$ or minimal brain)).tw. |
| 62 | or/59–61 |
| 63 | exp magnetic resonance imaging/ or exp nuclear magnetic resonance imaging/ |
| 64 | (magnetic resonance imag$ or magneti? transfer imag$ or ((mr or nmr) adj imag$) or mri$1).tw. |

| 65 | (positron-emission tomography or positron emission tomography or tomography, emission-computed).sh. |
|----|---|
| 66 | ((positron adj2 tomograph$) or (pet adj2 scan$)).tw. |
| 67 | exp computer assisted tomography/ or exp tomography, x-ray computed/ |
| 68 | ((comput$ adj2 tomograph$) or cat scan$).tw. |
| 69 | (single photon emission computer tomography or tomography, emission-computed, single-photon).sh. |
| 70 | (single photon emission comput$ tomograph$ or spect$1).tw. |
| 71 | exp electroencephalography/or exp electroencephalogram/ |
| 72 | ((brain adj (activity or wave or electric activit$)) or eeg$1 or electr$ encephalogram).tw. |
| 73 | neuroimag$.mp. |
| 74 | or/63–73 |
| 75 | (familial disease or family or family background or family characteristics or family life or heredity or relatives).sh. |
| 76 | (environment or environmental factor$ or environmental stress or family environment$ or home environment or social environment or environmental exposure).sh. |
| 77 | ((family or families or heredit$ or heritabl$) adj3 (adversity or contribut$ or effect$ or factor$ or influence$)).tw. |
| 78 | (environment$ adj3 (adversity or contribut$ or effect$ or factor$ or influence$)).tw. |
| 79 | (education$ adj3 (adversity or contribut$ or effect$ or factor$ or influence$)).tw. |
| 80 | or/75–79 |
| 81 | or/62, 74, 80 |
| 82 | or/29, 58, 81 |


| **Search: ADHD RCTs** | |
|---|---|
| **Interface:** OVID | **Databases:** MEDLINE, EMBASE, CINAHL, PsycINFO) |
| | **1. *Guideline topic search filter*** |
| 1 | (attenti$ or disrupt$ or impulsiv$ or inattenti$).sh. |

| 2 | ((attenti$ or disrupt$) adj3 (adolescen$ or adult$ or behav$ or child$ or class or classes or classroom$ or condition$ or difficult$ or disorder$ or learn$ or people or person$ or poor or problem$ or process$ or young-ster$)).tw. |
|---|---|
| 3 | disruptive$.tw,it,tm. |
| 4 | impulsiv$.tw. |
| 5 | inattentiv$.tw. |
| 6 | adhd.tw. |
| 7 | addh.tw. |
| 8 | ad hd.tw. |
| 9 | ad??hd.tw. |
| 10 | (attenti$ adj3 deficit$).tw. |
| 11 | hyperactiv$.mp. |
| 12 | (hyper adj1 activ$).tw. |
| 13 | hyperkin$.mp. |
| 14 | (hyper adj1 kin$).tw. |
| 15 | hkd.tw. |
| 16 | overactiv$.tw. not overactive bladder$.ti. |
| 17 | (over adj1 activ$).tw. not overactive bladder$.ti. |
| 18 | (minimal adj1 brain).tw. |
| 19 | or/1–18 |
| | **2. Randomised controlled trial search filter** |
| 20 | exp clinical trials/or exp clinical trial/ or exp controlled clinical trials/ |
| 21 | exp crossover procedure/or exp cross over studies/or exp crossover design/ |
| 22 | exp double blind procedure/ or exp double blind method/or exp double blind studies/or exp single blind procedure/or exp single blind method/or exp single blind studies/ |
| 23 | exp random allocation/or exp randomization/or exp random assignment/or exp random sample/or exp random sampling/ |
| 24 | exp randomized controlled trials/or exp randomized controlled trial/ |
| 25 | (clinical adj2 trial$).tw. |

| 26 | (crossover or cross over).tw. |
|----|-------------------------------|
| 27 | (((single$ or doubl$ or trebl$ or tripl$) adj5 (blind$ or mask$ or dummy)) or (singleblind$ or doubleblind$ or trebleblind$)).tw. |
| 28 | (placebo$ or random$).mp. |
| 29 | (clinical trial$ or random$).pt. or (random$ or clinical control trial).sd. |
| 30 | animals/not (animals/and human$.mp.) |
| 31 | animal$/not (animal$/and human$/) |
| 32 | (animal not (animal and human)).po. |
| 33 | (or/20–29) not (or/30–32) |
| 34 | case study/ |
| 35 | abstract report/ or letter/ |
| 36 | case report.tw. |
| 37 | letter.pt. |
| 38 | historical article.pt. |
| 39 | review$.pt. |
| 40 | 33 not (or/34–39) |
| 41 | and/19, 40 |
| 42 | remove duplicates from 42 |

| **Search: ADHD Systematic reviews** | |
|---|---|
| **Interface:** OVID | **Databases:** MEDLINE, EMBASE, CINAHL, PsycINFO, CDSR, DARE |
| | **1.** *Guideline topic search filter* |
| 1 | (attenti$ or disrupt$ or impulsiv$ or inattenti$).sh. |
| 2 | ((attenti$ or disrupt$) adj3 (adolescen$ or adult$ or behav$ or child$ or class or classes or classroom$ or condition$ or difficult$ or disorder$ or learn$ or people or person$ or poor or problem$ or process$ or youngster$)).tw. |
| 3 | disruptive$.tw,it,tm. |
| 4 | impulsiv$.tw. |

| 5 | inattentiv$.tw. |
|---|---|
| 6 | adhd.tw. |
| 7 | addh.tw. |
| 8 | ad hd.tw. |
| 9 | ad??hd.tw. |
| 10 | (attenti$ adj3 deficit$).tw. |
| 11 | hyperactiv$.mp. |
| 12 | (hyper adj1 activ$).tw. |
| 13 | hyperkin$.mp. |
| 14 | (hyper adj1 kin$).tw. |
| 15 | hkd.tw. |
| 16 | overactiv$.tw. not overactive bladder$.ti. |
| 17 | (over adj1 activ$).tw. not overactive bladder$.ti. |
| 18 | (minimal adj1 brain).tw. |
| 19 | or/1–18 |
| | **2. Systematic review search filter** |
| 20 | exp meta analysis/or exp systematic review/or exp literature review/or exp literature searching/or exp cochrane library/or exp review literature/ |
| 21 | ((systematic or quantitative or methodologic$) adj5 (overview$ or review$)).mp. |
| 22 | (metaanaly$ or meta analy$).mp. |
| 23 | (research adj (review$ or integration)).mp. |
| 24 | reference list$.ab. |
| 25 | bibliograph$.ab. |
| 26 | published studies.ab. |
| 27 | relevant journals.ab. |
| 28 | selection criteria.ab. |
| 29 | (data adj (extraction or synthesis)).ab. |
| 30 | (handsearch$ or ((hand or manual) adj search$)).ti,ab. |
| 31 | (mantel haenszel or peto or dersimonian or der simonian).ti,ab. |

| 32 | (fixed effect$ or random effect$).ti,ab. |
|----|------------------------------------------|
| 33 | ((bids or cochrane or index medicus or isi citation or psyclit or psychlit or scisearch or science citation or (web adj2 science)) and review$).mp. |
| 34 | (systematic$ or meta$).pt. |
| 35 | or/20–34 |
| 36 | and/19, 35 |

# APPENDIX 9:

# CLINICAL STUDY INFORMATION DATABASE

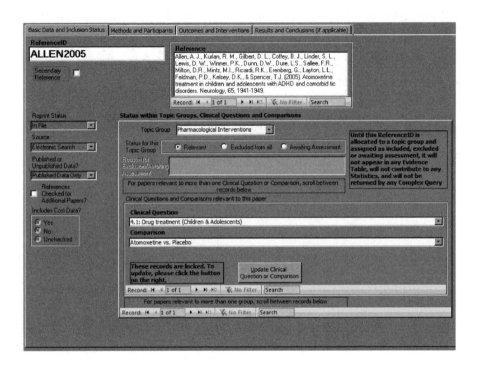

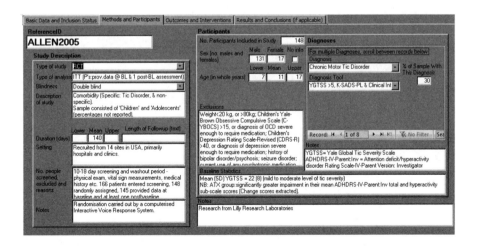

*Appendix 9*

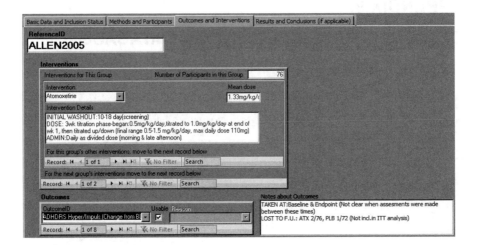

# APPENDIX 10:

# QUALITY CHECKLISTS FOR DIAGNOSTIC STUDIES, CLINICAL STUDIES AND REVIEWS

The methodological quality of each study was evaluated using dimensions adapted from SIGN (SIGN, 2001). SIGN originally adapted its quality criteria from checklists developed in Australia (Liddel *et al.*, 1996). Both groups reportedly undertook extensive development and validation procedures when creating their quality criteria. For information about how to use these checklists please see *The Guidelines Manual*[56] (NICE, 2006c).

| Quality checklist for a systematic review or meta-analysis | | | |
|---|---|---|---|
| Study ID: | | | |
| Guideline topic: | | Key question no: | |
| Checklist completed by: | | | |
| **SECTION 1: INTERNAL VALIDITY** | | | |
| **In a well-conducted systematic review:** | | **In this study this criterion is:** *(Circle one option for each question)* | |
| 1.1 | The study addresses an appropriate and clearly focused question. | Well covered Adequately addressed Poorly addressed | Not addressed Not reported Not applicable |
| 1.2 | A description of the methodology used is included. | Well covered Adequately addressed Poorly addressed | Not addressed Not reported Not applicable |
| 1.3 | The literature search is sufficiently rigorous to identify all the relevant studies. | Well covered Adequately addressed Poorly addressed | Not addressed Not reported Not applicable |
| 1.4 | Study quality is assessed and taken into account. | Well covered Adequately addressed Poorly addressed | Not addressed Not reported Not applicable |
| 1.5 | There are enough similarities between the studies selected to make combining them reasonable. | Well covered Adequately addressed Poorly addressed | Not addressed Not reported Not applicable |

---

[56]Available from: www.nice.org.uk

| SECTION 2: OVERALL ASSESSMENT OF THE STUDY | |
|---|---|
| 2.1 | How well was the study done to minimise bias? *Code* + +, + *or* – | |

| Quality checklist for an RCT | |
|---|---|
| Study ID: | |
| Guideline topic: | Key question no: |
| Checklist completed by: | |

| SECTION 1: INTERNAL VALIDITY | | |
|---|---|---|
| **In a well-conducted RCT study:** | **In this study this criterion is:** *(Circle one option for each question)* | |
| 1.1 | The study addresses an appropriate and clearly focused question. | Well covered    Not addressed<br>Adequately addressed    Not reported<br>Poorly addressed    Not applicable |
| 1.2 | The assignment of subjects to treatment groups is randomised. | Well covered    Not addressed<br>Adequately addressed    Not reported<br>Poorly addressed    Not applicable |
| 1.3 | An adequate concealment method is used. | Well covered    Not addressed<br>Adequately addressed    Not reported<br>Poorly addressed    Not applicable |
| 1.4 | Subjects and investigators are kept 'blind' about treatment allocation. | Well covered    Not addressed<br>Adequately addressed    Not reported<br>Poorly addressed    Not applicable |
| 1.5 | The treatment and control groups are similar at the start of the trial. | Well covered    Not addressed<br>Adequately addressed    Not reported<br>Poorly addressed    Not applicable |
| 1.6 | The only difference between groups is the treatment under investigation. | Well covered    Not addressed<br>Adequately addressed    Not reported<br>Poorly addressed    Not applicable |
| 1.7 | All relevant outcomes are measured in a standard, valid and reliable way. | Well covered    Not addressed<br>Adequately addressed    Not reported<br>Poorly addressed    Not applicable |
| 1.8 | What percentage of the individuals or clusters recruited into each treatment arm of the study dropped out before the study was completed? | |

| 1.9 | All the subjects are analysed in the groups to which they were randomly allocated (often referred to as intention-to-treat analysis). | Well covered<br>Adequately addressed<br>Poorly addressed | Not addressed<br>Not reported<br>Not applicable |
|---|---|---|---|
| 1.10 | Where the study is carried out at more than one site, results are comparable for all sites. | Well covered<br>Adequately addressed<br>Poorly addressed | Not addressed<br>Not reported<br>Not applicable |
| **SECTION 2: OVERALL ASSESSMENT OF THE STUDY** | | | |
| 2.1 | How well was the study done to minimise bias?<br>*Code + + , + or –* | | |

| **Quality checklist for a cohort study**[57] | |
|---|---|
| Study ID:<br>Guideline topic:<br>Checklist completed by: | Relevant questions: |
| **SECTION 1: INTERNAL VALIDITY** | |

| **In a well conducted cohort study:** | | **In this study the criterion is:** (*Circle one option for each question*) | |
|---|---|---|---|
| 1.1 | The study addresses an appropriate and clearly focused question. | Well covered<br>Adequately addressed<br>Poorly addressed | Not addressed<br>Not reported<br>Not applicable |
| SELECTION OF SUBJECTS | | | |
| 1.2 | The two groups being studied are selected from source populations that are comparable in all respects other than the factor under investigation. | Well covered<br>Adequately addressed<br>Poorly addressed | Not addressed<br>Not reported<br>Not applicable |
| 1.3 | The study indicates how many of the people asked to take part did so, in each of the groups being studied. | Well covered<br>Adequately addressed<br>Poorly addressed | Not addressed<br>Not reported<br>Not applicable |

[57]A cohort study can be defined as a retrospective or prospective follow-up study. Groups of individuals are defined on the basis of the presence or absence of exposure to a suspected risk factor or intervention. This checklist is not appropriate for assessing uncontrolled studies (for example, a case series where there is no comparison [control] group of patients).

| 1.4 | The likelihood that some eligible subjects might have the outcome at the time of enrolment is assessed and taken into account in the analysis. | Well covered Adequately addressed Poorly addressed | Not addressed Not reported Not applicable |
|---|---|---|---|
| 1.5 | What percentage of individuals or clusters recruited into each arm of the study dropped out before the study was completed? | | |
| 1.6 | Comparison is made between full participants and those lost to follow-up, by exposure status. | Well covered Adequately addressed Poorly addressed | Not addressed Not reported Not applicable |
| ASSESSMENT | | | |
| 1.7 | The outcomes are clearly defined. | Well covered Adequately addressed Poorly addressed | Not addressed Not reported Not applicable |
| 1.8 | The assessment of outcome is made blind to exposure status. | Well covered Adequately addressed Poorly addressed | Not addressed Not reported Not applicable |
| 1.9 | Where blinding was not possible, there is some recognition that knowledge of exposure status could have influenced the assessment of outcome. | Well covered Adequately addressed Poorly addressed | Not addressed Not reported Not applicable |
| 1.10 | The measure of assessment of exposure is reliable. | Well covered Adequately addressed Poorly addressed | Not addressed Not reported Not applicable |
| 1.11 | Evidence from other sources is used to demonstrate that the method of outcome assessment is valid and reliable. | Well covered Adequately addressed Poorly addressed | Not addressed Not reported Not applicable |
| 1.12 | Exposure level or prognostic factor is assessed more than once. | Well covered Adequately addressed Poorly addressed | Not addressed Not reported Not applicable |
| CONFOUNDING | | | |
| 1.13 | The main potential confounders are identified and taken into account in the design and analysis. | Well covered Adequately addressed Poorly addressed | Not addressed Not reported Not applicable |

| STATISTICAL ANALYSIS | |
|---|---|
| 1.14 | Have confidence intervals been provided? | |

## SECTION 2: OVERALL ASSESSMENT OF THE STUDY

| 2.1 | How well was the study done to minimise the risk of bias or confounding, and to establish a causal relationship between exposure and effect? *Code + + , + or –* | |
|---|---|---|

| **Quality checklist for an RCT** | |
|---|---|
| Study ID | |
| Guideline topic | Key question no: |
| Checklist completed by: | |

## SECTION 1: INTERNAL VALIDITY

| **In a well conducted diagnostic study:** | | **In this study the criterion is:** (*Circle one option for each question*) | |
|---|---|---|---|
| 1.1 | The nature of the test being studied is clearly specified. | Well covered  Adequately addressed  Poorly addressed | Not addressed  Not reported  Not applicable |
| 1.2 | The test is compared with an appropriate gold standard. | Well covered  Adequately addressed  Poorly addressed | Not addressed  Not reported  Not applicable |
| 1.3 | Where no gold standard exists, a validated reference standard is used as a comparator. | Well covered  Adequately addressed  Poorly addressed | Not addressed  Not reported  Not applicable |
| 1.4 | Patients for testing are selected either as a consecutive series or randomly, from a clearly defined study population. | Well covered  Adequately addressed  Poorly addressed | Not addressed  Not reported  Not applicable |
| 1.5 | The test and gold standard are measured independently ('blind') of each other. | Well covered  Adequately addressed  Poorly addressed | Not addressed  Not reported  Not applicable |

| 1.6 | The test and gold standard are applied as close together in time as possible. | Well covered | Not addressed |
| | | Adequately addressed | Not reported |
| | | Poorly addressed | Not applicable |
| 1.7 | Results are reported for all patients who are entered into the study. | Well covered | Not addressed |
| | | Adequately addressed | Not reported |
| | | Poorly addressed | Not applicable |
| ASSESSMENT | | | |
| 1.8 | A pre-diagnosis is made and reported. | Well covered | Not addressed |
| | | Adequately addressed | Not reported |
| | | Poorly addressed | Not applicable |
| **SECTION 2: OVERALL ASSESSMENT OF THE STUDY** | | | |
| 2.1 | How reliable are the conclusions of this study? *Code + + , + or −* | | |
| 2.2 | Is the spectrum of patients assessed in this study comparable with the patient group targeted by this guideline in terms of the proportion with the disease, or the proportion with severe versus mild disease? | | |

# APPENDIX 11:

# SEARCH STRATEGIES FOR THE IDENTIFICATION OF HEALTH ECONOMICS EVIDENCE

Search strategies for the identification of health economics and quality-of-life studies.
1  *General search filters (see Appendix 8)*
2  *Health economics and quality-of-life search filters*

## MEDLINE, EMBASE, PsycINFO, CINAHL – OVID INTERFACE

1  exp "costs and cost analysis"/or "health care costs"/
2  exp health resource allocation/or exp health resource utilization/
3  exp economics/or exp economic aspect/or exp health economics/
4  exp value of life/
5  (burden adj5 (disease or illness)).tw.
6  (cost$ or economic$ or expenditure$ or price$1 or pricing or pharmacoeconomic$).tw.
7  (budget$ or fiscal or funding or financial or finance$).tw.
8  (resource adj5 (allocation$ or utilit$)).tw.
9  or/1–8
10  (value adj5 money).tw.
11  exp quality of life/
12  (quality$ adj5 (life or survival)).tw.
13  (health status or QOL or well being or wellbeing).tw.
14  or/9–13

Details of additional searches undertaken to support the development of this guideline are available on request.

# APPENDIX 12:

# QUALITY CHECKLIST FOR FULL ECONOMIC EVALUATIONS

**Author:**                    **Date:**

Title:

| | Study design | Yes | No | NA |
|---|---|---|---|---|
| 1 | The research question is stated | ❑ | ❑ | |
| 2 | The viewpoint(s) of the analysis are clearly stated | ❑ | ❑ | |
| 3 | The alternatives being compared are relevant | ❑ | ❑ | |
| 4 | The rationale for choosing the alternative programmes or interventions compared is stated | ❑ | ❑ | |
| 5 | The alternatives being compared are clearly described | ❑ | ❑ | |
| 6 | The form of economic evaluation used is justified in relation to the question addressed | ❑ | ❑ | |
| | **Data collection** | | | |
| 1 | The source of effectiveness data used is stated | ❑ | ❑ | |
| 2 | Details of the design and results of the effectiveness study are given | ❑ | ❑ | ❑ |
| 3 | The primary outcome measure(s) for the economic evaluation are clearly stated | ❑ | ❑ | |
| 4 | Methods to value health states and other benefits are stated | ❑ | ❑ | |
| 5 | Details of the subjects from whom valuations were obtained are given | ❑ | ❑ | |
| 6 | Indirect costs (if included) are reported separately | ❑ | ❑ | ❑ |
| 7 | Quantities of resources are reported separately from their unit costs | ❑ | ❑ | |
| 8 | Methods for the estimation of quantities and unit costs are described | ❑ | ❑ | |

| 9 | Currency and price data are recorded | ❏ | ❏ | |
|---|---|---|---|---|
| 10 | Details of currency of price adjustments for inflation or currency conversion are given | ❏ | ❏ | ❏ |
| 11 | Details of any models used are given | ❏ | ❏ | ❏ |
| 12 | The choice of model used and the key parameters on which it is based are justified | ❏ | ❏ | ❏ |
| | **Analysis and interpretation of results** | | | |
| 1 | Time horizon of costs and benefits is stated | ❏ | ❏ | |
| 2 | The discount rate(s) is stated | ❏ | ❏ | ❏ |
| 3 | The choice of rate(s) is justified | ❏ | ❏ | ❏ |
| 4 | An explanation is given if costs or benefits are not discounted | ❏ | ❏ | ❏ |
| 5 | Details of statistical tests and confidence intervals are given for stochastic data | ❏ | ❏ | ❏ |
| 6 | The approach to sensitivity analysis is given | ❏ | ❏ | |
| 7 | The choice of variables for sensitivity analysis is given | ❏ | ❏ | |
| 8 | The ranges over which the variables are varied are stated | ❏ | ❏ | |
| 9 | Relevant alternatives are compared | ❏ | ❏ | |
| 10 | Incremental analysis is reported | ❏ | ❏ | ❏ |
| 11 | Major outcomes are presented in a disaggregated as well as aggregated form | ❏ | ❏ | |
| 12 | The answer to the study question is given | ❏ | ❏ | |
| 13 | Conclusions follow from the data reported | ❏ | ❏ | |
| 14 | Conclusions are accompanied by the appropriate caveats | ❏ | ❏ | |

# APPENDIX 13:
# DATA EXTRACTION FORM FOR
# ECONOMIC STUDIES

**Reviewer:**                                               **Date of Review:**

**Authors:**

**Publication Date:**

**Title:**

**Country:**

**Language:**

**Economic study design:**

❑ CEA          ❑ CCA

❑ CBA          ❑ CA

❑ CUA

❑ CMA

**Modelling:**

❑ No                                          ❑ Yes

**Source of data for effect size measure(s):**

❑ Meta-analysis

❑ RCT

❑ Quasi experimental study

❑ Cohort study

❑ Mirror image (before-after) study

❑ Expert opinion

Comments:_____

**Primary outcome measure(s) (please list):**

_____

**Interventions compared (please describe):**

Treatment:_____

Comparator:_____

**Setting (please describe):**

_____

_____

**Patient population characteristics (please describe):**

_____

_____

_____

**Perspective of analysis:**

❑  Societal                                ❑  Other: _____

❑  Patient and family

❑  Healthcare system

❑  Healthcare provider

❑  Third-party payer

**Time frame of analysis:** _____

**Cost data:**

❑  Primary                                ❑  Secondary

If secondary please specify: _____

**Costs included:**

Direct medical                Direct non-medical        Lost productivity

❑ direct treatment          ❑ social care               ❑ income forgone due
❑ inpatient                    ❑ social benefits              to illness
❑ outpatient                   ❑ travel costs              ❑ income forgone due to
❑ day care                     ❑ caregiver                    death
❑ community health care        out-of-pocket           ❑ income forgone by
❑ medication                   ❑ criminal justice             caregiver
                               ❑ training of staff

Or

❑ staff
❑ medication

❑ consumables
❑ overhead
❑ capital equipment
❑ real estate                    Others:_____

**Currency:**_____        **Year of costing:** _____

**Was discounting used?**

❑ Yes, for benefits and costs        ❑ Yes, but only for costs        ❑ No

Discount rate used for costs:_____

Discount rate used for benefits: _____

**Result(s):**

_____
_____
_____
_____

**Comments, limitations of the study:**

_____
_____
_____

Quality checklist score (Yes/NA/All): ....../....../......

# APPENDIX 14:

# EVIDENCE TABLES FOR ECONOMIC STUDIES

| Study and country | Intervention details | Study population / Study design / Data sources | Study type | Costs: description and values / Outcomes: description and values | Results: Cost effectiveness | Comments / Internal validity (Yes/No/NA) |
|---|---|---|---|---|---|---|
| Donnelly et al., 2004<br><br>Australia | Interventions: Methylphenidate Dexamfetamine<br><br>Comparator: Standard practice (contact with health services but no medication) | Australian children aged 4–17 years who seek care for ADHD in 2000 but do not receive stimulants (N = 21,000)<br><br>Decision-analytic modelling<br><br>Source of clinical effectiveness data: meta-analysis of RCTs<br><br>Source of resource use and measure of severity of ADHD: National Survey of Mental Health and Wellbeing<br><br>Source of unit costs: national sources | Cost-utility analysis | Costs: healthcare costs<br>● Drug acquisition costs<br>● Healthcare professional contacts (GPs, paediatricians, psychiatrists)<br><br>Mean incremental cost versus standard practice (N = 21,000):<br>Methylphenidate: $1.7million<br>Dexamfetamine: $7million<br><br>Primary outcome: DALYs averted<br><br>Mean % of years lived with disability avoided with intervention versus standard practice (N = 21,000):<br>Methylphenidate: 25<br>Dexamfetamine: 23 | Methylphenidate versus standard practice: $15,000/ DALY saved (95% CI: $9,100 to $22,000)<br><br>Dexamfetamine versus standard practice: $4,100/ DALY saved (95% CI: Dexamfetamine dominant to $14,000)<br><br>Dexamfetamine dominated methylphenidate (equally effective but cheaper) | Perspective: health-care sector (overall government and patient)<br><br>Currency: Aus $<br><br>Cost year: 2000 DALYs generated using previously published disability weights and the 'survey severity method'<br><br>Time horizon: 1 year Discounting: not needed<br><br>Internal validity: 25/4/6 |

| | Intervention/Comparator | Type of analysis | Costs and outcomes | Results | Other details |
|---|---|---|---|---|---|
| Gilmore & Milne, 2001 UK | Intervention: Methylphenidate<br><br>Comparator: No treatment (placebo)<br><br>Children aged 6–12 years with hyperkinetic disorder<br><br>Decision-analytic modelling<br><br>Source of clinical effectiveness data: literature review<br><br>Resource use estimates: expert opinion<br><br>Source of unit costs: national sources and local trust tariffs | Cost-utility analysis | Costs: healthcare costs<br>• Drug acquisition costs<br>• Outpatient clinic costs<br><br>Mean cost per 100 children:<br>Methylphenidate: £51,930<br>Placebo: 0<br><br>Primary outcome: QALYs<br>Mean QALYs per 100 children:<br>Methylphenidate: 94.06<br>Placebo: 88.4 | Methylphenidate versus placebo:<br>£9,177/QALY<br><br>Range of ICER in sensitivity analysis:<br>from £5,782 to £29,049/QALY | Perspective: NHS<br>Currency: UK £<br>Cost year: 1997<br>QALYs generated using the IHRQL<br>Time horizon: 1 year<br>Discounting: not needed<br>Internal validity: 28/1/6 |
| King et al., 2006 UK | Interventions:<br>Methylphenidate-IR<br>Methylphenidate-MR-8 hours<br>Methylphenidate-MR-12 hours<br>Atomoxetine<br>Dexamfetamine<br>Plus all the above<br><br>Children aged 6 years with ADHD<br><br>Decision-analytic modelling<br><br>Source of clinical effectiveness data: systematic literature review | Cost-utility analysis | Costs: healthcare costs<br>• Drug acquisition costs<br>• Healthcare professional contacts (psychiatrists, paediatricians, GPs)<br>• Laboratory testing<br><br>Mean cost per child:<br>Active treatment sequences: ranging from £1,098 | Analysis including sequences of medication alone plus no treatment:<br>Dexamfetamine-[methylphenidate-IR]-atomoxetine was dominant (remained in most scenarios explored) | Perspective: NHS and Personal Social Services<br>Currency: UK £<br>Cost year: 2003<br>QALYs based on EQ-5D questionnaires (Coghill et al., 2004)<br>Time horizon: 1 year (secondary analysis: |

Continued

| Study and country | Intervention details | Study population Study design Data sources | Study type | Costs: description and values Outcomes: description and values | Results: Cost effectiveness | Comments Internal validity (Yes/No/NA) |
|---|---|---|---|---|---|---|
| | medications combined with behavioural therapy<br><br>Comparator: No treatment (placebo)<br><br>Strategies assessed: 37 strategies in total, consisting of 18 possible sequences of three active treatments, 18 respective sequences of combination thera-pies, plus no treatment | and meta-analysis; mixed treatment comparison model<br><br>Source of resource use estimates: expert opinion<br><br>Source of unit costs: national sources | | (Dexamfetamine-[methylphenidate-IR]-atomoxetine) to £1,563 (atomoxetine-[methylphenidate-MR-12 hours]-dexamfetamine) No treatment: £1,223<br><br>Primary outcome: QALYs<br><br>Mean QALYs per child: Active treatment sequences: ranging from 0.8273 ([methylphenidate-MR-8hrs]-atomoxetine-dexamfetamine) to 0.8289 (dexamfetamine-[methylphenidate-IR]-atomoxetine) No treatment: 0.7727 | Probabilistic analysis: Dexamfetamine-[methylphenidate-IR]-atomoxetine most likely cost-effective option for WTP between 0 and £60,000/QALY<br><br>Sub-analysis including combination strategies: all therapies except two were ruled out by dominance; of the two remaining: Combination (dexamfetamine-atomoxetine-[methylphenidate-MR-8 hours]) versus dexamfetamine-[methylphenidate-IR]-atomoxetine: £1,241,570/QALY | 12 years)<br>Discounting: only in secondary analysis, 6% in costs and 1.5% in benefits; not needed in the primary analysis<br>Internal validity: 26/4/5 |

| Lord & Paisley, 2000 UK | Intervention: Combination therapy: Methylphenidate and behavioural therapy<br><br>Comparator: Behavioural therapy | Children with ADHD<br><br>Decision-analytic modelling<br><br>Source of clinical effectiveness data: the MTA study<br><br>Source of resource use estimates: expert opinion<br><br>Source of unit costs: national sources | Cost-effectiveness analysis | Costs: healthcare costs<br>• Drug acquisition costs<br>• Costs of pharmacotherapist (Behavioural therapy costs omitted – common in two arms)<br><br>Incremental cost of combo versus behavioural therapy: £750<br><br>Primary outcome: SMD in the SNAP-IV score<br><br>SMD of combo versus behavioural therapy: 0.47 | Combination versus behavioural therapy: £1,596/SMD<br><br>Range of ICER in sensitivity analysis: from £694 to £4,545/SMD | Perspective: NHS<br>Currency: UK £<br>Cost year: 1999<br>Time horizon: 14 months<br>Discounting: not needed<br>Internal validity: 26/1/8 |
| The MTA Co-operative study<br><br>Jensen et al., 2005<br>Foster et al., 2007<br><br>US | Intervention: Medication management<br>Intensive behavioural treatment<br>Combination therapy<br><br>Comparator: Community care, including some medication | Children aged 7–9.9 years with ADHD combined type (ADHD-all)<br><br>Source of clinical effectiveness and resource use data: six-site RCT (N = 579)<br><br>Source of unit costs: national sources | Cost-effectiveness analysis | Costs: healthcare costs<br>• Drug acquisition costs<br>• Healthcare professional contacts (psychiatrists, psychologists, paediatricians)<br><br>Teacher and teachers' aides costs<br><br>Mean cost per child (ADHD-all): Medication management: $1,180; intensive behavioural | Jensen et al.:<br>ADHD-all:<br>BT dominated by medication management versus community care: $360 per normalised child<br><br>Combination therapy versus medication management: $55,253 per normalised child | Perspective: Third party payer<br>Currency: US$<br>Cost year: 2000<br>Time horizon: 14 months<br>Discounting: not needed<br>Internal validity: 22/4/9 |

*Continued*

| Study and country | Intervention details | Study population<br>Study design<br>Data sources | Study type | Costs: description and values<br>Outcomes: description and values | Results:<br>Cost effectiveness | Comments<br>Internal validity (Yes/No/NA) |
|---|---|---|---|---|---|---|
| | | | | treatment: $6,988; combination therapy: $8,827; community care: $1,071<br><br>Primary outcome:<br>Jensen et al. (2005): proportion of 'normalised' children; normalisation defined by a score 0 or 1 on the SNAP scale<br><br>Proportion of normalised children in ADHD-all: Medication management: 56%; intensive behavioural treatment: 34%; combination therapy: 68%; community care: 25%<br><br>Foster et al. (2007): change on CIS ES<br><br>Mean change on CIS ES (per child with pure ADHD without coexisting conditions): Medication management: −0.92; intensive behavioural treatment: −0.70; combination therapy: −0.86; community care: −0.60 | Foster et al. (2007): Results presented as CEACs for ADHD-all and ADHD with and without coexisting conditions<br><br>ADHD-all:<br>Medication management cost effective at WTP up to roughly $55,000 per CIS ES; at higher WTP, combination therapy cost effective<br><br>Pure ADHD:<br>Medication management cost effective at any WTP<br><br>ADHD-internalising disorder:<br>Medication management cost effective at low WTP; intensive behavioural | |

470

| Study | Intervention/Comparator | Study type | Patients/Model | Costs | Results | Perspective |
|---|---|---|---|---|---|---|
| | | | | | treatment cost effective at higher WTP ADHD-externalising disorder: Medication management cost effective at low WTP; combination therapy cost effective at higher WTP ADHD-both internalising and externalising disorders: Medication management cost effective at low WTP; results unclear at high WTP | |
| Narayan & Hay, 2004 US | Intervention: Methylphenidate-IR Amphetamine/ dexamfetamine mixed salts Comparator: No treatment | Males aged 9 years, weighing 28 kg, with uncomplicated ADHD Decision-analytic modelling Source of clinical effectiveness data: | Cost-utility analysis | Costs: healthcare costs (drugs, outpatient visits, laboratory tests), school administration costs, out-of-pocket expenses Mean cost per child: Methylphenidate-IR: $3,053; amphetamine/dexamfetamine: | Methylphenidate dominated by amphetamine/dexa mfetamine Amphetamine/ dexamfetamine versus no treatment: $21,957/QALY | Perspective: stated as societal but indirect costs not included Currency: US$ Cost year: 2003 QALYs generated using the IHRQL Time horizon: 1 year |

*Continued*

| Study and country | Intervention details | Study population Study design Data sources | Study type | Costs: description and values Outcomes: description and values | Results: Cost effectiveness | Comments Internal validity (Yes/No/NA) |
|---|---|---|---|---|---|---|
| | | literature review Source of costs: literature review and national sources | | $3,000 No treatment: $994 Primary outcome: QALYs Mean QALYs per child: Methylphenidate-IR: 0.838; amphetamine/dexamfetamine: 0.889 No treatment: 0.798 | One-way sensitivity analysis: compliance is the major driver of the results | Discounting: not needed Internal validity: 23/6/6 |
| Zupancic et al., 1998 Canada | Intervention: Methylphenidate Dexamfetamine Pemoline Psychological therapy Combination of methylphenidate and psychological therapy Comparator: No active treatment | Males aged 9 years, weighing 28 kg, with ADHD Decision-analytic modelling Source of clinical effectiveness data: systematic literature review and meta-analysis Source of resource use estimates: published survey and expert opinion Source of unit costs: national sources | Cost-effectiveness analysis | Costs: direct healthcare costs • Drug acquisition costs • Laboratory testing costs • Healthcare professional contacts (GPs, paediatricians, psychiatrists, psychologists) • Costs of parent and teacher training • Cost of toxic hepatitis caused by pemoline Mean cost per child: No active treatment: $128; methylphenidate: $559; dexamfetamine: $566; pemoline: $829; psychological therapy: £1,946; combination: $2,505 | Methylphenidate dominated all strategies except pemoline; result remained through most sensitivity analyses Methylphenidate versus no treatment: $64 per point change in CTRS score Pemoline versus methylphenidate: $246 per unit change in CTRS score | Perspective: Third party payer (ministry of health) Currency: Can$ Cost year: 1997 Time horizon: 1 year Discounting: not needed Internal validity: 27/0/8 |

Primary outcome: Change in the CTRS

Mean change in CTRS score per child:

No active treatment: 0; methylphenidate: 6.7; dexamfetamine: 4.7; pemoline: 7.8; psychological therapy: 0.3; combination: 3.8

# APPENDIX 15:

# FOCUS GROUP STUDY OF CHILDREN

# AND YOUNG PEOPLE'S EXPERIENCE

# OF PSYCHOSTIMULANT MEDICATION

**Perceptions, knowledge and attitudes towards psychostimulant stimulant medication for ADHD: a focus group study of children and young people diagnosed with ADHD**

Dr Ilina Singh (IS)
London School of Economics and Political Science

Sinead Keenan
London School of Economics and Political Science

Dr Alex Mears
Healthcare Commission

7 December 2007

## INTRODUCTION

Stimulant medication is a widespread and generally supported treatment for ADHD. While the benefits are well recognised, so are the negative side effects (Kutcher *et al.*, 2004; DuPaul & Barkley, 1990)[58]. In addition to understanding the clinical and cost-effectiveness aspects of the use of these interventions, an important function of developing this guideline is capturing the voice of the service user; this is particularly pertinent where the user is a young person.

In order to capture a sufficient breadth of context and depth of understanding it was decided to use a qualitative methodology, the focus group. The following sections contain an in-depth consideration of the use of this methodology with young people as participants, a comparison of quantitative and qualitative methodologies, a review of the little literature available on young people's experience of medication for ADHD, supplemented by a broader consideration of young people's experiences of medication for other conditions.

It is important to understand that the current research investigated the perceptions, knowledge of and attitude to stimulant medication for ADHD as a primary focus, rather than a broader consideration of the diagnostic process and use of other interventions.

---

[58]References for this study can be found at the end of this appendix.

The latter are peripherally considered, however, both in the following review of literature and in the experimental phase.

## Using qualitative research methods in young people

The use of qualitative methods with young people has been recognised as a valuable route to a closer understanding of children's perspectives of their illness experience (Woodgate, 2000). These methods tend to yield information that is more of a reflection of the perspectives of the child participants, rather than those of the adult researchers (Woodgate, 2000). There are, however, considerations attached to the use of these techniques in young people, over and above those inherent with this kind of data collection. Curtin (2001) highlights the need to examine perceptions of children's competence, consider the inequality of power between the child and adult participants and bridge the generational differences in communication styles. There is also a need to consider the reconciliation between the requirements of the sponsors of the research and the ideals of participation (Hill *et al.*, 1996). Ireland and Holloway (1996) also highlight the asymmetrical relationship between researcher and participants and they consider the difficulties relating to access to participants, as well as ethical and developmental issues. They highlight the requirement for adequate safeguards and an awareness of the potential hazards. Kortesluoma and colleagues (2003) assert that there is very little guidance available for conducting this kind of research; the empirical and conceptual foundation for child interviewing is not very clear. The method chosen should suit both the purpose and context.

Taken together, the literature forms a narrative that has a clear message: extra care is required both in the design and execution of data collection methods to ensure that information gathered is robust and usable and that all ethical considerations relating to the vulnerable participant group are met. Much of what has been written describes the potential hazards around interviewing young people. While our chosen focus group methodology shares many of these, some are lessened (that is, the power inequality), although there are others that must be taken into consideration which are extensions of generic focus group issues. These are not considered in the literature, so have been taken into account by the research team through extrapolation of knowledge from both arenas.

In order to ensure that competing needs of the research sponsors and ethical consideration were reconciled, our research proposal was reviewed by the GDG, a nationally sanctioned ethics committee and local research and development committees. The research team undertaking the focus groups were experienced both in qualitative methodologies and working with young people, and carefully researched the issues described above prior to data collection.

## Young people's experience of stimulant medication

As highlighted above, the importance of the service user's voice has been recognised in the methodology for this guideline. It is important, when preparing for a focus group, to understand whatever previous research has contributed to the knowledge of the subject area, to give a structure to the issues to be considered, and to identify what gaps in knowledge exist to give focus to the investigation.

As Kendall and colleagues (2003) have pointed out: 'rarely are children's and adolescents' perspectives heard in regard to ADHD'. In recognition of the paucity of research in this field, Kendall and colleagues (2003) collected qualitative data from 39 children and young people with a diagnosis of ADHD regarding their perceptions and experiences of living with the disorder. Their findings showed that taking pills was a common theme. Both positive and negative aspects of pill-taking were mentioned. For example, many of the children spoke of how much the medication helped them in terms of controlling their hyperactivity, increasing their concentration, improving their school grades and helping them to be better behaved. When children were asked what helped the most with managing their ADHD, the majority reported that it was the medicine.

Participants also mentioned negative aspects of pill-taking, for example pills tasting bad and side effects including stomach aches and headaches. Significantly, what was of more concern to the participants was the stigma associated with taking pills to manage their behaviour. Children mentioned not wanting anybody to know that they took pills for fear of being laughed at. A number of participants also talked about not wanting to take medication because they did not like the change it made in them. According to one participant: 'I don't like it. I just want to be myself. My Mom makes me take it so I can focus… but I just want to be myself'. Other comments included: 'It just like changes me… it makes me awful, like this way… It's like, I don't like to play that much anymore' and 'I don't take [Ritalin] anymore. I didn't like how I felt on it. I felt real depressed on it.'

Recent research has investigated potentially mitigating factors. Meaux and colleagues (2006) conducted qualitative interviews to explore the factors contributing to whether or not children and young people continue to use prescription stimulant medications as they progress through developmental stages. Although this research was conducted with college students (n = 15), their reflections on taking medications as children are revealing.

The data revealed a 'trade-off' between the positive and negative effects of the medication. Participants unanimously confirmed that stimulant medications improved their concentration and focus. The greatest benefits mentioned by participants were being able to study longer, completing more school work and improving reading comprehension. However, all of the participants described negative physiological and psychological side effects of stimulant medication. Several felt the medication made them less sociable: 'It made me feel like I didn't have friends. I didn't ever really play that much'. Others described medication as 'taking away from the person I am'. Interestingly, participants who were diagnosed with ADHD later and began taking stimulant medications later were more positive and insightful in their perception of general social effects than those who were diagnosed in early elementary school.

Talking about their experiences and feelings about having to take medication during the school day evoked strong emotions. The sense of stigma was reiterated in this study, with most participants describing the frustration, anger, sadness and embarrassment regarding having to leave their classroom to take medication. The authors comment how medication may in fact make children with ADHD more aware of their differences and difficulties, leading to decreased initiative and feelings of self-worth. In some cases the feeling of being different eventually led them to stop taking their medication.

While participants who were diagnosed in elementary school seemed to have their identity defined by ADHD and viewed medication as 'changing who they were', participants who were diagnosed later described themselves as having 'strong person-alities' and viewed medication as a means to manage the challenges of ADHD. This comparison should be treated with caution however given the limited sample size. Meaux and colleagues (2006) conclude that higher levels of education about prescrip-tion medication and more careful management are required to reduce side effects and minimise the risks of misuse.

The 'trade-off' between the positive and negative dimensions of stimulant medications has also been echoed in other studies. Of 102 participants surveyed, Efron and colleagues (1998) found that most children in their study viewed medica-tion effects favourably, although a substantial proportion experienced their medication adversely. Side effects were found to be the main determinant of children's perceptions of negative impact. In a study of mother and child perceptions of stimulant medica-tion, McNeal and colleagues (2000) found that mothers perceived the medication to be more beneficial than did the children. It is worth noting that children's views about the benefits of medication became more positive as their concern about the problems associated with the condition increased.

One other piece of research directly gathered data on young people's knowledge of and attitude to stimulant medication. This study, conducted by Baxley and colleagues in 1978, is concerned with the views of participants with 'hyperactive child syndrome' (a diagnostic category preceding ADHD). The researchers found that the young people were generally knowledgeable about their medication, yet had a mixed attitude to having to take it and associated not taking it with certain negative consequences. Many of the issues raised in this study and those outlined above are explored further in the current research.

## Self-perception in young people with ADHD

A number of papers consider the issue of self-perception among hyperactive children from differing perspectives. While this is not directly relevant to our methodology, it provides valuable background about young people with ADHD. What follows is a chronology of this research.

Hoza and colleagues (1993) found that there was no difference between young people with ADHD and those without in comparisons of self-perceived competence and global self-worth (when internalising symptomatology was taken into account). Furthermore, they found that while the ADHD-diagnosed children showed higher scores on the Children's Depression Inventory, this difference was not significant when behaviour, school and social problems were excluded. Self-perceptions may be used to mediate performance in challenging academic and social situations. In another study, Dumas and Pelletier (1999) showed that children with ADHD perceive themselves as less competent in all areas of self-perception tested (scholastic competence, social acceptance, behavioural conduct) apart from athletic competence. This would seem to directly contradict Hoza and colleagues' findings 6 years earlier.

Krueger and Kendall (2001) found that the sense of self of a young person diagnosed with ADHD is distorted, and that the development of self has been disrupted because of the neurobiology of the ADHD and the environmental factors associated with the parenting of a difficult child. Significantly, it was found that young people defined themselves in terms of their ADHD traits and symptoms and did not perceive themselves as being distinct from the disorder. In other words, their experience of ADHD was intrinsically related to their identity. Therapeutic interventions to address self-function are recommended to aid the stabilisation of the self.

Adding a further dimension, Frame and colleagues (2003) showed that participation in a school-based, nurse-led support group was associated significantly with increases in scores on four self-perception sub-scales (social acceptance, athletic competence, physical appearance and global self-worth). Hoza and colleagues (2004) found that children with ADHD are more likely to over-estimate their competence in comparison with an adult's assessment. Barber and colleagues (2005), in contrast with Hoza and colleagues' 1993 study, found that children with ADHD had lower self-perception scores than those without the condition. This is attributed to the cumulative effect of years of low self-esteem and negative self-perception. They suggest that support groups and behavioural training may be a route to improving self-esteem and self-perception.

Other papers investigated the effect of medication on aspects of performance. Medication versus placebo was found to increase correspondence between participant's self-evaluations and performance of a task, although generally effort or ability were significantly more likely to be attributed as the cause (Millich *et al.*, 1989). This finding was confirmed by Pelham and colleagues (2002), who additionally found that medication improved behaviour (this was not related to expectancy), and that failure was attributed to the difficulty of the task and the effects of medication.

**Young people's experience of medication for other conditions**

Since the theoretical background relating to children's experience of medication for ADHD is less prolific, it was thought advisable to widen the consideration of literature to include young people's experience of medication for other conditions. It was thought that the issues of stigma, labelling and difference would be common or at least similar to those experienced by children prescribed stimulants for ADHD. A study by McElearney and colleagues (2005) compared the knowledge and perceptions of their respective medications of young people with ADHD with young people with epilepsy. More of the stimulant group (40% versus 32.5%) categorised themselves as non-compliant. There was a significant difference between the two groups in regard to confiding in friends about their medication. A greater number of the epilepsy group (55% versus 32.5%) reported they would tell a friend about their medication, indicating perhaps that ADHD is a more stigmatising illness than epilepsy.

More generally, Riis and colleagues (2007) found that healthy young people were more reluctant to take any medication that would alter fundamental traits (such as social comfort) than to take those that improve non-fundamental traits (for example, the ability to concentrate). Implications for ADHD stimulant medication are clear, although research would need specifically to test this hypothesis in that group to ensure that confounding factors do not reduce, remove or even reverse the observed effect. Buston and Wood (2000) found a number of reasons why young people with asthma would not comply with their medication regimen: they felt it was ineffective; they were exhibiting denial of their condition; inconvenience; fear of side effects; embarrassment or laziness. This is in spite of a belief in the importance of the medication, usually following a negative experience of non-compliance. Barriers exist, however, leading to lack of compliance. This paper shows that the relationship between compliance drivers and non-compliance drivers is complex, and will be investigated during the current study.

## Summary

The literature considered above gives a useful if far from comprehensive view of young people with ADHD and their relationship with prescribed medication. This is a poorly researched and therefore little understood area, and there is a clear need for the current research, especially in the context of the NICE guideline.

## METHOD

### Sample

The sample consisted of 16 children (14 boys and two girls) who ranged in age from 9 to 15 years old. All participants were attending state schools, and with the exception of one child who was of mixed race, all the children were white. Fifty per cent of the children were living in two-parent homes and 37% were living in single-mother homes. Two children lived with their father and one child lived with his grandmother. Educational achievement and type of employment were used as indicators of socio-economic status.[59] A majority of parents had completed O-levels; one parent had attended university. Seventy-two per cent of parents' job types ranged from semi-skilled to skilled work. A majority of mothers did not report having employment.

Child participants had all been diagnosed with ADHD and all were taking stimulant medication. Participants were recruited from clinics at three hospitals: Richmond

---

[59]Data was only available on mothers. Fathers' educational achievement and job types would be more reliable indicators of socio-economic status.

Royal Hospital, London, The Maudsley Hospital, London and Queen's Medical Centre, Nottingham.


## Data collection

Semi-structured focus groups were used to collect data about how children and young people experience stimulant medication. Allowing children to describe their experiences through qualitative interviews has been found to be both reliable and valid (Deatrick & Faux, 1991; Sorensen, 1992). Furthermore, there is compelling evidence to suggest that children are competent research participants (Singh, 2007b). Children's competence as research participants is supported by the literature on children's capacity and competence as patients. Children have been found to be capable of understanding the complexities of their condition; they have the capacity to give informed consent to invasive treatments, to contribute to deliberations over treatment strategies and, in the case of diabetic children, to take responsibility for administering their own treatment (Alderson *et al.*, 2006; Bluebond-Langner *et al.*, 2005).

Thirteen children were interviewed as part of a series of focus groups. Three children were interviewed one-to-one, either because they were unable to attend the focus groups or because of a preference to be interviewed individually. Participants were interviewed in a room based at the hospital clinic. Interviews lasted approximately one hour. Written informed consent was obtained from one parent and also from the participant. Parents were also asked to complete a basic demographic questionnaire.

*Focus group methodology*
Focus groups are a widely used method in qualitative health research. They are often used when the research aim is to gather information in a little-understood or under-researched area. Focus groups elicit a range of experiences, opinions and feelings about a topic (Krueger & Casey, 2000). The interaction in focus groups can result in enhanced disclosure, as participants challenge each other's perceptions and opinions. Focus groups with children are less commonly used in social science health research; however, market research with children, including market research around health and well being, more commonly uses a focus group approach (for example, Caruana & Vassallo, 2003). Focus groups with children provide access to children's own language and concepts, and encourage elaboration of children's own concerns and agendas. The collective nature of focus group discussion is often said to provide 'more than the sum of its parts' (Wilkinson, 1998). Interactive data result in enhanced disclosure, better understanding of participants' own agendas, the production of more elaborated accounts and the opportunity to observe the co-construction of meaning in action. Focus groups are, then, an ideal method for exploring people's own meanings and understandings of health and illness.

*Interviews*
Interviews were conducted in a conversational style and included a standard set of open-ended questions (the complete topic guide is reproduced at the end of this appendix).

### Figure 1:  Principle areas of investigation

- Children's understanding of ADHD diagnosis and behaviours
- Children's perceptions of how tablets helped them (or not)
- Children's experiences of stigma
- Children's experiences of non-drug interventions for ADHD behaviours
- Impact of tablets on children's perceptions of personal agency
- Children's experiences of psychiatric services

The first half of the interview involved posing broad questions that were followed by more specific probe questions. Principle areas of investigation are listed in Figure 1.

The second half of the interview involved a set of games and a vignette which provided children with the opportunity to elaborate their experiences and perceptions of medication in more creative and imaginative ways. The primary aims in this section of the interview were to:

a. Contextualise children's perceptions of tablets within their perceptions/under-standings/experiences of other means of improving behaviour.

b. Elicit ideas from children about resources that could help them have more posi-tive experiences of ADHD diagnosis and medication.

The following methods were used in the second half of the interview (see the topic guide at the end of this appendix for further elaboration).

1. Children were asked to compare how the experience of taking tablets was similar to, or different from, doing other things that were commonly considered good for them (see Figure 2).

2. Children were asked to respond to a vignette that elicited their ideas about what sorts to things can help a child's behaviour (see Figure 3).

3. Children were asked to think up and discuss an invention that could help children with ADHD.

### Figure 2:  How do tablets compare?

Let's imagine there are other things you could do that helped you with your behaviour. How are these the same as, or different from, taking your tablets? Which would you rather be doing?
- Piano lessons
- Vitamins
- Eating green vegetables
- Brain implant

### Figure 3:  Interventions vignette

Your favourite sports hero/heroine drops by one night wanting advice from you. He/she has a son who is having difficulty with his behaviour, especially his attention, focus, concentration. The doctor thinks the child has ADHD. Your sports hero/heroine wants to know what kinds of things he/she can do to help the child's behaviour get better. Let's make a list of things we know that can help this child.

4. Children were asked to place in order of rank a list of items that described common concerns voiced by school-age children. Each item was written on a separate card and children were asked to put the cards in order, from what they worried about most to what they worried about least. The list included the following items: global warming, having ADHD, taking tablets, exams, homework and friendships.

Global warming and exams were included on the list because these concerns were found to be significant sources of anxiety in a recent large cohort study of school-age children in the UK (Alexander & Hargreaves, 2007).

**Data analysis**

All interviews were digitally recorded and transcribed and were analysed using rigorous qualitative coding practices that meet established criteria of validity and relevance to qualitative health research (Mays & Pope, 2000). Focus groups were coded using content analysis. The coding process captured the data on two analytic levels: individual concepts were coded first, then these concepts were grouped together under higher-order themes. Systematic coding meant that it was possible to code at both the individual level and at the group level. Group-level data were represented in the frequency with which concepts and themes were expressed by group members. Transcript excerpts elucidated the meaning of codes.

A coding frame was drawn up by the lead author (IS) and validated within a coding team. The coding team applied the same codes to a transcript in order to discuss their definition and validity. This discussion resulted in refinements to the structure of categories and sub-categories, as well as refinements to individual codes. The coding team was able to reach agreement on the validity of a majority of codes.

**RESULTS**

**I.    ADHD behaviours**

Throughout the interviews and focus groups, children identified a broad range of behaviours as symptoms of ADHD (see Figure 4). This range maps on to the symptoms outlined in DSM-IV and ICD-10. The most frequently discussed types of behaviours were impulsiveness, physical aggression and hyperactivity. Children discussed impulsiveness in terms of 'an inability to restrain themselves from verbal or physical reactions'. Impulsiveness frequently overlapped with physical aggression, which children discussed as 'punching', 'kicking', 'pulling hair', usually of other children, but also sometimes of adults. Anger was an important motivating emotion in these activities, but children also frequently reported feeling regret for their actions immediately afterwards. Hyperactivity was discussed in strong terms by children, including 'going mental', 'mad', 'berserk' and 'nuts'. Children felt these types of behaviours to be particularly annoying to others.

**Figure 4:  ADHD behaviours and their qualities**

| Behaviours associated with ADHD | Qualities of ADHD behaviours |
|---|---|
| • Hyperactivity | • Out of control |
| • Difficulty concentrating | • Overwhelming |
| • Difficulty with organisation | • Angry |
| • Physical impulsiveness | • Frustrating |
| • Verbal impulsiveness | • Powerful |
| • Physical aggression | • Fun |
| • Verbal aggression | • A release |
| • Disruptive | • Sad |
| • Difficulty making friends | • Difficult |
| • Difficulty learning | |
| • Inability to sit still | |
| • Frustration | |
| • Poor at sports | |
| • Good at sports | |

Behaviours identified as symptomatic of ADHD were also frequently discussed in terms of their positive dimensions. Hyperactivity especially was 'fun', 'feels good' and 'lets off steam'. Children felt 'powerful' when acting aggressively and 'hyper'; in some cases, children thought these behaviours gave them increased credibility with peers. Peers were thought to fear how out-of-control and overwhelming children with ADHD could be. Children were able to perceive the tension between their experiences of the more negative and more positive aspects of their ADHD symptomatic behaviours. The majority of participants were not disturbed by this tension.

## II.    Tablets: perception of impacts

Children discussed a range of ways in which their tablets helped them (see Figure 5). Tablets were discussed primarily in terms of their impact on social behaviour, and less in terms of their impact on school work and school-related functioning. The positive effects of the tablets on behaviour were reported most clearly and consistently by children with aggression problems (see Text box 1). They reported that tablets helped them not to feel *'angry'*, helped to calm them down and to 'think first' before acting out. Children felt that these positive effects had an associated positive impact on their ability to make and retain friendships.

The most noticeable impact of tablets in the classroom context was their perceived effect on disruptive behaviour. Many children reported that tablets helped them to be less disruptive in the classroom. Disruptiveness was discussed both in terms of verbal disruptiveness ('I'm always talking when I shouldn't be') and physical disruptiveness ('I can't sit still'). Most groups had to be encouraged to identify other ways in which tablets might have an impact on school work and school-related functioning. Children thought that tablets had a positive effect on their ability to focus and to concentrate on work. This positive impact overlapped with children's improved ability to contain

## Figure 5: Areas in which tablets help

- Concentration
- Impulsiveness
- Physical aggression
- Peer relationships
- Relationship with teacher
- Performance on tests
- School marks
- Relationship with parents
- Relationship with siblings
- Writing
- Reading
- Maths
- Homework
- Behaviour towards teacher
- Self-confidence
- Self-esteem

## Text box 1: Perceived impact of tablets on anger

**Male child:**

It's like a wall between the rest of my body and my anger, and it's like a thousand to one against – with my anger. And I can't – just can't control it until I've took my tablets or until I get home.

their physical and verbal energies ('I can sit there and do my work better'). Children also reported that aspects of their school work, such as writing and maths, had improved as a result of tablets. Some children reported receiving better marks in school and on standardised tests as a result of taking tablets.

However, discussion of the positive impacts of tablets on school work was frequently associated with individual and collective disagreement as to the validity of a particular impact. For example, some children felt that tablets had a positive impact on reading, writing and maths and others did not. The degree of effects on school work and school-related functioning was also debated. For example, some children felt that tablets did improve their focus and concentration on school work, but they also still reported having significant trouble in this area.

## III.    Attitudes toward tablets

*i. Basic knowledge about tablets*
Children's knowledge of the name of their tablets and frequency of dosing was generally good. Most children were able to identify both. Children's knowledge of their dosage level was weaker, and was often expressed in terms of how many tablets they

**Figure 6: Expressed attitudes toward tablets**

- Normal
- Easy
- Ok-tasting
- Known risks
- Familiar
- Best alternative
- Essential
- Necessary
- Bad tasting
- Annoying
- Change a person

had to take in one day. A few children identified their tablets as 'stimulants' and discussed stimulants as 'real drugs'. Most children, but not all, understood that their tablets had a primary impact on the brain.

*ii. Expressed attitudes*

Generally, children had positive attitudes toward their medication for ADHD (see Figure 6). Most children felt taking this medication was 'necessary' for them, and it had become a 'normal' part of their lives. They resisted alternatives to medication largely because of an unwillingness to experiment with something different; children felt their tablets were 'familiar', 'relatively easy to take' and 'safe'. When asked to consider how a list of non-medical means of improving behaviour (see Section IV. ii) might match up against tablets in terms of efficacy, all children felt that tablets were the most efficacious form of treatment for ADHD behaviours. They also felt that tablets were an 'essential part' of treatments that incorporated non-medical means of improving behaviour.

Children did not report having strong anxieties about taking medication. When asked to rank a list of stressors from least to most anxiety-provoking, tablets were consistently at or near the bottom (see Figure 7).

**Figure 7: Contextualising the burden of ADHD diagnosis and medication**

Here are some things children worry about. (Stressors were written on individual cards). Can you line them up for me in order of the things you worry about most, to the things you worry about least? You can line them up and then see if it's right. If not you can discuss and rearrange things.

Global warming
Having ADHD
Taking tablets
Exams
Homework
Friendships

In the context of this generally positive attitude, more negative reactions to medication were also frequently expressed. The most frequently expressed reaction was also the most difficult for children to explain: a feeling that tablets were 'annoying'. Participants appeared to have a shared understanding of this experience of tablets, even though the experience was difficult to communicate to others. The annoying nature of tablets was most often related to the 'need to take them'. It was unclear whether it was the routine of taking tablets (such as, daily dosing, remembering to take tablets, the taste of tablets); the requirement to take them (for example, not having a choice); or the more existential meaning of the need for tablets (for example, having a mental disorder, being 'different') that was most distressing to children. All these dimensions were inherent to varying degrees in the expressed experiences of tablets being annoying.

*iii. Relationship of tablets to sense of self*

Almost all children believed that they needed to be on their medication for ADHD. Perceptions of the need for tablets ranged from medium to high. If a child raised a question about his/her need for medication, other children would frequently challenge the child's view. Understanding of how long it was necessary to stay on medication was not as frequently shared. Some children felt that they would 'grow out of ADHD'; others felt it was a life-long illness. Some children made reference to the fact that adult ADHD was now a recognised disorder. Most children felt it would become possible to cope with ADHD behaviours without the help of medication. Older children were more likely than younger children to question the need for life-long medication, and more likely than younger children to talk about a desire to come off medication in the near future.

Children tended to have a continuous, rather than a dichotomous, sense of themselves on and off tablets. Only a few children expressed feeling that they were 'a different person' on and off medication; for example, being a 'Jekyll and Hyde'. On further probing, such initial dichotomous statements were amended into continuous self-descriptions.

Most children expressed ambivalent self-conceptions on and off medication. For example, some children felt they were 'more fun' off medication; but these same children knew that when they were more 'free' they were also potentially 'more annoying' to others and more 'out of control'. Some children described themselves as 'more normal' off medication, which was a positive self-description. However, they also described their normal selves as 'berserk' and 'mental', which was 'fun' in certain situations, but 'horrible' in others. Children had a good understanding of the context-bound nature of how their behaviours would be interpreted. Their evaluations of their own behaviours as well as their evaluations of the need for tablets were strongly associated with their understanding of context.

*iv. Experience of side effects*

The most commonly discussed side effects of tablets were problems with appetite and sleep. A few children had experienced 'acting like a zombie' on certain medications and/or at certain dosage levels. For most children side effects were not expressed as severe problems, even if in some cases children reported getting extremely little sleep. In the context of the group discussion, side effects were reported with a degree of authority and even pride, which may have militated against fuller discussion of how difficult these experiences actually were.

*v. Compliance*

Compliance with medication was reported to be generally good, especially among the younger children. Older children were more likely to have experimented with not taking their medication to see whether anyone would notice, and to see how well they themselves could control their behaviours. Other reasons for not taking medication were related to medication being 'annoying'. Some children said that sometimes they just 'couldn't be bothered' to take their medication. A majority of children in this study were responsible for remembering to take their medication. Younger children were more likely to forget to take their medication and to need assistance with the responsibility of remembering to take it. A majority of children took medication all the time. A few children reported taking drug holidays at weekends and school holidays. A few children felt they had the option to stop taking tablets if they wanted to.

Children's compliance with medication was apparently tacitly monitored by their peer group. Children reported relatively frequent occurrences of friends asking if they had taken their medication – either as a reaction when the index child was exhibiting troublesome behaviours or as an encouragement to forgo medication (when friends thought that medication had inhibiting effects that made the index child less fun to be with).

## IV.     Alternatives to medication

*i. Experience of non-drug interventions*

Few children reported experiences of non-drug interventions that were memorable or productive in their view. Some children received additional support in the school day; three children reported having received counselling. Two children reported that counselling was helpful to them. A majority of parents of child participants were currently, or had previously, experimented with a range of non-drug interventions including Omega 3, elimination of E-numbers from the diet, 'IQ vitamins' and a low sugar/low caffeine diet. Children tended to be aware of these interventions but expressed no strong opinions about them. Several children reported that they had begun sports programmes that helped 'release energy' and made them 'feel good'. These programmes included boxing and football.

*ii. Children's ideas for non-drug interventions*

In response to a vignette, children were asked to brainstorm means of helping a child with ADHD symptoms manage their behaviour (see Figure 3 above). Children came up with answers easily and there was agreement within and across groups as to the efficacy of the proposed methods. The most frequently mentioned methods were playing sports, drawing/doodling and stress balls. Specific sports included boxing and football, as mentioned above. Two children mentioned a punching bag. One child said 'fighting' was helpful, by which he may have meant boxing. Less frequently mentioned non-drug methods of managing behaviour were reading, watching television and playing computer games.

When asked to compare the probable effectiveness of non-drug methods with the effectiveness of tablets, none of the participants felt non-drug methods were more effective than drug intervention. All participants felt that non-drug methods would be most effective if used in conjunction with medication.

*iii.  Inventions for ADHD children*
All groups and individuals were asked to think of something they would want to invent, to help children with ADHD (see Figure 8).

**Figure 8:  Inventions probe**

> Let's imagine you are an inventor and wanted to create a way to help children with ADHD. What might you invent?

Several children discussed alternative drug delivery systems, including 'better tasting drugs', less frequently administered drugs and drug dosing on demand. This last was described by one participant as a 'scratch dot' which could be scratched in the moment that the drug was needed, to deliver an immediate dose for an hour or two. The desire for a drug that had a short-term, targeted effect was also associated with a desire for a drug that didn't have pervasive effects: 'I wish it only affected the parts of me that need it'. Other children reported being glad that they only needed to take medication once a day, and were happier knowing that 'it's always working in me'.

Another major category of response to this question was desire for a means of communicating to others what it was like to have ADHD. Proposed methods of communication included a 'book about kids with ADHD' and a 'video about ADHD' (see Text box 2).

**Text box 2: Interactive ADHD video game**

> **Male child:**
>
> [I would invent] a video game where you actually took a picture of yourself and then put it into the game. And then you actually were this character running round, doing stuff that children do in a day so then these people could actually play on it... people who haven't got this thing [ADHD] that we've got can actually have a go and see what our life is like and so they would actually know how we feel. So then they'll learn not to treat us in a way that's different to everybody else... You can have, like, other characters that have been nasty to you without your tablets. You could have a level without your tablets and with, so then they'd know the difference with your tablets and without.

## V.    Agency

Agency is defined as the degree to which an individual feels he/she can affect behaviours, people, circumstances and/or events.

*i.  Personal agency over behaviours*
All children in this study reported feeling that their behaviours were a problem to some degree. No children attributed these problem behaviours solely to their ADHD diagnosis or to a lack of tablets. Frequently, when an individual child made such attributions he/she would be challenged by the group. All children admitted using their diagnosis as an 'excuse' for their behaviours at some point. Children felt that tablets helped them with their behaviours, as outlined above; however, no child reported feeling that tablets entirely resolved their problem behaviours. Children generally reported 'feeling responsible' for management of their behaviours, and felt that tablets assisted them to some degree with self-management.

*ii.  Agency over definition of behaviours*
Agency over definition of their behaviours was a greater problem for many children. In general, children did not report feeling that they had a voice in how their behaviours were classified and defined. They agreed that some of their behaviours caused problems, and referred to 'my ADHD'. However, many children were aware of the contextual nature of the interpretation of behaviours, but this only conferred agency on a child in situations when peer-generated social codes had more moral authority than adult-generated behavioural prohibitions. A frequently mentioned example of such a situation was bullying that involved denigration of or disrespect for a child's family. In such circumstances there was general agreement among participants that aggressive retaliation was socially and morally justified. Children sometimes used their ADHD and/or lack of tablets as an excuse for their behaviour following the fight. This can be seen as a strategic use of a particular interpretation of their behaviour. Children defined this sort of retaliation in moral terms, even if the impulsive, aggressive behaviours were also indicative of clinical symptoms. Children rarely reported feeling regret over their behaviours following such incidents (see Text box 3).

**Text box 3: Moral dimensions of aggressive impulses**

---

**Male child:**

Sometimes I play basketball and I don't take my tablets and I might get into a fight and then I might do something really dumb... I don't necessarily like to fight. When I take my tablets I can't fight for my whole life. When I take them they make me, like, so calm I won't do anything... [Another time someone said] 'Hopefully when your sister's born she'll be born with Down's Syndrome because you're spastic.' I got so angry so then in school I just got him and then I didn't stop punching him until he – until I, like, smashed up his nose and stuff because I got so angry because I could take anything that comes in if they say it to me, but about my family I can't take it.

---

Lack of agency in the definition of their behaviours was most frequently experienced in the classroom. Children felt that teachers were unfairly focused on their behaviour, assuming that they would cause more problems than other children. Children felt this was a result of having a diagnosis of ADHD. Some children felt 'watched' by teachers who were evaluating whether or not their behaviours were a sign that they had forgotten to take their medication. Children also experienced teachers as being able to define their behaviours according to the needs of teachers, rather than the needs of children. For example, some children felt that teachers attributed behaviours to ADHD as a way of explaining behaviours away. This was contrasted with teachers assessing the ways in which children with ADHD might be helped through structural changes in the classroom and/or the school day.

*iii. Agency over the future*
Children generally felt that they would be able to exercise choices with regard to their future, although they also tended to acknowledge their limitations. Many children were concerned about whether they would need to keep taking their tablets as young people and adults. All children in this study felt that this decision would eventually be their own decision to make.

## VI. STIGMA

*i. Stigma associated with tablets*
Experiences of stigma related to directly to medication were less frequently expressed than experiences of stigma related more generally to ADHD diagnosis and behavioural symptoms. Tablet-related experiences of stigma had an impact on children's sense of self in that these experiences often involved name-calling and bullying, for example, 'druggie' and 'tablet boy' (see Text box 4). Children reported 'feeling bad' about being called names and they generally associated experiences of stigma with feelings of low self-confidence and low self-esteem. Children frequently got into fights as a result of being verbally bullied. Children felt exposed by the need to take

**Text box 4: Bullying and retaliation related to tablets**

---

**Male child 1:** Someone says, 'Oh, you're a druggie addict,' so I just smacked him one.

**Interviewer:** A drug addict?

**Male child 2:** I get that. I get that. I did. A boy came up... 'Why are you on drugs?' I said, 'They're not drugs. Even if they were drugs, I wouldn't bring them into school. I'd probably have them at home.'

**Male child 1:** So I says – he says – 'Why are you a drug addict?' I says, 'I'm not.' He says, 'Yes you are.' So I just smacked him one and he went, 'No you're not,' went off crying.

---

medication, especially if they needed to take tablets during the school day. The need to take tablets made them 'feel different' in a negative way.

### ii.  *Stigma associated with ADHD behaviours and diagnosis*

In general, stigma associated with ADHD behaviours and diagnosis was expressed as the primary experience of stigma. Two participants kept their diagnosis secret from friends and members of the extended family. All children reported feeling that their ADHD behaviours gave them 'bad reputations' with peers, teachers and parents of peers. There was general agreement that children with ADHD were thought to be 'dumb'. A majority of children reported being called names and bullied about their ADHD behaviours and/or ADHD diagnosis and need for tablets.

Children reported that the negative assumptions of others about them were especially burdensome. They felt they received negative differential treatment because of their diagnosis. Both girls in the study (in separate groups) reported feeling that teachers ignored them completely because of their ADHD diagnosis. They felt the teachers had 'given up' on them. In general children felt there was a lack of empathy and a lack of understanding about children with ADHD. They felt peers and teachers were 'unkind'; and they reported experiences of feeling 'different' and 'isolated'.

### iii.  *Protections against stigma*

All children in this study reported having close friendships that helped to protect them from bullying. In several cases, friends who knew about the index child's ADHD diagnosis would 'come to the rescue' of the index child in a fight that resulted from bullying. The rescue often manifested as an effort to get the index child to 'stop and to think' about what he/she was doing. Other times friends would simply 'drag' the index child away from the situation (see Text box 5).

ADHD diagnosis could be turned around to serve as a protection in situations that arose as a result of stigma. For example, friends would use the ADHD diagnosis to frighten off a name-calling bully; for example, 'he told them I had ADHD and I was

### Text box 5: Peer protection and ADHD as an excuse

---

**Male child 1:**   If someone starts on me and I know I'm going to start on them. And they know to ask – and then my friends will help – come in and back me up. Otherwise I get them on the floor and I knee them in the back... My friends will say, 'He's got ADHD.'

**Male child 2:**   I kept butting this boy in the head... You can't help it.

**Interviewer:**   Is that what you say? But do you believe that?

**Male child 1:**   No, oh...

**Male child 2:**   No I just use it.

**Interviewer:**   You're using it as an excuse then?

**Male child 3:**   Sometimes.

---

crazy'. Frequently, ADHD was used as 'an excuse' following a fight; for example, 'I couldn't stop because of my ADHD'. Almost all children in the study acknowledged using ADHD as an excuse to get out of situations like this.


## VII. Discussion

Children who participated in this study had a generally positive experience of tablets. This does not mean that they liked being on medication; rather that they were willing to put up with the 'annoying' dimensions of taking medication in return for the perceived benefits. Medication was not viewed as a panacea; children had reasonable understanding and expectations of their medication. Individually and collectively children associated their tablets primarily with helping to improve their social behaviours, and, consequently, their relationships with peers. While improvements in school work and school functioning were often noted, these received less attention than improvements in social behaviour. Similarly, side effects of medication were commonly experienced in this group of children, particularly appetite suppression and insomnia. However, side effects did not make up a major theme of children's discussions individually or collectively. All children interviewed felt that they needed to be on their tablets; older children were more likely to be looking ahead to a time when they could manage without tablets.

Children had varied experiences of both formal and informal non-drug interventions aimed at helping them with their ADHD symptoms. With the exception of sports, particularly boxing, few of these interventions were thought to be very effective. All children in the study believed medication to be the most effective available treatment for their ADHD symptoms. However, children also understood that ADHD diagnosis and effective drug treatment did not mean that they were absolved of responsibility or of agency in their behaviours.

One of the most strongly stated, and most resonant, desires communicated by this group of children was for better public understanding of ADHD. Children felt this would create empathy for their situations and relieve them of some of the stigma of negative assumptions attached to ADHD diagnoses. Experiences of stigma because of ADHD behaviours and diagnosis were common; experiences of stigma related directly to ADHD medication were less frequently expressed by children in this study. Experiences of stigma, such as bullying, name-calling, negative assumptions and differential treatment were distressing to children, and negatively affected their self-evaluations, self-esteem and self-confidence. Close friendships were an important protective factor against the initiation and/or continuation of fights that arose as a result of the child with ADHD being bullied. These friendships were mentioned as or more often as medication, as factors that helped children to restrain their impulse to fight and/or to continue fighting.

Findings in this study are similar to other recent qualitative findings (Singh, 2007a; 2007b) that do not find strong support for concerns that children taking stimulant medication for ADHD are ethically compromised. A major ethical concern has been that stimulant medication potentially endangers children's agency (for example, President's Council on Bioethics, 2003), but children in this study expressed a significant degree of agency over their behaviours. A frequent topic of discussion among boys in particular was the moral dimension of the decision to fight or not to fight. Certain provocative comments (for example, about a boy's family) made it morally compromising not to fight the name-caller, even if it was socially inappropriate to fight in the playground. Children expressed a significant trust in their personal agency when discussing a process of making moral assessments of situations and choosing and judging their behaviour according to these assessments.

Similarly, concerns that taking medication could confer significant stigma on children (for example, Conrad, 2006) were not supported by this study. While children reported experiences of stigma as a direct result of taking tablets, experiences of stigma as a result of ADHD diagnosis and symptomatic behaviours were far more frequently described. Feelings of being different and feeling alienated were also more strongly connected with diagnosis and ADHD behaviours, than with the need for medication. To the extent that medication helps to alleviate some ADHD symptoms and helps to foster peer relationships, it would appear that the social benefits of medication outweigh the social burdens.

In view of the distress many children experienced in relation to ADHD diagnosis, ADHD behaviours and tablets, it is troubling that only one child in this study viewed their clinical encounters within child psychiatry services as having a therapeutic component. While no child had any strong complaints about services, several children reported not being able to get in to see a clinician and feeling that they would like more time with a psychiatrist. Some children felt that clinicians didn't really care about them. A majority of children felt appointments were routine and boring, and that appointments were primarily for medication checks and prescriptions.

Sport, especially boxing, is clearly considered therapeutic by boys with ADHD, especially those with aggression problems (Singh, 2007a). Many children in this study reported being kept inside during lunch time as punishment for their disruptive behaviours. Such punishment is counter-productive for this group of children because they need to 'let off steam' in order to better manage their behaviours. Clinical work with children, families and schools could emphasise and encourage the positive aspects of sport for this group of children.

There are few qualitative studies involving children with ADHD, and even fewer studies that attempt an in-depth investigation of children's experiences of medication. The controversial nature of ADHD diagnosis and drug intervention for young children has the potential for fuelling unproductive polemic debates about the safety, efficacy and/or validity of medication for young children. In view of this background, it is important to attempt to contextualise the discussions with children in this study. One means of contextualisation is to examine the relative significance of matters discussed with children in this study. How much do children worry about their ADHD diagnoses and their tablets, when compared with other things children reportedly worry a great deal about?

ADHD and medication were important aspects of this group of children's lives. All children reported various daily reminders of the burden of mental disorder and the need to take medication. However, when compared with a list of other stressors, 'ADHD diagnosis' and 'taking tablets' were not what children in this study reported they were worrying about most. Younger children worried most about friendships and global warming, while older children were most anxious about exams and friendships. While friendships and academic performance are often a problem for children with ADHD, these concerns are not uniquely related to having ADHD. A large cohort of children in the UK identified these concerns as their primary sources of anxiety (Alexander & Hargreaves, 2007). In the present study, ADHD diagnosis was ranked as more worrying than taking tablets for ADHD by almost all children. Results from this study therefore consistently suggest that children have relatively more positive experiences of medication when compared with more negative experiences of ADHD diagnosis and behavioural symptoms.

## VIII.   Limitations

This study is based on focus groups and a small number of individual interviews with 16 children in the UK. While all interviews and the analysis were intensive, systematic and rigorous, findings have within-group validity, and should be generalised with caution. The importance of certain themes may have been amplified by the particular dynamics of groups made up largely of young boys, who gave honest answers to questions but also wished to impress each other and the interviewer. In addition, this study, as is the case with many studies in psychiatry, may have attracted a group of children with a certain range of experiences with ADHD diagnosis and medication. Selection bias cannot be ruled out as a factor in these findings. Only two girls participated in the study (12%), and both were teenagers. Therefore the analysis is heavily skewed towards boys' experiences of ADHD diagnosis and medication. This study does not adequately capture experiences that might be unique to girls with ADHD.

## REFERENCES

Alderson, P., Sutcliffe, K. & Curtis, K. (2006) Children's consent to medical treatment. *Hastings Centre Report, 36*, 25–34.
Alexander, R. & Hargreaves, L. (2007) *Community Soundings: the Primary Review Regional Witness Sessions.* Cambridge: University of Cambridge Faculty of Education.
Barber, S., Grubbs, L. & Cottrell, B. (2005) Self-perception in children with attention deficit/hyperactivity disorder. *Journal of Pediatric Nursing, 20*, 235–245.
Baxley, G. B., Turner, P. F. & Greenwold, W. E. (1978) Hyperactive children's knowledge and attitudes concerning drug treatment. *Journal of Pediatric Psychology, 3*, 172–176.
Bluebond-Langner, M., DeCicco, A. & Belasco, J. (2005) Involving children with life-shortening illnesses in decisions about participation in clinical research: a proposal for shuttle diplomacy and negotiation. In *Ethics and Research with Children* (ed E. Kodish), pp. 323–344. Oxford: Oxford University Press.
Buston, K. & Wood, S. (2000) Non-compliance amongst adolescents with asthma: listening to what they tell us about self-management. *Family Practice, 17*, 134–138.

Caruana, A. & Vassallo, R. (2003) Children's perception of their influence over purchases: the role of parental communication patterns. *Journal of Consumer Marketing*, *20*, 55–66(12).

Conrad, P. (2006) *Identifying Hyperactive Children: the Medicalization of Deviant Behavior*. London: Ashgate.

Curtin, C. (2001). Eliciting children's voices in qualitative research. *American Journal of Occupational Therapy*, *55*, 295–302.

Deatrick, J. A. & Faux, S. A. (1991) Conducting qualitative studies with children and adolescents. In *Qualitative Nursing Research: A Contemporary Dialogue* (ed J. M. Morse), pp. 185–203. Newbury Park, CA: Sage.

Dumas, D. & Pelletier, L. (1999) A study of self-perception in hyperactive children. *MCN: The American Journal of Maternal/Child Nursing*, *24*, 12–19.

DuPaul, G. J. & Barkley, R. A. (1990) Medication therapy. In *Attention-Deficit Hyperactivity Disorder: A Handbook for Diagnosis and Treatment* (ed. R. A. Barkley). New York: Guilford Press.

Efron, D., Jarman, F. & Barker, M. (1998) Child and parent perceptions of stimulant medication treatment in attention deficit hyperactivity disorder. *Journal of Paediatrics and Child Health*, *34*, 288–292.

Frame, K., Kelly, L. & Bayley, E. (2003) Increasing perceptions of self-worth in preadolescents diagnosed with ADHD. *Journal of Nursing Scholarship*, *35*, 225–229.

Hill, M., Laybourn, A. & Borland, M. (1996) Engaging with primary-aged children about their emotions and well-being: methodological considerations. *Children and Society*, *10*, 129–144.

Hoza, B., Pelham, W. E., Milich, R., *et al.* (1993) The self-perceptions and attributions of attention deficit hyperactivity disordered and nonreferred boys. *Journal of Abnormal Child Psychology*, *21*, 271–286.

Hoza, B., Gerdes, A. C., Hinshaw, S. P., *et al.* (2004) Self-perceptions of competence in children with ADHD and comparison children. *Journal of Consulting and Clinical Psychology*, *72*, 382–391.

Ireland, L. & Holloway, I. (1996) Qualitative health research with children. *Children and Society*, *10*, 155–164.

Kendall, J., Hatton, D., Beckett, A., *et al.* (2003) Children's accounts of attention-deficit/hyperactivity disorder. *ANS Advances in Nursing Science*, *26*, 114–130.

Kortesluoma, R. L., Hentinen, M. & Nikkonen, M. (2003) Conducting a qualitative child interview: methodological considerations. *Journal of Advanced Nursing*, *42*, 434–441.

Krueger, M., & Kendall, J. (2001) Descriptions of self: an exploratory study of adolescents with ADHD. *Journal of Child and Adolescent Psychiatric Nursing*, *14*, 61–72.

Krueger, R. A. & Casey, M. A. (2000) *Focus Groups: A Practical Guide to Applied Research*. London: Sage.

Kutcher, S., Aman, M., Brooks, S. J., *et al.* (2004) International consensus statement on attention-deficit/hyperactivity disorder (ADHD) and disruptive behaviour disorders (DBDs): clinical implications and treatment practice suggestions. *European Neuropsychopharmacology*, *14*, 11–28.

Mays, N. & Pope, C. (2000) Qualitative research in health care: assessing quality in qualitative research. *British Medical Journal*, *320*, 50–52.

McElearney, C., Fitzpatrick, C., Farrell, N., *et al.* (2005) Stimulant medication in ADHD: what do children and their parents say? *Irish Journal of Psychological Medicine*, *22*, 5–9.

McNeal, R. E., Roberts, M. C. & Barone, V. J. (2000) Mothers' and children's perceptions of medication for children with attention-deficit hyperactivity disorder. *Child Psychiatry and Human Development*, *30*, 173–187.

Meaux, J., Hester, C., Smith, B., *et al.* (2006) Stimulant medications: a trade-off? The lived experience of adolescents with ADHD. *Journal for Specialists in Pediatric Nursing*, *11*, 214–226.

Milich, R., Licht, B. G., Murphy, D. A., *et al.* (1989) Attention-deficit hyperactivity disordered boys' evaluations of and attributions for task performance on medication versus placebo. *Journal of Abnormal Psychology*, *98*, 280–284.

Pelham, W. E., Hoza, B., Pillow, D. R., *et al.* (2002) Effects of methylphenidate and expectancy on children with ADHD: behavior, academic performance, and attributions in a summer treatment program and regular classroom settings. *Journal of Consulting and Clinical Psychology*, *70*, 320–335.

President's Council on Bioethics (2003) *Beyond Therapy: Biotechnology and the Pursuit of Happiness*. Washington, D.C.: Dana Press.

Riis, J., Simmons, J. & Goodwin, G. (2007) Preferences for psychological enhancements: the reluctance to enhance fundamental traits. *Social Science Research Network*. Available at: http://papers.ssrn.com/so13/papers.cfm?abstract_id=967676

Singh, I. (2007a) Clinical implications of ethical concepts: moral self-understandings in children taking methylphenidate for ADHD. *Clinical Child Psychology and Psychiatry*, *12*, 167–182.

Singh, I. (2007b) Capacity and competence in children as research participants. *EMBO Reports*, *8*, 35–39.

Sorensen, E. (1992) Qualitative research with children as informants. Paper presented at Western Institute of Nursing, San Diego, California. Abstract in *Communicating Nursing Research*, *25*, 328.

Wilkinson, S. (1998) Focus groups in health research: exploring the meanings of health and illness. *Journal of Health Psychology*, *3*, 329–348.

Woodgate, R. (2000) Part I: an introduction to conducting qualitative research in children with cancer. *Journal of Pediatric Oncology Nursing*, *17*, 192–206.

## FOCUS GROUPS TOPIC GUIDE

Welcome

Names

Why we are here:

*To talk about your experiences with tablets for ADHD*

*We are here to learn from you. Your job is important: what you say to us today will help doctors all over the UK better understand how to help children with ADHD.*

There are NO right or wrong answers.

No reason to feel embarrassed – everyone here is friendly and wants to hear from you.

The RULES:

YOU ARE THE EXPERTS

DON'T INTERRUPT OTHERS

SPEAK LOUDLY AND CLEARLY

(explain that this is for good politeness and for good quality recording!)

**Questions:**

**I.**
1. So, what is ADHD?
2. Why do you think you need to be taking tablets for ADHD?

**PROBE: Types of behaviours**

3. In what ways do you think the tablets have helped you?

**PROBE: behaviour, school work, social life, self-esteem**

4. Have the tablets caused you any problems?

**PROBE: stigma, alienation, side effects, shame**

5. Does anyone else know you have ADHD or take tablets for ADHD?
6. Other than taking tablets, do you get any special help from teachers or other doctors?

**PROBE: educational help, counselling, psychotherapy, have parents received any help?**

7. Do you think you need to take tablets?

**PROBE: Experimentation with not taking meds? Efforts to discontinue meds? For how long do you believe you will need to take these tablets? What other sorts of things help you with your behaviour?**

8. What would happen if you said you didn't want to take your tablets anymore right now?
9. What's it like going to see the doctor who gives you the prescription for your tablets?

**PROBE: comfort level, interaction, anxiety**

## II.    Games

A. Let's imagine there are other things you could do that helped you with your behaviour. How are these the same as, or different from, taking your tablets? Which would you rather be taking? (PROBE EACH ITEM)
   a.  piano lessons
   b.  vitamins
   c.  eating green vegetables
   d.  brain implant

B. VIGNETTE
   Your favourite sports hero/heroine rings your house one night wanting advice from you. This person has a son who is having the sorts of difficulties a child with ADHD has. The sports hero/heroine wants to know what kinds of things he/she can do, to help his/her child.
1. Let's make a list of all the things we know that can help a child's behaviour.


**PROBE: Have you tried this? What's it like?**

2. Can you line up all these ways of helping, from the thing that you think is best to the thing you think is worst?
   ● In what ways are these best and worst? For example, most effective, least effective; nicest to take; least nice to take, and so on.
   ● Where do tablets fit into this list?
C. Let's imagine you are an inventor and wanted to create a way to help children with ADHD. What might you invent?
D. Here are some things children worry about. Can you line them up for me in order of the things you worry about most, to the things you worry about least? You can line them up and then see if it's right. If not you can rearrange things!
   Global warming
   Having ADHD
   Taking tablets
   Exams
   Homework
   Friendships

## III.    FINAL QUESTIONS

1. If there were more tablets that made it easier for you in other ways, for example, tablets to improve your memory, would you want to take them too?
2. Anything else you would want doctors, parents or other kids to know about taking tablets for ADHD?

# APPENDIX 16: ADHD CONSENSUS CONFERENCE

## PART 1: SUMMARIES OF PRESENTATIONS PROVIDED BY THE ADHD CONSENSUS CONFERENCE SPEAKERS, 17 OCTOBER 2006

### 1.1 THE VALUE AND LIMITATIONS OF THE CONCEPTS OF ADHD AND HYPERKINETIC DISORDER IN GUIDING TREATMENT - A CLINICIAN'S PERSPECTIVE

*Dr David Coghill*
*Senior Lecturer in Child and Adolescent Psychiatry, Division of Pathology and Neuroscience (Psychiatry), University of Dundee.*

The presentation will look at the value and limitation of ADHD as a concept and develop ideas by looking at the questions posed in the outline of the position statement.

#### 1.1.1 To what extent do the phenomena of overactivity, inattentiveness and impulsiveness cluster into a particular disorder that can be distinguished from others and from normal variation?

*Internal validity*

Inattention, overactivity and impulsivity are all continuous variables which appear to be complex characteristics distributed throughout the population with a fairly normal distribution; these are normally distributed characteristics which therefore blend into the normal. The distinction of what is and what is not normal has to be, by definition, arbitrary.

Factor analysis suggests that their distribution is not random but shows a strong coherence with each other and far less coherence with behaviours characteristic of other conditions such as phobia aggression or anxiety.

#### 1.1.2 At what level, and in what circumstances, do these become impairing for the person?

To some extent where to draw the line as to when symptoms and behaviour are impairing is arbitrary, as it is on a continuum. Symptoms must be related to impairment.

The key issue is, how do symptoms relate to impairment? Impairment can be measured in several ways; however the Children's Global Assessment Scale (C-GAS) provides a relatively simple and valid measure, scored from 0–100 with 0 indicating the most severe impairment and 100 the most healthy and well-functioning child.

DSM-IV field trials used a C-GAS score of ≤60 (which implies impairment requiring specific treatment) and determined that five ADHD symptoms were required to be present to reach this cut-off. To avoid false positives the number was increased to six or more symptoms of inattention or hyperactivity/impulsivity.

Problems occur with children whose impairment arising from their ADHD symptoms is really quite severe, but who technically do not meet the diagnostic criteria.

### 1.1.3    Impact of ADHD on overall functioning

An important part of impairment arising from ADHD is its breadth, including impact on:
● social, academic and interpersonal domains
● the family
● ideas of self-worth.
What is particularly interesting to a clinician is how to reduce the functional impairments consequent to these symptoms and any comorbidities.

### 1.1.4    Impact of untreated and under-treated ADHD

Apart from the impact on the individual, ADHD has an impact on the following areas:
● The healthcare system: 50% increase in bike accidents, 33% increase in emergency room visits, 2 to 4 times more vehicle accidents.
● School and occupation: 46% expelled, 35% drop out and lower occupational status.
● Family: 3 to 5 times increase in parental divorce or separation and 2 to 4 times increase in sibling fights.
● Employer: increase in parental absenteeism and decrease in productivity.
● Society: twice the risk of substance misuse, earlier onset and individuals are less likely to quit in adulthood.

Children with ADHD are in the bottom 5% of children in terms of quality of life.

### 1.1.5    The clinical picture for the individual

The symptoms of inattention, hyperactivity and impulsivity combined with a number of psychiatric coexisting conditions such as oppositional defiant disorder and conduct disorder lead to a number of psychosocial impairments across a number of domains: self, school (or work), home and social.

### 1.1.6    Is there is evidence for a characteristic pattern of developmental changes, or outcome(s)?

ADHD symptoms were designed for primary school children, and an adult with ADHD is a child with ADHD who has grown up but continues to have problems. The symptoms experienced by these groups will differ; the levels of symptoms and impairment may not necessarily change at the same rate. Although individuals may have symptoms throughout their life they may not demonstrate impairment until later in life.

In children the pattern of symptoms/behaviours is characterised by motor hyper-activity, aggressiveness, low levels of tolerance, impulsiveness and being easily distracted. In adults the pattern is characterised by: inattentiveness, shifting activities, being easily bored, impatience and restlessness.

There is a characteristic pattern of developmental changes. During the pre-school years the child may show some level of behavioural disturbance. Once at school, academic, social and self-esteem problems begin to manifest themselves. As an adolescent, additional issues surrounding smoking and injury begin to appear and by the time the individual is of college age, a pattern of academic failure, occupational difficulties, substance misuse, injury and low self-esteem is apparent. As an adult, relationship problems will also occur.

### 1.1.7 Is there a specific response to clinical, educational and/or other interventions?

Home- and school-based behavioural treatments and treatment with methylphenidate, dexamfetamine, atomoxetine and several other drugs reduce symptoms and improve functioning. Treatment with other psychoactive medications such as SSRIs or antipsychotics does not have the same effect.

### 1.1.8 Is there evidence for a consistent heritability, neurobiological or other causality?

We do not know the cause of ADHD. Given that the causes are multifactorial, leading to a common behavioural phenotype, to search for a cause is probably not going to bear fruit.

ADHD aggregates in families with three to five times increased risk in first-degree relatives; twin studies suggest considerable heritability with between 65 and 90% of the phenotypic variance explained by genetic factors. There are also associations with a range of environmental risks (mainly non-shared factors) such as pre- and perinatal complications, low birth weight, prenatal exposure to benzodiazepines, alcohol and nicotine, and brain diseases and injuries.

Gene-environment interactions are likely to play a significant part. Genetic variations cause functional abnormalities in both dopaminergic and noradrenergic neurotransmission within frontostriatal pathways. This in turn leads to deficits in executive and reward-related functioning and subsequently the behavioural manifestations of ADHD.

Finally in terms of response to medication, children with ADHD performed as poorly on a memory task as elderly people with Alzheimer's disease, and reverted back to normal with one dose of medication.

### 1.1.9 The value of the concept of ADHD

● Reliability and validity is well established.

- It defines a group of children with considerable impairment.
  - It also defines those with symptoms but no impairment.
- These impairments affect not only the person with the diagnosis but also their family and community.
- It defines a group that has a high risk of suffering from a wide range of other difficulties.
- It provides a starting point from and an anchor on which clinicians can base their assessments.
- It defines a group which responds to (and will benefit from) treatment.
- It defines a group with a disability that is currently under-recognised and under-treated in the UK.
- It defines a group whose numbers are relatively stable across time and across cultures.
- It does not assume pathophysiology where this is not warranted but has strong associations with a range of biological measures for example, heritability, pathophysiology and neuropsychology.
- The diagnoses are now almost universally used in research studies into the causes, associations and treatment of ADHD. This provides a strong link between scientific research and clinical practice.

### 1.1.10    The limitations of the concept of ADHD

- It can lead to dispute and misunderstanding concerning the 'correct' system.
- Categorical definition of a dimensional concept.
  - Cut offs are arbitrary with a big impact on prevalence.
- Inattentiveness symptoms are not adequately defined.
- It defines a heterogeneous group.
- It can be misused if impairment is not adequately considered.
- The exclusion of comorbid forms within the ICD-10 criteria is not helpful when that is the picture of the case in front of you.
- It can lead to difficulties in identifying those requiring treatment.
  - For example, those with subthreshold symptoms but considerable impairment.
- Research has tended to focus on pure ADHD with much less information on those with comorbidity.
- Research has tended to concentrate on reduction in core symptoms rather than on the broader outcomes of impairment, quality of life and comorbidity.
- Neither is adequate for understanding pre-school or adult populations and have limitations with respect to adolescents.

## 1.2    THE CASE FOR WIDER RECOGNITION OF ADHD – FROM A PAEDIATRIC PERSPECTIVE

*Dr G. D. Kewley*

*Consultant Paediatrician/Physician, Director of Learning Assessment and Neurocare Centre, Horsham, West Sussex*

### 1.2.1    Previous significant under-recognition of ADHD

As noted with concern by the author in 1998 (Kewley, 1998)[60] there was continuing under-recognition of ADHD, because of i) persistent reliance on the ICD-10 hyperkinetic terminology; ii) psychosocial-only causes were seen as being solely responsible for all children's behavioural problems; iii) the copious myth and misinformation and the professional and societal ignorance about ADHD, its nature and complications persisted; and iv) there were divisions between professional groups, fixed professional beliefs, theoretical standpoints and a tendency to debate over the heads of the sufferers. Despite the fact that ADHD was the most referenced childhood condition in the Index Medicus during the 1970s and 1980s (Cantwell, 1996), the above difficulties had meant that ADHD was not validated in the UK until the NICE report of 2000 (Lord & Paisley, 2000), was significantly under-recognised and was very slow to be considered as part of the provision of effective child, adolescent and adult mental health services. Although since 2000 there has been an improvement in recognition and validity of ADHD, all of the above problems persist and affect the recognition and provision of effective children's mental health services today. Clinical experience and review of international literature concluded that DSM-IV-R had been a much more effective way of providing effective services. The NICE (2000) report noted that medication usage, however, is but one means of reflecting the increased recognition and diagnosis of ADHD.

### 1.2.2    Guidelines

It was noted that over the past 8 years there has been a degree of convergence between the DSM-IV-R and hyperkinetic (ICD-10) approaches to the diagnosis of ADHD (Swanson *et al.*, 1998). The publications of the Eunithydes Group (Banachewski *et al.*, 2006; Taylor *et al.*, 2004) in recent years have led to a much more clinically relevant evidence-based approach. In clinical practice it has become increasingly realistic to use European guidelines to guide patient management. Previously such guidelines had been more theoretical than practical and clinicians had tended to rely more on North American guidelines, such as the Texas Algorithms (Pliszka *et al.*, 2000) and those from the American Association of Child and Adolescent Psychiatry. Recent

---

[60]References for this paper can be found at the end of the section.

European guidelines have been increasingly relevant in guiding audit and helping manage patient care. However, there remains a need for guidelines for complex case management and for working between professional groups such as the youth justice system, social workers, substance misuse services, and so on. It was also clear that both paediatricians and child psychiatrists had a role in managing children and adolescents with ADHD.

### 1.2.3 Professional and societal recognition of the progression and life span issues of ADHD – relevance to guideline development

Many international studies have emphasised the long-term difficulties of having untreated ADHD (see Figure 1) and the need for differing professional bodies to work together. For example the British Cohort Study (Brassett-Grundy & Butler, 2004) in a 30-year prospective longitudinal study showed that people with childhood ADHD were significantly more likely to face a wide range of negative outcomes at age 30, spanning domains of education, economic status, housing, relationships, crime and health and that their adult lives were typified by social deprivation and adversity. This British study reflects a number of international studies.

Such long-term studies confirm the vulnerability created by ADHD. They emphasise the need for wider recognition of ADHD in relation to criminal behaviour, school under-achievement and exclusion, special schooling provision, workplace issues, teenage pregnancies, motor vehicle accidents and gambling. Another related issue is that many older people, who were educated before the recognition of ADHD as a

**Figure 1: Likely progression of children with untreated ADHD**

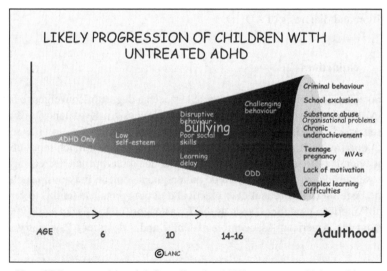

Key: ODD = oppositional defiant disorder; MVA = motor vehicle accidents

valid condition, still have ongoing, impairing symptomatology as older adolescents or adults.

One such subgroup of particular concern comprises those with long-term difficulties arising from ADHD and related difficulties who have entered the youth justice system. The risk factors for such youths are having ADHD with associated early onset of disruptive behaviour disorder, substance use disorder and/or bipolar disorder.

There are many studies in the criminology literature, which tend to run in parallel to ADHD literature (Farrington, 1996; Moffitt *et al.*, 1996). For example the UK National Epidemiologic Study in 1999 (Stephenson & Goodman, 2001) showed that 6% of 5- to 10-year-old boys have conduct disorder, a high percentage of whom entered the youth justice system. Other studies show that up to 90% of those with early conduct disorder have coexisting ADHD (McArdle *et al.*, 1995). Studies raise the possibility of effective medical treatment as part of an overall package of help. Many studies also show a significantly high incidence of ADHD in the juvenile offender population (Rosler *et al.*, 2004). It would be helpful for guidelines to be established, not only with the medical profession but also with other professions such as the Youth Justice Board, social services, tertiary education, teenage pregnancy initiatives and so on.

Approximately 200,000 youths enter the youth justice system annually (The Home Office, 2003). The Asset-Young offender assessment profile showed that up to 75% of such youths considered themselves to be excessively impulsive (Youth Justice Board, 2006). Studies have also shown that re-offending rates can be reduced from approximately 60 to 10% with effective multimodal management including management of ADHD (McCallon, 2000). There is a strong case to be made for guidelines within education and the healthcare profession that link much better with the youth justice and substance misuse services. Consideration is currently being given to whether or not responsibility for such youths could be with education and health rather than primarily with the Home Office and Youth Justice Board (Allen, 2006).

### 1.2.4    Summary

Despite greatly improved recognition of ADHD in recent years, it would appear it is still currently under-recognised both in terms of incidence, treatment and effective management, especially if DSM-IV-R criteria are to be used.

Paediatricians and child psychiatrists have a part to play in the diagnosis and management of the condition, as do many other professional groups.

Guidelines for the management of adult ADHD should also be developed.

Future guidelines, if they are to be more representative of children's mental health issues, and of the progression of ADHD, should be developed not only for the medical profession, as per the NICE guidelines, but also in conjunction with other service providers, such as education, youth justice and substance misuse services.

Broader recognition of the reality, the impact on the family, the chronic course and lifespan issues are essential with regard to public policy development, as an issue of social reform and in the development of effective child, adolescent and adult mental health and educational services.

## 1.2.5    References

Allen, R. (2006) *From Punishment To Problem Solving: A New Approach to Children in Trouble*. London: Centre for Crime and Justice Studies. Available at: http://www. crimeandjustice.org.uk

Banaschewski, T., Coghill, D., Paramala, S., *et al.* (2006) Long acting medications for hyperkinetic disorders: a systematic review and European treatment guideline. *European Child and Adolescent Psychiatry, 15*, 476–95.

Brassett-Grundy, A. & Butler, N. (2004) *Prevalence and Adult Outcomes of Attention-Deficit/Hyperactivity Disorder: Evidence From a 30-Year Prospective Longitudinal Study*. London: Bedford Group for Lifecourse and Statistical Studies. Available at: http://www.ioe.ac.uk/bedfordgroup/publications/ADHD_outcomes_2408.pdf

Cantwell, D. P. (1996) Attention deficit disorder: a review of the past 10 years. *Journal of the American Academy of Child and Adolescent Psychiatry, 35*, 978–987.

Farrington, D. (1996) *Understanding and Preventing Youth Crime*. York: York Publishing Services in association with the Joseph Rowntree Foundation.

Home Office, The (2003) *Youth Justice: The Next Steps*. London: The Home Office.

Kewley, G. D. (1998) Personal paper: attention deficit hyperactivity disorder is underdiagnosed and undertreated in Britain. *British Medical Journal, 316*, 1594–1596.

Lord, J. & Paisley, S. (2000) *The Clinical Effectiveness and Cost-Effectiveness of Methylphenidate for Hyperactivity in Childhood, Version 2*. London: National Institute for Clinical Excellence.

McArdle, P., O'Brien, G. & Kolvin, I. (1995) Hyperactivity: prevalence and relationship with conduct disorder. *The Journal of Child Psychology and Psychiatry, 36*, 279–303.

McCallon, D. (2000) Diagnosing and treating ADHD in a men's prison. In *The Science, Treatment and Prevention of Antisocial Behaviours: Application to the Criminal Justice System* (ed. D. H. Fishbein), 17.1–17.21. Kingston, New Jersey: Civic Research Institute.

Moffitt, T. E., Caspi, A., Dickson, N., *et al.* (1996) Childhood-onset versus adolescent-onset antisocial conduct in males: natural history from age 3 to 18. *Development and Psychopathology, 8*, 399–424.

Pliszka, S. R., Greenhill, L. L., Crismon, M. L., *et al.* (2000) The Texas Children's Medication Algorithm Project: report of the Texas Consensus Conference Panel on medication treatment of childhood attention-deficit/hyperactivity disorder. Parts I & II. *Journal of the American Academy of Child and Adolescent Psychiatry, 39*, 908–927.

Rosler, M., Retz, W., Retz-Junginger, P., *et al.* (2004) Prevalence of attention deficit-/hyperactivity disorder (ADHD) and comorbid disorders in young male prison inmates. *European Archives of Psychiatry and Clinical Neuroscience, 254*, 365–371.

Stephenson, J. & Goodman, R. (2001) Association between behaviour at age 3 years and adult criminality. *British Journal of Psychiatry, 179*, 197–202.

Swanson, J. A., Sargeant, E., Taylor, E. J., *et al.* (1998) Hyperkineses and ADHD. *The Lancet, 351*, 429–433.

Taylor, E., Doepfner, M., Sergeant, J., *et al.* (2004) European clinical guidelines for hyperkinetic disorder – first upgrade. *European Child and Adolescent Psychiatry, 13, Suppl. 1*, 1–30.

Youth Justice Board (2006) *Asset-Young Offender Assessment Profile.* Available at: http://www. yjb.gov.uk/en-gb/practitioners/Assessment/Asset.htm

## 1.3     CONCEPT OF HYPERKINETIC DISORDER AND ADHD AND ITS TREATMENT IMPLICATIONS

*Dr Paramala J. Santosh*
*Clinical Lecturer in Child and Adolescent Psychiatry, Institute of Psychiatry*

### 1.3.1     Introduction

This presentation will look at hyperkinetic disorder and ADHD. If you are looking at the symptom counts in the DSM, you need a greater number of symptoms than in the ICD-10 in order to make a diagnosis. However, an assumption that this means identifying fewer cases using DSM would be incorrect.

In hyperkinetic disorder, filters are applied, starting with the exclusion of anxiety and depression. You also need pervasiveness (symptoms across two settings) and impairment. (DSM focuses on impairment rather than symptoms across two settings.) Applying these filters mean that you will have a smaller number with hyperkinetic disorder as a diagnosis, as opposed to ADHD.

### 1.3.2     The MTA study

The MTA study (MTA Co-operative Group, 1999a & b; 2004a & b) can be used to show how figures can change by just using different criteria; for example the percentage of children diagnosed would vary whether parent, teacher or combined reports were used. Impairment and how you rate it and at what degree of impairment you say 'it is important and needs treatment' is relevant, because it is a question of how you set the threshold: that changes the numbers very dramatically. Differences in rates of diagnoses can therefore be explained by the way in which diagnostic criteria are applied.

### 1.3.3     Summary of the MTA study

This study was looked at to see whether the use of hyperkinetic disorder versus ADHD has an influence in terms of outcomes and treatment. (One factor to consider when looking at this study is that the intensity of the treatments used may not be transferable to clinical settings.)

The target population was children with a DSM-IV diagnosis of ADHD (combined type) plus a wide range of comorbid conditions and demographic characteristics. There were 579 individuals in the study group. The treatment strategies used in the randomly allocated groups were:

- behavioural management (parent training, child-focused, school-based)
- medication management (methylphenidate, if titration unsuccessful open titration of dextroamphetamine, pemoline, imipramine)
- combined treatment
- community care.

The combined treatment (medication plus behavioural intervention) was the most effective.

The next question to be asked was whether the MTA findings of combined ADHD could be generalised to hyperkinetic disorder. Starting with the initial 579 children with the diagnosis of ADHD (combined type), 147 were excluded for anxiety/depression. Of those remaining, once other filters were applied, 145 had a diagnosis of hyperkinetic disorder.

*Hyperkinetic disorder*

One of the main findings was that if you had hyperkinetic disorder, then using stimulants would be a good option as you had a higher chance of responding to medication. Children with hyperkinetic disorder are prescribed stimulants; this will also be the case for children with oppositional defiant disorder/conduct disorder (behavioural therapy is not used).

*Anxiety and depression*

If you had anxiety and depression, it is the combined treatment that was important; not just the behavioural intervention, but behavioural plus medication would be better than medication alone.

*Mild or 'borderline' ADHD*

You could get the same response with either behavioural intervention or stimulant use. The treatment recommendation for 'borderline' ADHD is behavioural therapy, then stimulants. If this is not effective the diagnosis is reviewed.

*Non-hyperkinetic disorder*

The one thing that stood out clearly in the data set was that inattention being reported in schools actually seemed to be a predictor that medication helped the inattention in school. Here medication should be a reasonable choice.

*Health economics*

Medication usage was effective in terms of treatment and even the community care as usual was beneficial. If you look at intensive behavioural therapy versus community care, then if you had a diagnosis of hyperkinetic disorder, it was almost costing twice as much as the ADHD construct. If you had hyperkinetic disorder or hyperkinetic conduct disorder, the likelihood of the behavioural strategy alone working over the medication is going to be less cost effective.

Even the intensive behavioural strategy used in this study was never more effective than medication.

### 1.3.4    What are practical applications of the MTA study in clinical practice?

Possible models include:
- telephone-based medication monitoring and stabilisation clinic – Cambridge International Primary Programme (CIPP)
- 1-week MTA titration phase strategy
- day-patient observation with differing doses of stimulants
- intense monitoring offered only when routine treatment fails.

Do these strategies matter when we now have long-acting drugs?

NICE guidelines should also be trying to look at how clinicians can be helped to do better clinical monitoring and titrating, as opposed to just deciding whether someone needs to receive a drug or not.

### 1.4    PREDICTIVE VALIDITY OF BROAD VERSUS NARROW CLASSIFICATION OF HYPERACTIVITY

*Dr Russell Schachar, MD, FRCP(C)*
*Department of Psychiatry, Neurosciences and Mental Health Research Institute, The Hospital for Sick Children, University of Toronto, Ontario, Canada*
Address for correspondence: R. Schachar, The Hospital for Sick Children, 555 University Avenue, Toronto, M5G 1X8, Canada, russell.schachar@sickkids.ca

At one extreme of the debate about the validity of the diagnosis of childhood hyperactivity are those who assert that the diagnosis is invalid no matter what criteria are applied. More often, however, the question is framed around the appropriate breadth of the diagnosis. Some hold that only a narrowly defined syndrome such as hyperkinetic disorder as defined in ICD-10 has diagnostic validity and that a more broadly defined syndrome such as ADHD as defined in DSM-IV captures a group of children who either has no disorder whatsoever or a group who is similar to children with other and presumably more valid and clinically meaningful diagnoses such as conduct disorder. Figure 1 shows several hypothetic functions relating severity of the phenotype on the y axis and accumulating underlying risk on the x axis. A narrowly defined diagnostic entity is shown by the smaller oval, a broadly defined entity by the larger oval.

In Model A, risk accumulates slowly without behavioural, cognitive or other manifestations until some threshold is exceeded. Beyond that threshold, the disorder is manifest and further risk does not substantially alter the phenotype. This is essentially the pathogen-disease model of disorder.

Model B shows a variation of the first function. At some level of the trait, there is a substantial increase in the expression of the disorder just as in model A. But in model B, the narrowly defined entity misses many individuals with risk who are captured

## Figure 1: Models relation phenotype and risk

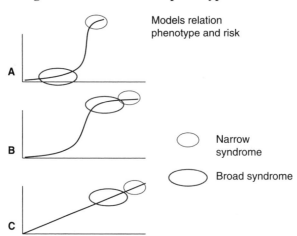

by the broader criteria. The big difference between broad and narrow entities is prevalence although the narrow entity could show more risks depending on the slope of the function relating risk to symptoms over the hypothetical diagnostic threshold. According to this model, both the broadly and the narrowly defined entities are different from unaffected individuals.

Model C shows a different function in which phenotypic expression increases linearly with increasing risk. There is no point at which there is a substantial and discontinuous increase in phenotypic expression with accumulating risk. Accordingly, a disorder defined narrowly by the presence of severe expression (the most symptomatic, the most impaired, those with the most evidence of some underlying pathogen or dysfunction) would differ in degree rather than in kind from a more broadly defined entity. Under these circumstances, there can be no easy solution to the classification problem. There will always be individuals who fall just below the boundary of the category and sub-threshold cases will differ only in degree from supra-threshold cases. Under these circumstances, factors other than validity of the defined entity will determine where the threshold is set. ICD-10 criteria are narrower than those for DSM in terms of pervasiveness, the range of symptoms required for criteria to be met (symptoms of inattention, hyperactivity *and* impulsiveness) and treatment of comorbidity.

We evaluated these models by assessing the predictive validity of hyperkinetic disorder and ADHD in a sample of approximately 1000 consecutive referrals to a specialty clinic for attention, learning and behaviour problems. First, we compared children who met criteria for hyperkinetic disorder, ADHD-combined subtype, ADHD-inattentive subtype, ADHD-hyperactive impulsive subtype and controls on a range of clinical and cognitive characteristics. Then we excluded cases with any comorbid condition (conduct disorder or oppositional disorder, generalised or separation anxiety disorder, reading disability) and compared hyperkinetic disorder, ADHD, and control groups once again. Only one in ten cases that met criteria for ADHD also fulfilled criteria for hyperkinetic disorder. The hyperkinetic disorder group was more severe in that they exhibited a greater number of parent- and teacher-rated symptoms followed by the ADHD-combined subtype, ADHD-hyperactive impulsive subtype and ADHD-inattentive subtype groups in descending order. Despite differences in symptoms severity and pervasiveness, hyperkinetic disorder, ADHD-combined subtype, ADHD-inattentive subtype and ADHD-hyperactive impulsive subtype differed little in teacher- and parent-rated impairment, exposure to psychosocial adversity (for example, low socioeconomic status, single parent-headed homes, and so on), recurrence risk for ADHD in first-degree family members, comorbidity (except for lower rate of conduct disorder in the ADHD-inattentive subtype group), intelligence, reading scores, and measures of working memory (digit span backward) and inhibitory control (stop signal reaction time in the stop task). All of these groups had more deviant or extreme scores in each of these characteristics than did controls. After excluding comorbidity, hyperkinetic disorder, ADHD and conduct disorder groups differed little in recurrence risk for ADHD in family members, exposure to psychosocial adversity, intelligence, digit span backwards, and reading performance; all three of these groups differed from controls. Hyperkinetic disorder was marked by more severe inhibitory control deficit than the ADHD, conduct disorder and control groups. The hyperkinetic disorder, conduct disorder and ADHD groups were more impaired according to parent and teacher ratings. In addition, parents rated the conduct disorder group as more impaired than the hyperkinetic disorder and ADHD groups whereas teachers rated the hyperkinetic disorder group as more impaired than the ADHD and conduct disorder groups.

In summary, these results support the predictive validity of both the narrowly (hyperkinetic disorder, ICD-10) and the broadly (ADHD, DSM-IV) defined entities and reject the hypothesis that either broadly or narrowly define hyperactivity or both are invalid clinical entities or nothing more than that which is predicted by their common comorbidities (Model A). There was only minimal evidence in these data for a quantitative increase in the severity of associated risks with increase in severity or pervasiveness (Model C). There was a trend for inhibitory control to be worse in hyperkinetic disorder compare with ADHD-combined subtype, ADHD-hyperactive impulsive subtype, and ADHD-inattentive subtype groups in that order. These results do not isolate a unique feature of childhood hyperactivity. In conclusion, the most clearly supported model is Model B which posits that both the broadly and the narrowly defined entities exceed the threshold for a valid diagnostic entity.

Finally, it should be recalled that in North America the small subgroup of narrowly defined hyperkinetic disorder cases would all meet criteria for ADHD; the predictive validity of the later group will be more marked than was found in this study where hyperkinetic disorder cases were separated from ADHD. By contrast, in the UK and other countries which follow ICD-10 diagnostic practice, at least nine of ten impaired children will not receive a diagnosis. More than half of these cases do not receive any other diagnosis and will therefore not receive a diagnosis commensurate with the seriousness of their disorder.

## 1.5 SOCIAL AND CULTURAL ISSUES IN ADHD DIAGNOSES AND PSYCHOSTIMULANT TREATMENT

*Dr Ilina Singh*
*Wellcome Trust University Lecturer in Bioethics and Society, The London School of Economics and Political Science*
**Professor Nikolas Rose**
*Professor of Sociology, Convenor of Department of Sociology, The London School of Economics and Political Science*

Reliable diagnosis rates for ADHD are difficult to find in any national context. It is also difficult to know the true epidemiology of ADHD in any national context, and prevalence rates vary widely, from 0.5 to 26% in the UK; and from 2 to 18% in the US. There is, however, good systematic data on worldwide consumption of methylphenidate (and dexamfetamine), collected by the United Nations International Narcotics Control Board. There is also detailed data available from IMS Health.

Both these sources demonstrate an enormous variation in global consumption of methylphenidate. Average consumption rates increased dramatically between 1999 and 2003, averaging five- to seven-fold increases. There are many possible explanations for this variation, including (and not limited to) true epidemiological variation across countries in ADHD, the impact of national prescribing practices, medical training, parenting ideology, drug policies, health insurance, educational practices, teaching, and so forth. The bottom line is this: we don't know why this variation exists.

The global variation in stimulant drug consumption does point to the fact that social and cultural factors are key to understanding patterns and trends in ADHD diagnoses and psychostimulant treatment. This does **not** mean that ADHD may not also have an organic aetiology. Socio-cultural analysis can make an important contribution to identifying and evaluating key environmental factors that shape ADHD diagnosis and stimulant drug treatment patterns.

It is unclear which level of socio-cultural analysis would be most useful. Potential analyses cover a wide range of targets: from a macro-level study of by-nation variation in methylphenidate consumption, to a micro-level study of the beliefs and practices of individual teachers and psychiatrists in local settings.

Evidence of socio-cultural factors in ADHD diagnosis and treatment can inform the guideline by providing understanding of the pathway to diagnosis of ADHD, and the key consequences of diagnosis of ADHD for the child and family. This is particularly important now that ADHD is no longer understood as a disorder of childhood. There is little or no long-term data on the 'career' of the ADHD patient. We need to understand more about this career in order to assess the risks and benefits of (1) a narrow versus wide diagnosis and (2) recommendations of long-term drug treatment.

We also need to avoid mistakenly attributing to the child consequences of social situations and cultural forces. This means we must have better (objective, sound and uniform) diagnoses for ADHD. However, even if this can be realised, in the absence of a biological marker for ADHD, there will always be an inherent dilemma about whether to cast the ADHD net widely or narrowly (by supporting a wide or a narrowly constructed diagnostic guideline). The costs and benefits of either approach must be very carefully weighed.

## 1.6 CATEGORICAL MODELS OF ATTENTION DEFICIT/ HYPERACTIVITY DISORDER: A CONCEPTUAL AND EMPIRICAL ANALYSIS

*Professor Edmund Sonuga-Barke*
*Professor in Psychology, Convenor of the Developmental Brain Behaviour Unit, University of Southampton*

In this presentation we explored the status of categorical models of ADHD as they underpin current diagnostic formulations in the DSM-IV and the ICD-10 and anchor debate about future revisions of these manuals. The presentation draws on the ideas published in a published journal article (Sonuga-Barke, 1998).[61] The presentation had three major elements. Part one involved a discussion of the defining role of diagnostic systems in clinical and scientific practice related to ADHD. We reviewed the historical development of the role of diagnostic systems and their political and economic foundations. Part two was a review of three major themes relating to categorical models of childhood disorder.

First, we discussed the inevitability of categorisation in clinical practice given the imperative to identify those individuals in need of intervention, that is, clinicians are inevitably categorisers and so categorical diagnostic systems go with the grain of clinical practice. Furthermore, we highlight the social-psychological basis of categorical models of disorder by arguing that clinicians, like other humans, when faced with challenge of understanding complex human behaviour, tend to use heuristic devices that involve inferring traits on the basis of behavioural observations and drawing categorical boundaries even when these are not obviously present.

Second, we examined the relationship between clinical categorisation and science. Here we focused on the role that the values and assumptions inherent in categorical diagnostic systems and the way that influence scientific practice – the hypotheses that are tested and the methods that are used to test them. In assuming that disorders, such as ADHD, are discrete entities qualitatively different from the normal variation of behaviour we bias our search for categorical boundaries between normality and abnormality and over-interpret evidence in favour of the validity of conditions. However, there is a need for a bridge of common meaning between the 'laboratory' and the 'clinic' and categorical diagnostic models support this vital function.

Third, we considered the different ways that one could respond to this recognition of the role of assumptions in the scientific study of categorical models of disorder. After considering a number of options (including the rejection of diagnostic approaches on the grounds that they are social constructions) we argued that Meehl's (1992) scientific realism whereby scientific assumptions are turned into specific testable hypotheses was the most valuable approach. The hypothesis that ADHD is a true category, or as Meehl (1992) calls it, a *taxa*, has not been tested sufficiently to date. However, genetics studies using DF analyses that look at the relationship between symptom severity and heritability do not support the taxa hypothesis of ADHD. More recent and more sophisticated

---

[61]References for this paper can be found at the end of the section.

studies using advanced taxonomic analyses also find no evidence for the existence of an ADHD taxa (for example, Haslam *et al.*, 2006; Frazier *et al.*, 2007). It appears that ADHD is better modelled as a continuous trait rather than a discrete category.

We concluded by highlighting the dilemma between this empirical reality (that ADHD is better regarded as the extreme of normal variation rather than a distinct category) and the practical necessity and psychological inevitability that clinicians will make categorical decisions. We concluded by highlighting concerns over the transparency, communicability and implementability of a dimensional system for the diagnosis of ADHD while accepting that it may be a better model for science. Adopting such a model in future diagnostic formulations may run the risk of dismantling the bridge of meaning between clinic and lab – paradoxically inhibiting the process of diagnostic refinement and so the relevance of scientific findings to clinical practice.

## REFERENCES

Haslam, N., Williams, B., Prior, M., *et al.* (2006) The latent structure of attention-deficit/hyperactivity disorder: a taxometric analysis. *Australian and New Zealand Journal of Psychiatry, 40*, 639–647.

Frazier, T. W., Youngstrom, E. A., Naugle, R. I. (2007) The latent structure of attention-deficit/hyperactivity disorder in a clinic-referred sample. *Neuropsychology, 21*, 45–64.

Meehl, P. E. (1992) Factors and taxa, traits and types, differences of degree and differences in kind. *Journal of Personality, 60*, 117–174.

Sonuga-Barke, E. J. S. (1998) Categorical model in child psychopathology: a conceptual and empirical analysis. *The Journal of Child Psychology and Psychiatry, 39*, 15–133.

## 1.7    ARGUMENTS AGAINST THE USE OF THE CONCEPT IN CLINICAL PRACTICE: INCLUDING WHETHER IT SHOULD BE USED NEVER OR SPARINGLY

*Dr Sami Timimi*
*Consultant Child Psychiatrist, Lincolnshire Partnership NHS Trust*

The main problem with current theory and practice in ADHD is the prevalence of the underlying assumption that ADHD is a genetic neurodevelopmental disorder and that clinicians have valid and reliable ways of identifying what behaviours are the result of such neurodevelopmental disabilities in any individual child. This narrow biomedical construction causes a polarisation of views and attitudes with proponents of this view claiming 'there is no such disagreement [about ADHD being a valid disorder]—at least no more so than there is over whether smoking causes cancer, or whether a virus causes HIV/AIDS' (Barkley, 2002);[62] while opponents claim, 'It's as

---

[62]References for this paper can be found at the end of the section.

simple as this: if no physical examination, lab test, X-ray, scan or biopsy shows an abnormality in your children, your child is normal' (Baughman,1998).

Current evidence does not support a simplistic view of ADHD type behaviours. Genetic studies have relied on poor standards of evidence (such as the disputed 'equal environment' assumption), and have failed to replicate genetic associations consistently, thus the null hypothesis stands – no genes exist for ADHD. Similarly, neuroimaging studies suffer from serious methodological failings and interpretive inadequacies; thus there are currently no neurological markers for ADHD (nor are there likely to be). Conceptual problems are endemic in ADHD; these include: high comorbidity, cross-cultural variations among raters and the rated, the behaviours are qualitatively common behaviours leading to large variations in prevalence, the gender distribution and the circularity of construct (the behaviours define the disorder, the disorder defines the behaviours).

The most important implication of the dominance of biological theory in ADHD is that it has led to a rapid rise in the use of biological remedies as the first-line and often only treatment for those diagnosed with ADHD. This is problematic. Although stimulants have proven efficacy (up to 4 weeks), the long-term outcome literature available does not support stimulants being effective in the long term (an important finding given that many end up on stimulants for many years). Current treatment protocols have come to rely too heavily on the MTA study (1999). However this had major methodological and interpretive flaws, with the 24-month follow-up study (MTA, 2004) having less positive findings for medication, with children on medication experiencing significant side effects. Indeed William Pelham, who was on the board of the MTA studies, recently concluded: 'No drug company in its literature mentions the fact that 40 years of research says there is no long-term benefit of medications. That is something parents need to know.' (Quoted in Hearn, 2004). The literature on medication has exaggerated stimulants' effectiveness and minimised its risks (which include serious risks such as cardiac disease, psychosis and sudden death).

However, we still have the reality that many children and many families are struggling to understand and deal with a range of behavioural and educational problems that we currently call ADHD. Some appear to benefit from diagnosis and prescription of medication, but we must balance this with our social responsibility for public health.

Alternative and useful ways forward can be found through incorporating discourses and research from related fields such as philosophy and transcultural/anthropological psychiatry which can provide both theory and practice with conceptual and practical tools to engage with questions of values, ethics, diversity and the changing nature of the challenges and circumstances that children and families live in.

The implications of this line of thinking are many. For the purposes of guidelines in diagnosing ADHD this means that ADHD should *not* be viewed as neurodevelopmental; diagnosis should come under the remit of mental health *not* paediatrics; the diagnosis should be reserved for more serious cases that are not responding to a variety of currently available clinical approaches, and when a diagnosis is made this should *not* lead to a long-term prescription.

**REFERENCES**

Baughman, F. A. (1998) The totality of the ADD/ADHD fraud. *National Institutes of Health, Consensus Conference on ADHD.* Video available at http://www.adhdfraud.com

Barkley, R. (2002) International Consensus Statement on ADHD. *Clinical Child and Family Psychology Review*, 5, 89–111.

Hearn, K. (2004) Here kiddie, kiddie. Available at http://alternet.org/drugreporter/20594/ [accessed June 2005].

MTA Co-operative Group (1999) A 14 month randomized clinical trial of treatment strategies for attention deficit/hyperactivity disorder. *Archives of General Psychiatry*, 56, 1073–1086.

MTA Co-operative Group (2004) National Institute of Mental Health Multimodal Treatment Study of ADHD follow-up: 24-month outcomes of treatment strategies for attention-deficit/hyperactivity disorder. *Pediatrics*, 113, 754–761.

## PART 2: DRAFT DIAGNOSIS CHAPTER (PART 1) SENT TO PEER REVIEWERS[63]

**Part I - Validity of the ADHD diagnosis**

### 1.1    INTRODUCTION

This guideline is applicable to people above the age of three and of all levels of intellectual ability who show symptoms of hyperactivity, impulsivity or inattention to a degree that impairs their academic progress, mental development, personal relationships, or physical or mental health. This includes people with ADHD whether or not they have other comorbid mental disorders or whether the ADHD symptoms result from genetic, physical environmental or social environmental causes. This chapter sets out to look at the issues of diagnostic categorisation and assessment that should trigger the use of this guideline. First, we address the validity of DSM-IV ADHD and ICD-10 hyperkinetic disorder as diagnostic categories. Second, a guidance for clinical practice is provided.

### 1.2    THE VALIDITY OF ADHD AS A DIAGNOSTIC CATEGORY

The Guideline Development Group (GDG) acknowledged at the outset that the use of the diagnosis of ADHD has been the subject of considerable controversy and debate and that the diagnosis itself has varied across time and place as diagnostic systems

---

[63]This is a reproduction of the document that was sent to peer reviewers. As this was in draft form it contains some typographical and grammatical errors.

have evolved (Rhodes *et al.*, 2006). Points of controversy identified by the GDG included the reasons for the wide variation in prevalence rates reported for ADHD and the nature of the aetiological risk factors for ADHD.

The GDG wished to evaluate evidence for the validity of the diagnostic category of ADHD and formulate a position statement. It was recognised that defining psychiatric disorders is a difficult process due to the overlapping nature of behavioural and psychiatric syndromes, the complexity of the aetiological processes and the lack of a 'gold standard' such as a biological test – in this regard ADHD is no different from other common psychiatric disorders. Furthermore, in keeping with other common behavioural disorders there is no clear distinction between the clinical condition and the normal variation in the general population (see Section A3 [1.4.3]). This is comparable to normal variation for medical traits such as hypertension and type II diabetes, as well as psychological problems such as anxiety. Controversial issues surround changing thresholds applied to the definition of illness as new knowledge and treatments are developed (Kessler *et al.*, 2003 and the extent to which functioning within the 'normal cultural environment' should determine clinical thresholds (Sonuga-Barke, 1998; Rosenman, 2006). As a result of considering these issues, a central question for this chapter is to delineate the level of ADHD symptoms and associated impairments required to trigger the use of this guideline.

It was recognised from the start that undertaking a systematic review of diagnostic categories is not a straightforward exercise for behavioural and psychiatric disorders because in most cases definitive diagnostic tests for the presence or absence of disorder do not exist. The relative lack of a validated reference standard (indicated by SIGN diagnostic study quality assessment, see Appendix A[64]) means that the question of validity for the diagnosis of ADHD needs to draw on evidence from a wide range of sources. There is also potential for ascertainment bias particularly in clinic-referred populations and considerable variation by clinical and demographic subgroups, disease prevalence and severity, and use of different behavioural and symptom measures (Whiting *et al.*, 2004). The GDG wish to emphasise that psychiatric nosology is a dynamic and developing field and changes are to be expected over time as more data are accrued.

To ensure that a transparent, structured approach was taken, the GDG agreed to use one similar to the Washington University Diagnostic Criteria (Feighner *et al.*, 1972). This approach involves setting out criteria for validating a particular disorder and seeing how far a particular set of phenomena is consistent with those criteria. Using these criteria as a framework, this chapter sets out to answer the following questions:

A: To what extent do the phenomena of hyperactivity, impulsivity and inattention, which define the current DSM-IV and ICD-10 criteria for ADHD and hyperkinetic disorder, cluster together in the general population and into a particular disorder that can be distinguished from other disorders and from normal variation?

B: Is the cluster of symptoms that defines ADHD associated with significant clinical and psychosocial impairments?

---

[64]Appendices A-J referenced here are not reproduced in this publication. Please contact the authors if you would like copies of these appendices.

C: Is there evidence for a characteristic pattern of developmental changes, or outcomes associated with the symptoms, that define ADHD?

D: Is there consistent evidence of genetic, environmental or neurobiological risk factors associated with ADHD?

These questions were taken to relate to both DSM-IV ADHD and ICD-10 hyperkinetic disorder criteria. Hyperkinetic disorder is a more restricted definition of ADHD that forms a subset of the DSM-IV combined subtype of ADHD. The term 'hyperactivity' has been used in some studies to mean the cluster of hyperactive, impulsive and inattentive symptoms. In this guideline the term 'hyperactivity' is restricted to mean the combination of symptoms that defines overactive behaviour and the term 'ADHD symptoms' is used to refer to the combination of hyperactive, impulsive and inattentive symptoms.

## 1.3 METHODOLOGY

A literature search was conducted for existing systematic reviews and meta-analyses on CINAHL, EMBASE, MEDLINE, PsycINFO. The initial search found 5,516 reviews of which nine were relevant to the questions about ADHD and application of the Washington University Diagnostic Criteria. Where insufficient evidence was found from previous systematic reviews, a search for primary studies was carried out (see Appendix B). We selected reviews for inclusion in this chapter if they met the SIGN quality assessment criteria for systematic reviews and cohort studies. For diagnostic and factor analytic studies we established a set of criteria approved by NICE (Appendix C).

In addition to the review of the literature, a consensus conference was held to bring together experts in the field who held a range of views and could address the concept of ADHD from different perspectives. This provided an opportunity to debate the key issues surrounding the use of this diagnostic category and thereby to assist the GDG with the task of deciding what should trigger the use of the guideline and for whom the guideline is intended. A summary of the consensus conference is provided in an Appendix to this chapter (Appendix D).

## 1.4 REVIEWING THE VALIDITY OF THE DIAGNOSIS: SUMMARY OF THE EVIDENCE

A: To what extent do the phenomena of hyperactivity, impulsivity and inattention, which define the current DSM-IV and ICD-10 criteria for ADHD and hyperkinetic disorder, cluster together in the general population and into a particular disorder that can be distinguished from other disorders and from normal variation?

The evidence addressing this issue is divided into three main questions:

(A1) Do the phenomena of hyperactivity, inattention and impulsivity cluster together?

(A2) Are ADHD symptoms distinguishable from other conditions?

(A3) Are the phenomena of hyperactivity, inattention and impulsivity distinguishable from the normal spectrum?

### 1.4.1 (A1) Do the phenomena of hyperactivity, inattention and impulsivity cluster together?

No evidence was found from the systematic search of reviews that was of direct relevance to this question. This is because, despite a large primary literature, few systematic reviews in this area have been undertaken. Therefore a systematic search of factor-analytic studies was carried out. Additional factor-analytic and cross-sectional studies were identified by the GDG (Appendix E). None of these studies met the SIGN inclusion criteria that requires an appropriate reference standard for diagnostic measures, but did meet the extension to the SIGN criteria approved for this review: the aim of the question was to evaluate whether the phenomena of hyperactivity, inattention and impulsivity cluster together in the population, rather than to assess the accuracy of diagnostic tests.

The inclusion criteria for factor-analytic studies were defined as follows: (i) that the study addresses an appropriate and clearly focused question and (ii) that the sample population being studied was selected either as a consecutive series or randomly, from a clearly defined study population.

*Evidence*
Many factor analyses indicate a two-factor model; 'hyperactivity-impulsivity' and 'inattention'. This has been replicated in population-based studies (Lahey *et al.*, 1994; Leviton *et al.*, 1993; Wolraich *et al.*, 1996) and clinical samples (Bauermeister *et al.*, 1992; Lahey *et al.*, 1988; Pelham *et al.*, 1992). Single factor 'hyperactivity-impulsivity' is also supported by Dreger and colleagues' (1964) early study where the factor 'hyperactivity' was defined as 'impulsive, excitable hyperactivity'. More recent factor-analytic studies based on DSM-IV criteria support previous findings that the symptoms of inattention and hyperactivity-impulsivity are distinct symptom domains in children (Molina *et al.*, 2001; Amador-Campos *et al.*, 2005; Zuddas *et al.*, 2006) and adolescents (Hudziak *et al.*, 1998).

Looking specifically at children identified as having a behavioural problem Conners (1969) found 'hyperactivity' and 'inattention' as separate and distinct factors. The factor structure of adolescent self-report behavioural data was investigated by Conners and colleagues (1997) and found six factors including 'hyperactivity' and 'cognitive problems'. The 'hyperactivity' factor included characteristics such as being unable to sit still for very long, squirming and fidgeting and feeling restless inside when sitting still. The 'cognitive problems' factor consisted of having trouble keeping focused attention, having problems organising tasks and forgetting things that were learnt. Similar results were found in Conners and colleagues' (1998) further study were attentional problems that overlap with the DSM-IV criteria for inattentive subtype of ADHD, with a similar overlap between the factor items and DMS-IV criteria for hyperactivity-impulsivity [sic].

Some studies have identified three factors; 'hyperactivity' and 'impulsivity' as two distinct factors in addition to 'inattention' in both the general population (Gomez *et al.*, 1999; Glutting *et al.*, 2005) and clinical populations (Pillow *et al.*, 1998). However, Gomez and colleagues (1999) showed that the model fit for the three-factor solution was only marginally better than the two-factor model. In the study of Pillow and colleagues (1998) of boys with ADHD, the impulsive and hyperactive symptoms formed a single factor when oppositional-defiant and conduct disorder items were also included in the factor analysis.

Werry and colleagues (1975), however, found that hyperactivity, impulsivity and inattention formed a single factor using both population control and 'hyperactive' samples.

Using a latent class analysis (LCA) that identifies clusters of symptoms that group together, Hudziak and colleagues (1998) found that hyperactivity-impulsivity and inattention could exist as a 'combined' type latent class as well as separate hyperactive-impulsive and inattention latent classes. The latent classes map closely to the DSM-IV criteria, with DSM-IV combined type falling entirely within the severe combined type latent class. Individuals with the DSM-IV inattentive subtype fell either within the severe inattentive or the severe combined latent classes.

The clustering of hyperactivity, impulsivity and inattention appear to be stable across a number of countries. Ho and colleagues (1996) found separate robust dimensions for 'hyperactivity' (the combination of inattention and hyperactive-impulsive behaviour), 'antisocial' and 'neurotic' behaviour in a sample of 3,069 Chinese schoolboys. Correlations among different dimensions were similar to those reported in European and US samples. Taylor and Sandberg (1984) compared data from 437 English schoolchildren with published data from the US and New Zealand. They identified a factor of hyperactivity-inattention that was distinct from conduct disorder. The comparisons supported the view that English schoolchildren were similar to their contemporaries in the US and New Zealand with differences in prevalence rates between different countries accounted for by discrepancies in diagnostic practice.

In adult population samples a two-factor model has been identified (DuPaul *et al.*, 2001; Smith & Johnson, 2000) as well as a three-factor model (Kooij *et al.*, 2005). Glutting and colleagues (2005) assessed university students aged 17 to 22 using parent-rated information in addition to self-rated data. They reported slightly contrasting findings within each set of data; exploratory and confirmatory analysis showed that DSM-IV ADHD symptoms generated a three-factor model in the self-report data and a two-factor model in the parent-informant data.

Although most studies show separate factors for 'inattention' and 'hyperactivity-impulsivity', these are highly correlated in children (Gomez *et al.*, 1999) and adult samples (Kooij *et al.*, 2005).

There may be age-dependent changes in the factor structure. Bauermeister and colleagues (1992) found that there was a single 'attention/impulsivity-hyperactivity' factor in pre-school children, and separation into two factors in school-age children. Nearly all the studies of school-age children reported two factors. In contrast, the study from Glutting and colleagues (2005) using college students aged 17 to 22 found three factors, with the separation of hyperactive and impulsive symptoms. Similarly Kooij and colleagues (2005) using adult samples identified three separate factors.

*Summary*

Factor-analytic studies indicate that ADHD symptoms cluster together in general population samples. The number of factors varies between studies, with most finding two correlated factors for hyperactivity-impulsivity and inattention; others find that hyperactivity and impulsivity can be distinguished and a few find one combined factor of all three domains. These findings have been observed in both population and clinical samples and in a number of different cultural settings. LCA in population samples detects clustering of symptoms into groups that are similar but not identical to DSM-IV criteria for ADHD.

### 1.4.2    (A2) Are ADHD symptoms distinguishable from other conditions?

No systematic reviews were identified in the literature that addressed this question. The GDG considered that the most important and controversial distinction to be made was between ADHD and oppositional-defiant and conduct disorders. These are also the most commonly reported comorbid problems in children and adolescents diagnosed with ADHD and define a set of behaviours that might be difficult to distinguish from ADHD. It was therefore decided to restrict a formal literature search to identify studies that indicate whether a distinction can be made between ADHD, oppositional-defiant and conduct problems. Additional references were identified by the GDG members (see Appendix F).

### Evidence

*1.4.2.1    ADHD and oppositional-defiant and conduct problems*
Most of the studies using factor-analytic approaches for the analysis of ADHD symptoms report separate factors for hyperactivity-impulsivity, inattention and oppositional-defiant or conduct problems. These include most of the studies reviewed in the previous section on factor structure of ADHD symptoms (for example, Bauermeister *et al.*, 1992; Conners, 1969; Conners, 1997a & 1997b; Ho *et al.*, 1996; Pelham *et al.*, 1992; Taylor & Sandberg, 1984; Werry *et al.*, 1975; Wolraich *et al.*, 1996). These studies are highly consistent in being able to separate oppositional-defiant and conduct problems from hyperactivity-impulsivity and inattention. Although the symptoms fall into separate dimensions there are significant correlations between the behavioural factors.

Frouke and colleagues (2005) conducted a diagnostic study of 2,230 Dutch preadolescents from the general population. LCA revealed that ADHD symptoms clustered together with symptoms of oppositional-defiant disorder and conduct disorder. A further study from the Netherlands of disruptive behaviour in 636 7-year-old children (Pol *et al.*, 2003) came to similar conclusions. LCA using the same data identified three main classes of children with: (i) high levels of ODD (oppositional defiant disorder) and ADHD, (ii) intermediate levels of ODD and ADHD with low levels of CP (conduct problems) and (iii) low levels of all disruptive problems. No classes were identified with only ADHD, ODD or CP.

King and colleagues (2005a) identified seven distinct groups using a cluster analysis that identified discrete groups: ADHD with inattention (ADHD-I), ADHD with hyperactivity-impulsivity (ADHD-H/I), ADHD with both hyperactivity/impulsivity and inattention (ADHD-C), ADHD-C with oppositional defiant disorder, and ADHD-I with oppositional defiant disorder. For both the inattentive symptoms and combined inattentive/hyperactive-impulsive symptoms they found clustering either with or without symptoms of oppositional defiant disorder.

Latent dimension modelling by Ferguson and colleagues (1991) looking at children with ADHD and conduct disorder (CD) suggested that these could be seen as independent dimensions, although they are highly inter-correlated. However the two often occur independently of each other and only partially share aetiological factors.

ADHD can be a precursor of other problems. When ADHD and disruptive behavioural problems coexist the history usually suggests that symptoms of ADHD appear first before the development of disruptive behavioural problems. A follow-up of a community sample of children with ADHD symptoms but no oppositional behaviour between the ages of 7 and 17 revealed that children with ADHD symptoms could develop oppositional behaviour at a later stage, but that the reverse pathway from oppositional behaviour to ADHD was uncommon (Taylor *et al.*, 1996).

Population twin studies find that symptoms of ADHD are distinct from but share overlapping familial and genetic influences with conduct problems (Thapar *et al.*, 2001; Silberg *et al.*, 1996; Nadder *et al.*, 2002). Multivariate twin modelling suggests that while the genetic influences on conduct disorder are largely shared with those that influence ADHD, there are in addition important environmental factors that influence the risk for conduct problems but not ADHD (Thapar *et al.*, 2001). Nadder and colleagues (2002) conclude that the co-variation of ADHD and ODD/CD is the result of shared genetic influences with little influence from environmental factors. However there are substantial environmental influences on ODD/CD, especially when they are not accompanied by ADHD (Silberg *et al.*, 1996; Eaves *et al.*, 1997). The heritability of ADHD symptoms is also higher than that for ODD/CD symptoms in these studies.

### 1.4.2.2    ADHD and other co-occurring conditions

Population twin studies find that symptoms of ADHD are distinct from but share overlapping familial and genetic influences with other neurodevelopmental problems including reading difficulties (Gilger *et al.*, 1992; Willcutt *et al.*, 2000; Willcutt *et al.*, 2007), impaired general cognitive ability (Kuntsi *et al.*, 2004) and developmental coordination disorder (Martin *et al.*, 2006).

ADHD is reported to co-occur with personality disorder in young offenders (Young *et al.*, 2003). A prison survey found that 45% of incarcerated young adults had a previous history and persistence of ADHD symptoms (Rosler *et al.*, 2004). The distinction between ADHD and personality disorder in adults raises important nosological questions and remains poorly investigated.

Dysthymia, depression and anxiety symptoms and disorders are frequently associated with ADHD in adults. In the US National Comorbidity Survey, adults with ADHD had increased rates of mood disorders, anxiety disorders, substance misuse disorders and impulse control disorders (Kessler *et al.*, 2006).

*Summary*

In the majority of factor-analytic studies ADHD symptoms are found to represent separate but correlated factors from oppositional behaviour and conduct problems. When symptom clusters are considered, ADHD symptoms are often found to group together with oppositional behaviour. Longitudinal studies suggest that ADHD represents a separate condition that is a risk factor for the development of oppositional and conduct problems. Twin studies suggest overlapping genetic influences on ADHD and conduct problems but the genetic influences estimated by twin studies are greater for ADHD than ODD/CD and there are environmental influences on ODD/CD that do not act on ADHD. The correlation between ADHD and several neurodevelopmental traits (cognitive ability, reading ability, developmental coordination and pervasive developmental disorders) is due largely to the effects of shared genetic influences. In adults, co-occurring symptoms, syndromes and disorders are frequently found to exist alongside the core ADHD syndrome, but their distinction from ADHD and the reasons for high rates of co-occurrence are not well addressed in the current literature.

### 1.4.3    (A3) Are the phenomena of hyperactivity, inattention and impulsivity distinguishable from the normal spectrum?

No systematic reviews were identified that were of direct relevance to this question. The previous search for primary studies revealed two factor-analytic studies relevant to this question. Also, the GDG members identified further factor-analytic and genetic studies (see Appendix G).

*Evidence*

Many studies have found a strong correspondence between quantitative measures of ADHD and the categorical diagnosis (Biederman *et al.*, 1993; Bird *et al.*, 1987; Biederman *et al.*, 1996; Boyle *et al.*, 1997; Chen *et al.*, 1994; Edelbrock *et al.*, 1986). These studies show that children with ADHD appear to be at one extreme of a quantitative dimension and this on this [sic] quantitative dimension there is no obvious bi-modality that separates children with ADHD from non-ADHD children.

Twin studies using individual differences approaches (reviewed in Thapar *et al.*, 1999; Faraone *et al.*, 2005) and De Fries-Fulker extremes analysis (Gjone *et al.*, 1996; Levy *et al.*, 1997; Willcutt *et al.*, 2000; Price *et al.*, 2001) estimate similar heritability for ADHD symptoms from general population twin samples. These studies indicate that the genetic influences on ADHD are distributed throughout the population; there is no obvious threshold or cut-off between ADHD and the continuous distribution of symptoms in the population.

ADHD can be divided into multiple latent class groups distinguished on the basis of three symptom groupings: attention, hyperactivity-impulsivity and the combination of these two symptom domains. In addition, the symptom groups are separated on the basis of low, medium and high levels into distinct severity groups. Twin data from female adolescents in Missouri and children in Australia both found that a similar pattern of familial segregation for the latent classes suggesting that familial influences can distinguish between ADHD and the normal range of behaviour (Rasmussen *et al.*, 2004). These data provide some evidence for the distinction of ADHD into inattentive, combined and hyperactive-impulsive subtypes and suggest that ADHD might be distinguishable from the normal range on the basis of familial risks to siblings.

*Summary*

Most analytic approaches are unable to make a clear distinction between the diagnosis of ADHD and the continuous distribution of ADHD symptoms in the general population. Twin studies suggest that familial and genetic influences on groups with extremely high ADHD symptom scores are the same as those that influence ADHD symptom levels throughout the general population. LCA can however be used to distinguish groups with high, moderate and low ADHD symptom levels and suggests that these groups might be distinguished on the basis of familial risk factors. The current literature does not address the difference in interpretation of the latent class and quantitative approaches. The GDG concluded that on the basis of current evidence, ADHD was similar to other common medical and psychiatric conditions that represent the extreme of dimensional traits such as hypertension, obesity, anxiety and depression.

### 1.4.4 B: Is the cluster of symptoms that defines ADHD associated with significant clinical and psychosocial impairments?

There were no systematic reviews that addressed this question. A search for cohort studies was carried out and additional primary studies were identified by the GDG members (see Appendix H).

**Evidence**

*1.4.4.1 Academic difficulties*

Follow-up studies of people diagnosed with ADHD in childhood have consistently indicated impairment in their academic functioning. Children and adolescents with ADHD have been shown to have greater impaired attention, less impulse control, greater off-task, restless and vocal behaviour (Fischer *et al.*, 1990), poor reading skills (McGee *et al.*, 1992) and speech and language problems (Hinshaw, 2002) when compared with healthy controls. These impairments often lead to grade retention (Hinshaw, 2002) and to a lower probability of completing schooling when compared with children who do not have ADHD (Mannuzza *et al.*, 1993), suggesting potential long-term ramifications for vocational, social and psychological functioning into adulthood (Biederman *et al.*, 1996; Young *et al.*, 2005a & 2005b; Wilson & Marcotte, 1996).

An important question about educational impairment of children with ADHD is whether this is determined primarily by the presence of high levels of ADHD symptoms or the association with co-occurring conditions such as conduct disorder. Wilson and Marcotte (1996) found that the presence of ADHD in adolescents increased the risk for lower academic performance and poorer social, emotional and adaptive functioning, but that the additional presence of conduct disorder further increased the risk for maladaptive outcomes. In another study the association of conduct disorder with academic underachievement was found to be due to its comorbidity with ADHD (Frick *et al.*, 1991).

### 1.4.4.2    Family difficulties

Impaired family relationships have been reported in families of children with ADHD. Follow-up studies indicate that mothers of children and adolescents with ADHD have more difficulty in child behaviour management practices and coping with their child's behaviour (August *et al.*, 1998), and display higher rates of conflict behaviours, such as negative comments, social irritability, hostility and maladaptive levels of communication and involvement (August *et al.*, 1998; Fletcher *et al.*, 1996).

Family impairment also permeates the parent's lives. Parents of children with ADHD report having less time to meet their own needs, fewer close friendships, greater peer rejection and less time for family activities, which might lead to less family cohesion and a significant effect on the parent's emotional health (Bagwell *et al.*, 2001).

### 1.4.4.3    Social difficulties

Girls with ADHD tend to have fewer friends (Blachman & Hinshaw, 2002) and greater problems with peers and the opposite sex (Young *et al.*, 2005a & 2005b).

Hyperactive children with or without conduct problems have higher rates of problems with peers and higher rates of social problems because of lack of constructive social activities (Taylor *et al.*, 1996). In a study by Ernhardt and Hinshaw (1994) it was reported that a diagnosis of ADHD significantly predicted peer rejection; however aggressive and non-compliant disruptive behaviours were important and accounted for 32% of the variance in peer rejection.

### 1.4.4.4    Antisocial behaviour

Antisocial behaviour is more prevalent in children and adolescents with ADHD than non-ADHD groups. Some studies show increased rates of antisocial acts (for example, drug misuse) in comparison to children who do not have ADHD (Barkley *et al.*, 2004; Mannuzza *et al.*, 1998).

Follow-up studies have also shown that people with high levels of ADHD symptoms had significantly higher juvenile and adult arrest rates (Satterfield & Schell, 1997). Young adults with a diagnosis of 'hyperactivity' in childhood were more likely to have a diagnosis of antisocial disorder than healthy controls (32% versus 8%) and drug misuse (10% versus 1%) at follow-up (Mannuzza *et al.*, 1991).

ADHD is also a risk factor for psychiatric problems including persistent hyperactivity, violence, antisocial behaviours (Biederman *et al.*, 1996; Taylor *et al.*, 1996), (Taylor *et al.*, 1996) and antisocial personality disorder (Mannuzza *et al.*, 1998).

In a prospective follow-up of 103 males diagnosed with ADHD, the presence of an antisocial or conduct disorder almost completely accounted for the increased risk for criminal activities. Mannuzza and colleagues (2002) reported that antisocial disorder was more prevalent in children with pervasive and school-only ADHD. However,

Lee and Hinshaw (2004) reported that the predictive power of ADHD status to adolescent delinquency diminishes when key indices of childhood externalising behaviour related to ADHD are taken into account.

Boys with ADHD and high defiance ratings show significantly higher felony rates than healthy controls (Satterfield *et al.*, 1994). However, ADHD diagnosed in childhood increases the risk of later antisocial behaviour, even in the absence of comorbid ODD or CD (Mannuzza *et al.*, 2004).

### 1.4.4.5    Other problems
A 10-year prospective study of young people with ADHD found that the lifetime prevalence for all categories of psychopathology were significantly greater in young adults with ADHD compared with controls. This included markedly elevated rates of antisocial, addictive, mood and anxiety disorders (Biederman *et al.*, 2006b).

Both cross-sectional epidemiological studies and follow-up studies of children with ADHD show increased rates of unemployment compared with controls (Biederman *et al.*, 2006b; Kessler *et al.*, 2006; Barkley *et al.*, 2006). Adults with ADHD were found to have significantly lower educational performance and attainment, with 32% failing to complete high school; they had been fired from more jobs and were rated by employers as showing a lower job performance (Barkley *et al.*, 2006). The survey from Biederman and colleagues (2006b) showed that 33.9% of people with ADHD were employed full time versus 59% of controls.

### Summary
ADHD symptoms are associated with a range of impairments in social, academic, family, mental health and employment outcomes. Longitudinal studies indicate that ADHD symptoms specifically are associated with both current and future impairments; additional impairments also result from the presence of co-occurring conditions, in particular conduct problems. Adults with ADHD are found to have lower paid jobs and lower socioeconomic status. Impairment is an essential factor to be considered in the diagnosis of ADHD. While it is clear that the presence of high levels of ADHD symptoms is associated with impairment in multiple domains, it is not possible to delineate clearly a specific number of ADHD symptoms at which impairment arises.

### 1.4.5    C: Is there evidence for a characteristic pattern of developmental changes, or outcomes associated with the symptoms, that define ADHD?

The search for systematic reviews and meta-analyses identified one review that was of relevance to this question. Additional reviews and primary studies were identified by the GDG members (see Appendix I).

### Evidence
There is evidence for continuity of ADHD symptoms over the lifespan. Faraone and colleagues (2006) analysed data from 32 follow-up studies of children with ADHD

into adulthood. Where full criteria for ADHD were used approximately 15% of children were still diagnosed with ADHD at age 25. In addition, the meta-analysis found that approximately 65% of children by age 25 fulfilled the DSM-IV definition of ADHD 'in partial remission', indicating persistence of some symptoms of ADHD associated with continued clinically meaningful impairments.

Relative to controls, levels of overactivity and inattention are developmentally stable (Taylor *et al.*, 1996). Longitudinal studies of children with ADHD show similar rates of ADHD in adolescence (Biederman *et al.*, 1996; Faraone *et al.*, 2002; Molina & Pelham, 2003).

Population twin studies have also addressed the stability of ADHD symptoms throughout childhood and adolescence. Rietveld and colleagues (2004) reported that parent ratings of attentional problems were moderately stable from age three to seven, and greater stability from age seven to ten. They further showed that such stability appeared to be mediated largely by overlapping genetic influences such that most, but not all, genetic influences at one age influenced ADHD at another age. Price and colleagues (2005) reported similar findings with correlations around 0.5 between ADHD symptoms at ages 2, 3 and 4. This stability was estimated to be mediated 91% by genetic influences. Kuntsi and colleagues (2004) extended these data to age 8, and found similar moderate stability between the data for age 2, 3 and 4 and the data for age 8. Larsson and colleagues (2004) completed a similar longitudinal twin study of 8 to 13 year olds and found fairly high stability between the two ages; they further concluded that this stability was due to shared genetic effects. Change in symptoms between childhood and adolescence was thought to be due to new genetic and environmental effects that become important in adolescence.

In adolescence and adult life, symptoms of ADHD begin to associate with other diagnoses that are seldom made in childhood. Adolescent substance misuse, in particular, seems to be more common in people with the diagnosis of ADHD (Wilens *et al.*, 2003), though it is not yet clear whether it is the ADHD *per se* that generates the risk or the co-existent presence of antisocial activities and peer groups. The mechanisms involved can include one or more of the following: first, that individuals with ADHD may seek out highly stimulating or risky activities; second, that individuals with ADHD are exposed to higher levels of psychosocial risks for development of substance use disorders, resulting from educational and social impairments, social exclusion and antisocial behaviour associated with ADHD; third, that various substances, including cannabis, alcohol and stimulants can attenuate ADHD symptoms and are therefore sometimes used as a form of self-treatment.

*Summary*

There is evidence for the persistence of ADHD symptoms from early childhood through to adulthood. Longitudinal studies confirm that ADHD persists into adulthood but developmentally appropriate criteria have yet to be developed for ADHD in adults. Using child criteria, approximately 15% of children with ADHD retain the diagnosis by age 25 but a much larger proportion (65%) show persistence of symptoms with associated impairments. The profile of symptoms may alter with a relative persistence of inattentive symptoms compared with hyperactive-impulsive symptoms, however the evidence base for this conclusion is poor, using developmentally appropriate measures of hyperactivity-impulsivity in adults. There was no evidence to warrant a different diagnostic concept in childhood and in adulthood. Familial and genetic influences in ADHD symptoms appear to be stable through childhood and early adolescence, but there is a lack of data on the continuity of aetiological factors into adulthood.

### 1.4.6    D: Is there consistent evidence of genetic, environmental or neurobiological risk factors associated with ADHD?

The literature search identified seven systematic reviews and meta-analyses. GDG members identified additional reviews and primary studies (see Appendix J).

*Evidence*
Dickstein and colleagues (2006) completed a systematic meta-analysis of 16 neuro-imaging studies that compared patterns of neural activity in children and adults with ADHD and healthy controls. Their results indicated a consistent pattern of reduced frontal activity (hypoactivity) in people with ADHD.

Willcutt and colleagues (2005) reviewed 83 studies that had administered executive functioning measures and found significant differences between ADHD and non-ADHD groups where the former showed executive function deficits. The size of the difference between children with ADHD and unaffected controls while significant was moderate rather than large.

Differences in executive functioning between ADHD and non-ADHD groups have also been reported in adults (Hervey *et al.*, 2004; Boonstra *et al.*, 2005; Schoechlin & Engel, 2005) results of studies of ADHD in adults suggest a wide variety of general and specific performance on cognitive-experimental tasks that are similar to those seen in children. The review from Hervey and colleagues (2004) did not point to a domain-specific neuropsychological deficit, but rather multiple domains revealed some degree of impairment on at least a subset of the tests considered within each domain. The interpretation of these studies remains controversial but most authorities agree that both executive and non-executive processes are disrupted in people with ADHD. Recently it has emerged that the strongest and most consistent association with ADHD is for intra-individual variability (Klein *et al.*, 2006).

A systematic meta-analysis of molecular genetic association for associated markers in or near to the dopamine D4 (DRD4), dopamine D5 (DRD5) and dopamine transporter (DAT1) genes, found strong evidence for the association of DRD4 and DRD5 but not DAT1 (Li *et al.*, 2006).

A systematic review of 20 population twin studies found an average heritability estimate of 76%. In most cases, heritability in these studies is estimated from the difference in the correlations for ADHD symptoms between identical and non-identical twin pairs, as reported by parents and teachers: with the correlation for identical twin pairs in the region of 60–90% and for non-identical twin pairs being half or less than half of this figure in most studies (Faraone, 2005). Under the equal environment assumption for the two types of twin pairs heritability can be estimated as twice the difference in the two sets of correlations. Although some people question the assumption of 'equal environment' for identical and non-identical twins, this does not impact on the question of validity since the high twin correlations observed in these studies indicates that ADHD symptoms are highly familial. The equal environment assumption impacts on estimates of the proportion of the familial risk that is due to genes or equal environments (for example, Horwitz *et al.*, 2003). It should also be recognised that high heritability does not exclude the important role of environment acting through gene-environment interactions (Moffitt *et al.*, 2005).

Linnet and colleagues (2003) completed a systematic review of the evidence for association between prenatal exposure to nicotine, alcohol, caffeine and psychosocial stress. They concluded that exposure to tobacco smoke *in utero* is associated with an increased risk for ADHD. In contrast contradictory findings were found for the risk from prenatal maternal use of alcohol and no conclusions could be drawn from the use of caffeine. Studies of psychosocial stress indicated possible but inconsistent evidence for an association with ADHD.

*Summary*

There is consistent evidence of familial influences on ADHD symptoms in the general population. Under the equal environment assumption these familial influences are thought to be largely genetic in origin. Environmental measures associated with ADHD have been identified, the most certain being the association with maternal use of tobacco during pregnancy. It is not known whether these environmental risks represent direct or indirect risks through correlated environmental or genetic factors. Specific genetic variants that are associated with a small increase in the risk for ADHD have been identified in the dopamine D4 and close to the dopamine D5 receptor genes. Analysis of ADHD versus non-ADHD groups has identified consistent changes in brain function and performance on neurocognitive tests; however, differences from controls are not universal, do not characterise all children and adults with a clinical diagnosis of ADHD and do not usually establish causality in individual cases.

## 1.5     LIMITATIONS

In line with methodology agreed with NICE the approach adopted was initially to identify all available systematic reviews and meta-analytic studies that related to the questions on validity of the diagnosis. While this was possible for much of the neuro-biological and genetic and environmental data there were few systematic reviews in other areas such as the factor- or cluster-analytic studies. Where systematic reviews were not available for these studies of ADHD symptoms and studies that investigate the differentiation of ADHD from oppositional and conduct problems, systematic reviews of the primary literature were conducted. For other sub-questions addressed in this section the systematic evidence was supplemented with expert opinion, drawing on evidence known to members of the GDG. The lack of specific reference standards for the diagnosis of ADHD led to an adaptation of the SIGN criteria (see

Appendix A) to ensure sufficient quality of the data used to derive recommendations for this guideline.

When considering the Feighner criteria for validity of a psychiatric disorder, the question of whether there are specific responses to clinical, educational and other interventions for ADHD was excluded, since the data to answer this question was very limited. For example it was not possible to identify studies that investigated the effects of stimulant treatments in disorders other than ADHD and there were limited published data on the effects of stimulants in people who do not ADHD [sic]. A paper that did not meet the quality control criteria for the evidence sections of this chapter investigated the response to dexamfetamine and placebo in a group of 14 pre-pubertal boys who did not fulfil criteria for ADHD (Rapoport, 1978). When amphetamine was given, the group showed a marked decrease in motor activity and reaction time and improved performance on cognitive tests. The very small numbers used in this study and lack of further similar studies means that considerable caution must be taken in drawing firm conclusions. Nevertheless, the similarity of the response observed in children without ADHD to that reported in children with ADHD provides further evidence that the aetiological mechanisms that give rise to ADHD are similar to those that influence levels of ADHD symptoms through the population. However the key difference from treatment of people with ADHD is that the 'behavioural symptoms' that responded to medication were not causing impairment in the children in this study.

## 1.6    POSITION STATEMENT ON VALIDITY OF ADHD

Hyperactivity, inattention and impulsivity cluster together both in children and in adults and can be recognised as distinct from other symptom clusters, although they frequently co-occur alongside other symptom clusters.

Symptoms of ADHD appear to be on a continuum in the general population.

ADHD is distinguished from the normal range partly by the number and severity of symptoms and partly by the association with significant levels of impairment.

The importance of evaluating impairment and the difficulty in establishing recognised thresholds on the basis of symptom counts alone needs to be addressed. It is not possible to determine a specific number of symptoms at which impairment arises.

There is evidence for psychological, social and educational impairments in both children and adults with ADHD.

ADHD symptoms persist from childhood through to adulthood. In a significant minority, the diagnosis persists and in the majority, sub-clinical symptoms continue to be detectable.

In adults the profile of symptoms may alter with a relative persistence of inattentive symptoms compared to hyperactive-impulsive symptoms.

There is evidence of both genetic and environmental influences in the aetiology of ADHD. It is not known the extent to which there is diversity in the aetiology of the disorder.

Contemporary research suggests that environmental risks are likely to interact with genetic factors, but there is currently limited direct evidence to support this view.

There is evidence of genetic associations with specific genes, environmental risks and neurobiological changes in groups of children with ADHD. However, no neurobiological, genetic or environmental measure is sufficiently predictive to be used as a diagnostic test.

The diagnosis remains a description of behavioural presentation and can only rarely be linked to specific neurobiological or environmental causes in individual cases.

Hyperkinetic disorder (ICD-10) is a narrower and more severe subtype of DSM-IV combined type ADHD. It defines a more pervasive and generally more impairing form of the disorder. Both concepts are useful (Santosh *et al.*, 2005).

There was no evidence of a need to apply a different concept of ADHD to children and adults. However age-related changes in the presentation are recognised.

All current assessment methods have their limitations. There is evidence of the need for flexibility and for a consideration of levels of impairment in assessments and when deriving appropriate diagnoses.

## 1.7    CONSENSUS CONFERENCE

In addition to a review of published evidence on the question of validity, a consensus conference was held to bring together experts in the field with a range of views, in order to debate the key issues of the use of ADHD as a diagnostic category. The aim was to provide a range of contemporary perspectives that would assist the GDG with the task of deciding what should trigger the use of the guideline and for whom the guideline is intended (see Chapter 3, Methods used to develop this guideline). The speakers delivered a 15-minute presentation addressing the key questions relating to the validity of the ADHD diagnosis set out by the GDG followed by questioning from the GDG members and a subsequent discussion of the presentation among members of the GDG. Each presenter was subsequently asked to provide a summary of their presentation[65] and these are also presented in Appendix A.

### 1.7.1    Discussion on consensus conference presentation

Different presenters brought their own perspectives and this contributed to highlight the importance of a multi-disciplinary approach to the diagnosis and treatment of children with ADHD [sic]. The conference did not consider diagnosis and treatment of adults with ADHD. Here some of the issues that were raised, and the areas of controversy arising from differences in the perception of the different speakers at the consensus conference, are discussed.

The evidence presented at the consensus conference indicated that there was a high degree of unanimity across presenters (coming from a wide range of perspectives) about the fact that there is a group of people who could be seen as having

---

[65]These are reproduced in Part 1 of this appendix.

distinct and impairing difficulties and who should trigger the use of this guideline. While recognition of a particular group was agreed upon, uncertainty about the breadth of diagnosis was discussed, namely, whether the use of a narrow (ICD-10 hyperkinetic disorder) versus a broad (DSM-IV ADHD) diagnosis should be used. The problems of using a narrow diagnosis are: (i) the under-recognition of people that are in need of help and (ii) the lack of connection with the research literature, which is based mainly on broader definitions such as DSM-IV. It was established that the main differences between people falling into narrow or broad diagnoses are the breadth of symptoms (requirement for both inattentive, and impulsive-overactive behaviour versus only one domain being sufficient), more or less stringent criteria for situational pervasiveness and the requirement for no major coexisting conditions (apart from oppositional defiant or conduct disorder under ICD-10). Both groups present similar problems of impairment. Overall there was general agreement that both the use of broad (DSM-IV) ADHD diagnosis and narrow hyperkinetic disorder criteria were useful.

One of the major issues of controversy in the UK setting is the very high and variable prevalence rates reported in the literature. For example, recent prevalence figures range from 6.8 to 15.8 for DSM-IV ADHD (Faraone *et al.*, 2003) while the British Child and Mental Health Survey reported a prevalence of 3.6% in male children and less than 1% in female (Ford *et al.*, 2003). Reasons for this are discussed in Faraone and colleagues (2003) who conclude that prevalence rates derived from symptoms counts alone, or from ratings in one setting, were higher than those that took into account functional impairment. For example Wolraich and colleagues (1998) estimated prevalence to be 16.1% on the basis of symptom counts, but 6.8% when functional impairment was taken into account. A study in the UK that specifically addressed the role of impairment found that among 7 to 8 year olds 11.1% had the ADHD syndrome based on symptom count alone (McArdle *et al.*, 2004). In contrast, 6.7% had ADHD with Children's Global Assessment Scale scores (C-GAS: measuring impairment) less than 71 and 4.2% with C-GAS scores less than 61. When pervasiveness included both parent- and teacher-reported ADHD and the presence of psychosocial impairment prevalence fell lower to 1.4%. The literature on prevalence therefore indicates that the rate of ADHD is sensitive to the degree of impairment associated with the symptom criteria and the degree to which the disorder shows situational pervasiveness.

All the speakers acknowledged the importance of functional impairments in relation to diagnosis, in other words, that diagnostic thresholds should be based on pragmatic grounds such as impairment and the need for treatment. However, there was also agreement that defining suitable thresholds for impairment is difficult due to the breadth of areas in which people with ADHD can be impaired. The level and types of behaviour that define the normal range remain a contentious issue.

On considering when this guideline would be triggered, the GDG concluded that it would be difficult to be prescriptive for any individual case, but that measurement of impairment linked to the symptoms of ADHD is a key component of the decision. Significant problems can arise at various levels, including personal distress from symptoms of the disorder, difficulties in forming stable social relationships and emotional bonds, difficulties with education and long-term risk for negative outcomes such as emotional problems, antisocial behaviour and addiction disorders. The group concluded that treatment response should take into account the severity of the disorder in terms of clinical and functional impairments and evidence should be looked for on the impact of severity of the disorder on treatment response. Overall this is an area in which further research is required to investigate both the short- and long-term outcomes of ADHD and its relation to severity of the condition.

One of the areas of controversy highlighted in the consensus conference was the degree of impairment and severity of ADHD needed to trigger the diagnosis, and related to this, treatment with medication. There is concern in some quarters that the diagnosis automatically leads to treatment with medication and this is not always desirable when the breadth of the definition includes people who might gain substantial benefit from education or psychosocial interventions alone. However even the most ardent supporters of non-medical interventions in ADHD recognised the importance of medical treatment in the most severe cases. In this context the participants in the consensus conference made an important contribution by raising the question of suitable thresholds for 'significant impairments associated with ADHD symptoms' and hence the proportion of children fulfilling criteria for the disorder and triggering use of the guideline.

One conclusion is that the acceptable thresholds for impairment are largely driven by the contemporary societal view of what is an acceptable level of deviation from the norm and level of impairment that requires treatment. However the GDG did not consider that the diagnosis should be reserved only for the most serious cases, since the broader concept of ADHD is important in triggering educational and behavioural approaches in addition to medical approaches. The GDG concluded that defining appropriate thresholds of impairment associated with the disorder was important, but that treatment implications might be different for individuals falling above or below particular thresholds.

Confirmatory factor-analytic studies clarify that ADHD symptoms represent a distinct set of symptoms and behaviours that co-vary together in both clinical and control populations. However these cross-sectional studies are far less informative than longitudinal studies that can clarify the predictive outcomes of early ADHD. There are however a few studies that provide suitable data on the relative outcomes of ADHD and other disruptive disorders such as ODD, which are important in delineating specificity in the outcomes related to ADHD. The available evidence suggests that when considering the link between ADHD and conduct problems, ADHD comes first and conduct problems develop later. In contrast there is no evidence that conduct problems in the absence of ADHD lead to the later development of ADHD. The small number of suitable longitudinal outcome studies highlights an important area for future research.

The consensus conference also raised questions about the interpretation of family, twin and adoption studies and the relative contributions between genetic and environmental influences indicated by these studies. The argument against genetic influences is not strong unless one questions the conventional interpretation of twin data. But it is non-controversial that parent and teacher ratings of ADHD symptoms/behaviours show MZ correlations around 70 to 80% and DZ correlations around 20 to 40%;

numerous studies replicate this. The usual interpretation of these findings is that the difference in MZ and DZ correlations are mainly the result of genetic influences. The alternative argument that the equal environment assumption is incorrect leads to the conclusion that familial influences are important, but not necessarily genetic. Either way, it is non-controversial that ADHD is familial and this in itself is strong evidence that the construct is sufficiently delineated to show such clear familial effects; that is, that the level of ADHD symptoms in one child strongly predicts the level of ADHD symptoms in his or her siblings. Interestingly there are limited data from twin studies using ADHD cases (for example, concordance rates for the clinical disorder), so the literature mainly uses extremes analysis of rating scale data. Similarly there is a lack of twin data in adult populations.

The GDG agreed that polarised positions in this debate are not helpful since the contemporary understanding of complex behavioural disorders emphasises the importance of interactions between genes and environments. The GDG wishes to stress that the role of important genetic influences does not exclude an important role for environmental influences since individual differences in genetic risk factors are likely to alter the sensitivity of an individual to environmental risks. In this event, reducing environmental risk would be expected to reduce the risk for ADHD. Furthermore, the extent to which there are genetic influences has no direct bearing on the choice of treatment approaches since both medical and psychosocial interventions (or a combination of the two) could be important in improving treatment outcomes.

## 1.8    EVIDENCE SUMMARY

ADHD should be considered a valid clinical disorder that can be distinguished from co-occurring disorders and the normal spectrum.

ADHD is distinguished from the normal spectrum by the co-occurrence of ADHD symptoms with significant clinical, psychosocial and educational impairments. These impairments should be enduring and occur across multiple settings.

Hyperkinetic disorder is a valid diagnosis that identifies a sub-group of people with ADHD with severe impairment in multiple domains.

ADHD commonly persists throughout childhood and into adult life where it continues to cause considerable psychiatric morbidity.

The quality of the evidence included in this review was variable and lacked any 'gold standard' because no diagnostic tests for ADHD have been developed or tested. In the absence of a gold standard for the validity of diagnosis of ADHD or hyperkinetic disorder a lower level of evidence was included in this review.

Although the quality of individual studies included in this review was variable, evidence consistently showed that children and adults with ADHD had associated impairments.

**1.9    CLINICAL PRACTICE RECOMMENDATIONS**

1.9.1.1    For the diagnosis of ADHD or hyperkinetic disorder to be made, and for this guideline to be considered appropriate, the following criteria should be met:

● Symptoms of ADHD (DSM-IV) or hyperkinetic disorder (ICD-10) should be sufficient to reach a formal diagnosis in DSM-IV or ICD-10.

● ADHD should be considered in all age groups (children, adolescents and adults), with symptom criteria adjusted for age appropriate changes in behaviour.

● The level of impairment resulting from symptoms of hyperactivity and or inattention should be:

– at least moderately clinically significant on the basis of interview and or direct observation in multiple settings, and

– pervasive (occur in all important settings) including social, familial educational and or occupational settings.

1.9.1.2    In determining the clinical significance of impairments resulting from the symptoms of ADHD in children, the views of the child should be taken into account, wherever this is possible.

1.9.1.3    The diagnosis of ADHD should only be made by specialist psychiatrists or paediatricians following a full assessment of the child, adolescent or adult; including all relevant settings.

1.9.1.4    After making a diagnosis of ADHD or hyperkinetic disorder subsequent assessment and treatment should follow the guideline recommendations.

# PART 3: DIAGNOSIS POSITION STATEMENT (PART 1: VALIDITY) PEER REVIEWER CONSULTATION TABLE

**Stakeholder**
PR – Peer Reviewer
CC – Participant in Consensus Conference

| No | Type | Stakeholder | Section | Comments | Reference suggested & reason for inclusion/exclusion | Actions |
|----|------|-------------|---------|----------|------------------------------------------------------|---------|
| 20 | CC | David Coghill | 1.1 | The document uses both the DSM-IV term of ADHD and ICD-10 hyperkinetic disorder. It also, however, uses ADHD as an umbrella term. The GDG should agree on a nomenclature and clarify this at the beginning of the document something along the lines of 'we will use the terms ADHD (DSM-IV) and hyperkinetic disorder (ICD-10) when talking about the specific diagnostic categories, however when discussing the general disorder we will use ADHD as an umbrella term' (others have chosen to use 'AD/HKD' as the umbrella. To this could be added the paragraph on 'hyperactivity' in the last paragraph in Section 1.2. | No reference suggested. | Comment addressed, see Section 5.2 'ADHD and hyper-kinetic disorder'. |
| 78 | PR | Jonathan Leo | 1.1 | Just because we can diagnose a trait does not mean it is a disease. Your title could leave some people with the mistaken impression that if you can identify a trait and label it, that it can then be called a disease. The validity of the diagnosis – whether you can reliably identify it in some children – is an interesting | No reference suggested. | Comment addressed, see Sections 5.3 and 5.10. |

536

| No. | Type | Name | Section | Comment | Reference | Response |
|---|---|---|---|---|---|---|
| | | | | question, but in this document it is simply a distraction from the main question. The essential question for the NICE committee should be: Is the disease concept of ADHD valid? With that in mind Section 1.4.1, 1.4.2, 1.4.2.1, and 1.4.2.2 have little relevance. The most important Section, which most of my comments address, is 1.4.6. | | |
| 42 | PR | David Cottrell | 1.1 | This comment may be redundant as definitions may come earlier in the guide but reading this section in isolation I wanted to see a clearer definition of ADHD and HK disorder at the beginning of the chapter. | No reference suggested. | Comment addressed, see Section 5.2 'ADHD and hyperkinetic disorder'. |
| 21 | CC | David Coghill | 1.2 | Overall I feel this section needs considerable rewriting as it does not flow at all well. As such does not do justice to the rest of the document which is essentially well written and organised. I have made some suggestions in the text. | No reference suggested. | Comment addressed, see Sections 5.1 to 5.4. |
| 50 | PR | Stephen Faraone | 1.2 | You might note that the methodology used to create the Washington University Diagnostic Criteria has been widely accepted and that similar approaches have been used to validate categories for the Research Diagnostic Criteria, the DSM and the ICD criteria (when relevant validating data have been available). My point is that your choice of the WDC is far from arbitrary as there is some consensus as to what the 'rules of evidence' should be for asserting the validity of a psychiatric disorder. The intellectual foundation for all these criteria relies heavily on the | No reference suggested. | Comment addressed, see Section 5.4. |

*Continued*

**PART 3:** (*Continued*)

| No | Type | Stakeholder | Section | Comments | Reference suggested & reason for inclusion/exclusion | Actions |
|----|------|-------------|---------|----------|---------|---------|
| | | | | concept of 'construct validity' so well articulated by Paul Meehl decades ago. | | |
| 22 | CC | David Coghill | 1.2 para 2 | 'Furthermore, in keeping with other common behavioural disorders there is no clear distinction between the clinical condition and the normal variation in the general population.' <br><br>The meaning of this sentence is rather unclear. I think it is confusing (or maybe confounding?) symptoms and impairment and to do with the precise words used. There is a continuity of symptoms between those with the disorder and the population. However those with the clinical condition have both high levels of symptoms *and* impairment leading to a clearer 'distinction' between the two. Whilst this may seem trivial the actual sentence is contrary to the conclusions and will be picked up by those who wish to point out that NICE says 'there is no clear distinction between the clinical condition and the normal variation in the general population' without clarifying the context of the quotation. | No reference suggested. | Comment addressed, see Sections 5.3 (third paragraph) and 5.5.3. |
| 80 | PR | Jonathan Leo | 1.3 | I think that somehow you need to mention that your literature review was very selective and systematically ignored review articles that were critical of the ADHD diagnosis. As you are aware of both the controversy surrounding the diagnosis and those | References suggested: Gale (2006) Ritalin requests often deemed | References included in the NICE guideline as evidence (found by systematic searches or identified |

Continued

| | |
|---|---|
| authors who have addressed the problem, I am assuming that it was a conscious decision to ignore one side of the debate. There is a large body of literature that sees forces other than biology as the source for the dramatic rise in the diagnosis of ADHD. This literature comes from wide and varied sources and is representative of a large segment of the mainstream media and academia. Since one reason that NICE is taking on this difficult task is because the ADHD diagnosis is controversial, it does not make sense to simply ignore critical publications. Just summarising the reviews from mainstream psychiatry journals does not give a balanced view, especially when one considers that it is extremely difficult to get anything published in a psychiatry journal or medical journal that is critical of the ADHD diagnosis. You even acknowledge in one section of the document that, because there was limited data 'the systematic evidence was supplemented with expert opinion, drawing on evidence known to members of the GDG'.

By selectively choosing data in support of a particular point of view it suggests that your conclusions were made first, and the studies were then subsequently chosen to support your conclusion, and not the other way around, that a group of non-partisan academics analysed all the data and then came to a conclusion.

As just one example of how the debate is framed in academic journals, in 2002, a group of scientists | inappropriate. *Medscape*. Paper excluded: relevant to use of Ritalin, not validity of ADHD; not peer reviewed.

by GDG members) have to meet quality assessment criteria. This is explained in Chapter 3, Methods.

Comments addressed, see Section 5.9 for limitations of references included and last two paragraphs for use of stimulants.

The use of drug treatment (recommendations) is addressed in Chapter 10, Pharmacological treatment. |

| No | Type | Stakeholder | Section | Comments | Reference suggested & reason for inclusion/exclusion | Actions |
|---|---|---|---|---|---|---|
| | | | | published the International Consensus Statement on ADHD. The consensus statement had several surprising and remarkable declarations such as: 'Numerous studies of twins demonstrate that family environment makes no significant separate contribution to these traits' (which runs counter to the NICE document). 'One gene has recently been reliably demonstrated to be associated with this disorder…'. 'Neuroimaging studies of groups with ADHD also demonstrate relatively smaller areas of brain matter.' 'Most neurological studies find that as a group those with ADHD have less brain activity…' When a group of academicians sent a letter to the editor of *Child and Family Psychology Reviews* about the Consensus Statement, the editor responded that the letter could be published, but only if Dr. Barkley, the lead author of the Consensus Statement, was given the courtesy of having the last chance to respond. However, this was not a courtesy initially granted to the academicians critical of the rising diagnosis of ADHD, who Barkley and his co-authors compared to members of the flat-earth society. Thus, the authors of the Consensus Statement were given a second chance to cite evidence in support of the biological basis of ADHD, yet rather than cite several | | |

Continued

specific articles; they instead mentioned that there were hundreds and hundreds of articles. However, good science is not determined by how high the papers can be stacked but by the quality of the papers. To paint those concerned about the rising use of stimulants as somehow on the fringe, shows how isolated academicians can become from the general public. For the GDG to not acknowledge anyone critical of the diagnosis in their own review puts the GDG in the same category as the Consensus authors. Does NICE want to be in the same category?

Nowhere in the GDG document is there a discussion about the ethics of giving a performance-enhancing drug to improve academic success in school - a major reason the drug is used in the first place. For instance, take the announcement about a recent survey, 'Results of a survey of physicians suggest that parents often request a "behavioral drug", such as Ritalin, with the goal of enhancing their child's academic performance *rather than treating an illness.*' (Gale, 2006, italics added). The headlines expressed surprise at this practice, yet the practice of prescribing stimulants to improve academic performance is exactly why these medications are prescribed in the first place, and it is fully sanctioned by the medical community. According to Joseph Biederman, 'If a child is brilliant but is doing OK in school, that child may need treatment, which would result in performing brilliantly in school' (Gale, 2006). *In fact, no official organisation that supports the use of*

541

**PART 3:** (*Continued*)

| No | Type | Stakeholder | Section | Comments | Reference suggested & reason for inclusion/exclusion | Actions |
|---|---|---|---|---|---|---|
| | | | | *stimulants has ever said that using stimulants to improve academic performance is inappropriate. Even the GDG has not said this is inappropriate. Is it?* | | |
| 82 | PR | Jonathan Leo | 1.4 | In your framing of the question, you ask if environmental factors are associated with ADHD. You then address one review covering the evidence of prenatal exposure to drugs. Again you have systematically ignored a large body of evidence. Perhaps this section is the biggest flaw in your document. Any academic reading this discussion will have a hard time taking you seriously if you cannot think of a single environmental influence coming from the home or school environments that contributes to ADHD. Either you need to comment on this research or explain why you are ignoring it. For instance, a recent study showed that children from divorced families are twice as likely to be diagnosed with ADHD (Strohschein, 2007). And prior studies have shown that children from single family homes are more likely to be diagnosed with ADHD. For more information I have attached two tables and a discussion from Dr Nicky Hart at UCLA who addresses the differences in the ADHD diagnosis across the socioeconomic strata in England and Wales. The data will appear in a forthcoming book, *ADHD and Health Inequality.* | References suggested: Strohschein, L. A. (2007) Prevalence of methylphenidate use among Canadian children following parental divorce. *CMAJ: Canadian Medical Association Journal* 176, 1711–1714. Paper included. Hart, N. (in press) *ADHD and Health Inequality.* Macmillan. Paper excluded: not peer-reviewed. | Comment addressed, see Section 5.8. |

The statistical evidence generated by the British government as part of its policy making function runs against the impression that ADHD is best thought of as a bio-medical phenomenon. The social distribution of the disorder follows the contours of the class mortality gradient. In other words, it fits the classic profile of health inequality: low prevalence at the top, and high prevalence at the bottom of the social hierarchy. Children exhibiting the symptoms of emotional and conduct disorders, and those afflicted with the troubling symptoms of attention deficit and hyperactivity disorder are much more likely to be poor, to be raised by single and / or unemployed parents, to grow up in neighbourhoods scarred by the signs of under-privilege and to be exposed to stressful life events and social relationships in their early lives.

Figure 1 displays the class gradient of psychiatric morbidity as a whole in British children. The rate is around 4% among children in families where the main breadwinners are employed in higher professional occupations (for example, lawyers, doctors, professors). It is four times higher (16%) in families where parents are either chronically unemployed or have never worked at all.

This group includes single-parent families headed by young women with no labour market experience prior to becoming mothers. The rate of ADHD British style (hyperkinetic disorder) follows the same

PART 3: (*Continued*)

| No | Type | Stakeholder | Section | Comments | Reference suggested & reason for inclusion/exclusion | Actions |
|----|------|-------------|---------|----------|------------------------------------------------------|---------|
| | | | | | | |
| | | | | | | |

**Figure 1: Social class & mental health in childhood England & Wales 2004**

| | Higher profs | Higher manag-erial | Lower manag-erial/prof | Small employ-ers & self employm-ent | Lower supervi-sory technical occups | Intermed-iate occups | Semi-routine | Routine occups | Never worked/ long-term une-mployed |
|---|---|---|---|---|---|---|---|---|---|
| ■ Hyperkinetic disorder | 0.5% | 0.8% | 0.7% | 1.3% | 1.0% | 2.6% | 1.7% | 3.0% | 2.6% |
| ▨ Any mental disorder | 4.4% | 6.1% | 6.3% | 6.6% | 8.7% | 11.3% | 12.9% | 14.9% | 16.1% |

Source: Department of Health, 2004

course. It increases from 0.5% in professional families to 2.6% in households with no attachment to the labour market, a five-fold increase. In between these two poles of social privilege and under-privilege, the risk of mental disorder is around 6% in other middle class strata before 'jumping' to more than 8% in the lower supervisory/ technical occupations, from this point onwards, it rises steadily on each successive downward rung of the social hierarchy. If we take the lower supervisory occupational category in Figure 1, as the division between the middle (white collar) and working class (blue collar) strata of British society (containing respectively 56 and 44% of the population), we can conclude that social class is strongly associated with children's mental well-being. Working class kids face a much higher probability of experiencing the symptoms of mental disorder in all its forms than their peers in middle class homes, hyperkinetic disorder is no exception.

The occupational class gradient of ADHD can be translated to another variable representing the social and economic geography of health inequality. This variable is based on the ACORN classification which uses the census characteristics of the area where a child lives (the postal code) to summarise its salient social characteristics. Figure 2, classifies the same sample of children by the quality of their living environment. In a literal sense this variable represents the social and economic environment of daily life and therefore the differential opportunities for physical

*Continued*

| No | Type | Stakeholder | Section | Comments | Reference suggested & reason for inclusion/exclusion | Actions |
|---|---|---|---|---|---|---|
| | | | | and intellectual development in childhood.<br><br>Once again, we find the social gradient so typical in the health inequality research literature. The symptoms of childhood psychiatric morbidity in areas populated by wealthy families are only half the rate of areas where families with moderate means make their homes. The gap is even wider between the most advantaged and the least disadvantaged neighbourhoods and it apples to all mental disorders as well as hyperkinetic disorder.<br><br>**Figure 2: Health inequality in childhood and the social geography of disadvantage**<br><br> | | |

| | Wealthy achievers | Urban prosperity | Comfort-ably off | Moderate means | Hard pressed |
|---|---|---|---|---|---|
| Hyperkinetic disorder | 1.10% | 1.30% | 1.20% | 1.70% | 2.30% |
| Any mental disorder | 5.80% | 7.40% | 8.20% | 11.70% | 14.60% |

| | | | | | |
|---|---|---|---|---|---|
| 23 | CC | David Coghill | 1.4 general | I do not think that the whole issue of impairment is dealt with well in this section. It makes a significant appearance in the discussion of the Consensus Conference and in the recommendations however it does not read as if it was critically appraised and considered by the GDG. I think this needs to be remedied within 1.4. | No references suggested. | Comment addressed, see Section 5.6. |
| 43 | PR | David Cottrell | 1.4.1 | First paragraph after subheading 'Evidence'. I have a problem with the use of the word 'symptom', in this chapter. The issue of the diagnostic validity is a contentious one as illustrated by the lengths the GDG have gone to in consulting widely. 'Symptom' implies an illness or disorder about which someone is complaining. Question A in 1.2, repeated at the start of 1.4, and question A1 at the start of 1.4.1 are careful in using the neutral term 'phenomena' to describe the behaviours of interest. This seems appropriate given that the whole point of this chapter is to reach conclusions about whether ADHD is or is not a useful construct. To then use the word 'symptom' seems to suggest that the issue is already decided. Its use may be appropriate when referring to clinical samples but the use at the end of this paragraph relates to a study where the sample is unclear. This usage recurs in 1.4.1 and throughout the chapter. For example 1.4.3 has 'phenomena' in the title but then refers to 'continuous distribution of symptoms in the population' in paragraph 3. I will not list all examples here, and as stated above, 'symptom' | No references suggested. | Comment addressed, see Section 5.2 'Symptoms'. |

*Continued*

| No | Type | Stakeholder | Section | Comments | Reference suggested & reason for inclusion/exclusion | Actions |
|---|---|---|---|---|---|---|
| | | | | may be appropriate for research on clinical samples but I think language could be used more carefully and would advocate a word search of the document and consideration on each occasion of the word 'symptom' whether it is in fact the best word available. | | |
| 71 | CC | Sami Timimi | 1.4.1 | (A1) Do the phenomena of hyperactivity, inattention and impulsivity cluster together? The GDG conclude, 'The number of factors varies between studies, with most finding two correlated factors for hyperactivity-impulsivity and inattention; others find that hyperactivity and impulsivity can be distinguished and a few find one combined factor of all three domains' suggesting little consistency in the literature. | No references suggested. | Comment addressed, see Sections 5.5.1 and 5.10. |
| 24 | CC | David Coghill | 1.4.1 evidence section (should be 1.4.1.1?) | This section would be easier to read if it started with a comment along the lines of, 'There was strong evidence for clustering of symptoms in both population and clinical samples. Evidence for one, two and three factor models was found with most evidence supporting a two factor model'. | No references suggested. | Comment addressed, see Section 5.5.1 'Summary'. |
| 25 | CC | David Coghill | 1.4.1 summary | The possibility of different patterns across different age ranges should be mentioned in the summary | No references suggested. | Comment addressed, see Section 5.5.1 'Summary'. |

| 44 | PR | David Cottrell | 1.4.2 | First paragraph, definitions again – it might be helpful to briefly define 'oppositional defiant and conduct problems', perhaps in a box? I confess to being unsure what these are myself. Are 'conduct problems' the same as conduct disorder? If so why not use a term with an agreed definition? If not we need a definition. The terms oppositional defiant problems, conduct problems, ODD (without ever being given in full), conduct disorder and 'disruptive behavioural problems' are all used in Section 1.4.2.1. | No references suggested. | Comment addressed, see Sections 5.2 'Oppositional defiant disorder and conduct disorder'. |
| 72 | CC | Sami Timimi | 1.4.2 | (A2) Are ADHD symptoms distinguishable from other conditions? It is noted that 'Frouke and colleagues (2005) conducted a diagnostic study of 2,230 Dutch pre-adolescents from the general population. LCA revealed that ADHD symptoms clustered together with symptoms of oppositional-defiant disorder and conduct disorder. A further study from the Netherlands of disruptive behaviour in 636 7-year-old children (Pol *et al.*, 2003) came to similar conclusions' and 'Multivariate twin modelling suggests that while the genetic influences on conduct disorder are largely shared with those that influence ADHD' and 'ADHD is reported to co-occur with personality disorder in young offenders (Young *et al.*, 2003)' and 'Dysthymia, depression and anxiety symptoms and disorders are frequently associated with ADHD in adults.' The GDG's own evidence is suggesting high levels of comorbidity raising doubts about the specificity of ADHD symptoms. The GDG | No references suggested. | Comment addressed, see Section 5.5.2 'Summary' (third paragraph). |

**PART 3:** (*Continued*)

| No | Type | Stakeholder | Section | Comments | Reference suggested & reason for inclusion/exclusion | Actions |
|---|---|---|---|---|---|---|
| | | | | use a 'get out of jail card' by concluding that this is because 'Longitudinal studies suggest that ADHD represents a separate condition that is a risk factor for the development of oppositional and conduct problems.' However, only one reference is cited in support of this (and this was in a study in which the chair of the GDG is the lead author). | | |
| 62 | PR | Anita Thapar | 1.4.2.1 | 'There are in addition environmental factors that influence the risk for conduct problems but not ADHD'. Suggest delete 'but not ADHD' Twin studies show important E contribution. | No references suggested. | Comment addressed, see Section 5.8.2. |
| 63 | PR | Anita Thapar | 1.4.2.1 | 'The heritability of ADHD symptoms is also higher than that for ODD/CD symptoms in these studies'. Suggest delete that sentence. It is not scientifically sensible to compare heritability estimates as they are population specific. Also some of the most genetic syndromes (for example, in general medicine) can show lower heritability estimates. | No references suggested. | Comment addressed, see Section 5.8.2. |
| 29 | CC | David Coghill | 1.4.2.1 and sumary for 1.4.2 | Pervasive developmental disorders are mentioned in the summary but not in the main body of the text. If there is info re. PDD it should be discussed, if there is not this also should be mentioned. | No references suggested. | Comment addressed, see Section 5.5.2 'Summary'. |

| 26 | CC | David Coghill | 1.4.2.1 para 2 | This paragraph should make it clearer that these studies disagree with those cited in para 1 by attaching a statement to that effect before giving the evidence (it is interesting that these are the only two studies in this Section with n reported). | No references suggested. | Comment addressed, see Section 5.5.2, 'ADHD and oppositional defiant and conduct problems'. |
| 27 | CC | David Coghill | 1.4.2.1 para 2 | What is CP? | No references suggested. | Typing mistake, now reads 'CD' for conduct disorder. |
| 28 | CC | David Coghill | 1.4.2.1 para 4 | 'However the two often occur independently of each other and only partially share aetiological factors'. Should read: 'However the two often occurred independently of each other and only partially shared aetiological factors', as it is citing the finding of the study not a general finding. | No references suggested. | Comment addressed, see Section 5.5.2 'Summary'. |
| 7 | PR | Margaret Alsop | 1.4.2.2 | Due to our involvement within many working and commissioning groups, it has been highlighted by Youth Offending Teams (YOTs), probation services, prisons, young offenders institutes, police, Youth Inclusion Support Programmes (YISPs) Connexions Services, Young People's Supported Housing, Housing Advice, Young People leaving Care, drug advisory teams and the legal profession such as magistrates/judges that there is now a high percentage of individuals with ADHD or suspected ADHD reaching these services. According to the Cambridgeshire study in 1995, 90% of recidivist juvenile offenders had a conduct | References suggested: Cambridgeshire study (1995). Asked reviewer for full reference; no response. | Comment taken into consideration, see Sections 5.5.2 'ADHD and oppositional defiant and conduct problems', 'ADHD and other co-occurring conditions' and 5.6 'Antisocial behaviour'. |

*Continued*

551

| No | Type | Stakeholder | Section | Comments | Reference suggested & reason for inclusion/exclusion | Actions |
|---|---|---|---|---|---|---|
|  |  |  |  | disorder at age 7. Young offenders are now responsible for about a third of all the criminal convictions. A Youth Justice Board survey showed that the number of criminal offences committed by young people is probably far higher than the conviction rates suggest. |  |  |
| 64 | PR | Anita Thapar | 1.4.2.2 | 'Overlapping genetic influences on ADHD and conduct problems but the genetic influences estimated by twin studies are greater for ADHD than ODD/CD....' Delete part of sentence, 'but the genetic influences estimated by twin studies are greater for ADHD than ODD/CD'. See above for reason. | No references suggested. | Comment addressed, see Section 5.5.2 'Summary'. |
| 30 | CC | David Coghill | 1.4.3 | I feel this section should precede the current 1.4.2 as it would seem logical to sat does adhd separate from normality and if so does it separate from other disorders. [sic] | No references suggested. | The sequence used follows the Washington University Diagnostic Criteria sequence. |
| 31 | CC | David Coghill | 1.4.3 | It should be made clearer that the factor approaches can only deal with the symptom level. It does not take into account the whole issue of impairment. Impairment is discussed in some depth in Section 1.7.1 but I feel that it should be discussed or at least better acknowledged in Section 1.4. Again a failure to do so will lead to misuse of isolated sections of | No references suggested. | Comment addressed, see Section 5.5.3 'Summary' (last paragraph). |

| | | | | | | |
|---|---|---|---|---|---|---|
| | | | | the guidance out of context and could lead to misunderstandings. | | |
| 51 | PR | Stephen Faraone | 1.4.3 | I agree with the comments in this section. But one point is missing. I think that the studies which show ADHD to be an extreme of a quantitative trait have typically defined ADHD based on symptom criteria alone. Their results may have been different if impairment criteria were used to define disorder status. | No references suggested. | Comment addressed, see Section 5.5.3 'Summary' (last paragraph). |
| 65 | PR | Anita Thapar | 1.4.3 | '...high ADHD symptom scores are the same as those that influence ADHD symptom levels...' DF analysis can't distinguish this – shows that the magnitude of the heritability estimate is the same for high as for 'normal range'. Suggest reword to 'high ADHD symptoms scores are of the same magnitude as those that influence ADHD symptom levels...' | No references suggested. | Comment addressed, see Section 5.5.3. |
| 73 | CC | Sami Timimi | 1.4.3 | (A3) Are the phenomena of hyperactivity, inattention and impulsivity distinguishable from the normal spectrum? It is stated that, 'These studies show that children with ADHD appear to be at one extreme of a quantitative dimension and on this quantitative dimension there is no obvious bi-modality that separates children with ADHD from non-ADHD children.' It is also noted that 'there is no obvious threshold or cut-off between ADHD and the continuous distribution of symptoms in the population.' In the introduction to the document it is stated that 'in | No references suggested. | Comment addressed, see Section 5.5.3 'Summary'. |

*Continued*

553

| No | Type | Stakeholder | Section | Comments | Reference suggested & reason for inclusion/exclusion | Actions |
|----|------|-------------|---------|----------|-------------------------------------------------------|---------|
|  |  |  |  | keeping with other common behavioural disorders there is no clear distinction between the clinical condition and the normal variation in the general population.' The GDG conclude that, 'Most analytic approaches are unable to make a clear distinction between the diagnosis of ADHD and the continuous distribution of ADHD symptoms in the general population'. In other words the answer to question 1.4.3 is, according to the evidence presented, 'no'. |  |  |
| 74 | CC | Sami Timimi | 1.4.4 | Is the cluster of symptoms that defines ADHD associated with significant clinical and psychosocial impairments? The GDG provides evidence that is consistent with ADHD being associated with significant impairment. However, what is not properly addressed is the nature of this association and direction of causality. For example, with regards academic difficulties it is noted that, 'These impairments often lead to grade retention (Hinshaw, 2002), to a lower probability of completing schooling when compared with children who do not have ADHD (Mannuzza *et al.*, 1993)'. This association could be mediated by a third factor, such as lowered self-esteem, boy-unfriendly school curricula, frustration, learning difficulties, and so on, that leads to both ADHD symptoms and poor school performance. In family difficulties it is mentioned that, 'Follow-up studies | References suggested: attachment studies. Asked reviewer for full references, no response. | Comment addressed, see Sections 5.6 and 5.11. |

indicate that mothers of children and adolescents with ADHD have more difficulty in child behaviour management practices and coping with their child's behaviour (August et al., 1998), and display higher rates of conflict behaviours, such as negative comments, social irritability, hostility and maladaptive levels of communication and involvement (August et al., 1998; Fletcher et al., 1996). Family impairment also permeates the parent's lives. Parents of children with ADHD report having less time to meet their own needs, fewer close friendships, greater peer rejection, less time for family activities, which might lead to less family cohesion and a significant effect on the parent's emotional health (Bagwell et al., 2001).' A vast repertoire of attachment studies also suggest that this association might well indicate important causal factors for ADHD symptoms (that is, these family difficulties cause rather than are caused by ADHD, or more likely interact in varying degrees and combinations depending on the family and individual). With regard to antisocial behaviour the GDG notes, 'In a prospective follow-up of 103 males diagnosed with ADHD, the presence of an antisocial or conduct disorder almost completely accounted for the increased risk for criminal activities' and 'Lee and Hinshaw (2004) reported that the predictive power of ADHD status to adolescent delinquency diminishes when key indices of childhood externalising behaviour related to ADHD are taken into account'. Finally, discussion of

Continued

| No | Type | Stakeholder | Section | Comments | Reference suggested & reason for inclusion/exclusion | Actions |
|----|------|-------------|---------|----------|-----------------------------------------------------|---------|
| | | | | long-term outcome is difficult to interpret given that no information is provided by the GDG on the relationship of outcome to other factors known to be associated with poorer outcome such as social class, IQ, comorbid diagnoses and so on. | | |
| 32 | CC | David Coghill | 1.4.4 and 1.4.5 | I think that the substance misuse issues should be considered in 1.4.4 rather than 1.4.5. This Section should also comment on the interactions between early treatment with stimulants and later occurring substance misuse and include nicotine as a drug of misuse that attenuates ADHD symptoms. | No references suggested. | Comment addressed, see Section 5.6. |
| 8 | PR | Margaret Alsop | 1.4.4.2 | Whilst we agree in principle, our own personal experiences, our own personal experiences and that of having worked with and supported many families for over a decade through the ADHD Support Group, there are clear indications that parents are still being subjected to accusations of 'poor parenting'. As parents, not only are we dealing with the family members' needs, and those of siblings but also with professional bodies such as health, education and social care in which to access an appropriate multi-agency, multi-disciplinary service for the ADHD family member, no one body taking responsibility in which to meet the needs of those with ADHD or those of family members.<br>Such dealings may lead to conflict between parent | No references suggested. | Comment taken into consideration. |

| | | | | | |
|---|---|---|---|---|---|
| | | | carers and service providers, therefore having an impact on service delivery. A high percentage of parents and family members living with ADHD may be accessing mental health services for that of their own needs. | | |
| 45 | PR | David Cottrell | 1.4.4.2 | The other parts of 1.4.4 address the potential confounding influence of comorbid conduct disorder, this is not mentioned in this section on family difficulties. | No references suggested. | Comment addressed, see Section 5.6 'Family difficulties'. |
| 9 | PR | Margaret Alsop | 1.4.4.3 | Could it be that by the time the ADHD child is a teenager they may feel that they are somehow different from their friends, but may not understand why? To the ADHD adolescent, they often think that there is some kind of secret code going on between others. This ever widening void is being caused by their inability to learn the code of social cues–those nuances of physical expression and movement that carry half of any conversation and convey personal attitude, varying emotions and defence (or lack of it) between other conversing groups of people. The ADHD adolescent may have a two-way body language problem involving interpreting others and giving the right signals in return. They may try and copy those around them, without being aware of the subtle complexities or of what is or is not socially acceptable. 'Too many children fail to achieve their full potential and face involvement in crime, poor health, early unwanted pregnancies, substance misuse or | References suggested: Cross Cutting Review of Children at Risk (2002). Paper excluded: Not specific to ADHD; not peer reviewed. | See Section 5.6. |

*Continued*

**PART 3:** (*Continued*)

| No | Type | Stakeholder | Section | Comments | Reference suggested & reason for inclusion/exclusion | Actions |
|----|------|-------------|---------|----------|-------------------------------------------------------|---------|
| | | | | under-achievement in education because services fail to spot the emerging risks or to intervene early enough to coordinate the support necessary. We know that factors such as poverty, failure at school, mental health, family problems or antisocial behaviour can each be possible indicators of future problems'. (Cross Cutting Review of Children at Risk for the 2002 Spending Review). | | |
| 10 | PR | Margaret Alsop | 1.4.4.5 | Adults with ADHD we have found may have a criminal record of some sort, this highly impacting on their accessing appropriate adult educational programmes, many with no educational qualifications (under-achieving academically), poor record of school attendances or exclusions from education, all of which are contributing factors and play a major role in their employment or future employment status. Multi-agency working to include occupational therapists during transitional services would perhaps contribute towards meeting the needs of those with ADHD and working alongside future employers. | No references suggested. | Comment addressed, see Section 5.6 'Adolescent and adult problems'. |
| 52 | PR | Stephen Faraone | 1.4.4.5 | You might also mention the data showing ADHD patients to be at high risk for traffic citations and traffic accidents. You could also mention their increased healthcare utilisation. | References suggested: Risk for traffic accidents. Asked reviewer | Comment addressed, see Section 5.6 'Adolescent and adult problems'. |

| | | | | | for full references, no response. | |
|---|---|---|---|---|---|---|
| 11 | PR | Margaret Alsop | 1.4.5 | Many children accessing CAMHS or paediatric services may do so until aged 16–17 years. A high percentage of this group may not be referred onto the adult community mental health teams, therefore a child who has received a multi-agency as well as a medicinal approach to treatments for ADHD may well end up in that 'grey area' of their not accessing the appropriate healthcare and treatments could all be contributing factors to the possibility of their self-medicating on other substances. | No references suggested. | Comment taken into consideration. For recommendations on this matter refer to the NICE guideline. |
| 46 | PR | David Cottrell | 1.4.5 | First paragraph after subheading 'Summary', line 10 – is 'appropriate' correct? Earlier you say the evidence is poor and that developmentally appropriate criteria have yet to be developed. I suspect this should be 'inappropriate'. | No references suggested. | Comment addressed, see Section 5.7.2. |
| 53 | PR | Stephen Faraone | 1.4.5 | In the summary, the following sentence is not clear and should be re-worded: 'The profile of symptoms may alter with a relative persistence of inattentive symptoms compared with hyperactive-impulsive symptoms, however the evidence base for this conclusion is poor, using developmentally appropriate measures of hyperactivity-impulsivity in adults.' | No references suggested. | Comment addressed, see Section 5.7.2. |
| 54 | PR | Stephen Faraone | 1.4.5 | The summary states: 'There was no evidence to warrant a different diagnostic concept in childhood and in adulthood.' This seems a bit too strong. The | References suggested: Barkley's book: | Comment addressed, see Section 5.7.2. |

*Continued*

**PART 3:** *(Continued)*

| No | Type | Stakeholder | Section | Comments | Reference suggested & reason for inclusion/exclusion | Actions |
|---|---|---|---|---|---|---|
| | | | | DSM itself allows for a different diagnostic concept: (1) the category of in partial remission can be used for adults; (2) a subjective feeling of restlessness can be diagnostic of motor hyperactivity. Russ Barkley's new book (and some of his prior work) suggests that the current ADHD symptoms are not developmentally sensitive and there have been some initiatives to re-write the ADHD rating scale (for example, work by Spencer and Adler) so that the questions are more relevant to adults. Also, I think that the greater reduction of hyperactive-impulsive versus inattentive symptoms is more strongly supported than you suggest. But these are all, for sure, debatable points. | Paper excluded: not peer-reviewed. | |
| 55 | PR | Stephen Faraone | 1.4.5 | I don't understand the statement, 'there is a lack of data on the continuity of aetiological factors into adulthood.' Given that many of the known risk factors for ADHD occur very early in development (for example, genes, fetal toxic exposures), why would we think their effects turn off during adulthood? I think you mean that we know little about which risk factors modify the course of ADHD through adolescence into adulthood. Probably a re-wording is needed. | No references suggested. | Comment addressed, see Section 5.7.2. |
| 75 | CC | Sami Timimi | 1.4.5 | Is there evidence for a characteristic pattern of developmental changes, or outcomes associated with the | No references suggested. | Comment addressed, see Section 5.7.2. |

*Continued*

symptoms, that define ADHD? It is noted that 'Faraone and colleagues (2006) analysed data from 32 follow-up studies of children with ADHD into adulthood. Where full criteria for ADHD were used approximately 15% of children were still diagnosed with ADHD at age 25'. This is the only systematic review identified outside of point 1.4.6 (where seven were identified). This finding seems to suggest that 'characteristic' outcomes for those diagnosed with ADHD is far from established. Later the GDG speculates as to why rates of substance abuse are higher in those with ADHD symptoms (is this a 'characteristic' outcome?) stating: 'The mechanisms involved can include one or more of the following: first, that individuals with ADHD may seek out highly stimulating or risky activities; second, that individuals with ADHD are exposed to higher levels of psychosocial risks for development of substance use disorders, resulting from educational and social impairments, social exclusion and antisocial behaviour associated with ADHD; third, that various substances, including cannabis, alcohol and stimulants can attenuate ADHD symptoms and are therefore sometimes used as a form of self-treatment.' Whilst it is unclear why the GDG felt the need to speculate (without evidential references) on this issue, narrow linear biomedical paradigms seems to have allowed them to overlook fairly basic scientific issues. The relationship between ADHD and substance misuse that they are referring to is an association, and thus a third (or

**PART 3:** (*Continued*)

| No | Type | Stakeholder | Section | Comments | Reference suggested & reason for inclusion/exclusion | Actions |
|----|------|-------------|---------|----------|------------------------------------------------------|---------|
| | | | | more) factor may be responsible for both the substance misuse and ADHD symptoms (such as low self-esteem, family conflict, learning difficulties, comorbid conditions, and so on) making the required criteria of 'characteristic' difficult to establish. | | |
| 33 | CC | David Coghill | 1.4.5 summary | 'Using child criteria, approximately 15% of children with ADHD retain the diagnosis by age 25 but a much larger proportion (65%) show persistence of symptoms with associated impairments.' <br><br>Could read: 'Using child criteria, approximately 15% of children with ADHD retain the diagnosis by age 25 but a much larger proportion (65%) show some persistence of symptoms with significant associated impairments.' | No references suggested. | Comment addressed, see Section 5.7.2. |
| 35 | CC | David Coghill | 1.4.6 | Also the whole issue of heterogeneity at all levels of analysis needs to be discussed as this is central to the whole issue of what is ADHD. I guess the current conclusion would be something like: here are a group of symptoms that hold together pretty well that can be distinguished from normal and other disorders that cause impairment but seem to be the end point (behavioural phenotypic expression) of a wide range of different causal pathways. This would assist the discussion of diversity in Section 1.6. | No references suggested. | Comment addressed, see Section 5.8. |

| | | | | | | |
|---|---|---|---|---|---|---|
| 47 | PR | David Cottrell | 1.4.6 | Could/ should you define executive function for a lay readership? | No references suggested. | Comment addressed, see Section 5.8.1. |
| 56 | PR | Stephen Faraone | 1.4.6 | I suggest you include the following: Valera, E. M., Faraone, S. V., Murray, K. E., *et al.* (2007) Meta-analysis of structural imaging findings in attention-deficit/hyperactivity disorder. *Biological Psychiatry, 61,* 1361–1369. | References suggested: Valera, E. M., Faraone, S. V., Murray, K. E., *et al.* (2007) Meta-analysis of structural imaging findings in attention-deficit/ hyperactivity disorder. *Biological Psychiatry, 61,* 1361–1369. Paper included | Comment addressed, see Section 5.8.1 'Neuroimaging studies' |
| 57 | PR | Stephen Faraone | 1.4.6 | A more thorough review of the molecular genetics literature would implicate other genes but that is not essential to make your point. If you'd like to improve the review of environmental risk factors, you could consult: Banerjee, T. D., Middleton, F. & Faraone, S. V. (2007) Environmental risk factors for attention-deficit hyperactivity disorder. *Acta Paediatrica, 6,* 1269–1274. | References suggested: Banerjee, T. D., Middleton, F. & Faraone, S. V. (2007) Environmental risk factors for attention-deficit hyperactivity disorder. *Acta Paediatrica,* | Comment taken into consideration. |

*Continued*

563

PART 3: (Continued)

| No | Type | Stakeholder | Section | Comments | Reference suggested & reason for inclusion/exclusion | Actions |
|---|---|---|---|---|---|---|
| | | | | | 6, 1269–1274. Paper excluded: Review (no systematic search). | |
| 66 | PR | Anita Thapar | 1.4.6 | Li *et al.*, 2006: There have actually been a number of meta-analyses. Most but not all have found the same as Li *et al.* Might want to mention at least that there have been several. The point of contention is DAT, where most meta-analyses have found no association but some notably have, for example Weiss, S., Tzavara, E. T., Davis, R. J., *et al.* (2007) Functional alterations of nicotinic neurotransmission in dopamine transporter knock-out mice. *Neuropharmacology*, 52, 1496–508. Epub 24 Feb 2007. | References suggested: Weiss, S., Tzavara, E. T., Davis, R. J., *et al.* (2007) Functional alterations of nicotinic neurotransmission in dopamine transporter knock-out mice. *Neuropharmacology*, 52, 1496–508. Paper excluded: Only studies on humans considered. | Comment taken into consideration. |
| 67 | PR | Anita Thapar | 1.4.6 | '..acting through gene-environment interactions'. Add 'and gene-environment correlations (Jaffee & Price, 2007)'. Jaffee, S. R. & Price, T. S. (2007) Gene-environment correlations: a review of the evidence and | References suggested: Jaffee, S. R. & Price, T. S. (2007) Gene-environment | Comment taken into consideration, see Section 5.13. |

| | | | | | | |
|---|---|---|---|---|---|---|
| | | | | implications for prevention of mental illness. *Molecular Psychiatry, 12*, 432–442. Epub 16 Jan 2007. Review. | correlations: a review of the evidence and implications for prevention of mental illness. *Molecular Psychiatry, 12*, 432–442. Paper excluded: Review (no systematic search). | Comment addressed, see Section 5.8.1, 'Physical environmental risks'. |
| 68 | PR | Anita Thapar | 1.4.6 | Literature on prenatal stress? Few studies now on this and ADHD, even though not covered by Linnet study. Talge, N. M., Neal, C. & Glover, V. (2007) Antenatal maternal stress and long-term effects on child neurodevelopment: how and why? *The Journal of Child Psychology and Psychiatry, 48*, 245–61. Review. | References suggested: Talge, N. M., Neal, C. & Glover, V. (2007) Antenatal maternal stress and long-term effects on child neurodevelopment: how and why? *The Journal of Child Psychology and Psychiatry, 48*, 245–61. Paper included. | |
| 76 | CC | Sami Timimi | 1.4.6 | Is there consistent evidence of genetic, environmental or neurobiological risk factors associated with | No specific references suggested. | Comment addressed, see Section 5.9. |

*Continued*

**PART 3:** (*Continued*)

| No | Type | Stakeholder | Section | Comments | Reference suggested & reason for inclusion/exclusion | Actions |
|----|------|-------------|---------|----------|------------------------------------------------------|---------|
|    |      |             |         | ADHD? The GDG concludes, 'Specific genetic variants that are associated with a *small* increase in the risk for ADHD have been identified in the dopamine D4 and close to the dopamine D5 receptor genes. Analysis of ADHD versus non-ADHD groups has identified consistent changes in brain function and performance on neurocognitive tests; however differences from controls *are not universal, do not characterise all children and adults with a clinical diagnosis of ADHD, and do not usually establish causality in individual cases.*' [my italics] The GDG were provided with several papers providing a critical evaluation of research in this area. None were cited in this document. <br><br> The GDG after reviewing the evidence and mentioning that, 'The quality of the evidence included in this review was variable and lacked any "gold standard"' goes on to recommend that ADHD is valid and to make a diagnosis the following criteria should be met: 'Symptoms of ADHD (DSM-IV) or hyperkinetic disorder (ICD-10) should be sufficient to reach a formal diagnosis in DSM-IV or ICD-10. ADHD should be considered in all age groups (children, adolescents and adults), with symptom criteria adjusted for age appropriate changes in behaviour. The level of impairment resulting from symptoms of |  |  |

*Continued*

hyperactivity and or inattention should be at least moderately clinically significant on the basis of interview and or direct observation in multiple settings, and pervasive (occur in all important settings) including social, familial educational and or occupational settings.' This is essentially no different to current DSM-IV criteria and one wonders what the point of this expensive, time consuming exercise was if this is the best the GDG can come up with, particularly when the GDG provide little guidance as to how a clinician is to interpret words like 'moderately', and 'significant'. Given that the chair of the group is well publicised for believing that ADHD is under-diagnosed in the UK, and that using DSM-IV criteria gives prevalence rates of between 3 and 7%, this guideline is likely to result in an increase of ADHD diagnosis. Given these potentially far reaching implications for children and adults in this country and the tenuous evidential support in the document, the basis for the GDG's conclusions must be questioned.

The GDG states that, 'It was recognised that defining psychiatric disorders is a difficult process due to the overlapping nature of behavioural and psychiatric syndromes, the complexity of the aetiological processes and the lack of a "gold standard" such as a biological test—in this regard ADHD is no different from other common psychiatric disorders.

Furthermore, in keeping with other common behavioural disorders there is no clear distinction between the clinical condition and the normal variation

| No | Type | Stakeholder | Section | Comments | Reference suggested & reason for inclusion/exclusion | Actions |
|----|------|-------------|---------|----------|-----------------------------------------------------|---------|
| | | | | in the general population'. The phrase 'two wrongs don't make a right' came to mind on reading this. A get-out clause that because other psychiatric diagnoses are problematic constructs (and there is a large literature that attests to this), it is acceptable for a lowering of standards and evidential basis with which to evaluate ADHD, is a circular argument to excuse poor science and insufficient rigour.<br><br>The GDG states that, 'Furthermore, in keeping with other common behavioural disorders there is no clear distinction between the clinical condition and the normal variation in the general population (see Section A3). This is comparable to normal variation for medical traits such as hypertension and type II diabetes'. Such a spurious analogy reveals the extent to which the GDG has ignored one of the most important differences between physical states and psychiatric ones – meaning. 120/80 BP means the same whether it is measured in New York or New Delhi and reflects a physical state (universalism). Further, the pathophysiological processes resulting from high blood pressure are known and independent of the meaning any culture ascribes to symptoms (essentialism). This is not the case for behavioural presentations such as ADHD, which has varying interpretations and meanings, just as beliefs about | | |

Continued

what is a 'normal childhood' and 'normal child development' varies enormously over time and between cultures. It is of concern that the GDG seems unaware of the diverse literature (from disciplines such as transcultural psychiatry and psychology, philosophy, anthropology and sociology) criticising the inappropriate use of univeralist and essentialist models (drawn from the biomedical paradigm) in multicultural societies. This is considered a very basic error. Such an approach leads to institutional racism as it assumes that the beliefs and practices about children and childhood drawn from a narrow Western biomedical paradigm is the standard through which to judge those cultures who have differing beliefs and practices with regards their paradigms for understanding the nature of childhood, childhood problems and child care and rearing. This replicates the dynamics of colonialism and such attitudes being promoted for our institutional practices are simply unacceptable in modern multicultural Britain.

The most disappointing aspect of the document is the missed opportunity for a more erudite approach to the question of diagnosis. Given the poor quality of the document it is likely that the current GDG simply does not have the objectivity, knowledge, or sophistication to produce an evidence-based, ethical and progressive review and set of guidelines that could help curtail bad practice, but more importantly provide guidelines that take practice beyond current

| No | Type | Stakeholder | Section | Comments | Reference suggested & reason for inclusion/exclusion | Actions |
|---|---|---|---|---|---|---|
| | | | | simplistic paradigms to make it fit for the realities of multi-cultural 21ˢᵗ century Britain. Psychiatry has been increasingly grasping the complexity that comes from a territory that sits at the meeting point of many disciplines' discourses. Medicine too has increasingly grasped these cross-disciplinary perspectives leading to growth of practices such as narrative medicine and values-based medicine to try and encompass the subjective, cultural, social, political, economic and psychological influences on physical health and medical treatment. In this respect psychiatry should be providing a lead for the rest of medicine as we increasingly move away from redundant dualistic conceptualisations such as mind/body, nature/nurture and universal/relative and toward accepting multiplicity in a way that reflects the diverse nature of the client group we wish to assist. Engagement with these issues would lead to an ability to examine validity of ADHD from a number of angles, recognising that there are many different approaches to this question that reflect different values and aims. For example, in addition to scientific validity, there are considerations of pragmatics, utility, administrative, consistency, relevance, coherence, precision, fecundity, epistemic, ethical, ontological, and so on. Using these multiple positions | | |

| | | | | | | |
|---|---|---|---|---|---|---|
| | | | | would enable greater transparency and openness to the novel and more flexible guidelines that have greater likelihood of enabling more appropriate engagement with the diverse issues clients with ADHD symptoms present with. It is clear to this author at least, that the current GDG is simply not up to that task. | | |
| 81 | PR | Jonathan Leo | 1.4.6 | Comments on D4, D5, DAT1. Regarding your citation of specific genes involved in ADHD. The evidence is mixed at best. And furthermore any connection would only be an association not a cause. Regarding D4 (DRD4) you state there is strong evidence for an association but this is not representative of the scientific literature. According to Willcutt (whom you cite earlier): 'Similar to the results for DAT1, however, this result [DRD4] was not replicated in all samples and does not appear to be necessary or sufficient to cause ADHD. Moreover, the association with ADHD is much stronger in case-control comparisons than in family-based designs, suggesting that some significant results may be due to differences in gene frequencies in the populations from which the ADHD and comparison samples were drawn' (Faraone et al., 2001). In a detailed 2006 survey of the evidence in support of DRD4, DAT1, and other candidate genes, Waldman and Gizer (p. 421) concluded, 'It should be clear…that for each [ADHD] candidate genes studied, there is a mixed picture of positive and negative | References suggested: Waldman (2006) Asked reviewer for full reference; no response. Baumeister & Hawkins (2001) Asked reviewer for full reference; no response. Giedd (2001) Asked reviewer for full reference; no response. Sowell (2003) Asked reviewer for full reference; no response. | Comment addressed, see Appendix 17.1 'Study characteristics – Diagnosis' for information on funding of studies included, see Section 5.8 'Neuroimaging studies' for discussion of genetic studies. |

Continued

**PART 3:** (*Continued*)

| No | Type | Stakeholder | Section | Comments | Reference suggested & reason for inclusion/exclusion | Actions |
|---|---|---|---|---|---|---|
| | | | | findings.' Or as Willcutt stated: 'For 14 of the 27 candidate genes a significant association with ADHD has been reported in at least one study; however, virtually all of these results have been replicated inconsistently or await independent replication (Table 2). Moreover, each of these genes appears to account for a relatively small proportion of the variance in ADHD symptoms (for example., Faraone, Doyle, Mick, *et al.*, 2001), suggesting that none are likely to be necessary or sufficient to cause ADHD.' Or as Faraone has stated (2005, p. 1319) with regard to genome wide scans, 'The handful of genome wide scans that have been conducted thus far show divergent findings and are, therefore, not conclusive.' Regarding your summary of the genetic studies it would be more straightforward to say, 'At this point in time no genes for ADHD have yet been identified.' In advertisements for ADHD the supposed genetic basis for ADHD is often used to justify medical treatment. However, left unsaid in these same advertisements, is that a presumed genetic defect is in no way a necessary prerequisite to prescribe stimulants. As of now, the medical community finds it entirely acceptable to prescribe medication for psychological stress brought on by environmental stressors. One needs to look no further than foster care programmes | Castellanos (2002) Asked reviewer for full reference; no response. Pliszka, S. R., Glahn, D. C., Semrud-Clikeman, M., *et al.* (2006) Neuroimaging of inhibitory control areas in children with attention deficit hyperactivity disorder who were treatment naive or in long-term treatment. *American Journal of Psychiatry, 163*, 1052–1060. Paper included. Smith (2006) *Am J Psychiatry,* | |

572

Continued

| | |
|---|---|
| which medicate an inordinate number of children. Presumably the common factor in these children is not their genetic makeup but their common environmental triggers. Although ADHD is considered a genetic defect, looking for a common gene in foster home children to explain their behaviour would seem to be a fruitless effort. Conversely, the results of a survey of environmental stressors in their lives would probably be very fruitful. The diagnosis and medication of children in foster homes is perhaps the best example of how, genes and biology aside, it is an acceptable practice to medicate children whose behaviour is explained by the environment. | 163, 1033–1043. Paper to be included.<br><br>Tamm (2006) *Am J Psychiatry*, 163, 1033–1043. Paper to be included. |
| 'Although some people question the assumption of the equal environment assumption for identical and non-identical twins this does not impact on the question of validity since the high twin correlations observed in these studies indicates that ADHD symptoms are highly familial.'<br><br>This is a very confusing sentence as it mixes up 'familial' with 'genetic.' It appears to be written by someone who does not understand the genetic studies. The claim that high MZ concordance shows that ADHD is 'familial' is erroneous. MZ concordance for speaking Italian is 100%, but does this mean speaking Italian is a genetic trait? The EEA does not just have an *impact* on estimates of genetic factors–if it is false then the twin method is deeply flawed. 'There is consistent evidence of familial influences on ADHD symptoms in the general population. | Casey & Durston (2006) *Am J Psychiatry*, 163, 1033–1043. Paper excluded: not peer reviewed (editorial).<br><br>Volkow (2007) Asked reviewer for full reference; no response.<br><br>Carey (2005) Can brain scans see depression? *The New York Times*. Paper excluded: not peer reviewed; opinion paper. |

573

| No | Type | Stakeholder | Section | Comments | Reference suggested & reason for inclusion/exclusion | Actions |
|----|------|-------------|---------|----------|------------------------------------------------------|---------|
| | | | | Under the equal environment assumption these familial influences are thought to be largely genetic in origin.'<br><br>This is very problematic and should be reworded. The EEA pertains only to the twin method and not to family studies In addition, the document does not provide any citations that the EEA, which is counter intuitive, is correct.<br><br>The NICE document also makes the assumption that if it is genetic then it must be a disease. However, a host of other traits have also been investigated and these studies have determined that MZs have a higher concordance than DZs. For instance, twin studies have shown a heritability for loneliness (Boomsma *et al.* 2005), the frequency of orgasm in women (Daewood *et al.*, 2005), the results of the United States 2004 presidential election (Alford *et al.*, 2005), perfectionism (Tozzi *et al.*, 2004), and breakfast eating patterns (Keski-Rahkonen *et al.*, 2004) (cited in Joseph 2008). In 1990, Bouchard stated: 'For almost every behavioural trait so far investigated, from reaction time to religiosity an important fraction of the variation among people turns out to be associated with genetic variation. This fact need no longer be subject to debate'. Yet, if all our traits have a genetic basis then the genetic | | |

Continued

evidence of a trait does not automatically lead to 'it's a disease' declarations. What many ADHD researchers seem to be saying is, that by implicating genetics in the behavioural trait of attention, this is somehow evidence of a disease. If Bouchard is correct, and all our traits have a strong basis in genetics, then can individuals exhibiting extremes of other traits also fall into the diseased category? The slippery-slope analogy seems almost too obvious to mention here, and might seem trite, however this appears to be exactly the trap that the child psychiatry profession has fallen into regarding other conditions, for instance child-onset bipolar disorder. The NICE statement on ADHD should not be seen with blinders on, as their statements about what constitutes a 'disease' will surely be revisited in the years ahead as they face other instances where traits can be classified as a disease in need of medication. NICE's foray into ADHD is only the beginning.

1.4.6 Dickstein and colleagues completed a systematic meta-analysis of 16 neuroimaging studies that compared patterns of neuroactivity in children and adults with ADHD and controls. The GDG's position would be stronger if indeed there was a biological marker for ADHD, however to cite the Dickstein paper will be seen as a desperate grasp for evidence. Like much of the ADHD neuroimaging research, on the surface the Dickstein paper might appear to make the case that there is a visible organic pathology in the brains of children diagnosed with

**PART 3:** (*Continued*)

| No | Type | Stakeholder | Section | Comments | Reference suggested & reason for inclusion/exclusion | Actions |
|----|------|-------------|---------|----------|------------------------------------------------------|---------|
| | | | | ADHD, however a more in-depth view of the study reveals problems of experimental design that have plagued this entire body of research. The Dickstein paper is a meta-analysis of 16 ADHD imaging studies. Out of these 16 studies, four were used for a comparison of ADHD non-medicated to controls – the most important comparison. Interestingly, Dickstein *et al.* do not mention that two out of these four studies used the same ADHD subjects – the two studies were separate papers but came from the same research group. This is fairly obvious from reading the two studies, and was confirmed in an email to the lead author. Emails to the corresponding author of the Dickstein paper asking for clarification have gone unanswered. Double counting subjects is problematic for a meta-analysis, especially since Dickstein *et al.* did not mention it in their paper. Furthermore, even in the Dickstein analysis for the most important comparison in the study which was the non-medicated ADHD to controls the majority of the differences were for the most part not significant. It seems highly problematic for the NICE review to not mention this in their review. Although positive findings on neuroimaging studies of psychiatric disorders, including ADHD, are usually given wide coverage in scientific publications and the mass media, the fact remains that this body | | |

576

of research has not provided support for a specific 'biological basis' of ADHD. This is well noted by Baumeister and Hawkins (2001) who report, 'inconsistencies among studies raise questions about the reliability of the findings' (p. 2). Writing, for instance, about the tendency for studies to find decreases in the size and activity of the frontal lobes, Baumeister and Hawkins summarise that:

'Even in this instance, however, the data are not compelling. The number of independent replications is small, and the validity of reported effects is compromised by a lack of statistical rigor. For example, several of the major functional imaging studies failed to employ standard statistical controls for multiple comparisons. This means that many of the reported findings are almost certainly spurious. Moreover, considering the likely existence of bias toward reporting and publishing positive results, the literature probably overestimates the occurrence of significant differences between subjects with ADHD and control subjects' (p. 8, references omitted).

In addition, virtually all researchers in this field acknowledge that no brain scan can currently detect anomalies in any given individual diagnosed with a primary mental disorder, nor can it help clinicians to confirm such a diagnose. For example, in his authoritative *Handbook of Brain Imaging*, Bremner (2005) states:

'Unfortunately, we are not at a point where brain imaging can be used routinely for the diagnosis of

| No | Type | Stakeholder | Section | Comments | Reference suggested & reason for inclusion/exclusion | Actions |
|----|------|-------------|---------|----------|------------------------------------------------------|---------|
|    |      |             |         | psychiatric conditions. ... We still do not understand the patho-physiology or mechanisms of response to treatment for most of these disorders. ...Most studies of psychiatric patients have found that even when a particular finding characterized a patient group, there remained as many as a third of patients who scored in the range of the control subjects' (pp. 33–35). Similarly, in the case of ADHD, Giedd and colleagues (2001) conclude unequivocally that: 'If a child has no symptoms of ADHD but a brain scan consistent with what is found in groups of ADHD, treatment for ADHD is not indicated. Therefore, at the time of this writing, clinical history remains the gold standard of ADHD diagnosis' (p. 45). The Dickstein paper was funded by NIMH. Of interest to the NICE reviewers might be the 2003 paper by Sowell and colleagues also funded by NIMH. The Sowell study, involving 27 ADHD and 46 normal control subjects, reported that ADHD children had smaller frontal lobes compared to the control subjects, but overall the ADHD subjects had more cortical grey matter (Sowell *et al.*, 2003). This study's significance derives not necessarily from this result, but – as with several previous ADHD neuroimaging studies – from important comparisons that researchers could have made, but *did not*. One |  |  |

reason for bringing this study to your attention is because of your own acknowledgment in your previous reports about other conditions and treatments (the SSRIs for instance) that seeing the published data is not the same as seeing all the data, because the pharmaceutical companies do not publish all their studies. The same holds true for research into basic science topics, although in this case it is government-funded organisations that will not release data.

As in an earlier, similar paper by Castellanos and colleagues (2002), some of the ADHD subjects in the Sowell study were apparently medication-naïve. I say 'apparently' because specific descriptions were not provided: '15 of the 27 patients were taking stimulant medication at the time of imaging' (p. 1705). It is unclear how to categorise the remaining 12 patients. Did they have a history of medication use prior to the start of the study, and then stop taking their medication for 48 hours, or some other arbitrary time period before imaging? It is surprising that a study published in *The Lancet* could be so vague about one of the most important variables in the study. Conclusions based on a comparison of normal control subjects to medication-naïve ADHD subjects would be very different from conclusions based on a comparison of control subjects to ADHD subjects with varying durations of medication exposure or undergoing abrupt withdrawal.

The issue becomes considerably more muddled and confusing due to a brief concluding discussion

*Continued*

**PART 3:** (*Continued*)

| No | Type | Stakeholder | Section | Comments | Reference suggested & reason for inclusion/exclusion | Actions |
|----|------|-------------|---------|----------|------------------------------------------------------|---------|
| | | | | by Sowell and colleagues (2003) of the potential role of stimulant medication on their findings. The authors first appropriately acknowledged that, since 55% of their ADHD children were taking stimulants, 'the effects of stimulant drugs could have confounded our findings of abnormal brain morphology in children with [ADHD]' (p. 1705). The simplest way to properly evaluate this confounding effect would have been to compare the 15 medicated ADHD children with the 12 unmedicated ADHD children. However, Sowell and colleagues chose to not make that comparison: 'We did not directly compare brain morphology across groups of patients on and off drugs because the sample size was considerably compromised when taking lifetime history of stimulant drugs into account' (p.1705). The authors further explained that this comparison, between unmedicated and medicated, is not needed because a prior study by Castellanos and colleagues (2002) suggested that medications do not affect brain size.

Sowell and colleagues' methodological choice, and its justification, is both unconvincing and puzzling. First, although one can sympathise with their judgement that 'taking lifetime history of stimulant medication into account' compromised their sample size, this judgement ignores that for 30 years ADHD | | |

neuroimaging researchers have deemed it perfectly acceptable to compare ADHD subjects and normal controls *regardless of medication history*. Indeed, virtually all the studies that Sowell and colleagues cite to contextualise their own study and interpret their results exemplify this practice. Thus it is difficult to see why Sowell and colleagues would feel that they should not compare medicated and unmedicated ADHD subjects. Clearly, just as they acknowledged limitations to their main study results, Sowell and colleagues could have reported the results of the more specific comparison with an acknowledgement of the appropriate limitations. Second, Sowell and colleagues cite Castellanos and colleagues to support the methodological choice of not comparing medicated and unmedicated ADHD subjects. But, third and most important, Sowell and colleagues' data appear directly relevant to either support or refute the conclusions that Castellanos and colleagues (2002) drew from their comparison. In fact, the results of the Castellanos and colleagues' comparison of brain volumes of medicated and unmedicated ADHD children were deemed worthy of a major press release by the NIMH concerning stimulant drugs' effects on developing brains, yet the same comparison in the Sowell and colleagues study was considered insignificant and not even reportable.

Sowell and colleagues would not supply the information about the most important comparison in the study, and a subsequent Freedom of Information Act

*Continued*

**PART 3:** (*Continued*)

| No | Type | Stakeholder | Section | Comments | Reference suggested & reason for inclusion/exclusion | Actions |
|----|------|-------------|---------|----------|------------------------------------------------------|---------|
|    |      |             |         | Request to NIMH to release the information was denied. This was in spite of the fact that on their own website NIMH encourages their grant recipients to share data. One could say that NIMH's actions speak louder than their words. Given their own interest in the subject, possibly the NICE reviewers could request the data? In June 2006, the *American Journal of Psychiatry* published three articles (Pliszka *et al.*, 2006; Smith *et al.*, 2006; Tamm *et al.*, 2006) and an accompanying editorial about functional magnetic resonance imaging (Casey & Durston, 2006). The three studies conducted scans of children's brains during a specified task, and, importantly, all three studies had a group of medication-naïve ADHD children. However, when considered together, the three studies implicated an inordinate number of different brain regions, with little replication of the regions between studies. In brief, Smith and colleagues (2006) implicated the frontal, parietal, and temporal lobes, along with the striatum. Pliszka and colleagues (2006) implicated the anterior cingulate cortex and the left ventrolateral prefrontal cortex. Tamm and colleagues (2006) implicated the parietal lobes, the right precuneus, and the thalamus. One could almost ask: What area of the brain is not implicated? |  |  |

Continued

The accompanying editorial by Casey and Durston (2006) acknowledges these disparate findings, yet instead of looking at them as problematic for the ADHD neuroimaging field, Casey and Durston attempt to place the disparate findings within a theoretical construct that cognitive deficits in ADHD are due to a deficit in inhibitory control. They state: 'Identification of core processes involved in a disorder can move a field from a disparate set of data-driven findings to a more theoretically coherent collection of studies' (p. 957). Does Casey and Durston's model provide a solid base for ADHD researchers to move forward, or is their explanation of these 'disparate findings' an attempt at salvaging a lack of reproducibility within the ADHD neuroimaging field? The model as proposed by Casey and Durston is that, 'basic learning systems are important in signalling top-down systems to adjust behaviour when predicted outcomes are violated.' This appears to be little more than a very general statement about learning. As a general statement it is hard to argue with it, because it is so broad and all-encompassing that it makes room for almost every conceivable finding. But it does little to explain how upwards of 10–15% of the population has a disease. One test for whether a theory is too broad, is to ask: What empirical findings would negate the theory? Casey and Durston have not proposed any findings that would negate their theory, and, indeed, it is hard to imagine any that would negate it. For instance, in Figure 16

| No | Type | Stakeholder | Section | Comments | Reference suggested & reason for inclusion/exclusion | Actions |
|----|------|-------------|---------|----------|------------------------------------------------------|---------|
| | | | | of their article, Casey and Durston hypothesise the involvement of the prefrontal cortex, the basal ganglia, the parietal cortex, and the cerebellum in ADHD. Yet none of the three accompanying studies even suggested that the cerebellum was involved. Bringing the cerebellum into the picture without elaboration is also problematic because as Furman notes: 'of the five studies that examined total cerebellar volume, four are listed as showing an association of ADHD with decreased volume, while three do not.' And missing from Casey and Durston's schematic is the thalamus, which one study did implicate. Moreover, two of the studies were contradictory: Pliszka and colleagues found greater activity in ADHD subjects than controls in the inferior prefrontal cortex (p. 1059), while Smith and colleagues found less activity (underactivation) in the mesial and front-parietal-temporal brain regions during the go/no go and switch tasks for the ADHD children. Yet, interestingly, while the imaging data for the ADHD children differed in these two studies, there was no difference in performance on the specified tasks between the ADHD children and controls. None of these issues are raised by Casey and Durston, and we are unsure how they could be fitted into the proposed model. | | |

Perhaps the most significant aspect of putting forth such a highly theoretical model of ADHD is that Casey and Durston are implicitly acknowledging that the more practical aspect of developing an imaging scan as a diagnostic tool is becoming more and more unlikely.

A recent study by Volkow and colleagues (2007) utilised PET and compared dopamine transporter levels in 20 never medicated adults to 25 controls, and found that dopamine transporter levels were not positively correlated with the disease. In the NICE document, to your credit, you have few positive statements about this research, but on the other hand you do not come right out and acknowledge this. For instance, Volkow, in much more direct terms than NICE, has commented: 'it should be noted that the imaging studies are still not definitive because of the discrepancies in the findings.'

The necessary and definitive test to confirm the suggestion that ADHD children have a neuroanatomic pathology consists of using an appropriate brain scan to detect a difference between a 'typical' unmedicated ADHD child as found in the classroom, and a 'normal' child. There is virtual unanimity that this cannot be accomplished at present. Experiments with highly selective patient and control groups are, at best, only preliminary studies, and the findings of these studies must be called into question. Ruling out the effects of psychotropic medication is merely one of the tasks confronting

| No | Type | Stakeholder | Section | Comments | Reference suggested & reason for inclusion/exclusion | Actions |
|---|---|---|---|---|---|---|
| | | | | researchers conducting neuroimaging research with ADHD patients. Even if the field accomplishes this task, however, several other important tasks remain. One of these will involve trying to make sense of findings of brain abnormalities or differences among some individuals diagnosed with ADHD. In October 2005, for example, the *New York Times* published an article by Benedict Carey entitled 'Can brain scans see depression?' It contained interviews with prominent psychiatrists and child psychiatrists, many of whom have authored ADHD imaging papers. The *Times* article was notable for both its candour and frank assessment of the psychiatric neuroimaging field: 'Yet, for a variety of reasons, the hopes and claims for brain imaging in psychiatry have far outpaced the science, experts say.' And in the words of Paul Wolpe, a professor of psychiatry and sociology: 'The thing for people to understand is that right now the only thing imaging can tell you is whether you have a brain tumor.' A recent imaging study found a difference between the brains of conservatives and liberals. Does this difference equate to a disease? | | |
| 34 | CC | David Coghill | 1.4.6 evidence | I think this section would read better if it were reordered to deal with causal factors, that is genetic, environmental and then mediating factors. In addition | References suggested: Sonuga-Barke | Comment taken into consideration, see Section 5.8. |

| No. | Type | Name | Score | Comment | References | Response |
|---|---|---|---|---|---|---|
|  |  |  |  | to the mediating factors already discussed (functional imaging, neuropsychology) structural imaging and neurophysiology should be added). The neuropsychology section stresses executive functions too strongly (although these are the most well studied other functions like delay aversion [Sonuga-Barke], timing [Tannock & Smith], non-executive memory [Rhodes & Coghill] and as noted variability also contribute – and may actually prove to be more important than executive functions). On the other hand the statement, 'Recently it has emerged that the strongest and most consistent association with ADHD is for intra-individual variability (Klein et al., 2006)' is way too strong as it relies on only one study. A similar argument could be made for a range of different neuropsychological functions based on other comparative studies. | Asked reviewer for full reference; no response. Tannock & Smith Asked reviewer for full reference, no response. Rhodes & Coghill Asked reviewer for full reference; no response. | Comment addressed, see Section 5.9 (third paragraph). |
| 36 | CC | David Coghill | 1.5 | Whilst there are not many child studies where healthy kids or kids with other disorders have been given methylphenidate or dexamfetamine there are many such adult studies. My understanding is that these support the notion that these stimulants in these doses work the same in healthy people as they do in those with problems. | No references suggested. |  |
| 58 | PR | Stephen Faraone | 1.5 | You state: 'When considering the Feighner criteria for validity of a psychiatric disorder, the question of whether there are specific responses to clinical, educational and other interventions for ADHD was excluded, since the data to answer this question was | No references suggested. | Comment addressed, see Section 5.8. |

Continued

| No | Type | Stakeholder | Section | Comments | Reference suggested & reason for inclusion/exclusion | Actions |
|---|---|---|---|---|---|---|
| | | | | very limited.' I don't have the Feighner criteria in front of me but I thought that the idea was that the disorder showed a 'characteristic' response to treatment rather than a 'specific' response. For example, the fact the SSRIs treat depression, OCD and other anxiety disorders does not challenge the validity of any of these disorders. | | |
| 84 | PR | Jonathan Leo | 1.5 | Limitations. When discussing the effect of stimulants on people not diagnosed with ADHD, regarding the Rapoport study, you state, 'there were limited published data on the effects of stimulants in people who do not have ADHD.'<br><br>This is an incredible statement as it seems to be saying that we do not know the effect of stimulants on normal people. Underlying any discussion of ADHD (except for possibly the NICE document) and what every neuroscience researcher is aware of, is the understanding that the most straightforward experiment in all of neuroscience is the one seeking to determine if stimulant medication works, at least if one defines 'works' as a short-term improvement in attention span. Whether the subjects are male or female, whether they are pre-schoolers or geriatrics, whether they are diagnosed with ADHD or not, and whether the medication is provided by a doctor or a friend, it has been known for 75 years that stimulants | No references suggested. | Comment addressed, see Section 5.9. |

Continued

improve anyone's and everyone's ability to pay attention.

The GDG sidesteps the issue of the fact that the stimulants such as methylphenidate (Ritalin) have a universal effect by stating that they are going to discuss the treatment of ADHD in a subsequent document. (However, even this is problematic because the document brings up the Rapoport study at one point.) Talking about treatment with stimulants in a future document is fine, but while it might be convenient this does not justify, in the current document, ignoring the universal effect of the stimulants on the CNS – as this does relate to the disease concept. Unfortunately much of the press still falls back on the so-called 'paradoxical effect' that sees stimulants only effecting ADHD children. Rapoport's study shows this is false. Coffee drinkers also know this is false. Apparently one of the few organisations to not acknowledge this fact is the GDG.

Also regarding the Rapoport study, you state, 'The very small numbers used in this study and lack of further similar studies means that considerable caution must be taken in drawing firm conclusions.' Again, your double standard is evident. The NICE review suggests 'considerable caution' when drawing conclusions about a study looking at the effect of amphetamines on the normal brain. Yet, just one page before in the review, there seems to be no hesitation or 'caution' in your interpretation of the genetic studies, which have not discovered any ADHD genes, or

**PART 3:** *(Continued)*

| No | Type | Stakeholder | Section | Comments | Reference suggested & reason for inclusion/exclusion | Actions |
|---|---|---|---|---|---|---|
| | | | | the imaging studies, which are unable to distinguish ADHD children from controls. | | |
| 13 | PR | Margaret Alsop | 1.6 | It is felt that the evidence submitted by parents, carers and others caring for an individual diagnosed as having ADHD is clear evidence on the validity of ADHD. There seems to be clear indication that the evidence submitted by professionals and those within the GDG echoes that of parents, carers and individuals themselves. | No references suggested. | Comment taken into consideration. |
| 37 | CC | David Coghill | 1.6 | The comment that, 'In adults the profile of symptoms may alter with a relative persistence of inattentive symptoms compared to hyperactive-impulsive symptoms' does not really match up with the evidence described in Section 1.4.5 where it is suggested that evidence for this is weak and that relative to controls levels of overactivity stay high. Here would be a good place to dispel this notion of a true reduction in overactivity problems as one of the ADHD myths. | No references suggested. | Comment taken into consideration. |
| 38 | CC | David Coghill | 1.6 | 'There was no evidence of a need to apply a different concept of ADHD to children and adults. However age-related changes in the presentation are recognised.' Could be expanded to add: 'There was no evidence of a need to apply a different concept of ADHD to children and adults. However age-related changes in the presentation are recognised. These | No references suggested. | Comment addressed, see Section 5.12. |

| 83 | PR | Jonathan Leo | 1.6 | changes are not yet reflected within the various diagnostic criteria.'.<br><br>Position Statement on the Validity of ADHD. 'There is evidence of both genetic and environmental influences in the aetiology of ADHD....Contemporary research suggests that environmental risks are likely to interact with genetic factors....' Why is that whenever environmental influences are brought up that you feel the need to drop genetics into the discussion? When you say 'contemporary research suggests that environmental risks are likely to interact with genetic factors' what recent research are you referring to? You are making it sound like the ADHD genetic researchers have recently uncovered this startling fact. However, the fact that genes interact with the environment has been known for years.<br><br>According to Robert Sapolsky, 'Genes influence behaviour, the environment influences behaviour, and genes and environment interact – this view is one of the great scientific clichés of the 20th century.'<br><br>Commenting on the usefulness of the 'vulnerability – stress theory of mental disorders' that any potential harmful environmental influences only operate on those with faulty genes, Mary Boyle points out that the theory is an important mechanism for managing the potential threat posed to biological psychiatrists whenever non-biological conditions are implicated in the aetiology of psychological stress. The usefulness of the hypothesis lies partly in its | No references suggested. | Comment taken into consideration. |

*Continued*

**PART 3:** (*Continued*)

| No | Type | Stakeholder | Section | Comments | Reference suggested & reason for inclusion/exclusion | Actions |
|----|------|-------------|---------|----------|------------------------------------------------------|---------|
| | | | | lack of specificity – since the nature of the claimed vulnerability has never been discovered, anything can count as an instance of it. Its usefulness also lies in its seeming reasonableness (who could deny that biological and psychological or social factors interact?) and its inclusiveness (it encompasses both the biological and social – surely better than focusing on only one?) while at the same time it firmly maintains the primacy of biology, not least through word order, and potentially de-emphasises the environment by making it look as if the 'stress' part of the vulnerability – stress model consists of ordinary stresses which most of us would cope with, but which overwhelm only 'vulnerable' people. We are thus excused from examining too closely either the events themselves or their meaning to the 'vulnerable' person (Boyle, 2002).<br><br>Your document seems to be the perfect example of what Boyle is referring to. You maintain the primacy of biology with your wording, but as Boyle points out, the driving force behind your wording is not 'contemporary research' that has discovered an ADHD gene, but is the contrast between the genetic studies, that have failed to find a specific ADHD gene or even a gene of modest effect, and studies implicating environmental factors. If you had | | |

*Continued*

| 88 | PR | Jonathan Leo | 1.6 | discovered a gene, then you would not be talking about the vulnerability-stress hypothesis. Again, take the example of foster care homes where an inordinate number of children are diagnosed with ADHD (and other conditions). Clearly this data points to environmental influences on ADHD, no matter what genes a child is born with.<br><br>As the data from Nicky Hart shows, there appears to be a strong role for socioeconomic strata. If we follow your logic, then the increased prevalence of children with smaller brains and less electrical activity (according to the current concept of ADHD) in the lower socioeconomic strata must be qualified with the statement that their smaller brains are due to faulty genes being influenced by the environment. | |
| | | | | Position Statement on Validity of ADHD. 'ADHD is distinguished from the normal range partly by the number and severity of symptoms and partly by the association with significant levels of impairment.'<br><br>Your statement points out why the diagnosis varies so much from one country to another, from one doctor's practice to another, from one school to another, and from one household to another. Take the 2004 guidelines on the diagnosis of ADHD from the American Academy of Pediatricians. Take item 2 on their questionnaire as an example:<br><br>2) Six (or more) of the following symptoms of hyperactivity-impulsivity have persisted for at least | No references suggested. |
| | | | | | Comment taken into consideration. |

**PART 3:** (*Continued*)

| No | Type | Stakeholder | Section | Comments | Reference suggested & reason for inclusion/exclusion | Actions |
|----|------|-------------|---------|----------|------------------------------------------------------|---------|
| | | | | 6 months to a degree that is maladaptive and inconsistent with developmental level: *Hyperactivity* a) Often fidgets with hands or feet or squirms in seat b) Often leaves seat in classroom or in other situations in which remaining seated is expected c) Often runs about or climbs excessively in situations in which it is inappropriate (in adolescents or adults, may be limited to subjective feelings of restlessness) d) Often had difficulty playing or engaging in leisure activities quietly e) Is often 'on the go' or often acts as if 'driven by a motor' f) Often talks excessively Note that every item on the list uses the term 'often', a very unscientific term. How does one quantify 'often'. Since 'often' is in the eye of the beholder and can vary from one doctor's office to the next it is easy to see how this document has little teeth to it. Apparently as long as one adult decides that the child 'often' fidgets, then the child can be labelled and medicated. It is easy to see how a parent who does not get a diagnosis from one doctor can simply go to another doctor with different ideas about what | | |

| | | | | | | |
|---|---|---|---|---|---|---|
| 39 | CC | David Coghill | 1.7.1 | 'often' means. As an example of how the general public sees through a document like this take this example provided by the late Kevin McCready (2002): 'In an episode of *The Sopranos*, the popular and critically acclaimed HBO series about a New Jersey mobster and his family, the primary character, Tony Soprano, is called into a meeting with school officials, including the school psychologist. Tony is told that his son has been determined to "have" ADHD. He asks how this has been determined and is told there is a set of criteria, which the psychologist then begins to itemise. The third criterion on the list is "tends to fidget." The poorly educated, psychologically unsophisticated, working class gangster looks at directly at the psychologist and asks simply in his earthy "Jersey" accent: "What constitutes a fidget?"' There may be little to admire about a man who makes his living illegally, but at least he "gets it."'. It is easy to see how guidelines that use the word 'often' mean very little. Is NICE going to develop more stringent guidelines? | No references suggested. | Comment addressed, see Section 5.12. |
| 59 | PR | Stephen Faraone | 1.7.1 | The term 'medical treatment' should be replaced by 'pharmacological treatment' or 'drug treatment'. | No references suggested. | Comment addressed, see Section 5.13.1. |
| | | | | I don't understand the following sentence: 'The group concluded that treatment response should take into account the severity of the disorder in terms of clinical and functional impairments and evidence should be looked for on the impact of severity of the disorder on treatment response.' | | |

*Continued*

**PART 3:** (*Continued*)

| No | Type | Stakeholder | Section | Comments | Reference suggested & reason for inclusion/exclusion | Actions |
|---|---|---|---|---|---|---|
| 69 | PR | Anita Thapar | 1.7.1 | 'The argument against genetic influences is not strong unless one questions the conventional interpretation of twin data' and continuing paragraph. Contribution of genetic influences doesn't rest purely on twin studies of ADHD. There have been five adoption studies all showing familial clustering due to genetic influences (refer to any review on ADHD genetics).<br><br>Thapar, A., Langley, K., Owen, M. J., *et al.* (2007) Advances in genetic findings on attention deficit hyperactivity disorder. *Psychological Medicine, 17*, 1–12.<br><br>Khan, S. A. & Faraone, S. V. (2006) The genetics of ADHD: a literature review of 2005. *Current Psychiatry Reports, 8*, 393–397. Review. | References suggested: Thapar, A., Langley, K., Owen, M. J., *et al.* (2007) Advances in genetic findings on attention deficit hyperactivity disorder. *Psychological Medicine, 17*, 1–12. Paper excluded: Review (no systematic search).<br><br>Khan, S. A. & Faraone, S. V. (2006) The genetics of ADHD: a literature review of 2005. *Current Psychiatry Reports, 8*, 393–397. Paper excluded: Review (no systematic search). | Comment addressed, see Section 5.8 and throughout the chapter. |

| 85 | Jonathan Leo | PR | 1.7.1 | 'The level and types of behaviour that define the normal range remain a contentious issue.' The current GDG believes that children with ADHD have an organic brain deficiency, resulting from a genetic defect that in the future, once the technology is available, will be detected by a brain scan. However nowhere in the document has NICE answered the controversial question: How many children have this defect? The obvious problem being that as the percentage of children taking Ritalin escalates, the harder it is to make the case that they have a disease. If, as in some school districts, upwards of 17% of the boys are prescribed Ritalin, this would suggest that the boundaries for normalcy have become narrower. As often happens after statistics documenting the increasing use of stimulants for younger and younger children make the headlines, many of the opinion leaders in the psychiatry community state that there is a problem with 'over-prescribing' or 'misdiagnosis', yet none of | References of individual studies were hand searched and those meeting the quality assessment criteria were included [Sprich et al., 2000]. References suggested: Johnson (2006) Study: ADHD drugs send thousands to ERs. Paper excluded: not peer reviewed. Nakamura (2002) Attention deficit/ hyperactivity disorders: are children being overmedicated? NIMH. Paper excluded: not peer reviewed; opinion paper. | Comments taken into consideration. |

*Continued*

**PART 3:** (*Continued*)

| No | Type | Stakeholder | Section | Comments | Reference suggested & reason for inclusion/exclusion | Actions |
|---|---|---|---|---|---|---|
| | | | | these leaders, or any of the major psychiatric organisations, has issued guidelines on how to identify this large group of 'misdiagnosed' children, nor have they clarified what they consider to be improper uses of prescribed stimulant medication (Johnson, 2006; Nakamura, 2002). No matter where NICE draws the line between normal and ADHD, whether it classifies 2%, 5% or 7% as having the disease, there will, by definition, be children who are inappropriately taking stimulant medication. Based on what criteria will NICE decide who these misdiagnosed children are? For instance, if according to NICE 7% of British children have ADHD then what if 10% are taking medication? How will doctors identify the 3% of misdiagnosed children?<br><br>The dilemma for medical professionals who want to go beyond simply talking about misdiagnosed children and to actually identifying these children is that, without an objective biological marker demarcating the line between the 'correctly' and 'incorrectly' diagnosed, the sole criterion for determining the appropriateness of stimulant treatment comes down to: Are the adults in the child's life satisfied with the medication's effect? Presumably there are not many parents unhappy with the medication's effects, who still continue to medicate their children. | Case study & editor comments, *Pediatrics* (1999) Asked reviewer for full reference; no response. | |

598

Continued

None of the medical professionals who talk about misdiagnosis has ever elaborated on how they plan to tell all these parents of misdiagnosed children that they should not be medicating their children, even though the medication is doing exactly what the medical community says it should be doing.

As an example of the forces at work in the diagnosis of an individual child with ADHD, take a case study in the journal *Pediatrics*. In 1999, the editors elicited commentaries from several prominent physicians about the case of a teenage boy who had been taking Ritalin for several years. The editors saw the boy's scenario as an interesting case, worthy of commentary from a group of prominent child psychiatrists. But in an ironic twist of fate, they have unintentionally provided a much more interesting case study. From a sociological point of view the subject of the case was not the boy, but, instead, was the doctors and the editors. The case provides an excellent example of: (1) how a major determination in the diagnosis of ADHD is adult satisfaction, (2) how the medical community fully supports the use of stimulant medication as a performance enhancing drug, (3) how the same mindset that approves of using one psychotropic drug easily leads to the use of multiple medications and (4) how the main stream medical journals have given little attention to the ethical implications of controlling and altering children to meet the demands of our contemporary educational/cultural system.

PART 3: (*Continued*)

| No | Type | Stakeholder | Section | Comments | Reference suggested & reason for inclusion/exclusion | Actions |
|----|------|-------------|---------|----------|---------------------------------------------------|---------|
| | | | | 'The 15-year-old boy announced to his parents and his pediatrician that he wanted to stop taking his medication: "I don't need it. . .I'm fine. . .I don't see why I should take it." He purposefully did not take the medication for a few weeks and he said he could not tell the difference. . . . However, his parents observed that his test results, when off the medication, were below his standard scores. . . . They also noted that he was more distractible and less attentive when doing his homework during that time' (Cohen & Leo, 2002).<br><br>As stated by the physicians, the most important variable in determining whether this boy should keep taking his medication was the parental satisfaction with the medication, and the subsequent commentaries all focused on how to convince the boy to continue taking his medication. The boy's wishes were not something to be listened to, but rather something to be managed, whether through dialogue or with another medication. As an example of polypharmaceuticals for children one of the commentators even suggested that the boy's reluctance to keep taking his Ritalin suggested this was a sign that he needed another medication. Thus the boy, who wants go off his one medication, would instead get two medications. None of the | | |

*Continued*

| No. | | Name | Section | Comment | | |
|---|---|---|---|---|---|---|
| 86 | PR | Jonathan Leo | 1.7.1 | commentators in the *Pediatrics* article contemplated that the boy's wishes might be legitimate, but more importantly, as a sign of how one-sided the issue has become in the medical community, *the editors* did not give space to a single commentator who questioned the ethics of giving a medication to improve grades.<br><br>As an example of who the experts in America are diagnosing with ADHD take this example from the Department of Psychiatry at New York University: 'Sarah chooses to sit in the back of the classroom and much of the time she's doodling in her notebook or staring out of the window. She seldom completes assignments and often forgets to bring the right book to class. Her desk is a mess and she generally can't find what she is looking for. Then she gets weepy and says that nobody understands her.' This 14-year-old girl is crying out 'please understand me'. The New York University experts' response is to label her with ADHD. Medication will surely follow. Examples like this and the others I have cited, which come from those who strongly believe that ADHD is biological, are just more examples of how little science is involved in the ADHD diagnosis.<br><br>'The GDG wish to stress that the role of important genetic influences does not exclude an important role for environmental influences since individual differences in genetic risk factors are likely to alter the | References suggested: Andreasen (1984) *The Broken Brain.* | Comments taken into consideration. |

**PART 3:** (*Continued*)

| No | Type | Stakeholder | Section | Comments | Reference suggested & reason for inclusion/exclusion | Actions |
|----|------|-------------|---------|----------|------------------------------------------------------|---------|
| | | | | sensitivity of an individual to environmental risks.' This is confusing because earlier in the document the only environmental influences that you mentioned were prenatal exposure to drugs such as nicotine. What environmental influences are you referring to here? 'Furthermore, the extent to which there are genetic influences has no direct bearing on the choice of treatment approaches since both medical and psychosocial interventions could be important in improving treatment outcomes.' Let's be honest here, the idea that ADHD is due to genetics is one of the most common reasons cited by the pharmaceutical companies and the psychiatric profession as evidence that ADHD is a biological disease, like diabetes. And diseases are treated with medications. Your statement is even going against much of modern day psychiatry. According to Nancy Andreasen, in *The Broken Brain*, the biological model of mental illness can be summed up as follows: '(1) The major psychiatric illnesses are diseases, (2) These diseases are caused principally by biological factors and most of these reside in the brain,…and (4) The treatment of these diseases emphasises the use of somatic therapies.' As another example of this type of thinking, take the recent comments by Stephen Faraone in *Science*. In a discussion of 'ADHD genes' he stated: 'My hope is | Paper excluded: book (not peer-reviewed).<br><br>Faraone, *Science.* Asked reviewer for full reference; no response.<br><br>Brown (2003). New attention to ADHD genes. *Science.*<br><br>Paper excluded: not peer reviewed. Hartmann (1996). Asked reviewer for full reference; no response. | |

602

that once we've discovered those genes, we'll be able to do a prospective study of kids at high versus low genetic risk. That's when you'll see environmental factors at work.' But certainly one can still see environmental factors at work in children without knowing their genotype. Yet, even more confusing is Faraone's next comment. According to the reporter, 'Eventually, he [Faraone] adds, environmental changes could play an important role in treating some ADHD patients' (Brown, 2003, p. 160). Eventually? Why do we need to wait? Why not implement the changes right now? Changing the environment is exactly what many people opposed to stimulants have been saying for years. Faraone's take on the aetiology of ADHD is strikingly similar to Thom Hartmann's view. Both believe that ADHD is a biological, hereditary trait (Hartmann, 1996). Where they differ is that Faraone, and other biological psychiatrists, see these children as dysfunctional, with a genetic defect in need of medication. The other group sees the children as having different genes, at one end of the spectrum, and that what is needed is a different environment (Hartmann, 1996). One purpose of the genetic studies, which the pharmaceutical companies, and the psychiatry profession, have propagated, is to imply that, because it's genetic that drugs are needed. For instance, Faraone states: 'Many parents are reluctant for their children to take psychotropic medication and others find it difficult to maintain the prescribed regimes. These problems are

| No | Type | Stakeholder | Section | Comments | Reference suggested & reason for inclusion/exclusion | Actions |
|----|------|-------------|---------|----------|---------------------------------------------------|---------|
| | | | | mitigated by discussing the genetic etiology of ADHD' (Faraone, 1996, p. 598). | | |
| | | | | If you are going to acknowledge that knowing about genetics has nothing to do with treatment than you should be ready to answer the general public and politicians when they ask: Then why are you doing this research? If knowing about genetics has no benefit to the patient, then one possibility for this line of research is to justify current practices. If ADHD does not have a strong genetic influence then giving a medication would be seen as very problematic, and would call into question the entire practice of medicating children with stimulants. If I were you I would delete this line about genetics and treatment. | | |
| 60 | PR | Stephen Faraone | 1.8 | You state, 'The quality of the evidence included in this review was variable and lacked any "gold standard" because no diagnostic tests for ADHD have been developed or tested.' I suggest you be clear what you mean by 'gold standard.' I think you mean a laboratory test of some sort. Although I'm probably in the minority, I think that the DSM-IV diagnosis of ADHD as made by a competent health professional is a pretty good gold standard inasmuch as it is reproducible with high reliability and has clinical implications. The inter-rater reliability of the ADHD diagnosis is not much worse than, for example, many | No reference suggested. | Comment addressed, see Section 5.3. |

| | | | | | | | |
|---|---|---|---|---|---|---|---|
| | PR | 89 | Jonathan Leo | 1.8 | accepted 'gold standard' diagnoses made by radiologists. | No references suggested. | Comment addressed, see Section 5.14. |
| | | | | | Evidence Summary. In your summary, after 22 pages of discussion about the evidence, you do not cite any direct evidence that ADHD results from a biological, hereditary defect. However, you do not come right out and acknowledge this lack of evidence. The 1998 National Institutes of Health conference was much more direct when it said, 'there are no data to indicate that ADHD is due to a brain malfunction.' | | |
| | PR | 87 | Jonathan Leo | 1.9 | 'ADHD should be considered in all age groups (children adolescents, and adults), with symptom criteria adjusted for age appropriate changes in behaviour.' And also in 1. 6, 'There was no evidence of a need to apply a different concept of ADHD to children and adults.' There is an important point to be mentioned here that the NICE document ignores. Allowing adults, who can make their own decisions, to take stimulants is one matter, however it is an entirely separate matter when it comes to children. The ethical questions surrounding the use of Ritalin are becoming more significant as once-medicated children are now reaching adulthood. According to a recent survey in the *LA Times*, a significant number of these adults are deciding to discontinue their medication (Healy, 2006b). The *LA Times* article quotes a 27-year-old girl who reflects back on the years she was medicated, 'It was kind of weirdly | Healy (2006) The Ritalin kids grow up: many of the ADD generation say no to meds. *LA Times*. Paper excluded: not peer reviewed; relevant to treatment not validity. | Comment taken into consideration. |

*Continued*

605

**PART 3:** *(Continued)*

| No | Type | Stakeholder | Section | Comments | Reference suggested & reason for inclusion/exclusion | Actions |
|---|---|---|---|---|---|---|
| | | | | amazing.... You get excited about monotonous work, honestly. Like, translating Spanish becomes totally fun ...The thing is, it works. But why are we forcing people to be in that position that they should like something that they wouldn't ordinarily' (Healy, 2006). In just three short sentences this 27-year-old girl goes right to the heart of the ethical dilemma of stimulant medication: Is it right to medicate people so that they do well in school? How is it that a lay person can go right to the heart of the issue while a committee of physicians with years of training can produce a document that ignores this key point? Why are questions like this not raised by academicians in medical journals, or by the GDG? | | |
| 40 | CC | David Coghill | 1.9.1.1 | I felt that these were rather weakly described and a bit 'fluffy' for want of a better word. It is really saying you should use the diagnostic criteria, you should actually count the symptoms you should be clear about impairment and you should consider ADHD diagnosis in all ages. I think it just needs some re-wording to make it snappier.<br><br>Also it could benefit from starting off with a *very* clear and strong statement saying that the diagnostic categories of ADHD and hyperkinetic disorder are considered valid and should be used. This is a very important message to clinicians, the public, the government, the press, and so on. | No references suggested. | Comment addressed, see Sections 5.14 and 5.15. |

| | | | | | | |
|---|---|---|---|---|---|---|
| 48 | PR | David Cottrell | 1.9.1.1 | Will you be able to operationally define 'moderately clinically significant' impairment? | No references suggested. | Comment addressed, see Section 5.15.2 (C) 'How should impairment be judged?' |
| 1 | CC | Edmund Sonuga-Barke | General | This seems a very accurate and sensible document. | No references suggested. | Comment taken into consideration. |
| 2 | CC | Russell Schachar | General | I read the document with great interest and think that it is a solid contribution to the ongoing debate about ADHD/HKD. Given that the document is based on a review of reviews, it is not altogether easy to judge how the summary statements were reached, but they look appropriate. | No references suggested. | Comment taken into consideration. |
| 3 | CC | Geoff Kewley | General | I felt the review was a reasonable summary of discussion and have nothing else to add. | No references suggested. | Comment taken into consideration. |
| 4 | PR | Margaret Alsop | General | We are concerned with processes preceding and following diagnosis rather than diagnosis. The concept of ADHD is multi-faceted, therefore no individual discipline is likely to be competent to identify, assess and intervene alone. As such diagnosis becomes a mechanical feature in a holistic process involving a range of professionals. A child psychiatrist or paediatrician should normally make the formal diagnosis. However, a diagnosis should only be considered valid if it is made on the basis of evidence that a particular agency is pertinent; that agency should be involved as appropriate. Medical practitioners also have a significant role to play in | No references suggested. | Comment addressed, see Section 5.15. |

*Continued*

**PART 3:** (*Continued*)

| No | Type | Stakeholder | Section | Comments | Reference suggested & reason for inclusion/exclusion | Actions |
|----|------|-------------|---------|----------|------------------------------------------------------|---------|
| | | | | diagnosis and assessment in order to rule out physical factors which may lead to the symptoms similar to those of ADHD. | | |
| 5 | PR | Margaret Alsop | General | If these guidelines are intended to be accessible to professionals and parents from a range of disciplines who might first identify, or have concerns about, problems that may or may not result in an ADHD diagnosis, their first efforts are likely to be of a broadly psychosocial nature (that is, behavioural/cognitive and educational interventions). Currently different professionals use different terminology to describe the phenomenon of ADHD (for example, hyperkinetic disorder, behavioural problems). The use of different terms is not helpful to professionals, children, young people, adults or their families: therefore an attempt should be made in this document to be consistent in the use of terms that have been selected for their clarity and acceptability to a wide range of professionals. There are significant differences, sometimes of an ideological nature between different professional groups (Cooper, 1997; Hughes, 1999; Maras & Redmayne, 1997). These differences can be exaggerated through training and practice and are often reflected in different professional perceptions and | References suggested: Cooper (1997). Asked reviewer for full reference; no response. Hughes (1999). Asked reviewer for full reference; no response. Maras & Redmayne (1997). Asked reviewer for full reference; no response. | Comment taken into consideration. |

| | | | | | | |
|---|---|---|---|---|---|---|
| | | | | views of ADHD. Differences can sometimes result in confusion, misunderstandings and conflict and may have an adverse influence on the effectiveness of multi-disciplinary/agency working. However, there is also much common ground among professionals, especially in terms of sought after outcomes of intervention. ADHD by its very nature demands a multi-agency response and provides an opportunity for medical, educational, psychological, social care and other professionals to work together. | | |
| 6 | PR | Margaret Alsop | General | We note that there is no reference made in relation to transition between CAMHS into the adult CMHT. There is clear evidence to indicate that a high percentage of those diagnosed with ADHD in childhood will not have any appropriate transitional plan in place, therefore it is important that an appropriate multi-agency response for transitional arrangements are identified.<br>(Social Exclusion Unit – Transitions Young Adults with Complex Needs) | No references suggested. | Comment addressed, see NICE guideline 'Transition to adult services'. |
| 12 | PR | Margaret Alsop | General | The following statistics provides an overview of the numbers of children facing particular risk factors out of a total population of children in England of 12 million:<br>A. In 2000, 2.7 million children lived in low income families.<br>B. Up to 75,000 children may be missing from school rolls. | No references suggested. | Comment taken into consideration. |

*Continued*

**PART 3:** (*Continued*)

| No | Type | Stakeholder | Section | Comments | Reference suggested & reason for inclusion/exclusion | Actions |
|----|------|-------------|---------|----------|------------------------------------------------------|---------|
| | | | | C. Around ten per cent of children aged 5 to 15 have a mental disorder of sufficient severity to cause them distress or to have considerable effect on the way they live and 20% of children suffer from mental health problems. <br> D. One in nine children run away from home for at least a night. <br> E. One in ten families in England and Wales report incidences of domestic violence in a year. <br> F. In 2000 there were 91,400 conceptions to girls aged under 20. <br> G. At the end of September 2001 there were approximately 5,400 households with children in bed and breakfast accommodation. <br> H. There are approximately 300,000 children with disabilities in England; 110,000 of these are severely disabled. <br> I. 26,800 children and young people are on the child protection register. <br> J. 58,900 children and young people are in public care. <br> K. 11,000 young people aged 15–20 are in young offenders institutions. <br> Our concerns are, how many of these include those with ADHD or possible ADHD? <br> *Figures released by the Children and Young People's Unit on 6th September 2002, www.cypu.gov.uk* | | |

| | | | | |
|---|---|---|---|---|
| 14 | PR | Margaret Alsop | General | That the assessment, diagnosis and treatment for ADHD should be delivered throughout the lifespan, services delivery should be multi-agency, multi-model and incorporate professionals from many services such as: health, education, social care, behaviour support, parenting programmes, adult community mental health, community care, prison healthcare providers, housing, employment agencies and those within the criminal justice system. Our belief is that the term EBD (emotional and behavioural difficulties) should not be used in relation to service delivery for those already diagnosed as having ADHD. Within many services the term used for those with ADHD is described as having EBD, therefore access to a full multi-agency approach may not be forthcoming. We understand that this request may be out of the remit of the GDG and NICE but would still therefore like to request it for inclusion and consideration. | No references suggested. | Comment taken into consideration. |
| 15 | PR | Margaret Alsop | General | Not being qualified nor trained in medicine, I do not consider it appropriate for contributions from non-medically trained individuals to be included. I can only go on experiences as a parent-carer of a young adult (25 years old ) his having been un-medicated for the first 14 years of his life and as to how medications have now turned his life around and made him feel totally inclusive to society and not another statistic within our penal system or another fatality of drug abuse/overdose. | No references suggested. | Comment taken into consideration. |

*Continued*

611

**PART 3:** (*Continued*)

| No | Type | Stakeholder | Section | Comments | Reference suggested & reason for inclusion/exclusion | Actions |
|----|------|-------------|---------|----------|-------------------------------------------------------|---------|
| 16 | PR | Margaret Alsop | General | It is felt that the assessments for ADHD in children should be conducted through a 'core diagnostic' team, this way it is multi-agency, multi-model and will rule out/include any other underlying difficulties such as ASD, learning difficulties, dyslexia, and so on.<br><br>During my own experiences, those diagnosed with ADHD as children have received a dual diagnosis of ADHD and ASD in later adolescence or adulthood. | No references suggested. | Comment addressed, see Section 5.15. |
| 17 | CC | David Coghill | General | In general I very much agree with the way that the issues are addressed and the conclusions reached. Overall this is a well-structured document and reaches some clear conclusions. I think that the sample comment given above applies to this document and that, 'The guideline highlights throughout the document where there are gaps in the evidence to support clinical practice. Although these areas are in the main text of the document, it would be helpful if there could be an additional section at the end of each chapter with areas where further research would be helpful. This would support the research agenda and maximise resources.' | No references suggested. | Comment taken into consideration. |
| 18 | CC | David Coghill | General | Will the appendices detailing the literature be in tabular form showing sample size, and so on? As it would be very helpful to be able to see this information. | No references suggested. | Comment addressed, see Appendix 17.1 'Study characteristics – Diagnosis'. |

| | | | | | |
|---|---|---|---|---|---|
| 19 | CC | David Coghill | General | I have marked up minor comments on wording and so on in the document itself. | No references suggested. | Comments taken into consideration. |
| 41 | PR | David Cottrell | General | I found this to be a well written and coherent account of diagnostic validity issues. Given the potentially diverse readership of NICE guidelines and the complexity of the literature I thought the language clear and the research explained well.<br><br>The questions to be addressed and the methods used are set out clearly towards the end of Section 1.3 and in 1.3. The methods are appropriate for the questions asked. My comments are largely about the use of language and presentation. I have no substantive disagreement with the case that is presented. | No references suggested. | Comments taken into consideration. |
| 49 | PR | David Cottrell | General | 1.2. Third paragraph, line 8 – I think this should be 'particularly' but the whole sentence is clumsily worded and obscures meaning.<br>1.4.1. Second paragraph after subheading 'Evidence' – the final sentence is not grammatical and again obscures meaning.<br>1.4.3. First paragraph after subheading 'evidence', line 5 – presumably 'that on this' not 'this on this'.<br>1.5. Second paragraph, line 7 – 'who do not ADHD' does not make sense<br>1.7.1. First sentence is ungrammatical.<br>There are other minor typos in the document but those above have the potential to distort the meaning of the text. | No references suggested. | Comment addressed, see Section 5.3. |

*Continued*

| No | Type | Stakeholder | Section | Comments | Reference suggested & reason for inclusion/exclusion | Actions |
|----|------|-------------|---------|----------|------------------------------------------------------|---------|
| 61 | PR | Stephen Faraone | General | The following article should be of interest to you: Faraone, S. V. (2005) The scientific foundation for understanding attention-deficit/hyperactivity disorder as a valid psychiatric disorder. *European Child and Adolescent Psychiatry, 14*, 1–10. | References suggested: Faraone, S. V. (2005) The scientific foundation for understanding attention-deficit/ hyperactivity disorder as a valid psychiatric disorder. *European Child and Adolescent Psychiatry, 14*, 1–10. Paper excluded: opinion paper. | Comment taken into consideration. |
| 70 | CC | Sami Timimi | General | I wish to make the following points on the above document: The document states in its introduction that, 'The Guideline Development Group (GDG) acknowledged at the outset that the use of the diagnosis of ADHD has been the subject of considerable controversy and debate' and 'The relative lack of a validated reference standard (indicated by SIGN diagnostic study quality assessment, see Appendix A) means that the | No references suggested. | Comment addressed, see Sections 5.3 and 5.9. |

question of validity for the diagnosis of ADHD needs to draw on evidence from a *wide range of sources'* [my italics]. Despite this the subsequent discussion of the evidence included no references drawn from authors who are critical of the concept of ADHD, despite the group being provided with a number of scientific reviews from such authors. The references included repeatedly cited research by a small number of researchers and research groups (including from the chair of the group) known to be supporters of the concept of ADHD. This suggests that the document lacks balance and is ideologically biased toward literature that confirms the majority of GDG members' views.

Many members of the GDG have previously written papers or otherwise collaborated with the chair of this group. The fact that there is not one academic/ practitioner who is able to represent the other side of this debate is reflected in the one-sided document the GDG has produced. It is my opinion that the conflict of interest in this group is to an extent that is unacceptable given the importance of their task.

It isn't clear why the GDG decided to use the Washington University Diagnostic Criteria beyond the unexplained 'ensure that a transparent, structured approach was taken' nor is it evident whether any other systematic approach or framework was considered. However, even with these criteria, the interpretation of the GDG that the evidence they present is

*Continued*

| No | Type | Stakeholder | Section | Comments | Reference suggested & reason for inclusion/exclusion | Actions |
|----|------|-------------|---------|----------|------------------------------------------------------|---------|
| | | | | sufficient to support the validity of ADHD using these criteria is open to question. | | |
| 77 | CC | Sami Timimi | General | There is clear evidence in the document that the GDG has displayed unacceptable bias in its preferred paradigm for analysing the literature, in its selection of literature and in its interpretation of the literature they selected. The fact that most of the academic members of the GDG have previously published papers with the chair of the group and that the group does not include any members with a more critical stance, strengthens the impression that the levels of bias result from conflicts of interest that are seriously unethical. The conclusions are thus not valid and could lead to serious deficiencies in practice and provide poor protection for patients, possibly exposing many more children to significant harm. The document should not be accepted. The GDG should be dismantled, a new chair appointed and a new GDG convened with a more equitable balance of opinion reflected in its membership. | No references suggested. | Comment addressed, see Sections 5.3 and 5.9, as well as Chapter 3, Methods. |
| 79 | PR | Jonathan Leo | General | Take a trait – any trait, either physical or behavioural. Given normal biological variability, if the trait is measured and subsequently plotted on a graph there will be a spectrum. Some are tall and some are short, some have long legs and some have short legs, or | No references suggested. | Comment taken into consideration. |

Continued

some have a longer attention span than others.

Variability of a trait is not proof of a disease.

Take a drug's effect. There are certain drugs that have an effect on human traits. Alli, a new diet drug, will help people lose weight – no matter what their weight to begin with. There are also drugs that have an effect on an individual's behaviour, no matter what their behaviour to begin with. Take the stimulants, for example: response to a drug with a universal effect, like the stimulants, is not proof of a disease. (See the GDG comments page 17 Section 1.5 limitations.)

These are the two most common reasons cited as evidence for a biological basis of ADHD. The dilemma for NICE is to go beyond this. As it is stands now, NICE's conclusion that the ADHD diagnosis is valid is primarily based on the flawed premise that variability of a trait is proof of a disease. Even your own 'Evidence Summary', basically says it is a trait, which in your opinion should be called a disease, at one end of the spectrum. In the summary you do not (or cannot) cite a single scientific study or even an area of study confirming that ADHD is primarily a problem of biology.

If traits can be called diseases then where does this stop? A recent Op-Ed article in the New York Times addresses the problem of pathologising traits:

'It may seem baffling, even bizarre, that ordinary shyness could assume the dimension of a mental disease. But if a youngster is reserved, the odds are high that a psychiatrist will diagnose social anxiety

**PART 3:** (*Continued*)

| No | Type | Stakeholder | Section | Comments | Reference suggested & reason for inclusion/exclusion | Actions |
|---|---|---|---|---|---|---|
| | | | | disorder and recommend treatment. How much credence should we give the diagnosis? Shyness is so common among American children that 42 percent exhibit it. And, according to one major study, the trait increases with age. By the time they reach college, up to 51 percent of men and 43 percent of women describe themselves as shy or introverted. Among graduate students, half of men and 48 percent of women do. Psychiatrists say that at least one in eight of these people needs medical attention' (Lane, 23 September, 2007). | | |
| | | | | In the future will NICE have a committee deciding if 'Is shyness a valid diagnosis?' According to the logic of the current document that identifying a trait is somehow proof of a disease the answer would appear to be 'yes'. | | |
| 90 | PR | Jonathan Leo | General | Conclusion: The NICE document provides no new insight into the diagnosis of ADHD. It has systematically ignored one side of the debate and has simply summarised the views of those involved with the ongoing medication of children. The flaws are neither subtle nor minor, nor can they be rectified with editing. The entire approach of the panel is flawed. I am not privy to the make-up of the panel but it appears that the panel had no members with a broad societal view of the ADHD diagnosis – if it | No references suggested. | Comment taken into consideration. |

did, then they were ignored. In all your discussions you seem to have one standard for biology and one for the environment. Marginal imaging studies, that compared medicated ADHD children to controls, and genetic studies, which have not found an ADHD gene, are given credence, while you cannot even cite a study linking the environment to ADHD.

The other side of the debate, that variability of a trait, and the universal effect of stimulants, are not good evidence for justifying the belief that, upwards of 10 to 15% to of the world's children have an organic brain defect, is simply not presented. Likewise the ethics surrounding the diagnosis are ignored in the NICE document. If the NICE statement on ADHD is approved no one should be surprised when 5 years from now more British children are being prescribed stimulants. In no way should the current NICE document be considered a fair and all encompassing view of the ADHD phenomena. On the surface, it is a document couched in the language of science, but when one looks deeper at the scientific studies there is little evidence to support the disease concept of ADHD.

**Margaret Alsop**
Executive Director, Dorset ADHD Support Group

**Dr David Coghill**
Senior Lecturer in Child and Adolescent Psychiatry, Division of Pathology and Neuroscience (Psychiatry), University of Dundee

**Professor David Cottrell**
Professor of Child and Adolescent Psychiatry, Associate Professor of Psychology, University of Leeds

**Dr Stephen Faraone**
Professor of Psychiatry and of Neuroscience and Physiology, SUNY Upstate Medical University

**Dr Geoff Kewley**
Consultant Paediatrician/Physician, Director of Learning Assessment and Neurocare Centre, Horsham, West Sussex

**Dr Jonathan Leo**
Associate Professor of Anatomy, Western University of Health Sciences, California

**Dr Russell Schachar**
Department of Psychiatry, Neurosciences and Mental Health Research Institute, The Hospital for Sick Children, University of Toronto, Ontario, Canada

**Professor Edmund Sonuga-Barke**
Professor in Psychology, Convenor of the Developmental Brain Behaviour Unit, University of Southampton

**Professor Anita Thapar**
Professor, Department of Psychological Medicine, Cardiff University School of Medicine

**Dr Sami Timimi**
Consultant Child Psychiatrist, Lincolnshire Partnership NHS Trust

# 14.  REFERENCES

Abikoff, H., Hechtman, L., Klein, R. G., *et al.* (2004a) Symptomatic improvement in children with ADHD treated with long-term methylphenidate and multimodal psychosocial treatment. *Journal of the American Academy of Child and Adolescent Psychiatry, 43,* 802–811.

Abikoff, H., Hechtman, L., Klein, R. G., *et al.* (2004b) Social functioning in children with ADHD treated with long-term methylphenidate and multimodal psychosocial treatment. *Journal of the American Academy of Child and Adolescent Psychiatry*, *43*, 820–829.

Achenbach, T. M. & Rescorla, L. A. (2001) *Manual for the ASEBA School-age Forms and Profiles.* Burlington: University of Vermont, Research Center for Children, Youth, and Families.

Achenbach, T. M., Dumenci, L. & Rescorla, L. A. (2003) DSM-oriented and empirically based approaches to constructing scales from the same item pools. *Journal of Clinical Child and Adolescent Psychology, 32,* 328–340.

Adey, P., Hewitt, G., Hewitt, J., *et al.* (2004) *The Professional Development of Teachers: Practice and Theory.* London: Kluwer.

Adler, L., Dietrich, A., Reimherr, F. W., *et al.* (2006a) Safety and tolerability of once versus twice daily atomoxetine in adults with ADHD. *Annals of Clinical Psychiatry, 18,* 107–113.

Adler, L. A., Sutton, V. K., Moore, R. J., *et al.* (2006b) Quality of life assessment in adult patients with attention-deficit/hyperactivity disorder treated with atomoxetine. *Journal of Clinical Psychopharmacology, 26,* 648–652.

AGREE Collaboration (2003) Development and validation of an international appraisal instrument for assessing the quality of clinical practice guidelines: the AGREE project. *Quality and Safety in Health Care, 12,* 18–23.

Alderson, P., Sutcliffe, K. & Curtis, K. (2006) Children's consent to medical treatment. *Hastings Centre Report, 36,* 25–34.

Alderson, R. M., Rapport, M. D. & Kofler, M. J. (2007) Attention-deficit/hyperactivity disorder and behavioral inhibition: a meta-analytic review of the stop-signal paradigm. *Journal of Abnormal Child Psychology, 35,* 745–758.

Alexander, R. & Hargreaves, L. (2007) *Community Soundings: the Primary Review Regional Witness Sessions.* Cambridge: University of Cambridge Faculty of Education.

Allen, A. J., Kurlan, R. M., Gilbert, D. L., *et al.* (2005) Atomoxetine treatment in children and adolescents with ADHD and comorbid tic disorders. *Neurology, 65,* 1941–1949.

Altshuler, D. & Daly, M. (2007) Guilt beyond a reasonable doubt. *Nature Genetics, 39,* 813–815.

Amador-Campos, J. A., Forns-Santacana, M., Martorell-Balanzo, B., *et al.* (2005) Confirmatory factor analysis of parents' and teachers ratings of DSM-IV symptoms of attention deficit hyperactivity disorder in a Spanish sample. *Psychological Reports, 97,* 847–860.

Aman, M. G., Mitchell, E. A. & Turbott, S. H. (1987) The effects of essential fatty acid supplementation by Efamol in hyperactive children. *Journal of Abnormal Psychology, 15*, 75–90.

American Academy of Child and Adolescent Psychiatry (2007) Practice parameter for the assessment and treatment of children and adolescents with attention deficit/hyperactivity disorder. *Journal of the American Academy of Child and Adolescent Psychiatry, 46*, 894–921.

American Psychiatric Association (2000) *Diagnostic and Statistical Manual of Mental Disorders: Text Revision* (4th edn, text revision). Washington, DC: American Psychiatric Association.

Antrop, I., Roeyers, H., Van Oost, P., *et al.* (2000) Stimulation seeking and hyperactivity in children with ADHD. *The Journal of Child Psychology and Psychiatry, 41*, 225–232.

Antshel, K. M. & Remer, R. (2003) Social skills training in children with attention deficit hyperactivity disorder: a randomized-controlled clinical trial. *Journal of Clinical Child and Adolescent Psychology, 32*, 153–165.

Applegate, B., Lahey, B. B., Hart, E. L., *et al.* (1997) Validity of the age-of-onset criterion for ADHD: a report from the DSM-IV field trials. *Journal of the American Academy of Child and Adolescent Psychiatry, 36*, 1211–1221.

Armstrong, F. (2003) *Spaced Out: Policy, Difference and the Challenge of Inclusive Education.* London: Kluwer.

Arnold, L. E., Kleykamp, D., Votolato, N. A., *et al.* (1989) Gamma-linolenic acid for attention-deficit hyperactivity disorder: placebo-controlled comparison to D-amphetamine. *Biological Psychiatry, 25*, 222–228.

Arnold, L. E., Elliot, M., Sachs, L., *et al.* (2003) Effects of ethnicity on treatment attendance, stimulant response/dose, and 14-month outcome in ADHD. *Journal of Consulting and Clinical Psychology, 71*, 713–727.

Aubrey, C., Godfrey, R. & Manigan, S. (2007) *Overcoming Barriers to Learning: How do we include young children with moderate learning difficulty?* Paper presented at the 12th Biennial Conference for Research on Learning and Instruction, Budapest, August 2007.

August, G. J., Braswell, L. & Thuras, P. (1998) Diagnostic stability of ADHD in a community sample of school-aged children screened for disruptive behavior. *Journal of Abnormal Child Psychology, 26*, 345–356.

Avramidis, A., Bayliss, P. & Burden, R. (2000) A survey into mainstream teachers' attitudes towards the inclusion of children with special educational needs in the ordinary school in one local education authority. *Educational Psychology, 20*, 191–211.

Bagwell, C. L., Molina, B. S. G., Pelham, W. E., *et al.* (2001) Attention-deficit hyperactivity disorder and problems in peer relations: predictions from childhood to adolescence. *Journal of the American Academy of Child and Adolescent Psychiatry, 40*, 1285–1292.

Bailey, S. (2006) ADHD - what's in a name? Paper presented at the British Education Research Association Conference, Warwick, England, 6–9 September 2006.

Available at: http://www.leeds.ac.uk/educol/documents/157738.htm [accessed June 2008].

Bambinski, L. M., Hartsough, C. S. & Lambert, N. M. (1999) Childhood conduct problems, hyperactivity-impulsivity, and inattention as predictors of adult criminal activity. *The Journal of Child Psychology and Psychiatry, 40*, 347–355.

Barbaresi, W. J. & Olsen, R. D. (1998) An ADHD educational intervention for elementary schoolteachers: a pilot study. *Journal of Developmental and Behavioral Pediatrics, 19*, 94–100.

Barbaresi, W. J., Katusic, S. K., Colligan, R. C., *et al.* (2007) Long-term school outcomes for children with attention-deficit/hyperactivity disorder: a population-based perspective. *Journal of Developmental and Behavioral Pediatrics, 28*, 265–273.

Barkley, R. A. (1990) *Attention Deficit Disorder: A Handbook for Diagnosis and Treatment.* New York: Guilford Press.

Barkley, R. A. (1997) *ADHD and the Nature of Self-Control.* New York: Guilford.

Barkley, R. A. & Cox, D. (2007) A review of driving risks and impairments associated with attention-deficit/hyperactivity disorder and the effects of stimulant medication on driving performance. *Journal of Safety Research, 38*, 113–128.

Barkley, R. A. & Murphy, K. R. (1998) *Attention-Deficit Hyperactivity Disorder: a Clinical Workbook* (2nd edn). New York: Guilford Press.

Barkley, R. A., Fischer, M., Edelbrock, C. S., *et al.* (1990a) The adolescent outcome of hyperactive children diagnosed by research criteria: I. An 8 year old prospective follow up study. *Journal of the American Academy of Child and Adolescent Psychiatry, 29*, 546–557.

Barkley, R. A., McMurray, M. B., Edelbrock, C. S., *et al.* (1990b) Side effects of methylphenidate in children with attention deficit hyperactivity disorder: a systemic, placebo-controlled evaluation. *Pediatrics, 86*, 184–192.

Barkley, R. A., Shelton, T. L., Crosswait, C., *et al.* (2000) Multi-method psycho-educational intervention for preschool children with disruptive behavior: preliminary results at post-treatment. *The Journal of Child Psychology and Psychiatry, 41*, 319–332.

Barkley, R. A., Fischer, M., Smallish, L., *et al.* (2004) Young adult follow-up of hyperactive children: antisocial activities and drug use. *The Journal of Child Psychology and Psychiatry, 45*, 195–211.

Barkley, R. A., Fischer, M., Smallish, L., *et al.* (2006) Young adult outcomes of hyperactive children: adaptive functioning in major life activities. *Journal of the American Academy of Child and Adolescent Psychiatry, 45*, 192–202.

Barry, T. D., Lyman, R. D. & Klinger, L. G. (2002) Academic underachievement and attention deficit/hyperactivity disorder: the negative impact of symptom severity on school performance. *Journal of School Psychology, 40*, 259–283.

Bauermeister, J. J., Alegria, M., Bird, H. R., *et al.* (1992) Are attention-hyperactivity deficits unidimensional or multidimensional syndromes? Empirical findings from a community survey. *Journal of the American Academy of Child and Adolescent Psychiatry, 31*, 423–431.

Bauermeister, J., Matos, M., Reina, G., *et al.* (2005) Comparison of the DSM-IV combined and inattentive types of ADHD in a school-based sample of Latino/ Hispanic children. *The Journal of Child Psychology and Psychiatry, 46*, 166–179.

Bauman, A. (2007) Stigmatization, social distance and exclusion because of mental illness: the individual with mental illness as a 'stranger'. *International Review of Psychiatry, 19*, 131–135.

Bekle, B. (1994) Knowledge and attitudes about attention-deficit hyperactivity disorder (ADHD): a comparison between practicing teachers and undergraduate education students. *Journal of Attention Disorders, 7*, 151–161.

Benjamin, S., Nind, M., Hall, K., *et al.* (2003) Moments of inclusion and exclusion: pupils negotiating classroom contexts. *British Journal of Sociology of Education, 24*, 547–558.

Bereket, A., Turan, S., Karaman, M. G., *et al.* (2005) Height, weight, IGF-I, IGFBP–3 and thyroid functions in prepubertal children with attention deficit hyperacticity disorder: effect of methylphenidate treatment. *Hormone Research, 63*, 159–164.

Berlin, J. A. (2001) Does blinding of readers affect the results of meta-analyses? *The Lancet, 350*, 185–186.

Berwid, O. G., Curko Kera, E. A., Marks, D. J., *et al.* (2005) Sustained attention and response inhibition in young children at risk for attention deficit/hyperactivity disorder. *The Journal of Child Psychology and Psychiatry, 46*, 1219–1229.

Biederman, J., Faraone, S. V., Keenan, K., *et al.* (1992) Further evidence for family-genetic risk factors in attention deficit hyperactivity disorder: patterns of comorbidity in probands and relatives psychiatrically and pediatrically referred samples. *Archives of General Psychiatry, 49*, 728–738.

Biederman, J., Faraone, S. V., Doyle, A., *et al.* (1993) Convergence of the child behavior checklist with structured interview-based psychiatric diagnoses of ADHD children with and without comorbidity. *The Journal of Child Psychology and Psychiatry, 34*, 1241–1251.

Biederman, J., Milberger, S., Faraone, S. V., *et al.* (1995) Family-environment risk factors for attention-deficit hyperactivity disorder: a test of Rutter's indicators of adversity. *Archives of General Psychiatry, 52*, 464–470.

Biederman, J., Faraone, S., Milberger, S., *et al.* (1996) A prospective 4-year follow-up study of attention-deficit hyperactivity and related disorders. *Archives of General Psychiatry, 53*, 437–446.

Biederman, J., Swanson, J. M., Wigal, S. B., *et al.* (2005) Efficacy and safety of modafinil film-coated tablets in children and adolescents with attention-deficit/hyperactivity disorder: results of a randomized, double-blind, placebo-controlled, flexible-dose study. *Pediatrics, 116*, e777–e784.

Biederman, J., Mick, E., Surman, C., *et al.* (2006a) A randomized, placebo-controlled trial of OROS methylphenidate in adults with attention-deficit/hyperactivity disorder. *Biological Psychiatry, 59*, 829–835.

Biederman, J., Petty, C., Fried, R., *et al.* (2006b) Impact of psychometrically defined deficits of executive functioning in adults with attention deficit hyperactivity disorder. *American Journal of Psychiatry, 163*, 1730–1738.

Biederman, J., Monuteaux, M. C., Spencer, T., *et al.* (2008) Stimulant therapy and risk for subsequent substance use disorders in male adults with ADHD: a naturalistic controlled 10-year follow-up study. *American Journal of Psychiatry, 165*, 597–603.

Birnbaum, H. G., Kessler, R. C., Lowe, S. W., *et al.* (2005) Costs of attention deficit-hyperactivity disorder (ADHD) in the US: excess costs of persons with ADHD and their family members in 2000. *Current Medical Research and Opinion, 21*, 195–206.

Blachman, D. R. & Hinshaw, S. P. (2002) Patterns of friendship among girls with and without attention-deficit/hyperactivity disorder. *Journal of Abnormal Child Psychology, 30*, 625–640.

Bloomquist, M. L., August, G. J. & Ostrander, R. (1991) Effects of a school-based cognitive-behavioral intervention for ADHD children. *Journal of Abnormal Child Psychology, 19*, 591–605.

Bluebond-Langner, M., DeCicco, A. & Belasco, J. (2005) Involving children with life-shortening illnesses in decisions about participation in clinical research: a proposal for shuttle diplomacy and negotiation. In *Ethics and Research with Children* (ed E. Kodish), pp. 323–344. Oxford: Oxford University Press.

Bohnstedt, B. N., Kronenberger, W. G., Dunn, D. W., *et al.* (2005) Investigator ratings of ADHD symptoms during a randomized, placebo-controlled trial of atomoxetine: a comparison of parents and teachers as informants. *Journal of Attention Disorders, 8*, 153–159.

Boonstra, A. M., Oosterlaan, J., Sergent, J. A., *et al.* (2005) Executive functioning in adult ADHD: a meta-analytic review. *Psychological Medicine, 35*, 1097–1108.

Bor, W., Sanders, M. R. & Markie-Dadds, C. (2002) The effects of the Triple P-Positive Parenting Program on preschool children with co-occurring disruptive behavior and attentional/hyperactive difficulties. *Journal of Abnormal Child Psychology, 30*, 571–587.

Botting, N., Powls, A., Cooke, R. W. I., *et al.* (1997) Attention deficit hyperactivity disorders and other psychiatric outcomes in very low birth weight children at 12 years. *The Journal of Child Psychology and Psychiatry, 38*, 931–941.

Boyle, M. H., Offord, D. R., Racine, Y. A., *et al.* (1997) Adequacy of interviews vs. checklists for classifying childhood psychiatric disorder based on parent reports. *Archives of General Psychiatry, 54*, 793–799.

Bradley, C. (1937) The behavior of children receiving benzedrine. *American Journal of Psychiatry, 94*, 577–585.

Bramham, J., Young, S., Bickerdike, A., *et al.* (2008) Evaluation of group cognitive behavioural therapy for adults with ADHD. *Journal of Attention Disorders*, Epub 1087054708314596v1.

Brazier, J. & Roberts, J. (2004) The estimation of a preference-based measure of health from the SF-12. *Medical Care, 42*, 851–859.

Brazier, J., Usherwood, T., Harper, R., *et al.* (1998) Deriving a preference-based single index from the UK SF–36 Health Survey. *Journal of Clinical Epidemiology, 51*, 1115–1128.

British Medical Association & the Royal Pharmaceutical Society of Great Britain (2007) *British National Formulary (BNF)* 54. London: British Medical Association & Royal Pharmaceutical Society of Great Britain.

British Medical Association, the Royal Pharmaceutical Society of Great Britain & the Royal College of Paediatrics and Child Health, *et al.* (2005) *BNF for Children.* London: BMJ Pub.Group.

Brookes, K.-J., Mill, J., Guindalini, C., *et al.* (2006) A common haplotype of the dopamine transporter gene associated with attention deficit hyperactivity disorder and interacting with maternal use of alcohol during pregnancy. *Archives of General Psychiatry, 63*, 74–81.

Brown, G. L., Hunt, R. D., Ebert, M. H., *et al.* (1979) Plasma levels of d-amphetamine in hyperactive children. *Psychopharmacology, 62*, 133–140.

Brown, R. T., Wynne, M. E. & Slimmer, L. W. (1984) Attention deficit disorder and the effect of methylphenidate on attention, behavioral, and cardiovascular functioning. *Journal of Clinical Psychiatry, 45*, 473–476.

Brown, R. T., Wynne, M. E. & Medenis, R. (1985) Methylphenidate and cognitive therapy: a comparison of treatment approaches with hyperactive boys. *Journal of Abnormal Child Psychology, 13*, 69–87.

Brown, R. T., Perwein, A., Faries, D. E., *et al.* (2006) Atomoxetine in the management of children with ADHD: effects on quality of life and school functioning. *Clinical Pediatrics, 45*, 819–827.

Brown, T. E. (1996) *Brown Attention-Deficit Disorder Scales.* San Antonio, Texas: The Psychological Corporation, Harcourt Brace.

Brown, T. E. (2001) *Brown Attention-Deficit Disorder Scales for Children.* San Antonio, Texas: The Psychological Corporation, Harcourt Brace.

Buhrmester, D., Whalen, C. K., Henker, B., *et al.* (1992) Prosocial behaviour in hyperactive boys: effects of stimulant medication in comparison with normal boys. *Journal of Abnormal Child Psychology, 20*, 103–121.

Bukstein, O. (2006) Substance use disorders in adolescents with attention-deficit/ hyperactivity disorder. *Adolescent Medicine: State of the Art Reviews, 19*, 242–253.

Burd, L., Klug, M. G., Coumbe, M. J., *et al.* (2003a) Children and adolescents with attention deficit-hyperactivity disorder: 1. Prevalence and cost of care. *Journal of Child Neurology, 18*, 555–561.

Burd, L., Klug, M. G., Coumbe, M. J., *et al.* (2003b) The attention-deficit hyperactivity disorder paradox: 2. Phenotypic variability in prevalence and cost of comorbidity. *Journal of Child Neurology, 18*, 653–660.

Burgess, I. (2002) Service innovations: attention-deficit hyperactivity disorder: development of a multi-professional integrated care pathway. *Psychiatric Bulletin, 26*, 148–151.

Bussing, R., Gary, F. A., Leon, C. E., *et al.* (2002) General classroom teachers' information and perceptions of attention deficit hyperactivity disorder. *Behavioral Disorders, 27*, 327–339.

Butter, H. J., Lapierre, Y., Firestone, P., *et al.* (1983) A comparative study of the efficacy of ACTH4–9 analogue, methylphenidate, and placebo on attention deficit disorder with hyperkinesis. *Journal of Clinical Psychopharmacology, 3*, 226–230.

Camp, B. & Bash, M. A. (1981) *Think Aloud: Increasing Social and Cognitive Skills - A Problem-Solving Program for Children: Primary Level.* Champaign, Illinois: Research Press.

Canino, G., Shrout, P. E., Rubio-Stipec, M., *et al.* (2004) The DSM-IV rates of child and adolescent disorders in Puerto Rico: prevalence, correlates, service use, and the effects of impairment. *Archives of General Psychiatry, 61*, 85–93.

Carter, C. M., Urbanowitz, M., Hemsley, R., *et al.* (1993) Effects of a food diet in attention deficit disorder. *Archives of Disease in Childhood, 69*, 564–568.

Caruana, A. & Vassallo, R. (2003) Children's perception of their influence over purchases: the role of parental communication patterns. *Journal of Consumer Marketing, 20*, 55–66.

Casat, C. D., Pleasants, D. Z. & Fleet, J. V. W. (1987) A double-blind trial of bupropion in children with attention deficit disorder. *Psychopharmacology Bulletin, 23*, 120–121.

Castellanos, F. X., Giedd, J. N., Elia, J., *et al.* (1997) Controlled stimulant treatment of ADHD and comorbid Tourette's syndrome: effects of stimulant and dose. *Journal of the American Academy of Child and Adolescent Psychiatry, 36*, 589–596.

Cephalon UK Limited (2008) *Provigil 100 mg Tablets, Provigil 200 mg Tablets.* Summary of Product Characteristics. Available at: http://emc.medicines.org.uk

Chan, E., Zhan, C. & Homer, C. J. (2002) Health care use and costs for children with attention-deficit/hyperactivity disorder: national estimates from the medical expenditure panel survey. *Archives of Pediatrics and Adolescent Medicine, 156*, 504–511.

Chen, W. J., Faraone, S. V., Biederman, J., *et al.* (1994) Diagnostic accuracy of the child behavior checklist scales for attention-deficit hyperactivity disorder: a receiver-operating characteristic analysis. *Journal of Consulting and Clinical Psychology, 62*, 1017–1025.

Cochrane Collaboration (2005) Review Manager (RevMan) [computer program]. Version 4.2.5 for Windows. Oxford: The Cochrane Collaboration.

Coghill, D., Spende, Q., Barton, J., *et al.* (2004) *Measuring Quality of Life in Children with Attention-Deficit-Hyperactivity Disorder in the UK.* Poster presented at 16th World Congress of the International Association for Child and Adolescent Psychiatry and Allied Professions (IACAPAP), 22–26 August 2004, Berlin, Germany.

Coghill, D., Spiel, G., Baldursson, G., *et al.* (2006) Which factors impact on clinician-rated impairment in children with ADHD? *European Child and Adolescent Psychiatry, 13 (Suppl. 1)*, 117–129.

Compas, B. E., Benson, M., Boyer, M., *et al.* (2002) Problem-solving and problem-solving therapies. In *Child and Adolescent Psychiatry* (4th edn) (eds M. Rutter & E. Taylor), pp. 938–948. Oxford: Blackwell.

Conners, C. K. (1969) A teacher rating scale for use in drug studies with children. *American Journal of Psychiatry, 126*, 884–888.

Conners, C. K. (1980) *Food Additives and Hyperactive Children.* New York: Plenum.

Conners, C. K. (1997) *Conners Rating Scales-Revised (CRS-R).* North Tonawanda, New York: Multi-Health Systems.

## References

Conners, C. K. & Taylor, E. (1980) Pemoline, methylphenidate, and placebo in children with minimal brain dysfunction. *Archives of General Psychiatry, 37,* 922–930.

Conners, C. K., Goyette, C. H., Southwick, D. A., *et al.* (1976) Food additives and hyperkinesis: a controlled double-blind experiment. *Pediatrics, 58,* 154–66.

Conners, C. K., Casat, C. D., Gualtieri, C. T., *et al.* (1996) Bupropion hydrochloride in attention deficit disorder with hyperactivity. *Journal of the American Academy of Child and Adolescent Psychiatry, 34,* 1314–1321.

Conners, C. K., Wells, K. C., Parker, J. D. A., *et al.* (1997) A new self-report scale for assessment of adolescent psychopathology: factor structure, reliability, validity, and diagnostic sensitivity. *Journal of Abnormal Child Psychology, 25,* 487–497.

Conners, C. K., Sitarenios, G., Parker, J. D. A., *et al.* (1998) Revision and restandardization of the Conners Teacher Rating Scale (CTRS-R): factor structure, reliability and criterion validity. *Journal of Abnormal Child Psychology, 26,* 279–291.

Cooper, P. & Ideus, K. (1996) *Attention Deficit/Hyperactivity Disorder: A Practical Guide for Teachers.* London: David Fulton.

Corkum, P. V., McKinnon, M. M., Mullane, J. C. (2005) The effect of involving classroom teachers in a parent training program for families of children with ADHD. *Child and Family Behavior Therapy, 27,* 29–49.

Costello, A. J., Edelbrock, C. S., Kalas, R., *et al.* (1982) *NIMH Diagnostic Interview Schedule for Children.* Bethesda, Maryland: NIMH.

Couture, C., Royer, E., Dupuis, F. A., *et al.* (2003) Comparison of Quebec and British teachers' beliefs about, training in and experience with attention deficit hyperactivity disorder. *Emotional Behavioural Difficulties, 8,* 284–302.

Cuffe, S. P., Moore, C. G. & McKeown, R. E. (2005) Prevalence and correlates of ADHD symptoms in the national health interview survey. *Journal of Attention Disorders, 9,* 392–401.

Cunningham, C. & Boyle, M. (2002) Preschoolers at risk for attention-deficit hyperactivity disorder and oppositional defiant disorder: family, parenting, and behavioural correlates. *Journal of Abnormal Child Psychology, 30,* 555–569.

Curtis, D. F., Pisecco, S., Hamilton, R. J., *et al.* (2006) Teacher perceptions of classroom interventions for children with ADHD: a cross-cultural comparison of teachers in the United States and New Zealand. *School Psychology Quarterly, 21,* 171–196.

Curtis, L. & Netten, A. (2006) *Unit Costs of Health and Social Care.* Canterbury: Personal Social Services Research Unit. Available from: http://www.pssru.ac.uk/

Dahl, R., Pelham, W. & Wierson, M. (1991) The role of sleep disturbances in attention deficit disorder symptoms: a case study. *Journal of Pediatric Psychology, 16,* 229–239.

Dall'Alba, G. & Sandberg, J. (2006) Unveiling professional development: a critical review of stage models. *Review of Education Research, 76,* 383–412.

Dalsgaard, S., Mortensen, P. B., Frydenberg, M., *et al.* (2002) Conduct problems, gender and the adult psychiatric outcome of children with attention-deficit hyperactive disorder. *British Journal of Psychiatry, 181,* 416–421.

Deatrick, J. A. & Faux, S. A. (1991) Conducting qualitative studies with children and adolescents. In *Qualitative Nursing Research: a Contemporary Dialogue* (ed J. M. Morse), pp. 185–203. Newbury Park, California: Sage.

DeBar, L. L., Lynch, F. L. & Boles, M. (2004) Healthcare use by children with attention deficit/hyperactivity disorder with and without psychiatric comorbidities. *Journal of Behavioral Health Services and Research, 31*, 312–323.

De Civita, M., Regier, D., Alamgir, A. H., *et al.* (2005) Evaluating health-related quality-of-life studies in paediatric populations: some conceptual, methodological and developmental considerations and recent applications. *Pharmacoeconomics, 23*, 659–685.

Deeks, J. J. (2002) Issues in the selection of a summary statistic for meta-analysis of clinical trials with binary outcomes. *Statistics in Medicine, 21*, 1575–1600.

Department of Health (2004) *National Service Framework for Children, Young People and Maternity Services. The Mental Health and Psychological Well-being of Children and Young People.* London: HMSO.

De Ridder, A. & De Graeve, A. (2006) Healthcare use, social burden and costs of children with and without ADHD in Flanders, Belgium. *Clinical Drug Investigation, 26*, 75–90.

DerSimonian, R. & Laird, N. (1986) Meta-analysis in clinical trials. *Controlled Clinical Trials, 7*, 177–188.

DfES (2001) *Special Educational Needs Code of Practice.* Reference dfes/581/2001. Available at: http://publications.teachernet.gov.uk/eOrderingDownload/DfES%200581%20200MIG2228.pdf [accessed April 2007].

Dickstein, S. G., Bannon, K., Castellanos, F. X., *et al.* (2006) The neural correlates of attention deficit hyperactivity disorder: an ALE meta-analysis. *The Journal of Child Psychology and Psychiatry, 47*, 1051–1062.

Dolan, P. (1997) Modelling valuations for EuroQol health states. *Medical Care, 35*, 1095–1108.

Donnelly, M., Haby, M. M., Carter, R., *et al.* (2004) Cost-effectiveness of dexamphetamine and methylphenidate for the treatment of childhood attention deficit hyperactivity disorder. *Australian and New Zealand Journal of Psychiatry, 38*, 592–601.

Döpfner, M., Breuter, D., Schürmann, S., *et al.* (2004) Effectiveness of an adaptive multimodal treatment in children with attention-deficit hyperactivity disorder: global outcome. *European Child and Adolescent Psychiatry, 13 (Suppl. 1)*, i117–i129.

Dreger, R. M., Lewis, P. M., Rich, T. A., *et al.* (1964) Behavioral classification project. *Journal of Consulting Psychology, 28*, 1–13. *Journal of the American Academy of Child and Adolescent Psychiatry, 31*, 210–218.

Dretzke, J., Frew, E., Davenport, C., *et al.* (2005) *The Effectiveness and Cost-Effectiveness of Parent Training/Education Programmes for the Treatment of Conduct Disorder, Including Oppositional Defiant Disorder, in Children.* Health Technology Assessment, 9. Tunbridge Wells: Gray Publishing.

Dreyfus, H. L. & Dreyfus, S. E. (1986) *A Phenomenology of Skill Acquisition as a Basis For A Merleau-Pontian Non-Representationalist Cognitive Science.*

Unpublished manuscript, University of California, Berkley, Department of Philosophy.

Drummond, M. F. & Jefferson, T. O. (1996) Guidelines for authors and peer reviewers of economic submissions to the *British Medical Journal. British Medical Journal, 313*, 275–283.

Dulcan, M. & Popper, C. W. (1991) *Concise Guide to Child and Adolescent Psychiatry.* Washington: American Psychiatric Press.

DuPaul, G. J. & Eckert, T. L. (1997) The effects of school-based interventions for attention deficit hyperactivity disorder: a meta analysis. *School Psychology Review, 26*, 5–27.

DuPaul, G. J., Reid, R., Power, T. J., *et al.* (1998) *ADHD Rating Scale-IV.* New York: Guilford Press.

DuPaul, G. J., McGoey, K. E., Eckert, T. L., *et al.* (2001) Preschool children with attention deficit / hyperactivity disorder: impairments in behavioral, social, and school functioning. *Journal of the American Academy of Child and Adolescent Psychiatry, 40*, 508–515.

Eaves, L. J., Silberg, J. L., Meyer, J. M., *et al.* (1997) Genetics and developmental psychopathology: 2. The main effects of genes and environment on behavioral problems in the Virginia twin study of adolescent behavioral development. *The Journal of Child Psychology and Psychiatry, 38*, 965–980.

Eccles, M., Freemantle, N. & Mason, J. (1998) North of England evidence based guideline development project: methods of developing guidelines for efficient drug use in primary care. *British Medical Journal, 316*, 1232–1235.

Edelbrock, C. (1986) Behavioral ratings of children diagnosed for attention deficit disorder. *Psychiatric Annals, 16*, 36–40.

Edelbrock, C., Costello, A. J., Dulcan, M. K., *et al.* (1986) Parent-child agreement on child psychiatric symptoms assessed via structured interview. *The Journal of Child Psychology and Psychiatry, 27*, 181–190.

Efron, D., Jarman, F. C. & Barker, M. J. (1998) Child and parent perceptions of stimulant medication treatment in attention deficit hyperactivity disorder. *Journal of Paediatrics and Child Health, 34*, 288–292.

Egger, J., Carter, C. M., Graham, P. J., *et al.* (1985) Controlled trial of oligoantigenic treatment in the hyperkinetic syndrome. *The Lancet, 1*, 540–545.

Eli Lilly and Company Ltd (2008) *Strattera 10 mg, 18 mg, 25 mg, 40 mg, 60 mg or 80 mg Hard Capsules.* Summary of Product Characteristics. Available at: http://emc.medicines.org.uk

Epstein, J. N., Johnson, D. & Conners, C. K. (2001) *CAADID: Conners Adult ADHD Diagnostic Interview for DSM-IV Technical Manual.* North Towanda, NY: Multihealth Systems.

Epstein, J. N., Willoughby, M., Valencia, E. Y., *et al.* (2005) The role of children's ethnicity in the relationship between teacher ratings of attention-deficit/hyperactivity disorder and observed classroom behavior. *Journal of Consulting and Clinical Psychology, 73*, 424–434.

Ernhardt, D. & Hinshaw, S. P. (1994) Initial sociometric impressions of attention-deficit hyperactivity disorder and comparison boys: predictions from social behaviors and from nonbehavioral variables. *Journal of Consulting and Clinical Psychology, 62*, 833–842.

Eysenck, N. T. & Rachman, S. T. (1971) The application of learning theory to child psychiatry. In *Modern Perspectives in Child Psychiatry* (ed T. C. Howells), pp. 104–169. New York: Brunner/Mazel.

Famularo, R., Kinscherff, R. & Fenton, T. (1992) Psychiatric diagnoses of maltreated children: preliminary findings. *Journal of the American Academy of Child and Adolescent Psychiatry, 31*, 863–867.

Faraone, S. V. (2005) The scientific foundation for understanding attention-deficit/hyperactivity disorder as a valid psychiatric disorder. *European Child and Adolescent Psychiatry, 14*, 1–10.

Faraone, S. V. & Biederman, J. (2005) What is the prevalence of adult ADHD? Results of a population screen of 966 adults. *Journal of Attention Disorders, 9*, 384–391.

Faraone, S., Biederman, J. & Monuteaux, M. C. (2002) Further evidence for the diagnostic continuity between child and adolescent ADHD. *Journal of Attention Disorders, 6*, 5–13.

Faraone, S. V., Sergeant, J., Gillberg, C., *et al.* (2003) The worldwide prevalence of ADHD: is it an American condition? *World Psychiatry, 2*, 104–113.

Faraone, S. V., Perlis, R. H., Doyle, A. E., *et al.* (2005) Molecular genetics of attention-deficit/hyperactivity disorder. *Biological Psychiatry, 57*, 1313–1323.

Faraone, S. V., Biederman, J. & Mick, E. (2006) The age-dependent decline of attention deficit hyperactivity disorder: a meta-analysis of follow-up studies. *Psychological Medicine, 36*, 159–165.

Farrington, D. P. (1994) *Delinquency Prevention in the First Few Years of Life.* Plenary Address from 4th European Conference on Law and Psychology, Barcelona, Spain.

Farrington, D. P. (1995) The Twelfth Jack Tizard Memorial Lecture. The development of offending and antisocial behaviour from childhood: key findings from the Cambridge Study in Delinquent Development. *The Journal of Child Psychology and Psychiatry, 36*, 929–964.

FDA (2004) Review of AERS data for marketed safety experience during stimulant therapy: death, sudden death, cardiovascular SAEs (including stroke). Meeting report.

FDA (2008a) FDA asks attention-deficit hyperactivity disorder (ADHD) drug manufacturers to develop patient medication guides. http://www.fda.gov/cder/drug/infopage/ADHD/default.htm [accessed January 2008].

FDA (2008b) FDA alert for healthcare professionals: Adderall and Adderall XR (amphetamine). http://www.fda.gov/cder/drug/InfoSheets/HCP/AdderallHCP Sheet.pdf [accessed January 2008].

Fehlings, D. L., Roberts, W., Humphries, T., *et al.* (1991) Attention deficit hyperactivity disorder: does cognitive behavioral therapy improve home behavior? *Journal of Developmental and Behavioral Pediatrics, 12*, 223–228.

Feighner, J. P., Robins, E., Guze, E. B., *et al.* (1972) Diagnostic criteria for use in psychiatric research. *Archives of General Psychiatry, 26*, 57–63.

*References*

Feldman, H., Cumrine, P., Handen, B. L., *et al.* (1989) Methylphenidate in children with seizures and attention-deficit disorder. *American Journal of Diseases in Children, 143*, 1081–1086.

Fennell, D. & Liberato, A. (2007) Learning to live with OCD: labelling, the self, and stigma. *Deviant Behavior, 28*, 305–331.

Ferguson, D. M., Horwood, L. J. & Lloyd, M. (1991) Confirmatory factor models of attention deficit and conduct disorder. *The Journal of Child Psychology and Psychiatry, 32*, 257–274.

Findling, R. L., Short, E. J. & Manos, M. J. (2001) Short-term cardiovascular effects of methylphenidate and Adderall. *Journal of the American Academy of Child and Adolescent Psychiatry, 40*, 525–529.

Findling, R. L., Quinn, D., Hatch, S. J., *et al.* (2006) Comparison of the clinical efficacy of twice-daily Ritalin and once-daily Equasym XL with placebo in children with attention-deficit/hyperactivity disorder. *European Child and Adolescent Psychiatry, 15*, 450–459.

Firestone, P., Kelly, M. J., Goodman, J. T., *et al.* (1981) Differential effects of parent training and stimulant medication with hyperactives: a progress report. *American Academy of Child Psychiatry, 20*, 135–147.

Firestone, P., Crowe, D., Goodman, J. T., *et al.* (1986) Vicissitudes of follow-up studies: differential effects of parent training and stimulant medication with hyperactives. *American Journal of Orthopsychiatry, 56*, 184–194.

Fischer, M., Barkley, R. A., Edelbrock, C. S., *et al.* (1990) The adolescent outcome of hyperactive children diagnosed by research criteria: II. Academic, attentional, and neuropsychological status. *Journal of Consulting and Clinical Psychology, 58*, 580–588.

Fischer, M., Barkley, R. A., Smallish, L., *et al.* (2007) Hyperactive children as young adults: driving abilities, safe driving behavior, and adverse driving outcomes. *Accident Analysis and Prevention, 39*, 94–105.

Fletcher, K. E., Fischer, M., Barkley, R. A., *et al.* (1996) A sequential analysis of the mother-adolescent interactions of ADHD, ADHD / ODD, and normal teenagers during neutral and conflict discussions. *Journal of Abnormal Child Psychology, 24*, 271–297.

Flynn Pharma Ltd (2007a) *Medikinet Tablets.* Summary of Product Characteristics. Available at: http://emc.medicines.org.uk

Flynn Pharma Ltd (2007b) *Medikinet XL.* Summary of Product Characteristics. Available at: http://emc.medicines.org.uk

Fonagy, P., Target, M., Cottrell, D., *et al.* (2002) *What Works for Whom? A Critical Review of Treatments for Children and Adolescents.* New York: Guilford Press.

Ford, T., Goodman, R. & Meltzer, H. (2003) The British Child and Adolescent Mental Health Survey 1999: the prevalence of DSM-IV disorders. *Journal of the American Academy of Child and Adolescent Psychiatry, 42*, 1203–1211.

Ford, T., Goodman, R. & Meltzer, H. (2004) The relative importance of child, family, school and neighbourhood correlates of childhood psychiatric disorder. *Social Psychiatry and Psychiatric Epidemiology, 39*, 487–496.

Foster, E. M., Jensen, P. S., Schlander, M., *et al.* (2007) Treatment for ADHD: is more complex treatment cost-effective for more complex cases? *Health Services Research, 42*, 165–82.

Fowler, M. & the National Education Committee (1992) *CH.A.D.D. Educator's Manual: an In-Depth Look at Attention Deficit Disorders from an Educational Perspective.* Plantation, Florida: CH.A.D.D.

Frazier, T. W., Youngstrom, E. A., Glutting, J. J., *et al.* (2007) ADHD and achievement: meta analysis of the child, adolescent, and adult literatures and a concomitant study with college students. *Journal of Learning Disabilities, 40*, 49–65.

Frick, P. J., Lahey, B. B., Kamphaus, R. W., *et al.* (1991) Academic underachievement and the disruptive behavior disorders. *Journal of Consulting and Clinical Psychology, 59*, 289–294.

Frouke, E. P. L., Ferdinand, R. F. & Oldehinkel, A. J. (2005) Classes of adolescents with disruptive behaviors in a general population sample. *Social Psychiatry and Psychiatric Epidemiology, 40*, 931–938.

Furukawa, T. A., Barbui, C., Cipriani, A., *et al.* (2006) Imputing missing standard deviations in meta-analyses can provide accurate results. *Journal of Clinical Epidemiology, 59*, 7–10.

Gadow, K. D., Sverd, J., Sprafkin, J., *et al.* (1999) Long-term methylphenidate therapy in children with comorbid attention-deficit hyperactivity disorder and chronic multiple tic disorder. *Archives of General Psychiatry, 56*, 337–338.

Galloway, D., Leo, E. L., Rogers, C., *et al.* (1995) Motivational styles in English and mathematics among children identified as having special educational needs. *British Journal of Educational Psychology, 65*, 477–487.

Gaub, M. & Carlson, C. L. (1997) Behavioural characteristics of DSM-IV ADHD subtypes in a school-based population. *Journal of Abnormal Child Psychology, 25*, 103–111.

Gerring, J. P., Brady, K. D., Chen, A., *et al.* (1998) Premorbid prevalence of ADHD and development of secondary ADHD after closed head injury. *Journal of the American Academy of Child and Adolescent Psychiatry, 37*, 647–654.

Gilger, J. W., Pennington, B. F. & DeFries, J. C. (1992) A twin study of the etiology of comorbidity: attention-deficit hyperactivity disorder and dyslexia. *Journal of the American Academy of Child and Adolescent Psychiatry, 31*, 343–348.

Gilmore, A. & Milne, R. (2001) Methylphenidate in children with hyperactivity: review and cost analysis. *Pharmacoepidemiology and Drug Safety, 10*, 85–94.

Gittelman-Klein, R., Klein, D. F., Abikoff, H., *et al.* (1976a) Relative efficacy of methylphenidate and behavior modification in hyperkinetic children: an interim report. *Journal of Abnormal Child Psychology, 4*, 361–379.

Gittelman-Klein, R., Klein, D. F., Katz, S., *et al.* (1976b) Comparative effects of methylphenidate and thioridazine in hyperkinetic children. I. Clinical results. *Archives of General Psychiatry, 33*, 1217–1231.

Gittelman-Klein, R., Landa, B., Mattes, J. A., *et al.* (1988) Methylphenidate and growth in hyperactive children. *Archives of General Psychiatry, 45*, 1127–1130.

Gjone, H., Stevenson, J. & Sundet, J. M. (1996) Genetic influence on parent-reported attention-related problems in a Norwegian general population twin sample.

*Journal of the American Academy of Child and Adolescent Psychiatry, 35*, 588–596.

GlaxoSmithKline UK (2008) *Zyban 150 mg Prolonged Release Film-Coated Tablets.* Summary of Product Characteristics. Available at: http://emc.medicines.org.uk

Glutting, J. J., Youngstrom, E. A. & Watkins, M. W. (2005) ADHD and college students: exploratory and confirmatory factor structures with student and parent data. *Psychological Assessment, 17*, 44–55.

Goffman, E. (1968a) *Asylums: Essays on the Social Situation of Mental Patients and Other Inmates.* Harmondsworth: Penguin.

Goffman, E. (1968b) *Stigma: Notes on the Management of Spoiled Identity.* Harmondsworth: Penguin.

Gomez, R., Harvey, J., Quick, C., *et al.* (1999) DSM-IV AD/HD: confirmatory factor models, prevalence, and gender and age differences based on parent and teacher ratings of Australian primary school children. *The Journal of Child Psychology and Psychiatry, 40*, 265–274.

Gonzalez, L. O. & Sellers, E. W. (2002) The effects of a stress-management program on self-concept, locus of control, and the acquisition of coping skills in school-age children diagnosed with attention deficit hyperactivity disorder. *Journal of Child and Adolescent Psychiatric Nursing, 15*, 5–15.

Goodman, R. (2001) Psychometric properties of the Strengths and Difficulties Questionnaire. *Journal of the American Academy of Child and Adolescent Psychiatry, 40*, 1337–1345.

Gowers, S., Thomas, S. & Deeley, S. (2004) Can primary schools contribute effectively to Tier I Child Mental Health Services? *Clinical Child Psychology and Psychiatry 9*, 419–425.

GRADE Working Group (2004) Grading quality of evidence and strength of recommendations. *British Medical Journal, 328*, 1490–1497.

Gray, J. & Sime, N. (1988) A report for the committee of inquiry into discipline in schools. Part 1: Findings from the national survey of teachers in England and Wales. In *The Elton Report (1989). Enquiry into Discipline in Schools.* London: HMSO.

Green, H., McGinnity, A., Meltzer, H., *et al.* (2005) *Mental Health of Children and Young People in Great Britain, 2004.* A survey carried out by the Office for National Statistics on behalf of the Department of Health and the Scottish Executive. Basingstoke: Palgrave Macmillan.

Green, V. A., O'Reilly, M., Itchon, J., *et al.* (2004) Persistence of early emerging aberrant behavior in children with developmental disabilities. *Research in Developmental Disabilities, 26*, 47–55.

Greenberg, L. M., Deem, M. A. & McMahon, S. (1972) Effects of dextroamphetamine, chlorpromazine, and hydroxyzine on behavior and performance in hyperactive children. *American Journal of Psychiatry, 129*, 44–51.

Greenhill, L. L., Findling, R. L., Swanson, J. M., *et al.* (2002) A double-blind, placebo-controlled study of modified-release methylphenidate in children with attention-deficit/hyperactivity disorder. *Pediatrics, 109*, E39.

Greenhill, L. L., Muniz, R., Ball, R. R., *et al.* (2006) Efficacy and safety of dexmethylphenidate extended-release capsules in children with attention-deficit/hyperactivity disorder. *Journal of the American Academy of Child and Adolescent Psychiatry, 45,* 817–823.

Gross-Tsur, V., Manor, O., van der Meere, J., *et al.* (1997) Epilepsy and attention deficit hyperactivity disorder: is methylphenidate safe and effective? *Journal of Pediatrics, 130,* 40–44.

Gudex, C., Dolan, P., Kind, P., *et al.* (1996) Health state valuations from the general public using the Visual Analogue Scale. *Quality of Life Research, 5,* 521–531.

Guevara, J. P. & Mandell, D. S. (2003) Costs associated with attention deficit hyperactivity disorder: overview and future projections. *Expert Review on Pharmacoeconomics and Outcomes Research, 3,* 201–210.

Guevara, J., Lozano, P., Wickizer, T., *et al.* (2001) Utilization and cost of health care services for children with attention-deficit/hyperactivity disorder. *Pediatrics, 108,* 71–78.

Hagerman, R. J. (1999) Psychopharmacological interventions in fragile x syndrome, fetal alcohol syndrome, Prader-Willi syndrome, Angelman syndrome, Smith-Magenis syndrome, and velocardiofacial syndrome. *Mental Retardation and Developmental Disabilities Research Reviews, 5,* 305–313.

Hakkaart-van Roijen, L., Zwirs, B. W. C., Bouwmans, C., *et al.* (2007) Societal costs and quality of life of children suffering from attention deficient hyperactivity disorder (ADHD). *European Child and Adolescent Psychiatry, 16,* 316–326.

Hankin, C. S. (2001) ADHD and its impact on the family. *Drug Benefit Trends, 13* (Suppl. C), 15–16.

Hankin, C. S., Wright, A. & Gephart, H. (2001) The burden of attention deficit/ hyperactivity disorder. *Drug Benefit Trends, 13,* 7–14.

Harley, J. P., Ray, R. S., Tomasi, L., *et al.* (1978) Hyperkinesis and food additives: testing the Feingold hypothesis. *Pediatrics, 61,* 818–827.

Hartl, T., Duffany, S., Allen, G., *et al.* (2005) Relationships among compulsive hoarding, trauma, and attention-deficit/hyperactivity disorder. *Behaviour Research and Therapy, 43,* 269–276.

Hazell, P. L. & Stuart, J. E. (2003) A randomized controlled trial of clonidine added to psychostimulant medication for hyperactive and aggressive children. *Journal of the American Academy of Child and Adolescent Psychiatry, 42,* 886–894.

Hechtman, L. & Weiss, G. (1983) Long-term outcome of hyperactive children. *American Journal of Orthopsychiatry, 53,* 532–541.

Heinrich, H., Gevensleben, H. & Strehl, U. (2006) Annotation: Neurofeedback – train your brain to train behaviour. *The Journal of Child Psychology and Psychiatry, 48,* 3–16.

Hemmer, S. A., Pasternak, J. F., Zecker, S. G., *et al.* (2001) Stimulant therapy and seizure risk in children with ADHD. *Pediatric Neurology, 24,* 99–102.

Hervey, A. S., Epstein, J. N. & Curry, J. F. (2004) Neuropsychology of adults with attention-deficit /hyperactivity disorder: a meta-analytic review. *Neuropsychology, 18,* 485–503.

Higgins, J. P. T. & Thompson, S. G. (2002) Quantifying heterogeneity in a meta-analysis. *Statistics in Medicine, 21,* 1539–1558.

Hill, J. C. & Schoener, E. P. (1996) Age-dependent decline of attention deficit hyperactivity disorder. *American Journal of Psychiatry, 153*, 1143–1146.

Hinnenthal, J. A., Perwien, A. R. & Sterling, K. L. (2005) A comparison of service use and costs among adults with ADHD and adults with other chronic diseases. *Psychiatric Services, 56*, 1593–1599.

Hinshaw, S. P. (2002) Preadolescent girls with attention-deficit/hyperactivity disorder: I. Background characteristics, comorbidity, cognitive and social functioning, and parenting practices. *Journal of Consulting and Clinical Psychology, 70*, 1086–1098.

Hinshaw, S. P. (2005) The stigmatization of mental illness in children and parents: developmental issues, family concerns, and research needs. *The Journal of Child Psychology and Psychiatry, 46*, 714–734.

Hirayama, S., Hamazaki, T. & Terasawa, K. (2004) Effect of docosahexaenoic acid-containing food administration on symptoms of attention-deficit/hyperactivity disorder: a placebo-controlled double-blind study. *European Journal of Clinical Nutrition, 58*, 467–473.

HMSO (1989) *The Elton Report. Enquiry into Discipline in Schools.* London: HMSO.

Ho, T. P., Leung, P. W. L., Luk, E. S. L., *et al.* (1996) Establishing the constructs of childhood behavioral disturbance in a Chinese population: a questionnaire study. *Journal of Abnormal Child Psychology, 24*, 417–431.

Hoath, F. E. & Sanders, M. R. (2002) A feasibility study of enhanced group Triple P—Positive Parenting Program for parents of children with attention-deficit/hyperactivity disorder. *Behaviour Change, 19*, 191–206.

Hoofdakker, B. J., van den, Veen-Mulders, L., van der, Sytema, S., *et al.* (2007) Effectiveness of behavioural parent training for children with ADHD in routine clinical practice: a randomized controlled study. *Journal of the American Academy of Child and Adolescent Psychiatry, 46*, 1263–1271.

Horwitz, A. V., Videon, T. M., Schmitz, M. F., *et al.* (2003) Rethinking twins and environments: possible social sources for assumed genetic influences in twin research. *Journal of Health and Social Behavior, 44*, 111–129.

House of Commons Education and Skills Committee (2006) *Special Educational Needs: Third Report of Session 2005-06.* Vol. 1. Available at: http://www.publications.parliament.uk/pa/cm200506/cmselect/cmeduski/478/478i.pdf

Hudziak, J., Heath, A. C., Madden, P. F., *et al.* (1998) *Latent class and factor analysis of DSM-IV ADHD: a twin study of female adolescents.* Journal of the American Academy of Child and Adolescent Psychiatry, *37*, 848–857.

Hughes, L. & Cooper, P. (2006) *Understanding and Supporting Children with ADHD: Strategies for Teachers, Parents and other Professionals.* London: Paul Chapman.

Ialongo, N. S., Lopez, M., Horn, W. F., *et al.* (1994) Effects of psychostimulant medication on self-perceptions of competence, control, and mood in children with attention deficit hyperactivity disorder. *Journal of Clinical Child Psychology, 23*, 161–173.

Information Centre, The (2006) *Prescription Cost Analysis England 2006.* The Information Centre, Prescribing Support Unit, NHS. Available at: http://www.ic.nhs.uk/webfiles/publications/pca2006/PCA_2006.pdf

Jacobs, B. W. (2002) Individual and group therapy. In *Child and Adolescent Psychiatry* (4th edn) (eds M. Rutter & E. Taylor), pp. 983–997. Oxford: Blackwell.

Jadad, A. R., Moore, R. A., Carroll, D., *et al.* (1996) Assessing the quality of reports of randomised clinical trials: is blinding necessary? *Controlled Clinical Trials, 17*, 1–12.

Jaffee, S. R. & Price, T. S. (2007) Gene-environment correlations: a review of the evidence and implications for prevention of mental illness. *Molecular Psychiatry, 12*, 432–442.

Janssen-Cilag Ltd (2008a) *Concerta XL 18 mg Prolonged-Release Tablets, Concerta XL 36 mg Prolonged-Release Tablets.* Summary of Product Characteristics. Available at: http://emc.medicines.org.uk

Janssen-Cilag Ltd (2008b) *Concerta XL 27 mg Prolonged-Release Tablets.* Summary of Product Characteristics. Available at: http://emc.medicines.org.uk

Jensen, P. S., Martin, D. & Cantwell, D. P. (1997a) Comorbidity in ADHD: implications for research, practice, and DSM-V. *Journal of the American Academy of Child and Adolescent Psychiatry, 36*, 1065–1079.

Jensen, P. S., Arnold, L. E., Swanson, J. M., *et al.* (1997b) 3-year follow-up of the NIMH MTA study. *Journal of the American Academy of Child and Adolescent Psychiatry, 46*, 989–1002.

Jensen, P. S., Hinshaw, S. P., Kraemer, H. C., *et al.* (2001) ADHD comorbidity findings from the MTA study: comparing comorbid subgroups. *Journal of the American Academy of Child and Adolescent Psychiatry, 40*, 147–158.

Jensen, P. S., Garcia, J. A., Glied, S., *et al.* (2005) Cost-effectiveness of ADHD treatments: findings from the multimodal treatment study of children with ADHD. *American Journal of Psychiatry, 162*, 1628–1636.

Jensen, P. S., Arnold, L. E., Swanson, J. M., *et al.* (2007) 3-year follow-up of the NIMH MTA study. *Journal of the American Academy of Child and Adolescent Psychiatry, 46*, 989–1002.

Jerome, L., Habinski, L. & Segal, A. (2006) Attention-deficit/hyperactivity disorder (ADHD) and driving risk: a review of the literature and a methodological critique. *Current Psychiatry Reports, 8*, 416–426.

Johnston, C. & Mash, E. J. (2001) Families of children with attention-deficit/hyperactivity disorder: review and recommendations for future research. *Clinical Child and Family Psychology Review, 4*, 183–207.

Joint Formulary Committee (2008) *British National Formulary 55.* London: Pharmaceutical Press.

Joint Royal College of Paediatrics and Child Health/Neonatal and Paediatric Pharmacists Group Standing Committee on Medicines (2000) *The Use of Unlicensed Medicines or Licensed Medicines for Unlicensed Applications in Paediatric Practice: Policy Statement.* London: Royal College of Paediatrics and Child Health.

Joyce, B. & Showers, B. (1980) Improving inservice training: the messages of research. *Educational Leadership, 37*, 379–385.

Kapalka, G. M. (2005) Avoiding repetitions reduces ADHD children's management problems in the classroom. *Emotional and Behavioural Difficulties, 10*, 269–279.

*References*

Kaplan, B. J., McNicol, J., Conte, R. A., *et al.* (1989) Dietary replacement in preschool-aged hyperactive boys. *Pediatrics, 83*, 7–17.

Keith, R. (1994) A*uditory Continuous Performance Test.* San Antonio, Texas: Psychological Corporation.

Kelleher, K. J., McInerny, T. K., Gardner, W. P., *et al.* (2000) Increasing identification of psychosocial problems: 1979–1996. *Pediatrics, 105*, 1313–1321.

Kelleher, K. J., Childs, G. E. & Harman, J. S. (2001) Healthcare costs for children with attention-deficit/hyperactivity disorder. *TEN: The Economics of Neuroscience, 3*, 60–63.

Kelsey, D. K., Sumner, C. R., Casat, C. D., *et al.* (2004) Once-daily atomoxetine treatment for children with attention-deficit/hyperactivity disorder, including an assessment of evening and morning behavior: a double-blind, placebo-controlled trial. *Pediatrics, 114*, e1–e8.

Kendall, J., Hatton, D., Beckett, A., *et al.* (2003) Children's accounts of attention deficit/hyperactivity disorder. *Advances in Nursing Science, 26*, 114–130.

Kendall, P. & Braswell, L. (1982) *Cognitive Behavioural Therapy for Impulsive Children.* New York: Guilford Press.

Kendall, P. & Finch, A. (1978) A cognitive-behavioural treatment for impulsivity: a group comparison study. *Journal of Consulting and Clinical Psychology, 46*, 110–118.

Kendall, P. & Wilcox, L. (1980) A cognitive-behavioural treatment for impulsivity: concrete versus conceptual training in non-self-controlled problem children. *Journal of Consulting and Clinical Psychology, 48*, 80–91.

Kessler, R. C., McGonagle, K. A., Zhao, S., *et al.* (1994) Lifetime and 12-month prevalence of DSM-III-R psychiatric disorders in the United States: results from the National Comorbidity Survey. *Archives of General Psychiatry, 51*, 8–18.

Kessler, R. C., Merikangas, K. R. & Berglund, P. (2003) Mild disorders should not be eliminated from the *DSM-V. Archives of General Psychiatry, 60*, 1117–1122.

Kessler, R. C., Adler, L., Ames, M., *et al.* (2005) The prevalence and effects of adult attention deficit/hyperactivity disorder on work performance in a nationally representative sample of workers. *Journal of Occupational and Environmental Medicine, 47*, 565–572.

Kessler, R. C., Adler, L., Barkley, R., *et al.* (2006) The prevalence and correlates of adult ADHD in the United States: results from the national comorbidity survey replication. *American Journal of Psychiatry, 163*, 716–723.

King, S., Waschbusch, D. A., Frankland, B. W., *et al.* (2005a) Taxonomic examination of ADHD and conduct problem comorbidity in elementary school children using cluster analyses. *Journal of Psychopathology and Behavioral Assessment, 27*, 77–88.

King, S., Griffin, S., Hodges, Z., *et al.* (2005b) *Assessment Report: Attention Deficit Hyperactivity Disorder – Methylphenidate, Atomoxetine and Dexamfetamine (Review).* Available at: http://www.nice.org.uk/guidance/index.jsp?action= download&o=33226 [accessed January 2008].

King, S., Griffin, S., Hodges, Z., *et al.* (2006) *A Systematic Review and Economic Model of the Effectiveness and Cost-Effectiveness of Methylphenidate, Dexamfetamine and Atomoxetine for the Treatment of Attention Deficit*

*Hyperactivity Disorder in Children and Adolescents.* Health Technology Assessment, 10. Tunbridge Wells: Gray Publishing.

Klein, C., Wendling, K., Huettner, P., *et al.* (2006) Intra-subject variability in attention-deficit hyperactivity disorder. *Biological Psychiatry, 60,* 1088–1097.

Klein, R. G. & Abikoff, H. (1997) Behavior therapy and methylphenidate in the treatment of children with ADHD. *Journal of Attention Disorders, 2,* 89–114.

Klein, R. G. & Mannuzza, S. (1991) Long-term outcome of hyperactive children: a review. *Journal of the American Academy of Child and Adolescent Psychiatry, 30,* 383–387.

Kollins, S., Greenhill, L., Swanson, J., *et al.* (2006) Rationale, design, and methods of the preschool ADHD treatment study (PATS). *Journal of the American Academy of Child and Adolescent Psychiatry, 45,* 1275–1283.

Kooij, J. J. S., Burger, H., Boonstra, A. M., *et al.* (2004) Efficacy and safety of methylphenidate in 45 adults with attention-deficit/hyperactivity disorder: a randomised placebo-controlled double-blind cross-over trial. *Psychological Medicine, 34,* 973–982.

Kooij, J. J., Buitelaar, J. K., Van Der Oord, E. J., *et al.* (2005) Internal and external validity of attention-deficit hyperactivity disorder in a population-based sample of adults. *Psychological Medicine, 35,* 817–827.

Korkman, M., Kirk, U. & Kemp, S. (1998) *NEPSY: A Developmental Neuropsychological Assessment.* San Antonio, Texas: Psychological Corporation.

Krueger, R. A. & Casey, M. A. (2000) *Focus Groups: A Practical Guide to Applied Research.* London: Sage.

Kuntsi, J., Eley, T. C., Taylor, A., *et al.* (2004) Co-occurrence of ADHD and low IQ has genetic origins. *American Journal of Medical Genetics, 124B,* 41–47.

Kupietz, S. S., Winsberg, B. G., Richardson, E., *et al.* (1988) Effects of methylphenidate dosage in hyperactive reading-disabled children: I. Behavior and cognitive performance effects. *Journal of the American Academy of Child and Adolescent Psychiatry, 27,* 70–77.

Kurlan, R., Goetz, C. G., McDermott, M. P., *et al.* (2002) Treatment of ADHD in children with tics: a randomized controlled trial. *Neurology, 58,* 527–536.

Lahey, B. B., Pelham, W. E., Schaughency, E. A., *et al.* (1988) Dimensions and types of attention deficit disorder. *Journal of the American Academy of Child and Adolescent Psychiatry, 27,* 330–335.

Lahey, B. B., Applegate, K., McBurnett, J., *et al.* (1994) DSM-IV field trials for attention deficit hyperactivity disorder in children and adolescents. *American Journal of Psychiatry, 151,* 1673–1685.

Lahti, J., Raikkonen, K., Kajantie, E., *et al.* (2006) Small body size at birth and behavioural symptoms of ADHD in children aged five to six years. *The Journal of Child Psychology and Psychiatry, 47,* 1167–1174.

Laing, A. & Aristides, M. (2005) *Attention Deficit Hyperactivity Disorder (ADHD) in Adults: SF–6D Utilities from SF–36 Scores in a Randomised trial.* Poster presented at 8th Annual European Congress of the International Society for Pharmacoeconomics and Outcomes Research (ISPOR), 6–8 November 2005, Florence, Italy.

Lambert, N. (2005) The contribution of childhood ADHD, conduct problems, and stimulant treatment to adolescent and adult tobacco and psychoactive substance abuse. *Ethical Human Psychiatry and Psychology, 7*, 197–221.

Larsson, J. O., Larsson, H. & Lichtenstein, P. (2004) Genetic and environmental contributions to stability and change of ADHD symptoms between 8 and 13 years of age: a longitudinal twin study. *Journal of the American Academy of Child and Adolescent Psychiatry, 43*, 1267–1275.

Lee, S. S. & Hinshaw, S. P. (2004) Severity of adolescent delinquency among boys with and without attention deficit hyperactivity disorder: predictions from early antisocial behavior and peer status. *Journal of Clinical Child and Adolescent Psychology, 33*, 705–716.

Leibson, C. L., Katusic, S. K., Barbaresi, W. J., *et al.* (2001) Use and costs of medical care for children and adolescents with and without attention-deficit/hyperactivity disorder. *The Journal of the American Medical Association, 285*, 60–66.

Lerer, R. J., Lerer, M. P. & Artner, J. (1977) The effects of methylphenidate on the handwriting of children with minimal brain dysfunction. *Journal of Pediatrics, 91*, 127–32.

Leviton, A., Guild-Wilson, M., Neff, R. K., *et al.* (1993) The Boston teacher questionnaire. 1. Definition of syndromes. *Journal of Child Neurology, 8*, 43–53.

Levy, F., Dumbrell, S., Hobbes, G., *et al.* (1978) Hyperkinesis and diet: a double-blind crossover trial with a tartrazine challenge. *The Medical Journal of Australia, 1*, 61–64.

Levy, F., Hay, D. A., McStephen, M., *et al.* (1997) Attention-deficit hyperactivity disorder: a category or a continuum? Genetic analysis of a large-scale twin study. *Journal of the American Academy of Child and Adolescent Psychiatry, 36*, 737–744.

Li, D., Sham, P. C., Owen, M. J., *et al.* (2006) Meta-analysis shows significant association between dopamine system genes and attention deficit hyperactivity disorder (ADHD). *Human Molecular Genetics, 15*, 2276–2284.

Liddel, J., Williamson, M. & Irwig, L. (1996) *Method for Evaluating Research and Guideline Evidence.* Sydney: New South Wales Health Department.

Linnet, K. M., Dalsgaard, S., Obel, C., *et al.* (2003) Maternal lifestyle factors in pregnancy risk of attention deficit hyperactivity disorder and associated behaviors: review of the current evidence. *American Journal of Psychiatry, 160*, 1028–1040.

Lloyd, G., Stead, J. & Cohen, D. (eds) (2006) *Critical New Perspectives on ADHD.* London: Routledge.

Long, N., Rickert, V. I. & Ashcraft, E. W. (1993) Bibliotherapy as an adjunct to stimulant medication in the treatment of attention-deficit hyperactivity disorder. *Journal of Pediatric Health Care, 7*, 82–88.

Lord, J. & Paisley, S. (2000) *The Clinical Effectiveness and Cost-Effectiveness of Methylphenidate for Hyperactivity in Childhood, Version 2.* London: NICE.

Manly, T., Robertson, I. H., Anderson, V., *et al.* (1998) *Test of Everyday Attention for Children.* Bury St Edmunds: Thames Valley Test Company.

Mann, T. (1996) *Clinical Guidelines: Using Clinical Guidelines to Improve Patient Care Within the NHS.* Leeds: NHS Executive.

Mannuzza, S., Klein, R. G., Bonagura, N., *et al.* (1991) Hyperactive boys almost grown up. *Archives of General Psychiatry, 48,* 77–83.

Mannuzza, S., Klein, R. G., Bessler, A., *et al.* (1993) Adult outcome of hyperactive boys: educational achievement, occupational rank, and psychiatric status. *Archives of General Psychiatry, 50,* 565–576.

Mannuzza, S., Klein, R. G., Bessler, A., *et al.* (1998) Adult psychiatric status of hyperactive boys grown up. *American Journal of Psychiatry, 155,* 493–498.

Mannuzza, S., Klein, R. G. & Moulton, J. L. (2002) Young adult outcome of children with 'situational' hyperactivity: a prospective, controlled follow-up study. *Journal of Abnormal Child Psychology, 30,* 191–198.

Mannuzza, S., Klein, R. G., Abikoff, H., *et al.* (2004) Significance of childhood conduct problems to later development of conduct disorder among children with ADHD: a prospective follow-up study. *Journal of Abnormal Child Psychology, 32,* 565–573.

Mannuzza, S., Klein, R. G., Truong, N. L., *et al.* (2008) Age of methylphenidate treatment initiation in children with ADHD and later substance abuse: prospective follow-up into adulthood. *American Journal of Psychiatry, 165,* 604–609.

Marshall, R. M., Schafer, V. A., O'Donnell, L., *et al.* (1999) Arithmetic disabilities and ADHD subtypes: implications for DSM-IV. *Journal of Learning Disabilities, 32,* 239–247.

Martin, N. C., Piek, J. P. & Hay, D. (2006) DCD and ADHD: a genetic study of their shared aetiology. *Human Movement Science, 25,* 110–124.

Mattes, J. A. & Gittelman, R. (1981) Effects of artificial food colorings in children with hyperactive symptoms: a critical review and results of a controlled study. *Archives of General Psychiatry, 38,* 714–718.

Matza, L. S., Secnik, K., Rentz, A. M., *et al.* (2005) Assessment of health states utilities for attention-deficit/hyperactivity disorder in children using parent proxy report. *Quality of Life Research, 14,* 735–747.

Mautner, V. F., Kluwe, L., Thakker, S. D., *et al.* (2002) Treatment of ADHD in neurofibromatosis type I. *Developmental Medicine and Child Neurology, 44,* 164–170.

McArdle, P., Prosser, J., Kolvin, I. (2004) Prevalence of psychiatric disorder: with and without psychosocial impairment. *European Child and Adolescent Psychiatry, 13,* 347–353.

McCann, D., Barrett, A., Cooper, A., *et al.* (2007) Food additives and hyperactive behaviour in 3-year-old and 8/9-year-old children in the community: a randomised, double-blind, placebo-controlled trial. *The Lancet, 3,* 1560–1567.

McDonagh, M. S., Peterson, K., Dana, T., *et al.* (2007) *Drug Class Review on Pharmacologic Treatments for ADHD.* Available at: http://www.ohsu.edu/drugeffectiveness/reports/final.cfm [accessed July 2008].

McElearney, C., Fitzpatrick, C., Farrell, N., *et al.* (2005) Stimulant medication in ADHD: what do children and their parents say? *Irish Journal of Psychological Medicine, 22,* 5–9.

McGee, R., Williams, S., Bradshaw, J., *et al.* (1985) The Rutter scale for completion by teachers: factor structure and relationships with cognitive abilities and family adversity for a sample of New Zealand children. *The Journal of Child Psychology and Psychiatry, 26*, 727–739.

McGee, R., Williams, S. & Feehan, M. (1992) Attention deficit disorder and age of onset of problem behaviors. *Journal of Abnormal Child Psychology, 20*, 487–502.

McGee, R., Prior, M., Williams, S., *et al.* (2002) The long-term significance of teacher-rated hyperactivity and reading ability in childhood: findings from two longitudinal studies. *The Journal of Child Psychology and Psychiatry, 43*, 1004–1017.

McLeer, S. V., Callaghan, M., Henry, D., *et al.* (1994) Psychiatric disorders in sexually abused children. *Journal of the American Academy of Child and Adolescent Psychiatry, 33*, 313–319.

Meaux, J., Hester, C., Smith, B., *et al.* (2006) Stimulant medications: a trade-off? The lived experience of adolescents with ADHD. *Journal for Specialists in Pediatric Nursing, 11*, 214–226.

Meichenbaum, D. (1977) *Cognitive Behaviour Modification: An Integrative Approach.* New York: Plenum.

Meichenbaum, D. & Goodman, J. (1971) Training impulsive children to talk to themselves: a means of developing self-control. *Journal of Abnormal Psychology, 77*, 115–126.

Meo, A. & Parker, A. (2004) Teachers, teaching and educational exclusion: pupil referral units and pedagogic practice. *International Journal of Inclusive Education, 8*, 103–120.

Merrell, C. & Tymms, P. (2001) Inattention, hyperactivity and impulsiveness: their impact on academic achievement and progress. *British Journal of Educational Psychology, 71*, 43–56.

Merrell, C. & Tymms, P. (2002) *Working with Difficult Children in Years 1 and 2: A Guide for Teachers.* Durham: CEM Centre, University of Durham.

Merrell, C. & Tymms, P. (2005a) Rasch analysis of inattentive, hyperactive and impulsive behaviour in young children and the link with academic achievement. *Journal of Applied Measurement, 6*, 1–18.

Merrell, C. & Tymms, P. (2005b) *A Longitudinal Study of the Achievements, Progress and Attitudes of Severely Inattentive, Hyperactive and Impulsive Young Children.* Paper presented at the Annual Conference of the British Educational Research Association, University of Glamorgan, September 2005.

MHRA (2002) Zyban (bupropion hydrochloride) – safety update, 26 July 2002. Available at: http://www.mhra.gov.uk/Safetyinformation/Safetywarningsalerts andrecalls/Safetywarningsandmessagesformedicines/CON2015725 [accessed April 2008].

Michelson, D., Faries, D., Wernicke, J., *et al.* (2001) Atomoxetine in the treatment of children and adolescents with attention-deficit/hyperactivity disorder: a randomized, placebo-controlled, dose-response study. *Pediatrics, 108*, E83.

Michelson, D., Allen, A. J., Busner, J., *et al.* (2002) Once-daily atomoxetine treatment for children and adolescents with attention deficit hyperactivity disorder: a randomized, placebo-controlled study. *American Journal of Psychiatry, 159*, 1896–1901.

Michelson, D., Adler, L., Spencer, T., *et al.* (2003)[66] Atomoxetine in adults with ADHD: two randomized, placebo-controlled studies. *Biological Psychiatry, 53*, 112–120.

Michelson, D., Buitelaar, J. K., Danckaerts, M., *et al.* (2004) Relapse prevention in pediatric patients with ADHD treated with atomoxetine: a randomized, double-blind, placebo-controlled study. *Journal of the American Academy of Child and Adolescent Psychiatry, 43*, 896–904.

Mick, E., Biederman, J., Faraone, S. V., *et al.* (2002) Case-control study of attention deficit hyperactivity disorder and maternal smoking, alcohol use and drug use during pregnancy. *American Journal of Child and Adolescent Psychiatry, 41*, 378–385.

Moffitt, T. E. (1990) Juvenile delinquency and attention deficit disorder: boys' developmental trajectories from age 3 to 15. *Child Development, 61*, 893–910.

Moffitt, T. E., Caspi, A. & Rutter, M. (2005) Strategy for investigating interactions between measured genes and measured environments. *Archives of General Psychiatry, 62*, 473–481.

Molina, B. S. G. & Pelham, W. E. (2003) Childhood predictors of adolescent substance use in a longitudinal study of children with ADHD. *Journal of Abnormal Psychology, 112*, 497–507.

Molina, B. S. G., Smith, B. H. & Pelham, W. E. (2001) Factor structure and criterion validity of secondary school teacher ratings of ADHD and ODD. *Journal of Abnormal Child Psychology, 29*, 71–82.

Molina, B. S. G., Flory, K., Hinshaw, S. P., *et al.* (2007) Delinquent behaviour and emerging substance use in MTA at 36 months: prevalence, course, and treatment effects. *Journal of the American Academy of Child and Adolescent Psychiatry, 46*, 1–11.

Mortimore, P., Sammons, P., Stoll, L., *et al.* (1988) *School Matters: The Junior Years.* Wells, Somerset: Open Books.

MTA Co-operative Group (1999a) A 14-month randomized clinical trial of treatment strategies for attention-deficit/hyperactivity disorder. *Archives of General Psychiatry, 56*, 1073–1086.

MTA Co-operative Group (1999b) Moderators and mediators of treatment response for children with attention-deficit/hyperactivity disorder. *Archives of General Psychiatry, 56*, 1088–1096.

MTA Co-operative Group (2004a) National Institute of Mental Health multimodal treatment study of ADHD follow-up: 24-month outcomes of treatment strategies for attention-deficit/hyperactivity disorder. *Archives of General Psychiatry, 56*, 1088–1096.

MTA Co-operative Group (2004b) National Institute of Mental Health multimodal treatment study of ADHD follow-up: changes in effectiveness and growth after the end of treatment. *Pediatrics, 113*, 762–769.

---

[66]This is the reference for MICHELSON2003A and MICHELSON2003B.

Muthukrishna, N. (2006) Inclusion and exclusion in school: experiences of children labelled 'ADHD' in South Africa. In *Critical New Perspectives on ADHD* (eds G. Lloyd, J. Stead & D. Cohen), pp. 96–114. Abingdon: Routledge.

Nadder, T. S., Rutter, M., Silberg, J. L., *et al.* (2002) Genetic effects on the variation and covariation of attention deficit-hyperactivity disorder (ADHD) and oppositional-defiant disorder/conduct disorder (ODD/CD) symptomatologies across informant and occasion of measurement. *Psychological Medicine, 32,* 39–53.

Narayan, S. & Hay, J. (2004) Cost effectiveness of methylphenidate versus AMP/DEX mixed salts for the first-line treatment of ADHD. *Expert Review of Pharmacoeconomics and Outcomes Research, 4,* 625–634.

National Institutes of Health (1998) *NIH Consensus Development Conference: Diagnosis and Treatment of Attention Deficit Hyperactivity Disorder,* 16–18 November, William H. Natcher Conference Centre, National Institutes of Health, Bethesda, Maryland.

Neuman, R. J., Lobos, E., Reich, W., *et al.* (2007) Prenatal smoking exposure and dopaminergic genotypes interact to cause a severe ADHD subtype. *Biological Psychiatry, 61,* 1320–1328.

Newcorn, J. H., Michelson, D., Kratochvil, C. J., *et al.* (2006) Low-dose atomoxetine for maintenance treatment of attention-deficit/hyperactivity disorder. *Pediatrics, 118,* e1701–e1706.

Newcorn, J. H., Kratochvil, C., Allen, A. J., *et al.* (2008) Atomoxetine and osmotically released methylphenidate for the treatment of attention deficit hyperactivity disorder: acute comparison and differential response. *American Journal of Psychiatry, 165,* 721–730.

NHS Health and Social Care Information Centre (2006) *Prescription Cost Analysis England 2005.* London: NHS Health and Social Care Information Centre, Health Care Statistics.

NHS Information Centre (2007) *Prescription Cost Analysis England 2006.* London: NHS Information Centre, Prescribing Support Unit.

NICE (2004) *Guide to the Methods of Technology Appraisal. National Institute for Clinical Excellence.* London: NICE. Available from: www.nice.org.uk

NICE and SCIE (2006a) *Parent-Training/Education Programmes in the Management of Children with Conduct Disorders.* Technology Appraisal 102. London: NICE. Available at: www.nice.org.uk/TA102

NICE (2006b) *Methylphenidate, atomoxetine and dexamfetamine for the treatment of attention deficit hyperactivity disorder in children and adolescents.* Technology Appraisal 98. London: NICE. Available at: www.nice.org.uk/TA98

NICE (2006c) *The Guidelines Manual.* London: NICE. Available from: www.nice.org.uk

Novartis Pharmaceuticals UK Ltd (2007) *Ritalin.* Summary of Product Characteristics. Available at: http://emc.medicines.org.uk

Nussbaum, N. L., Grant, M. L., Roman, M. J., *et al.* (1990) Attention deficit and the mediating effect of age on academic and behavioural variables. *Journal of Behavioural and Developmental Pediatrics, 11,* 22–26.

O'Connor, T. G., Heron, J., Golding, J., *et al.* (2002) Maternal antenatal anxiety and children's behavioural/emotional problems at 4 years. Report from the Avon Longitudinal Study of Parents and Children. *British Journal of Psychiatry, 180*, 502–508.

O'Connor, T. G., Heron, J., Golding, J., *et al.* (2003) Maternal antenatal anxiety and behavioural/emotional problems in children: a test of a programming hypothesis. *The Journal of Child Psychology and Psychiatry, 44*, 1025–1036.

Office for National Statistics (2007) *T 03: England and Wales; Estimated Resident Population by Single Year of Age and Sex; Mid–2006 Population Estimates.* London: Office for National Statistics. Available from: http://www.statistics.gov. uk/statbase/ssdataset.asp?vlnk=9659&More=Y

Olfson, M., Gameroff, M. J., Marcus, S. C., *et al.* (2003) National trends in the treatment of attention deficit hyperactivity disorder. *American Journal of Psychiatry, 160*, 1071–1077.

Ornoy, A., Segal, J., Bar-Hamburger, R., *et al.* (2001) Developmental outcome of school-age children born to mothers with heroin dependency: importance of environmental factors. *Developmental Medicine and Child Neurology, 43*, 668–675.

O'Shaughnessy, T., Lane, K., Gresham, F., *et al.* (2003) Children placed at risk for learning and behavioural difficulties: implementing a school-wide system of early identification and intervention. *Remedial and Special Education, 24*, 27–35.

Owens, E. B., Hinshaw, S. P., Kraemer, H. C., *et al.* (2003) Which treatment for whom for ADHD? Moderators of treatment response in the MTA. *Journal of Consulting and Clinical Psychology, 71*, 540–552.

Paloyelis, Y., Mehta, M. A., Kuntsi, J., *et al.* (2007) Functional MRI in ADHD: a systematic literature review. *Expert Review of Neurotherapeutics, 7*, 1337–1356.

Palumbo, D., Spencer, T., Lynch, J., *et al.* (2004) Emergence of tics in children with ADHD: impact of once-daily OROS methylphenidate therapy. *Journal of Child and Adolescent Psychopharmacology, 14*, 185–194.

Paterson, R., Douglas, C., Hallmayer, J., *et al.* (1999) A randomised, double-blind, placebo-controlled trial of dexamphetamine in adults with attention deficit hyperactivity disorder. *Australian and New Zealand Journal of Psychiatry, 33*, 494–502.

Pelham, W. E. (1986) The effects of psychostimulant drugs on learning and academic achievement in children with attention-deficit hyperactivity disorders and learning disabilities. In *Psychological and Educational Perspectives on Learning Disabilities* (eds J. K. Torgesen & B. Wong), pp. 259–295. New York: Academic Press.

Pelham, W. E. & Gnagy, E. M. (1999) Psychosocial and combined treatments. *Mental Retardation and Developmental Disabilities Research Reviews, 5*, 225–236.

Pelham, W. E. & Murphy, H. A. (1986) Attention deficit and conduct disorder. In *Pharmacological and Behavioural Treatment: an Integrative Approach* (ed M. Hersen), pp. 108–148. New York: John Wiley & Sons.

Pelham, W. E., Gnagy, E. M., Greenslade, K. E., *et al.* (1992) Teacher ratings of DSM-III-R symptoms for the disruptive behavior disorders. *Journal of the American Academy of Child and Adolescent Psychiatry, 31*, 210–218.

Pelham, W. E., Foster, E. M. & Robb, J. A. (2007) The economic impact of attention-deficit/hyperactivity disorder in children and adolescents. *Journal of Pediatric Psychology, 32*, 711–727.

Perring, C. (1997) Medicating children: the case of Ritalin. *Bioethics, 11*, 228–240.

Pfiffner, L. J. & McBurnett, K. (1997) Social skills training with parent generalization: treatment effects for children with attention deficit disorder. *Journal of Consulting and Clinical Psychology, 65*, 749–757.

Philbrick, D., Tymms, P. & Woodcock, S. (eds) (2004) *A Multi-Agency Approach to Difficulties Associated with Attention, Hyperactivity and Impulsiveness: Framework and Guidance 2004*. Durham: Durham County Council, NHS, CEM Centre.

Pillow, D. R., Pelham, W. E., Hoza, B., *et al.* (1998) Confirmatory factor analyses examining attention deficit hyperactivity disorder symptoms and other childhood disruptive behaviors. *Journal of Abnormal Child Psychology, 26*, 293–309.

Pineda, D. A., Lopera, F., Palacio, J. D., *et al.* (2003) Prevalence estimations of attention-deficit/hyperactivity disorder: differential diagnoses and comorbidities in a Colombian sample. *International Journal of Neuroscience, 113*, 49–71.

Pliszka, S. R., Browne, R. G., Olvera, R. L., *et al.* (2000) A double-blind, placebo-controlled study of Adderall and methylphenidate in the treatment of attention-deficit/hyperactivity disorder. *Journal of the American Academy of Child and Adolescent Psychiatry, 39*, 619–626.

Pliszka, S. R., Glahn, D. C., Semrud-Clikeman, M., *et al.* (2006) Neuroimaging of inhibitory control areas in children with attention deficit hyperactivity disorder who were treatment naive or in long-term treatment. *American Journal of Psychiatry, 163*, 1052–1060.

Poduska, J. M. (2000) Parents' perceptions of their first graders' need for mental health and educational services. *Journal of the American Academy of Child and Adolescent Psychiatry, 39*, 584–591.

Pol, A. C., Verhulst, F. C., van der Ende, J., *et al.* (2003) Classes of disruptive behaviour in a sample of young elementary school children. *The Journal of Child Psychology and Psychiatry, 44*, 377–387.

Polanczyk, G., Silva de Lima, M., Horta, B. H., *et al.* (2007) The worldwide prevalence of ADHD: a systematic review and metaregression analysis. *American Journal of Psychiatry, 164*, 942–948.

Poulton, A. (2006) Growth and sexual maturation in children and adolescents with attention deficit hyperactivity disorder. *Current Opinion in Pediatrics, 18*, 427–434.

Power, T. J., Hess, L. E. & Bennett, D. S. (1995) The acceptability of interventions for attention-deficit hyperactivity disorder among elementary and middle school teachers. *Journal of Developmental and Behavioral Pediatrics, 16*, 238–243.

Pratt, T. C., Cullen, F. T., Blevins, K. R., *et al.* (2002) The relationship of attention deficit hyperactivity disorder to crime and delinquency: a meta-analysis. *International Journal of Police Science and Management, 4*, 344–360.

Price, T. S., Simonoff, E., Waldman, I., *et al.* (2001) Hyperactivity in preschool children is highly heritable. *Journal of the American Academy of Child and Adolescent Psychiatry, 40*, 1362–1364.

Price, T. S., Simonoff, E., Asherson, P., *et al.* (2005) Continuity and change in preschool ADHD symptoms: longitudinal genetic analysis with contrast effects. *Behavior Genetics, 35*, 121–132.

Prosser, B. (2006) *ADHD: Who's Failing Who?* Sydney: Finch Publishing.

Psychogiou, L., Daley, D. M., Thompson, M. J., *et al.* (2007) Mothers' expressed emotion toward their school-aged sons. Associations with child and maternal symptoms of psychopathology. *European Child and Adolescent Psychiatry, 16*, 458–464.

Purdie, N., Hattie, J. & Carroll, A. (2002) A review of the research on interventions for attention deficit hyperactivity disorder: what works best? *Review of Educational Research, 72*, 61–99.

Rabinowitz, E. (2004) Recreation interventions for individuals with attention deficit hyperactivity disorder. *American Journal of Recreation Therapy, 3*, 31–35.

Ramsay, J. R. & Rostain, A. L. (2003) A cognitive therapy approach for adult attention deficit/hyperactivity disorder. *Journal of Cognitive Psychotherapy: an International Quarterly, 17*, 319–333.

Rapoport, J. L. (1978) Dextroamphetamine: cognitive and behavioral effects in normal prepubertal boys. *Science, 199*, 560–563.

Rasmussen, E. R., Neuman, R. J., Heath, A. C., *et al.* (2004) Familial clustering of latent class and DSM-IV defined attention-deficit/hyperactivity disorder (ADHD) subtypes. *The Journal of Child Psychology and Psychiatry, 45*, 589–598.

Read, J. (2007) Why promoting biological ideology increases prejudice against people labeled 'schizophrenic'. *Australian Psychologist, 42*, 118–128.

Reimherr, F. W., Hedges, D. W., Strong, R. E., *et al.* (2005) Bupropion SR in adults with ADHD: a short-term, placebo-controlled trial. *Neuropsychiatric Disease and Treatment, 1*, 245–251.

Rey, J. M., Walter, G., Plapp, J. M., *et al.* (2000) Family environment in attention deficit hyperactivity, oppositional defiant and conduct disorders. *Australian and New Zealand Journal of Psychiatry, 34*, 453–457.

Rhodes, S. M., Coghill, D. R. & Matthews, K. (2006) Acute neuropsychological effects of methylphenidate in stimulant drug-naive boys with ADHD II: broader executive and non-executive domains. *The Journal of Child Psychology and Psychiatry, 47*, 1184–1194.

Richardson, A. (2004) Long-chain polyunsaturated fatty acids in childhood developmental and psychiatric disorders. *Biomedical and Life Sciences, 39*, 1215–1222.

Richardson, A. J. & Montgomery, P. (2005) The Oxford–Durham study: a randomized, controlled trial of dietary supplementation with fatty acids in children with developmental coordination disorder. *Pediatrics, 115*, 1360–1366.

Richardson, A. & Puri, B. (2002) A randomized double-blind, placebo-controlled study of the effects of supplementation with highly unsaturated fatty acids on ADHD-related symptoms in children with specific learning disabilities. *Progress in Neuro-Psychopharmacology and Biological Psychiatry, 26*, 233–239.

Rieppi, R., Greenhill, L. L., Ford, R. E., *et al.* (2002) Socioeconomic status as a moderator of ADHD treatment outcomes. *Journal of the American Academy of Child and Adolescent Psychiatry, 41*, 269–277.

Rietveld, M. J. H., Hudziak, J. J., Bartels, M., *et al.* (2004) Heritability of attention problems in children: longitudinal results from a study of twins, age 3 to 12. *The Journal of Child Psychology and Psychiatry, 45*, 577–588.

Risch, N. & Merikangas, K. (1996) The future of genetic studies of complex human diseases. *Science, 273*, 1516–1517.

Robertson, I. H., Ward, T., Ridgeway, V., *et al.* (1994) *The Test of Everyday Attention.* Bury St Edmunds: Thames Valley Test Company.

Robins, L. N., Helzer, J. E., Croughan, J., *et al.* (1981) National Institute of Mental Health diagnostic interview schedule: its history, characteristics and validity. *Archives of General Psychiatry, 38*, 381–389.

Rodriguez, A. & Bohlin, G. (2005) Are maternal smoking and stress during pregnancy related to ADHD symptoms in children? *The Journal of Child Psychology and Psychiatry, 46*, 246–254.

Ronald, A., Simonoff, E., Kuntsi, J., *et al.* (2008) Evidence for overlapping genetic influences on autistic and ADHD behaviours in a community twin sample. *The Journal of Child Psychology and Psychiatry, 49*, 535–542.

Rosenhan, D. (1973) On being sane in insane places. *Science, 179*, 250–258.

Rosenman, S. (2006) Reconsidering the attention deficit paradigm. *Australasian Psychiatry, 14*, 127–132.

Rosler, M., Retz, W., Retz-Junginger, P., *et al.* (2004) Prevalence of attention deficit-/hyperactivity disorder (ADHD) and comorbid disorders in young male prison inmates. *European Archives of Psychiatry and Clinical Neuroscience, 254*, 365–371.

Rosvold, H. E., Mirsky, A. F., Sarason, I., *et al.* (1956) A continuous performance test of brain damage. *Journal of Consulting Psychology, 20*, 343–350.

Roy, P., Rutter, M. & Pickles, A. (2000) Institutional care: risk from family background or pattern of rearing? *The Journal of Child Psychology and Psychiatry, 41*, 139–149.

Rugino, T. A. & Samsock, T. C. (2003) Modafinil in children with attention-deficit hyperactivity disorder. *Pediatric Neurology, 29*, 136–142.

Rutter, M. & O'Connor, T. G. (2004) Are there biological programming effects for psychological development? Findings from a study of Romanian adoptees. *Developmental Psychology, 40*, 81–94.

Rutter, M., Cox, A., Tupling, C., *et al.* (1975) Attainment and adjustment in two geographical areas. I: the prevalence of psychiatric disorder. *British Journal of Psychiatry, 126*, 493–509.

Rutter, M., Maughan, B., Mortimer, P., *et al.* (1979) *Fifteen Thousand Hours.* London: Open Books.

Safren, S. A., Otto, M. W., Sprich, S., *et al.* (2005) Cognitive-behavioral therapy for ADHD in medication-treated adults with continued symptoms. *Behaviour Research and Therapy, 43*, 831–842.

Sanders, M. R., Mazzucchelli, T. G. & Studman, L. (2004) Stepping Stones Triple P – An evidence-based positive parenting program for families with a child who has a disability: its theoretical basis and development. *Journal of Intellectual and Developmental Disability, 29*, 1–19.

San Roman, P. (2007) Multi-agency assessment pathway approach to difficulties of attention/overactivity (including AD/HD): a community pilot. In *National ADHD Conference*. Edinburgh: University of Edinburgh.

Santosh, P. J., Taylor, E., Swanson, J., *et al.* (2005) Refining the diagnoses of inattention and overactivity syndromes: a reanalysis of the multimodal treatment study of attention deficit hyperactivity disorder (ADHD) based on ICD–10 criteria for hyperkinetic disorder. *Clinical Neuroscience Research, 5*, 307–314.

Satterfield, J. H. & Dawson, M. E. (1971) Electrodermal correlates of hyperactivity in children. *Psychophysiology, 8*, 191.

Satterfield, J. H. & Schell, A. (1997) A prospective study of hyperactive boys with conduct problems and normal boys: adolescent and adult criminality. *Journal of the American Academy of Child and Adolescent Psychiatry, 36*, 1726–1735.

Satterfield, J. H., Cantwell, D. P., Saul, R. E., *et al.* (1973) Response to stimulant drug treatment in hyperactive children: prediction from EEG and neurological findings. *Journal of Autism and Childhood Schizophrenia, 3*, 35–48.

Satterfield, J., Swanson, J., Schell, A., *et al.* (1994) Prediction of antisocial behavior in attention-deficit hyperactivity disorder boys from aggression/defiance scores. *Journal of the American Academy of Child and Adolescent Psychiatry, 33*, 185–190.

Sayal, K., Taylor, E., Beecham, J., *et al.* (2002) Pathways to care in children at risk of attention-deficit hyperactivity disorder. *The British Journal of Psychiatry, 181*, 43–48.

Sayal, K., Goodman, R. & Ford, T. (2006a) Barriers to the identification of children with attention deficit/hyperactivity disorder. *The Journal of Child Psychology and Psychiatry 47*, 744–750.

Sayal, K., Hornsey, H., Warren, S., *et al.* (2006b) Identification of children at risk of attention deficit/hyperactivity disorder: a school-based intervention. *Social Psychiatry and Psychiatric Epidemiology, 41*, 806–813.

Schab, D. W. & Trinh, N. H. T. (2004) Do artificial food colors promote hyperactivity in children with hyperactive syndromes? A meta-analysis of double-blind placebo-controlled trials. *Journal of Developmental and Behavioral Pediatrics, 25*, 423–434.

Schacher, R. & Tannock, R. (2002) Syndromes of hyperactivity and attention deficit. In *Child and Adolescent Psychiatry* (4th edn) (eds M. Rutter & E. Taylor), pp. 399–418. Oxford: Blackwell.

Schachar, R. J., Tannock, R., Cunningham, C., *et al.* (1997) Behavioral, situational and temporal effects of treatment of ADHD with methylphenidate. *Journal of the American Academy of Child and Adolescent Psychiatry, 36*, 754–763.

Scheff, T. (1975) Labelling mental illness. In *Mental Health Matters* (ed T. C. Heller). London: Macmillan.

Schlander, M. (2007) Impact of attention-deficit/hyperactivity disorder (ADHD) on prescription drug spending for children and adolescents: increasing relevance of health economic evidence. *Child and Adolescent Psychiatry and Mental Health, 1*, doi:10.1186/1753-2000-1-13.

Schlander, M., Schwartz, O., Hakkart-van Roijen, L., *et al.* (2006a) *Cost-Effectiveness of Clinical Proven Treatment Strategies for Attention-Deficit/*

*Hyperactivity Disorder (ADHD) in the United States, Germany, The Netherlands, Sweden, and United Kingdom.* Poster presented at 9th Annual European meeting of the International Society for Pharmacoeconomics and Outcomes Research (ISPOR), 29–31 October 2006, Copenhagen, Denmark.

Schlander, M., Schwartz, O., Hakkart-van Roijen L., *et al.* (2006b) *Functional Impairment of Patients with Attention-Deficit/Hyperactivity Disorder (ADHD): An Alternative Cost-Effectiveness Analysis of Clinically Proven Treatment Strategies Based upon the NIMH MTA Study.* Poster presented at 9th Annual European meeting of the International Society for Pharmacoeconomics and Outcomes Research (ISPOR), 29–31 October 2006, Copenhagen, Denmark.

Schlander, M., Schwartz, O., Foster, E. M., *et al.* (2006c) *Cost-Effectiveness of Clinically Proven Treatment Strategies for Attention-Deficit/Hyperactivity Disorder (ADHD): Impact of Co-existing Conditions.* Poster presented at 9th Annual European meeting of the International Society for Pharmacoeconomics and Outcomes Research (ISPOR), 29–31 October 2006, Copenhagen, Denmark.

Schmidt, M. H., Mocks, P., Lay, B., *et al.* (1997) Does oligoantigenic diet influence hyperactive/conduct-disordered children: a controlled trial. *European Child and Adolescent Psychiatry, 6*, 88–95.

Schmitt, B. (1975) The minimal brain dysfunction myth. *American Journal of Diseases of Children, 129*, 1313–1318.

Schoechlin, C. & Engel, R. R. (2005) Neuropsychological performance in adult attention-deficit hyperactivity disorder: meta-analysis of empirical data. *Archives of Clinical Neuropsychology, 20*, 727–744.

Schwab-Stone, M., Fisher, P., Piacentini, J., *et al.* (1993) The Diagnostic Interview Schedule for Children-Revised Version (DISC-R): II. Test-retest reliability. *Journal of the American Academy of Child and Adolescent Psychiatry, 32*, 651–657.

Schwab-Stone, M., Fallon, T., Briggs, M., *et al.* (1994) Reliability of diagnostic reporting for children aged 6–11 years: a test-retest study of the Diagnostic Interview Schedule for Children-Revised. *American Journal Psychiatry, 151*, 1048–1054.

Sciutto, M. J., Terjesen, M. D. & Frank, A. S. B. (2000) Teachers' knowledge and misperceptions of attention-deficit/hyperactivity disorder. *Psychology in the Schools, 37*, 115–122.

Scott, S. (2002) Parent training programmes. In *Child and Adolescent Psychiatry* (4th edn) (eds M. Rutter & E. Taylor), pp. 949–967. Oxford: Blackwell.

Secnik, K., Swensen, A. & Lage, M. J. (2005a) Comorbidities and costs of adult patients diagnosed with attention-deficit hyperactivity disorder. *Pharmacoeconomics, 23*, 93–102.

Secnik, K., Matza, L. S., Cottrell, S., *et al.* (2005b) Health state utilities for childhood attention-deficit/hyperactivity disorder based on parent preferences in the United Kingdom. *Medical Decision Making, 25*, 56–70.

Silberg, J., Rutter, M., Meyer, J., *et al.* (1996) Genetic and environmental influences on the covariation between hyperactivity and conduct disturbance in juvenile twins. *The Journal of Child Psychology and Psychiatry, 37*, 803–816.

Singh, I. (2003) Boys will be boys: fathers' perspectives on ADHD symptoms, diagnosis, and drug treatment. *Harvard Review of Psychiatry, 11*, 308–316.

Singh, I. (2004) Doing their jobs: mothering with Ritalin in a culture of mother-blame. *Social Science and Medicine, 59*, 1193–1205.

Singh, I. (2005) Will the 'real boy' please behave: dosing dilemmas for parents of boys with ADHD. *The American Journal of Bioethics, 5*, 1–14.

Singh, I. (2006) A framework for understanding trends in ADHD diagnosis and stimulant drug treatment: school and schooling as a case study. *BioSocieties, 1*, 439–452.

Singh, I. (2007) Capacity and competence in children as research participants. *EMBO Reports, 8*, 35–39.

Smith, E. V., Jr. & Johnson, B. D. (2000) Attention deficit hyperactivity disorder: scaling and standard setting using Rasch measurement. *Journal of Applied Psychological Measurement, 1*, 3–24.

Sonuga-Barke, E. J. S. (1998) Categorical model in child psychopathology: a conceptual and empirical analysis. *The Journal of Child Psychology and Psychiatry, 39*, 115–133.

Sonuga-Barke, E. J. (2003) The dual pathway model of AH/HD: an elaboration of neuron-developmental characteristics. *Neuroscience and Biobehavioural Reviews, 27*, 593–604.

Sonuga-Barke, E. J., Minocha, K., Taylor, E. A., *et al.* (1993). Inter-ethnic bias in teachers' ratings of childhood hyperactivity. *British Journal of Developmental Psychology, 11*, 187–200.

Sonuga-Barke, E. J., Daley, D., Thompson, M., *et al.* (2001) Parent-based therapies for preschool attention-deficit/hyperactivity disorder: a randomized, controlled trial with a community sample. *Journal of the American Academy of Child and Adolescent Psychiatry, 40*, 402–408.

Sorensen, E. (1992) Qualitative research with children as informants. *Communicating Nursing Research, 25*, 328.

Sparks, G. M. (1986) The effectiveness of alternative training activities in changing teaching practices. *American Educational Research Journal, 23*, 217–225.

Spencer, T. J., Biederman, J., Harding, M., *et al.* (1996) Growth deficits in ADHD children revisited: evidence for disorder-associated growth delays? *Journal of the American Academy of Child and Adolescent Psychiatry, 35*, 1460–1469.

Spencer, T., Heiligenstein, J. H., Biederman, J., *et al.* (2002)[67] Results from 2 proof-of-concept, placebo-controlled studies of atomoxetine in children with attention-deficit/hyperactivity disorder. *Journal of Clinical Psychiatry, 63*, 1140–1147.

Spencer, T., Biederman, J., Wilens, T., *et al.* (2005) A large, double-blind, randomised clinical trial of methylphenidate in the treatment of adults with attention-deficit/hyperactivity disorder. *Biological Psychiatry, 57*, 456–463.

Sprague, R. L. & Werry, J. S. (1971) Methodology of psychopharmacological studies with the retarded. In *International Review of Research in Mental Retardation*, vol. 5. (ed N. R. Ellis), pp. 148–220. New York: Academic Press.

---

[67]This is the reference for SPENCER2002A, 2002B and 2002C.

*References*

Sprich, S., Biederman, J., Crawford, M. H., *et al.* (2000) Adoptive and biological families of children and adolescents with ADHD. *Journal of the American Academy of Child and Adolescent Psychiatry, 39,* 1432–1437.

Sterman, M. B. (1996) Physiological origins and functional correlates of EEG-rhythmic activities: implications for self-regulation. *Biofeedback and Self-Regulation, 21,* 3–33.

Stevens, L., Zhang, W., Peck, L., *et al.* (2003) EFA supplementation in children with inattention, hyperactivity, and other disruptive behaviors. *Lipids, 38,* 1007–1021.

Stevens, S. E., Sonuga-Barke, E. J., Kreppner, J. M., *et al.* (2008) Inattention/overactivity following early severe institutional deprivation: presentation and associations in early adolescence. *Journal of Abnormal Child Psychology, 36,* 385–398.

Stevenson, C. S., Whitmont, S., Bornholt, L., *et al.* (2002) A cognitive remediation programme for adults with attention deficit hyperactivity disorder. *Australian and New Zealand Journal of Psychiatry, 36,* 610–616.

Stevenson, C. S., Stevenson, R. J. & Whitmont, S. (2003) A self-directed psychosocial intervention with minimal therapist contact for adults with attention deficit hyperactivity disorder. *Clinical Psychology and Psychotherapy, 10,* 93–101.

Stier, A. & Hinshaw, S. (2007) Explicit and implicit stigma against individuals with mental illness. *Australian Psychologist, 42,* 106–117.

Stoops, W. W., Glaser, P. E., Fillmore, M. T., *et al.* (2004) Reinforcing, subject-rated, performance and physiological effects of methylphenidate and d-amphetamine in stimulant abusing humans. *Journal of Psychopharmacology, 18,* 534–543.

Stowe, C. D., Gardner, S. F., Gist, C. C., *et al.* (2002) 24-hour ambulatory blood pressure monitoring in male children receiving stimulant therapy. *The Annals of Pharmacotherapy, 36,* 1142–1149.

Swanson, J. M., McBurnett, K., Wigal, T., *et al.* (1993) Effect of stimulant medication on children with attention deficit hyperactivity disorder: a review of reviews. *Exceptional Children, 60,* 154–162.

Swanson, J. M., McBurnett, K., Christian, D. L., *et al.* (1995) Stimulant medication and treatment of children with ADHD. In *Advances in Clinical Child Psychology,* vol. 17 (eds T. H. Ollendick & R. J. Prinz), pp. 265–322. New York: Plenum Press.

Swanson, J. M., Kraemer, H. C., Hinshaw, S. P., *et al.* (2001) Clinical relevance of the primary findings of the MTA: success rates based on severity of ADHD and ODD symptoms at the end of treatment. *Journal of the American Academy of Child and Adolescent Psychiatry, 40,* 168–179.

Swanson, J. M., Greenhill, L. L., Lopez, F. A., *et al.* (2006) Modafinil film-coated tablets in children and adolescents with attention-deficit/hyperactivity disorder: results of a randomised, double-blind, placebo-controlled, fixed-dose study followed by abrupt discontinuation. *Journal of Clinical Psychiatry, 67,* 137–147.

Swanson, J. M., Elliott, G. R., Greenhill, L. L., *et al.* (2007) Effects of stimulant medication on growth rates across 3 years in the MTA follow-up. *Journal of the American Academy of Child and Adolescent Psychiatry, 46,* 1014–1026.

Swensen, A. R., Birnbaum, H. G., Secnik, K., *et al.* (2003) Attention-deficit/hyperactivity disorder: increased costs for patients and their families. *Journal of the American Academy of Child and Adolescent Psychiatry, 42*, 1415–1423.

Talge, N. M., Neal, C. & Glover, V. (2007) Antenatal maternal stress and long-term effects on child neurodevelopment: how and why? *The Journal of Child Psychology and Psychiatry, 48*, 245–261.

Taylor, E. (1986) Overactivity, hyperactivity and hyperkinesis: problems and prevalence. In *The Overactive Child: Clinics in Developmental Medicine* No. 97 (ed. E. Taylor). London & Oxford: Mac Keith Press & Blackwell.

Taylor, E. & Sandberg, S. (1984) Hyperactive behavior in English schoolchildren: a questionnaire survey. *Journal of Abnormal Child Psychology, 12*, 143–156.

Taylor, E. & Sonuga-Barke, E. (2008) Disorders of attention and activity. In *Rutter's Child and Adolescent Psychiatry* (5th edn) (eds M. Rutter, E. Taylor, J. S. Stevenson, *et al.*). London: Blackwell.

Taylor, E. A., Schachar, R., Thorley, G., *et al.* (1986) Conduct disorder and hyperactivity: I. Separation of hyperactivity and antisocial conduct in British child psychiatric patients. *British Journal of Psychiatry, 149*, 760–767.

Taylor, E., Sandberg, S., Thorley, G., *et al.* (1991) *The Epidemiology of Childhood Hyperactivity*. Oxford: Oxford University Press.

Taylor, E., Chadwick, O., Heptinstall, E., *et al.* (1996) Hyperactivity and conduct problems as risk factors for adolescent development. *Journal of the American Academy of Child and Adolescent Psychiatry, 35*, 1213–1226.

Taylor, E., Doepfner, M., Sergeant, J., *et al.* (2004) European clinical guidelines for hyperkinetic disorder: first upgrade. *European Child and Adolescent Psychiatry, 13, Suppl. 1*, 1–30.

Thapar, A., Holmes, J., Poulton, K., *et al.* (1999) Genetic basis of attention deficit and hyperactivity. *British Journal of Psychiatry, 174*, 105–111.

Thapar, A., Harrington, R. & McGuffin, P. (2001) Examining the comorbidity of ADHD-related behaviours and conduct problems using a twin study design. *British Journal of Psychiatry, 179*, 224–229.

Thompson, A. L., Molina, B. S., Pelham, W., Jr., *et al.* (2007) Risky driving in adolescents and young adults with childhood ADHD. *Journal of Pediatric Psychology, 32*, 745–759.

Thorell, L. (2007) Do delay aversion and executive function deficits make distinct contributions to the functional impact of ADHD symptoms? A study of early academic skills deficits. *The Journal of Child Psychology and Psychiatry, 48*, 1061–1070.

Timimi, S. (2006) Why diagnosis of ADHD has increased so rapidly in the west: a cultural perspective. In *Rethinking ADHD* (eds S. Timimi & J. Lee) Hampshire: Palgrave Macmillan.

Toren, P., Eldar, S., Sela, B. A., *et al.* (1996) Zinc deficiency in attention deficit hyperactivity disorder. *Biological Psychiatry, 40*, 1308–1310.

Tutty, S., Gephart, H. & Wurzbacher, K. (2003) Enhancing behavioral and social skill functioning in children newly diagnosed with attention-deficit hyperactivity disorder in a pediatric setting. *Journal of Developmental and Behavioral Pediatrics, 24*, 51–57.

Tymms, P. & Merrell, C. (2006) The impact of screening and advice on inattentive, hyperactive and impulsive children. *European Journal of Special Needs Education, 21*, 321–337.

UCB Pharma Limited (2005) *Dexedrine Tablets 5 mg.* Summary of Product Characteristics. Available at: http://emc.medicines.org.uk

UCB Pharma Limited (2006) *Equasym 5 mg, 10 mg and 20 mg Tablets.* Summary of Product Characteristics. Available at: http://emc.medicines.org.uk

UCB Pharma Limited (2008) *Equasym XL 10 mg, 20 mg or 30 mg Capsules.* Summary of Product Characteristics. Available at: http://emc.medicines.org.uk

Urbano, F. J., Leznik, E. & Llinás, R. R. (2007) Modafinil enhances thalamocortical activity by increasing neuronal electrotonic coupling. *Proceedings of the National Academy of Sciences of the United States of America, 104*, 12554–12559.

Valera, E., Faraone, S., Murray, K., *et al.* (2007) Meta-analysis of structural imaging findings in attention-deficit/hyperactivity disorder. *Biological Psychiatry, 61*, 1361–1369.

Van den Bergh, B. R. & Marcoen, A. (2004) High antenatal maternal anxiety is related to ADHD symptoms, externalizing problems, and anxiety in 8- and 9-year-olds. *Child Development, 75*, 1085–1097.

Van Lier, P. A. C., Verhulst, F. C., van der Ende, J., *et al.* (2003) Classes of disruptive behaviour in a sample of young elementary school children. *The Journal of Child Psychology and Psychiatry, 44*, 377–387.

Verhulst, F. C. & van der Ende, J. (2002) Rating scales. In *Child and Adolescent Psychiatry* (eds. M. Rutter & E. Taylor), pp. 70–86. Oxford: Blackwell.

Villalba, L. (2006) *Safety Review: Sudden Death with Drugs Used to Treat ADHD.* Available at: http://www.fda.gov/OHRMS/DOCKETS/AC/06/briefing/2006–4210b_07_01_safetyreview.pdf

Voigt, R. G., Llorente, A. M., Jensen, C. L., *et al.* (2001) A randomized, double-blind, placebo-controlled trial of docosahexaenoic acid supplementation in children with attention-deficit/hyperactivity disorder. *Journal of Pediatrics, 139*, 189–196.

Volkow, N. D., Wang, G. J., Fowler, J. S., *et al.* (1998) Dopamine transporter occupancies in the human brain induced by therapeutic doses of oral methylphenidate. *American Journal of Psychiatry, 155*, 1325–1331.

Volkow, N. D., Wang, G. J., Fowler, J. S., *et al.* (2004) Evidence that methylphenidate enhances the saliency of a mathematical task by increasing dopamine in the human brain. *American Journal of Psychiatry, 161*, 1173–1180.

Wallander, J. L., Schmitt, M. & Koot, H. M. (2001) Quality of life measurement in children and adolescents: issues, instruments, and applications. *Journal of Clinical Psychology, 57*, 571–585.

Walter, H. J., Gouze, K. & Lim, K. G. (2006) Teachers' beliefs about mental health needs in inner city elementary schools. *Journal of the American Academy of Child and Adolescent Psychiatry, 45*, 61–68.

Wang, Y., Zheng, Y., Du, Y., *et al.* (2007) Atomoxetine versus methylphenidate in paediatric outpatients with attention deficit hyperactivity disorder: a randomized, double-blind comparison trial. *Australian and New Zealand Journal of Psychiatry, 41*, 222–230.

Webster-Stratton, C. (1981) Videotape modeling: a method of parent education. *Journal of Clinical Child Psychology, 10*, 93–98.

Weiss, G. & Hechtman, L. T. (1993) *Hyperactive Children Grown Up: ADHD in Children, Adolescents and Adults* (2nd edn). New York: Guilford Press.

Weiss, G., Kruger, E., Danielson, U., *et al.* (1975) Effect of long-term treatment of hyperactive children with methylphenidate. *Canadian Medical Association Journal, 112*, 159–165.

Weiss, M. & Murray, C. (2003) Assessment and management of attention-deficit hyperactivity disorder in adults. *Canadian Medical Association Journal, 168*, 715–722.

Weiss, M., Trokenberg-Hechtman, L. & Weiss, G. (1999) *ADHD in Adulthood: a Guide to Current Theory, Diagnosis, and Treatment*. Baltimore: Johns Hopkins University Press.

Weiss, M., Tannock, R., Kratochvil, C., *et al.* (2005) A randomized, placebo-controlled study of once-daily atomoxetine in the school setting in children with ADHD. *Journal of the American Academy of Child and Adolescent Psychiatry, 44*, 647–655.

Wells, K. C., Pelham, W. E., Kotkin, R. A., *et al.* (2000) Psychosocial treatment strategies in the MTA study: rationale, methods, and critical issues in design and implementation. *Journal of Abnormal Child Psychology, 28*, 483–505.

Wender, P. H. (1998) Attention-deficit hyperactivity disorder in adults. *Psychiatric Clinics of North America, 21*, 761–774.

Wernicke, J. F., Faries, D., Girod, D., *et al.* (2003) Cardiovascular effects of atomoxetine in children, adolescents, and adults. *Drug Safety, 26*, 729–740.

Wernicke, J. F., Adler, L., Spencer, T., *et al.* (2004)[68] Changes in symptoms and adverse events after discontinuation of atomoxetine in children and adults with attention deficit/hyperactivity disorder: a prospective, placebo-controlled assessment. *Journal of Clinical Psychopharmacology, 24*, 30–35.

Werry, J. S., Sprague, R. L. & Cohen, M. N. (1975) Conners' teacher rating scale for use in drug studies with children: an empirical study. *Journal of Abnormal Child Psychology, 3*, 217–229.

Whalen, C. K. & Henker, B. (1991) Therapies for hyperactive children: comparisons, combinations, and compromises. *Journal of Consulting and Clinical Psychology, 59*, 126–137.

Whalen, C. K., Henker, B., Collins, B. E., *et al.* (1979) A social ecology of hyperactive boys: medication effects in structured classroom environments. *Journal of Applied Behavior Analysis, 12*, 65–81.

Whiting, P. F., Rutjes, A. W. S., Reitsma, J. B., *et al.* (2004) Sources of variation and bias in studies of diagnostic accuracy: a systematic review. *Annals of Internal Medicine, 140*, 189–202.

---

[68]This is the reference for WERNICKE2004A and 2004B.

## References

Wilcutt, E., Doyle, A. E., Nigg, J. T., *et al.* (2005) Validity of the executive function theory of attention deficit/hyperactivity disorder: a meta-analytic review. *Biological Psychiatry, 57,* 1336–1346.

Wilens, T. E., McDermott, S., Biederman, J., *et al.* (1999) Cognitive therapy for adults with ADHD: a systematic chart review of 26 cases. *Journal of Cognitive Psychotherapy, 13,* 215–226.

Wilens, T. E., Spencer, T. J., Biederman, J., *et al.* (2001)[69] A controlled clinical trial of bupropion for attention deficit hyperactivity disorder in adults. *American Journal of Psychiatry, 158,* 282–288.

Wilens, T. E., Faraone, S. V., Biederman, J., *et al.* (2003) Does stimulant therapy of attention-deficit/hyperactivity disorder beget later substance abuse? A meta-analytic review of the literature. *Pediatrics, 111,* 179–185.

Wilens, T. E., Haight, B. R., Horrigan, J. P., *et al.* (2005a) Bupropion XL in adults with attention-deficit/hyperactivity disorder: a randomised, placebo-controlled study. *Biological Psychiatry, 57,* 793–801.

Wilens, T., McBurnett, K., Stein, M., *et al.* (2005b) ADHD treatment with once-daily OROS methylphenidate: final results from a long-term open label study. *Journal of the American Academy of Child and Adolescent Psychiatry, 44,* 1015–1023.

Wilens, T. E., McBurnett, K., Bukstein, O., *et al.* (2006) Multisite controlled study of OROS methylphenidate in the treatment of adolescents with attention-deficit/ hyperactivity disorder. *Archives of Pediatrics and Adolescent Medicine, 160,* 82–90.

Wilens, T. E., Adler, L. A., Adams, J., *et al.* (2008) Misuse and diversion of stimulants prescribed for ADHD: a systematic review of the literature. *Journal of the American Academy of Child and Adolescent Psychiatry, 47,* 21–31.

Wilkinson, S. (1998) Focus groups in health research: exploring the meanings of health and illness. *Journal of Health Psychology, 3,* 329–348.

Willcutt, E. G., Pennington, B. F. & DeFries, J. C. (2000) Twin study of the etiology of comorbidity between reading disability and attention-deficit/hyperactivity disorder. *American Journal of Medical Genetics, 96,* 293–301.

Willcutt, E. G., Pennington, B. F., Olsen, R. K., *et al.* (2007) Understanding comorbidity: a twin study of reading disability and attention-deficit/hyperactivity disorder. *American Journal of Medical Genetics, 144B,* 709–714.

Williams, J. I., Cram, D. M., Tusig, F. T., *et al.* (1978) Relative effects of drugs and diet on hyperactive behaviors: an experimental study. *Pediatrics, 61,* 811–817.

Wilson, J. M. & Marcotte, A. C. (1996) Psychosocial adjustment and educational outcome in adolescents with a childhood diagnosis of attention deficit disorder. *Journal of the American Academy of Child and Adolescent Psychiatry, 35,* 579–587.

Wolraich, M. L., Hannah, J. N., Pinnock, T. Y., *et al.* (1996) Comparison of diagnostic criteria for attention-deficit-hyperactivity-disorder in a country-wide sample. *Journal of the American Academy of Child and Adolescent Psychiatry, 35,* 319–324.

---

[69]This is the reference for WILENS2001A.

Wolraich, M. L., Hannah, J. N., Baumgaertel, A., *et al.* (1998) Examination of DSM-IV criteria for attention deficit/hyperactivity disorder in a county-wide sample. *Journal of Developmental and Behavioral Pediatrics, 19,* 162–168.

Wolraich, M., Lambert, E., Baumgaertel, A., *et al.* (2003) Teachers' screening for attention deficit/hyperactivity disorder: comparing multinational samples on teacher ratings of ADHD. *Journal of Abnormal Child Psychology, 31,* 445–455.

Wolraich, M. L., Lambert, E. W., Bickman, L., *et al.* (2004) Assessing the impact of parent and teacher agreement on diagnosing attention-deficit hyperactivity disorder. *Journal of Developmental and Behavioural Pediatrics, 25,* 41–47.

Wolraich, M. L., McGuinn, L. & Doffing, M. (2007) Treatment of attention deficit hyperactivity disorder in children and adolescents: safety considerations. *Drug Safety, 30,* 17–26.

Woods, S. P., Lovejoy, D. W. & Ball, J. D. (2002) Neuropsychological characteristics of adults with ADHD: a comprehensive review of initial studies. *The Clinical Neuropsychologist, 16,* 12–34.

World Federation for Mental Health (2005) *Without Boundaries: Challenges and Hopes for Living With ADHD. An International Survey.* Available at: http://www.wfmh.org/

World Health Organization (1992) *The ICD–10 Classification of Mental and Behavioural Disorders: Clinical Descriptions and Diagnostic Guidelines.* Geneva: World Health Organization.

Wright, P., Turner, C., Clay, D., *et al.* (2006) *The Participation of Children and Young People in Developing Social Care.* London: SCIE.

Young, S. (1999) Psychological therapy for adults with Attention Deficit Hyperactivity Disorder. *Counselling Psychology Quarterly, 12,* 183–190.

Young, S. (2002) A model of psychotherapy for adults with ADHD. In *Clinical Interventions for Adult ADHD: A Comprehensive Approach* (eds S. Goldstein & A. Teeter). pp. 147–163. Orlando, Florida: Harcourt Academic Press.

Young, S. (2007a) Psychological therapy for adults with attention deficit hyperactivity disorder. In *Handbook of Attention Deficit Hyperactive Disorder* (eds M. Fitzgerald, M. Bellgrove & M. Gill). Chichester: John Wiley.

Young, S. (2007b) Forensic aspects of ADHD. In *Handbook of Attention Deficit Hyperactive Disorder* (eds M. Fitzgerald, M. Bellgrove & M. Gill). Chichester: John Wiley.

Young, S. & Bramham, J. (2007) *ADHD in Adults: a Psychological Guide to Practice.* Chichester: John Wiley & Sons.

Young, S., Toone, B. & Tyson, C. (2003) Comorbidity and psychosocial profile of adults with attention deficit hyperactivity disorder. *Personality and Individual Differences, 35,* 743–755.

Young, S., Heptinstall, E., Sonuga-Barke, E. J. S., *et al.* (2005a) The adolescent outcome of hyperactive girls: self-report of psychosocial status. *The Journal of Child Psychology and Psychiatry, 46,* 255–262.

Young, S., Heptinstall, E., Sonuga-Barke, E. J. S., *et al.* (2005b) The adolescent outcome of hyperactive girls: interpersonal relationships and coping mechanisms. *European Child and Adolescent Psychiatry, 14,* 245–253.

*References*

Young, S., Bramham, J., Gray, K., *et al.* (2008a) The experience of receiving a diagnosis and treatment of ADHD in adulthood. A qualitative study of clinically referred patients using interpretative phenomenological analysis. *Journal of Attention Disorders*.

Young, S., Bramham, J. & Gray, K. (2008b) The experience of receiving a diagnosis and treatment of ADHD in adulthood from a partner's perspective. A qualitative study of partners of clinically referred patients using interpretative phenomenological analysis. *Journal of Attention Disorders* (in press).

Zentall, S. S. (1993) Research on the educational implications of attention deficit hyperactivity disorder. *Exceptional Children, 60*, 143–153.

Zuddas, A., Marzocchi, G. M., Oosterlaan, J., *et al.* (2006) Factor structure and cultural factors of disruptive behavior disorders symptoms in Italian children. *European Psychiatry, 21*, 410–418.

Zupancic, J. A. F., Miller, A., Raina, P., *et al.* (1998) Economic evaluation of pharmaceutical and psychological/behavioural therapies for attention-deficit/hyperactivity disorder. In *A Review of Therapies for Attention Deficit/Hyperactivity Disorder* (eds A. Miller, S. K. Lee, P. Raina, *et al.*), pp. 132–162. Ottawa: Canadian Coordinating Office for Health Technology Assessment.

# 15.   ABBREVIATIONS

| | |
|---|---|
| ADD | attention deficit disorder |
| ADDISS | Attention Deficit Disorder Information and Support Service |
| ADHD | attention deficit hyperactivity disorder |
| ADHD-C | ADHD with both hyperactivity/impulsivity and inattention |
| ADHD-H/I | ADHD with hyperactivity-impulsivity |
| ADHD-I | ADHD with inattention |
| ADHD-RS (-P; -IV) | ADHD Rating Scale (-Parent; -IV) |
| AERS | Adverse Event Reporting System |
| AGREE | Appraisal of Guidelines for Research and Evaluation Instrument |
| AISRS | Adult ADHD Investigator System Report Scale |
| AMED | Allied and Complementary Medicine Database |
| AMHS | adult mental health services |
| ASQ (-P; -T) | Abbreviated Symptom Questionnaire (-Parents; -Teachers) |
| | |
| BNF | *British National Formulary* |
| bpm | beats per minute |
| | |
| CA | cost analysis |
| CAARS (-Inv) | Conners' Adult ADHD Rating Scale (-Investigator rated) |
| CAMHS | child and adolescent mental health services |
| CATQ | Conners' Abbreviated Teacher Questionnaire |
| CBA | cost-benefit analysis |
| CBCL (-P; -T) | Child Behaviour Checklist (-Parent; -Teacher) |
| CBT | cognitive behavioural therapy |
| CCA | cost-consequences analysis |
| CDSR | Cochrane Database of Systematic Reviews |
| CEA | cost-effectiveness analysis |
| CEACs | cost-effectiveness acceptability curves |
| C-GAS | Children's Global Assessment Scale |
| CGI (-ADHD-S; -I) | Clinical Global Impression (-ADHD-Severity; -Improvement) |
| CI | confidence interval |
| CINAHL | Cumulative Index to Nursing and Allied Health Literature |
| CIS ES | Columbia Impairment Scale Effect Size |
| CMA | cost-minimisation analysis |
| CMHT | community mental health team |
| CNS | central nervous system |
| CPQ | Conners' Parent Questionnaire |
| CPRS (-R; -S) | Conners' Parent Rating Scales (-Revised; -Short form) |

*Abbreviations*

| | |
|---|---|
| CPTQ (-P; -T) | Conners' Parent-Teacher Questionnaire (-Parent; -Teacher) |
| CRS | Conners' Rating Scales |
| CSM | Committee on Safety of Medicines |
| CTQ | Conners' Teacher's Questionnaire |
| CTRS (-R; -HI) | Conners' Teacher Rating Scales (-Revised; -Hyperactivity Index) |
| CUA | cost-utility analysis |
| | |
| DALY | Disability Adjusted Life Years |
| DARE | Database of Abstracts of Reviews of Effects |
| DAT | dopamine transporter |
| DF | De Fries-Fulker analysis |
| DfES | Department for Education and Skills (now the Department for Children, Schools and Families) |
| DPICS | Dyadic Parent–Child Interaction Coding System |
| DRD4/5 | dopamine D4/D5 |
| DSM-III (-R) | *Diagnostic and Statistical Manual of Mental Disorders* (3rd edition) (-Revised) |
| DSM-IV (-TR) | *Diagnostic and Statistical Manual of Mental Disorders* (4th edition) (-Text Revision) |
| | |
| ECBI | Eyberg Child Behaviour Inventory |
| EEG | electro-encephalography |
| EMBASE | Excerpta Medica database |
| EQ-5D | Euro-Qol 5-Dimension |
| ER | empirical reviews |
| ERIC | Educational Resources Information Center |
| ERP | event related brain potential |
| | |
| 5HT | 5-hydroxytryptamine |
| FDA | Food and Drug Administration (US) |
| fMRI | functional magnetic resonance imaging |
| | |
| GDG | Guideline Development Group |
| GP | general practitioner |
| GRADE | Grading of Recommendations: Assessment, Development, and Evaluation |
| GRP | Guideline Review Panel |
| HMSO | Her Majesty's Stationery Office |
| HRQoL | health related quality of life |
| | |
| ICD-9 | *International Classification of Diseases* (9th revision) |
| ICD-10 | *International Classification of Diseases* (10th revision) |

| | |
|---|---|
| ICER | incremental cost-effectiveness ratio |
| IHRQL | Index of Health Related Quality of Life |
| IOWA | IOWA oppositional/defiant subscale |
| IR | immediate-release |
| | |
| K | number of studies |
| KS1 | key stage 1 |
| | |
| LCA | latent class analysis |
| LEA | local education authority |
| | |
| MBD | minimal brain dysfunction |
| MD | mean difference |
| MEDLINE | Compiled by the US National Library of Medicine and published on the web by Community of Science, MEDLINE is a source of life sciences and biomedical bibliographic information |
| MHRA | Medicines and Healthcare Products Regulatory Agency |
| MR | modified-release |
| MRC | Medical Research Council |
| MRI | magnetic resonance imaging |
| MTA | Multimodal Treatment Study of Children with ADHD |
| | |
| N | number of participants |
| NCCMH | National Collaborating Centre for Mental Health |
| NHS | National Health Service |
| NHS EED | National Health Service Economic Evaluation Database |
| NICE | National Institute for Health and Clinical Excellence |
| NIMH | National Institute of Mental Health |
| NNT (-B; -H) | number needed to treat (benefit; harm) |
| NSF | National Service Framework |
| | |
| OHE HEED | Office of Health Economics, Health Economics Evaluation Database |
| OS | observational studies |
| | |
| p | probability |
| PET | positron emission tomography |
| PI | principal investigator |
| PILOTS | An electronic index to the worldwide literature on post-traumatic stress disorder |
| PIPS | performance indicators in primary schools |
| PsycINFO | An abstract (not full text) database of psychological literature from the 1800s to the present |

| PUFA | polyunsaturated fatty acids |
|---|---|
| QALY | quality adjusted life year |
| QT | the interval between Q and T waves in an electrocardiogram |
| RCT | randomised controlled trial |
| RR | relative risk |
| SCIE | Social Care Institute for Excellence |
| SEN | special educational needs |
| SENCO | special educational needs coordinator |
| SF (-36; -6D) | Short Form (-36; -6D) |
| SG | Standard Gamble |
| SIGLE | *System for Information on Grey Literature in Europe* |
| SIGN | Scottish Intercollegiate Guidelines Network |
| SKAMP | Swanson, Kotkin, Agler, McFlynn and Pelham test |
| SMD | standardised mean difference |
| SNAP | Swanson, Nolan and Pelham checklist |
| SNRI | serotonin and noradrenaline reuptake inhibitor |
| SR | systematic review |
| SSRI | selective serotonin reuptake inhibitor |
| TA | technology appraisal |
| TCA | tricyclic antidepressants |
| TG | topic group |
| TQ | Teacher Questionnaire |
| TTO | Time Trade-Off |
| WMD | weighted mean difference |
| WTP | willingness-to-pay |
| Y2 | year 2 |